GunDigest BOOK OF
SIG SAUER®

2nd Edition

Massad Ayoob

Published by

Gun Digest® Books, an imprint of F+W Media, Inc.
Krause Publications • 700 East State Street • Iola, WI 54990-0001
715-445-2214 • 888-457-2873
www.krausebooks.com

To order books or other products call toll-free 1-800-258-0929
or visit us online at www.gundigeststore.com

A word on terminology. Over the years, the company in question has been known variously as SIG Sauer, SIG-Sauer, and most recently SIG SAUER. To avoid confusion, and because it seemed that SIG-Sauer was the presentation of the name that most customers would be most familiar with, we went that route. If a quote or reprint from a given period used a different spelling, it was left that way in this book to remain true to the original.

ISBN-13: 978-1-4402-3914-4
ISBN-10: 1-4402-3914-2

Cover & Interior Design by Tom Nelsen
Edited by Corrina Peterson

Printed in the United States of America

Acknowledgments

In writing the Second Edition of this book a bit more than a decade after the first, I have all the more people to thank.

At SIG, past and present: Ron Cohen, the CEO who more than once has taken time to share his view of the company now, and his vision for it in the future. Ted Rowe, who godfathered the .357 SIG cartridge when he was with the company. Matt McLearn, who had a similar role when SIG went into the 1911 sphere. Joe Kiesel, Jeff Creamer, Tim Butler, and Ethan Lessard for sharing their vast knowledge of the design and engineering side of things at SIG. Laura Burgess, Paul Erhard, and Bud Fini who shepherded generations of marketing at SIG and were all unfailingly cooperative with us writers, and uniformly excellent ambassadors for the company they served. At the SIG Academy: Bank Miller, George Harris, Wes Doss, Scott Reidy and many more who over the years made their school into what Ron Cohen called the soul of SIG. Particular thanks to a couple of SIG staffers whose patience with me went above and beyond the call of duty: Kathy McQueeney, who handles the flow of the test guns, and Rance Deware, my instructor at SIG armorer's school. Given that I have a mechanical IQ of about 50, Rance must have felt like Anne Sullivan teaching Helen Keller.

On the publisher's end, thanks go to Don Gulbrandsen, who assigned me to write the First Edition; Kevin Michalowski, who edited that edition; and the long-suffering Corrina Peterson, who edited this Second Edition.

Staff trainers at LFI and MAG contributed greatly. In alphabetical order they include Sally Bartoo, Steve Denney, Rick Devoid, Mike Izumi, Andy Kemp, Dennis Luosey, Tara and Al Miller, Steve Sager, and Jeff Williams.

I appreciate what I learned of SIG-Sauer innards from two past masters who have specialized in modifying this gun: John Quintrall, who has retired from gunsmithing, and Ernest Langdon, who thankfully has not.

Many friends and colleagues are quoted in this book, and a decade after the first edition it saddens me that some are no longer with us. They include, in alphabetical order: Jim Andrews, Peter Brookesmith, Ray Chapman, Wiley Clapp, Dean Grennell, Roy Huntington, Chuck Karwan, Richard Law, Evan Marshall, Tim Mullin, Walt Rauch, Ed Sanow, Ned Schwing, Dave Spaulding, Chuck Taylor, and Duane Thomas.

I can't name the people who gave me inside stuff on the JSSAP's exhaustive test of SIG verus Beretta, nor the SEALs and SAS guys who told me how much they liked the SIG P226, and why. Police instructors aren't supposed to be seen as endorsing product, so I can't publicly name most of them who gave me input on their departments' long and extensive experience with these guns. These people know who they are, and I publicly thank them now, as I did in the First Edition.

Perhaps most of all I want to thank the countless cops, servicemen, and armed citizens who have gone through my classes, first at Lethal Force Institute and now at Massad Ayoob Group, with SIG-Sauer pistols. Each of them was a piece in the jigsaw puzzle of what I was able to put together in both editions about how these guns work in many different hands. In the First Edition, I wrote, "It's good to know that those SIG-Sauer bearing hands belong to a wide variety of good men and women who use them in the righteous cause of the protection of the innocent."

That has not changed since, and I don't think it ever will.

Massad Ayoob
Live Oak, Florida
2014

Contents

Introduction 5

Chapter 1: **The SIG P220** 18

Chapter 2: **The SIG P225** 36

Chapter 3: **The SIG P226** 39

Chapter 4: **The SIG P227** 62

Chapter 5: **The SIG P228** 72

Chapter 6: **The SIG P229** 77

Chapter 7: **The SIG .380s: The P232 and P230** 88

Chapter 8: **The SIG P238** 96

Chapter 9: **The SIG P239** 101

Chapter 10: **The SIG P245** 108

Chapter 11: **The SIG P250** 114

Chapter 12: **The SIG P290** 126

Chapter 13: **The SIG P320** 136

Chapter 14: **The SIG X-Six** 139

Chapter 15: **The SIG Pro** 152

Chapter 16: **SIGs That Are Sweet, Not Sauer** 158

Chapter 17: **SIGARMS' Hammerli Trailside** 163

Chapter 18: **GSR: The SIG 1911** 169

Chapter 19: **Manipulation of the Pistol** 189

Chapter 20: **Shooting the SIG-Sauer Pistol** 218

Chapter 21: **Holstering the SIG-Sauer** 229

Chapter 22: **Don't Let Your SIG Go Sour** 242

Chapter 23: **The Custom SIG** 251

Chapter 24: **Competing with the SIG** 259

Chapter 25: **The SIG in Training** 266

Chapter 26: **Ammunition for the SIG-Sauer** 275

Chapter 27: **Seasons of the SIG** 284

Introduction

It was an honor to be asked to write the *Gun Digest Book of SIG-Sauer*. These are handguns with which I've had a long and most agreeable acquaintance. My work, as a firearms and deadly force instructor and as a writer/tester for gun magazines, has brought me into contact with more of them than I can count. It brings me into contact with lots of other fine guns, too, and that's been useful in putting the SIG pistols in context.

When it was announced at an executive meeting at SIG that I'd be writing this book, one fellow blurted, "They can't let him write it! He's a *Glock* guy!"

After I stopped laughing, I realized he was partly right. I *am* a Glock guy. I'm also a Colt and Smith and Ruger guy, and a Beretta, Browning, and HK guy … and yes, a SIG guy too. Damn it, I'm a *gun* guy.

And that's the angle from which this book comes. I was hired by Krause Publications, not SIG. I'm not here to sell the guns. I'm here to tell you what we've learned about them. I've shot SIGs in matches, carried them on and off duty, taught classes with them, and kept them for home defense. But far more has been learned from the collective experience of law enforcement and military, and a vast nation of law-abiding armed citizens.

Sure, I've carried the SIG-Sauer from Alaska to Miami, but it's a lot more important to know that SEAL Teams and SAS troopers have used them from Arctic cold to desert sands, and found them not wanting. One of the most popular law enforcement sidearms of modern times – probably the second most popular in the U.S. right now, outsold only by the Glock – the SIG has proven itself accurate, ergonomic, and above all, reliable and safe.

SAFETY

Colt's classic 1911 pistol did not become drop-safe until the Series 80 firing pin safety, nor Browning's High Power until the introduction of the Mark III series in the late 1980s. Smith & Wesson's double-action autos did not get passive firing pin safeties to prevent inertia discharge until their second generation, and the Glock did not become 100 percent safe against impact discharge until 1990. The SIG-Sauers were drop-safe from the beginning. Some pistols require the trigger to be pulled on an empty chamber to begin the disassembly process, which has led to the occasional negligent discharge

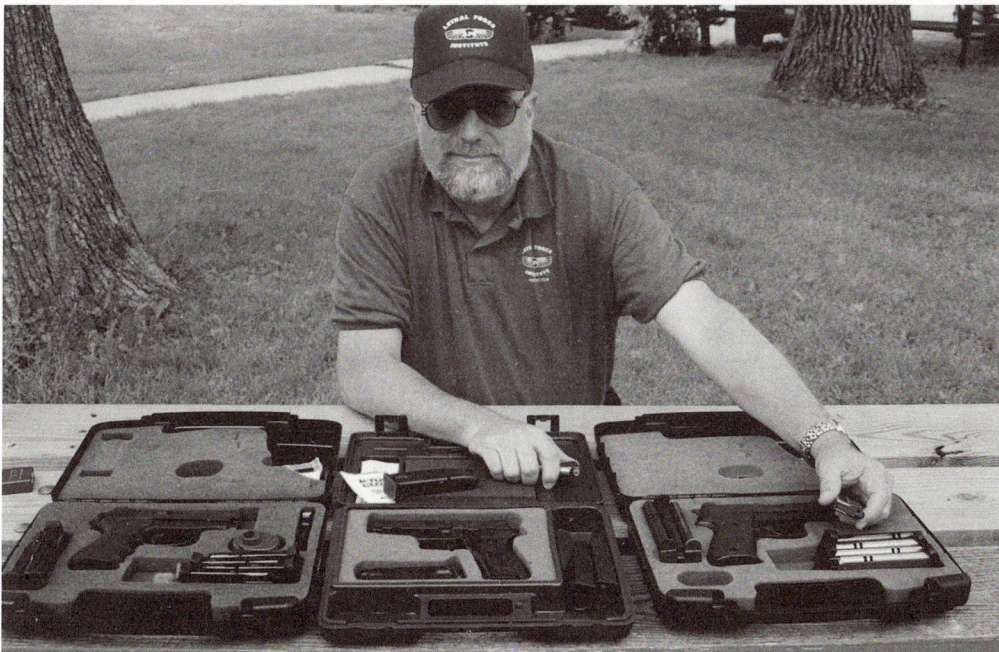

Once you appreciate a SIG-Sauer, you won't be satisfied with just one. Firearms instructor Steve Denney with just the three SIGs he takes on the road while teaching; cases contain spare .40 S&W and .357 SIG barrels for further versatility.

SIG-Sauer evolves the product as they find better ways to build guns. Left, an early P226 with separate breechface block, internal extractor, hollow pins. Right, current P226 with accessory rail, milled steel slide, solid pins, heavy-duty modern extractor.

Note that you can see daylight through the hollow slide pin of this older SIG. Current production uses stronger solid pins.

It's a stretch to call the SIG-Sauer "southpaw-unfriendly," and this book explains the left-handed manual of arms for this pistol.

with a missile in the launch tube, but SIG-Sauer disassembly requires that the slide be locked open before takedown can even begin.

For many in law enforcement and the military, the long, heavy pull of a double-action trigger to fire the first shot is seen as a bulwark against accidental discharge. It is easy enough to shrug and say, "Just keep your finger out of the trigger guard until you're going to shoot," but that's too pat an answer. Take a walk through a video store and look at how many of the video and DVD jackets portray someone holding a gun...and notice how many depict the actor with his finger on the trigger. This sort of subliminal conditioning, along with a childhood of playing with toy guns, has left many people with a finger-on-the-trigger habit that takes a lot of time to train away. A firm resistance to an unintended pull is some degree of a safety net, and the SIG-Sauers have that.

I can think of three good-sized police departments who won't buy or authorize SIGSauers because these pistols do not have thumb safeties. Those three agencies require all personnel to carry their pistols on-safe. The SIG design parameter from the beginning was for these to be point-and-shoot pistols, simple to learn and simple to operate. It was felt that with a drop-safe gun, a manual safety was redundant, and not in keeping with the principle later heard at SIGARMS Academy, "**S**imple **I**s **G**ood." Although a few SIGs with magazine disconnector safeties were made up per government requests the SIG-Sauer has always been "an automatic that you shoot like a revolver."

RELIABILITY

There will be comments from knowledgeable sources in this book about the final duel between SIG and Beretta for the U.S. military contract in the 1980s. It should not be taken as Beretta-bashing. After all, Beretta won. The final tests showed them neck and neck for reliability at virtually faultless levels. In 9mm service pistols, the comparison between the SIG P226 and the Beretta 92 is much like a comparison of the BMW and the Audi automobiles. In each case, both machines operate at the highest level of reliability and performance. Little things will dictate the choice. If you prefer to carry your pistol on-safe, you want a Beretta 92F. If you prefer to carry off-safe, you probably want a SIG P226, because it can't be found unexpectedly on-safe at the worst possible time. While Beretta offers the decock-only G-series, I don't find its operation nearly as ergonomic as the SIG's.

While I am one of those who likes the idea of an on-safe pistol, primarily from the handgun retention standpoint, the absence of that feature is not necessarily a deal-breaker. The selection of any firearm is going to be a balance of perceived needs with the features of the given gun. The SIG has a lot going for it, and should not be discarded from consideration because it does not have one particular feature.

WARTS AND ALL

This book will cover each of the SIG-Sauers, no holds barred. The good, the bad, and the ugly. No one has ever accused a SIG-Sauer of being a sleek or pretty gun. It's a tool, and a heavy-duty one at that. There is the occasional ammo incompatibility with this or that model, and these will be discussed with a view toward prevention and rectification.

SIG has been good about listening to constructive criticism and responding to it positively. One model would sometimes cycle too fast and fail to pick up the next round when loaded with +P+ ammo. That model is no longer imported. Another came with magazines that could jam during a slide-lock reload when wide-mouth hollow-points were used. Those magazines are no longer furnished with SIGARMS pistols.

One model was known to occasionally suffer frame cracks when fired extensively with hot loads. It was beefed up and the problem was solved. The hollow slide pins on the P226 used to start to work their way out in the course of long shooting sessions – I remember pounding them back in place with a plastic Kubotan – but SIG replaced them with solid pins in the mid-1990s and cured the problem. SIG grip screws had an irritating habit of loosening up in the course of intensive firearms training...and damn it, they still do.

SIGs are designed to function – and to interface with the human hand – in the nastiest weather. The author has just come in from firing a 60-shot qualification course in freezing rain, but the target score is a perfect 300. Ergonomics of the P226 were critical to success; Blackhawk combat shooting gloves helped too.

In their first incarnations, the P220 American and the P226 had magazine release springs sufficiently light as to be occasionally culpable in unintended dropping of magazines. For years, I advised students to replace them with aftermarket springs offered for the purpose by Trapper Gun in Michigan, and did so with my own. SIG fixed that problem quietly in the mid-1990s.

Some criticisms levied against the SIG-Sauer are simply unfounded. A good example is the allegation that they are not southpaw-friendly. I think we can prove in this book that it's no trick at all for a left-handed shooter to manipulate the SIG-Sauer swiftly, positively, and effectively. Some make a big deal out of transitioning from a double-action first shot to single-action follow-ups. It's easy, and this book will show you how to do it. It's all a matter of knowing the correct techniques.

HAVE IT YOUR WAY

Europeans as a group can sometimes be arrogant about what they choose to sell to Americans, vis-à-vis what those Americans ask them for. The people at SIG and Sauer have listened to the Yanks better than most. Those of us who've watched the SIG-Sauer pistols evolve over the years see this in a number of ways. Nowhere is it more graphic than in the development of no fewer than three significantly different trigger systems.

The standard SIG duty pistol is a traditional double-action (TDA), the first shot requiring a long, relatively heavy pull of the trigger. Subsequent shots offer a short, light trigger pull as the pistol cocks itself with each cycle. This is the overwhelming preference of military and civilian purchasers. It has also proven to be the most popular among police, though by a lesser margin.

ATF, FBI, DEA, IRS, Secret Service, Air Marshals, U.S. Marshals, and others have acquired SIGs by the thousands, and to the best of my knowledge all or virtually all have been TDA. Back around 1990, Supervisory Special Agent John Hall – then head of the FBI's elite Firearms Training Unit, and the man most responsible for bringing semiautomatics to rank and file Bureau agents – explained to me his rationale for favoring the TDA firing system. Recognizing that the main reason for double-action in a service auto is to reduce the likelihood of accidental discharges, he said, "The great majority

Three SIG P226s. Top, early production with internal extractor, folded chrome molybdenum slide. Center, current production, milled and blackened stainless slide, traditional configuration. Below, current production with integral accessory rail.

of accidental discharges occur with the first round. When it comes time to fire a second shot, the agent is in a gunfight, and I want that shot to be as easy as possible to put in the right place." Frankly, I find it hard to refute that argument, and all the SIGs I personally choose to carry are in the TDA format.

Next came DAO, the double-action-only trigger system. Where TDA is self-cocking during fire, the DAO is self-decocking. For decades before autoloaders replaced revolvers in the holsters of most American cops, police departments of New York City, Los Angeles, Miami, and others rendered their sixguns double-action-only. They had discovered that the hair trigger effect of a cocked gun could precipitate an accidental discharge, and that even the presence of single-action capability could bring a false accusation that an officer had cocked a gun and set the stage for a negligent shooting. The double-action-only concept was soon applied to autos.

The DAO SIG was pretty much the standard gun without a single-action mechanism. The stroke was full length and the same weight as the first shot on a TDA gun. Many officers found it tiresome, and few civilians wanted anything to do with it. Beretta's DAO, their D-series, had a lighter trigger pull thanks to the elimination of a single-action sear in its mechanism, and Smith & Wesson designed a new action entirely for this market with a shorter, lighter double-action stroke.

Several departments chose the SIG version. One example was the Ohio State Patrol, which adopted the P226DAO in caliber .40 S&W. The nation's two largest municipal police departments also went DAO. On both agencies, officers purchase their own guns off an approved list, and in both cases the SIG made the list. NYPD authorizes three DAO 9mms, and the P226DAO immediately became the "prestige gun" on that force. SIG has even produced what might be called an "NYPD Special," a P226DAO produced to the exacting demands of the end users in the Big Apple. Chicago PD authorizes 9mm or .45, and both the P226DAO and the P220DAO are very well represented there.

The third variation is the DAK, which stands for "double-action, Kellerman." Explains Joe Kiesel, Technical Director at SIGARMS, "Harald Kellerman is in charge of engineering on all the Classic pistols at Sauer, and he was the one who supervised development of the new design. As the slide comes forward, the hammer comes to rest in a slightly pre-cocked position. The trigger pull is a very comfortable 6.6 to 7 pounds. If the shooter should fail to return the trigger all the way forward under extreme stress, he will still be able to fire, although the pull will now be about 8.5 pounds. In dry fire, or if he has a bad primer, the hammer will go all the way forward. The shooter will have a second-strike capability as in our TDA and DAO guns, but the pull will be heavier, again about 8.5 pounds."

This has proven to be a much more "shooter-friendly" trigger than SIG's traditional DAO.

The DAO is visibly distinguishable from the TDA only in that it has an empty space on the frame where the traditional gun would have a decocking lever. The DAK gun also comes *sans* decock lever, and in addition can be identified by a smaller, more rounded hammer configuration. When the hammer is all the way forward, as in dry fire, it disappears within the silhouette of the pistol.

Noted gun expert Walt Rauch, not usually a fan of conventional DAO semiautomatics, has had good things to say about the DAK. So, I suspect, did the late Chuck Karwan, the gun-wise author of the third edition of the *Gun Digest Book of Combat Handgunnery*"; Chuck hated the conventional SIG DAO trigger mechanism. Tactical firearms expert John Farnam absolutely raves about the DAK, and considers it a most valuable option. On all SIG-Sauers, no matter what the trigger mechanism, the takedown lever and slide release lever are all in the same place, except for the .380s, which do not have slide lock levers.

The SIG remains extremely popular with the police establishment. I've worked on the range with SIG-carrying cops from Australia, Belgium, Canada (where RCMP SWAT was the first to get them), Denmark, Germany, Great Britain, and of course Switzerland, as well as the USA. When one department adopts these guns and has tremendous success with them, you see the brand spread in the region. Around the Dallas area, you see more SIGs on cops' hips than anything else. The SIG-Sauer is the predominant sidearm I see cops wearing when in Virginia. Indeed, whole regions are dominated by SIGs.

A VERY BRIEF HISTORY

This particular book was never conceptualized as a history of SIG, the SIG-Sauer collaboration, or SIGARMS. It's a user's guide, not a collector's reference. **S**chweizerische **I**ndustrie **G**esselschaft (meaning, literally, "Swiss Industrial Company") of Neuhausen am Rheinfall, Switzerland built a long and honorable history as one of the world's most respected arms makers. Their first, classic pistol, in production for more than half a century, is the beautifully crafted and famously accurate P210. Though the SIGs have a Teutonic aura today due to the Sauer influence, there's also a Gallic thread in its history. A key element of the P210 is a slide that runs inside rather than outside the frame rails, and SIG licensed the patent for this, originally granted to Charles Gabriel Petter of France's Societe Alsacienne de Construction

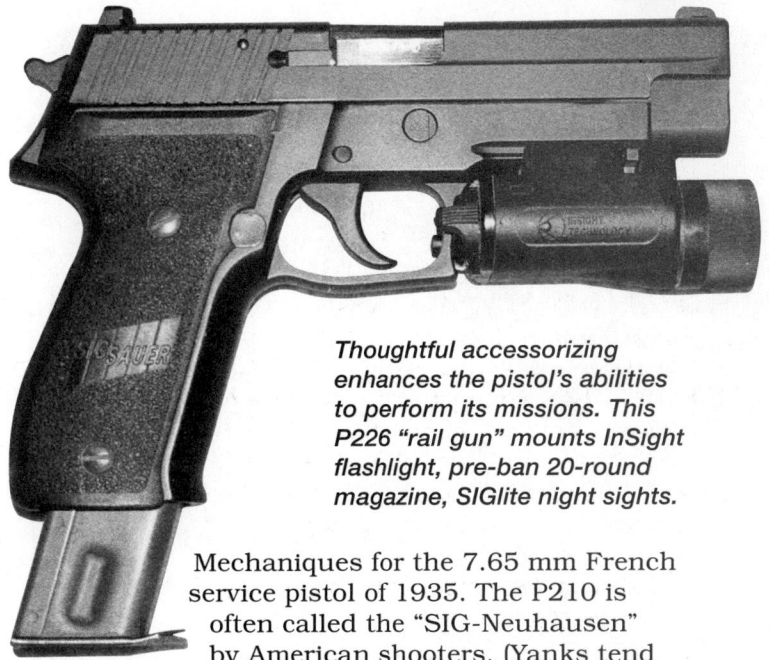

Thoughtful accessorizing enhances the pistol's abilities to perform its missions. This P226 "rail gun" mounts InSight flashlight, pre-ban 20-round magazine, SIGlite night sights.

Mechaniques for the 7.65 mm French service pistol of 1935. The P210 is often called the "SIG-Neuhausen" by American shooters. (Yanks tend to pronounce it "*New*-howzen," but those who've been there say "*Noy*-hawzen.") SIG began arms making in 1860, producing muzzle-loaders, and around 1865 perfected a breech-loading military rifle. It was SIG that manufactured the bolt-action Vetterli rifle, which changed the face of military small arms in 1869; before WWI, SIG was building the Mondragon automatic rifle for international military contracts. The P210, which was born in 1947, was actually SIG's first handgun.

J. P. Sauer & Sohn (not "Sauer & Son," as commonly misquoted in the U.S. gun press) is located in Eckenfoerde in what at the time of their link-up with SIG was known as West Germany. They had produced modern, high quality pistols before WWII. Sauer stood ready in the early 1970s when SIG approached them with a design for a highly reliable, modern service pistol which could be cheaply mass-produced but whose reliance on sheet metal stampings would be antithetical to the "Swiss watch of the pistol world" image that had been so carefully cultivated for the P210. The SIG-Sauer collaboration was born.

SIG absorbed the famous precision gun manufacturer Hammerli in 1971, and annexed J. P. Sauer in 1974. The SIG-Sauer concept was now locked in place.

In turn, SIG-Sauer begat SIG as an American branch for sales and, ultimately, manufacturing. Much assembly is now done at the SIGARMS plant in New Hampshire, and slides and frames for the P226 and P229 pistols are now manufactured there. (That had been true of the P239 as well, and may be again, but at this writing SIGARMS tells me that they are so overwhelmed with production demand for the 226 and 229 that the

9

SIG-Sauers deliver two ingredients of Jeff Cooper's defensive handgun recipe: Accuracy...

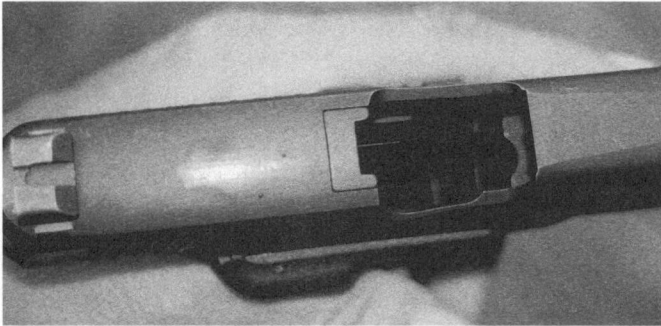

Continuing SIG-Sauer evolution. The breechblock is fitted into the stamped slide of this early P226...

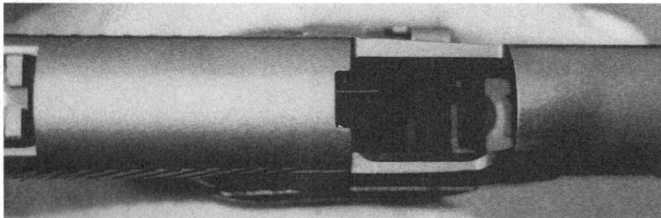

... and milled from a solid block of stainless steel which was then blackened in this later version of same pistol.

... and Power. Speed is up to you.

P239 components are currently being produced by Sauer.) Hammerli, famous for the accuracy of their precision target pistols, produces the barrels. This is doubtless one reason why the SIG-Sauer guns are so accurate. By the 21st Century, the Mauser trademark, the exciting Blaser rifle, and assorted shotguns had also come into the SIG family.

As the years went on, the European Community concept encroached more and more around and even in what some consider the last truly free country on the Continent, Switzerland. There were those among the decision makers at SIG who felt that the future did not bode well for either the political correctness or the profitability of the gun industry, which was only a part of SIG's business. Enter Michael Lueke (pronounced Loo-Kay) and Thomas Ortmeier, German entrepreneurs who had become wealthy in the textile business, establishing the flourishing European firm TWE Technische Weberei GmbH & Co. Rifle enthusiasts and hunters, they at first wanted to purchase the rights to the ingenious Blaser hunting rifle. They ended up with a package deal, purchasing SIGARMS, Blaser, Hammerli, Mauser, Sauer, and the SIG assault rifle line. Those assault rifles are, in my opinion, quite possibly the finest in the world. It is Lueke and Ortmeier who are steering the SIG-Sauer pistols through their second quarter-century of triumphant performance.

FROM THE AUTHOR'S PERSPECTIVE

If we're going to show the subject warts and all, we should do the same with the author. I've been shooting handguns for about 45 years at this writing, and SIG-Sauers, since they came out in the U.S. I've carried the P226 9mm and P220 .45 in uniform, and those and others as a plainclothes officer and off-duty armed citizen. I've taught the use of the SIG on four continents (including the nation of Switzerland). The very first Lethal Force Institute class I taught included one, a Browning BDA .45 in the hands of a capable student of the gun named Shelley Ivey, and the SIG has been a constant presence among the student body ever since.

I've shot matches with them, legally carried them concealed in the four corners of the United States and in between, and monitored their large-scale use in more police departments than I can remember. I've taught shooting classes, and taken them, with the SIG-Sauer. I've come to respect these pistols. The first fully automatic firearm my younger daughter ever fired was a *Sturmgewehr 90*, the splendid Swiss assault rifle produced by SIG, when she accompanied me to Switzerland at the age of 11 while I was teaching there for the International Association of Law Enforcement

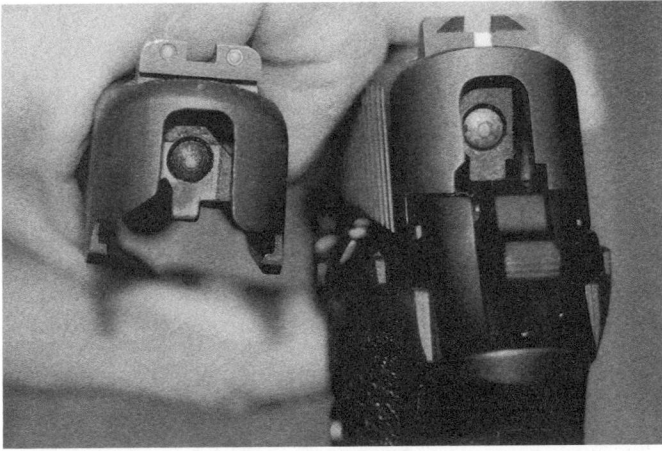

Left, heavy-duty sheet metal stamping was the method of production for this early P226 slide; the slide on the new production pistol at right is machined from a solid block of steel.

Firearms Instructors. When I was gone on long trips, the pistol my gun-savvy wife of 30 years chose to keep at her bedside was my SIG P226 DAO with an extended magazine loaded with 20 rounds of 9mm +P+. You could say that I have a lot of positive memories of SIGSauers.

This book focuses on the development, selection, and safe and effective use of the SIGSauer pistols. There will be only brief attention paid to the other SIG handguns: the legendary SIG-Neuhausen P210, the sweet little Hammerli Trailside .22 which was so particularly well suited to smaller sport shooters, and the latest, the well-conceived and executed SIG GSR 1911. The Mauser M2, which has been marketed by SIG, is left out entirely. Despite its excellent accuracy potential, its poor human engineering, second-rate workmanship, lack of reliability, and minimal projected service life don't make it fit to appear in the pages of book concerning SIG. Also absent is the .22 Mosquito, with which I saw many reliability issues. I don't have any say what goes into the SIG catalog, but I do have a say on what goes into this book, which is why we'll focus on the proven and enduring excellence of the true SIG-Sauer pistols.

Massad Ayoob
Concord, NH, U.S.A.
November, 2003

SIG-SAUER HANDGUNS IN 2014: A TEN-YEAR UPDATE FROM THE CEO

This being a second edition, it seemed logical to start with an update of what's been happening with SIG pistols since the first edition ten years ago. The author sat down with Ron Cohen, CEO of SIG-Sauer, at his executive office in Exeter, New Hampshire, in the summer of 2013, to catch up.

Ron has been in the firearms business officially since the early 1990s, mostly on the defense side and often involving heavier armament than what SIG has traditionally manufactured. In terms of small arms, Ron's career traces back to his time in the 1990s with Kimber. He is remembered there for popularizing the concept of an out-of-the-box 1911 pistol already fitted with the throated barrel, good sights, and beavertail grip safeties most knowledgeable users had been retrofitting to such pistols. Ron remembers now that this concept "was laughed upon by Colt and others, but apparently it was successful." It was in late 2004 that he came to SIG.

"I've worked in firearms construction for 18 years now," he said. "Part of that I was in military service. Firearms have been part of my life since (I was) 6 or 7." His firearms experience as an adult was mostly on the military side, Cohen explains. He says with a smile, "I'm enjoying myself tremendously at SIG."

The SIG's .22 Mosquito is available in a wide array of variations. This is the Mosquito Carbon.

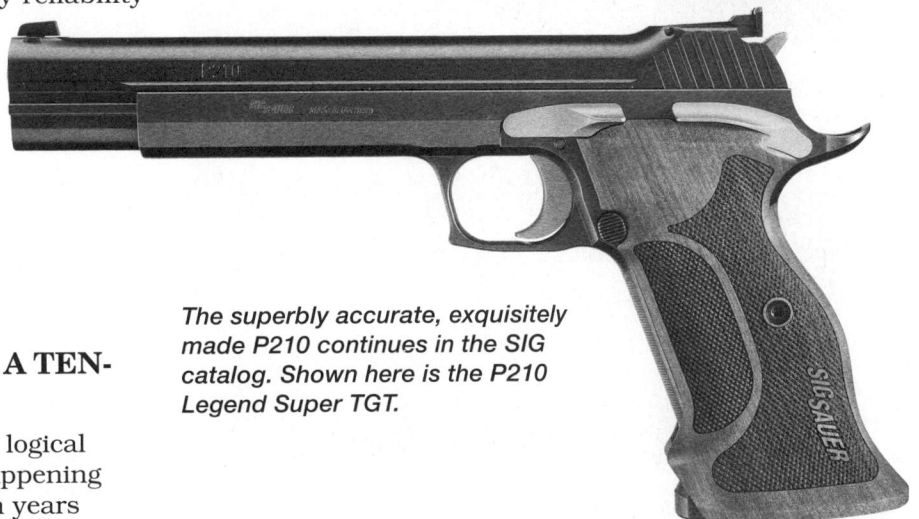

The superbly accurate, exquisitely made P210 continues in the SIG catalog. Shown here is the P210 Legend Super TGT.

1911 production has grown greatly since this book's first edition. These are on display in the luxurious SIG SAUER Pro Shop.

■ The Last Ten Years

"SIG since late '04 has undergone probably most unique transformation of any company in firearms business," Ron told me. His feeling is that the whole industry has changed quite a bit in the last few years in terms of tremendous growth, but he adds that "SIG is unparalleled" in that respect. The SIG facility in Exeter, he explained, "went from light manufacturing to a company that has grown thirteen, fourteen times in the last eight years." While SIG is seen as a Swiss-German entity by most of the world, he reports that the New Hampshire operation is "now manufacturing about 90% of SIG's worldwide output."

Pro Shop is well-appointed, well-stocked, and well-staffed.

Ron explained that while the NH factory used to manufacture only the P226 and P229, it now manufactures some thirteen platforms. Ron explains that these include the 1911 series, the P238 .380, the P938 single action 9mm, and the 516, 716, and 556 rifles. "The list goes on and on," Cohen says proudly. He adds, "SIG (in New Hampshire) went from ninety people in 2004 to (by summer of 2013) about nine hundred people."

The history of Cohen's stewardship is a history of increasing production while maintaining quality. He commented in his light but distinctive Israeli accent, "The theory that you can make in America a Chevy but not a Mercedes, is wrong. SIG, which we like to compare to Mercedes, makes the finest 226s and rifles that can be made, right here in New Hampshire. The growth of the company could not happen without the talent we have found here in the US. The design ability, not just manufacturing – we have, more than any other company, focused on design and new platforms in (both the) rifle and pistol sides. SIG up 'til now grew about twelve times what it was in 2004. We have just warmed up."

Cohen continued, "We have in the pipeline today unique, innovative, transformational products. We are at the beginning, not the end of a certain curve. We cater to the US commercial side, (but still maintain a) strong focus on law enforcement, military special ops ... A lot of growth is from penetrating those special units. (In) our commercial market, consumers are benefiting from the fact that we build a system and test it with the mindset that a Navy SEAL (or) a Secret Service guy will have to use that gun. We want any handgun to last 20,000 rounds. We want to get to 10,000 rounds without a single failure. Some of our clients will take a gun and shoot it 20,000 rounds without fail, which is incredible and unheard of. When we service the special units that way, everyone else benefits. We are continually pushing the quality of firearms that we wouldn't have believed we could do ten years ago."

Ron gives credit to the engineers, the machinists, the assemblers, the quality control personnel, and everyone else involved in manufacturing a SIG. "It has to be perfect," he exclaims whether it's a Navy SEAL or a cop or what Cohen calls "a concerned citizen" who ends up using the given firearm.

Consumer feedback is monitored closely in the executive offices at SIG. "It gives us great pleasure to hear from customers," Ron told me. "One customer in a foreign country (was) issued a specific firearm for political reasons. This man in last six months sits in my office, says he was just sent to combat and prior ditched (his) issue firearm and took a SIG because 'when it counts you need a SIG.' This is a guy telling me our tag line, basically. You go home very happy after a day like that. Our people here live for that day."

Assessing the company's pattern of growth, Ron commented, "I think right now we have grown in the LE sector (domestic), internationally, and US consumer. Growth (among) US consumers is dramatically higher in its pace compared to other sectors, even though these other sectors have grown very well."

▓ Plant Expansion

In the course of preparing this Second Edition, I was given an extensive tour of both the Exeter plant and the vast new plant just outfitted in nearby Newington, New Hampshire.

Explained Cohen, "The Newington facility? In early 2011, we were looking at (moving) everything there. Newington facility is three times bigger than Exeter facility and thus (would have) enabled us to consolidate under one roof. In view of our immense growth in last two years, Newington is now just an expansion of the current operation. The Newington facility is already full. We are now at a point where we are planning future growth of the company beyond both facilities. (The Newington plant) will be the most advanced firearms facility in the US today. The best technology. Top range builders, (and a) unique range."

The CEO added, "We need to use the best technology to make the best firearms. We don't spare a penny when we build the infrastructure. The Newington facility is a celebration of talent and machinery that you cannot find in other places in the US today.

"Most of what we do in Newington is the metal cutting. Rows and rows of CNC, computer numeric controlled machines, the most advanced

The new plant in Newington, NH represents vast expansion of production.

in the marketplace. (Add to that the) ability of our manufacturing department to use these machines to push the envelope. We are constantly evolving our ability to increase output and quality at the same time. As your quality gets better, you can get more parts with less wasted time. Broaching machines, forging machines, grinding machines." Economies of scale and of worker time allow more focus on assembly and inspection.

▓ On The Sig Academy

The SIG Academy has expanded greatly over the years, the jewel in its crown being the sumptuously appointed Pro Shop at the original, expanded Academy building. The training center is, says Cohen, "one of our biggest secrets. The academy in our eyes is the window to SIG. When we are able to bring anybody, concerned citizen or police officer or Navy SEAL or Federal Air Marshal or foreign dignitary, (to) spend half a day with us in the Academy... after that half day (they) get an idea what SIG is about."

And what *do* they find SIG is about? Ron Cohen answers, "Professionalism. High end products, tested and not just sold. You see what the product can do in the harshest testing environment. The Academy is a laboratory for weapon performance, and a showplace for tactics, marrying men and machines, teaching them use of the machines and best tactics for using those machines. Simunition™, live ammunition, video scenarios." He counts off the facilities: "twenty-one ranges, indoor to thousand meter sniper range. We have the shoot houses, streets you can shoot 360 degrees in, amphibious training, you name it we have it. About 2000 students per month, several classes going per day.

We think it is the most advanced training facility now available in the United States."

"We are very proud of the Academy," the CEO concludes. "It's a window to SIG's soul."

Ron explains that the Academy staff consists of about 47 trainers, all top instructors from either SWAT or military special units. "Exceptional human beings," he says with a proud smile. "Not here to show how good they are, but to show you how good *you* can be. My kids go there. My fifteen-year-old daughter can hit head plates at 800 yard like a born sniper. No arrogance, just that we love what we do and spread that to those willing to listen. Concerned citizen classes will be Mercedes and pickups, men and women, young and old. Not intimidating. It's a pleasure. All my kids study there."

Unlike some gun company execs, Ron Cohen carries a pistol himself. When asked what his favorite carry sidearm is, he bursts out laughing. "We always have that dilemma, what do you like? The gun has to fit your hand, not your ego. I personally like a 229 with e2 grips, that's the gun I love, but when I hold a 1911 there's something unique. A 238 makes me feel like an excellent shot. It depends what day you ask me."

■ Into The Future

SIG has obviously changed a lot in the last decade, which logically begged the question, what about the *next* decade?

"I will start by saying I think we're just warming up," began Cohen. "We're competing in a world of large companies that have been doing what they're doing for many generations. SIG is in many ways the newcomer. Our investments in engineering as a percentage of our business is double that of the average gun company in America. In our case, if you look at our last five years of new products we've brought to the table, you can get a glimpse of what we're looking at for the future. The MPX (in submachine gun and carbine formats), which I think will shape the next twenty years of sub-guns, I think that product is going to be in essence a new category of business in firearms. (In the conventional paradigm, the) consumer can buy handgun, rifle, shotgun. MPX is not clear to me what it is when I come into the store, is it handgun or rifle or both? In essence, a (semi-automatic) carbine that can be shot as a pistol and converted to SBR (short barrel rifle) and multiple calibers. It

A vast array of expensive state of the art machinery has enhanced quality while keeping cost down, says SIG SAUER's CEO.

This barrel will soon be inside a new SIG SAUER pistol.

is the first piston-driven submachine gun the world has ever seen. It is a fine-tuned race car that you can only enjoy when you actually operate it.

"Our marketing program will be changing directions in ground breaking ways that I think will take SIG to another category of business we have not been in. I think we are in the forefront of a major revolution in our rifle development. We view SIG as starting new categories of business. We are excited about the future domestic and abroad, and expect to expand those horizons tremendously in years to come."

2014 SIG-SAUER UPDATE: THE WORD FROM THE INSIDERS

When I was at the plant in New Hampshire researching for this second edition of *Gun Digest Book of SIG-Sauer*, I made a point of picking the brains of engineers, production executives, and marketing people as well as the CEO. I had questions about quality control, product decisions, and more. What follows is an extrapolation of the answers I received.

■ What Are The Most Popular Sigs In The Us Today?

The answers I received frankly surprised me. The top-selling SIG lines in the USA today at this writing turn out to be, in order:

1. P238
2. P938
3. P226
4. P229
5. 1911

Itty-bitty .380s are huge in this country right now. Witness the spectacular sales of the Ruger LCP, the Kel-Tec P3AT, and the S&W Bodyguard380 and more. With good sights and its good 1911-ish trigger, the .380 caliber SIG P238 is obviously getting its share of that market. This pistol is

essentially a reprise of the old Colt Mustang. Indeed, it apparently inspired Colt to re-introduce the Mustang .380 itself, and to follow recently with a polymer frame version.

"Slim-nine" pistols chambered for the 9mm Luger cartridge are likewise huge – witness the rush to buy S&W Shields and Springfield Armory XDS pistols. Since many shooters are inclined toward non-polymer designs, perhaps I shouldn't have been so surprised that the sweet little single action 9mm P938 is now in second place for SIG.

■ What's Up With Sig 1911S Since The First Edition?

The 1911 line at SIG has added a conventional "John Moses Browning-lookin'" slide on several models. They also have versions with the rounded butt pioneered by Ed Brown with his Bobtail design. However, the distinctive "SIG-style" slides of Matt McLearn's original interpretation of "a 1911 by SIG" still account for about 80% of the SIG 1911 production line.

I learned that the single most popular finish of the many that SIG has taken to offering across their handgun product line is, for the 1911 series, Cerakote in Flat Dark Earth. Their Scorpion line has been a big hit among 1911 enthusiasts, too.

■ What Caused The P250'S Growing Pains?

If you've read the new chapter on the polymer-framed P250 pistol, you're aware that there were problems which had to be worked out with design improvements. Sources at SIG confirmed that, as I experienced, the problems centered on trigger bar design; early in production, the company found in endurance testing that the single "lowest round count part" was the trigger bar spring. That has been tweaked and fixed, I'm told. In current P250 production, the part most likely to break and need replacement is the slide catch lever, where breakage has been found to sometimes occur starting at around the 14,000 round level on the subcompact .40 calibers, which apparently receive the most brutal parts buffeting during the firing cycle.

I've noted elsewhere that I don't care for the P250's rear sight design, which can't be drifted for point of aim/point of impact correction if windage is off. One senior SIG engineer explained that the sight sits in a U-notch instead of a dovetail because it performs the additional function of holding the extractor assembly in place. This allows a firing pin safety weighing only .7 grams, while that of the P-series is around eleven grams. Making this part lighter allows the P250 to pass "drop tests" from higher thresholds.

I asked why no major police departments seem to have bought the P250 and was told that the P250 has been adopted for the Netherlands' national police force. What, I asked, was the story behind the P250 being dropped at the last minute by the Federal Air Marshals, who had announced the intention of adopting it to replace their P229s in .357 SIG? I had been told by some among the Feds that trigger bar breakage in the .357 SIG P250s had been the problem, but SIG execs told me their understanding was that the FAMs preferred the self-cocking mechanism of their familiar P229 traditional double actions to the double action pull for every shot which characterizes the P250. The Federal Air Marshals are, after all, famous for what many

consider to be the fastest and most challenging qualification course in law enforcement today. The air marshals wound up replacing their old P229 .357s with identical new ones.

The P250 has not been a best-seller, but is selling steadily enough to remain in the line. Subcompact, compact, and full size P250 pistols remain in production in a full range of calibers: 9mm Luger, .40 S &W, .357 SIG, and .45 ACP. Indeed, by the time this second edition hits print, there should be a .380 ACP P250 on the market. At the request of a minority of potential purchasers, SIG also offers a P250 variation with a manual safety, which is mounted on the slide. Many feel a thumb safety lever is unnecessary on a hammer-fired, double action only pistol such as the P250. One rationale for the manual safety version is the handgun retention factor; a manual safety slows down a gun-snatcher's ability to instantly shoot the legitimate owner with his or her own gun.

■ P228 And M11A1?

The once-popular P228 double stack compact 9mm, adopted years ago for plainclothes military police work as the M11, has been phased out in favor of the M11A1. The original P228, I was told, "is not an active product, though the original M11 will still be made in Germany as needed for the Department of Defense." On the market now for consumers is the replacement gun, the M11A1. Where the P228 had a two-piece carbon steel slide, the slide of the M11A1 is a single piece of stainless steel. This 9mm comes standard with fifteen-round magazine and short trigger reset. The internal phosphating that helped distinguish the earlier M11 from the commercial P228 remains in the M11A1. One SIG insider describes the M11 as "essentially, a P229, non-railed."

The New Jersey State Police were for some time the only troopers in the US still carrying 9mm as standard, and they famously adopted the P228 and gave it rave reviews. A SIG executive tells me that NJSP has replaced the P228 with the P229 with light rail.

The folded slide design of the original double action SIGs has at last been consigned to the museum; a SIG exec assured me that by the time this second edition came out, the last folded slide will have been produced.

■ What's Made Where?

The long-ago promise that the classic German-made SIGs would eventually be manufactured in the US has apparently been fulfilled. Of the pistols now in the SIG catalog, I was told that the only ones now being made in Europe are the .22 Mosquito, the .22

Creative use of modular construction allows an almost infinite variety of tactical settings at SIG SAUER Academy.

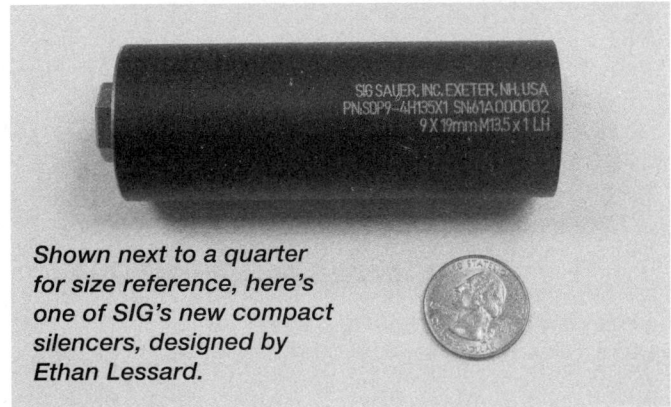

Shown next to a quarter for size reference, here's one of SIG's new compact silencers, designed by Ethan Lessard.

Ethan Lessard of SIG SAUER, widely proclaimed a genius by other engineers in the firearms industry. He was the lead designer of the new P320.

caliber 1911 (which comes with internal firing pin safety), the great old Swiss-designed P210, and the X-series Mastershop deluxe pistols.

■ P-Series Single Actions...Why?

Beginning with the P220 SAO, single action only SIG-Sauers were built on double action pistol frames. The design was originally for MARSOC, the Marine Special Operations Command. This RFI (request for information) eventually led to the adoption of an updated Colt Government Model .45 for the USMC, but it turned out that the P220 SAO fit the needs of the shooter who liked the idea of a cocked and locked single action .45 auto, but for whatever reason did not care for the 1911 design. These pistols turned out to work remarkably well.

A P226 SAO was introduced in 2013, in 9mm. One exec says, "I see its market as competition. It's an advanced user's gun, a niche gun."

■ What Led To The P290 Rs?

The original P290 pocket pistol generated some complaints about inadvertent magazine drops, sharp edges on the slide stop, and hammer bite. The RS variation answered those concerns, and also

gave re-strike capability in the event of a misfire.

The P290 RS, when I visited, was scheduled to be introduced in 2014 in caliber .380. The rationale was not only milder recoil, but a much lighter recoil spring which would allow the slide to be more easily operated by users with weak or injured hands.

■ What's The Story On Quality Control?

We hear complaints about SIG QC on gun forums, notably sigforum.com, now and then. However, the same is true of the brands of choice at coltforum.com, smith-wessonforum.com, etc. It is the nature of brand fans to imprint on the first ones they fell in love with, and sometimes be overly critical of later models. In the ten years between these two editions, I did personally encounter more defective SIGs than in the past: one P250 with broken trigger bar, another that came with the wrong magazines, and a couple of P-series guns whose sights weren't right.

The SIG folks I talked to were adamant that proportional to their large production volume today, their quality control and frequency of repair is better than ever.

■ Why Sig Silencers?

With a lot of its business going to free world government entities including our own, SIG was getting an increasing number of tenders for large numbers of firearms equipped with sound suppressors. Having learned in the past that outside vendors don't always deliver products that are "up to spec," the company decided to make their own. One of their most brilliant American engineers, Ethan Lessard, led the design team.

Introduced in 2013, the already extensive SIG-Sauer line of sound suppressors includes rifle and handgun models, centerfire and .22 rimfire, and even a short "can" for SIG's new 9mm submachinegun. The .22 unit has a particularly ingenious Lessard design feature which allows unusually easy cleaning.

Chapter 1
The SIG P220

A writer owes his readers a disclosure as to his biases toward this and his prejudices against that. Let me open this chapter by confessing that the P220 is my very favorite SIG pistol, and indeed, one of my all-time favorite handguns. Extraordinarily accurate, very reliable, and easy to handle and shoot, one of the P220's cardinal attributes is the cartridge for which it is chambered: the .45 ACP.

The gun was introduced in 1976, the first of the SIG-Sauer line. Essentially designed by Schwe tzerische Industriale Gesselcraft and manufactured by Sauer, it was chambered initially for the 9mm Parabellum cartridge and then almost immediately for .45 ACP and .38 Super for the American market. The 9mm P220 was immediately adopted by the armed forces of Japan, and of Switzerland, where it remains the standard military sidearm of Europe's safest and most neutral country.

In 1977, Browning contracted with SIGSauer to produce the gun under their name as the BDA (Browning Double Action). It was introduced as such to the American market, where it received a mixed welcome. The gun experts loved it, instantly appreciating its smooth action, good trigger, reliability, and ingenious design. The purchasing public was less enthusiastic. They associated the Browning name with traditional, Old World guns crafted of fine blue steel and hand-rubbed walnut. Here was a modern pistol with flat gray finish and checkered plastic stocks, with an aluminum frame and a slide made of metal folded over a mandrel. It was as if Jeep had produced a fine four-wheel-drive vehicle under the aegis of Rolls-Royce: though the quality and function were there, the "look," the *cachet,* were not what the buyers associated with that particular brand image.

Before long, SIG had decided to import the guns into the United States on their own and under their own name, establishing SIGARMS in Virginia. (Much later, SIGARMS would move to Exeter, New Hampshire.) It was at this point that SIG sales apparently took off. If the public would buy a machine that was rugged and precision-made, but not fancy, from Jeep but not from Rolls-Royce, then the same public would buy a rugged, precision-made but not fancy P220 that was marked SIG-Sauer instead of Browning.

The Huntington Beach, California Police Department adopted the BDA in .45 ACP and had great luck with it. Their experience was widely publicized in both gun magazines and law enforcement professional journals. In the late 1970s, only a minority of American police carried semiautomatic pistols. Many gun-wise cops wanted auto pistols and didn't trust the 9mm ammo of the day; they wanted .45s. Until the P220, the only gun that fit the bill was the Colt 1911 type pistol. Some forward-thinking departments adopted the Colt – LAPD SWAT, several small departments in California, a couple of county sheriff's departments in

Arizona – and many more made the Colt .45 optional. However, the mainstream of American police decision makers were leery about authorizing their personnel to carry a pistol that was perpetually cocked, and some worried that having to manipulate a safety catch would get in the way of a quick response when the officer needed it. The Browning BDA was obviously the answer, and changing its name to SIG P220 didn't change that answer. When the BDA as such was discontinued, Huntington Beach recognized that the P220 was exactly the same gun, right down to complete parts interchangeability; they bought P220s and used them interchangeably with the BDA pistols already in hand.

Police interest in autos was soaring. One sore point was that Americans habituated to American-style guns wanted a magazine release that worked quickly with a push-button behind the trigger guard. The BDA and the first SIG-Sauers had the European style magazine release, a spring-loaded securing clip at the heel of the butt. Police firearms instructors tended to be the department gun buffs, familiar with the 1911 and similar pistols from their time in other provinces of the world of the gun, and they clamored to SIG-Sauer for a pistol that ejected its magazines in the fashion to which they were accustomed. After all, speed of reloading was seen as one of the cardinal advantages of a semiautomatic pistol over a revolver; it was natural for the cops to want the fastest magazine release and therefore the fastest emergency reload possible.

SIG-Sauer listened and responded. In the early 1980s, they redesigned the P220 with an oval, grooved button behind the trigger guard to dump the magazine. While they were at it, they changed the shape of the grips, bringing the lower rear of the grip frame backward into an arch that widened toward the bottom. It filled the hand more substantially than the thinner and flatter-backed grip shape of the original P220. The change was analogous to Colt's switch in the

Top: The dust cover of P220 ST is grooved to accept accessories such as this InSights M3 flashlight.

The author's Langdon Custom P220 ST is shown here with stocks by Nill.

1920s, at the request of the U.S. Army Ordnance Board, from the flat-backed mainspring housing of the original 1911 pistol to the arched housing of the 1911A1.

It was what the cops wanted, and SIG P220 sales skyrocketed. The .38 Super had never been popular in America except for a brief period between its introduction in the late 1920s and when it was eclipsed by Smith & Wesson and Winchester's joint introduction of the .357 Magnum revolver and cartridge. Only a few hundred .38 Super BDAs had been sold, and the caliber remained similarly moribund in the P220 configuration. While all P220 sales to the world's military had been in the 9X19 NATO chambering, I'm not aware of a single American police department that adopted either the BDA or the P220 in 9mm or .38 Super (though Secret Service would look very closely at the latter). No, it was the .45 that American cops wanted.

With the changed grip shape and side-button release, the new gun was designated the P220 American.

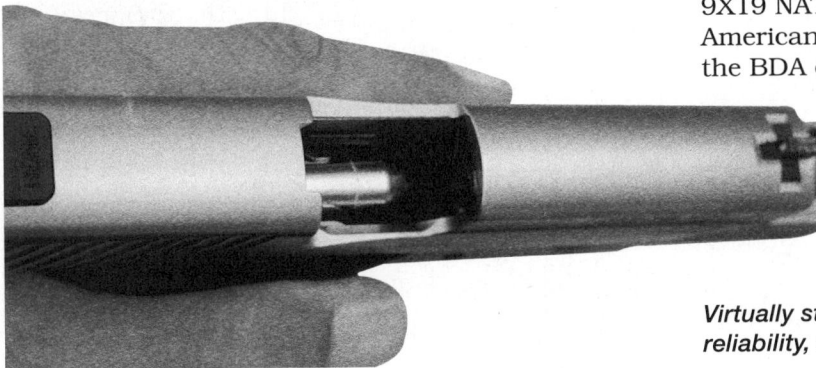

Virtually straight-line feed is a key to the PP220's famous reliability, especially with hollow-point ammunition.

This standard P220 has earned the author's smug smile. The one-hole group in the neck of target was made by 12 200-grain bullets fired in less than 20 seconds from 7 yards, including a reload.The tight cluster in the target's chest was from one-shot draws averaging around a second at 4 yards. This is proof of the P220's shootability.

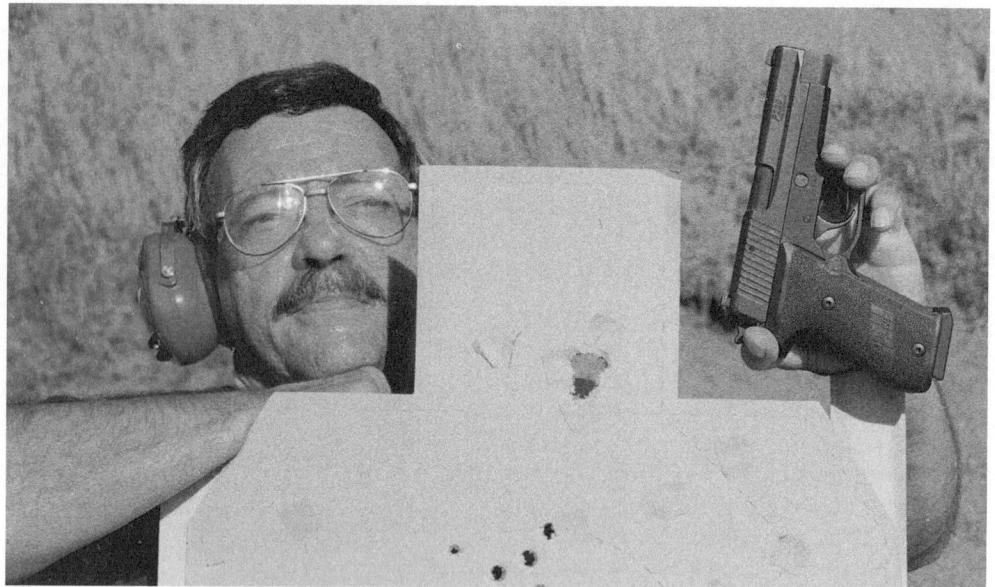

IDPA Stock Service Pistol Master Steve Sager tries his hand with a P220. The spent casing visible above his head shows immediacy of the shot, but the muzzle is still on target.

Accordingly, the original would become known as the P220 European or P220-E. Its sales in the U.S. would wither and die, with the American style roaring forward in sales to police and civilians alike; the 1911's influence was even stronger in the latter sector of the U.S. handgun market.

Countless police departments, including the state troopers of Texas (who used it exclusively) and of Arizona, adopted the P220. The latter gave their highway patrolmen the choice of the eight-shot .45 P220 or the 16shot 9mm P226. The overwhelming majority chose the P220 .45.

In 1988, the FBI for the first time authorized rank and file agents to carry semiautomatic pistols. At first, only two guns were authorized, both in 9mm: the SIG and the Smith & Wesson. Shortly thereafter, the forward-thinking head of the Firearms Training Unit at FBI's Academy in Quantico, John Hall, convinced the Director to also approve the .45 ACP in the same two already-

approved brands of pistol. FBI agents rushed to purchase their own SIG P220s, which were both more compact than the all-steel Smith & Wesson Model 645 that had been introduced in 1983, and much lighter. The P220 .45 was the choice of Special Agent Edmundo Mireles, who had emerged as the hero of the infamous shootout in Miami, which had led to the Bureau's approval of semiautomatics. Mireles had ended that gunfight with .38 Special bullets delivered to the head/neck area of the two cop-killers involved, and was clicking his revolver's hammer on six spent cartridges at the end of the drawn-out death duel.

P220 ATTRIBUTES

The P220 always fit most hands well. It always had good sights compared to most of its competition. And, of course, there was the reliability factor. The gun was and is extremely reliable.

Right: *Whether steel- or alloy-framed, P220s are accurate with a variety of ammunition. +P should be used sparingly in aluminum-framed guns.*

Below: *The accessory rail of the P220 ST is a great addition.*

The P220, even with an aluminum frame and powerful .45 ammo, is comfortable for a week of intensive firearms training.

But the gun had other advantages, too. High among these was the double-action first shot mechanism. Police chiefs had been leery about carrying cocked and locked guns. The long, heavy double-action pull required to initially unleash the firepower of the P220 was much like that of the revolvers that were so much a part of their institutional history. Cops in general and police chiefs in particular were and still are much more comfortable with a double-action like the 220.

Most 1911 pistols of the period were not "throated" by their manufacturers to feed wide-mouth hollow-point bullets, the choice of most police and gun-wise private citizens. Engineered with a nearly straight-line feed, the P220 was reliable with almost every hollow-point bullet.

There was also the accuracy factor. The SIG-Sauer pistols are famous for accuracy across the board, but the P220 may be the most accurate of them all. I have twice put five rounds from a P220 into one inch at 25 yards. Both times, the ammunition was Federal 185-grain JHP, which the manufacturer used to mark on the box as "Match Hollow Point." It was certainly truth in advertising. One of those guns was a well-worn P220 European, the other, a brand new P220 American. I later hit the 1-inch mark at 25 yards with a 5-inch SAO P220 and inexpensive MagTech 230 grain FMJ.

Almost every credentialed tester has noted the P220's extraordinary accuracy. In his book *The 100 Greatest Combat Pistols*, defensive firearms expert Timothy J. Mullin had this to say about the P220. "All SIG pistols and products are fine weapons, but this one is particularly impressive. My groups were so remarkable that I tested again at 25 and at 50 yards – and the results were just as superb. I placed five shots into a little more than 2 inches, and I pulled one of those shots. Four shots went into roughly 1-1/4 inches." (1) A fan of SIG's compact single-stack 9mm, Mullin added, "Although the P220 is not as good as a P225, I would rate it the top weapon that I tested *in .45 ACP."* (Mullin's emphasis.) (2)

My friend Chuck Taylor is one of the leading authorities on combat handguns and the author of a great many articles and multiple books on the topic. When he wrote the fourth edition of *The Gun Digest Book of Combat Handgunnery* he had the following to say about the P220 .45.

This LFI student has topped his class more than once with his ergonomic SIG P220 American. He is about to fire all center hits strong-hand-only...

...and does the same weak-hand-only, with good recoil control. Note spent casing passing the target to the right of the gun.

"First appearing almost two decades ago as the Browning BDA, the P220 in its current American version is regarded by many as being *the* state-of-the-art .45 auto. Indeed, its popularity is exceeded only by that of the Colt M1911 Government Model, whose king-of-the-hill status the P220 is now seriously challenging, especially in law enforcement circles." Chuck continued, "The P220 is a simple design, perhaps as simple as a handgun can be and still work. Its human engineering is excellent because, like its baby 9mm brothers, the P225 and

P226, its controls are placed where they can be readily operated, something exceptional for a DA auto. Furthermore, its mechanical performance leaves nothing to be desired. It is probably the best DA self-loader around...In summary, the P220 is an excellent example of how good a DA auto can be. As such, it is well worth its not-inconsequential price and clearly a handgun upon which one could with confidence bet his life." (3)

Many double-action semiautomatics had a DA trigger pull that was heavy, rough, or downright

Current magazines make the P220 reliable with eight in the stack and a ninth in the launch tube.

lousy. The SIG's double action pull was excellent, probably "best of breed." It was the standard by which the competition was judged. Once the first shot had been fired, it went to single-action, where the trigger press was a clean, easy 4 to 6pounds or so. The distance the trigger had to move forward to re-set the sear was just enough to give a buffer against unintentional discharges under stress, but not so great that it appreciably slowed down the shooter's rate of fire.

With a 4.41-inch barrel, the SIG was a little longer in that dimension than the 4.25-inch Colt Commander, but more than half an inch shorter than the 5-inch Government Model. The Commander, originally introduced in lightweight format in 1949, weighed 26.5 ounces unloaded and held the same number of .45, .38 Super, or 9mm rounds as the P220. Later offered as the steel-framed Combat Commander, the Colt put on an additional 10 ounces in that format. The lightweight Commander was dubbed by one of its greatest advocates, Col. Jeff Cooper, as "a gun designed to be carried much and shot seldom." Most who had fired it considered it much more unpleasant to shoot than its big brother, the full-sized, all-steel Government Model.

Thus it was that the cops and the shooting public were delighted to discover that the SIG P220, which like the lightweight Commander had an aluminum frame, wasn't anywhere near as difficult to shoot as the alloy-framed Colt. A major reason for the perception of the Commander's vicious recoil was that, until the 1990s, its manufacturer furnished it with a short, stubby-tanged grip safety that bit

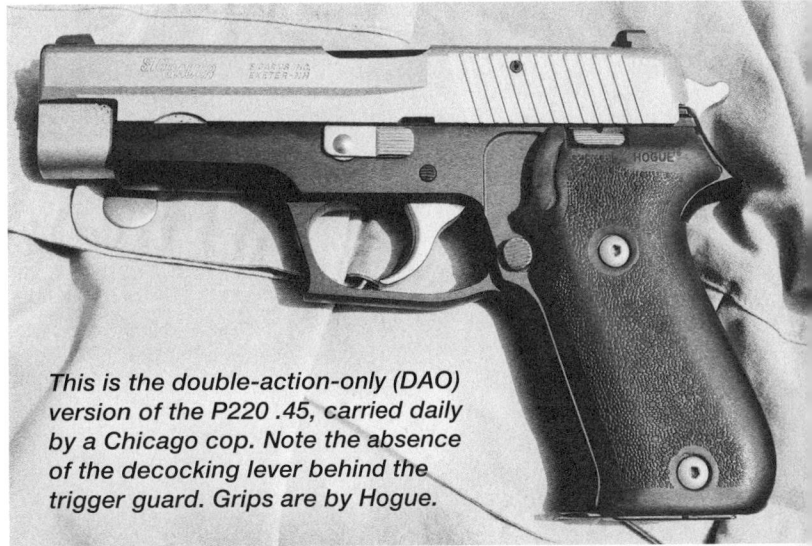

This is the double-action-only (DAO) version of the P220 .45, carried daily by a Chicago cop. Note the absence of the decocking lever behind the trigger guard. Grips are by Hogue.

painfully into the web of the hand whenever the gun was fired.

By contrast, the P220 was much rounder and more friendly to the hand. Nothing bit the shooter. In the P220, the low-pressure .45 cartridge simply drives the slide back with a gentle bump. Even though the slide of a 1911 pistol sits lower to the hand and should jump less since it has more leverage, anything that causes pain to the hand will magnify the shooter's sense of recoil, and increase his likelihood of flinching and blowing each shot.

The P220 weighs a tad less than a lightweight Commander, 25.7 ounces unloaded. Yet most officers found it at least as pleasant to shoot as the full size 1911A1 in the all-steel configuration, which weighed some 39.5 ounces. Only when a

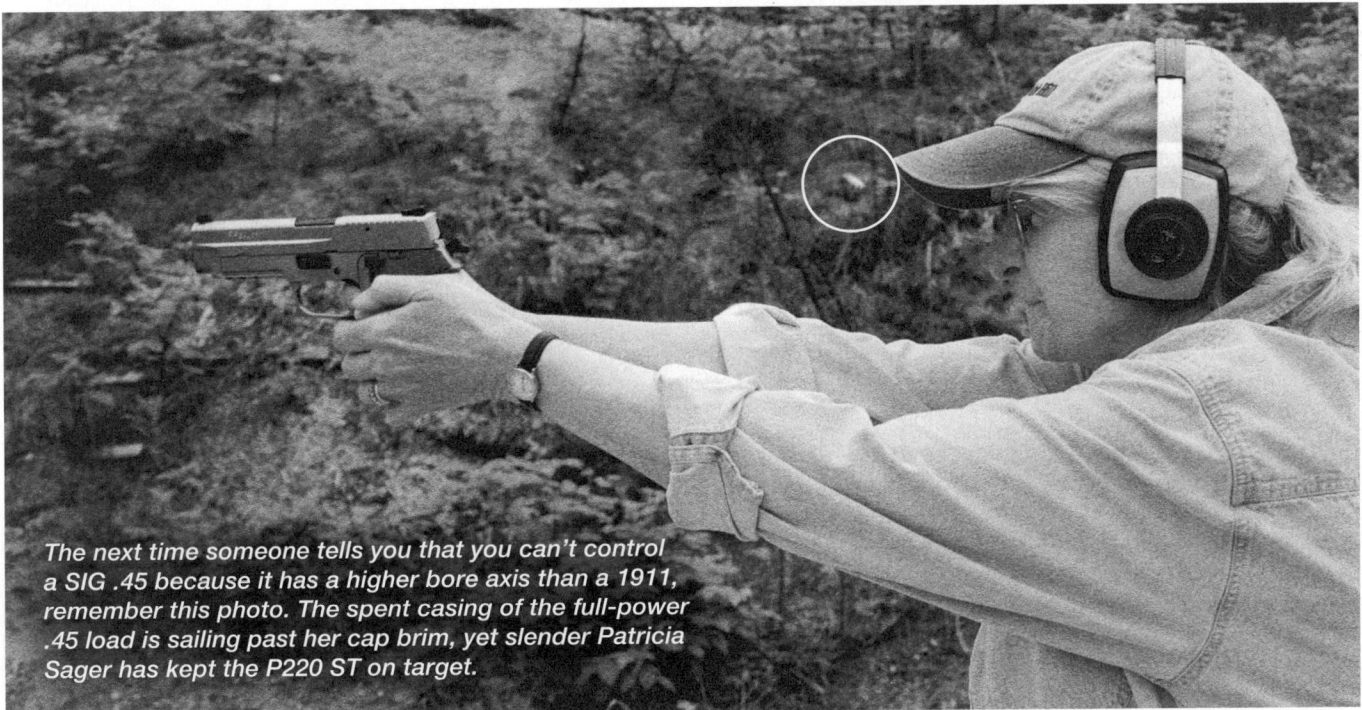

The next time someone tells you that you can't control a SIG .45 because it has a higher bore axis than a 1911, remember this photo. The spent casing of the full-power .45 load is sailing past her cap brim, yet slender Patricia Sager has kept the P220 ST on target.

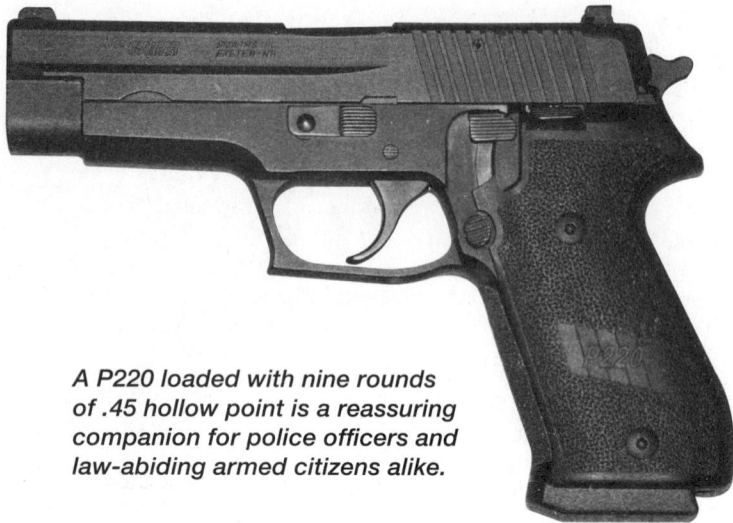

A P220 loaded with nine rounds of .45 hollow point is a reassuring companion for police officers and law-abiding armed citizens alike.

custom gunsmith (or, beginning in the 1990s, the manufacturers) put a beavertail grip safety on the lightweight 1911 did it become as comfortable to shoot as a P220, and allow the shooter to take advantage of the reduced muzzle jump potential afforded by its lower bore axis. However, none of this changes the other SIG attributes that made the P220 a favorite.

A lightweight service pistol is especially important in law enforcement. The duty belt carries a great deal of equipment. The author has seen duty belts weighing in the 15- to 20-pound range once festooned with multiple handcuffs, a full-sized baton, heavy flashlight, portable radio, and ammunition. The pistol is a significant part of the load, and any reduction in weight is appreciated. The weight of the duty belt is one reason why back problems in general and lower back problems in particular seem to be an occupational hazard of the street cop.

The pistol in its uniform holster rides near the edge of the hip, and on some individuals with some uniform designs, can directly contact the ileac crest of the hip. The potential for fatigue and discomfort is obvious. Reducing the weight of the duty .45 from 39.5 ounces to 25.7 (the same round-count of the same ammunition adds the same weight to either) results in a 13.8-ounce weight saving – almost a pound – at a critical point.

Now, let's look at plainclothes wear, whether in a detective assignment or off duty. The dress type belt, even a dress gunbelt, does not support the weight of the holstered gun as efficiently as the big, 2-1/4-inch-wide Sam Browne style uniform belt. A heavy gun becomes all the more noticeable. For generations, officers carried little 2-inch .38 caliber revolvers as off-duty guns, simply for their light weight and convenience. However, they paid the price of a caliber that offered minimum acceptable power, especially when the ammunition was fired

from a short barrel. They paid the price of a reduced in-gun cartridge capacity, only five to six rounds. They paid the price of a gun that kicked hard despite that minimum acceptable power level, and a gun that was difficult to shoot fast and straight, particularly at small targets or at longer range.

Now, the P220 .45 gives the plainclothes officer a much more attractive option. While not so small overall as a snubby .38, it is very flat. It fires the much more powerful .45 ACP cartridge, but despite its greater power it kicks less and is more pleasant to shoot than most snubbies. It is about the same weight as the six-shot Smith & Wesson Model 10 or Model 64 Military & Police revolver with a 2-inch barrel. And, of course, it is much faster to reload, and its flat magazines are much more discreet and comfortable to carry than speedloaders for a revolver when concealment is the order of the day.

With an inside-the-waistband holster and proper clothing, the P220 virtually disappears into concealment. With a well-designed scabbard riding on the outside of the belt, it is almost as easy to hide. The fact that a single pistol with which the officer is intensively trained could be used on or off duty, in uniform or in plainclothes, is another big factor in the P220's favor when police departments look at purchasing new sidearms.

The P220-E is a particular favorite of mine. Back in the 1980s I discovered that, just as the flat housing of the original 1911 pistol fits my hand better than the arched housing of the later A1, the slimmer, flatter-backed shape of the original SIG P220 grip frame seemed more comfortable in my hand than that of the later P220.

However, there is another reason I was partial to the P220-E. In the Northern New England area where I have spent my now almost 40 years as a police officer, it is not uncommon for the wind chill factor to bring the temperature to 30 degrees below zero or worse in deep winter. This requires heavy gloves. I had found over the years that bulky gloves could sometimes cause a shooter to unintentionally activate a side-mounted magazine release button. This did not occur with a gun that had a butt-heel magazine release, like the P220-E or the BDA that preceded it. I special-ordered a P220-E .45 from SIG, and was told that it would probably be the last one brought into the country. (I'm told that the firm later changed its mind and brought in a few more in dribs and drabs, as the limited stateside demand warranted.)

This became my favorite winter gun for many years. On patrol when department regulations allowed it, and on my own time always, the P220-E was part of my cold-weather gear. Since the P220 American's magazine was the same as the European's but with four engagement holes cut in the sides (two on each side, to mate with the side button mag release, which could be easily converted for left hand use), the new magazines fit my old gun. The reverse was not true. This was because the European style mags did not have a cutout in which the side-button mechanism of the P220 American could engage. Much later, when SIG's current eight-round mags came out with bumper pads running front to back, it turned out that they would not be compatible with the European or BDA magazines. This was because the rear of the extended bottom of the magazine could not engage the butt heel release device.

The butt-heel release is a second or so slower for speed reloading than the American style. Certainly, there are situations in which a second can make all the difference; Americans are acutely conscious of that, and this is why SIG makes the American style P220. However, I found that with heavy snowmobile gloves on, the cruder gross motor movements of pushing back the latch with the free hand thumb and ripping the spent magazine out were actually more easily accomplished than finding the magazine release button with a thumb encased in a heavy glove that blunted the sense of touch and limited the thumb's range of movement. In short, in heavy winter garb, I was able to reload the P220-E as fast, or very slightly faster, than the P220 American.

THE P220'S "OTHER" CALIBERS

While we Americans have directed most of our attention to the .45 caliber P220 – after all, the .45 ACP has been called "the classic American cartridge" – the P220 has racked up an enviable reputation in its other calibers as well. On more than one occasion I've taught in Switzerland. There are some police departments there that issue the P220 in 9X19mm, though the higher capacity P226 seems to be far more common in Swiss law enforcement. More to the point, though, the P220 9mm has been the national standard Swiss military sidearm for many years.

Switzerland is a nation of shooters. It is well known that the Swiss militia constitutes the entire able-bodied male population of the nation (Swiss women may join voluntarily, though it is not required) and that all are issued what may be the finest assault rifle in the world, SIG's Stg.90.

The *Sturmgewehr 90* is a superb, state-of-the-art assault weapon. However, the Swiss public takes marksmanship as one of their national sports, and most of that marksmanship is done with military weapons of various ages. Virtually every Swiss village I passed through had a 300-meter rifle range, and the ranges stay in constant, heavy use. In rifle matches, the ancient Schmidt-Rubin 7.5 mm straight-pull bolt-action rifle is still used to compete against the ultra-modern SIG Stg. 90.

I say all this to lead up to a point. The Swiss have a lot of pistol matches, too. As you might expect they fare well in ISU (International Shooting Union) Olympic-style target sports, and also have a well-established contingent of practical shooters who belong to IPSC (the International Practical Shooting Confederation). However, a good deal of their handgun competition also involves national standard military weapons. Over the course of the 20th Century, Swiss military-issue handguns have included such fabulously accurate weapons as the Luger pistol, the exquisite SIG-Neuhausen P210, and only since the latter quarter of that century the SIG P220 9mm.

And there was one thing I couldn't help but notice. The 9mm P220 keeps up with the famously

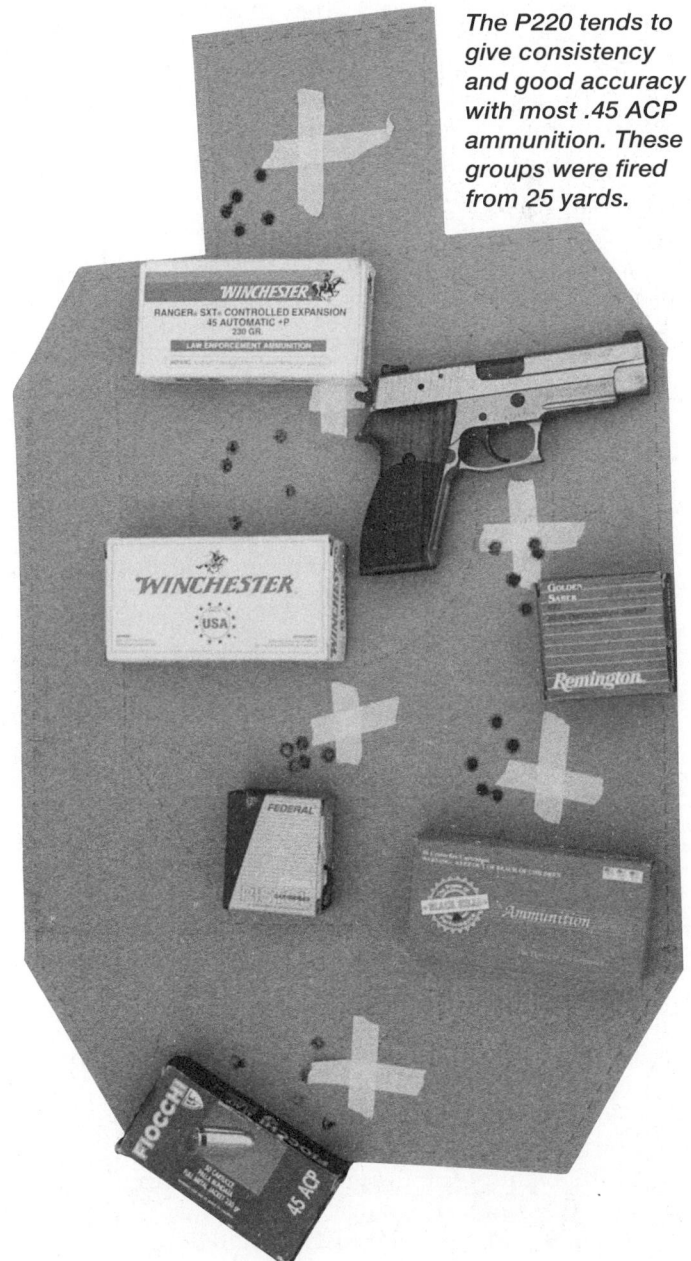

The P220 tends to give consistency and good accuracy with most .45 ACP ammunition. These groups were fired from 25 yards.

accurate P210! This, clearly, is testimony to the P220 9mm's match-grade accuracy, which is achieved without compromising total reliability, even with some very old pistols that have fired countless thousands of rounds over the decades.

The .38 Super P220 did not prove popular at all. In the United States, at least, it had always been a specialist's cartridge. Handgun enthusiasts appreciated its flat trajectory. Handgun hunters appreciated its inherent power. Cops in the Depression years liked its deep penetration against criminals' "bullet-proof vests" and automobiles of the period. But no one liked its mediocre accuracy.

The reason was that the .38 Super was not a true "rimless" auto pistol cartridge, but instead featured a semi-rimmed case. From its introduction in the late 1920s until the coming of the SIG-Sauer engineers, Colt and every other manufacturer cut the chambers of their .38 Supers to headspace on the rim. The chamber in SIG-Sauer P220 in .38 Super was cut to headspace at the case mouth, which allowed more consistent and solid chambering. Thus did the Browning BDA/SIG P220 become the first truly accurate factory-produced .38 Super pistol. The same headspacing was developed by gun barrel genius Irv Stone, the founder of Bar-Sto, and when put in 1911 target pistols resulted in the .38 Super cartridge's renaissance in the shooting world, specifically in practical pistol competition.

It has been reported that the P220 has been produced in very small quantities in caliber .30 Luger. I cannot speak to its accuracy as I have never seen one, let alone tested one. I am not aware of any nation or agency that has adopted the P220 in that caliber. Thus, its accuracy remains an unknown quantity, at least to this author.

IDIOSYNCRASIES

In earlier models, there were some specimens in .45 caliber which did not feed one particular cartridge in one particular situation. The round was the old "flying ashtray," a short and very wide 200-grain hollow-point from CCI Speer, who called it at various times the Lawman load and the Inspector load. It was notorious for jamming 1911 .45 pistols. The SIG would normally feed it just fine, but with some of the seven-round magazines, if the pistol was reloaded from slide-lock, the short Speer 200-grain would take a little dip coming off the magazine's follower and strike low enough on the feed ramp to cause a six o'clock jam.

Most simply got by with another brand of ammo. My own solution was to load my personal P220 with the eight of the flying ashtrays, one in the pipe and seven in the mag, and then load the spare magazines with some other type of JHP round. My

P220 *never* failed to feed this infamous gun-jammer once it was loaded into the P220 and the first round was chambered.

Over the years, the problem has resolved itself with new designs. The current 200-grain CCI Speer .45 offering, the Gold Dot bullet, does not seem to have any problem feeding in late model SIGs. I think it's a combination of the improved fourth-generation P220 .45 magazine, and better feeding characteristics of the Gold Dot 200-grain bullet compared to the conventional jacketed hollow-point which preceded it.

Chuck Taylor is a contemporary and observed the same thing. He wrote in his edition of *The Gun Digest Book of Combat Handgunnery*, "My P220 shoots very well indeed, with three-shot Ransom Rest 25-meter groups averaging slightly over 2 inches. I've also had no functioning problems whatsoever with the gun, although in some of the earlier versions, some problems were reported with several styles of JHP bullet. SIG Sauer, to their credit, immediately relieved the front of the magazine body to allow better bullet clearance, which solved the problem nicely." (4)

P220 .45 MAGAZINES

About those four generations of P220 .45 magazines. They go like this:

First generation: Seven-round BDA/European style. Will only work in P220s with butt-heel magazine release.

Second generation: Seven-round P220 American style. Will work in American, European, and BDA model .45s.

Third generation: The so-called "DPS Magazine." A P220 American mag with the same flat-bottom floorplate as the first two generations, but modified in spring and follower to take an eighth round. These were created for the Texas Department of Public Safety when they adopted the P220 American .45, and reportedly, Texas DPS had great success with them. Personally, I have never trusted a magazine designed for seven rounds, which then had an eighth forced into it; we fool Mother Nature at our peril.

The eighth cartridge in a magazine originally designed for seven put the rounds so tightly in the stack inside the magazine that there was no flex in the spring. This meant that if the P220 was reloaded with the slide forward, either in administrative loading getting ready for duty or in a tactical reload with a live round already in the chamber, the shooter really had to *slam* the magazine in to make certain that it locked in place. After experimenting with the DPS magazine, I went back to the earlier ones. Police had already cautiously waited for decades to switch from revolvers to autos because of fears of reliability.

Their mantra had been, "Six for sure beats 14 maybe." My reasoning as to P220 magazines was similar: "Seven for sure beats eight maybe."

Fourth generation: Eight-round current production. These are unquestionably the finest .45 caliber magazines ever made for the P220 pistol. They are crafted of stainless steel, always a bonus when a gun and its spare magazines are carried in hostile environments, which can be rain and snow attacking guns holstered outside the clothing, or heat and humidity and salty, corrosive human sweat when the pistol is carried concealed. Moreover, the Gen Four SIG P220 .45 magazines are extended very slightly at the bottom, into a hollow floorplate. This does two good things. First, the buffer pad on the floorplate makes magazine insertion easier and more positive, especially under stress. Second, the added space inside the floorplate allows the eighth round to be stored there without too rigid a spring stack or undue pressure on the magazine springs. These are what I now carry in my P220 .45.

A word on aftermarket magazines. I normally trust only the magazines the gunmaker sells with its firearms. For the P220 .45, I trust Sauer-made SIG magazines and I trust Mec-Gar magazines. This may be seen as a redundancy, since Mec-Gar produces SIG's magazines for them. The currently imported Novak's P220 magazine seems to work well. ACT in Italy produces it. While marketed as an eight-round mag and having an extended floorplate, I've nonetheless found that some will comfortably hold all eight and some are better carried with seven rounds, at least when new.

Many shooters have found full P220 .45 mags hard to unload, at least for the topmost cartridge or two. Here's the secret. Hold the loaded magazine in one hand and pinch the thumb and forefinger of the other hand beneath the nose of the cartridge on top, applying upward pressure. Now use the thumb of the magazine-holding hand to push the cartridge forward. It will come out much easier. Repeat if necessary for the next cartridge or two; after that, spring pressure will be relieved and the thumb alone will be able to slide the rest of the rounds out easily.

VARIATIONS

Though many considered the P220 a compact handgun, many who owned them wanted one even smaller for deeper concealment. This wish was granted by SIG in the form of the excellent little P245, a pistol that differs sufficiently from the P220 that it is treated separately in this book.

Stainless steel P220s have also been produced. Basically the same gun as the original, but heavier, they differ only in handling qualities and, of course, in adding one more option of corrosion resistance to the many finishes which are discussed in the segments of this book devoted to accessories and customizing.

The first of these guns was the P220 Sport, introduced to the public in 1999. I was at a conference of the firearms press conducted by SIGARMS in conjunction with the NRA Show and Annual Meeting in Philadelphia in 1998, where we were given a chance to play with advance versions of this gun.

Fitted with a long muzzle weight-*cum*-compensator, and with an all-steel frame of stainless alloy, this handsome pistol sports a 5.5-inch barrel and weighs some 44 ounces. With the added weight and the comp, recoil and muzzle jump are greatly reduced. The exquisite accuracy of the earlier P220s was clearly present in this .45. It was introduced with grooves on the dust cover (front of frame) to accept additional weights and other accessories proprietary to SIGARMS.

Three generations of the SIG P220 .45. From left: P220 "European," P220 "American," and P220 ST.

27

I liked the gun, but found it a bit big for my tastes and needs. Like many, I just said, "Make us a regular P220 with this frame, and groove the dust cover to accept more common accessories, like the M-3 flashlight."

SIG listened. The 21st Century saw the P220 ST, exactly the gun described above. Though the first models had reliability problems (and, I thought, below-P220-standard accuracy), this was traced to the use of a stainless steel barrel. SIG solved the problem by installing their conventional chrome molybdenum steel barrel within the stainless slide.

Now, we had a truly meaningful option within the P220 line. There were those of us accustomed by years of wearing Colt Government .45s that weighed 39 or so ounces, and didn't mind the fact that this was the weight of the all-steel P220 ST. In return, we got the recoil reduction and added durability that came with all-steel construction. Before, SIG engineers had been leery about recommending +P .45 ACP ammo for these guns. I saw very few aluminum P220 frames crack after continuous shooting with +P, which brings the ACP up to a power level comparable to a full-power 10mm Auto cartridge, which is infamously brutal to even full-size .45 caliber guns. With the ST variation, my sources at SIG tell me that they just don't see a problem.

References

1. Mullin, Timothy J., "The 100 Greatest Combat Pistols," Boulder, CO: Paladin Press, 1994, P.315.
2. *Ibid. P.316.*
3. *Taylor, Chuck, The Gun Digest Book of Combat Handgunnery, Fourth Edition, Iola, WI: Krause Publications, 1997, P.224-225.*
4. *Ibid., P.225.*

Early P220 European. Note pointed-tip hammer, butt heel magazine release, no magazine release button on side.

MODERN CLASSICS: THE SIG P220 .45

The gun that made the .45 Auto truly acceptable to modern police, accuracy and reliability have made this a classic sidearm with many roles. A gun that will last for generations, it has experienced multiple generations itself.

Introduced in 1976 as a single-stack 9mm with a butt heel magazine release, the SIG-Sauer P220 was quickly adopted as the standard service pistol of Switzerland. There was, of course, a home court advantage: SIG stands for Schweizerische Industrie Gesselschaft, which in direct translation from German means Swiss Industrial Company. The P220 was designed by SIG in Switzerland, and manufactured by Sauer of Germany. With its long history of peaceful neutrality secured by a citizenry heavily armed by its government, Switzerland has a similarly long history of choosing particularly fine small arms.

Within a year, Browning had contracted with SIG to build this pistol in more powerful chambering, branding it as the Browning BDA, which redundantly stood for Browning Double Action. Where the BDA captured interest stateside was with the .45 ACP version. Over the years, a handful of cops had been permitted to carry cocked and locked 1911 .45 autos, but most chiefs (and a good number of handgun-owning citizens) were horrified at the concept of a duty handgun carried visibly cocked in its holster. The BDA of course lived up to its name. It was a double action design, meaning that the hammer could be down at rest in the officer's exposed holster, like the service revolver it replaced. That put some fears "at rest," too. The BDA was approved by forward-thinking police departments such as that of Huntington Beach, California. (Double action S&W .45 autos, starting with the Model 645, were still years away, as was the Glock, whose G21 in the same caliber would not appear until 1990.) Indeed, the success of the SIG-made double action .45 very likely hastened the introduction of that first S&W .45 auto. Thus, one can honestly suggest that the SIG P220/Browning BDA was the pistol that made the .45 auto generally acceptable in mainstream American law enforcement.

Browning's customer base had been accustomed to finely polished blue steel and handsome checkered walnut; the flatter, grayer finish and plastic grip panels of this European-made service pistol apparently caused a mass outbreak of cognitive dissonance among Browning's fan base, which ignored the BDA in droves. SIG responded with a corporate shrug, returned the name SIG-Sauer P220 to the pistol, and continued to market it, under its own name.

In both police and private citizen circles, the desirability and therefore the popularity of the P220 were greatly enhanced by SIG's introduction of what was then called the P220 American in the early 1980s. The key change was replacing what was perceived as an "old fashioned, European style" butt-heel magazine release with one more in keeping with Yankee tastes: a push button located behind the trigger on the left side of the frame, exactly where had been on the 1911 since, well, at least 1911. (And on the German Luger pistol before that.)

At the same time, SIG changed the grip configuration of the P220. The result was a little bit fuller grasp, with a curve that descended outward on the lower rear edge. As an analogy, consider the original slim-handled P220 with the butt heel release as comparable to the original 1911 pistol, with its flat mainspring housing, and the more curving back of the P220 American as the analog to the arched mainspring housing of a 1911-A1. In any case, this redesign kicked popularity of the P220 .45 into high gear.

Over the years, the P220 design slowly, incrementally matured. Some subtle changes were made in the 1990s to the fire control system. The company switched from hollow pins and folded metal slides to solid pins and milled steel slides. It took them until the 1990s, but they finally figured out that the magazine release springs on the 220 American were a little light, and prone to accidental dropping. The sharply pointed hammer spur of the early P220, which could dig mercilessly into "muffin tops" when the gun was holstered tight to the waist, gave way to a gentler, rounded profile.

In the late 1990s and even more in the two thousands, SIG experimented with expanding the line. There were short barrel versions, the P245 and the P220 Carry. There were five-inch "longslides." (Yeah, I know...but since the P220's traditional barrel length has been 4.4" since its inception, for that gun a five-inch barrel *does* make it a longslide.)

The P220 has been produced on special order with a magazine disconnector safety, not a standard item on SIG-Sauers by any means.

Midway through the first decade of the 20th century, the firm debuted the P220 SAO. Yep, you read it correctly: SAO, as in Single Action Only. It was the first P220 to be so configured, and also the only one to be commercially offered with a manual thumb safety. This pistol's is ambidextrous and frame mounted, pressed down for "fire" and up for "safe." On two out of three, I found it stiff to on-safe left-handed, but for off-safe on either side and for on-safe with the right thumb, they always seemed perfectly adjusted. I thought these were

P220 European.

The classic: The aluminum-frame P220 American .45. Note different grip shape, and 1911-style magazine release, compared to original European style.

Current P220 ST with all stainless steel frame, Nill grips, and an upgrade by Ernest Langdon.

P220 ST fitted with SIG's own .22 LR conversion unit.

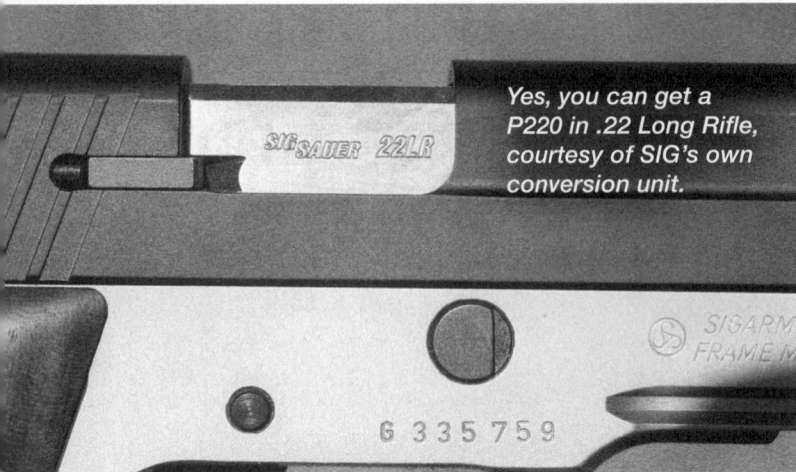

Yes, you can get a P220 in .22 Long Rifle, courtesy of SIG's own conversion unit.

P220 .22 conversion unit, seen from the front.

neat pistols, and bought more than one of them. Because of the big trigger guard, it was one single action auto I found particularly comfortable with in winter with heavy gloves on. A gun-wise friend who works as an appellate attorney in New Mexico has one of these, and it has become a staple in his "concealed carry rotation."

A big advance was the P220 ST, introduced early in the 20th century. Shortly before the turn of that century, SIG had produced the all-steel P220 Sport with 5.5-inch barrel. It shot sweet, but just seemed to be too *big.* The market was much more receptive to the P220, which had the conventional service pistol's 4.4-inch barrel length. Its solid steel frame wasn't any big deal to those of us who'd grown up carrying all-steel five-inch 1911 .45s, and it had the added advantage of being railed for light/laser attachments.

The weight of the P220 ST dampened muzzle jump. It also made the gun rugged enough that SIG-Sauer was finally comfortable approving it for +P .45 ACP ammunition, something I don't believe they ever did for the aluminum frame P220s.

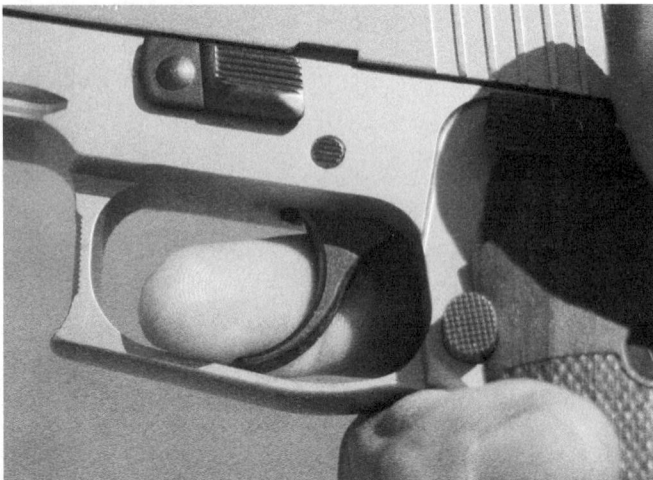

Short trigger installation by Ernest Langdon has reduced and improved the trigger reach on this late model P220.

P220 CALIBERS

The single-stack 9mm version of the P220, of course, won the title of official Swiss military sidearm. Oddly enough, Japan adopted the exact same gun in that caliber as a military pistol.

I'm told that a handful of these pistols have also been produced in .30 Luger. Never saw one, though, and SIG couldn't find me a 7.63mm Luger barrel for a P220 when I tried to get one.

The Browning BDA was produced in .38 Super... for only a few hundred units, I'm told. It was the first *accurate* factory-produced .38 Super, because it was the first to headspace on the case mouth as is customary for auto pistol cartridges, instead of on the "semi-rim" with which that cartridge was designed, and for which it was headspaced, circa 1929. Today, all .38 Supers are made that way. Some American style P220s were subsequently produced for the Super round, and were reportedly tested by US Secret Service, but this caliber just never caught on in this particular gun.

Once the P220 came out with a stainless steel frame as the P220 ST, it was obvious it was going to be able to withstand hotter loads. There are SIG fans, and there are 10mm Auto fans...and, inevitably, there was some crossover between the two. At the spirited shooting forum **www.sigforum. com,** demand arose for a P220 ST chambered for the potent 10mm. It has been answered by Bruce Gray of GrayGuns (grayguns.com). I first got to know Bruce when he and I shot together on the "pro tour" with the Heckler & Koch factory team under John Bressem. A fine man, and a very skilled shooter and instructor, Bruce is also one of the top pistolsmiths around for SIG-Sauers. At this writing, Bruce is taking orders for a limited number of custom SIG-Sauer P220 ST pistols that will leave GrayGuns chambered for full power 10mm Auto.

Finally, SIG-Sauer itself offers a .22 Long Rifle conversion kit for the P220. I ordered one as soon

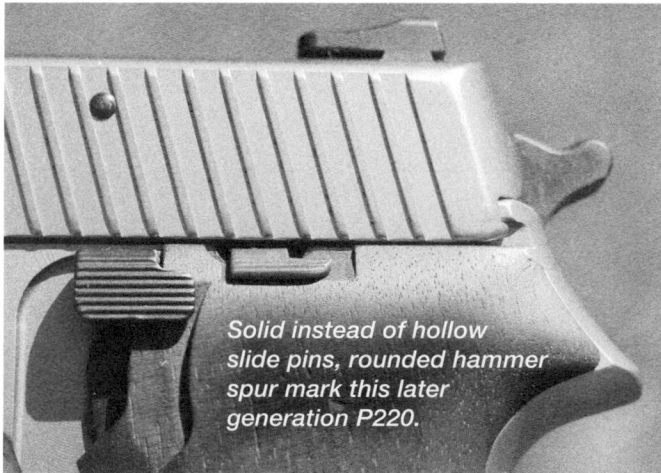

Solid instead of hollow slide pins, rounded hammer spur mark this later generation P220.

Light rail on this recent model P220 is a useful update.

as I saw it, and am glad I did. I have been extremely pleased with its reliability and accuracy.

All that said, though, the SIG P220 is seen primarily in the United States as a .45 auto. Of the many law enforcement agencies that adopted it or approved it over the years, while a great many issued (and many still issue) the P220 in .45 ACP, I don't know of a single one that has issued it as a required duty pistol in any other caliber.

P220 RELIABILITY

Two questions tend to come up in regard to any defense/service pistol that fires the .45 ACP. One is, "Will it feed every conceivable .45 ACP hollow point round?" The other is, "Is it rated for Plus-P ammunition?"

I found over the years that about the only JHP load with which the SIG .45 wouldn't run just fine was the old 200 grain Speer load, known as the "Inspector" back in the day. Its nose cavity yawned so wide that gun writer and reloading expert Dean Grennell famously nicknamed it "the flying ashtray." Exacerbating the problem was that the short, wide bullet made for a short, relatively wide *cartridge*, in terms of overall dimensions.

Even so, in all the P220s I shot, that load would only jam when you were reloading from slide-lock. The topmost cartridge – not always, but now and then – would catch on the feedway. I found that if I inserted a magazine with the slide closed, then racked the slide to chamber that topmost round, it would go into the chamber just fine. I'd then withdraw the magazine and top it off. The gun would then fire all eight rounds with perfect reliability. (Remember, we only had seven-round magazines for these guns back then.) Since that Speer load was "the hot setup" back in the eighties, I carried it loaded with that ammo with perfect confidence and then simply used a different JHP round in the backup magazines.

The P220 .45 magazines evolved over the years, going through at least four generations. First came

was the smooth-front mag, needing no cutouts for a side release since it was the catch at the heel of the butt which held it in place. The next evolution was the first magazine for the P220 American. It had notches on both sides along its front edge (to allow for the magazine release catch being reversed for southpaws). This P220 American magazine would work just fine in a BDA or P220 European pistol with the butt catch, but not vice versa, since the earlier mags had no notches with which to engage the internal portion of the P220 American's side-button magazine release. The next generation had a different follower to bring the seven-round capacity up to eight cartridges, and was known among SIG fans as the DPS magazine because it was created for the Texas Department of Public Safety when that agency adopted the P220 .45 as standard issue. You can't fool Mother Nature: I found it very difficult to get the eighth round into a DPS magazine, and a nightmare to get it back out without the amateur's technique of hand-cycling the live cartridges through the pistol's action. The cramped stack of cartridges

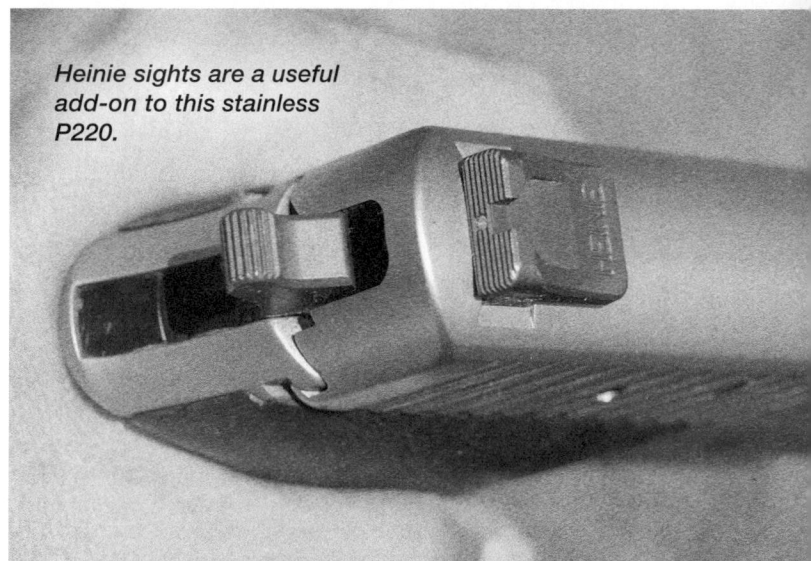

Heinie sights are a useful add-on to this stainless P220.

also eliminated the last bit of flexibility inside the magazine, and you practically had to hammer a full DPS mag into a P220's butt to get it seated. SIG quickly realized that this was unacceptable, and evolved the current magazine, lengthened with a protuberance that doubled as extra space inside and a bumper pad outside, as its floorplate. This accommodated the eighth round very comfortably, and is my choice today in any American style P220. It won't work with the old BDA or P220-E pistols, though, because the magazine extends down below the locking point of those old guns' butt-mounted magazine catches.

P220 ACCURACY

All who've seriously tested the P220 .45 have come away with an extremely positive impression of its inherent accuracy. (There was a small batch of early P220 ST pistols that got out with crappy barrels, but SIG got on top of that and rectified it quickly.) I've found several 4.4-inch and 5-inch P220s that would put five shots in an inch or slightly less at 25 yards from a solid bench rest. Usually, those groups were accomplished with 185 grain Federal JHP, a load that used to be marked "Match Hollow Point" on the package, for very good reason. I've seen one P220 SAO break that magic inch at 25 yards with generic 230 grain hardball.

PROVEN WHERE IT COUNTS

The P220 is a shootable, ergonomic pistol. It has no sharp edges to bite the hand. A few years ago, if for no other reason than to prove it could be done, National IDPA Stock Service Pistol Champion Ernest Langdon shot a National event with a SIG P220, firing double action every first shot, in the Custom Defense Pistol division against all the easy-trigger

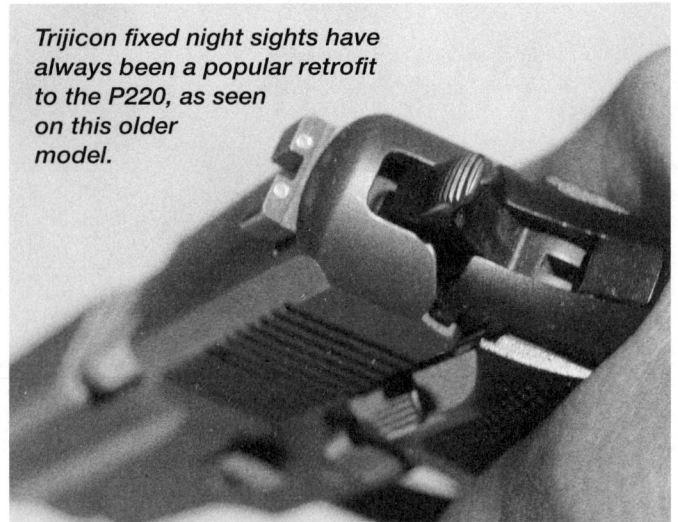

Trijicon fixed night sights have always been a popular retrofit to the P220, as seen on this older model.

1911 pistols. Darned if he didn't win *that* national championship with the SIG, too.

Properly executed, a combat match is a microcosmic test of street survival abilities. When those situations have come up in the real world, the SIG P220 has likewise acquitted itself well. With swift, sure handling, a high order of reliability, and accuracy-delivering ergonomics, the P220 has saved many a good guy's – and gal's – life.

One of our graduates in California was a police officer who was sucker punched by a burglary suspect. She fell to a sitting position, and saw the man reaching for a 9mm in his waistband. Recently trained to fire from awkward positions, she cleared her P220 from its duty holster and, before he could shoot her, center-punched him with a 230 grain hollow point. He collapsed, and died; she survived with a broken nose.

Another officer was stepping out of his patrol car when a suspect swung a semiautomatic rifle up at him. Ducking for cover, the lawman fired from a bent-over position with his P220 horizontal to the ground.

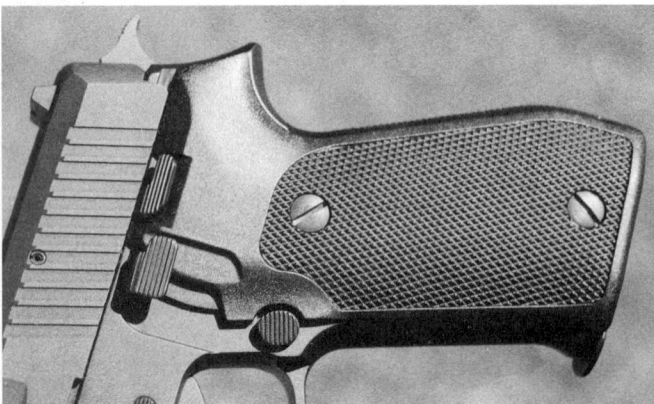

The first P220 Americans still had the pointy tip hammer, but a larger butt with more curve where it met the heel of the shooter's hand, and of course the push-button magazine, were distinguishing features.

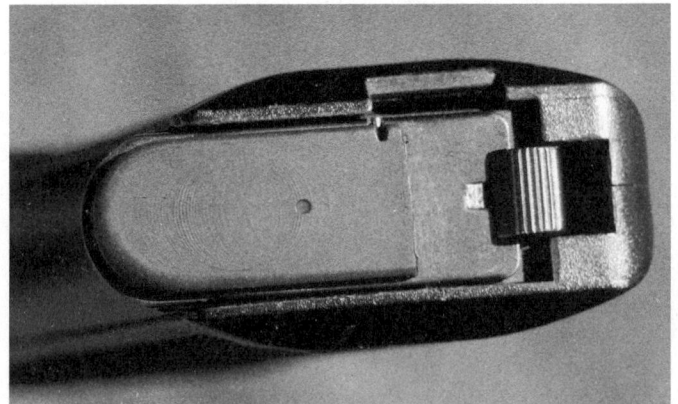

Butt heel release catch was a distinguishing feature of the original P220 and the Browning BDA. Magazine buttplate pad has had to be cut to allow the butt catch to work.

No matter: its fire went true to the center of the gunman's torso. The perp was down and done, and the officer survived unscathed.

In Florida, a friend of mine who is a K9 officer cornered an armed man who decided to shoot it out. The lighting conditions were poor, but the natural pointing characteristics of his P220 paid off, and my friend killed the assailant before the man could shoot him.

Private citizens have likewise used the SIG P220 to good effect. A powerful, enraged man in Louisiana overpowered a police officer and was in the act of taking his service pistol, with the obvious intent of murdering him with it. An armed citizen intervened, drawing his personal SIG .45 and killing the madman with accurate fire from his P220, saving the officer's life. In New Hampshire, a citizen saw a man shoot a local police officer in the back. The citizen grabbed the officer's P220 .45, and shot and killed the suspect. The officer's wounds proved to be unsurvivable, but the private citizen's ability to use the officer's P220 .45 effectively took a cop-killer permanently off the street, only moments after his murderous act.

IN SUMMARY

Trends have lately gone toward polymer pistols in both the law enforcement sector and the world of the law-abiding armed citizen, and even SIG is aggressively marketing its own ingenious polymer handgun, the P250. Nonetheless, the SIG P220 .45 is present in several forms on SIG-SAUER's website and in their catalog. A great many law enforcement officers still carry it by choice, as do many private citizens.

Tastes and trends change. But when something works well for its intended task...well, that just never changes.

Yep, that's a cocked and locked SIG P220 .45, the SAO (Single Action Only) variation.

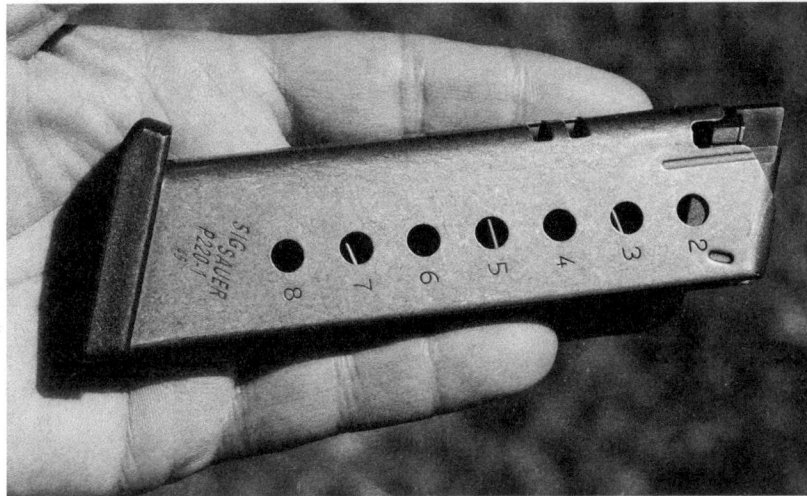

Current generation P220 magazines are extremely reliable, come with bumper pads, and hold 8 rounds, with one more in the pistol's chamber.

A recent variation of the P220 with beavertail grip frame.

The SIG P220 Compact is an extremely viable carry gun.

Caught by fast lens in mid-firing cycle, Mas finds the P220 conversion unit "a hoot to shoot."

.22 LR CONVERSION UNITS FROM SIG-SAUER

These things work, and they come at just the right time in the "ammo drought."

A few years ago, at a SIG gun writers' conference in Exeter, NH, I was delighted to see that the company was introducing .22 Long Rifle conversion kits for their popular classic series pistols. Ammo prices had gone through the roof, and something that would give cheap trigger time was most welcome. The panic buying and hoarding that came along later, after the election of Barack Obama, led to an ammo

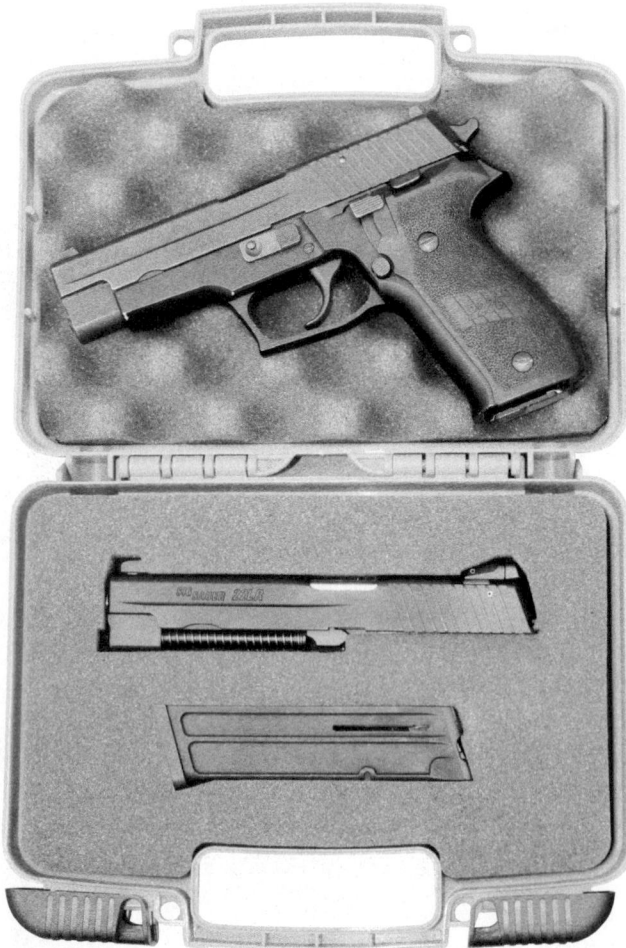

SIG P226 9mm, above, with .22 conversion unit.

Converted P220 was tested with these two flavors of Winchester .22 LR. Surprisingly, high speed outshot the T22 load, but both functioned 100%.

drought that made these devices even more valuable. .22 ammo prices may be up some, but at least you can usually *get* the stuff.

I ordered one each, for my P226 9mm and my P220 ST .45. Testing the conversion on the 9mm for another magazine, I experienced zero malfunctions using Remington Golden Bullet ammo, which a friend at the factory had recommended. At 25 yards, groups ran right about two inches. This particular SIG does just over an inch at that distance with the 9mm ammo it likes best, Federal 115 grain 9BP hollow point and Winchester 147 grain subsonic JHP, and I was perfectly happy with two-inch groups for cheap practice with the .22 conversion unit. Reliability was flawless.

I threw the P220 conversion unit on my ST (stainless) .45 frame and, for the test, returned to the 25-yard bench with a couple of Winchester rimfire loads. The pistol had experienced a very few stoppages when breaking it in with a different brand, but the conversion unit liked the Winchester ammo and ran 100% on both flavors. T-22 target ammo, standard velocity with a 40 grain lead bullet, did exactly two and a half inches for all five shots, but showed more promise since four of those were in 1.30" and the best three in 1.15". High Velocity .22 LR actually shot better, with all five shots in 1.45" and the best three of them in the same 1.15" as the T-22's tightest three-shot cluster.

Neither unit came out of the box shooting spot on to the sights. The P220 unit, for instance, went high left. Fortunately, these come with neat adjustable sights and it's no trick at all to zero them.

With a lighter slide operable by the feeble .22's recoil, the pistol with the conversion unit doesn't have exactly the same balance it has in "fighting configuration," but it does have the exact same trigger pull. Right up until the recoil starts, it's extremely relevant training. Draw to the shot. Precision shot placement. Coming up from low ready. And don't forget reaction targets: "plinkin' steel" for .22 rimfire costs *much* less than for centerfire, and is much more conveniently portable because it's so much lighter. These .22 conversion units are also great for introducing new shooters to your centerfire SIG-Sauer pistols.

Each conversion unit comes with one magazine built of sturdy synthetic. While the slide won't automatically lock back empty, you can lock it back manually for inspection when you go downrange or are ready to pack up for the day.

At a reasonable suggested retail, these SIG-Sauer conversion units come at just the right time to help you alleviate the ammo crunch and the ammo price hikes at the same time. If you shoot regularly, the ammunition savings will quickly pay for the conversion unit.

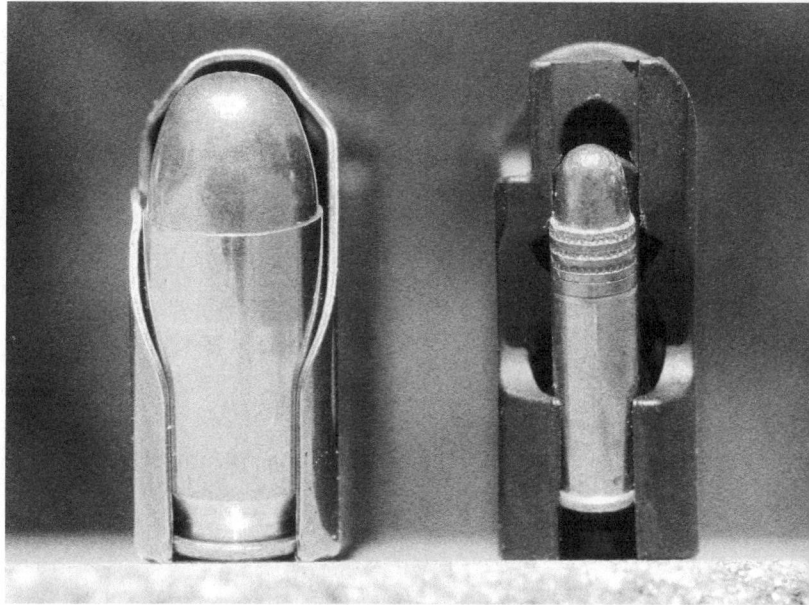

230 grain hardball .45 ACP training round in P220 mag, left, dwarfs .22 LR round in conversion kit's magazine, right. .22 offers super-cheap shooting and virtually non-existent recoil, plus much quieter report.

Target loads (left) and high velocity (right) yielded identical "best 3" group measurements from 25 yards.

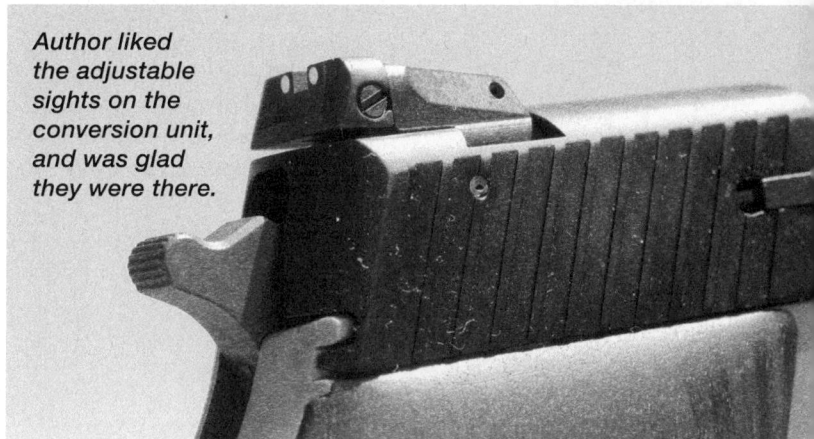

Author liked the adjustable sights on the conversion unit, and was glad they were there.

Chapter 2
The SIG P225

SIG-Sauer's second pistol was the P225. The German government was looking for a compact law enforcement pistol in 9mm Parabellum, and high magazine capacity was not a priority. SIG's answer, the P225, became a modern classic overnight. It was widely adopted in German law enforcement, and struck a responsive chord in the U.S. market as well.

Mechanically, Wiley Clapp in *The Gun Digest Book of 9mm Handguns* aptly described the P225: "The 225 is a version of the 220 in which the length and height measurements have been reduced. A 225 will measure about three-quarters of an inch less in length and about a half inch less in height. Aside from the more compact dimensions, the 225 differs in the contour of the grip and trigger guard. The grip has been altered in an altogether pleasing fashion. It is slightly slimmer, but more significantly, it is attractively rounded at the lower rear of the butt. The overall impression is quite different from the 220." (1)

The P225 has been made only in one caliber; 9mm Parabellum. It contains eight rounds in its single-stack magazine and a ninth in its chamber. The magazines are slim, flat, and easy to conceal. So, of course, is the gun itself.

WHEN HANDLING CHARACTERISTICS DECIDE THE ISSUE

Numerous law enforcement agencies have adopted this gun in Europe, and many have authorized it in the United States. It is particularly suitable for officers with small hands. The shorter reach to the trigger is a boon for shooters with short fingers.

In a federal lawsuit entitled *Judy Cangealose v. Department of Justice, Janet Reno, and FBI*, I was hired on behalf of a female FBI agent trainee who was fired for failing to qualify with her issue service weapon at the FBI Academy in Quantico. At the time (and now, for that matter) Cangealose would have had the option of carrying a compact 9mm pistol such as the SIG P225 or the S&W Model 3913 while on duty. One element of the lawsuit was that she should have been allowed to use such a pistol at the Academy. Instead, the Bureau issued Cangealose – a slender, petite woman with very small hands – a relatively huge, heavy 10mm semiautomatic. She could not reach the trigger in a manner that gave her proper control of the pistol.

In preparation for the trial, I took Ms. Cangealose to the range with, among other guns, a SIG-Sauer P225. She fired a number of exercises from the required FBI qualification curriculum. The P225 fit her perfectly, and she passed with flying colors. I testified to this under oath in deposition. Knowing where it was going, FBI and the Department of Justice settled out of court for a significant amount of money just before the trial got underway.

The P225 was by no means limited to petite females in its appeal. A number of highly trained men find its ergonomics, even more than its compact size, make the P225 not only their favorite SIG, but sometimes, their personal carry gun.

Tim Mullin raved about the P225 in his book *The 100 Greatest Combat Pistols*. "The P225 is an excellent weapon," he wrote. "Because of the single-column magazine, the grip on the P225 is sufficiently shallow and narrow to allow you to get a good grip on a weapon (unlike the P226), and it has a good feel to it... All in all, I would rate this pistol very highly." (2)

Roy Huntington has been a well-known commentator on police firearms and the law enforcement training scene for many years. His 20-year career with the San Diego Police Department

encompassed a number of assignments, including a stint on the Harbor Patrol, where he became the model for a character in a Joseph Wambaugh novel. Now retired from police work and serving as the editor of *American Handgunner* magazine, Roy worked on a department that limited pistol choice to 9mm at that time and issued 147-grain subsonic ammunition, but gave the officers a number of weapons choices within those parameters. The SIG-Sauer pistol is extremely popular among San Diego cops who buy their own guns. In fact, the P229 9mm is currently the standard-issue sidearm there and Roy purchased his own P225.

Well trained at Thunder Ranch and a number of other schools he attended on his own, Huntington was well aware that shot placement was more important than round count or caliber. He perceived himself as having short fingers, and didn't feel that the larger girth of a pistol frame housing a double-stack magazine gave him the exact grasp he wanted for maximum control of his shots at high speed. Modified slightly over the years by the best custom gunsmiths, Huntington's SIG-Sauer P225 was his choice of a duty weapon. He never felt handicapped in terms of firepower with nine rounds in the gun and a pair of spare magazines on his belt, and never regretted his choice of duty sidearm.

Lt. Dave Spaulding of the Montgomery County, Ohio Sheriff's Department is another lawman with a very long resume in firearms training. He has served with me for many years on the Firearms Committee of the American Society for Law Enforcement Training. Dave had broad discretion in choice of sidearm for most of his career. For many years, his choice of duty weapon was also the SIG P225. Like Roy, he had his pistol lightly customized and action-tuned for maximum performance over the years, a prerogative each man enjoyed because each had purchased his duty weapon out of his own pocket. Though he does not have particularly small hands, Dave also appreciates a pistol that lets you get a good bit of flesh and bone wrapped around the "handle," and gives you a reach to the trigger that affords you maximum leverage in high-speed shooting. It was this that made the P225 so appealing to Dave Spaulding.

Unlike Roy, however, Dave didn't finish his career with the P225. While Roy was happy with the performance of the Winchester OSM (Olin Super Match) subsonic 147-grain hollow-point issued by his department, Dave's agency had less satisfactory experiences with it. After an egregious stopping failure Dave, who was in a position to do something about it, got the department into hotter loads with lighter bullets and higher velocities. Eventually, he just decided to go with a .40 caliber service pistol.

The first of the SIG-Sauer pistols to get the American style push-button magazine release located behind the trigger, the P225 is an ergonomic pistol that seems to make a friend of everyone who shoots it. The accuracy is right up there with the SIG-Sauer tradition. In the *Gun Digest Book of 9mm Handguns* the P225 delivered 2.25-inch groups with Winchester Silvertip 115-grain JHP, 2.5-inch groups with Federal 9BP 115-grain JHP, and 2.75-inch groups with Federal full-metal-jacket ball ammo weighing 123 grains. This very consistent shooting was done at 25 yards. (3)

The book also illustrated that the 9mm cartridge is less sensitive than some others to velocity loss from shorter barrels. The barrel length of a P225 is 3.86 inches. Notes co-author Wiley Clapp, "An interesting thing happens when you compare the velocities that were obtained in the 225 with those of the 226. There is no statistically significant difference. But there is about three quarters of an inch difference in the barrel length. If you need the concealability of the shorter 225 , you are sacrificing nothing in the performance of typical ammunition. If you have to have the larger capacity of the 226 with its 15 shots, so be it. Still, you could take the bottom half of a 226 (fifteen-shot

magazine) and graft on the top half of a 225 (short barrel and slide) – you'd get the best of both – call it a 225-1/2 ." (4)

Some perceived the 9mm Parabellum chambering itself to be a shortcoming of this gun. Noted Clapp, "...the gun would sell like hotcakes if it were to be made in .45 ACP or 10 mm auto, at least in the United States." (5) There is reason to believe that the folks at SIG, Sauer, and SIGARMS all had the same assessment. When the next compact SIG came out, the P239, it was chambered for .40 Smith & Wesson and .357 SIG as well as 9mm Parabellum.

The P239 would cast a dark cloud over the P225. It was seen as a more modern gun, and optionally, a more powerful one, and therefore more desirable. The most recent *Gun Digest* does not list the P225. Imports to the United States dried up some time ago.

A decade ago, then-SIGARMS Technical Director Joe Kiesel told me, "The P225 is still produced, and will be with us for some time to come. A variant of the P225 is the P6, the German Army pistol, and for that contract alone it can be expected to remain in production. It hasn't been imported to the U.S. for years, for the simple reason that since the introduction of the P239, there has been virtually no demand for the P225."

The P239 is a superb pistol. There is much that it can do that the P225 cannot, such as fire more powerful ammunition. Still, there is a combination of classic lines and exquisite feel in the hand that will make the P225 much missed in some U.S. shooting circles. If you can find a good used one, you'll probably not be sorry if you buy it.

IDIOSYNCRASIES

Over the years, I received complaints occasionally from owners of the P225 that when they loaded it with hot, high-velocity ammunition such as the Cor-Bon 115-grain JHP at 1,350 feet per second nominal velocity, the pistol would occasionally fail to pick up a round. What apparently was happening was that the extremely powerful round was driving the short, light slide rearward so fast, allowing it to snap back forward with commensurately greater momentum, that the slide would close over the top of the magazine before the topmost cartridge could be picked up. The result would be a "click" instead of a "bang" at the next pull of the trigger, because the hammer would fall on an empty chamber.

I never personally experienced this with a P225, and I never heard of it happening with a P228, which also has a short slide. Apparently, the strong spring in the double-stack magazine of the P228 was always able to push the next round up into place so fast that the fastest slide couldn't beat it. The P225 magazine, being a single-stack that required less spring tension, was the only gun I heard of this happening with. The subsequent P239 does not seem to have ever had this problem.

When Spaulding was carrying a P225 on Montgomery County, the agency for some time had both Cor-Bon and Winchester 115-grain +P+ ammunition for the 9mm guns, and he had no problem running plenty of it through his. This incompatibility is apparently a rare one. If you carry hot loads in your P225, be certain to run a lot of them through to ensure proper functioning. If the problem does show up, the best bet would probably be to throttle back to a standard pressure 115-grain hollow-point Winchester Silvertip or Federal 9BP.

References

1. Grennell, Dean A., and Clapp, Wiley, "The Gun Digest Book of 9mm Handguns," Northbrook, IL: DBI Books, 1986, P.147.
2. Mullin, Timothy J., "The 100 Greatest Combat Pistols," Boulder, CO: Paladin Press, 1994, P.187.
3. Grennell and Clapp, *op.cit.* P.207.
4. *Ibid.*
5. (5) *Ibid.*

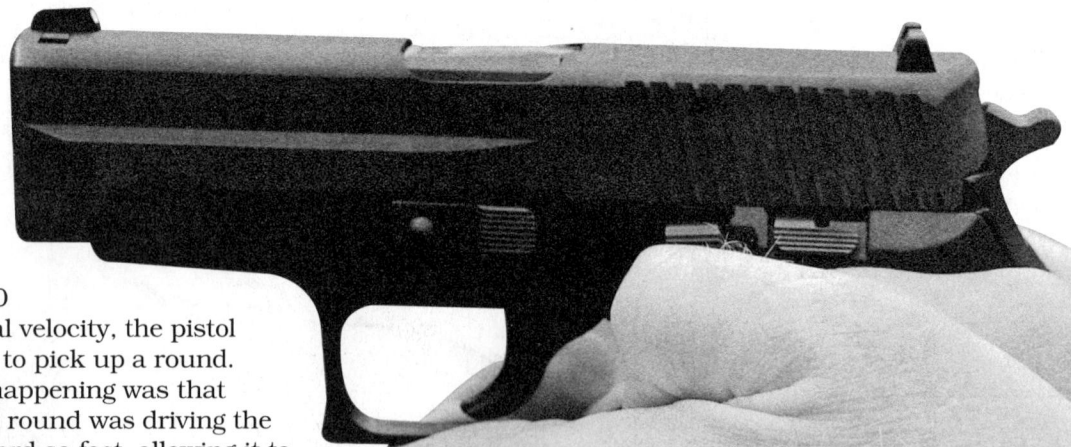

The P225 in an average size man's hand. One of the most ergonomic modern auto pistols ever made, it is particularly suitable to those with small hands and/or short fingers.

Chapter 3
The SIG P226

Developed for the military, the P226 became a premier police service pistol.

Introduced in 1983, the P226 evolved from the P220 as a large-capacity 9mm. It was SIG's entry in the U.S. trials for what would become the nation's new military service pistol. When those grueling and comprehensive tests were done, only two handguns stood at the top of the heap: The SIG P226 and the Beretta 92F.

Beretta won the contract. Some said that they had underbid SIG, either on the pistols themselves or on the combined package including magazines, parts, and accessories. Others hinted darkly that a deal had been brokered. Rumor had it that the U.S. wanted to place cruise missiles in Italy, and that Italy in return wanted a fat contract for their military arms industry, which included Beretta.

One thing is certain: the SIG came through the test with flying colors. Even Beretta fans do not attempt to debate the fact that the SIG P226 at the very least tied their favorite gun. Firearms historian Larry Wilson wrote the following in *The World of Beretta: An International Legend.*

"In winning the contract," Wilson stated flatly, "the Beretta was one of only two candidates to complete satisfactorily the testing program. The other finalist was the Swiss-German firm of SIG-Sauer." (1)

Let's look at the perspectives of some other authorities. Vietnam combat vet and world-renowned authority on military small arms Chuck Karwan commented, "The P226 9mm was designed specifically to compete in the U.S. trials to replace the M1911A1 .45. It was co-winner of the trials but lost in the final bidding process to the Beretta M92F. Many, including the author, felt that the P226 was the better pistol." (2)

Another noted handgun expert, Tim Mullin, has this to say about the P226 in those U.S. military trials, "This is the pistol the U.S. military forces actually wanted when they adopted a 9X19mm pistols. ...(it was the choice of) many elite military units, the most famous being the Navy SEALS. After they broke the M92 repeatedly, they refused delivery of any more Beretta pistols and bought SIG P226 pistols instead. This pistol is also used by many federal law enforcement agencies." (3)

Chuck Taylor is another highly respected authority on combat handguns. His take on the JSSAP trials goes thus, "(The P226) was originally designed to satisfy the criteria of the infamous U.S. military Joint Service Small Arms Program handgun trials, wherein many 'in the know' claim that the P226 actually outperformed the eventual choice, the Beretta M92." (4) Appropriately enough, Taylor's comments on the SIG P226 appear on p. 226 of the book in question, the fourth edition of the *Gun Digest Book of Combat Handgunnery.*

All these authorities have good opinions of the P226 pistol, and all are on record

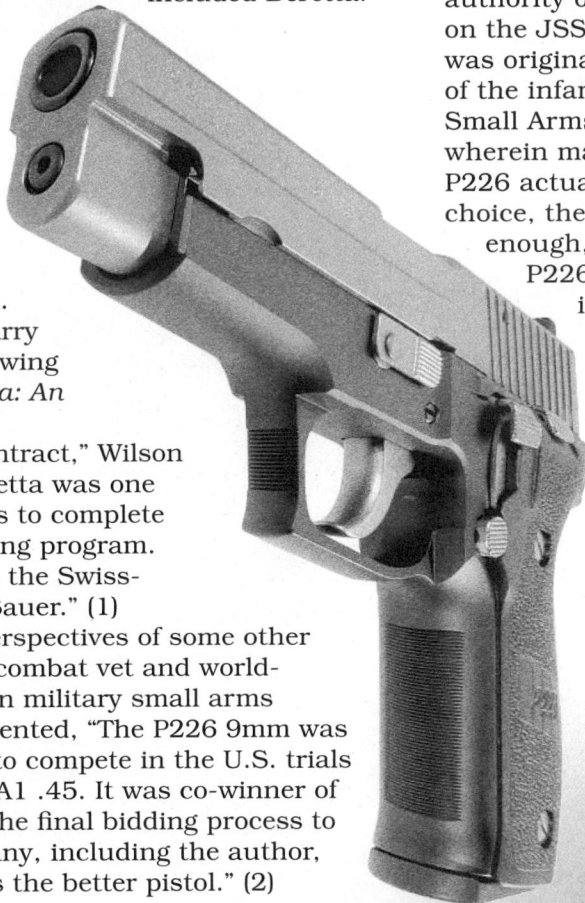

Three generations of the 9mm SIG-Sauer P226. Top, the first classic: note unique checkering pattern on grips, internal extractor, hollow slide pin. Center, the next generation: note cobblestone pattern of grip roughening, external extractor, solid slide pin. Below, the latest: same as center gun, but with Picatinny accessory attachment rail integral to dust cover of frame.

explaining why. "...while I feel the concept around which the modern high-capacity auto is based to be dreadfully ill-advised, I also feel that the P226 is one of the best-designed and best-built examples of the breed," says Taylor. "It is extremely well made and finished, featuring a black anodized frame and Parkerized slide, and presents a formidable appearance, backed by solid functionality. It is one of the most accurate self-loaders I have ever fired and possesses well-conceived human engineering features."

Continues Taylor, "Its decocking lever and slide lock/release are all centrally located for quick, easy manipulation. In addition, it feeds most anything you care to stuff into the magazine, including the latest exotic JHP designs. It field strips in less than five seconds. A rebounding hammer and white-

dot-front, white-outline-rear sight combination completes its formidable package...One of the most user-friendly large-capacity DA autos produced, the P226 also points well and presents few edges to cut skin or abrade concealment clothing.

"So," he concludes, "if you're one of those who prefers a large-capacity auto, you can't really go wrong with the P226. In fact, while it's certainly no secret that I'm not an advocate of the concept, I find the P226 to be a pleasant gun to shoot and prefer it hands-down over all other large-capacity DA 9mm pistols. It isn't a cheap gun, but it's well worth its price." (5)

"The SIG pistols of any style are always quite accurate," explains Mullin. "They vary from excellent to outstanding in my experience." He concludes, "I agree with the SEALS: if you can, pick the SIG over the Beretta...You can't go wrong by selecting this pistol if you are looking for a full-size battle pistol." (6)

Karwan quantifies his appreciation of the big SIG 9mm. "Of all the high-capacity 9mm pistols,

Top, P226 from the early 1980s. This one has been retrofitted with short-reach trigger and Crimson Trace LaserGrips, and Trijicon night sights installed aftermarket in the mid-80s. Below, its successor: this is the "rail gun" variation, with SIGLite night sights and standard length trigger. Both of these specimens are chambered for 9mm.

the P226 has one of the most comfortable and naturally pointing grip shapes. The trigger reach is a little long for some people with small hands but SIG offers an optional short trigger to help in that regard. With good ammunition the P226 is on the average one of the most accurate service pistols on the market. Its double-action trigger is quite smooth and reasonably light, making the transition from a long double-action first shot to the subsequent single-action shots easy to accomplish...The P226 is expensive compared to some of its competition but it is a superbly made, very accurate, and very reliable fighting handgun." (7)

Wiley Clapp brings both police and military experience to the table when he evaluates handguns, which is something he has done successfully full-time for a number of years now. In the *Gun Digest Book of 9mm Handguns*, he wrote, "Apparently the (P226's) magazine was designed with considerable care, as the gun fired without a single glitch in the course of hundreds of rounds. When the magazine design is increased to nearly double capacity, the butt becomes thicker. In the 226, the thickening of the butt section is far less objectionable than in other guns, because the butt has been subtly re-contoured. The bulk is held to a

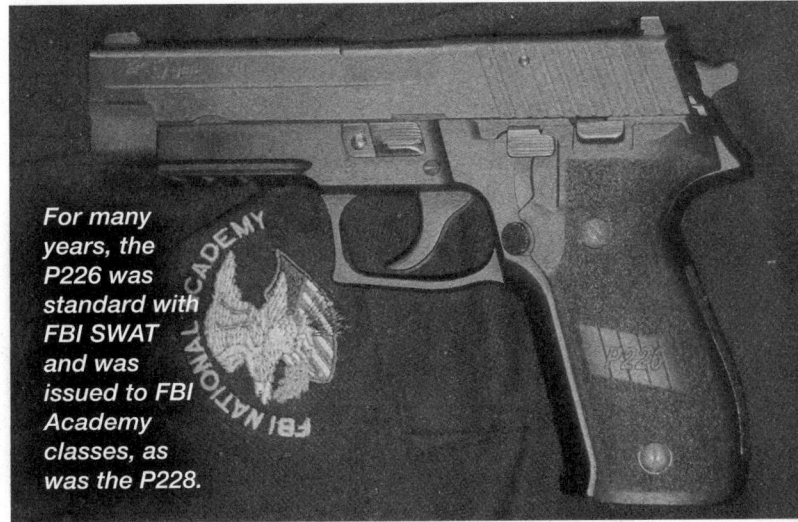

For many years, the P226 was standard with FBI SWAT and was issued to FBI Academy classes, as was the P228.

minimum and the more rounded butt actually feels better than the original 220. That is not usually the case when a single-column design is altered to a double."

Clapp goes on to say, "I fired the 226 extensively for this book. In the course of several hundred rounds downrange, I came to appreciate another feature of the pistol. The sights are excellent,

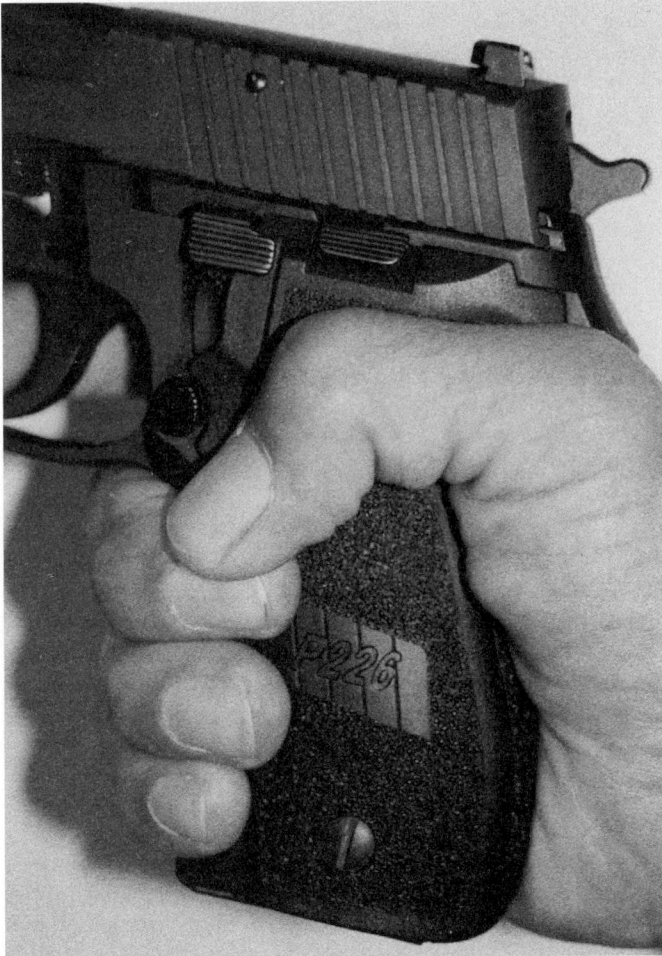

Above: The difference between two generations of P226. First Gen, top: Note that extractor is invisible, concealed inside the slide mechanism, and that the slide pin which holds the extractor is hollow. Current Gen, below, has beefed up extractor mounted outside the slide and securely pinned in place, and a solid steel pin has replaced the hollow one in slide.

Left: Since the thumb does not have to manipulate a safety catch on the frame or the slide, shooter with SIG P226 can take this extremely powerful "master grip" with thumb curled down and actually touching middle finger. It's the strongest start for handgun retention if there's a struggle for the gun, and no grasp is stronger when a pistol is fired one hand only. When thumb is curled down, it cannot ride the slide lock lever and prevent the slide from staying open on the last round, a common problem with some other right-handed grasp techniques.

among the best to be found on any of the myriad of handguns on today's market. They are big enough to be seen, with a wide, deep notch and a prominent front ramped blade. Some versions of the SIG-Sauer pistols have sights highlighted with dots for better sight acquisition in low light situations. I don't care for them. Double-action autoloaders have traditionally poor trigger pulls, at least in the DA mode. The 226 defies tradition in that the double-action pull on this pistol is very good. Once that first double-action shot is gone, the single-action trigger action for subsequent shots is fairly light, with only a small amount of creep. As the test results show, the 226 pistol is accurate, too." (8)

POLICE HISTORY

When the big wave of police adoptions of high-capacity 9mm autos to replace traditional service revolvers hit in the early 1980s, SIG was there at the right time, in the right place, with the right product. The P226 took off like a rocket. What had started as a three-way race between Beretta, SIG, and Smith & Wesson would soon become a wider field as Glock and Ruger entered the market.

Competition was fierce. There were major departments that approved or adopted all these brands. However, as an instructor teaching nationwide and around the world at that time, it was my perception that the SIG pulled ahead, with the P226 being the top seller during that period.

The Feds went to the SIG big time in the 1980s. It was one of the very first autoloaders authorized by the FBI for field personnel, and the P226 quickly replaced the high-capacity 9mm auto by another maker on the SWAT teams in every local FBI office in the land. The Bureau had input from British SAS, which traded their trademark Browning Hi-Power 9mm autos for the P226, citing its greater durability and reliability. The ATF and the DEA adopted the SIG, too. So did Secret Service and Sky Marshals, though they both went with the smaller P228 version. The U.S. Marshal's Service at that time gave its deputy federal marshals wide latitude in their choice of personal sidearm, and a huge number bought SIGs, often the P226.

The wartime draftee training doctrine of the military, the KISS principle ("Keep It Simple, Stupid!") had rightly or wrongly become part and parcel of most American police handgun training. It was felt that there were enough new skills to learn in transitioning from a revolver to a semiautomatic pistol without throwing in one more, such as the manipulation of a thumb safety.

If the pistol came with a lever on the slide that performed the dual functions of a manual safety catch and a decocking lever, recruits were told that it was a decocking lever only. But, it wasn't. If the officer used the typical U.S. military slide manipulation technique of grasping it overhand and jerking it to the rear, his thumb on one side and finger on the other tended to push the slide-mounted lever down into the "safe" position. Since he had been taught that the lever was a decocker, not a safety, by definition that officer had not been taught how to rapidly and reflexively off-safe an on

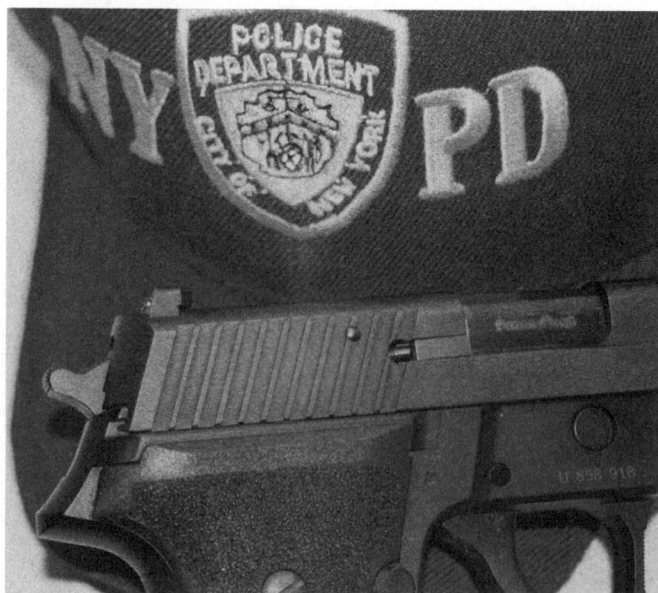

SIG P226 DAO is one of three 9mm pistols authorized by the New York City Police Department, and is seen by many officers as the most prestigious of the uniform guns on their "approved" list. It is almost certainly the most accurate of those three, as well.

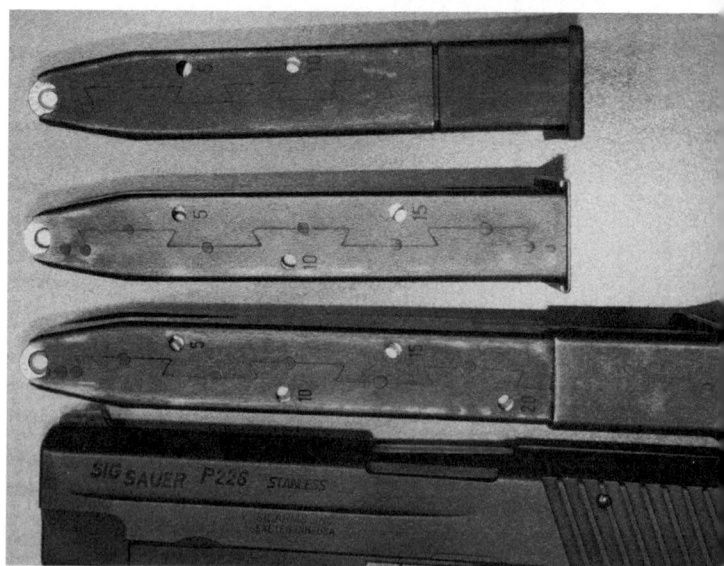

Three styles of 9mm SIG P226 magazine. Top, a ten round "Clinton magazine," once required for officers on NYPD, and useful for training or IDPA competition. Center: original 15 round SIG-Sauer P226 magazine. Below: Extended 20-round SIG P226 mag, popular with SWAT and Britain's SAS.

The P226 is an extremely controllable gun, particularly in 9mm. The 9mm brass in the air shows that Ayoob is firing rapidly, but note that the muzzle of the SIG is still dead on target for the next shot. Stance is the aggressive StressFire version of the Isosceles, and grasp is the "wedge hold."

safe gun. Thus, he would stand there pulling the trigger and wonder why his pistol was not firing.

My feeling was that if the lever was going to be used only as a decocker, it should function only as a decocker. The rest of the police community came to agree with me. The SIG-Sauer, unlike its competitors with similar double-action first shot pistols (later known as TDA, or Traditional Double Action), had a "slick slide." It was simply not possible to inadvertently on-safe a SIGSauer, because there was no such device on the pistol.

Moreover, the SIG's decocking lever was behind the trigger on the frame, not on the slide. This is a more ergonomic placement. Beretta, Ruger, and S&W eventually offered decocker-only models in which the slide-mounted lever was spring-loaded and could not go "on safe." Nonetheless, there were two downsides to that design. One was that many officers found it awkward to reach their thumb to the slide to decock, and much more natural to bring the thumb down behind the trigger guard to perform the same function with a SIG. (A left-handed officer with a SIG would use the trigger finger to decock.) The other was that a palm-down slide manipulation could inadvertently decock a gun with a slide-mounted lever when the officer didn't intend for that to happen, as when reloading or clearing a malfunction. This could be confusing in a high-stress situation...and it

couldn't happen with a SIG. S&W copied the SIG-style decocking lever on the ill-fated Model 1076 10mm they developed for the FBI, and put it on some of their other TDA models (distinguishable by the suffix "26" in their model numbers). However,

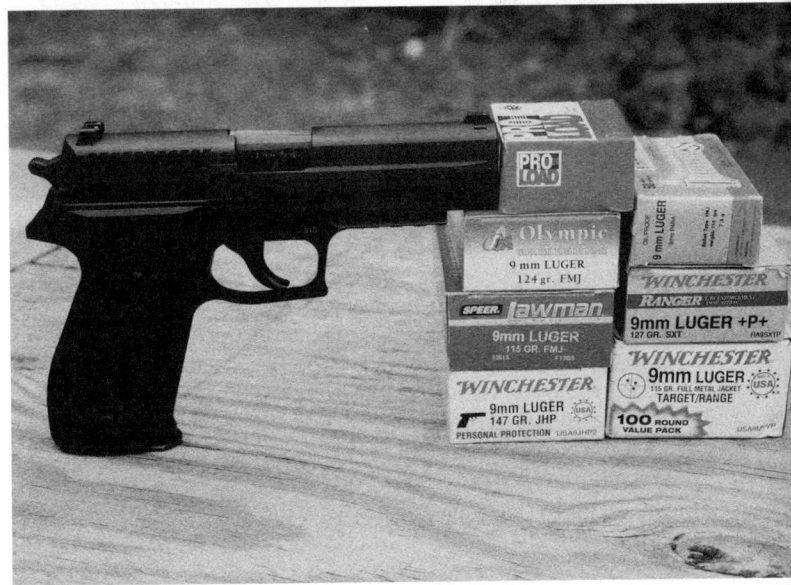

Author finds the P226 an accurate pistol in general, and likes the fact that it gives consistent accuracy with a broad range of ammo, as with this 9mm example.

that version of the S&W decocker proved to be problematic, and S&W soon stopped making guns that way.

The possibility of accidentally engaging the safety of a pistol with a slide-mounted lever was not just theoretical. Circa 1990 in Dade County, Florida, such an incident occurred in a gunfight. Dade County had authorized their deputies to purchase SIG, Beretta, or S&W 9mm autos, and in transition training the deputies were taught to treat the slide-mounted levers on the latter brands as decockers, not safeties.

The time came when a deputy with a new Beretta was the first to respond to a psycho firing a shotgun in a public place. When the shotgunner came at him, the officer fired one round and missed. Still new to the semiautomatic, he failed to return the trigger far enough forward to re-set it for the second shot, and when he pulled the trigger, the gun of course did not fire. Thinking it had jammed, he racked the slide with his non-dominant hand as he had been taught, clearing a live round from the chamber and cycling another one in. However, his hand had inadvertently pushed the lever down into the "safe" position as he performed the stoppage clearance drill. Now, as he attempted to fire on the gunman who was rapidly closing on him, the trigger moved uselessly under his finger. His life was saved when another policeman, off duty at the scene and armed with a slick-slide 9mm, shot and killed the gunman just in time.

It should be noted that in writing the above, I am not condemning the concept of a safety/decock lever. I am simply saying that if the decision is made to carry the gun off safe, the gun probably should not have an "on safe" option at all. Moreover, that

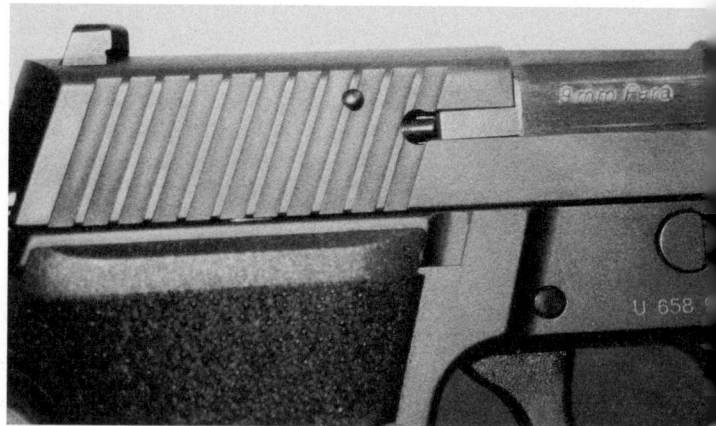

9mm Parabellum was the original chambering for the P226, and is still extremely popular.

Current "stippling" on grips instead of checkering pattern is extremely popular among P226 fans. The purpose is a non-slip grasp in the most stressful situations.

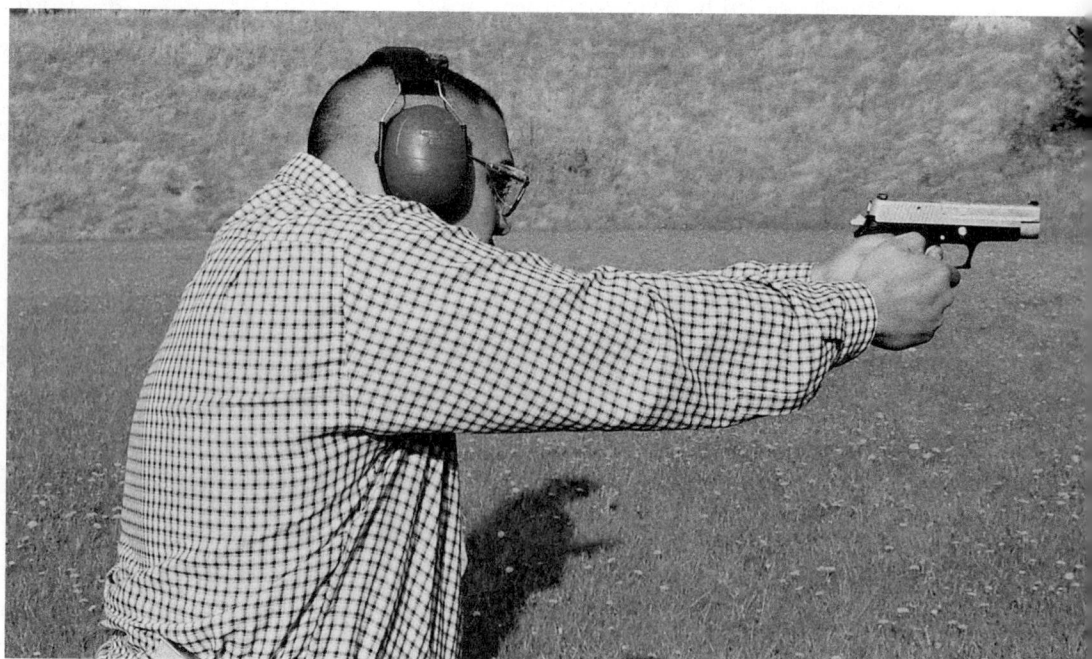

This P226 9mm is in its second generation of protecting the public. Originally issued to a trooper by the Michigan State Police, it was traded in when MSP upgraded to the more powerful .40 caliber version of the P226. This officer purchased it second hand, and wears it to work daily today. It still delivers excellent accuracy and, as he demonstrates, excellent control.

if the design chosen is "decocker-only," the frame-mounted decocker as on the SIG makes more sense for more people than does a decocker mounted on the slide. I've carried the Beretta, the Ruger, and the S&W TDA autos on duty, but always carried them on-safe and always practiced the off-safing movement as part of the draw, and taught it to my officers who also carried that type of gun.

The SIG, of course, had other attributes. No competitive gun had a better trigger in terms of smoothness of the first double-action shot and controllability of single-action follow-up shots. The trigger re-set of the SIG-Sauer was just right for police work: Not so long as to be ungainly, but not so short as to allow a shaky hand to fire an additional shot unintentionally after the need to shoot had ended.

There was the reliability factor, too. The SIG was simply extraordinary in this regard. The good "feel" and "pointability" repeatedly cited by the authorities quoted above made for good, fast shooting in the hands of the average cop. Competence and confidence were both enhanced by this.

The SIG's inherent accuracy put it in the forefront, too. The experts cited above told you the straight stuff about that. In my job teaching nationwide, I got to not only intensively test every 9mm out there, but got to observe a great number of them in the hands of officers and instructors. As a rule, the SIG P226 would group tighter than the Glock, the Ruger, and the Smith & Wesson service pistols. Only the Beretta and two of HK's entries, which eventually numbered four, could keep up. The VP70Z, a machine pistol designed for cheap mass-manufacture turned into a cheap semiautomatic pistol, was never in the same ballpark with the SIG for accuracy, reliability, or ergonomics, and was soon mercifully discontinued. The current HK USP is a good gun, and spectacularly accurate in .45 ACP, but not so accurate in the 9mm specimens I've seen. The P9S, discontinued in the 1980s, would stay with or even exceed the SIG-Sauer for accuracy in 9mm, but design quirks such as requiring a pull of the trigger to decock made it unworkable for American law enforcement. The HK P7, then and now, could be expected to keep pace with the SIG in the accuracy department, but its unique squeeze-cocking mechanism turned off as many police departments as its very high price.

Thus, if you're talking about maximum accuracy in a 9mm service pistol, and you want traditional design plus high reliability plus affordability, you're down to a two-horse race: SIG and Beretta. The two are almost indistinguishable in this regard, each occasionally beating the other, but if it came down to the wire I would have to admit that in my

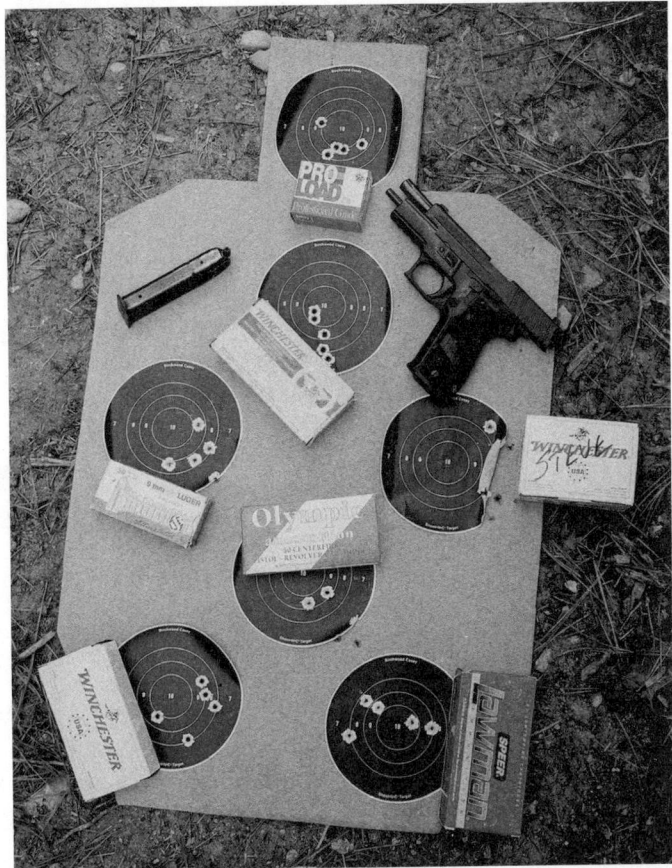

Author found extremely uniform accuracy with a wide variety of 9mm ammo when shooting this P226 from the "auto hood position" at 25 yards.

Accuracy is the P226's calling card. Behold a one-inch five-shot group, fired at 25 yards from a bench rest with the most popular .357 SIG duty load, the Speer Gold Dot 125-grain jacketed hollow point (JHP).

45

The P226 Rail model set up for home defense or police tactical work. InSight M3 tactical flashlight is mounted to the rail at the front of the dust cover, and a 20-round extended magazine is locked in place.

Many state police agencies have issued the .357 SIG P226 to their uniformed troopers. These guns combine great power with extraordinary accuracy, very good controllability, and the highest order of reliability. Full cartridge capacity is 13 rounds in the magazine and one more in the firing chamber.

The P226 Rail's trademark is this extended dust cover portion of the frame.

experience the average SIG P226 9mm will, just by a hair, shoot a little tighter than the average Beretta.

The P226 has a distinguished history in American law enforcement. It has been the service gun of the state police in Massachusetts, Michigan, and other states. Arizona troopers used to have a choice between two SIGs, the P226 in 9mm and the P220 in .45.

At this writing the Orlando, Florida Police Department, nationally famous for its professionalism and high-grade handgun training and performance, is still using the P226 9mm after many, many years. Their usual load has been a 124 to 127 grain bullet at 1220 to 1250 feet per second. In a long list of shootings, these rounds have stopped the bad guys with alacrity, curing the one thing that is really wrong with a 9mm, its

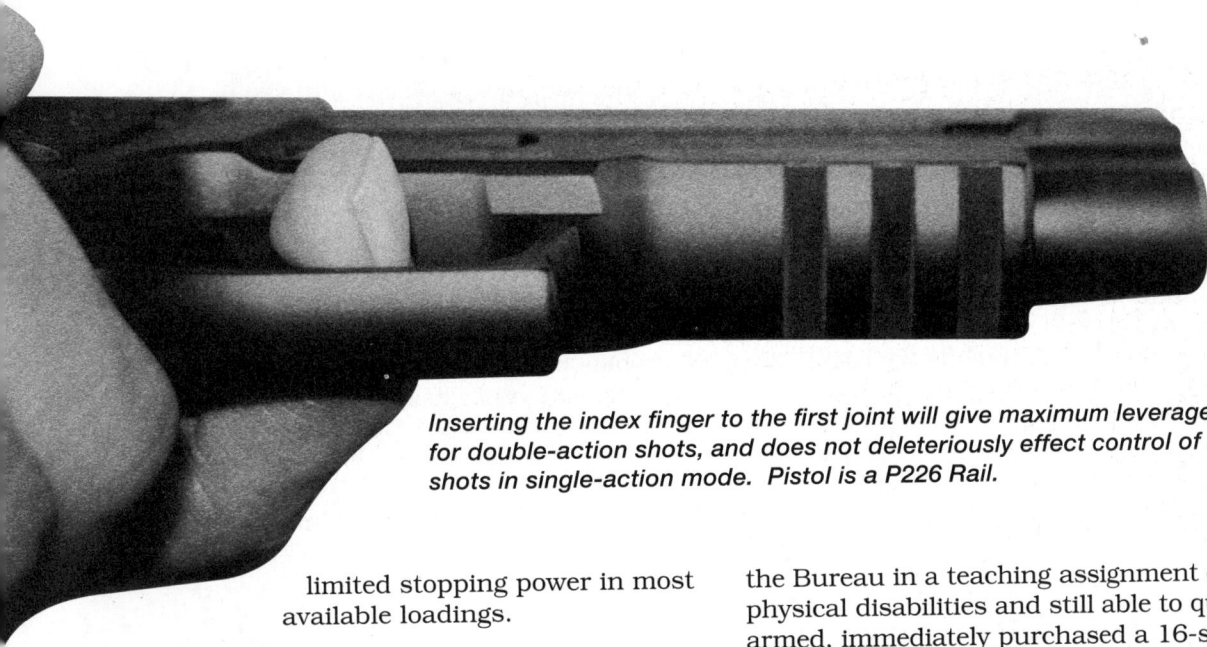

Inserting the index finger to the first joint will give maximum leverage on the trigger for double-action shots, and does not deleteriously effect control of subsequent shots in single-action mode. Pistol is a P226 Rail.

limited stopping power in most available loadings.

CHOICE OF EXPERTS

Supervisory Special Agent Gordon McNeill was team leader of the FBI stakeout group that engaged the armed robbery and murder suspects Edward Matix and Michael Platt on April 11, 1986, in a suburb of Miami, Florida. Armed with a short-barreled six-shot .357 revolver, he fired the opening police shots of the encounter. He wounded Matix, but emptied the gun. Between his fourth and fifth shot a .223 rifle bullet fired by Platt smashed McNeill's gun hand. Unable to reload his revolver due to his injuries, he was about to turn back to his vehicle to grab his shotgun when Platt loomed up and shot him in the neck. The bullet left him partially paralyzed for life.

Good sights are a feature on all the SIG-Sauer duty guns. This P226 benefits from night sights. Note proper grasp: web of hand high into the grip tang, and barrel in line with the long bones of the forearm.

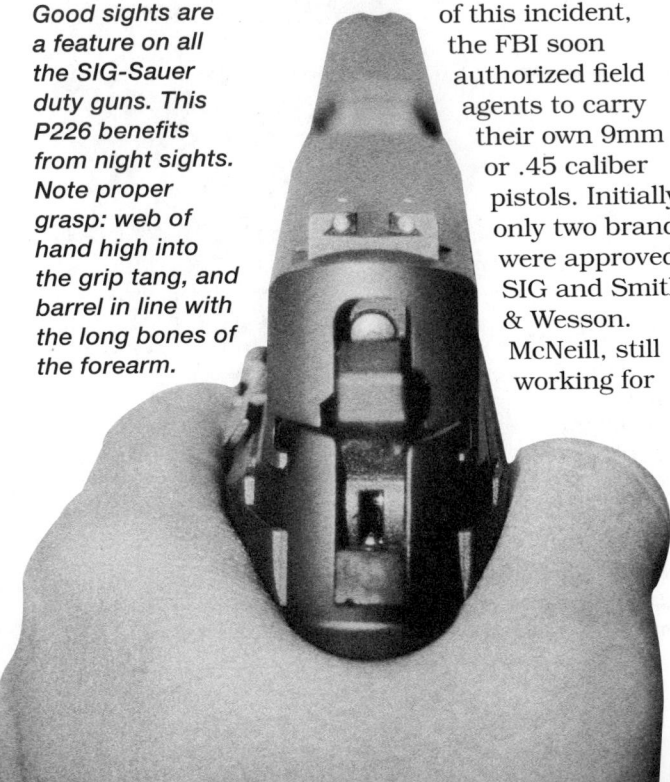

Largely as a result of this incident, the FBI soon authorized field agents to carry their own 9mm or .45 caliber pistols. Initially, only two brands were approved, SIG and Smith & Wesson. McNeill, still working for the Bureau in a teaching assignment despite his physical disabilities and still able to qualify to work armed, immediately purchased a 16-shot SIG-Sauer P226. After the horror of being helpless with an empty gun after six shots, Gordon McNeill wanted increased and highly reliable firepower on his side. No one in the world can blame him. His choice of pistol was an excellent one.

Evan Marshall has been a friend of mine for going on 40 years. A survivor of multiple armed encounters during his distinguished career with the Detroit Police Department, he has for many years kept a running tally of gunfight reports from around the country and the world, and attempted to assess how well different calibers and loads worked in actual shootouts. His work has been controversial, but based on all my input, his conclusions about the relative stopping power of 9mm and larger caliber hollow-points are pretty much on the mark. He has no problem at all carrying a 9mm so long as it is loaded with an efficiently opening bullet in the 115- to 127-grain weight range at +P or +P+ velocity. And I've often seen him carrying a 9mm SIG P226 as his primary weapon.

The late Robert Shimek was famous as an authority on classic handguns. What few of his readers knew was that he was also a career law enforcement officer. The gun that he carried on

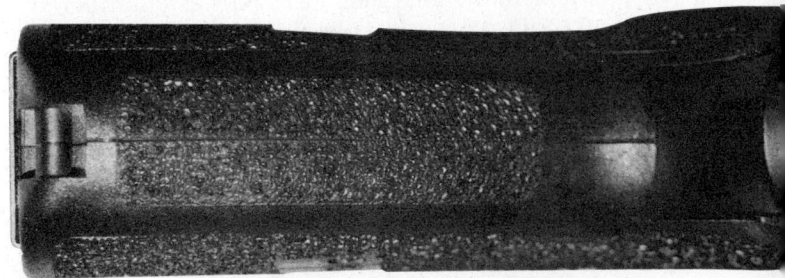

"Stippled" front strap and back strap aid in secure grasp under the most adverse conditions of climate, circumstances, and stress.

duty, right up through his retirement shortly before his untimely death, was a SIG-Sauer P226 9mm.

In police departments where there is a broad choice of options as to what gun to carry, it's always wise to look to see what the instructors are carrying. They see all the guns in action, and they know what works.

Consider NYPD. Requiring double-action-only 9mm pistols, the nation's largest police department (some 40,000 sworn officers) authorizes three specific make/models, one of which is the SIG P226 DAO. The SIG has become the "prestige gun" on that department. Its reliability is unbeaten, and it is more accurate than either of the other two approved pistols.

P226 CHOICES

Since the mid-1990s, the P226 has been available chambered for the .357 SIG and the .40 S&W. Each will hold two fewer of the large-diameter cartridges than the predecessor gun. Going from 16 of the 9mm rounds to 14 of the .40s or .357s is an upgrade as far as most people are concerned.

The .40 S&W cartridge in general is simply not the most accurate semiautomatic round available. That's as true in the SIG as anything else. I've found that it will certainly be accurate enough for police work or IDPA competition, but it does not deliver the same high order of accuracy in the P226 as does the 9mm Parabellum round.

The .357 SIG cartridge is something else, though. With its high energy and high terminal striking power comes also a high order of accuracy. Simply put, the .357 SIG is an inherently accurate cartridge.

George Harris, for many years head of SIG Academy, brought a lot of real-world experience to the ranges and classrooms. He has always been a strong proponent of the .357 SIG cartridge, and used to harvest his annual venison with a P226 in that caliber.

A few years ago, the Texas Department of Public Safety, which encompasses the state highway patrol, swapped the trusty P220 .45s they had carried for many years for P226 pistols chambered for .357 SIG. They have been delighted with the stopping power it has afforded their personnel in

several gunfights since. Anecdotal reports indicate that the bad guys go down a little faster to the .357 SIG than to even a .45 auto.

In one famous shooting, during the transition period between guns, two Texas highway patrolmen shot it out with a gunman ensconced in the cab of an 18-wheeler. The senior officer's P220 shot where he aimed it, but the wide, slow .45 slugs did not punch through the massive bodywork of the giant truck with enough authority to stop the offender. His rookie partner, however, was fresh from the academy with a newly issued P226 in .357 SIG. His 125-grain CCI Gold Dot bullets at 1350 feet per second drilled through the heavy cab and punched through their would-be killer's brain, ending the deadly battle instantly. When the department went to a 9mm pistol in early 2014, troopers requested permission to keep their SIG DAK P226 .357s.

The P226 is an eminently "shootable" pistol when the pressure is on. Firing in front of a large class of students to "set the pace," author shot this perfect 300 out of 300 score with sixty rounds of 9mm on the combat course. Thanks to the P226's consistency of performance, such a target is pretty much replicable on demand.

Left: As with other SIGs in these calibers, the same magazine is interchangeable between .357 SIG and .40 S&W P226s. In fact, all that needs to be swapped to change caliber is the barrel.

Most of them took advantage of that permission.

Steel-framed P226s are now available. I haven't really worked with them, except for the target model, which is just deliciously accurate and sweet to shoot.

PERSONAL PERSPECTIVE

If I sound high on the P226, it's not because it's one of my favorite guns and my second favorite SIG. Rather, those things are true because the gun has proven itself in the manner described above. I use the P226 in its original caliber, 9mm, for several reasons that may or may not be relevant to your own needs.

First, I'm on the road a lot teaching, and usually flying. The airlines at this writing limit you to 11 pounds of ammunition in checked baggage. Eleven pounds of ammo means a lot more 9mm rounds than .40 or .45 rounds. When the Twin Towers were hit on September 11, 2001, my wife and daughter

were in Nevada. Air travel shut down nationwide instantly, a situation that lasted for several days. Fortunately, I was able to fax my lovely bride a copy of her FFL, and she went to the nearest gun shop and bought the last suitable hardware that hadn't been cleaned off the shelf by panicky buyers. Ammo disappeared from dealers' shelves, too. They were stranded out there for a while. A lot of people had to make their way home on the ground, often hitch-hiking because the rental agencies had run out of automobiles, and the trains and buses were overloaded.

If I have to make a long journey on foot or by thumb in a time of national emergency, I would find it much more comforting to have a lot of ammo in my backpack rather than a little. Unlike most police officers with issue ammo, when I'm on my own time I can carry whatever I want. Those 127-grain +P+ Winchesters, or Evan Marshall's favorite 115-grain JHPs at 1300 or more feet per second, will get the job done quite nicely in 9mm.

Other more routine job-related requirements exist. If I have to buy training ammo on the road, 9mm is cheaper than anything else. If I have to ship thousands of rounds ahead to a training site, the lighter 9mm ammo costs less. I put a couple of thousand rounds of 9mm through my P226 at my last busman's holiday at Chapman Academy.

I also compete whenever I can. The SIG pistol is very well suited to IDPA, where it is shot in the Stock Service Pistol (SSP) category. There, 9mm pistols compete with those chambered for .40 S&W, .357 SIG, and .45 ACP. I see no reason at all to have a .45 that only holds eight or nine rounds when IDPA rules let me have 11 in an SSP gun, and my 9mm SIG will take that many. I see no reason, either, to contend with .45 caliber recoil when I can shoot just a little bit faster against the omnipresent clock with a 9mm.

Each of us has our own job to do, and we pick our tools accordingly. However, in its broad caliber range of 9mm Parabellum, .357 SIG, and .40 S&W, the SIG P226 can literally offer something for everyone.

Of the many variations of the P226, and among the four P226 9mms that now rest in my gun safe, the one I prefer to use is the newest, the "rail gun." The dust cover, or forward portion of the frame, is grooved to accept accessories such as an attached white light unit. ("White light" is the current way cool, high-speed, low-drag "tactical" terminology for "flashlight.") I travel with an InSight M3 light in my carry-on luggage. At night, when I go to bed, I slide the flashlight onto the P226. I also do a tactical reload and swap out the 15-round "carry magazine" of 9mm hot loads for a 20-round magazine of the same ammo.

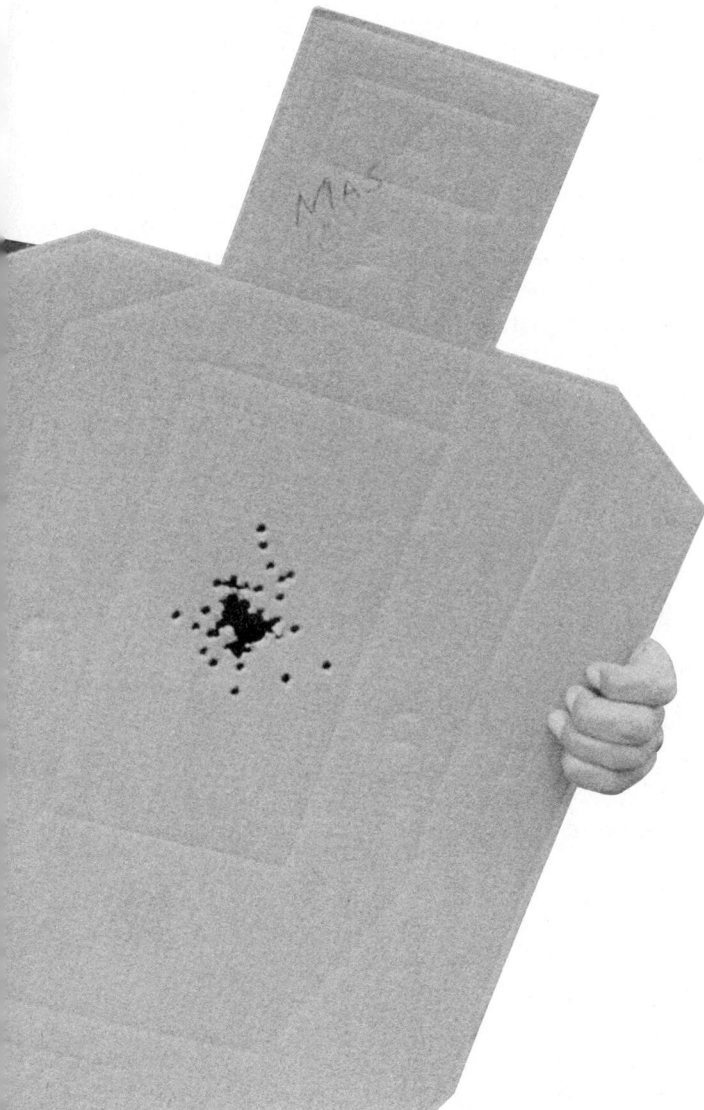

Do you wear a tactical load-bearing vest or magazine pouches to bed? Good. Neither do I. Police work has taught me that home invasions happen fast, and hotel room invasions happen faster because there's less space to act as a buffer zone. I like the idea of one practiced movement putting everything in my hand that I need. A pistol with powerful ammunition; an ample supply of that ammunition already on board; light attached, with which to find, identify and blind my opponent; and, as icing on the cake, SIG-Lite night sights.

Another special-purpose P226 has already been mentioned: The double-action-only model as required by Chicago PD. For the armed citizen as well, the DAO concept bears looking at, if only from its civil liability defensibility standpoint, which, to be frank, is why so many police chiefs have specified it.

E2 looks different, shoots great with 9mm ammo from 115 to 147 grains. Also available in .40 S&W and .357 SIG.

References

1. (1) Wilson,R.L.,*The World of beretta: An International Legend*, New York City: Random House, 2000, PP. 238-240.
2. (2)Karwan, Chuck, *The SIG-Sauer P226*, sidebar in Standard Catalog of Firearms,13th Edition, by Ned Schwing. Iola, WI: Krause Publications, 2002, P. 958.
3. (3)Mullin, Timothy J., "*The 100 Greatest Combat Pistols*," Boulder, CO: Paladin Press, 1994, P.381.
4. (4)Taylor, Chuck, *The Gun Digest Book of Combat Handgunnery, Fourth Edition*, Iola, WI: Krause Publications, 1997, P. 226.
5. (5)Taylor, *Ibid.*
6. (6)Mullin, *op.cit., P. 382.*
7. (7)Karwan, *op.cit.*
8. (8)Clapp, Wiley, The Gun Digest Book of 9mm Pistols, Northbrook, IL: DBI Books, 1986*, P. 209.*

SIG P226E2

The SIG P226 has been with us so long that the newest generation of pistoleros considers it "Old Skool." Yet, some proven designs are timeless, and in the world of handguns, the SIG P226 has earned enough chops to make it into that category.

SIG has of late introduced a plethora of variations in the Classic Line, most of them in the nature of cosmetic changes. The "E2" version goes way beyond that. Folks at SIG pronounce its name "E-squared" – you'll see that the "2" is reduced in size and lifted high at the end of the "E" to denote this in the slide stamp – and the intended meaning is "Ergonomics, multiplied."

The E2 mounts SIG's recent short-reset trigger, which combined with the short reach trigger option helps make this the most "shootable" P226 yet, and

I've been shooting them since they came out back in the eighties. So does a reshaping of the grip, which brings the web of the hand deeper into the pistol toward the trigger, and "lets you get more of your fingers around the gun."

Result? The shooter has proportionally more flesh and bone to wrap around the grip frame and stabilize the pistol. This helps keep it solidly on target, improves recoil control, and steadies the aim against the trigger pull, particularly for the first double action shot. Perhaps most important, it allows the index finger more reach to the trigger, giving that digit more leverage with which to smoothly, swiftly pull the trigger straight back. Thus, these seemingly subtle improvements go a disproportionally long way toward *making you shoot the gun better.*

The chopped and channeled P226 became the P224, available in configurations such as these from left to opposite page right.

OTHER CHANGES

Levers seem to have been expanded outward a little for easier reach by the thumb. The Classic Line SIG has always been prone to the thumb overriding the slide stop lever if the shooter fires right-handed with straight thumbs, and a wider lever will exacerbate this. I finally learned to simply curl my thumbs down as if shooting a revolver when running these guns, and whaddaya know, everything worked again.

There are few tests for a combat handgun more valid than shooting a combat handgun match, particularly when you're testing for ergonomics factors. There will be one hand and two hand, weak hand and strong hand shooting, draws to the shot, speed reloads and tactical reloads…and of course, there are targets you're expected to hit. I took the test E2 to a match sponsored by the First Coast IDPA Club in Jacksonville, Florida, in April 2010. A double action auto, the P226 would normally compete in Stock Service Pistol division, but my team already had members entered there, so I signed up to shoot it in Enhanced Service Pistol. This puts you against 1911 9mms and .38 Supers and such, with exquisite trigger pulls, but we were testing for *ergonomics*, right?

It was all there. The pistol seemed to come into line by itself. Recoil was quite manageable (it was a 9mm, after all). The slide always locked open, and the larger slide release lever really did come into its own for speeding timed reloads. The gun had delivered groups in the inch and a half range at 25 yards with 147 grain Winchester, so accuracy on the IDPA targets was no problem. Bottom line? I won the overall Enhanced Service Pistol Division with the double action SIG shooting in a "single action game." Better testament to the E2's ergonomics, I could not ask.

The test crew and I killed about a 500 round case of ammo – assorted jacketed hollow point, full metal jacket, and jacketed truncated cone, 115 to 147 grain – with this pistol, without a single malfunction

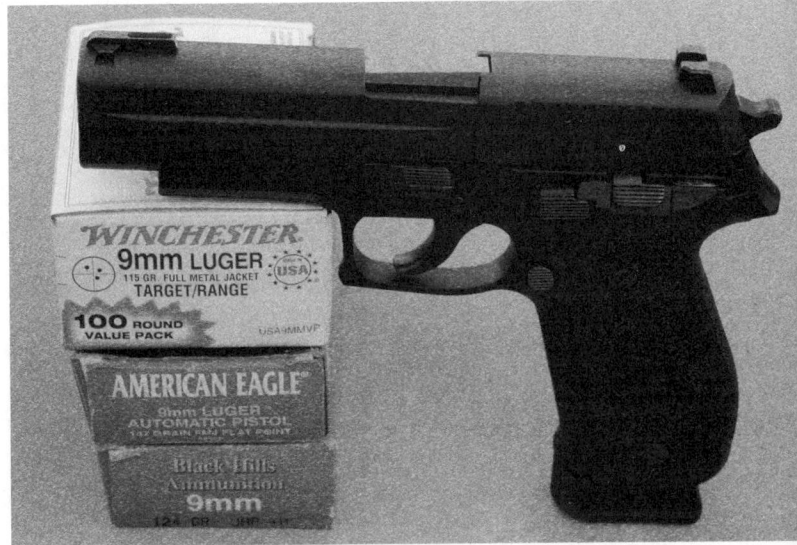

New 20-rd 9mm mag has enhanced P226 9mm.

Striking finish and high traction grips mark this XTM variation of the SIG P224.

51

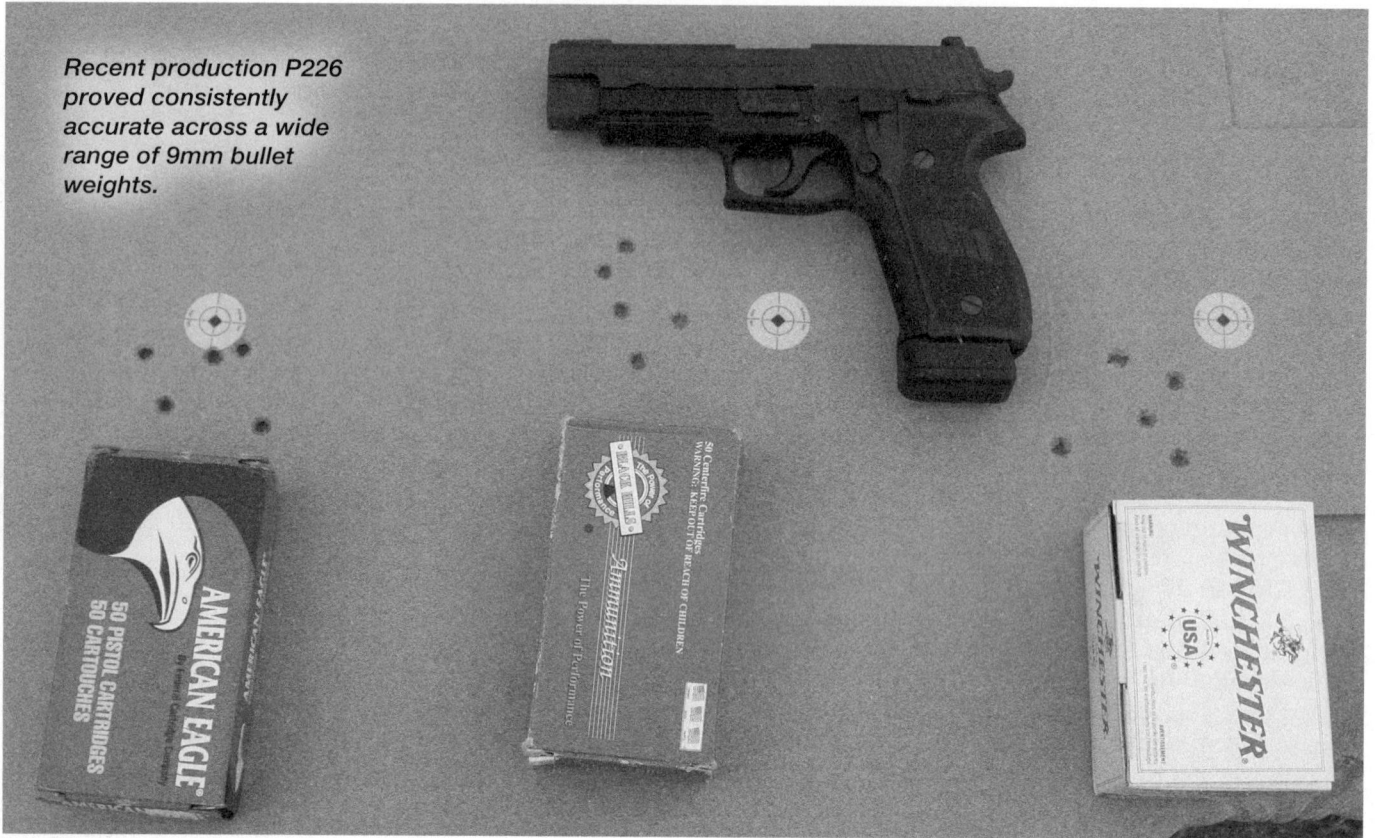

Recent production P226 proved consistently accurate across a wide range of 9mm bullet weights.

of any kind. That, of course, was no surprise with any kind of a SIG P226.

SIG has take a time proven classic and enhanced its ergonomics to make it shoot even better for more people, keeping its long-established accuracy and reliability.

NEW GENERATION SIG CLASSIC: THE E2

A new update makes one of our most proven service pistol better fit smaller hands.

25 yard group, Black Hills 124 grain JHP, SIG P226 9mm.

25 yard group, 125 grain Winchester FMJ, late model P226 9mm.

You don't need to be a Navy SEAL to protect your family with the MK25 Navy variation of the P226R.

Over the years, 9mm SIGs have turned out to be reliable and accurate with popular 147 grain subsonic ammo.

From left: original 15-rd mag, earlier 20-rd, and current 20-rd mag for 9mm P226.

The SIG P226 came very, *very* close to being the current US military service pistol instead of the Beretta 92. Cloned from the earlier single-stack magazine P220 pistol expressly for the US military contract, the P226 was a double-stack magazine version in 9mm that held 15 rounds in the magazine and a sixteenth in the firing chamber. Its relatively straight-line feed angle assured reliability with hollow point ammunition, endearing it to police and armed citizens alike. Despite its near-miss status with the US armed forces, the P226 was a solid hit with American law enforcement. The SIG brand remains today one of the most popular police handguns in this country, second only to the Glock. The P226 (and its smaller clone, the P229, which may actually outsell it) are still guns you can "ride the river with," as the late, great gunfighting expert Bill Jordan used to say.

Now part of SIG-Sauer's "classic" series, these guns are still seen in the holsters of some of America's largest law enforcement agencies. The double action only versions of the P226 are approved by NYPD and Chicago PD, and are approved (and have been issued) by FBI and DEA.

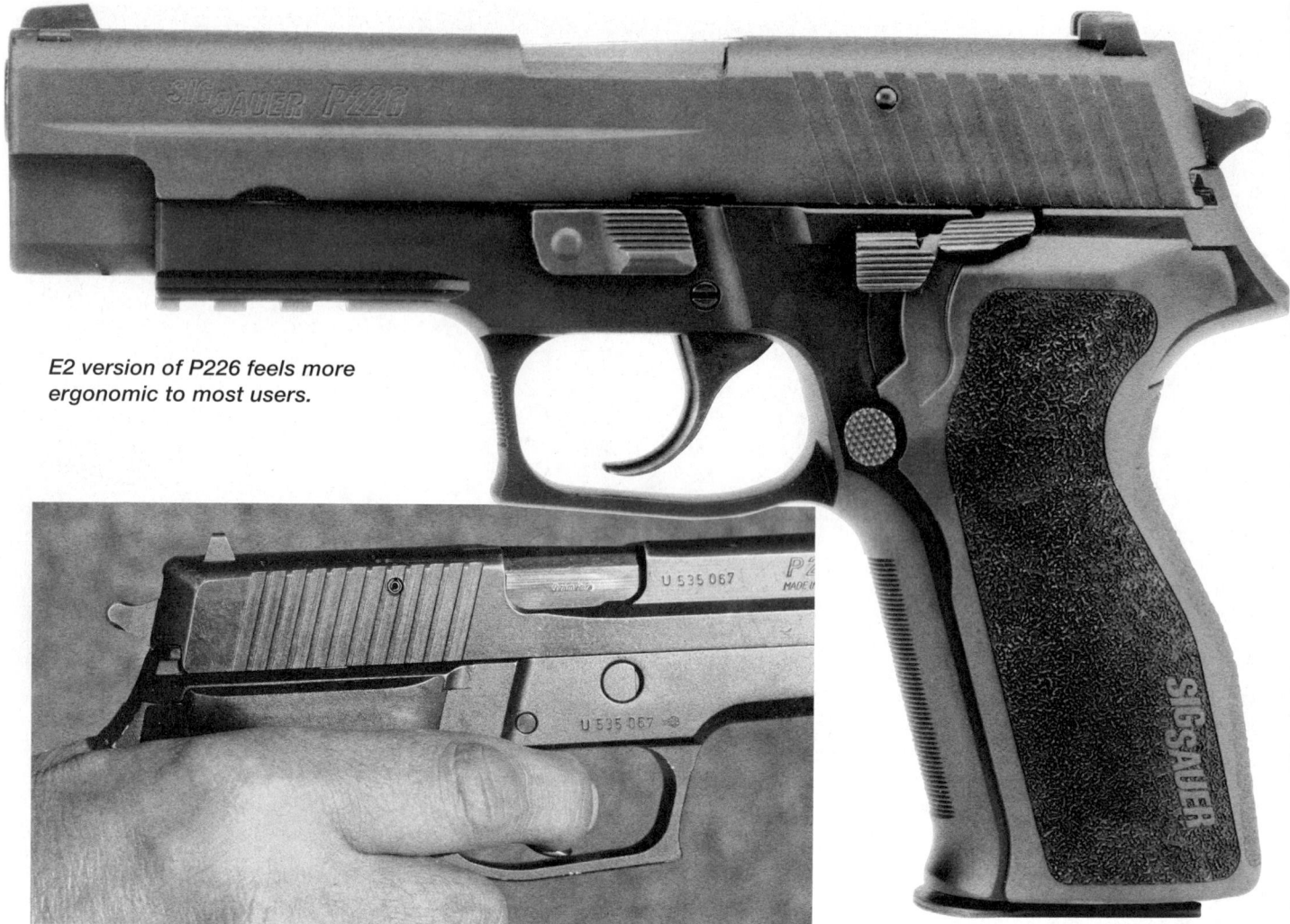

E2 version of P226 feels more ergonomic to most users.

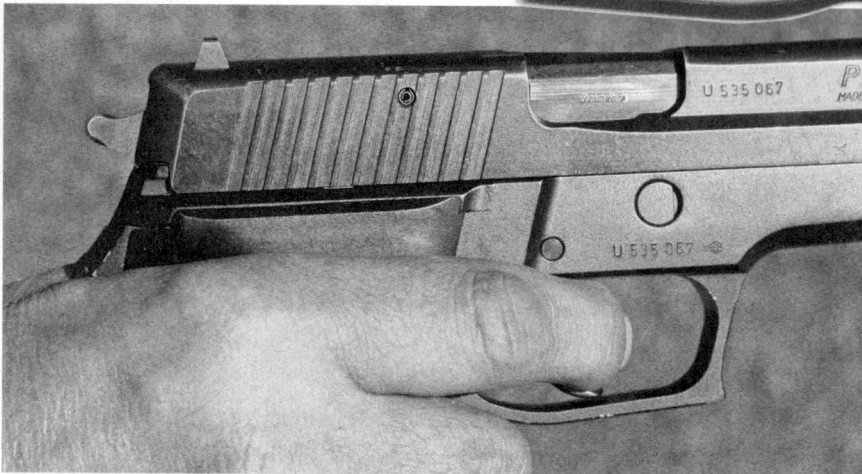

You don't understand the importance of the changed dimensions until you see (and especially, feel) the difference in a human hand. Here, Mas holds an older model P226. Pad of index finger is in contact in double action mode...

...but here, Mas' trigger finger is at the "double action sweet spot" with distal joint centered on trigger. In both cases, grip tang is centered on web of hand, and barrel is directly in line with long bones of the forearm.

The 9mm SIG P226 is the standard sidearm of the elite Navy SEALs, who have carried it since (as some would put it) Christ was a corporal (or in this case, a Petty Officer Third Class). The SIG P226 is the issue weapon of Great Britain's famed, elite SAS.

SIG has gone in multiple directions in their auto pistol design in the years since the P226 was introduced. Their polymer-framed version, first called the SIG-Pro, has met with more favor in some countries other than ours: France, for example, where the 9mm version is standard issue for the national police. A purpose-designed double action only polymer frame gun – the P250 with modular capability, which allows changing calibers, frames, and barrel/slide lengths with the same firing mechanism and the same serial number – has

*Right: The "E2" on the slide of the new SIG signals
a change far more important than cosmetics. E2
designation is pronounced "E-squared" at the factory.*

been adopted by the Federal Air Marshal service
in caliber .357 SIG. Yet the P226 remains, a
steadfast gun that is much beloved by those who
have actually used it in the field. Classic guns
have a way of doing that. Can anyone say, "1911"?
The same principle is at work with the P226: it
has done its job so very well over the years for
the old Jedi Masters, it survives because even the
"younglings" realize it has been proven to perform
very well in the wars of its time, and the nature of
those wars has not changed.

ENTER THE E2

At the SHOT Show in January 2010 in Las Vegas,
my old friend Dennis Carroll – a veteran Illinois
street cop now retired, and a champion combat
shooter, who now works for SIG – introduced me to
the E2. The "E2" designation stands for Enhanced
Ergonomics.

The enhancements are basically a short re-set
trigger, which has been there with SIG with these
guns for a while, *and* – yes, more important, cue

*Right: The short-reach trigger of the E2, seen at rest
in double action mode. Magazine release button is
reversible, as on earlier variants of the same pistol.*

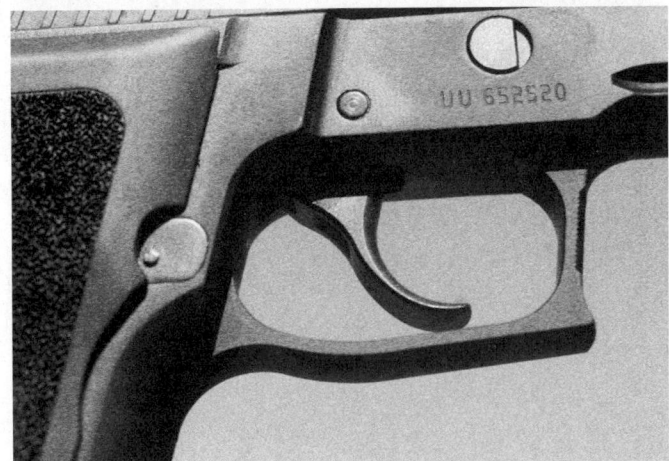

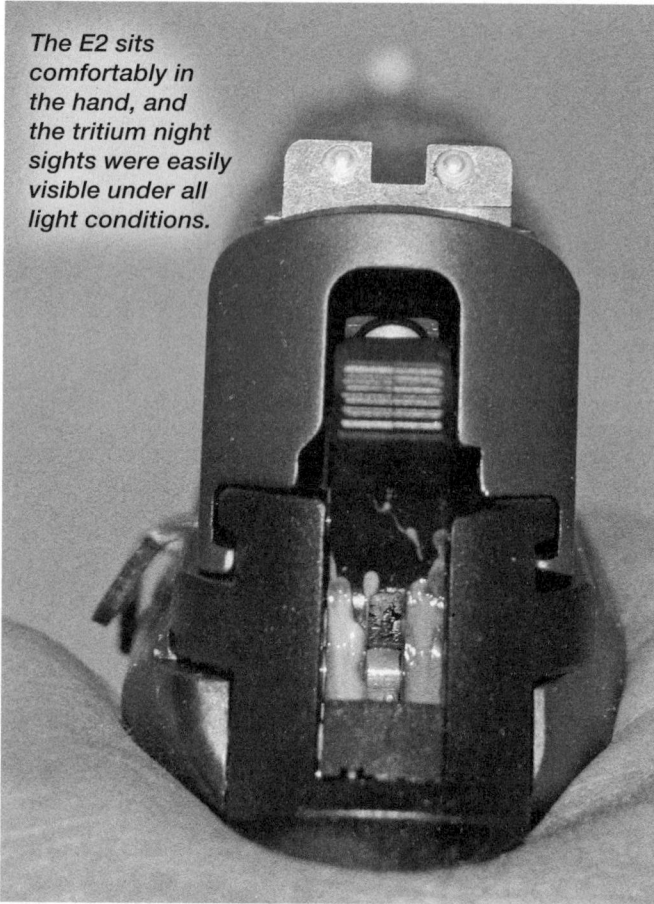

The E2 sits comfortably in the hand, and the tritium night sights were easily visible under all light conditions.

in the drum-roll here please – a grip-frame that is smaller in circumference and, *mainly*, which brings its back-strap more forward toward the trigger. This does two very important things: it gets more of the shooter's fingers around the frame to exert more stabilizing force during shooting, and it gets the shooter's finger "deeper into the trigger."

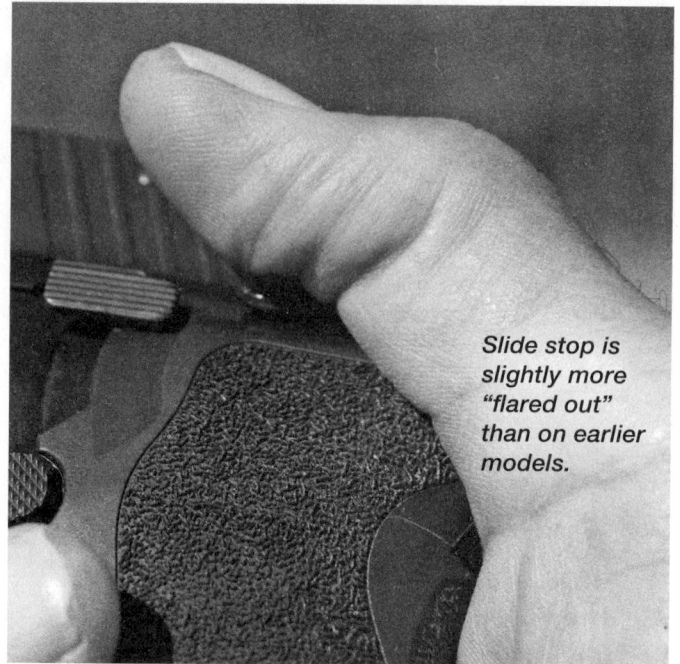

Slide stop is slightly more "flared out" than on earlier models.

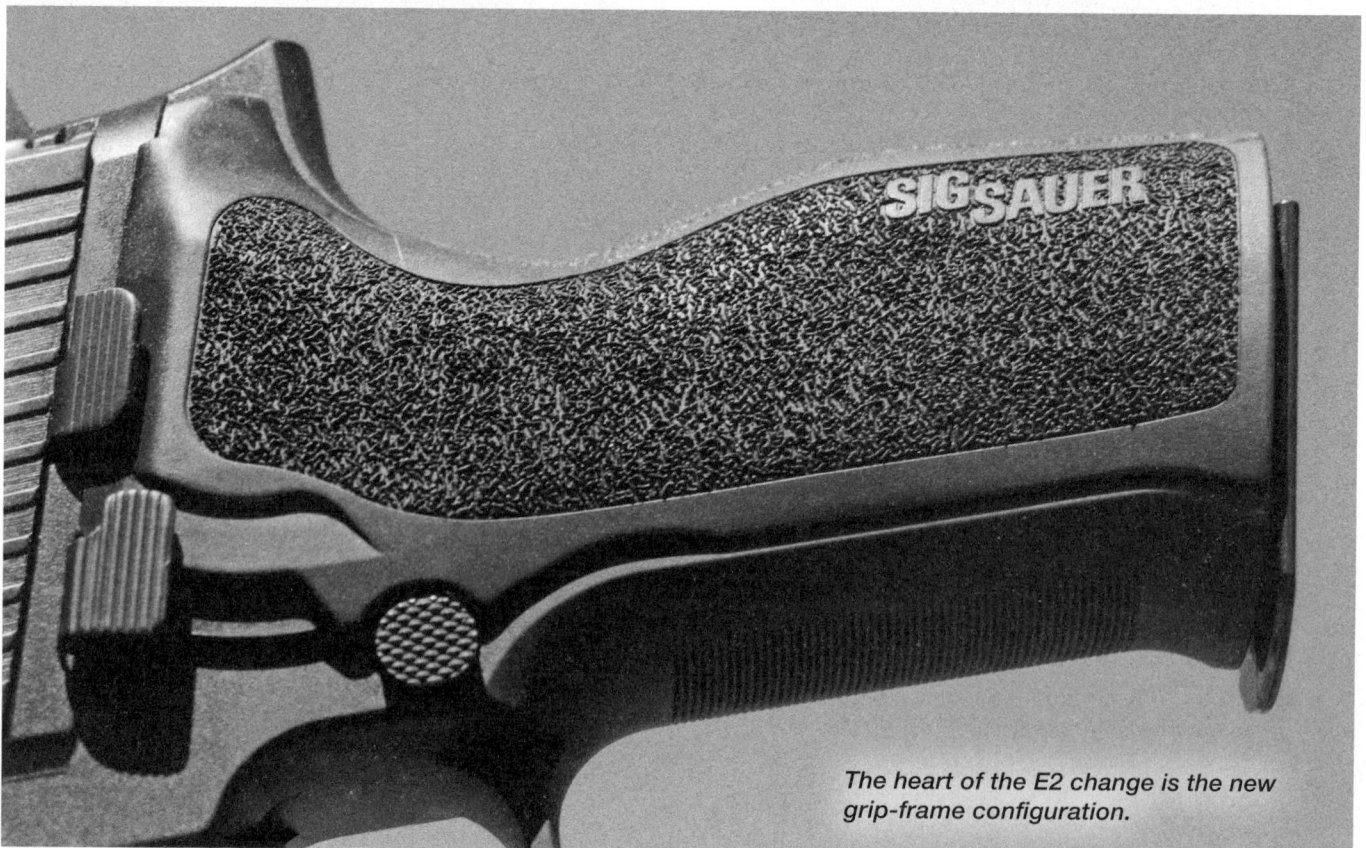

The heart of the E2 change is the new grip-frame configuration.

Using the 3-dot sight picture for aiming, the E2 delivered head shots 5 for 5 from 25 yards, out of the box.

The front night sight on the P226 E2 picked up fast under all light conditions. "Aiming dot" sits below top edge of front sight; post in notch sight picture sent shots low, but 3-dot alignment brought them center.

Let's talk about those little subtleties, which are far more important than they sound. The more flesh and bone that gets wrapped around the gun's "handle" during firing, the more strength the shooter can exert to stabilize the gun, proportionally speaking. This impacts recoil control in a positive way, because it gives the shooter a stronger grasp with which to hold the gun down against rearward forces as the shot is fired. It also has a profound effect on trigger control, because the more firmly the gun is held by the other four digits of the hand, the less that one finger controlling the trigger can jerk the gun off target if said finger gets all spastic under stress.

Now, let's talk about that fifth digit, the trigger finger. In the old days when all cops carried double action revolvers which required a long, heavy pull of the trigger for every shot fired if you wanted to hit quickly again and again, the Old Masters learned that the "sweet spot" for trigger control was not the tip or the pad of the finger as with a light-triggered single action target pistol, but the crease of the join between the distal and medial phalanges of that trigger finger. It simply gave

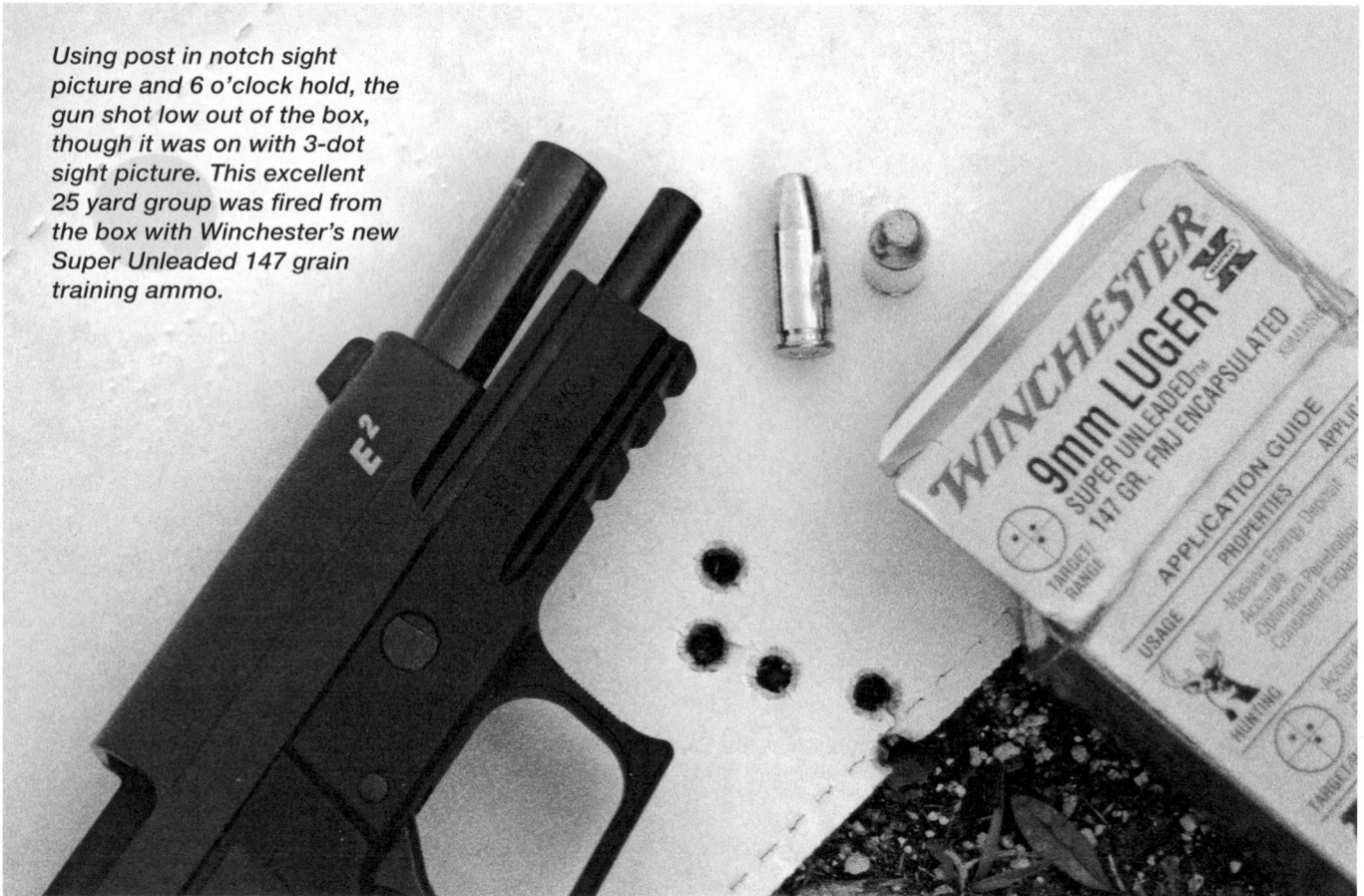

Using post in notch sight picture and 6 o'clock hold, the gun shot low out of the box, though it was on with 3-dot sight picture. This excellent 25 yard group was fired from the box with Winchester's new Super Unleaded 147 grain training ammo.

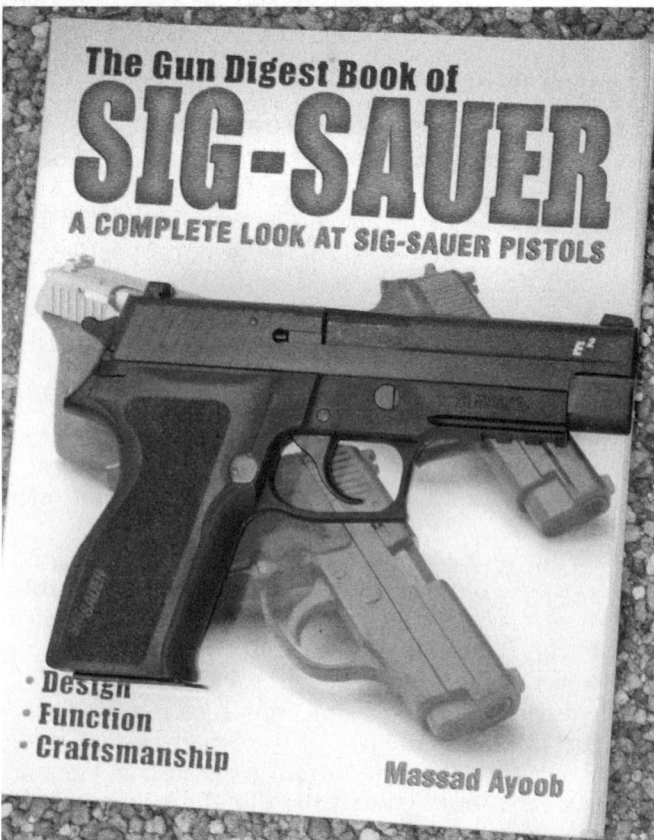

The Gun Digest Book of
SIG-SAUER
A COMPLETE LOOK AT SIG-SAUER PISTOLS

• Design
• Function
• Craftsmanship

Massad Ayoob

more leverage against a heavy resistance against which that finger was pulling. And, of course, it was understood since the 19th century if not earlier, that the barrel of the gun had to be in line with the long bones of the forearm for the gun to stay on target in rapid fire.

By shortening the index finger's reach to the trigger both fore and aft – In front, with the trigger that didn't extend so far forward as before, and in the back, with the newly trimmed backstrap of the E2 – the new gun better allows the shooter's hand to find that "sweet spot." This, in essence, is the core of the E2's appeal. Those who are deeply into the ergonomics of handguns will understand. So will those who shoot for money in competition, and are accustomed to combining maximum speed with maximum accuracy, with electronic timers recording the results and telling the final tale.

SHOOTING THE E2

The E2 is available in this writing in the full-size P226 format and the more compact P229

Left: The E2 was not available when Mas wrote First Edition of Gun Digest Book of SIG-Sauer. He feels the new gun is an important upgrade to a well-proven system.

Mas shoots an IDPA match with the test gun, using "mailbox" for cover. Spent casing from Shot 1 has just cleared chamber, but P226 E2 is already on target for Shot 2...

...and the camera "catches the fire" as the Shot 2 discharges and E2 begins to cycle next round into chamber. He felt "more hand around gun" gave more control of recoil.

configuration. Both guns are available in 9mm Parabellum, .40 S&W, and .357 SIG. Our test gun was a 9mm P226R E2 (the "R" stands for "rail," accepting a light, laser module, or combination thereof). I found that it fit my hand better than the multiple P226s I own, which I've come to appreciate, from earlier design formats.

Accuracy? I shot the test P226R E2 from the bench at 25 yards, and found that MagTech 115 grain JHP put five shots into 2.05 inches, with four of those in 1.30 inches and the best three in 1.25 inches, measured to the nearest 0.05 inch, center to center. Black Hills 124 grain JHP did 3.35 inches for five shots, with 1.50 inches for four of them and

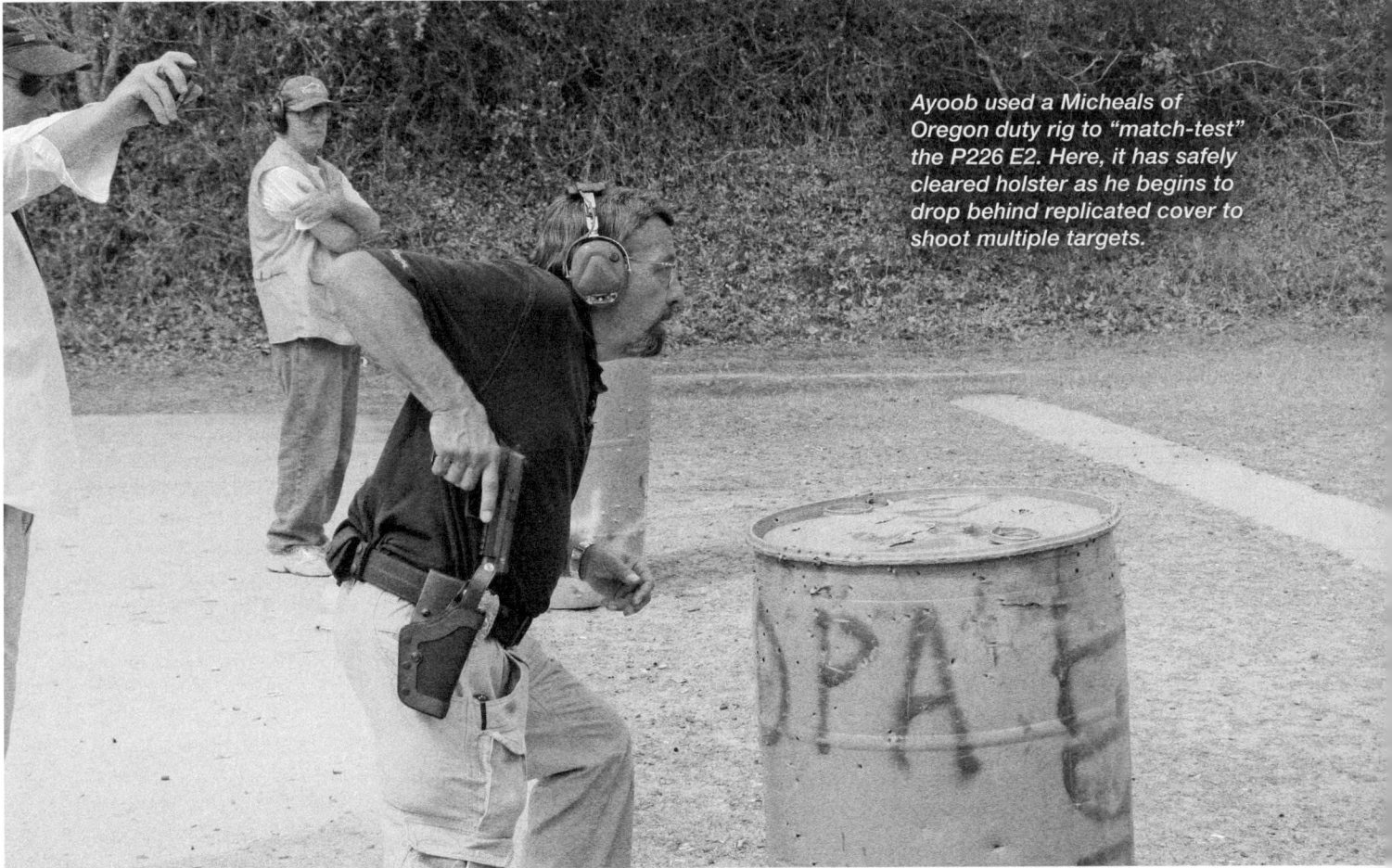

Ayoob used a Micheals of Oregon duty rig to "match-test" the P226 E2. Here, it has safely cleared holster as he begins to drop behind replicated cover to shoot multiple targets.

1.35 inches for the best three. Winchester's latest iteration of the 147 grain subsonic 9mm load they developed in the '80s, the Super Unleaded practice round, trumped everything else with five shots in 1.55 inches, and the best three of those in 0.75 inch. For those who came in late, the best three of a hand-held five-shot bench-rested group have proven to my satisfaction to factor out enough human error to give an excellent prediction of the gun's pure mechanical accuracy with all five shots from a machine rest.

Trigger pull has a lot to do with "practical accuracy." The P226 from its genesis was a standard for smoothness in double action pull. As it "cocks itself" in cycling for the next shot,

the single action pull of the SIG is still awfully nice, though it has historically had a long re-set. I believe this was part of its engineering parameters: as a military and police gun, its designers wanted to make sure that every shot fired after the first double-action round was intentional, and not caused by a quiver of a shaky trigger finger when that subsequent shot might no longer be justified.

RELIABILITY

Many of the folks on my "test crew" are SIG fans, and all were eager to check out the new E2 with their own ammo. (Sometimes, I feel like Tom

Sawyer whitewashing the fence in that old Mark Twain classic of the same name...) I figure about 500 rounds went through the test gun. No misfires, no misfeeds, no mis-anything...no problems, as we have learned to expect from the P226. The slide will fail to lock open if the right-handed shooter holds the slide-stop lever down with the right thumb...but that's the shooter's problem in my view, not the gun's.

E2 IN ACTION

I've carried P226s concealed all over the country, and in times past, in uniform. I noticed that part of the Enhanced Ergonomics seem to be extended slide stops and decocking lever on the E2. Cool for shooting, maybe...but the parts protruded just enough that the gun "stuck" in an inside the waistband holster made for the older series P226R. I shot an IDPA match with the test gun and had to fall back on the IDPA rule that allows those of us with badges to shoot with uniform duty rigs, so long as we use the security devices. Even so, the pistol did well for me; I had learned in accuracy testing to use the 3-dot sight picture because the gun hit low with a post-in-notch sight picture.

Bottom line? The E2 really is more "shootable" in most hands thanks to the reshaping, and is a genuine improvement to an already excellent modern classic among service pistols.

Chapter 4

The SIG P227

In firearms design, there is evolution and there is revolution. Evolution: you take a proven good thing and find ways to make it even better. Revolution: you come up with something pretty much new, and maybe even radical.

As I hope this book clearly shows, SIG Sauer has taken part in both. The P320 is certainly, at least for SIG, revolution. Let's look at an example of evolution, the SIG P227.

Essentially jacking up the barrel/slide assembly of a P220 and running something very much like a P226 frame under it, SIG created their first high capacity traditional double action service pistol in .45 ACP. This new model was dubbed the P227, and first appeared at the SHOT Show in Las Vegas in January of 2013. Getting production out took longer, but the pistol was a reality by mid-year.

In 2013, I tested a P227 for a cover story in *GUNS* magazine, scheduled to run with an early 2014 dateline. By then, the 227 was no longer new. Several shooters at **www.sigforum.com** wrote glowingly of their experiences with the P227s they'd bought, and I saw no criticisms, let alone horror stories.

It's no secret that when you buy a new model of anything, you become the "beta tester." Many seasoned shooters have learned not to be the first on their block to have the new goodie, and to let others be the guinea pigs who find the hidden problems that the engineers missed.

With the P227, we seem to have had enough already proven and de-bugged elements – the famously reliable P220 on the top end, a slightly modified P250 .45 magazine from the always reliable MecGar, and the long-proven double action/double stack SIG-Sauer frame – that when they all came together, they worked fine. The first year of the P227 in the marketplace is not yet complete at this writing, but so far, it has been smooth sailing for this pistol.

This writer's take on it is found here, in the story written for *GUNS* magazine:

SIG P227 .45

In the late 1970s, SIG contracted with Browning to produce their P220 pistol as the Browning BDA. It caught the imagination of American shooters. The Huntington Beach, California Police Department adopted it for their officers, and the die was cast: there was at last a .45 auto (that so many street cops wanted) which was double action and would be acceptable to police chiefs (many of whom

ACP cartridges in standard configuration, and the company offers a fourteen-round extended magazine. Counting the round in the chamber, this brings the firepower "up to speed" in the double-stack .45 ACP market, where the thirteen-plus-one round Glock 21 seems to be the current sales leader.

FIRST IMPRESSIONS

The easiest way for me to say it is, "If you've held the P226 with E2 ("Ergonomics squared") grip configuration, you've essentially held the P227. If you've shot the P220 .45, you've pretty much shot

SIG P227 Nitron was accuracy tested with these three loads at 25 yards.

were scared to death of issuing a cocked and locked 1911). A trend was started. Smith & Wesson finally got in gear with something they'd long been thinking of, a double action .45 auto, and a few years later the S&W Model 645 was introduced. Meanwhile, SIG listened to Yank cops (and civilians) who didn't care for the butt-heel magazine release of the original P220/Browning BDA, and the result was what was called then the P220 American, with a 1911-type push button mag release.

Ever since, the P220 .45 has been popular in America, among cops and armed citizens alike. From the beginning, it proved remarkably accurate, and thanks to its relatively straight line feed, remarkably reliable. As SIG found ways to build even better pistols, the P220 gained a forged slide instead of the "folded" style of the original German-made gun, and production was transferred to the American factory in Exeter, NH.

The one complaint the company got was in reference to the single-stack magazine. The P220 mag originally held seven rounds; the company redesigned for eight, making it a nine-shot pistol counting the round in the chamber. The trend was toward still higher firepower, though.

SIG listened, and 2013 saw the introduction of the latest evolution of the P220 series .45s, the P227. Its tapered magazine holds ten .45

Top, early P220E with "folded" slide and butt heel mag release. Center, Nill-gripped P220ST tuned by Ernest Langdon. Below, the latest evolution, the P227.

Finish wear soon became evident at left rear of P227's slide.

the P227." I honestly can't distinguish the P226 E2 from the P227 with my eyes closed by feel, and the always-controllable recoil of the P220 remains so in the larger capacity P227 .45.

About that double-stack magazine: if you noticed that it's remarkably similar to the .45 caliber P250 double action only SIG Sauer with polymer frame, well, that's not exactly a coincidence. It seems that SIG engineers saw no need to reinvent the wheel. My friend Chuck McDonald slightly modified some P250 .45 mags he had, and *voila:* they worked fine in his new P227, with which he is extremely happy.

A pleasant side effect of the tapered mag is that it facilitates reloading. The smaller top of the magazine is easier to insert in the relatively larger magazine well of the double-stack gun. For those of a competitive bent, the magazine release button is convertible and can be moved from the left side of the pistol to the right. I don't think that's a great idea for carry because if your side bumps into a hard object that hits the button, it can dislodge the magazine, but for competitors it does speed up the reload. As southpaws long ago discovered with 1911s and left-side mag release buttons, it's quicker

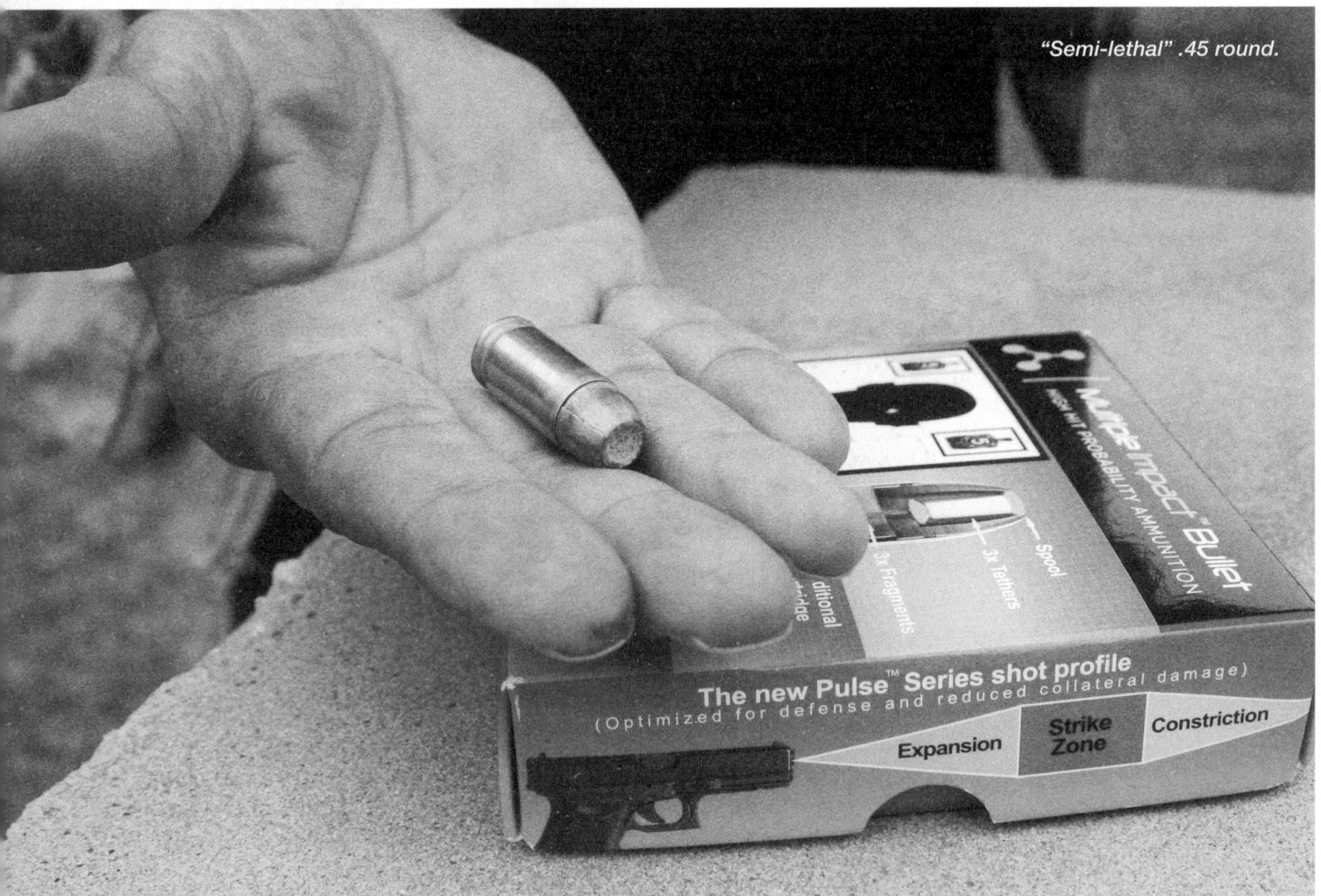

"Semi-lethal" .45 round.

The new Pulse™ Series shot profile
(Optimized for defense and reduced collateral damage)

Expansion   Strike Zone   Constriction

Mas test-fires "semi-lethal" round at 7 yards from P227 .45.

Result of single "semi-lethal" .45 round from P227 at 7 yards.

to just bring your trigger finger back out of the trigger guard and punch a button on the same side, than to turn your hand as many must to hit a left-side button with one's right thumb.

TRIGGER PULL

GUNS' test sample P227, serial number 51A000493, had a double action pull that measured 10.78 pounds on a Lyman digital trigger gauge, acquired from Brownell's. Single action pull ran 6.71 pounds. This was a bit over the factory spec, which is ten pounds even for double action mode and 4.4

pounds in single action, but is also in keeping with my experience with SIG-Sauers over the years.

Double action pull is smooth. This was expected. For many years, the SIG set the standard by which other double action autos' trigger strokes were judged. It was consistent all the way through the pull, with no staging and no "stacking," or increase in pressure near the end. In single action there's a fairly long re-set, perhaps to prevent nervous, twitchy hands from triggering unintentional extra shots. You can feel a very short roll before the single action shot breaks.

ACCURACY

Bench testing was done off a Caldwell Matrix rest on a concrete bench in Live Oak, Florida from 25 yards. Conventional jacketed hollow points were used in standard pressure 185 grain and 230 grain loadings, along with a 185 grain all copper hollow point at +P velocity.

The 185 grain Nosler Match Grade JHP, rated for 980 foot-seconds velocity (presumably from a 5-inch barrel), shot center for windage and just below the aiming dot with a post in notch sight picture. It turned out to shoot spot on for elevation if the Trijicon dots were used for aiming, instead of the conventional sight picture, since the dots sit below the top edges of front and rear sights. The five-shot group measured 1.90 inches. The best three hits among those was also measured, since experience has taught me that this will factor out unnoticed human error and give a good approximation of what the same gun and load would have done from a Ransom machine rest. That measurement was considerably under an inch, 0.85 inch to be exact.

The other 185 grain load in the test was the +P Barnes TAC-XPD, a fast-stepping all-copper hollow point. I've been impressed with how Barnes all-copper bullets "test" for terminal ballistics since they first came out as loaded .45 ACP in Taurus-branded boxes. It was "on" for elevation with post in notch sight picture at 25

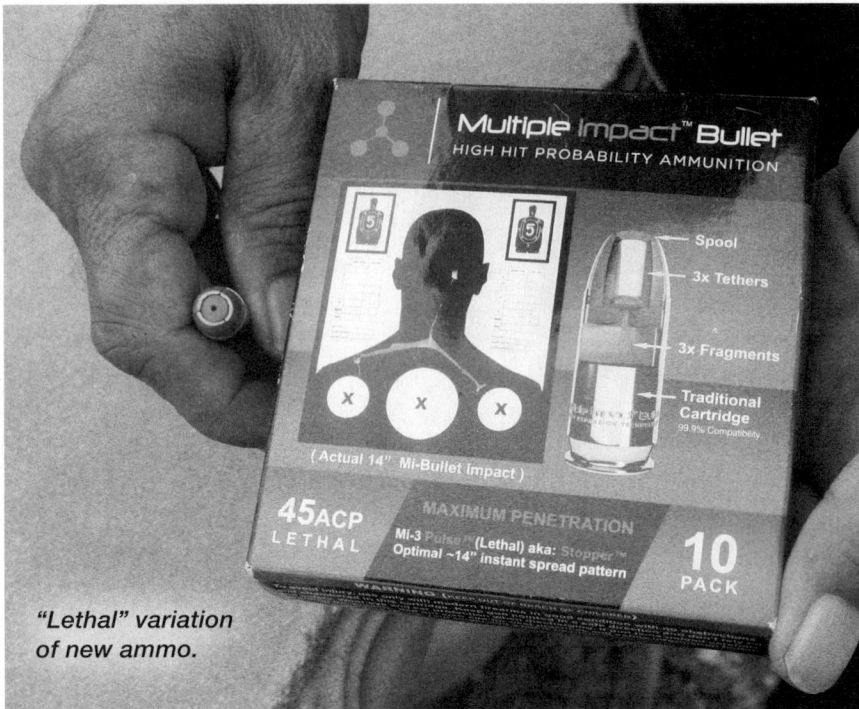

"Lethal" variation of new ammo.

Below: Mas fires "Lethal" variation of new load from 7 yards, with SIG P227.

Right: Result of one shot from Lethal strung-projectile load, 7 yards, from P227.

yards, if a whisker right. The five shots clustered in 2.05 inches (I measure to the nearest 0.05 inch), and the best three of those were in 1.10 inches.

Then came the star of the show, the Nosler Match Grade 230 grain JHP, rated for 830 feet per second (again, presumably, out of a 5-inch gun; the P227 tested here had a 4.4-inch barrel). The group formed a single small, angled slash in the target: two very tight doubles connected by a single smaller-looking .45 hole between them. The group measurement was a personal best in many decades of shooting SIG-Sauer pistols: right at seven-tenths of one inch for all five, measuring the bullet holes center to center. The best three of those, center to center, measured 0.40 inch, less than the diameter of a single .45 hole.

Allow me to ponder that with you. First, I feel an overwhelming urge to order a case of Nosler 230 grain Match jacketed hollow point. But, second, consider this. I've always found the P220 .45 to be the most accurate of SIG pistols. I've twice gotten groups an inch or less with them for all five shots at 75 feet, once with a 5" single action only model and inexpensive MagTech 230 hardball, and once with my old P220E (the "E" is for "European") with folded slide and butt-heel magazine release, and Federal 185 grain Match JHP.

With the P226 in .357 SIG, I was once able to put five shots in exactly an inch with Speer Gold Dot 125 grain bonded jacketed hollow point, at the Jim McLoud's Manchester Indoor Firing Line in Manchester, NH. Of the many P226s I've shot in 9mm, I've come achingly close to an inch, but was never quite able to make it.

Seven-tenths of an inch for five shots with a service pistol at 25 yards? I would dance in the streets if I wasn't too old to dance. Instead, I'll just brag about it here. I'm gonna frame that group.

BULLETS WITH STRINGS ATTACHED

We also had with us Multiple Impact ™ Bullet ammo. Ten rounds each of ".45 ACP semi-lethal" Mi3 Pulse ™ aka Stunner™ rounds, marked on the box "Optimal-14" instant spread pattern." I fired one round of this from the P227 SIG at seven yards. Three holes appeared, 7.2 inches apart in a catty-cornered Y-shaped incision resembling the cut the medical examiner makes when he does your autopsy. The strings attaching the three projectiles were left hanging in the target, one on the front and two out the back. The lower hole was the shape of a keyholed bullet, and the other two looked like stab wounds.

The other load was marked "45 ACP LETHAL: Mi3 Pulse™ aka: Stopper™, Optimal-14" instant spread pattern." The three projectiles created a couple of small "stab wounds" in the cardboard

185 grain Match Nosler JHP, 5 shots from 25 yard bench rest, SIG P227.

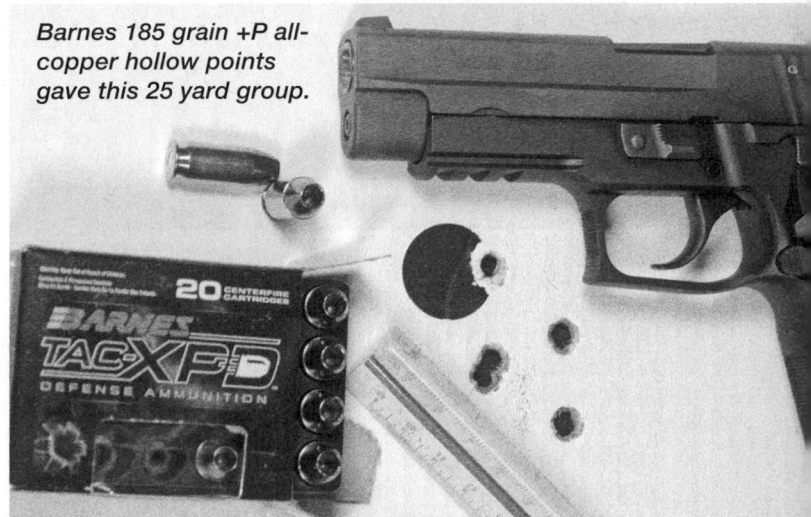

Barnes 185 grain +P all-copper hollow points gave this 25 yard group.

Nosler Match Grade 230 grain JHP resulted in 2 tight doubles connected by one more shot, measuring overall 0.70" center to center, from P227 at 25 yards.

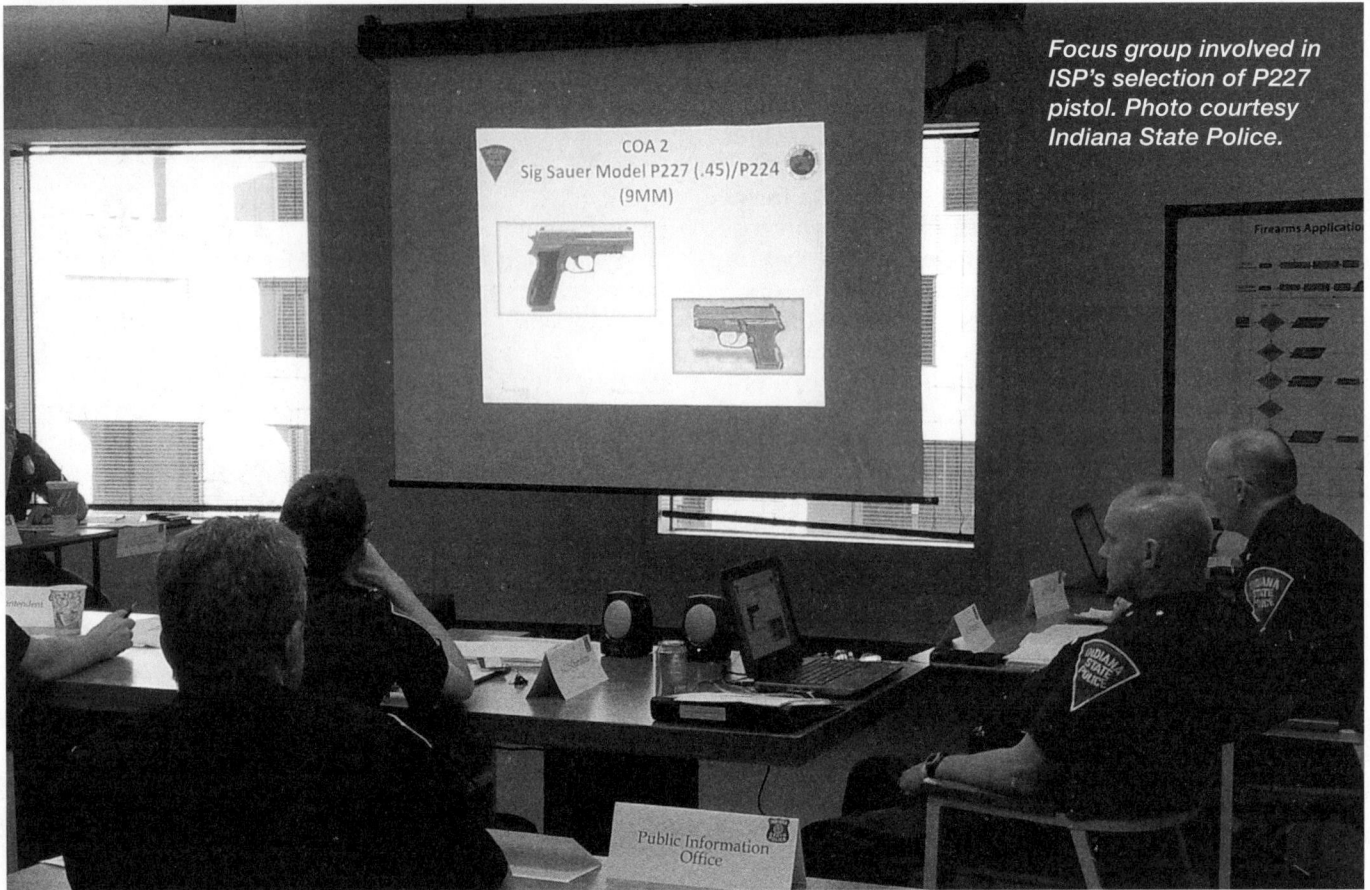

Focus group involved in ISP's selection of P227 pistol. Photo courtesy Indiana State Police.

target and one tiny bullet hole, grouping 8.8 inches apart center to center. Two of the threaded "tethers" managed to punch through the cardboard, while the third only indented the outer surface.

The ammo was provided to GUNS courtesy of Ballistic Concepts, LLC in Colorado. While I still blanch at the idea of trying to fire something "semi-lethal" out of an inherently lethal weapon, innovation is always worth a look.

P227 RELIABILITY

I've put a few hundred rounds now through a couple of P227s, one that I tested at the SIG Academy in Exeter in the summer of 2013, and the one in a Leather Arsenal inside the waistband holster on my hip as I write this while looking out the window and watching wind-driven snow falling in Iowa in November 2013. There has not been a single malfunction with any round I've run through this .45, including some, uh, unusual stuff.

The aforementioned Chuck McDonald ran more than 650 rounds through his P227 when he got it. His experience was like mine: zero malfunctions.

In June of 2013, I visited the Indiana State Police headquarters in Indianapolis, and debriefed personnel from Superintendent Doug Carter on down as to why they had become the first major police department in the nation to adopt the SIG P227 .45. From the top cop to the firearms instructors to the ERT (Emergency Response Team, aka SWAT) to the field troopers they had test the guns in contention, all had appreciated the power and the reliability. Indeed, it appears that reliability was the single biggest point that caused this agency to adopt the P227 as the first SIG in their history.

BOTTOM LINE

The only real complaint I have with this pistol is that the finish seems thin. It is starting to wear off on the left rear of the slide. There is no indication of corrosion yet, but this does not please. I'm also a bit disappointed that the test gun came with two ten-round magazines, and none of those appealing fourteen-rounders.

SIGs have never been cheap. MSRP is $993 for this P227 Nitron; add night sights such as those on our test pistol, and that goes up to $1,085.

I'll tell you right now, I think it's worth it. I like the ergonomics, the reliability, and the shootability. When you get a personal best for accuracy with a brand, it leaves an impression. There are no sharp edges to chafe either body or clothing after several days of constant concealed carry.

I am liking this pistol very much, and am thinking of buying it rather than letting it go back to SIG.

After all, SIG can make more...

In the *GUNS* story above, reference was made to the Indiana State Police adopting the P227. I visited them in June of 2013 to see how that went. It was a fascinating lesson in selecting equipment by letting both the resident experts and the end users have a say in the matter. My article on it appeared shortly thereafter in my Cop Talk column in *American Handgunner* magazine, where I've proudly served as Law Enforcement Editor for thirty-some years. That article follows here:

COP TALK: CALIBER CHOICE: A QUESTION OF CONFIDENCE

When a department adopts a new service pistol, perceptions of the rank and file are important.

In a world where one size does not fit all, standard issue police handgun choice can be controversial. This has certainly been true of the Indiana State Police, with more than 1300 armed and sworn personnel in the ranks of its uniformed troopers and plainclothes detectives.

In the last quarter century, the ISP has gone through half a dozen different types of handgun. The old standby .357 revolver with 125 grain Magnum loads was replaced in the 80s by a double action 9mm with 147 grain subsonic ammo. In the 90s, there was a switch to the same pistol in caliber .40 S&W, with 180 grain subsonic hollow points. Time went on, and in the new century a striker-fired polymer-framed .40 replaced the older style. Various issues caused another change, to the same model in 9mm. Toward the end of 2012, the department adopted a striker-fired .45 auto.

This was the situation faced in 2013 by newly appointed Superintendent Doug Carter, when it was determined that it was time for the agency to review its sidearm policy and start with the proverbial new sheet of paper. An Indiana state trooper in his younger days, Carter had become famous as the elected sheriff of Hamilton County, and one of his hallmarks had been responsiveness to his personnel on the street. Bringing the same approach to the Superintendent's office, he created an enhanced planning team to study the issue. Input encompassed the agency's firearms instructors, both at headquarters and post level, as well as the Emergency Response Team, ISP's full-time SWAT entity. Moreover, Carter made sure there were representatives of rank and file troopers and detectives from all five of the state's areas. "Our core tenet," the superintendent told American Handgunner, "is troopers first."

SIDES OF THE DEBATE

For ISP, the choice came down to 9mm or .45 ACP. When the agency first adopted autos, the troopers certainly appreciated soft recoil and sixteen rounds instead of six, but many were doubtful about the smallest caliber service pistol after the 125 grain .357 Magnum hollow point had proven itself spectacularly well on the street. That residual desire for more power had led to ISP's adoption of the .40 in the last decade of the 20th century. The subsequent return to the 9mm had drawn

From left: Col. Mark French, Superintendent Doug Carter, Lt. Col. Mark Smith discuss Indiana State Police choice of P227. Ayoob photo.

complaints from many troopers who had found a larger caliber pistol round comforting.

One point to which both sides stipulated was that the 147 grain Gold Dot 9mm duty load had not been a failure. There had been no horror stories of outlaws soaking up bullet after bullet and staying on their feet shooting at troopers. For this reason, and because the 9mm offered softer recoil and slightly higher cartridge capacity, there were some voices in ISP advocating for the smaller cartridge.

ERT, and many of the individual troopers who were into guns, took a different view. They felt that with the 230 grain .45 Gold Dot giving essentially the same tactical penetration as the 147   9mm but with a larger bullet, the .45 offered more of the same good thing. They saw all up-side and no down-side to a wider bullet that impacted more tissue. In a world where doctors often say a tenth of an inch makes the difference in whether a major organ or artery is damaged or not, the wider .45 slug was seen as a clear advantage.

What was the perception of the rank and file? "Many of the troops said they didn't care about the caliber, they just wanted a pistol that worked every time," one instructor told me. "But the ones who did care all seemed to want .45s. No one told us, '.45s are too powerful, we want something smaller.'" ISP's second in command, Col. Mark French, told me that the Superintendent "felt that most all the rank and file guys he spoke   to wanted a .45 also."

Confidence is inextricably intertwined with competence. One long-time Indiana trooper familiar with the controversy told me, "In the end, it was pretty clear that what it came down to was, the Superintendent wanted that trooper out there alone to have maximum confidence in what he or she was carrying." When I asked Superintendent Carter about that, he smiled and nodded in the affirmative.

Which, in the end, is why the .45 won out for the Indiana State Police. The contract has not been signed at this writing, but by the time you read this, the ISP is expected to be issuing the new SIG P227, its double-stack magazines loaded with 230 grain .45 ACP Speer Gold Dots. A quantity of subcompact P224 9mm SIGs will also be ordered for those personnel, such as the executive protection unit, who require an extremely concealable duty pistol.

The P227 can be seen as a P220 with larger magazine, or as a P226 chambered in .45 ACP.

In late November 04 2013, as deadline was closing on the Second Edition of "Gun Digest Book of SIG SAUER," I touched bases again with Col. Mark French of the Indiana State Police to see how the changeover to the P227 was progressing. He replied, "This week we received our first 50 P227s. A cadre of our senior firearms instructors flew to New Hampshire to randomly shoot a sampling of these 50. They also took in an overview of the manufacturing facility. All went very well. We are set to transition our firearms instructors (about 50 troops) beginning Dec 9th. From there, at the end of December, we will begin firearms training for about 70 recruits that we currently have in our State Police Academy. That will be our first transition phase other than instructors. After that we'll push out into the rest of the department, the entire roll out will take us several months into 2014. The transition will be a 4 day block of instruction, a large portion of our department have never been issued a DA / SA pistol so we want to slow down and get that trigger pull right."

All things considered, the P227 shows all the signs of "a new product done right." It's going to be a stellar addition to the SIG SAUER line.

Two inch groups like this at 25 yards are typical for SIG's new P227 .45.

Spent case in air, muzzle on target shows easy control of P227 with .45 hardball in hands of petite pistol champ Gail Pepin.

Chapter 5
The SIG P228

A MORE COMPACT VERSION OF THE P226 9MM, COMPLETE WITH THE BIGGER GUN'S RELIABILITY AND ACCURACY.

Introduced in 1988, the P228 is essentially a P226 9mm shortened at muzzle and butt for easier concealed carry. Despite a shorter (3.86-inch) barrel and proportionally shorter sight radius, the P228 delivers the same excellent accuracy of its big brother.

How accurate is that? I recently took a nearly new P228 to the range, equipped with a LaserMax sighting unit, which I turned off for the 25-yard accuracy testing. The 25-yard bench rest line I usually employ for this was in use, so I set up in one of the IDPA shooting bays, which had a Kriss-Kross barricade set up at the 25-yard line. This particular range prop gets its name from an IDPA match stage which forces the shooter to fire at three targets from each side of the barricade high, and each side of the barricade low, changing positions in a diagonal fashion. The cross beam marks the boundary between the high and the low positions. It is at a height where, with a minimum of contortions, I could brace the heel of the support hand on the cross beam and the back of that hand against the vertical portion of the wooden barricade at the same time. This allowed an unusually steady hold for a strong-side barricade position.

Five different loads were tested, running the gamut from 950 to 1250 feet per second in velocity and 147 to 115 grains in bullet weight, and encompassing four well-known brands. Each five-shot group was measured three times. The first measurement was all five shots, to indicate practical accuracy that could be expected in a solidly braced cover position. The second was the best three shots, always a good predictor of the gun's inherent mechanical accuracy with the given round since human error is largely accounted for. Finally, because this particular gun showed a very consistent "4+1" shot placement factor, the best four hits were also measured to get one more perspective on the gun's grouping tendencies. The results are shown above.

Ah, the unexpected changes and variables of shooting. Note that the ammo with the loosest overall group, PMC, also had the tightest measurement of 1/2 an inch in the Best 3 category with two shots in a

Brand	Load	5-Shot Group	Best 4 Shots	Best 3 Shots
Black Hills EXP	115-grain JHP+P	3-1/2"	2-3/8"	2-1/8"
PMC	115-grain JHP	4-1/2"	2-1/2"	1/2"
Remington	115-grain JHP	2-15/16"	1-5/8"	1-1/8"
Winchester Silvertip	147-grain JHP subsonic	2-7/8"	1-3/16"	11/16"
Winchester USA	147-grain TMJ subsonic	2.00"	1-5/16"	1-1/4"

This 2-inch group at 25 yards, fired from a barricade position with Winchester USA 147-grain subsonic, shows the P228's extraordinary accuracy.

tight double hole. Two out of five loadings gave Best 3 groupings of under an inch.

The "4+1" element was very consistent here, with the first hand-chambered shot always going higher than the subsequent four rounds that were automatically cycled into the firing chamber by the SIG's recoil-operated mechanism. The photos show that the groups tended to be larger in vertical measurement than in horizontal. The lateral measurement was only about 3/4 of one inch for the PMC, 2 inches for the Black Hills, and barely over an inch for the Remington, and so on.

The P228 was issued in the thousands by the FBI. Read the comments of Richard Law and Peter Brookesmith in *The Fighting Handgun* on the Bureau's temporary return to the 9mm after experiencing problems with their trademark 10mm. "The FBI, meanwhile, went back to 9mm after all, and in 1996 were issuing their agents with SIG-Sauer P228 pistols – a choice automatic, but not a .40." (1) Law and Brookesmith, it should be noted, are advocates of larger calibers.

The FBI was not the only Federal law enforcement agency to adopt the P228. So did the Internal Revenue Service for its armed enforcement personnel. The DEA issued a great many P228s, and a number of U.S. Marshals have carried that sidearm as well.

The U.S. military, however, made the most striking purchase of SIG P228s by the Federal government. In what many saw as confession and atonement for the decision that had been made in the service pistol trials, the P228 was designated the M11 and issued to CID (Criminal Investigation Division, the "detective branch" if you will of the Military Police). Firearms authority Tim Mullin had the following to say in his book *The 100 Greatest Combat Pistols*. "…(The) U.S. military really wanted the SIG P226 when it sought a 9X19mm pistol, but got stuck with the Beretta M9/M10. Well, some military units got around adopting the Beretta by opting for the SIG P226 anyway, rebuilding old Government Models (as did Delta), or buying Glock 21s, as did the Marine Corps."

Continues Mullin, "After the M9/M10 was adopted, all of a sudden it dawned on some people

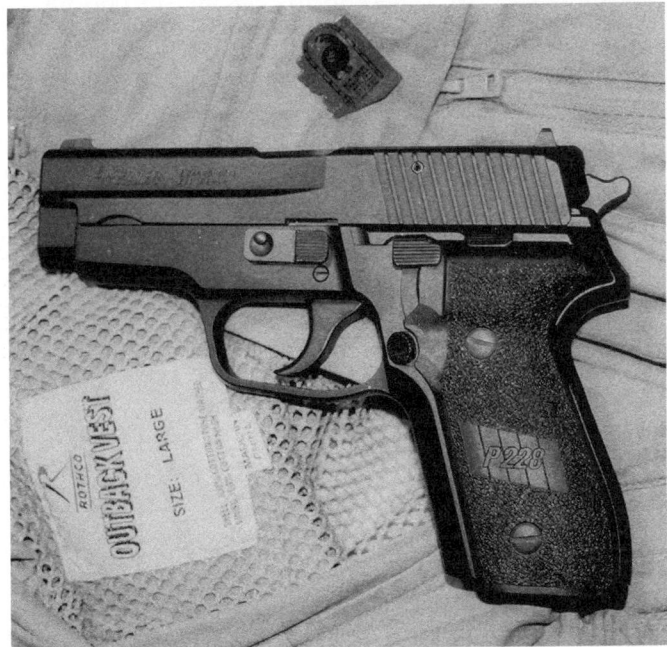

The P228 succeeded in its design parameter, which was to be a concealable handgun of adequate power with a substantial magazine reservoir. The Outback concealed carry vest has worked well for the author and many of his staff, associates, and students.

that this was a *big* pistol. There were many different pistols in the U.S. military inventory simply because big pistols don't work for every situation. But the military had spent a lot of money convincing Congress that it needed one caliber to rationalize ammunition control, 9X19mm. As soon as the call went out for a smaller pistol for women, criminal investigators, and others, the P228 was developed. Now, anyone who knows anything about guns knows that it is not the length of the barrel that makes it difficult to conceal a pistol, but rather its width. The P228 was shorter than the M9/10, but just as wide since it used a double-column magazine. If the military services needed a smaller weapon, you think they would have gone to the single-column version of the M92. Had they done that, the manual of arms training would have been the same. Instead, they adopted the P228, calling it the M11, which meant extra training. Of course, the P228 was merely a shortened version of the pistol they originally wanted, and that was probably the major element in the decision." (2)

When Britain's SAS adopted the P226 as its primary fighting pistol to replace its former trademark gun, the Browning Hi-Power, "the regiment" also acquired a quantity of the more compact P228s. Known to work in undercover/plainclothes modes against terrorists, they wanted a handgun which would be reasonably concealable yet eminently shootable under stress. By all reports, they are delighted with both the P226 and the P228 in their respective roles within SAS mission profiles. Observes Mullin, "The British Army made a better

decision in adopting the P226 for general use and the P228 for those requiring a smaller weapon. It would have been even better for it to have taken the P225, but high-capacity autoloaders are the rage for those who plan to miss a lot." (3)

The P228 was not limited to plainclothes operatives, however. Many police departments thought enough of the gun that they adopted it department wide, issuing it to uniformed officers as well as plainclothes investigators. The rationale was that with 14 shots (13 in the original pre-ban magazines and subsequent LEO magazines, and one more in the firing chamber), the P228 brought them nearly equal the firepower they would have been afforded with the larger SIG P226. They also had a pistol which, being shorter overall and particularly in the butt, was much more amenable to concealed carry.

This has several advantages. Many private citizens looking at police weapons purchases do not take into consideration that today's uniformed officer is tonight's off-duty cop, and tomorrow's plainclothes investigator. If you issue separate guns for uniform division and detective division, there are extra guns that must be accounted for to the bureaucracy. There are extra training hours and qualifications that must be scheduled when a uniformed patrolman is promoted to detective, or when a detective is promoted to sergeant and rotated back to uniformed patrol.

Some police departments still require their sworn personnel to be armed at all times when off duty except when they plan to consume significant quantities of alcohol. Most, at minimum, encourage off-duty carry. Only a handful of agencies (in the United States, at least) forbid their cops from carrying on their own time.

For the off-duty policeman and his department *and* his firearms instructors, having one gun for both plainclothes and uniform wear solves many problems. It guarantees that the officer will have maximum familiarity, confidence, and competence with the one gun he has trained with most, and carries all the time. It is one less gun to keep track of in terms of department records. It is one less set of skills the officer must learn, and one less set of qualifications that the often beleaguered range staff must put him through.

Consider the Vermont State Police. When they switched from the six-shot revolver, the pistol they adopted was the SIG P228. Troopers carried it in exposed duty holsters in uniform. Plainclothes officers carried it in concealed, safety-strapped holsters. And all sworn personnel, no matter what their assignment or daily dress code, had it to carry off duty.

The result was uniform competence and confidence with the State Police sidearm. The

This particular P228 shows "4+1 syndrome" with 147-grain subsonic ammo, but still shows splendid grouping potential.

troopers I talked with loved the pistol for its reliability, its good fit to the hand, its light weight on the hip during a long tour of duty, and its comfort and discretion in concealed carry. Similarly, the instructional staff sang its praises. The troops shot it well, found it quick and easy to learn, and were able to easily maintain it in perfect condition.

In the end, the only reason the Vermont State Police traded in their P228s was that the agency found the same fault with it that Law and Brookesmith had. It was a 9mm, and they decided that the more potent .40 S&W caliber would be a better choice. The VSP traded up to the SIG P229 in .40 caliber.

America's armed citizens also liked the P228. From the time of its introduction to the coming of the high-capacity magazine ban in 1994, we saw a great many of them in the civilian classes at Lethal Force Institute. The owners were usually licensed to carry concealed unless they came from a state with no provision for such a permit, and they appreciated the P228's concealability as much as any plainclothes cop, and found the small, high-capacity pistol substantial enough for the added function of home defense. Once again, the dual-purpose thing kicked in: The carry gun could also function admirably as the house gun.

After the Clinton magazine ban, we saw a shift in what might be called "SIG demographics" among the civilian students. Before, we had seen both the P226 and the P228 in copious numbers. Gradually, we saw the P226s replaced by P228s, P220 .45s, and P239s when the latter became available. The civilian market had decided, reasonably enough, that a full-size 10-plus-one-shot pistol was less efficient and therefore less desirable than a full-size 15-plus-one-shot pistol. The P228, on the other hand, suffered less by comparison. Proportionally, a 10-plus-one-shot compact pistol is not so much less efficient than a 13-plus-one-shot compact pistol.

However, while some citizens who formerly would have purchased P226s went to the P228, I had a sense that more were going to the P220 in .45 ACP and particularly the "personal size" P239 when it came out. A distinctly smaller gun than the P228 and holding only two less rounds of 9mm ammunition, the P239 in that caliber seemed a more advantageous design to a number of buyers who were interested in that caliber. The compactness of the P239 coupled with the power of its two other optional chamberings, .40 S&W and .357 SIG, switched still more buyers from the P228 to the P239.

Today, the excellent P228 has been superseded by SIG's M11A1 and P229 pistols. Even at inflated "post-ban" prices, pre-ban magazines of full capacity were absolutely worth it to private citizens

P228, below, is descended from the P226, above.

who appreciated the pistol's reliability, accuracy, compactness, and shooting characteristics.

The P228 is the concealed carry choice of John Hoelschen, a Special Forces trainer whose teaching encompasses CQB, unarmed combat, and field treatment of gunshot trauma. John has won the demanding National Tactical Invitational with his personal P228. When John Hoelschen talks, wise people listen. When he acts, wise people follow his actions.

For many years, the P228 was the preferred sidearm of Duane Thomas, a gun writer who shoots a lot, competes, and teaches. He performs well in all these endeavors, and he takes his personal self-defense very seriously. Duane spoke dryly of his P228's "almost boring reliability," and in the end, that says a lot.

P228 IDIOSYNCRASIES

All standard advice for the SIG-Sauer system applies. Remember that with the shorter grip frame, as with all auto pistols that have this feature, there is a chance of the flesh of the pinkie finger being pinched between the magazine floorplate and the bottom edge of the frame during a fast reload. Learn to keep that finger out of the way during the loading/reloading process.

SIG magazines are preferred. MecGar is the only other brand of magazine I would trust in the P228 pistol. SIG now offers an attachment for P226 magazines that allows them to fit in the P228 without a gap in the frame. The larger magazines work fine. This attachment gives the shooter a surer grip, and is also more esthetically pleasing. It has been suggested that this adapter also acts as a "magazine stop" to keep the mag from traveling too far upward when slammed into the gun. I suppose

P228 is shown with optional extended floorplate magazine...

... which when inserted, better fits the hands of some shooters.

that's true, but my experience is that even *trying* to jam the pistol by vigorously slamming a P226 magazine into a P228, I have been unable to cause a problem. The tapered magazine, by its nature, does not want to over-travel, a problem which occurs epidemically in short-butt 1911 compacts when loaded at slide-lock with singlestack Government Model magazines which do not have the natural detent effect of the double-stack SIG's tapered magazines. Because the P226 was in production much longer before the ban on full capacity magazines, there are more pre-ban P226 magazines than pre-ban P228 magazines available on the legal market.

Some shooters have commented that in general, the P226 action feels smoother and lighter than that of the P228. While that may have been true to a minor degree in the early days of the P228, in recent production runs the P226 and P228 are virtually indistinguishable from one another in this regard. Both are very smooth, with very crisp and controllable single-action pulls and a proper re-set distance for defensive work.

The P228 seems to be extraordinarily reliable with a broad range of ammunition. The 147-grain 9mm subsonic, which I've seen cause sluggish cycling and even malfunctions in some competitive brands, doesn't seem to bother any of the SIGs including this one. The 115-grain bullet at 1350 feet per second, which has established such an enviable "stopping power" record in real world shootings and test shootings of animals, works perfectly in the P228. This round has been known to occasionally cycle a P225's slide so fast that it will close before picking up the next round from its single-stack magazine. This does not seem to happen with the P228, whether you use pre-ban, post-ban, or LEO magazines. The military's hot NATO ammo – hotter than domestic +P+, if you look at the pressure tests – cycles just fine in the M11/P228, as the military has found for years. There are no reports from the military of the M11/P228 failing to stand up as expected to this high-powered ammunition.

Using the same ammunition, I don't find the P228 to kick any more than the P226. This sounds counter-intuitive, because the larger and heavier pistol is supposed to absorb more of the recoil impulse than the smaller and lighter one, but it's simply an honest and true observation. Some shooters even perceive that the P228 jumps less than its bigger brother, theorizing that the shorter slide is traveling less distance and therefore moving the pistol less during the cycling process. All this is highly subjective. Suffice to say that the P228 is an extremely light-kicking handgun.

IN SUMMARY

Well conceived and well executed, the SIG P228 is a splendid example of the compact, high-capacity double-action 9mm pistol. It is extremely reliable and eminently shootable. Delivering a 2-inch group for five shots from a barricade position, and showing potential for sub-1-inch groups at the same 25-yard distance, it is one of the most accurate of its breed. The P228 is, overall, an excellent handgun.

References

1. Law, Richard and Brookesmith, Peter, *The Fighting Handgun*, London: Arms and Armour Press, 1996, P. 157.
2. Mullin, Timothy J., *"The 100 Greatest Combat Pistols,"* Boulder, CO: Paladin Press, 1994, P.385.
3. Mullin, *Ibid.*

Chapter 6
The SIG P229

Smith & Wesson and Winchester jointly introduced the .40 S&W cartridge in January of 1990 at the SHOT (Shooting, Hunting and Outdoor Trade) Show in Las Vegas. I was there. Instantly, the industry jumped on the bandwagon of this new "compromise cartridge."

But not the *whole* industry. While some of the subsequently introduced .40 pistols were simply rechambered 9mms, SIG's research indicated that the high slide velocity and sharp pressure curve generated by the powerful new cartridge warranted a significant redesign before any new pistol should be chambered for it. SIG waited until their designers got it right. In 1992, when SIG introduced the P229 in that caliber, the wait was rewarded with a gun that *worked*.

The P229 is also available in .357 SIG (introduced in 1994) and 9mm Parabellum, but it has been overwhelmingly most popular in the .40 S&W chambering around which it was designed. Identical in height, length, and silhouette with the P228 9mm compact, the P229 is distinguished by a more rugged slide, which is slightly thicker and adds some weight to the pistol, which goes about an ounce and a half more on the scales than a P228. The 229's slide has narrower slide grasping grooves than other SIG-Sauer pistols, blended in with what might be called the "reinforcing band" of added metal along the bottom edge of the slide, which gives the slide and the pistol the necessary added weight. On some pistols, notably the CZ75 style with strong recoil springs, as in the European American Armory (EAA) Witness 10mm model, these smaller slide grooves can make for tenuous grasping and set the stage for fumbles during handling. The shape of the slide grasping grooves on the P229 is such that this does not seem to happen with the SIG pistol.

The slide differed not just in size and shape but in construction. A friend of mine, gun expert Walt Rauch, explains: "The SIG P229 is one of the compact versions of the SIG P226 with one major change from its close relatives, the P225 and P228. The P229 slide is machined from a billet of stainless steel and then blackened to match the frame. The others use slides formed from stamped steel with a steel breechblock pinned into the frame. The all-steel slide came about with the introduction of the .40 S&W cartridge to better handle this high-intensity round and increased the gun's weight by a little over an ounce."[1]

The P229 met with instant success in the law enforcement community. With 12 rounds of .40 S&W or .357 SIG ammo in the magazine or 13 rounds of 9mm, plus one more in the firing chamber, it more than doubled the cartridge capacity of the service revolvers it replaced. Like the P228, it was light and compact enough for plainclothes carry, making it a "gun for all seasons" suited to uniformed officer, detective, and

off-duty policeman alike. It merely offered more power in the same size package. Indeed, the Vermont State Police swapped their 9mm P228s for .40 caliber P229 pistols.

The P229 has earned an excellent reputation in all three of the calibers in which it is offered. The gun stands up well in constant training fire. Let's look at some major police departments that have adopted it in its various chamberings.

.40 S&W. The Sacramento County, California Sheriff's Department had good luck with its SIG pistols for many years. Up through the mid-1990s, deputies had the choice of the 16-shot 9mm P226 or the eight- or nine-shot (depending on the generation of the magazine) P220 .45, with the larger caliber SIG issued to the SWAT team. In the late 1990s, the department decided to split the difference and adopted the .40 caliber P229 as standard issue, though deputies are still allowed to carry the P226 or P220 if they prefer. The guns have worked out well. I was recently retained as an expert witness on behalf of two Sacramento County deputies who had shot a man who was wielding an edged weapon. Of the several shots fired, the great majority struck the target. SCSD's excellent training held for them; they immediately decocked

An interesting depiction of the P229 put forth by SIGARMS when the gun was introduced. Note the absence of markings on the pistol.

The P229 in .357 SIG has proven to be an awesomely effective manstopper on the street.

and safely holstered their weapons and offered what first aid they could to the neutralized subject. The suit against them was thrown out on a motion for summary judgment.

The Arizona Department of Public Safety did something very similar. They had long before traded in their S&W Model 15 Combat Masterpiece .38 Special revolvers for SIG pistols. Troopers and conservation officers were given their choice of the 9mm P226 or the P220 .45, with the overwhelming majority choosing the latter. There was pressure for uniformity, however, and again, the essential compromise nature of the .40 caliber round made itself felt. Like Sacramento County, Arizona DPS traded in both the P226 and the P220 for the P229 in .40, which became standard issue for all personnel. A 13-shot .40 caliber weapon split the difference between a 16-shot 9mm and an eight- or nine-shot .45.

Connecticut's state troopers were the second in the country to get semiautomatics, choosing a popular high-capacity 9mm. When the Connecticut State Police decided to power up from the 9mm to the .40 S&W cartridge, they changed gunmakers,

too. The pistol they chose was the SIG P229. After many years of satisfaction with the P229, Connecticut SP traded up to the SIG P220 because they wanted the larger .45 caliber round.

.357 SIG. The Delaware State Police had switched from revolvers to the compact Smith & Wesson 9mm auto, using the 147-grain subsonic hollow-point. They had loved the gun but hated the cartridge. When they decided to power up, an exhaustive test led DSP to the SIG P229 in caliber .357 SIG. It embodied the compactness and light weight the troopers had come to appreciate with their Smith & Wessons, with a .357 Magnum potency level. The Delaware troopers had just become the first major department to adopt the new pistol caliber. They would not be the last.

The Virginia State Police had, in the late 1980s, decided to follow the FBI's lead and adopt the 10mm Auto cartridge in the Smith & Wesson decocker pistol. As with the FBI, this proved to be a debacle. "Designed by committee," these guns in many of its production runs lacked the durability and reliability of other third-generation S&W service automatics. VSP dumped those guns and bought SIG 9mm pistols for all the troopers, stoking them with the 147-grain subsonic hollow-points that FBI was strongly recommending for the 9mm cartridge. In an experience that mirrored Delaware's, the troopers loved the reliable, accurate, easy-shooting guns, but learned from collected experience to distrust the cartridge. In a decision that also mirrored Delaware's, after a lengthy test/evaluation period and extensive research, Virginia State Police adopted the P229 in .357 SIG.

In a bigger state than Delaware, the .357 SIG quickly had a chance to strut its stuff. At an ASLET conference years later in Virginia, I was able to talk with troopers of varying ranks about the SIG .357s, and their approval was unanimous. "We had been having to hose pit bulls with most of a magazine of 9mm subsonics before they'd go down," said one source, "but with the P229 and the 125-grain Gold Dot .357 SIG rounds, one shot is usually enough now." Said another, "What's really most impressive is how many bad guys have gone down with a single, non-fatal hit," said another. "We're really impressed with the stopping power of the .357 SIG round."

Federal law enforcement has gone to the P229 in .357 SIG in a big way. This gun in this caliber is standard issue for the United States Secret Service, and for the Air Marshals. Issue ammunition is the fast 125-grain hollow-point, Speer's Gold Dot or Winchester's Ranger Talon. Both rounds have been issued by both agencies. Air Marshals have had no shootings yet, but shootings reported by Secret Service indicate that the superb stopping power for which they chose these guns was delivered on the street. Secret Service and Air Marshals had already had the P228 9mm for many years before switching to the P229 in .357 SIG.

9mm Luger. The slightly greater weight of the P229's slide reduces the recoil of the already light-kicking 9mm more than you might think. It's as if you were shooting a steel-frame 9mm. This has made it one of the favorite guns of IDPA shooters in the Stock Service Pistol category.

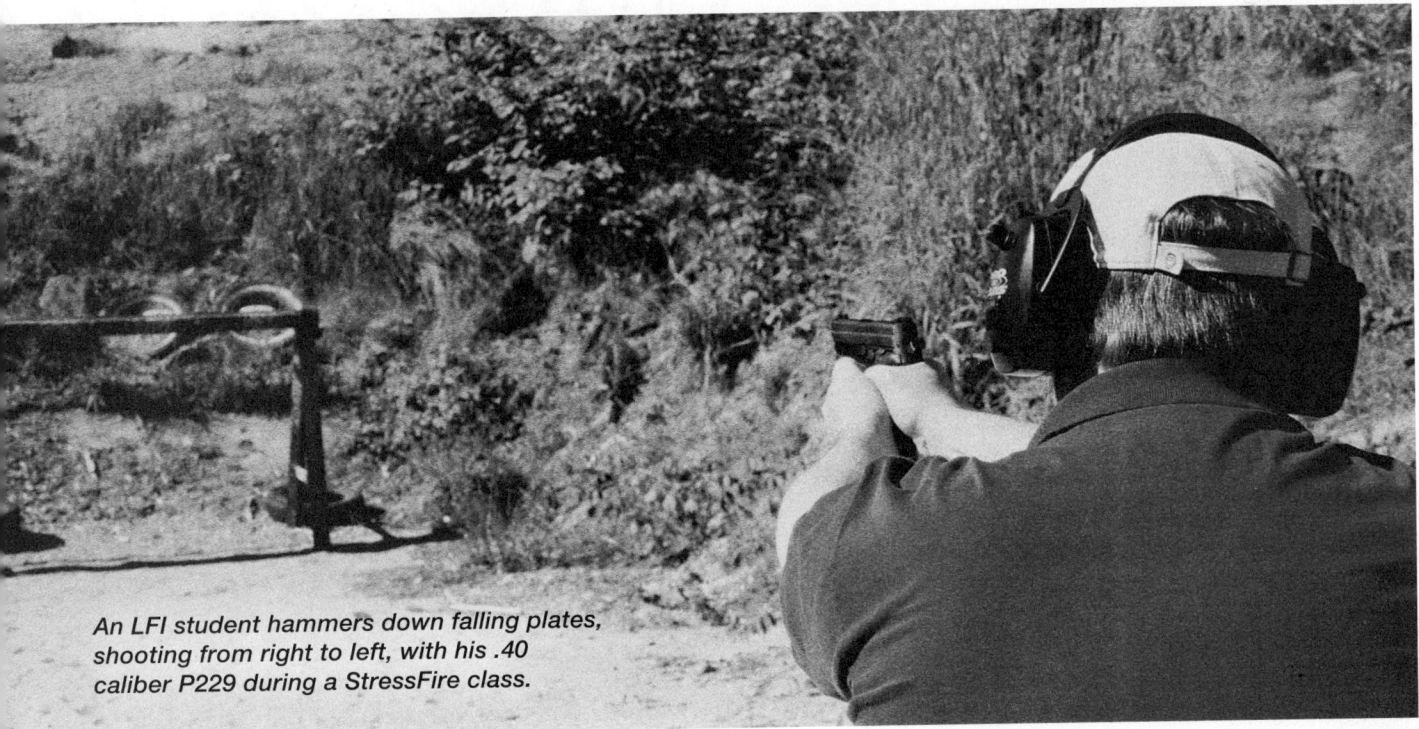

An LFI student hammers down falling plates, shooting from right to left, with his .40 caliber P229 during a StressFire class.

The San Diego Police Department was one of the few major PDs still requiring the 9mm for duty. For many, many years officers were issued the Ruger pistol but authorized to carry their own SIG, Beretta, or S&W 9mm autos. The SIGs were always extremely popular. About 12 years ago, the department switched to the P229 in 9mm as the standard-issue sidearm. San Diego cops tell me they've found the P229 to be every bit as reliable as the famously rugged Ruger, but easier to shoot well, with slightly lighter recoil and with better inherent accuracy.

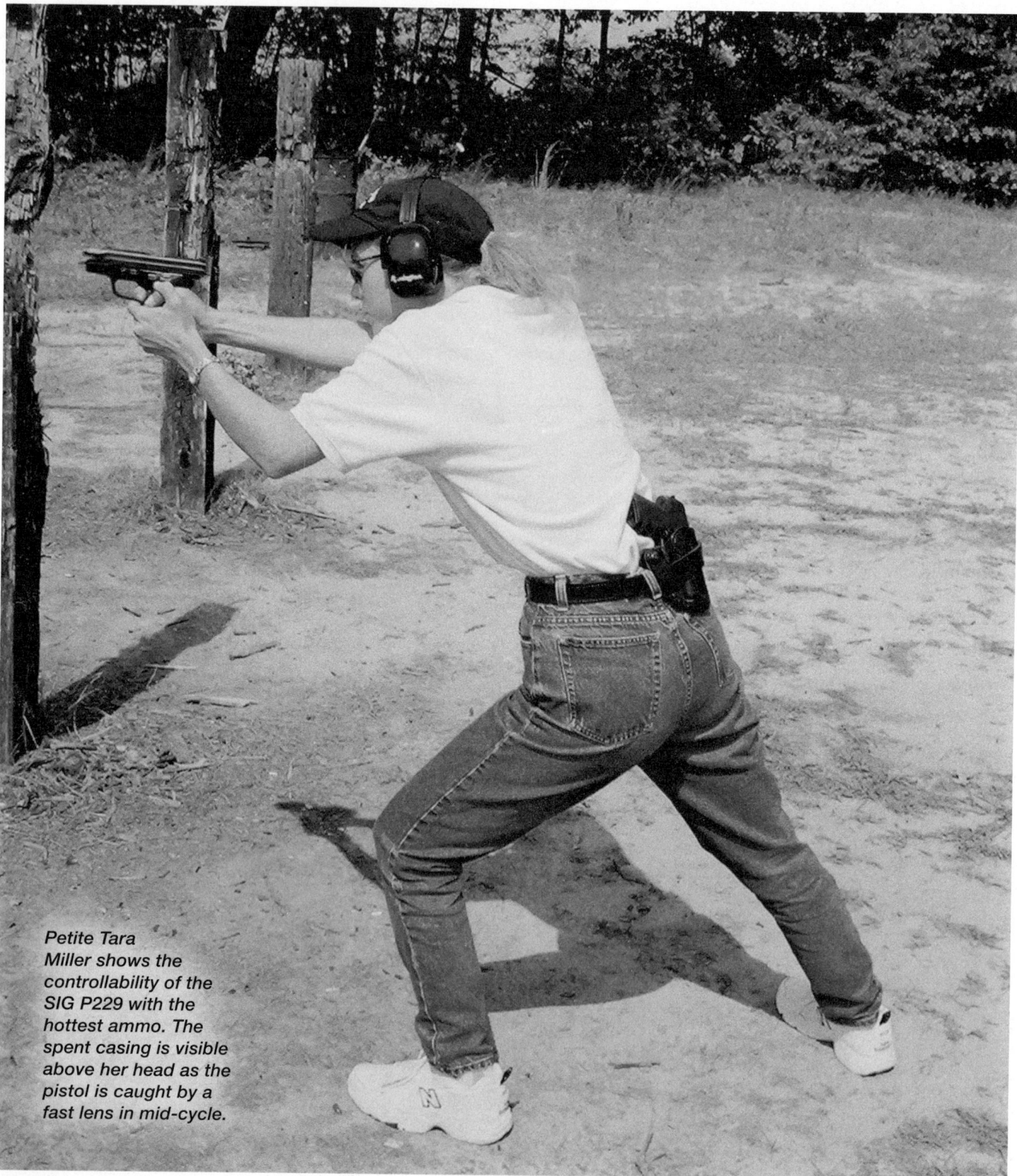

Petite Tara Miller shows the controllability of the SIG P229 with the hottest ammo. The spent casing is visible above her head as the pistol is caught by a fast lens in mid-cycle.

ACCURACY

In 1998, SIGARMS introduced the P229 Sport. Made with a stainless steel frame and fitted with a 4.8-inch barrel and recoil compensator, this adjustable-sight pistol is *sweet!* I did the introductory article on it for *Combat Handguns* magazine, and watched one of SIG's testers shoot groups with it that hovered around an inch at 25 yards.

It is not exactly clear what this particular SIG target pistol is best suited for. Chambered in .357 SIG, the P229 Sport is more powerful than necessary for IPSC, in which any competition category where you can use a compensated gun is one in which the double-action first shot would be more hindrance than help. The compensator makes it ineligible for IDPA matches.

The .357 SIG is certainly suitable for deer hunting. George Harris of SIGARMS Academy has for years taken his annual whitetail with a SIG .357 pistol, but he uses a street gun, not a target model.

Personally, I think the market for the P229 Sport is the connoisseur of fine firearms who simply enjoys a powerful pistol with moderated recoil and flat trajectory, which delivers superb accuracy and is shootable enough to let that accuracy translate to human hands. I don't see it so much as a competitor's gun, but rather, simply an enthusiast's gun.

However, you don't need the target model to get accuracy out of a P229. All you need is either the .357 SIG or the 9mm version of the standard model.

In .40, the P229 gives decent accuracy but not great accuracy. As commercially loaded, the .40 S&W cartridge simply is not among our most accurate rounds. I had a P229 .40 and liked it, but found that like most such guns I've tried, it grouped five shots into 3 to 4 inches at 25 yards. My P226s and P220s did much better, and I decided that for my own needs, the P229 in .40 caliber was redundant. My chief of police liked the gun, however, so I sold it to him for what I had in it. He carries it often as an off duty pistol. We later discovered that with Black Hills 165-grain EXP ammo, this particular P229 could deliver a "personal best" of about 2 inches for five shots at 25 yards. I've won three state championships with Black Hills 165-grain EXP .40 S&W ammunition. In the last several tests I've done of .40 caliber pistols, this has proven to be the most accurate round in seven or eight of them. Passing all the FBI Protocol tests with flying colors, and imbued with the superb match-grade quality control that has made Black Hills Ammunition famous, this cartridge is comprised of a 165-grain Speer Gold Dot bullet loaded to a nominal velocity of 1150 feet per second. Recoil is distinctly snappier than the typical first-generation 180-grain subsonic .40 JHP, but the improved performance is more than worth it.

In 9mm Luger, however, the P229 gives you the same delicious accuracy you can expect from its near-twin, the P228. And it does so with perceptibly less recoil. I think the 9mm P229, fitted with the short-reach factory option trigger, is close to ideal for the recoil-sensitive shooter.

In .357 SIG, however, the P229 reaches a newer and loftier level of accuracy. Yes, the expensive Sport model delivers those fabulous one-inch groups. However, the standard service model P229 .357 can be expected to deliver between 1 and 2 inches at 25 yards with the loads it likes best.

In each caliber, the P229 is something of a "niche gun." The P229 .40 may well be the most popular currently purchased police handgun in the SIG line and one of the most popular law enforcement handguns, period. It is compact, reliable, and user-friendly. The P229 9mm is one of the best possible choices for the recoil-sensitive shooter whose fingers are long enough to be comfortable around the grip-frame of a pistol with a double-stack magazine. The P229 in .357 SIG is arguably the best of the breed, with an optimum balance of weight and size with match-grade accuracy, superb shootability, and awesome power for self-defense.

References

1. Rauch Walter, "NewSigarms P229KDAO .40," *Combat Handguns* magazine, Feb. 2004, P. 13-14.

SIG P229R E2 9MM

Latest evolution of a popular favorite offers improved ergonomics in its latest evolution.

At the SHOT Show in January 2010, SIG's Dennis Carroll gave me a quick introduction to their new E2 concept. At SIG, they pronounce E2 "Ergonomics squared," and Dennis – an old friend from the firearms committee of the International Law Enforcement Educators and Trainers Association – put one of the guns in my hand to make the point. A much-reshaped grip configuration combines with SIG-Sauer's popular short-reach trigger to let the shooter get more flesh and bone

P229R E2 was tested with three distinctly different 9mm loads.

around the gun. This helps with recoil control, and with stabilizing the pistol against the sudden rearward pull of the trigger finger in rapid fire. It also "gets more finger on the trigger," affording the shooter better leverage. This is particularly important in double action fire.

The company got me a P226 E2 9mm pistol the first of the year, and I liked it very much. Shot it in an IDPA match, in fact, against tricked out 9mm 1911s and such in the Enhanced Service Pistol Division, and managed to win the division. That SIG E2 performed superbly.

Now comes the P229R E2. If you don't have your SIG decoder ring handy, "P229" denotes their medium size service pistol, one size smaller than the P226 if you will, and offered in the same choice of calibers: 9mm Luger, .40 S&W, and .357 SIG. The P229 was intended to be of a size substantial enough to qualify with easily and be suitable for a uniformed officer's service pistol, but also compact enough that the same officer could carry it in a plainclothes

assignment or off duty. SIG is the second most popular police pistol in the US, after the Glock, and the P229 is the most popular law enforcement handgun in the SIG catalog. It's carried by cops from New Hampshire's Atlantic Seaboard area to the San Francisco Bay, in its various calibers.

The "R" suffix stands for "Rail," and it's integral to the dust cover of the frame. These are becoming commonplace on police patrol now, and we're even seeing concealable holsters for them. Once the province of SWAT and K-9, this concept is a welcome one in patrol division, and also has useful applications for home defense so long as it's not used as a "search and find" light.

Finally, there's "E2," the whole "ergonomics squared" thing. Bud Fini at SIG tells me not to be surprised if the "E2" designation fades away as this treatment becomes standard instead of special option in the SIG Classic line. It has apparently met a wonderfully enthusiastic reception from law enforcement. Manchester, the largest city in New

Hampshire, is now protected by cops all carrying P229R E2 pistols in .40 S&W.

Bud pointed out to me that the variant of the P229 currently called the E2 has been lightly restyled to more resemble the P226, and that where before the P229 in 9mm had a subtly different frame than the .40 and .357, they're now all being produced on the same rugged frame.

TEST GUN

The test pistol, serial number AGU 05237, was chambered for 9mm and came with three fifteen-round magazines. It mounted Trijicon fixed night sights, and was assembled in "traditional double action" mode. Thus, only the first shot was double action, with the pistol cocking itself to single action for every subsequent shot. The decocking lever was in the usual place.

On the Lyman digital trigger pull weight scale from Brownell's, double action went ten pounds three ounces. With a very slow pull, a miniscule bit of scraping "creep" was barely palpable, but it disappeared as soon as the shooter started running the trigger back fast. In single action, pull weight averaged a hair over four and a half pounds, and squeezed off with a short, gentle roll that was conducive to the surprise break a marksman looks for. The trigger re-set is quicker than in SIG-Sauers of old, answering a long standing complaint from marksmanship purists.

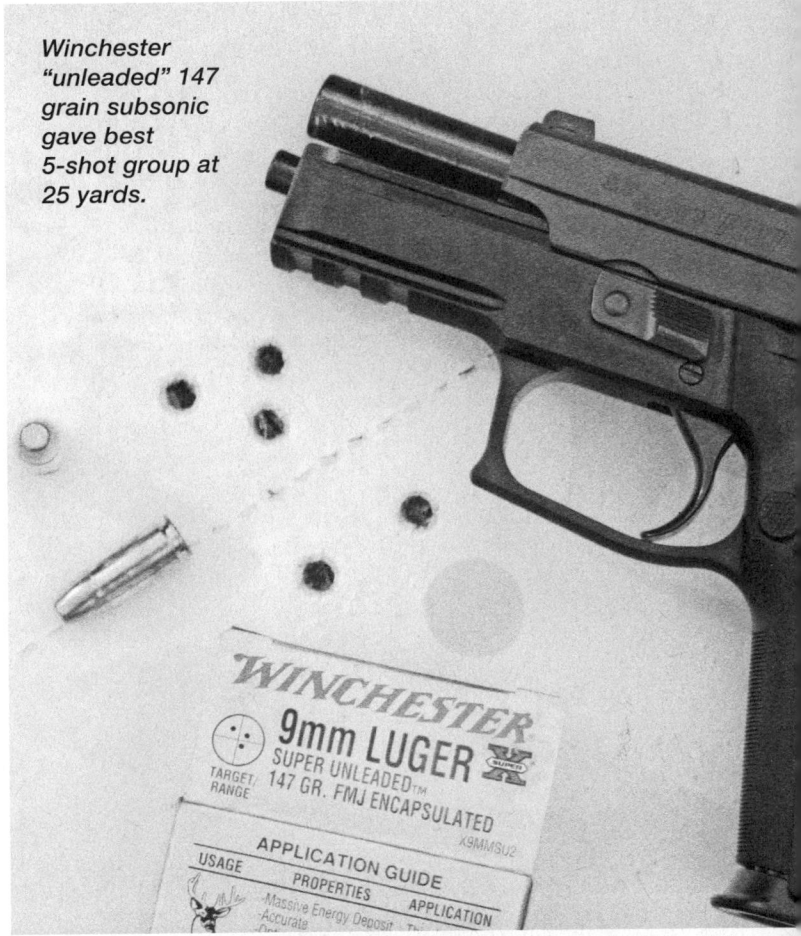

Winchester "unleaded" 147 grain subsonic gave best 5-shot group at 25 yards.

Black Hills 124 grain JHP gave the tightest "best 3" cluster at 25 yards with P229R E2.

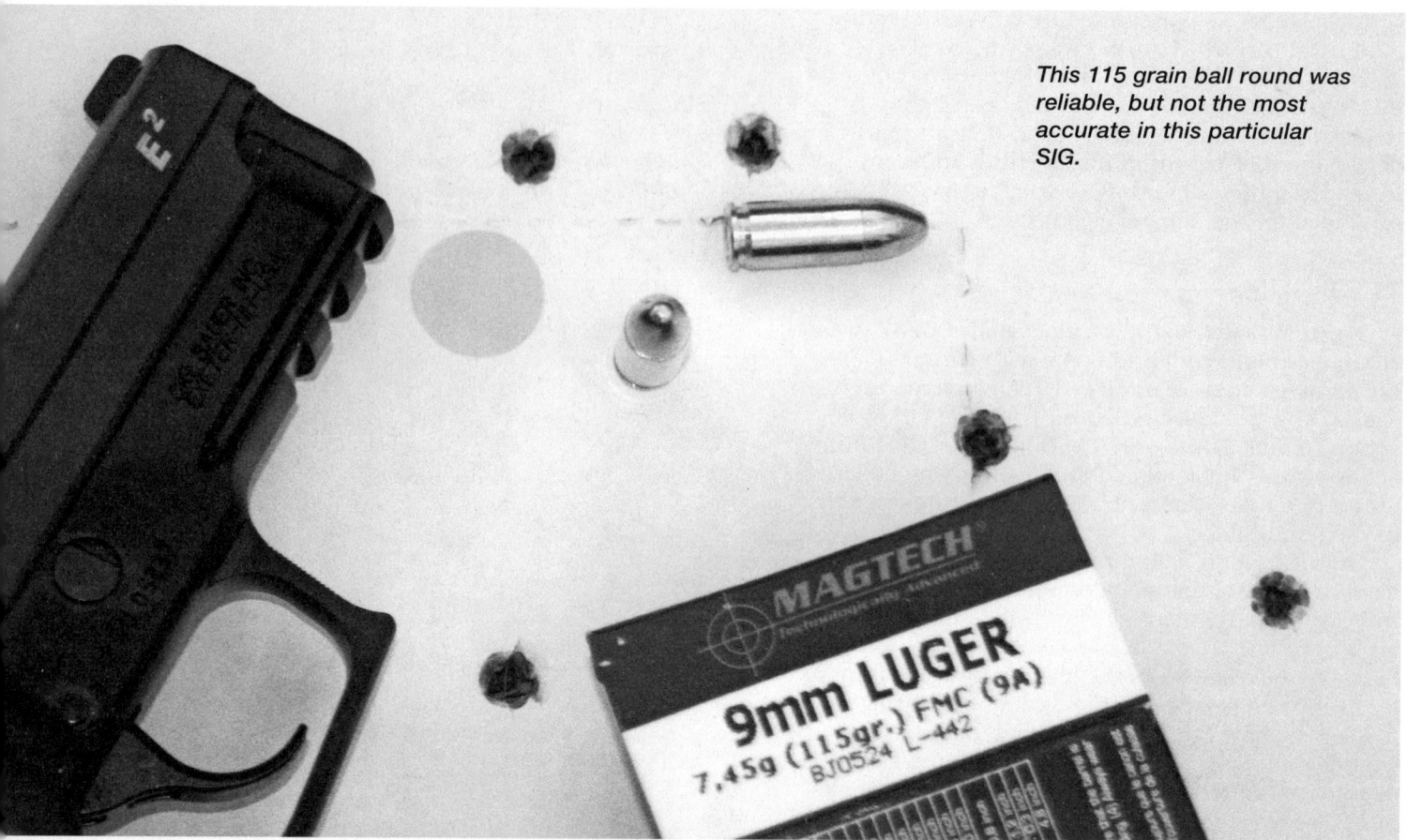

This 115 grain ball round was reliable, but not the most accurate in this particular SIG.

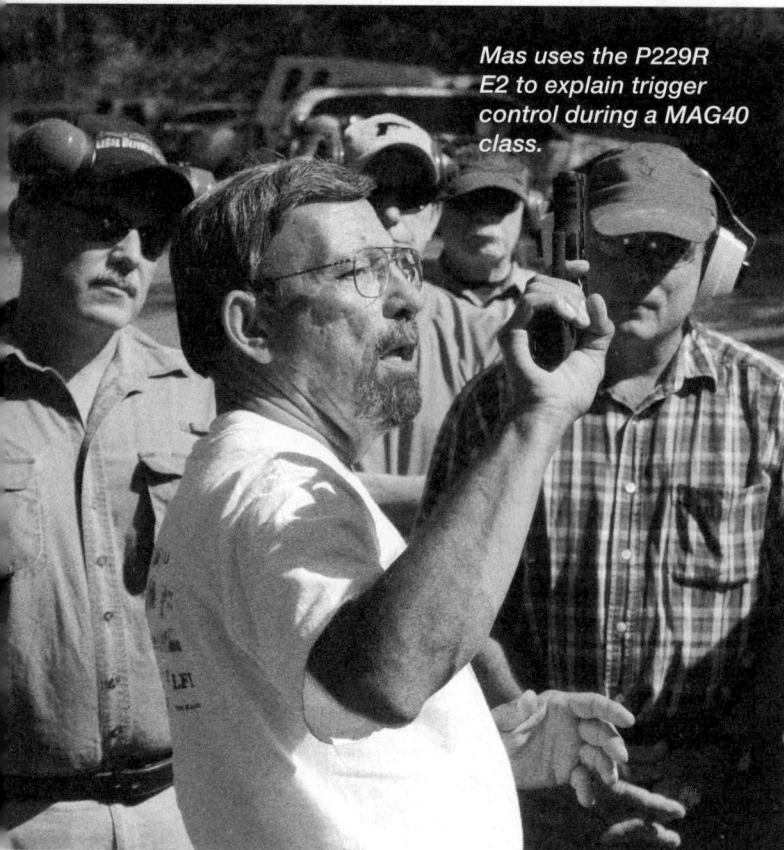

Mas uses the P229R E2 to explain trigger control during a MAG40 class.

The grip treatment is a very fine-grain stippling. "Like hard velvet," said my gun-savvy girlfriend, with her inimitable gift for description. It locks very solidly into the hand, with no felt slippage at all.

I have "average size adult male hands" (according to the hand size studies done by S&W for their Sigma project many years ago, anyway), and in these hands, this SIG fits with the barrel in line with the forearm and allows the distal joint of my trigger finger to just about reach the center of that short-reach trigger. That's the "sweet spot" for leverage when even one shot is going to require a fairly heavy trigger pull, and it made the P229R handle very well for me.

ACCURACY

I benched the P229R E2 at 25 yards with three different brands, bullet weights, and bullet configurations. Going in alphabetical order, Black Hills 124 grain 9mm jacketed hollow point has always been an accurate load, and the test gun put five rounds of it in two and a quarter inches center to center. I blame one shot for that, because four of those bullets went into 1.40 inches, and the best three were in 0.65 inch, the tightest three-shot cluster of the test.

P229 Elite .40 was reliable with 180, 155, and 165 grain duty loads.

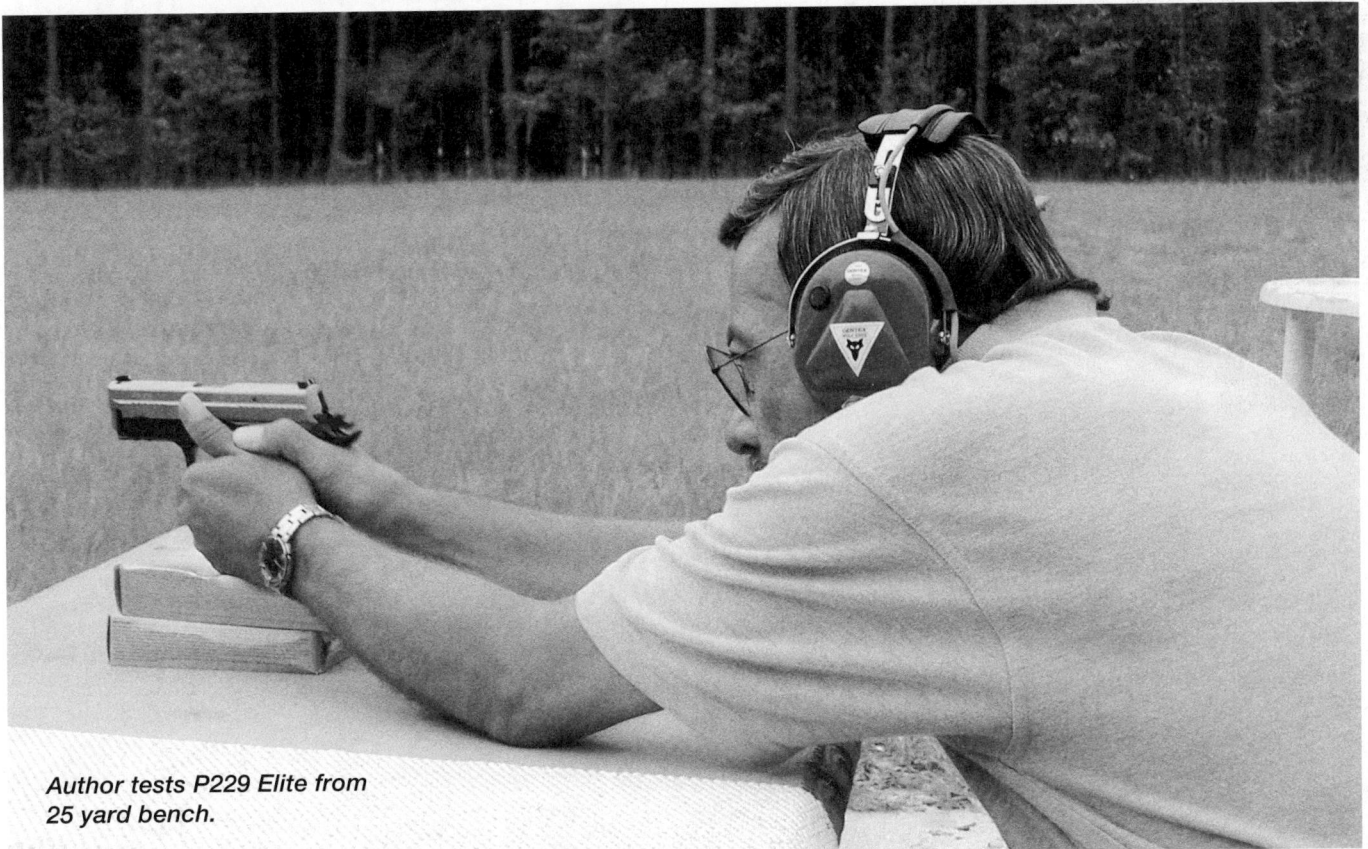

Author tests P229 Elite from 25 yard bench.

Right: 25-yard group with Winchester 155 grain Silvertip .40 S&W from P229 Elite.

Below Left: 25-yard group with P229 and .40 S&W 165 grain Winchester Ranger duty loads.

Below Right: This P229 Elite preferred some bullet weights over others for accuracy, but was reliable with all.

MagTech makes some very accurate ammunition, and I've done more than one gun test where it proved most accurate and beat much more expensive rounds. This particular gun, however, didn't especially like this 115 grain round nose full metal jacket configuration, throwing a 4.90-inch 5-shot group and putting the best three hits in 3.05 inches.

Winchester's 147 grain jacketed truncated cone Super-X Unleaded is the most accurate "lead-free" ammo I've ever shot, and it proved itself again with the tightest five-shot group of the day from the P229R E2: 2.05", with the best three almost as tight as the Black Hills at 0.75 inch.

RELIABILITY

In *shooting,* this pistol ran 100%. There were no failures to chamber, fire, or cycle in several hundred rounds and in multiple hands. This is what we've come to expect from decades of heavy use of SIG-Sauer pistols in police service worldwide...and in military service, with P226s in the hands of Navy SEALs and British SAS.

What we did run into was one significant problem in "administrative handling," the routine loading and unloading of the firearm. I discovered that when clearing a live round from the chamber, it just didn't want to leave. The cartridge stuck there at "needs two men and a boy to accomplish it" difficulty level for clearing the chamber. The first time it happened, I just got fed up after a bit and cleared the magazine, aimed the pistol at the backstop, and shot the chambered round outa there. I thought I had just run into an out of spec round. But then I tried it again to see, with another round from the same box...and it happened again. And then again with another brand.

I disassembled the pistol and ran a brass bristle brush through the chamber, thinking it might just be crud in there. Nope: same problem upon reassembly. I can only presume that the chamber

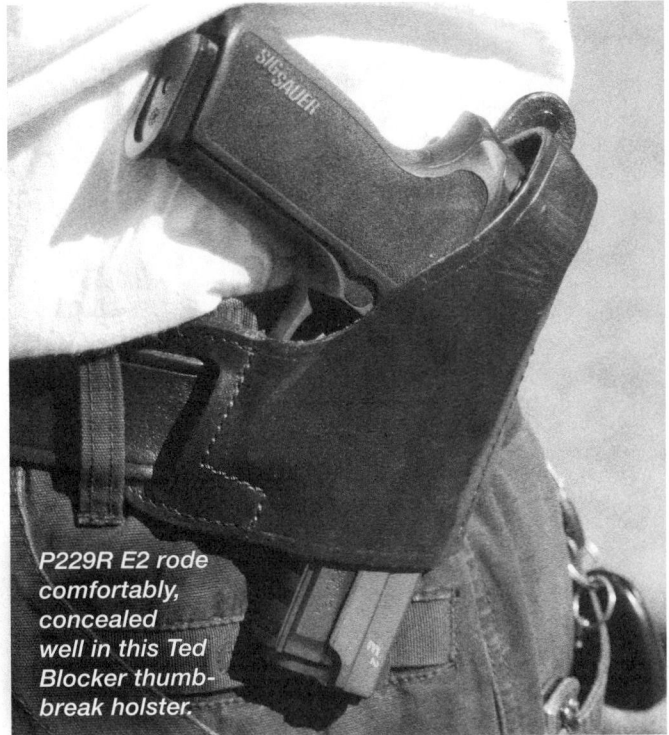

P229R E2 rode comfortably, concealed well in this Ted Blocker thumb-break holster.

wasn't as perfectly concentric as I've come to expect from SIG-Sauer pistols over the decades. If the gun was mine, I'd have sent it back to SIG in Exeter, NH; their customer service is excellent.

I've checked on the Internet and elsewhere and haven't seen anyone else mention such a problem, so I have to assume mine was an anomaly of this particular specimen.

BOTTOM LINE

If you like hammer-fired, double action autos – and there *are* lots of reasons to – check out the E2 series from SIG. The improvements in ergonomics are definitely there: I found that one needs to feel the gun, and *shoot* it, more than just look at it, to fully appreciate that.

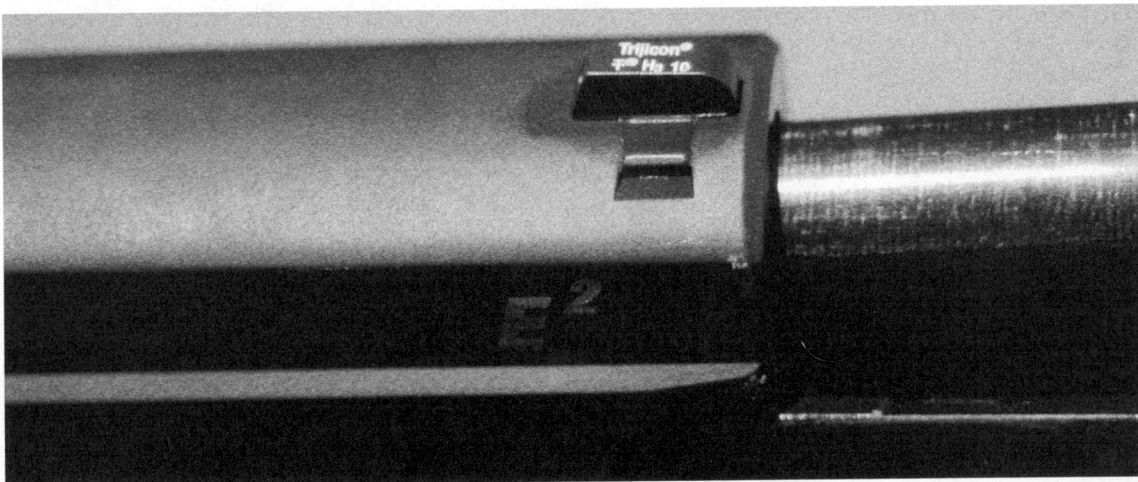

Trijicon night sights gave the E2 a good sight picture under all light conditions.

Chapter 7

SIG'S .380s: The P232 and P230

I n June, 2003 Trish Brown, a slender 26-year-old, stepped to the firing line for the qualification course that capped her 40 hours of training in an LFI-I class. She was the only female in class – something unusual for an LFI program – but her male classmates were supportive. Still, she had taken some ribbing about being the only person there shooting a "mouse gun": a .380 caliber semiautomatic pistol.

Sixty rounds later, a tie was announced for first place. Two shooters had scored 299 out of 300 on the demanding police-style qualification course, with an IDPA target whose maximum five-point scoring zone is only about half the size it would be on a regulation police silhouette. The winners were a tall, powerfully built ex-Marine with a target-grade 1911 .45 auto and Trish, with her SIG-Sauer P232 pocket pistol. All of a sudden, no one is teasing her about her .380 any more.

The SIG is universally recognized as one of the finest .380s ever made. Many experts consider it *the* best handgun ever produced in its caliber. With its barrel affixed to the frame, it offers superb inherent accuracy potential. Its low-pressure cartridge requires less mass of metal surrounding it, and consequently, it is the thinnest and "flattest" pistol in the SIG-Sauer line. Particularly in its aluminum-frame version it is extraordinarily comfortable to carry concealed for long periods of time. It shares the smooth, easy double-action trigger pull and crisp, clean single-action pull of its larger siblings. With no manual safety, it is quick to deploy. Unlike many .380 autos of both single- and double-action design, it was built to be safe to carry with a cartridge in the chamber. It is ready to fire swiftly and reactively by simply pulling the trigger, yet immune to an accidental discharge of the "intertia fire" type when dropped or struck.

This is a very important feature in a

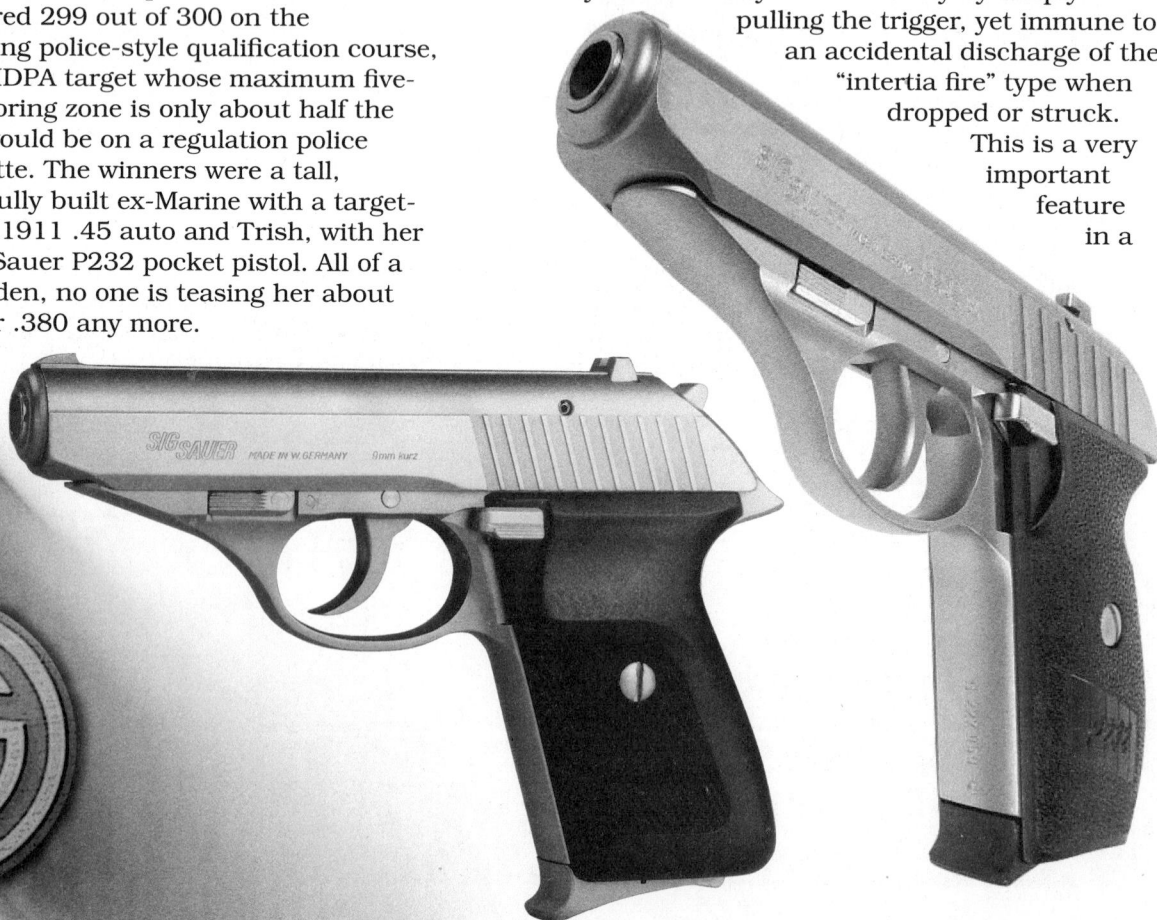

This is Trish, the young lady who tied for first place in her class with a superb 299/300 qualification score, using a SIG P232. In fact, she managed it twice in a row. The targets tell the tale.

"pocket auto." As their colloquial name implies, these handguns are designed to be carried in a trouser pocket or coat pocket, and because of their convenient size and light weight, they are often carried in a purse or fanny pack. A coat or pair of pants with a pistol still in the pocket may be tossed onto a bed or chair, miss, and hit the floor. A belt pack or purse may likewise be dropped to a hard surface. In any of these scenarios, a pistol that is not drop-safe may accidentally discharge. Thanks to its intelligent design in this regard, this is not possible with one of the SIG .380s, even with a round in the chamber.

Another design advantage of the P232 and P230 is the traditional SIG-Sauer decocking lever located behind the trigger guard on the left side of the frame. Even more than with the larger models, this is advantageous on the small guns because, especially in larger hands, pocket-sized pistols can be awkward to decock if the lever is located up on the rear of the slide.

P230 TO P232

The P230 was produced from 1976 to approximately 1998. For the worldwide market it was produced in four calibers. Notes gun expert Ned Schwing, "This is a semi-automatic, compact, pocket-type pistol chambered for .22 LR, .32 ACP, .380 ACP, and 9mm Ultra. It has a 3.62-inch barrel and either a 10-, 8-, or 7-round magazine, depending on the caliber chambered." (1)

The P232 is a sleek pistol, accurate for a "pocket gun."

For a .380, the P232 gives above average accuracy at 25 yards.

The 9mm Ultra P230 is a serious collector's item. For that matter, good luck finding a P230 in the United States in any caliber but .380. This was simply the caliber Yanks wanted if the gun was going to be the same size in .32 ACP anyway.

The blue version with an aluminum alloy frame weighed 16.2 ounces unloaded. SIG later introduced an all-stainless version, which tipped the scales at 20.8 ounces. They were equally smooth of action and equally accurate. Here we had a quandary. The stainless was less likely to rust when carried tight next to a hot, sweaty body, which is where particularly slim and flat auto pistols often wind up in real-world use. However, the lighter alloy frame just felt more comfortable in the same kind of carry.

For me, having one of each, the solution was simple enough. I put the stainless slide on the blue aluminum alloy frame. It gave me the best of all worlds, and the hybrid P230 functioned as if it had been made that way.

The P232, introduced in 1998, is an updated P230. Plastic checkered grips were replaced with plastic stippled ones, in keeping with a change all the way across the SIG-Sauer lineup. They really did feel better in the hand. The slide cuts were updated to a much more ergonomic and functional pattern. The decock lever spring was now attached to the frame in the same manner as bigger SIGs, which made detail stripping easier. The sights were redesigned to allow them to take Tritium inserts.

The basic function, accuracy, and reliability did

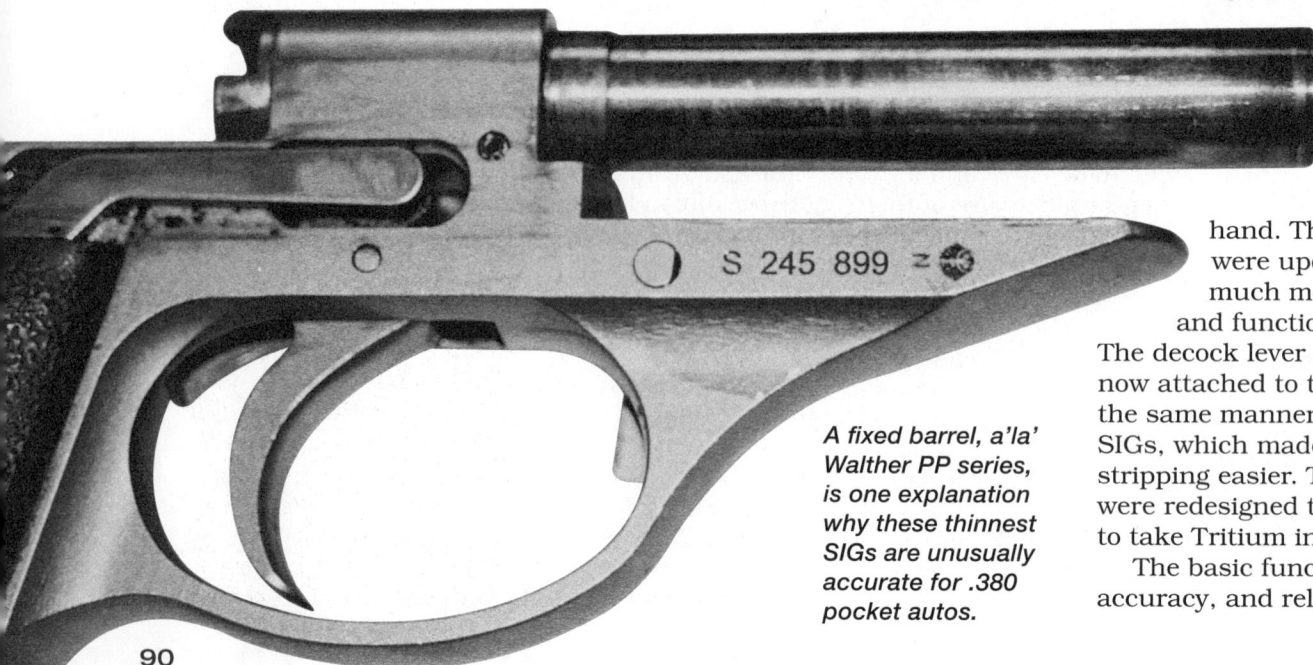

A fixed barrel, a'la' Walther PP series, is one explanation why these thinnest SIGs are unusually accurate for .380 pocket autos.

S 245 899

Homage to Walther PP/PPk is obvious when a SIG .380 is field stripped...

Brand	Bullet	5-Shot Group	Best 3 Shots
PMC	90-grain FMJ	3-13/16"	2-5/16"
Rem Golden Saber	102-grain JHP	3-5/8"	1-13/16"

not change appreciably between the two models. The P232 is generally encountered in the stainless format.

How accurate is the pistol? It won't give you the groups you'll expect from a P226 or a P220, but it will outshoot the great majority of .380 autos that are out there. One quick and dirty test at 25 yards with a well-used P232 gave these results:

HANDLING THE SIG .380

The P232 is the one SIG-Sauer still made with the European-style magazine release with the latch at the heal of the butt. Use the techniques for speed reloading and tactical reloading that are found in the chapter on manipulating the SIG-Sauer pistol. The butt release makes particular sense when a handgun this small is to be used in large hands. That is because a release button located behind the trigger guard on the frame, in the position Americans traditionally prefer, is all the more likely to be accidentally released by the normal grasp of a hand that may be literally too big for the pistol.

These guns have one design feature I don't care for, which they share with the Walther, the S&W Sigma, and many other .380s: they do not have a dedicated slide lock lever. If there should be

...but the fire control functions and even takedown latch are pure SIG-Sauer.

an extraction failure, resulting in a spent casing trapped in the firing chamber and held there under the great pressure of the slide pushing the next live round against it, the stoppage will be much more difficult to clear without a lever that can be used to mechanically lock the slide to the rear and relieve this pressure.

In this situation with a bigger SIG, you would simply retract the slide to the rear and thumb the slide lock lever upward. This would relieve slide pressure against the topmost round in the magazine and facilitate the removal of the magazine and manual ejection of the empty casing, to be followed by a reload to get the pistol back into action. Since the .380 SIG lacks this feature, such a stoppage must be handled differently.

With the .380 SIG, you would keep a firm grasp of the grip frame with the firing hand and use your

The fastest way to operate the release is this method shown by Jim McLoud, Jr. The thumb works the lever, while the middle finger pulls down on magazine's floorplate.

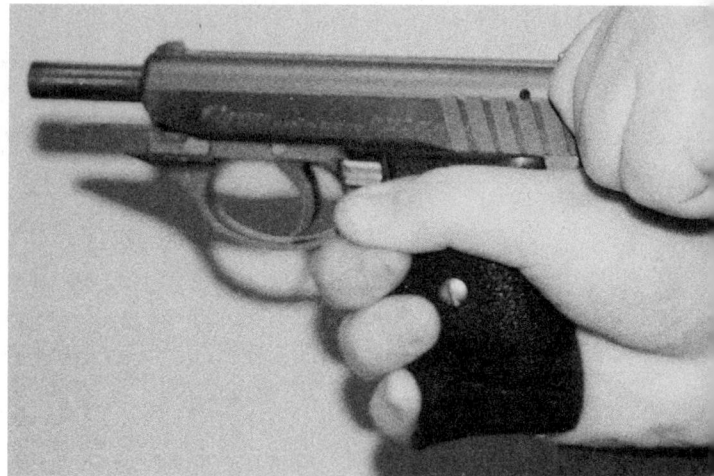

Since the neither P230 nor P232 comes with a slide stop lever, reload is completed by tugging back on the slide as shown and letting it fly forward to chamber a round.

support hand to draw the slide all the way back. Now, using the web of the firing hand under the frame's grip tang as a pivot point, you would pivot your firing hand up into the "armorer's grasp," as shown in accompanying photograph. The web of the hand is now clamped securely at the inside curve of the grip tang on the frame, while all four fingers now wrap around the slide from above, holding the slide back against the recoil spring's tension with a very firm grasp.

With the thumb of the free hand, you now push the butt heel magazine release backward, while your middle or index finger pulls downward on the lip of the magazine's floorplate. This will prove difficult, because in a malfunction of this type the topmost live cartridge in the magazine will have been pushed forward. The cartridge's rear end is still held firmly by the magazine's feed lips, while the front portion of its bullet is dragging on the pistol's feed ramp. Thus, a very forcible pull is required to extract the magazine. Once this is accomplished, the firing hand pivots back down into a firing grasp, holding the frame securely while the free hand activates the

slide. Work the slide until you see the spent casing fly clear (or three times, to fail-safe yourself in the dark). Then reload a fresh magazine, operate the slide one more time to chamber a round, and you're ready to fire again if it is still necessary to do so.

There is one more design feature not found on other SIG-Sauers that can prove to be problematical in shooting these smallest SIGs. In keeping with their need to be small and low-profile, they have a slide that is mounted very low on the frame. Thus, in all but the smallest hand, the sharp edge of the slide can bite the hand as the pistol cycles in firing. The contact point is usually at the proximal joint (base joint) of the firing thumb.

With a very fleshy hand or with a glove, this contact can slow down the slide sufficiently to jam the P230 or P232. With almost any hand, a long sequence of fire will result in laceration. We advise students with these pistols to proactively put a Band-Aid on the hand, with its padded portion covering the base joint at the point shown in photos. The bandage is applied prophylactically, as it were. As they say in safe sex lectures, "wrap that rascal."

High-traction slide grasping grooves and a heavy duty externally mounted extractor are hallmarks of the P232.

THE QUESTION OF CALIBER

It was mentioned earlier that the reader has a right to know the biases and prejudices of the writer. Just as I've made it clear that I'm biased toward the P220 .45, my favorite SIG, and toward the P226, my close second favorite, it's only fair to disclose that the P230 and P232 are my least favorite SIGs.

Part of that is a prejudice against its caliber. I was the guy who said, "Friends don't let friends carry mouse guns." While some gun experts list the .380 as a minimum caliber for self-defense, I'm among the many who draw the line just above it, preferring the 9mm Parabellum as the minimum standard for personal protection use in a semiautomatic pistol. There are simply too many cases that have occurred where the .380, a.k.a. "9mm Short," lived up to its alias and came up short in stopping power.

This is not to say that a .380 SIG can't save your life. Let's look at three instances where the SIG .380 did just that. In the first case, a particularly violent male suspect who attacked a female officer in Pennsylvania went for her service pistol. He was gaining control of the weapon and obviously intent on murdering her with her own gun when, in desperation, she pulled her backup, a SIG .380. She fired one shot into his brain, killing him instantly and just as quickly ending the murder attempt.

In the second case, a petite female came home and encountered a burglar in her Oregon home. He approached her menacingly with what appeared to be a weapon in his hand. Licensed to carry, she drew her SIG P230, leveled it at him, and did exactly as she had been trained at LFI. Neighbors heard her yell, "Don't move! Drop that weapon!" He ignored her commands and came at her, and she fired. Her first .380 JHP struck him

Recoil is mild in this blowback .380.

in the wrist, breaking it. He looked at her and said numbly, "You shot me." He then came at her again, and she fired a second time. He stopped and grimaced, then slowly put one hand on his chest where the bullet had struck center, punching through the aorta. Then he put his other hand on the same spot. Very slowly and carefully he sat down, then lay down. He closed his eyes...and did not open them again.

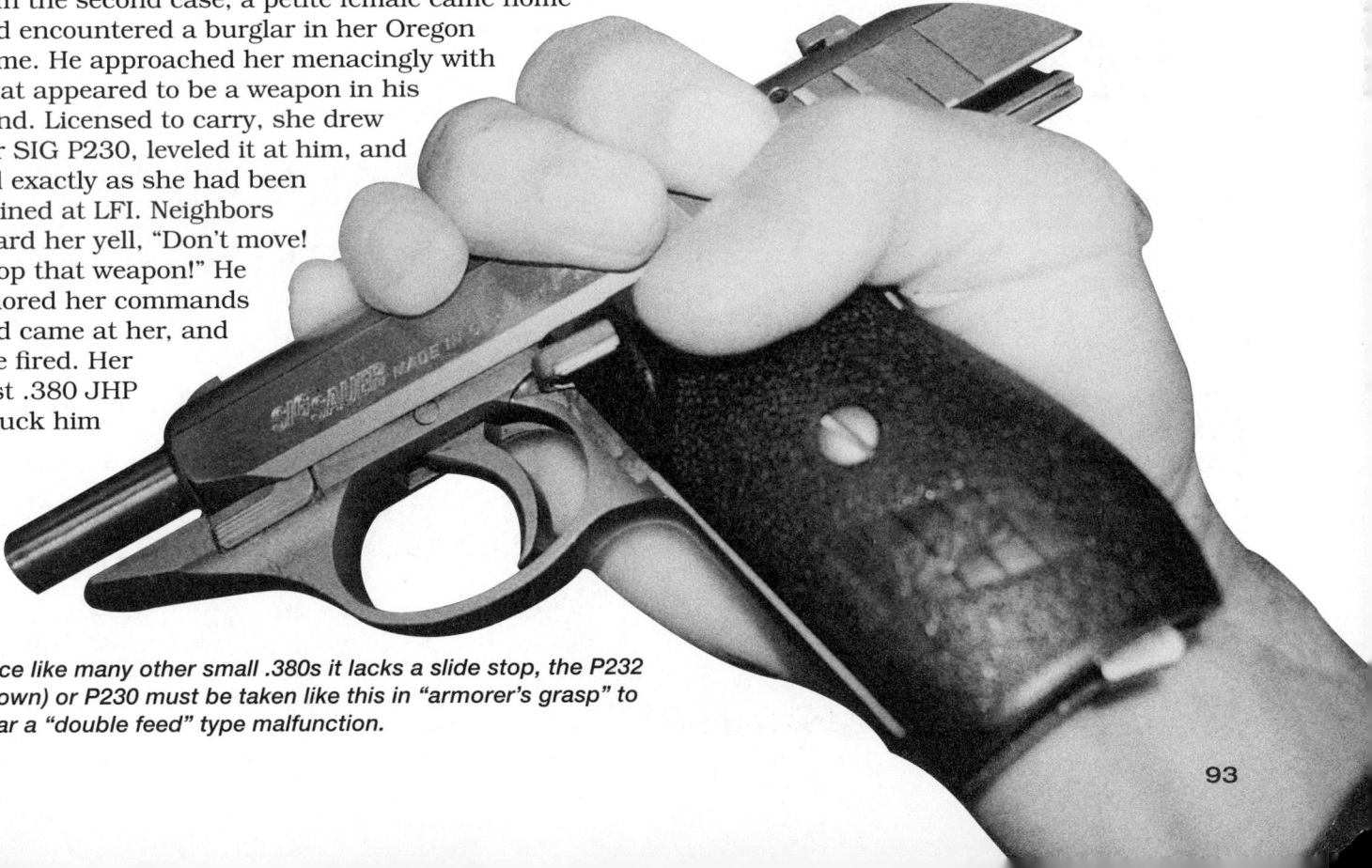

Since like many other small .380s it lacks a slide stop, the P232 (shown) or P230 must be taken like this in "armorer's grasp" to clear a "double feed" type malfunction.

In the third instance, a California deputy sheriff was off duty on medical leave subsequent to surgery for a severe injury to his right wrist. This was his gun hand. Uncertain whether the knitting joint could handle the recoil of his preferred on- and off-duty gun, a SIG P220 .45, he borrowed his wife's P230 to put in his fanny pack. He and his wife and young boys were spending a pleasant day with his elderly parents, safely plinking with .22 rifles on the parents' rural property, when a tall man burst onto the scene, raving obscenities and threats and trying to grab the loaded rifles away from the boys. The off-duty cop tried to stop him physically, but the man proved immune to kicks and, with only one functional arm, the deputy knew that grappling would be futile. He drew the SIG .380, identified himself as a law enforcement officer, and ordered the suspect not to move.

Instead the man lunged at him, going for his gun instead of the boys'. The officer fired as he tried to move away. Extremely well trained by the Sacramento County Sheriff's Department's elite staff, he was able to index the weapon as he fired, and even remembered "catching the link" of the sear mechanism as he delivered a stream of accurate fire. Every shot hit the man in the upper body. At last, the crazed man stopped, bending over with his hands on his knees like someone very tired, and breathing hard. He rocked back into a sitting position as if catching his breath, then went supine, and then lost consciousness. He did not awaken. It had taken seven solid hits from the .380 to stop him, and then not spectacularly.

All three incidents were ruled justifiable homicide. None went to trial in criminal court. The deputy in the last case was sued. I know this because I spoke for him at trial as an expert witness. I am happy to report that the jury came back with a total defense

At 25 yards, the P232 easily keeps five high-tech .380 Remington Golden Sabers in a palm-size group. The best three shots are under two inches.

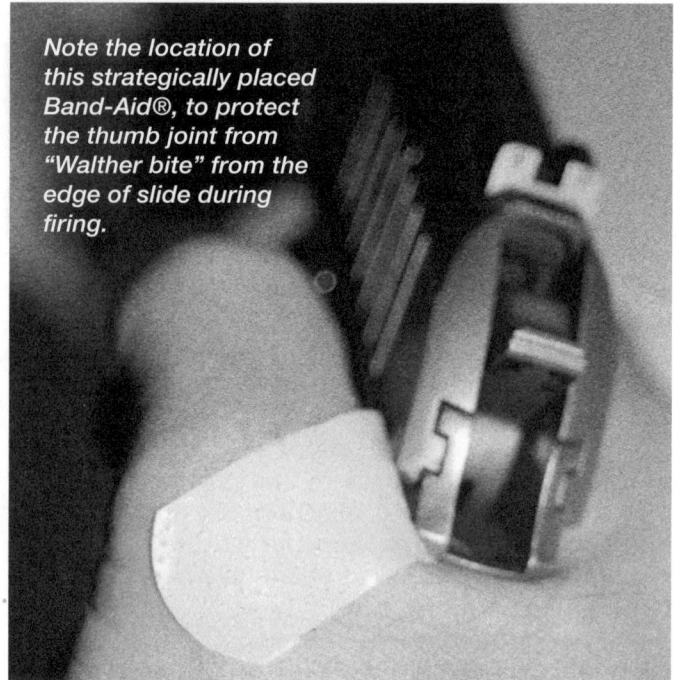

Note the location of this strategically placed Band-Aid®, to protect the thumb joint from "Walther bite" from the edge of slide during firing.

verdict, completely exonerating the deputy and his department. Today, retired from police work because of his injury and licensed to carry a gun, he wears his P220 .45 in a concealment holster and uses the .380 only for backup.

The only one-shot stop in the bunch was delivered by the female officer's brain shot. The two incidents in which the offenders were shot in the body with .380 hollow-points demonstrated what can only be called a disappointing level of stopping power.

Now you understand why I've been known to stand up in class with two SIG pistols. Raising

my P220 .45 I would say, "This is your brain." Raising my P230 .380 I would add, "This is your brain on drugs. Any questions?"

Idiosyncrasies

My other concern with the SIG .380 is that it doesn't quite live up to the reliability standards of its larger siblings in the SIG-Sauer family. While its fire control mechanism is pure SIG-Sauer, its operating mechanism appears to owe more to the Walther PP/PPK design of the late 1920s. This has certain advantages, notably the fixed barrel that is probably responsible for the splendid accuracy delivered by SIG and Walther .380s alike. However, both mechanisms also seem to experience more feeding malfunctions than you ever see with the larger SIG-Sauer combat pistols. Tightly fitted guns, these .380s have a tendency to choke on dirt. As noted in the maintenance chapter, these small pistols don't go long distances of hot and dirty firearms training as do the big SIGs. You probably want to disassemble, clean, and lubricate them every 200 rounds or so. Even Trish, the sharpshooting young lady with whom this chapter opened, experienced malfunctions with her P232 toward the end of the course when dirt built up in the little pistol. A field strip, cleaning, and re-lubrication put her gun right again, but it's something the shooter simply has to keep in mind.

On rare occasions I've seen a P230 that was simply a jam-omatic, even if it was clean. Each time, I advised the student to send the gun back to SIG and each time the company chose

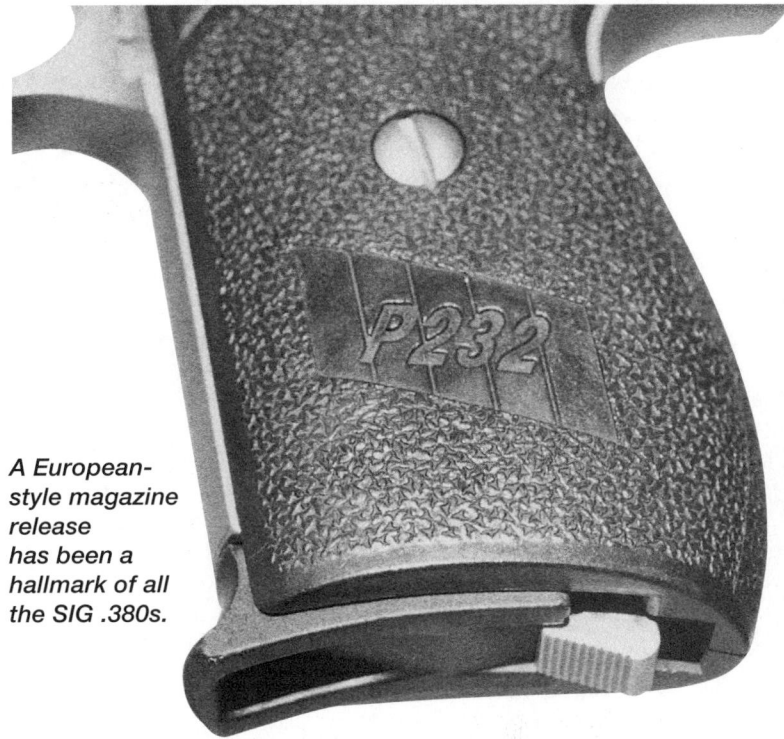

A European-style magazine release has been a hallmark of all the SIG .380s.

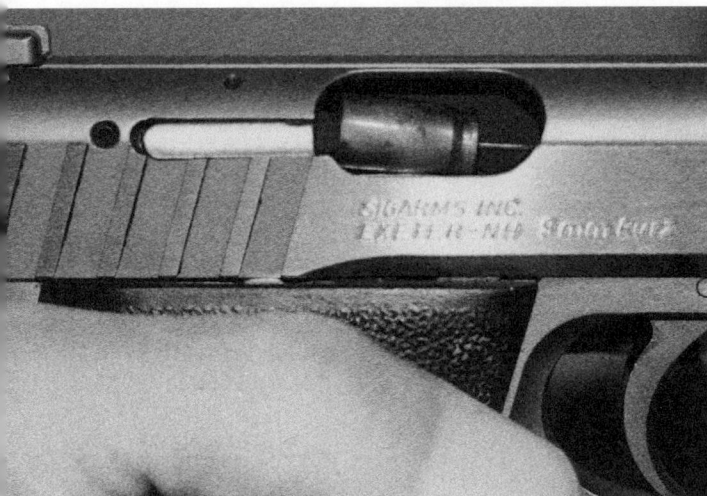

The author does not find the .380s as reliable as the larger SIGs. The hull from the last round has failed to clear the ejection port and ended up backwards atop magazine follower.

to replace the pistol at no cost with one that worked, rather than repair the problem gun.

I understand why so many people love the SIG .380. It fits the hand well, right until the shooting starts and the slide starts biting the hand. It is luxuriously flat, and therefore both easy and comfortable to conceal. However, we have to remember that the ultimate purpose of a defensive handgun is to get you through a gunfight, and here, *any* .380 can be wanting.

Personally, I think a SIG P239, in any of that reliable little gun's three more powerful calibers, will far better protect you. "Friends don't let friends carry mouse guns." End of editorial.

If you choose to carry a .380, the SIG is a good choice. Keep it clean. Train intensively; you will need surgically precise shot placement to turn off an aggressive attacker with this marginal ammunition. Fortunately, as noted above, the P230 and P232 are accurate as .380 pistols go, though neither is likely to produce the gilt-edged accuracy of, say, a P220 or a P226.

References

1. (1) Schwing, Ned, "2003 Standard Catalog of Firearms," Iola, WI: Krause Publications, 2002, P. 960.

Chapter 8

The SIG P238

When SIG introduced their tiny single action .380 auto in 2009, no one could have foreseen that by 2013 it would be the most popular pistol in the lineup. Here's my first look at it, done for On Target magazine:

SIG'S P238 .380

This micro-size, micro-power 1911 is the answer for many who must carry a tiny gun or none at all.

Introduced in January 2009, the SIG P238 is a single action .380 pistol looks remarkably like the reincarnation of the old Colt Mustang, though there are some differences both internally and externally. Essentially, from a shooter's perspective, it's a scaled-down 19ll. Size is reduced...

but, with its "9mm Short" cartridge, so of course is power.

I've shot several P238s now, and have been very much impressed with their reliability. With .380 ammo particularly hard to find the last couple of years, I wasn't able to get as much through the test sample, serial number DA018321, as I would have liked, but I can tell you that my friend Jim McLoud, who runs the Manchester Indoor Firing Line facility in Manchester, NH, had stockpiled enough ammo "before the crunch" that he put three thousand rounds through his personal P238, and didn't have a single malfunction.

In close, the accuracy is fine. At seven yards, every shot is in the heart in deliberate fire, and every shot in the brain case area in rapid fire if you know what you're doing. The big, blocky sights with Tritium inserts are a HUGE help here. I've found that it's important to verify your point of aim/point of impact with these guns. Jim's little P238 shot dead on to the sights, and at seven yards put every shot in one hole. However, it had been well broken in.

One P238 I tested for another magazine came out of the box with the rear sight too far over on one side, and the front sight too far over on the other side in its dovetail, with the result that the bullets were hitting the far edge of the silhouette target at 25 yards. A set of Advantage Tactical sights was retrofitted, solving the problem. This test pistol had the sights more tuned to the barrel's alignment, and shots went just a little high and slightly right. .380 pocket pistols are not made for service pistol accuracy

Gail Pepin is happy with the three tight groups she's shot with Jim McLoud's P238 at Manchester (NH) Indoor Firing Line. Check the target!

Great sight picture on our test P238...but notice how far to the right the rear sight is. That showed up profoundly in accuracy testing.

– that's why most gun magazines test them for that only at seven to 15 yards – but realizing that bad guys don't cut you slack before they shoot at you from across the parking lot, I test them at 25 yards anyway. With Remington 102 grain Golden Saber brass-jacketed hollow points, P238 number DA018321 put five shots in 4.40 inches from the 25 yard bench rest, with three of them in a much more reassuring 1.65 inches. Flat-nosed Winchester full metal jacket ball ammo planted five shots in a 2.25 inches high by 5.25 inches wide group at the same 75-foot distance, the gun supported by an MTM rest on a concrete bench.

Other P238s I've shot weighed out in the seven-pound range in terms of trigger pulls, but felt lighter; this particular specimen went 9.8 pounds average on the Lyman digital gauge from Brownell's, and felt every ounce of it. Release was clean, though. Recoil was negligible, and that's important because there are little .380s out there that tend to bite everything from the web of the hand to the trigger finger. This one was *sweet* to shoot. The night sights and big, blocky "daylight sight picture" made up for the heavy trigger. However, the thumb safety was difficult to on-safe, requiring two hands to git'r'done, while off-safing was smooth and easy.

Left to right, micro-size .380s are Kahr P380, Ruger LCP with Crimson Trace laser sight, and SIG P238.

Mas liked the group size of P238 at 7 yards...but note how far the group is to the right. Sights were off.

P238
Rosewood Tribal

P238
Black Diamond Plate

P238
White Pearl

P238 Extreme

938 BRG

P238
Tactical Laser

There were no malfunctions in the test. Slim and flat, weighing less than a pound before you load it with six little .380 rounds in the magazine and a seventh in the chamber, the P238 has made a lot of friends among those folks whose work rules and dress codes simply forbid them to carry anything bigger. Its short trigger reach, easy-working slide (if you cock the hammer before you chamber a round, to relieve mainspring pressure) and soft recoil make it attractive to those with arthritis, osteoporosis, or any other ailment that weakens hands and wrists. It's no wonder the gun dealers are telling me that P238s get sold to satisfied customers as soon as they come into the store.

Chapter 9
The SIG P239

S mith & Wesson's development of the Model 3913 traditional double-action pistol in the late 1980s – a flat, compact nineshot 9mm single-stack concealment gun – carved a new niche in the firearms market. A disproportionate number of gun experts chose it for personal carry, particularly in warm climates where a discreet profile was critical for an all-day "packing pistol."

It was endorsed by three of our top female instructors, all slim women who appreciated its attributes: Lyn Bates, Gila May-Hayes, and Paxton Quigley. Big John Taffin, a man famous for his erudition in the world of large, powerful six-shooters, chose the double-action-only version of this flat little 9mm, S&W's Model 3953, as the pistol to tuck into his waistband when he went into town in the warm weather. At a gun writers' conference in humid Florida, I found myself at a table with two respected colleagues, Walt Rauch and Frank James. As conversation progressed, we discovered something interesting: all of us were licensed to carry in the Sunshine State, and all three of us were wearing Smith & Wesson Model 3913s as we sat talking to one another in that tropical environment.

The success of this slick little S&W pistol was not lost on SIGARMS, who set about duplicating the concept with their own twist, knowing they'd have to improve on the Smith to displace it in the market. They worked long and hard, and the result, introduced in 1996, was the SIG P239.

In an absolutely brilliant marketing stroke, the P239 was marketed as the "personal-size" SIG. The ill-advised Clinton Crime Bill had passed a couple of years before, and the P228 and similar pistols were now necessarily sold with 10-round magazines instead of the 13-round magazines for which they had been designed. The market had responded: If people were going to buy small 9mm pistols of limited cartridge capacity, they wanted them proportionally smaller than before so as to at least get *something* out of the bad bargain. The flat, single-stack P239, sized perfectly to its cartridge capacity, appealed naturally to this reasonable thinking.

P239 ATTRIBUTES

The P239 came to a marketing table absolutely dominated by Smith & Wesson's Model 3913. What it brought to that table were two attributes: Superior accuracy and more powerful caliber options.

The Model 3913 was available only in 9mm Parabellum. Wayne Novak, the famous pistolsmith, managed to chamber two 3913s for the .40 S&W cartridge and make them work. He kept one, and the other is in the hands of my friend and colleague Charlie Petty. The work had been so difficult that Wayne didn't think it could affordably be made

In this petite female shooter's hands, a 9mm P239 proves to be the perfect self-defense handgun.

Wesson 5906 and the Ruger P89. Ruger never did enter the compact single-stack 9mm market, and Beretta's entry, the Model 92 Compact, was never as short or as flat as the 3913 or the P239, leaving the SIG and Smith marques to do battle for that lucrative corner of firearms sales.

I had always appreciated the good accuracy of the 3913. It was one of those rare cases where the shorter gun was more accurate than the long one; the 3913 was invariably more accurate than its big brother, the 5906. The latter gun would do 3 inches to 4 inches at 25 yards in most examples (though the expensive Performance Center semi-custom version that came later could crack an inch), but the 3913 would typically group five shots in about 2-1/2 inches at the same distance.

The P239 9mm could beat that. Not by a lot, but it could beat it.

Thus, the customer looking for a high-quality, totally reliable double-action 9mm concealed carry pistol with a flat profile, and satisfied with a 9-shot cartridge capacity with the gun fully loaded, now had a choice. Before, they'd had only the 3913; now they had the P239 on the table, too.

In 9mm, the choice was simple. Both had good actions, good trigger pulls, superb reliability. If you preferred a pistol you could carry on-safe, you would buy the Model 3913, whose slide-mounted lever functioned as both a decocker and a manual safety. If you preferred to carry without a manual safety engaged, the P239 was the more logical choice. Not only was its frame-mounted decocker more accessible to most shooters, but the SIG could not accidentally be put on-safe by an overhand slide manipulation, as could the S&W. If accuracy was your determining factor, the SIG would win the contest by a small margin.

available to the general public, and he never commercially offered the conversion. S&W did have a compact single-stack .40, but it was their Model 4013 on the .45 caliber Model 4516 frame, distinctly larger and thicker than either the 3913 or the P239. In the P239, the market now had a comparable size package to the 3913, not just in 9mm, but in .40 S&W and in .357 SIG.

And, finally, there was accuracy. In the bigger market battle already ongoing – that of the full-size, high-capacity 9mm service pistol – it had become clear that the SIG P226 and the Beretta 92 were demonstrably more accurate than the Smith &

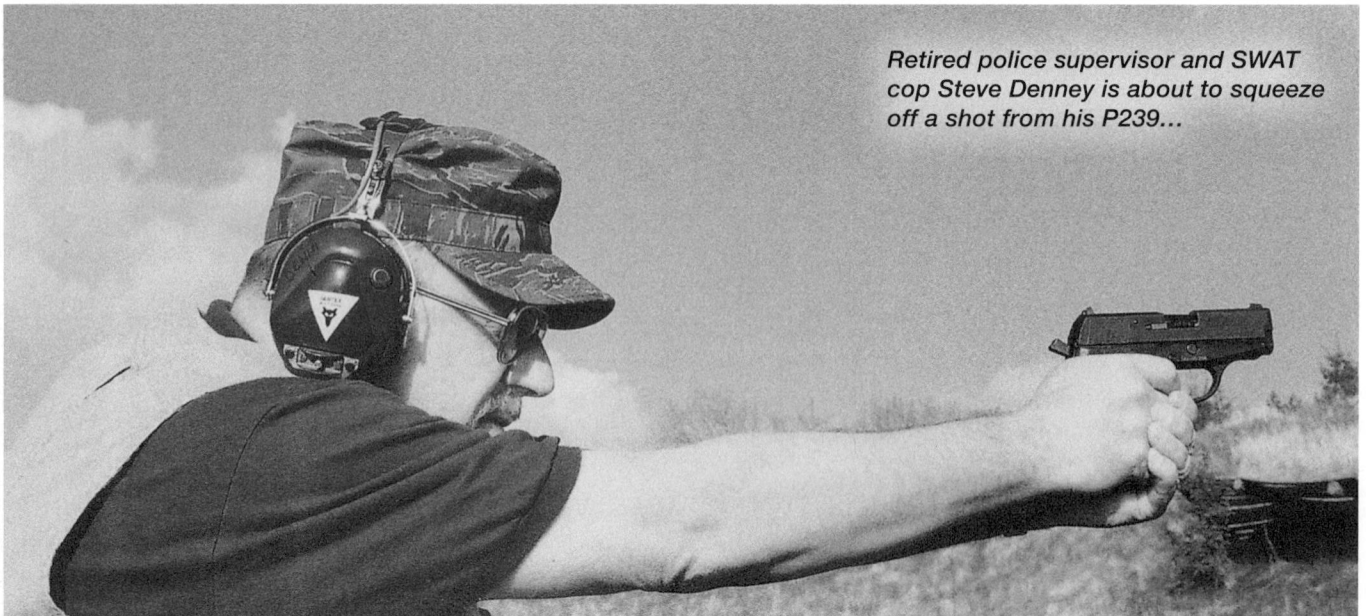

Retired police supervisor and SWAT cop Steve Denney is about to squeeze off a shot from his P239...

180-grain subsonic .40 bullet. On the other hand, a Pro-Load +P 135-grain .40 JHP traveling at 1300 feet per second can cause more damage than a 115-grain 9mm JHP at the same velocity. And a 125-grain .357 SIG bullet at 1350 or more feet per second can be reasonably expected to do a little more damage than either of the others.

The .40 S&W may be the most popular chambering for the P239, and most certainly an effective one. This specimen wears Hogue grips.

But, there was also that matter of power.

At the price of one cartridge in magazine capacity, you could get the P239 in .40 S&W or .357 SIG. Not until 2003 would Smith & Wesson offer the Model 3913's slim-line format in the .40 caliber, announced at a gun writers' conference S&W hosted in Springfield, Mass. in January of that year. Not until the fourth quarter of that year would S&W sort out the magazine problems and actually start shipping the gun they called the Model 4040. While they considered chambering it for .357 SIG, that has not yet been done at this writing.

For many, the greater power of the .40 S&W or the .357 SIG over the 9mm is the deciding factor. One must be careful with this decision, however. A properly selected 9mm round can be more potent than some .40 cartridges. The 115-grain 9mm in the +P or +P+ velocity range can do more damage than a

HAND FIT

The P239 has the shortest trigger reach of any double-action SIG. This makes it particularly suitable for the hands of petite women and anyone else with short fingers. Interestingly, this is the one pistol SIGARMS produces with the short-reach trigger as standard. On other models, the longer-reach trigger is the standard part unless the pistol is special ordered.

Some shooters with longer fingers actually find the short-reach trigger *too* short. No problem. The longer or shorter trigger can be retrofitted to these guns by a SIG armorer or by the factory if you wish to send it back. Armorer Rick Devoid notes that one of the most popular modifications he does on SIG pistols is the installation of the shorter reach trigger. However, he also does a land office business installing the longer-reach triggers on P239s that belong to shooters with large hands!

P239 VERSUS P225

The P239 essentially supplanted the P225 in the SIG line-up. It was slightly lighter, 25 ounces to the P225's 26.1 ounces. It was distinctly smaller:

...and with his strong stance he easily manages the recoil of a full power .357 SIG round, seen exiting the chamber of the pistol.

The 9mm P239 competes directly with this successful carry pistol, the Smith & Wesson Model 3913.

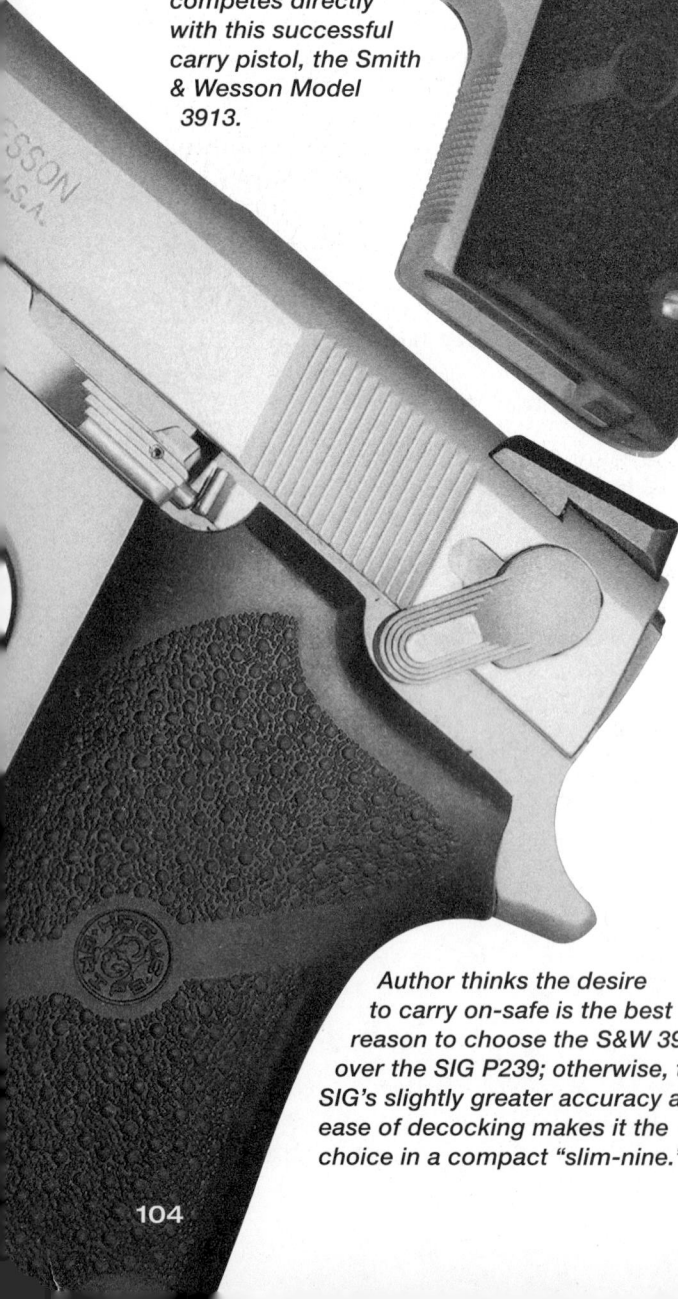

Author thinks the desire to carry on-safe is the best reason to choose the S&W 3913 over the SIG P239; otherwise, the SIG's slightly greater accuracy and ease of decocking makes it the choice in a compact "slim-nine."

the P225 is 7.1 inches long with a 3.86-inch barrel; the P239 is 6.6 inches long with a 3.6-inch barrel. In height, topstrap to butt, it measured virtually the same with the magazine in place. While the frame was shorter in this dimension on the P239 compared to the P225, the new gun had a flanged plastic buffer on the floorplate of the magazine, which gave the little finger something to hang onto. It also increased the height dimension to about the same as a P225 with its flat-bottomed magazine inserted. Recoil difference was virtually indistinguishable when the same 9mm ammo was fired in each gun.

For those who carried the hottest 9mm self-defense ammunition, the P239 had another big advantage over its older brother, the P225. I've heard numerous reports of P225s failing with hot 115-grain/1300+ fps 9mm ammunition when the powerful loads cycled the slide so fast that it couldn't pick up the next round on the single stack of cartridges, and closed on an empty chamber instead of a live round. I have never either seen or heard of such an occurrence with a P239 9mm pistol.

And, of course, there is the availability of the .40 S&W and .357 SIG caliber options with the P239, which never existed with the P225. As an added bonus, the P239 in calibers .40 or .357 is

Weighing barely 100 pounds, Tara Miller hammers five rounds of the most powerful .40 S&W ammo through her SIG P239 in one second, still maintaining recoil control. Note one spent casing airborne above gun, another behind it, and one more passing forward of her knee.

interchangeable; that is, you can put a .357 SIG barrel in your .40 or a .40 S&W barrel in your .357 SIG without changing anything else. Neither caliber will interchange with 9mm.

One who felt the P239 was a huge improvement over the P225 was Duane Thomas. Published in *Gun World* magazine, his article "Choosing a Compact Carry Pistol" was subtitled "Why this author thinks the SIG P239 is the best bet for most people."

Duane had this to say, among other things, about the P239 vis-à-vis its predecessor gun. "SIG can make the slide on a P239 shorter and narrower than a P225's and still have a functional gun because on a P239 that part is actually a solid, machined piece of stainless steel versus the hollow stamping with pinned-in-place breech block of the P225. Even though the P239's slide is smaller than the P225's, it weighs about the same, therefore slowing slide velocity to allow good cycle reliability. This also ensures the piece doesn't beat itself to death in short order as tends to happen on guns with really high-speed slide strokes." (1)

Thomas also wrote, "Speaking of reliability, in my experience I'd have to rate the P239 higher than the P225 in this critical area. I've owned two P225s and at one time was very impressed with this gun. That positive impression has waned as I've gained more experience with it. Both my P225s experienced serious functional problems as time went on. While attending and competing in numerous combat pistol matches, I've been able to watch several other people firing their P225s. I have yet to see anyone who was not having serious feed reliability problems with this gun. According to one competitor who had researched this matter thoroughly with the SIG warranty repair department while dealing with

With fifth hit in the white at 12 o'clock, this P239 has centered a nice group at 25 yards with Winchester's police-only Ranger .357 SIG ammo.

Above: Tucked away in a good inside-the-waistband holster, the P239 is a concealable package even for the very slender woman wearing it here.

Jim McLoud finds the recoil of the SIG P239 controllable in caliber .40 S&W.

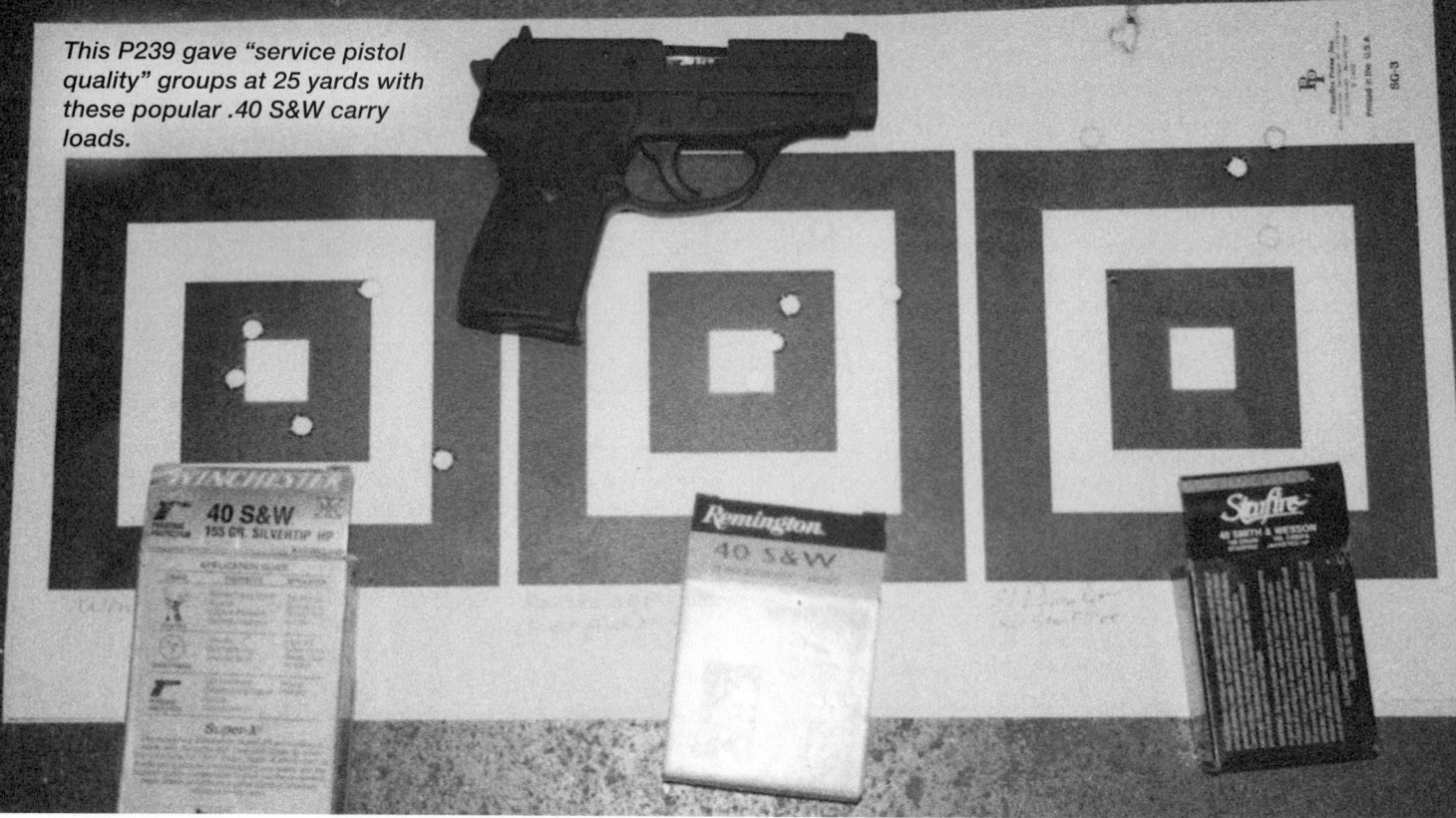

This P239 gave "service pistol quality" groups at 25 yards with these popular .40 S&W carry loads.

Two groups at 25 yards with .40 caliber P239, measuring about 1-1/2 inches, top, and 1-1/8 inches, below. Ammo is Black Hills with 180-grain Gold Dot bullet.

his own P225 woes, the problem is traceable to the P225s magazine feed lips. Only a minute spreading of the lips under hard use is required to cause rounds in the mag to simply not feed. Happened to me, happened to him, happened to another hapless P225er I watched struggling with his gun at a match. On the other hand I don't know anyone who's ever had a problem with a 9mm P239." (2)

The P225 jams that Duane Thomas describes are something I have not seen personally. However, I have had the same observation as he concerning the P239: total reliability, no breakage.

In any case, the P239 has well and truly replaced the P225 in the hearts, minds, and holsters of most SIG shooters. I used to see quite a few P225s at our LFI-I classes, where students tend to show up with their concealed carry guns. This past year, I kept count, and exactly *one* student brought a P225. It functioned perfectly and he had no problems with it. However, I lost count early on of the number who came to class with SIG P239s in the various calibers.

P239 ACCURACY

This "personal-size gun" delivers full-size accuracy. The S&W Model 3913 that was often my "summer pistol" for concealed carry would reliably shoot five 9mm bullets into 2-1/2 inches at 25 yards, and the P239 I tested when the new SIG came out shot better. I couldn't find the original article I wrote on the 9mm P239, and so default to Duane Thomas' story on the same make and model in the February, 2002 edition of *Gun World* magazine.

Duane has taken a couple of LFI classes with me, and I've shot a couple of matches with him. I know him and I know the pistol in question – both are very good – so I was not surprised with the results.

Thomas tested his SIG P239 9mm on an indoor range with only 50 feet of distance available, not the usual 75 feet (25 yards). He reported, "Best groups were evinced by Federal's famously accurate 115-grain 9BP with a group of 1 inch even, darn near perfectly regulated for windage and elevation, with three of the five rounds in one hole in the X-ring. But slightly larger was the 1-1/16-inch thrown by the Hornady 124grain XTPs. Marginally larger again were the Winchester 115-grain Silvertips at 1-1/8 inches. Several loads put four rounds into exceptional groups with a fifth opening up overall group size somewhat...The Speer 115grain Gold Dots put four rounds into a tight 7/8-inch group, with a fifth shot increasing the overall group to 111/16 inches. Another Gold Dot, the 147-grainer, put four rounds into 11/16 inches, a fifth coming in at 2-1/4 inches. And the Wolf hardball put four rounds into a nice, tight 1inch cluster with a fifth hole, alas, at 2-1/4 inches." (3) Adding half again the distance, Duane's fifty-foot groups would extrapolate to an inch and a half to two inches with most of those loads at 25 yards. This is about the performance I recall with my own test sample of the P239 in 9mm.

The 9mm is not the only accurate P239. For the purpose of this book, the following test was done in November 2003 at the Manchester Indoor Firing Line in Manchester, New Hampshire from the 25-yard bench. The pistols were heavily shot range rental guns, P239s chambered for .357 SIG and .40 S&W.

The P239 was aptly named the "personal-size" model by the SIGARMS people. It is extremely discreet and comfortable to carry. Recoil is trifling in 9mm, certainly manageable in .40 S&W, and not even that much of a challenge in .357 SIG. Its extreme popularity is well deserved.

References

1. Thomas, Duane "Choosing a Compact Carry Pistol, *Gun World* magazine, February 2002, P. 53.
2. *Ibid*, P. 54.
3. *Ibid*, P. 58-59.

Three variations on a theme include P239 pistols in, top to bottom, 9mm Parabellum, .40 S&W, .357 SIG. Identical in most dimensions, though the slide of the 9mm is very slightly lighter. The .357 and .40 can interchange calibers with replacement barrels, but neither is interchangeable with 9mm.

Chapter 10
The SIG P245

AT LAST: A SIG .45 COMPACT

Fans of the P220 .45 auto had long clamored for a compact version, a pistol that would be to the P220 as Colt's Officers ACP and Defender compacts were to the classic Colt Commander. SIGARMS answered that request in 1999.

I wrote what may have been the first published test on the new pistol, for *Guns* magazine. Since that time, SIGARMS has come up with a new incarnation of the eight-shot P220 magazine that does not have the problems I mentioned in 1999 that can be found in the earlier DPS magazine. They also have an attachment to make the longer .45 magazine fit better in the shorter-framed P245. A P245 may now be ordered with XS sights, the old "fast and close" Ashley Express concept. Other than that, nothing about the P245 has changed, and the 1999 article is reprinted below, with updated photos.

In double-action combat autos, one of the pistols to beat has always been the SIG-Sauer, imported into the United States by SIGARMS. Their P220 .45 auto has been around for more than 20 years. It debuted in this country as the Browning BDA, and when adopted by the Huntington Beach, California Police Department, it opened the U.S. police market to .45 automatics. Police executives of the period were still embroiled in ACLU hollow-point bullet controversies, still subject to a media that bitched at them for wanting ".45 caliber horse pistols" instead of traditional ".38 Police Specials," and were avoiding at all costs anything as militaristic as adopting what was then still the official U.S. armed services sidearm, the Colt 1911. Besides, a "cocked and locked" pistol gave non-gun-oriented police chiefs the heebie-jeebies, and still does.

The P220 won an enviable reputation for reliability, accuracy, and safety in service. It was one of the first .45 automatics approved by the FBI. More than one state police agency adopted it. The overall shape and aluminum alloy frame made it roughly equivalent in size and bulk to the lightweight Colt Commander in the same caliber. It was easy to carry and easy to shoot well.

The SIG's trigger pull, in both double- and single-action, became the standard of the double-action auto pistol industry. It was a superbly accurate weapon, outshooting every double-action .45 auto but the Ruger P-90, and even that gun, while equalling the P220, did not exceed

it for accuracy. The P220's almost straight-line feed angle let it feed hollow-points at a time when the paradigm .45 auto, the 1911, needed to be customized to feed any hollow-point but the Remington.

Suffice to say the P220 made a lot of friends in both the police sector and the private citizen market in the United States. I was one of them. I make my home in a part of the country whose winters make it a frozen wasteland and where for about four weeks annually, wind-chill factors in the "30 degrees below zero" range are not unheard of. I discovered that the butt-heel release of the European-style P220 made it work better in a heavily gloved hand than anything else. It became my pet carry gun for deep cold weather.

We of the unofficial "SIG P220 .45 Fan Club" had but one request, and it was one the SIG folks heard ad nauseam. "We love the gun... but when are you going to make it just a little bit smaller?"

SIG heard. SIG listened. SIG quietly went to work on it. And, just when we least expected it, SIG responded to our pleading with a pistol they call the P245.

P245 proved itself in cold-weather handling, and presents a significantly smaller size package than SIG's standard .45.

QUIET INTRODUCTION

I would like to tell you that SIG appreciated me being a longtime fan and sent me the first test gun for that reason. I would like to tell you that, since I live less than an hour's drive from the SIGARMS plant in Exeter, New Hampshire, my keen "trained investigator" instincts allowed me to smell it out before anyone else. I would like to tell you that and more, but I can't, because it would all be a crock of crap. Let me tell you what, as near as we can figure out, really happened.

The first shipment of guns came into the country. Somebody slipped somewhere at SIGARMS, and at least one shipment was sent out to a certain distributor who was backordered on the ever-popular full-size SIG .45. One such pistol found it's way to a San Diego gunshop. Cameron Hopkins, this publication's executive editor, walked into that shop and saw what appeared to be a shrunken P220 American (the P220 with the Yank-preferred side button magazine release) in the showcase. Hopkins went into high gear: one gun to Ichiro Nagata for his

incomparable photography, one to me some 3,000 miles away by Federal Express, and, oh yes, there was the matter of the deadline. "Yeah, Merry Christmas, yada yada, I need you to shoot hell out of this gun now!"

SURPRISING ACCURACY

So there I was, two days after Christmas, on a range that wasn't sub-zero yet but was damn sure sub-freezing, accuracy testing the P245. It was braced on a bench while I was down on both knees 25 yards from a backstop sufficiently frozen that at each shot, it sprayed particles of frozen dirt 75 feet back in protest. (Actually, this was a good thing.

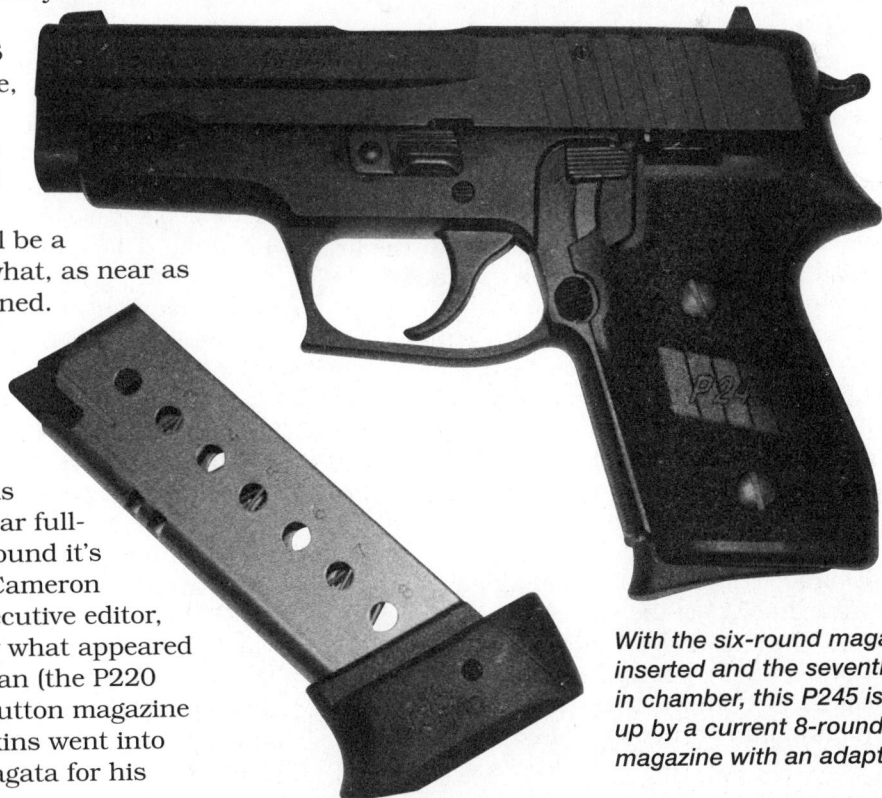

With the six-round magazine inserted and the seventh round in chamber, this P245 is backed up by a current 8-round P220 magazine with an adapter...

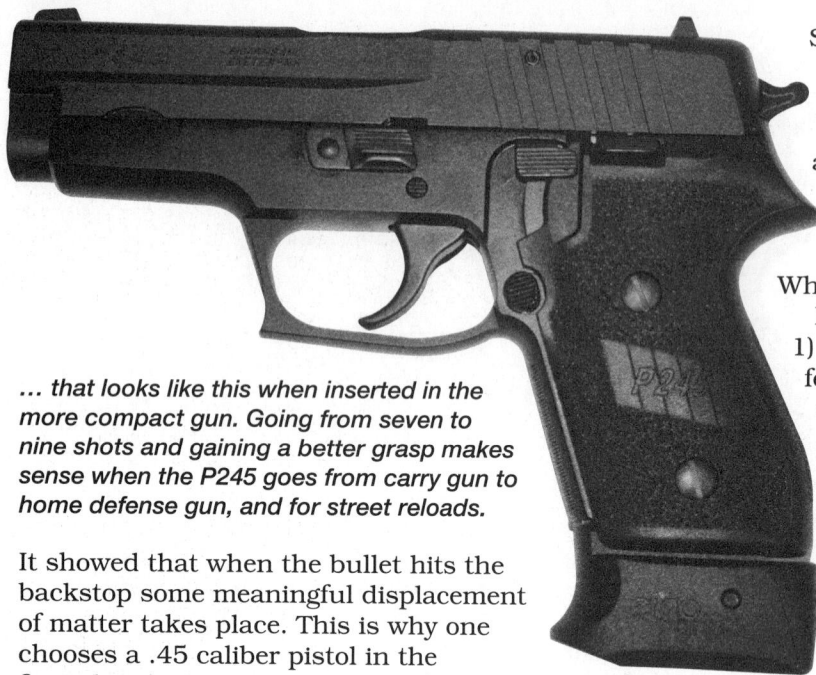

... that looks like this when inserted in the more compact gun. Going from seven to nine shots and gaining a better grasp makes sense when the P245 goes from carry gun to home defense gun, and for street reloads.

It showed that when the bullet hits the backstop some meaningful displacement of matter takes place. This is why one chooses a .45 caliber pistol in the first place.)

As you peruse the group sizes, bear in mind that the shooter was an aging, arthritic male descended from an anthropological background that is not genetically programmed to thrive in sub-freezing temperatures. His arthritic knees were in direct contact with frozen ground surface. He was not at his best. Read in a whimper if you wish.

Five shots were fired with each of six popular .45 ACP defense loads. Two measurements were then taken, each center-to-center in the bullet holes: the dispersal of all five shots, and the dispersal of the tightest three of those hits. The five-shot group gives you a prediction of what you can do if you keep your cool and are shooting from cover over a stone wall or something 25 paces from the threat. The three-shot group gives a pretty good idea of the inherent accuracy of the pistol/load combination. By taking the best three, you factor out two things: ever-present human error, and the fact that the first hand-cycled cartridge is usually in a very subtly different "battery" vis-à-vis how the parts wind up aligned after automatically cycling subsequent to a previous shot. This is why it is so common to see the first shot of the group hit a little away from where the subsequent shots go when accuracy-testing a semiautomatic pistol.

Results were as follows, with a shivering shooter firing at 25 yards with gloved hands, and all the rest of the cheap excuses:

The accuracy results are listed in alphabetical order. By the time I shot the last group, the Speer 200-grain, I was palpably shivering. An almost 4-1/2-inch group should be held against me, not the gun, but the significant thing is that the best three shots from that particular cluster measured seven-eighths of one inch center to center from 25 yards.

Suffice to say that under the circumstances, the P245 delivered superb accuracy. None of the ammunition used was "match-grade," no robot machine rest was involved, and the tester (me) was an aging feeb who was shivering from the cold for at least part of the shooting protocols. Anything unimpressive here, speaks to the shooter. What is impressive speaks to the pistol.

In past years, I have noted the following. 1) No double-action pistol exceeds the SIG for accuracy in .45ACP, and damn few even equal it. 2) Frankly, damn few custom 1911 .45s equal or exceed the SIG either. 3) The SIG P220 is the one service pistol that in my experience will not be made more accurate by installing a BarSto barrel. All I found was that my own old SIG with its factory barrel and a new P220 American would both do 7/8 inches with Federal Classic 185-grain JHP at 25 yards, and the BarSto would equal but not exceed that. And it might be as accurate with one or two more additional factory .45 combat loads, such as the Federal Hydra-Shok, which normally won't do under an inch in a factory SIG like it will in a BarSto 1911 barrel.

Let's stop here, and simply say that the P245 passed the accuracy test with flying colors.

SHOOTABILITY

Call it "ergonomics." Call it "human engineering." Call it "user-friendliness," or just call it "shootability" in shorthand. Whatever. The SIG P245 not only has it, but has it nailed down.

Take it out of the sleek new "double-lockable" box it's shipped in. Triple-check it unloaded, close your eyes, and run your hands over it. There are no sharp edges that will bite your hands while shooting. The stippling on the plastic grips gives you a sense of "permanent skateboard tape." However, it doesn't snag on fabric and lift the concealing garment when you carry the pistol hidden behind your hip.

It has big, blocky sights that even us old blind guys can see. The test pistol didn't have tritium night sight inserts but instead, the familiar SIG "von Stavenhagen pattern" of a white bar at the rear and a white dot up front, a dot the "i" kind of thing. I found it to work well shooting a qualification with the sun in my eyes on a cold winter day.

Shooting a qualification in front of somebody is a good way to test the human engineering of a pistol. No, "you ain't bein' shot at or nothin'," but there are elements of peer pressure and performance anxiety that create a microcosm of stress and some degree of "body alarm reaction." I remember shooting the first Bianchi Cup in 1979 with Jim Cirillo, the multiple shootout survivor of the famed NYPD Stakeout Squad, who told me then, "I never felt this much stress in any of my (expletive deleted) gunfights!"

RELIABILITY

The test of a .45 auto is, "will it feed the 'flying ashtray'?" This is what my friend Dean Grennell christened the 200-grain CCI-Speer hollow-point .45 ACP. The P245 fed it without a bobble, spitting three Gold Dot versions of that long-proven manstopper into seven-eighths of an inch, center-to-center, at 25 yards from a two-handed rest with gloves on. This wide-mouth "CCI trademark profile" bullet has put a lot of bad guys out of commission in actual shootings. I recall one slaughterhouse test in which several animals were killed with exotic 230-grain hollow-point .45 bullets like the Black Talon, the Hydra-Shok, and the extremely impressive StarFire. Then, almost as an afterthought, we did a steer with the load I was carrying in my issue 4-1/4-inch Ruger .45 auto, a 200-grain CCI "flying ashtray" loaded to 1,050 feet per second. The huge animal died instantly, its brain so devastated by intracranial pressure that the animal's eyes were bulged out of their sockets. The bullet had virtually 100 percent weight retention, and mushroomed to about an inch in diameter, which is something you don't often see.

The SIG P245 fed the "flying ashtray" without a hitch. It fed everything. The one malfunction experienced in several hundred rounds was a failure to eject with a 230-grain ball round, during accuracy testing where the shooter was firing with a relaxed grip and the shot in question was the final round in the gun. Simply reloading and jacking the slide cleared the weapon and brought it back up and running.

WEARING THE P245

New guns need new holsters. I tried several of mine, and the bottom line was, the P245 worked best out of a P220 holster. There will soon be numerous holsters made to fit this truncated P220.

Tiny Tara Miller demonstrates control of P245 lightweight compact with full power G.I. .45 hardball. Her whole 100 pounds or so is "into" the gun (note tautly flexed knee of rear drive leg), even with a spent casing at 1 o'clock above the gun, the muzzle still on the target.

Depending upon where you take your rearmost measurement from, the P245 is somewhere between half an inch and three quarters of an inch shorter than the P220. Unless you're wearing the wrong kind of holster in the wrong place, this won't matter much in terms of concealment.

Where the reduced dimensions of the P245 do matter in terms of concealment is in that often-

Manufacturer	Load	5-Shot Group	Best 3 Shots
Federal Classic	185-grain JHP	2-1/16"	1-3/8"
Pro-Load	230-grain FMJ	2-3/8"	1-1/8"
Pro-Load	185-grain JHP	3"	1-7/16"
Speer Gold Dot	200-grain JHP	4-7/16"	7/8"
Winchester Silvertip	185-grain JHP	2-1/2"	1-7/8"
Winchester	230-grain JHP	3-5/8"	1-5/8"

QUALIFYING WITH THE P245

Scene circumstance: Freezing, no gloves, sun in eyes.

Psychological circumstance: It's Christmas weekend, for goodness sake, just want to get home and be with the kids before the oldest has to go back to school.

Target: ISPC Brussels, with a 6-inch by 11-inch five-point zone that's a helluva lot tighter than the maximum five-point zone on an old FBI Colt silhouette, a new FBI "Q" silhouette, or the ever popular NRA Police Qualifier B-27 silhouette.

Course of fire: easy "off duty gun" course, 60 shots, times like 12 shots in 25 seconds from 7 yards.

Score: 60 Pro-Load 230-grain hardball and Winchester Silvertip 185-grain JHP in a centered group measuring 6-5/8 inches vertical by 4 inches horizontal. A total score of 299 out of 300, but I was holding too high in the "five zone." Shooter's fault, not gun's fault.

Points noted in qualification: If you shoot with the "high thumbs" position, a right-handed shooter's thumb rides the slide lock lever and the pistol won't lock open with empty. SIG-Sauer shooters have known this for 22 years. Get over it or shoot with thumbs curled down, which there's no reason not to do with the SIG pistol. The magazine release button needs a forcible stab to release. This is a good thing for those of us who carry guns in cold weather. It won't accidentally release in the two-handed grasp of a right-handed shooter, especially when wearing gloves, like the older "American-style" SIG pistols did. During reloading the magazine insertion needs to be forcible to get past the "sticky point" felt when reloading in slow motion. Duh. Who reloads in slow motion anyway? Not a problem of the gun, a problem of the shooter. Reload forcibly. Get over it. The trigger pull is consistent, clean, around 4.5 pounds in single-action and perhaps 12 to 13 pounds in double. There is a slight creep (palpable sense of trigger moving internal parts). But this is "good creep" rather than "bad creep," in that it gives you a sense of when the gun is about to go off, but does not have friction or drag points that pull the sights off target as the shot is about to be unleashed. The trigger reach could be a little shorter in the double-action mode, but is ideal for my "average adult male hand" in single-action. With a bare hand, the magazine extension makes the pistol fit my hand almost perfectly. With a glove on, the added bulk and thickness of my fingers is enough that it's a "two finger grasp" gun, with my little finger curled under the butt. Overall, this is not really a problem. The full size SIG for me is also an excellent fit in the gripframe bare handed, but with gloves the little finger hits the magazine lip about halfway, and I generally wind up shooting with the little finger curled underneath anyway when wearing snowmobile gloves.

Overall impression: This is a good little .45 auto.

misunderstood measurement called "height." Measured from the butt of the pistol to the top of the slide, this is the dimension that really matters when you carry the gun at your waist, and it's here that the P245 is distinctly shorter than its parent P220. The price you pay for that is "one round down." Yeah, I know, SIG created the "DPS" magazine for the Texas Department of Safety after they adopted the P220, and thus created the "eight-plus-one-shot SIG .45." Guys who have them show them to me as if they were revealing icons, since the eight-shot SIG .45 mag is rarely seen outside police departments.

Let's get real here. The compact SIG .45 holds six rounds in its magazine and a seventh in its firing chamber. The typical P220 you're likely to find will hold seven, plus one. I noticed that my one DPS eight-round magazine for the P220 "tightened the stack" so much with spring pressure that it took extra force for me to reload it into a SIG .45 whose slide was still forward on a live round, and I got to where, if I carried that magazine, I loaded it with only seven rounds just to make sure everything would work in an emergency.

So, you've got a .45 and you're down from eight or nine rounds to seven. Is this really a problem? For most of this century, U.S. military men carried seven-shot .45 automatics – the 1911 pistol with the generally ordered carry condition of empty chamber, and seven-shot magazine in place – and were considered to be the best-armed soldiers on the planet who had been issued "pistols only." These were men in combat zones. Should concealed carry of a seven-shot .45 that can fire its first shot instantly without having to work a slide be seen as a handicap in civilian, stateside America? I for one don't really think that's a problem.

FOR COMPARISON

	P245	P220
Overall length	7.28"	7.8"
Overall length	5.0"	5.6"
Unloaded weight	27.5 oz.	27.8 oz.
Width	1.34"	1.4"
Barrel length	3.9"	4.4"
Sight radius	5.7"	6.3"
Cartridge capacity	6+1	7+1
Caliber	.45 ACP	.45 ACP
Available as DAO?	Yes	Yes

BOTTOM LINE

I found the SIG P245 comfortable and concealable to carry, quick and easy to shoot, and more accurate than most would dare to have hoped.

SIG has a history of not being the first to jump on the bandwagon. They were the last of the big police pistol purveyors to come on line with a .40 S&W caliber handgun, because they waited until they had it down pat with total reliability. They waited to jump into the "plastic pistol market" longer than the rest, until their polymer-framed *sig pro* was totally debugged and ready to pass the torture tests, as it just did for the Drug Enforcement Administration a few months after this magazine gave it a clean bill of health.

SIG did the same with its compact P245. Unlike manufacturers who call press conferences about guns they haven't got working yet, SIG kept the long-demanded compact .45 under wraps until they were coming off the production line working 100 percent. They'd have kept it under wraps longer and gotten more feedback if Hopkins hadn't picked up on the P245 and "outed" it.

The bottom line is, the long-awaited compact SIG P220 .45 is here...it works...it has the fine accuracy and excellent reliability of its street-proven parent product... and it was worth the wait. They call it the "P245," and if you feel the traditional SIG double-action pistol concept and the .45 ACP cartridge coincide with your concealed handgun needs, you really should check it out.

Professional pistol packers like the nononsense look and non-reflective finish of the SIG P245.

Chapter 11
The SIG P250

SIG P250C: THE NEW MODULAR AUTO PISTOL

The polymer-framed Glock pistol had captured the police sales market in the mid-1980s, and dominated it by the '90s. The SIG-Pro series had not proven as popular with police stateside as in other countries. By mid-first-decade of the new millennium, SIG was ready to take another stab at the polymer pistol market. The result was the P250. My first write-up on it dates back to 2007, with my test of a compact model reprinted here from On Target magazine.

These days, SIG is big. Their guns are selling well. They're coming out with new models. The brand has gone from SIG-Sauer to SIGARMS to its latest incarnation, at least stateside, SIG-

SAUER. Newer than alphabet juggling, and a lot more important, is the company's latest new design, the P250.

And this one, folks, *is* something new. We're all accustomed by now to the little stamped metal serial numbers inset into polymer pistol frames. It was a bit of culture shock to see the one bearing the number EAU000664 staring out at me *through* a window in the polymer frame of the P250c test gun. Silly me, the number was *on* the "frame." It was just that it was on a steel frame *under* the polymer "outer frame."

This ingenious pistol, which is also the first SIG-SAUER design to have ambidextrous slide lock/slide release levers, has a steel fire control mechanism complete with serial number inside what the owner's manual says is a "grip module," even though it has trigger guard, dust cover, etc. Terminology is a wonderful thing. This concept will allow different length frames, different slides, different calibers...a new dimension in "interchangeability"! Unfortunately, we received no extra "grip modules," etc. for testing.

The gun is hammer fired, double action only, with second strike capability and a pretty sweet trigger stroke that averaged a little over seven pounds when pulled from center, and a little under seven when pulled from the toe of the trigger. The fixed tritium sights are unusual in that while the front sight is in a dovetail, the rear rests immovable in a U-shaped notch. Lateral adjustment is done by the unusual expedient of moving the front sight (in the direction opposite where you want the shots to go). Elevation is changed via optional sights of different heights, which seems unnecessarily tedious. The test gun tended to shoot low and very far right with a post-

The full size P250 sits well in the hand, with an ideal trigger reach for its double action only mechanism. The 4.5" barrel is longest yet offered on the P250 series.

in-notch sight picture, and on for elevation but still very far right with a three dot sight picture. The front sight was visibly well left of center in its notch when it came out of the box.

Recoil was soft, and muzzle jump barely noticeable despite a relatively high bore axis. Five shot groups were mediocre, below the high standard set by other SIG 9mms, running four inches for

This "unhappy face" group, fired from 25 yards with Winchester hardball, measures 2.05" and best three are in 0.65".

147 grain American Eagle, worse with Winchester white box, and a reassuring 2.90 inches with +P Black Hills 124 grain JHP. "Best three" clusters told a more promising story: 1.35 inches with the Black Hills, nine-tenths of one inch with Winchester 115 grain FMJ, and an incredible 0.45-inch center to center cluster with the AE 147 grain jacketed truncated cone, the latter including a double so tight we couldn't spot it until we turned the target over to examine the exit holes. Reliability was 100% with all three loads.

MSRP is $699. The SIG-SAUER P250's fascinating new design will interest the collector and also the shooter who needs different gun sizes with one serial number, for instance, in jurisdictions where only one "gun" is allowed on the carry license.

*SIG's radical P250 came out in 2007. The first ones weren't perfect, but were so promising that I gave the gun an Editor's Choice Award in the pages of **On Target** magazine, in the 2008 write-up that follows. There would be growing pains, and the gun would get better.*

SIG'S MODULAR P250 PISTOL

When I was young, grown-up "gun cranks" (as they often called themselves then) aspired to own

5-shot group with Black Hills' excellent duty load, a 230 grain JHP, measures 2" on the nose. Distance was 25 yards.

at least one specimen of every unusual handgun design. For example, a Luger, a Walter P-38, and a broomhandle Mauser were considered mandatory to a good collection. Those of that generation who are still around will doubtless want a SIG P250...and so will a lot of others, though perhaps for different reasons.

What sets the P250 apart is a totally modular system in which the fire control mechanism constitutes the firearm and bears the serial number, and what we would call the frame on any other pistol is a sort of polymer sleeve that encompasses this module. The gun can take longer or shorter barrel/slide assemblies, in a variety of calibers. This will make it particularly suitable for those in countries where the number of handguns owned is

The P250 worked perfectly with both FMJ and JHP 230 grain .45 ACP.

strictly limited, but a given approved handgun can be modified to the owner's content.

The P250 has a polymer, uh, frame, and this sort of production economy keeps its price reasonable. The retail tag is roughly that of a Glock, but the P250 comes with tritium night sights installed, a perk that normally adds $80 to $100 or more to competitive pistols' retail prices. This makes the new SIG all the more a good value. It also is completely ambidextrous, with reversible magazine release, and with slide lock levers on either side.

The P250 is outside hammer and double action only in design, with a *smoooooth* trigger stroke. It has "second strike" capability, meaning that a second pull of the trigger gives you another crack at discharging a misfired cartridge. There is debate as to whether that is useful or not, but what can't be debated is that this trigger mechanism allows dry fire practice without breaking your hold or your rhythm to pull the slide back to re-set the trigger between pulls.

The P250s I've shot have stayed inside the "4 inches at 25 yards" standard of accuracy for duty guns, but I haven't yet seen one that gives the gilt-edged accuracy of the older "classic line" SIG-Sauer pistols. I've seen two P226s in .357 SIG put five shots in an inch at the same distance, and I've seen more than two SIG P220s do the same with their favorite .45 ACP ammo. This is one of the things you're paying for with those higher-priced models.

P250s are eminently shootable, however. All of us on the test team liked their soft recoil (we've tested only the 9mm chambering so far). One shooter had brought his 15-year-old son along, and the lad shot the P250 better than his own self-cocking, name-brand traditional double action 9mm, with which he was much more familiar. I haven't seen a P250 skip a beat yet in terms of reliability, either. Give one a try...I think you'll like this new concept, too.

I had been looking forward to testing the P250 in .45 ACP, and finally got the chance to do so in 2009. Here's my report on that, from **On Target** *magazine.*

SIG P250 .45 SERVICE PISTOL

As the SIG P250 line expands, the guns are getting better, and this longer barreled .45 is a clear example.

The first thing I noticed when the modular SIG P250 started coming into this country was that while its claim to fame was that it could be morphed into different sizes and calibers bearing the same serial number, the pistol itself was perfectly good as a stand-alone. Mixing older-generation outside hammer design with revolver-like double action only trigger pull, it was both simple and reliable. The early ones had mediocre accuracy and poorly fitted sights

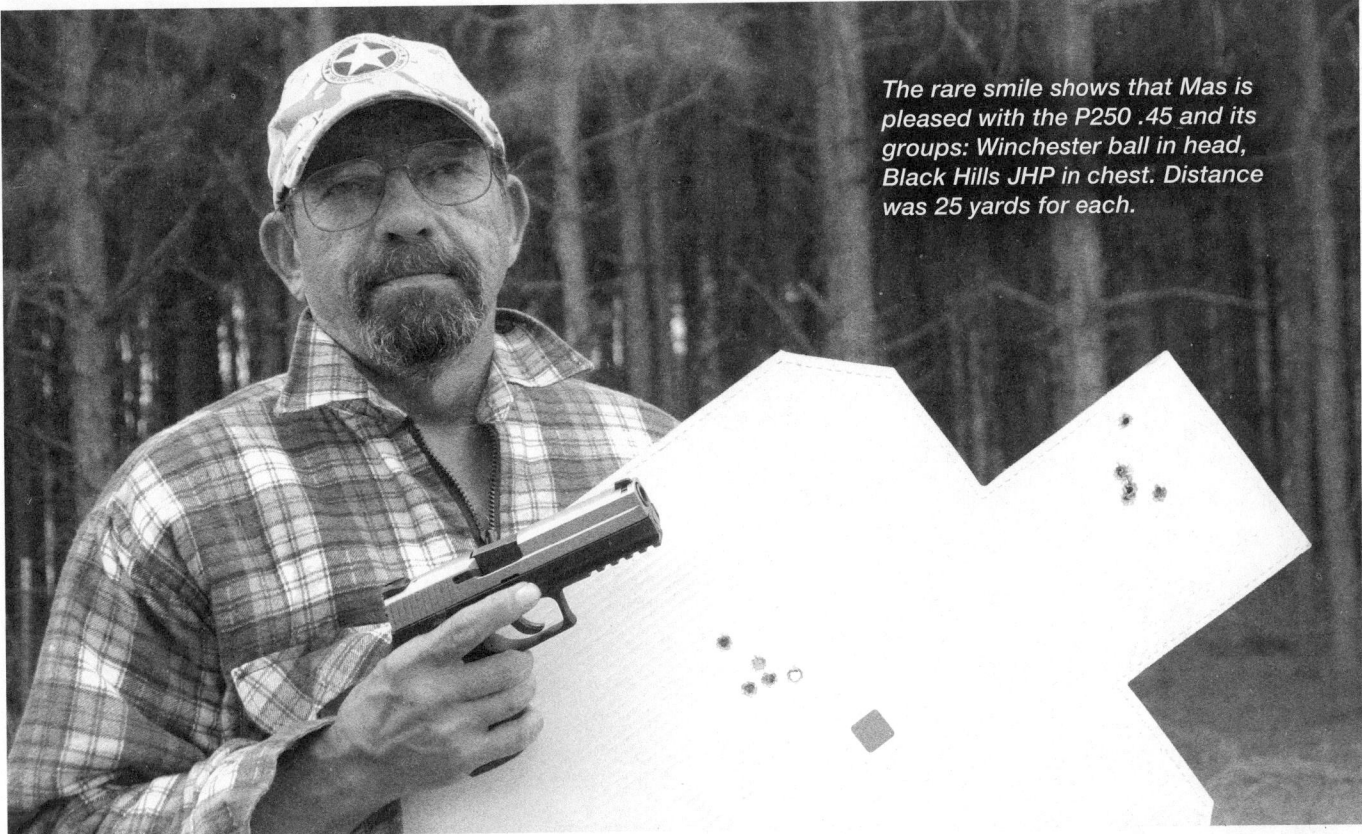

The rare smile shows that Mas is pleased with the P250 .45 and its groups: Winchester ball in head, Black Hills JHP in chest. Distance was 25 yards for each.

for SIGs, but that got dramatically better with time.

The first one I shot in caliber .45 ACP, which may have been the first to leave the factory, was a compact model. I liked its handling. I didn't like that they'd put the wrong sights on it, and its elevation was *way* off from point of aim at point of impact. Now comes *On Target's* latest test sample, a service-size P250 in .45 ACP with a 4.5" barrel. (4.7", actually, if you measure to the back of the barrel hood instead of the back of the chamber.)

With a lightly stippled grip-frame that stays put in the hand, and a well-shaped backstrap that distributes recoil into the hand, the P250 was a pussycat to shoot with full power, standard pressure .45 ACP ammunition. The DAO trigger pull reminds you of a good revolver: smooth, even, and no "stacking" or pressure increase toward the end of the firing stroke. Trigger pull weight ran about eight pounds, heavier than most P250s I've shot, but was smooth enough not to be problematic.

My first, very early P250 had the wrong sights. This one was only a little low with post in notch sight picture, and spot on for elevation when aiming with the three dots, which usually raises point of impact. It shot very slightly left for me. The shape of the fixed rear sight on the P250 doesn't lend itself to drifting, but it would be no trick to drift the *front* sight in its dovetail to correct this.

I used two proven brands of standard pressure 230 grain .45 ACP for accuracy testing off the 25-yard bench. Black Hills jacketed hollow point put five holes exactly two inches apart center to center. Four of those hits were in 1.20 inches and the best three, in 0.95 inch. Inexpensive Winchester "white box" USA brand 230 grain full metal jacket put five hits in 2.05 inches, with the best four in 1.15 inches and the best three in 0.65 inch! In a double action only .45 with economy ammo, I think that's worth its exclamation point. A few months before, when I was having dinner with SIG-Sauer CEO Ron Cohen, he told me he believed the P250 was capable of holding at inch at 25 yards. Those "best three" measurements seem to fulfill his promise.

There were no malfunctions, unless you count the slide stop locking the slide open inadvertently on recoil, which seems to happen with these guns if the shooter's thumb rides the slide stop. So, curl the thumb down and it won't happen. With a slide stop on either side, and no manual safety or decocking levers, it's very southpaw friendly. The P250s have all come in with one magazine apiece (the one with the test .45 took ten rounds) so I didn't have enough mags to shoot it in a match, or I would have. Night sights were standard when the P250 was introduced, but were not present on this test .45. Coming with a light rail integral, and adding its unique modularity features to its sales package, I think the P250 .45 is going to be very competitive in its market. It's certainly an impressive "shooter."

SIG SAUER
P250® Caliber X+CHANGE™ Kit

Replacement Assembly Includes: Barrel, Recoil Spring/Guide,
Slide with SIGLITE® Night Sights, and Magazine.

Barrel

Recoil
Spring/Guide

SIGLITE®
Night Sights

Slide Finish:
Stainless or Nitron™

Magazine

Above: Caliber change kit is integral part of the P250 theme, but Mas says it's a fine stand-alone pistol.

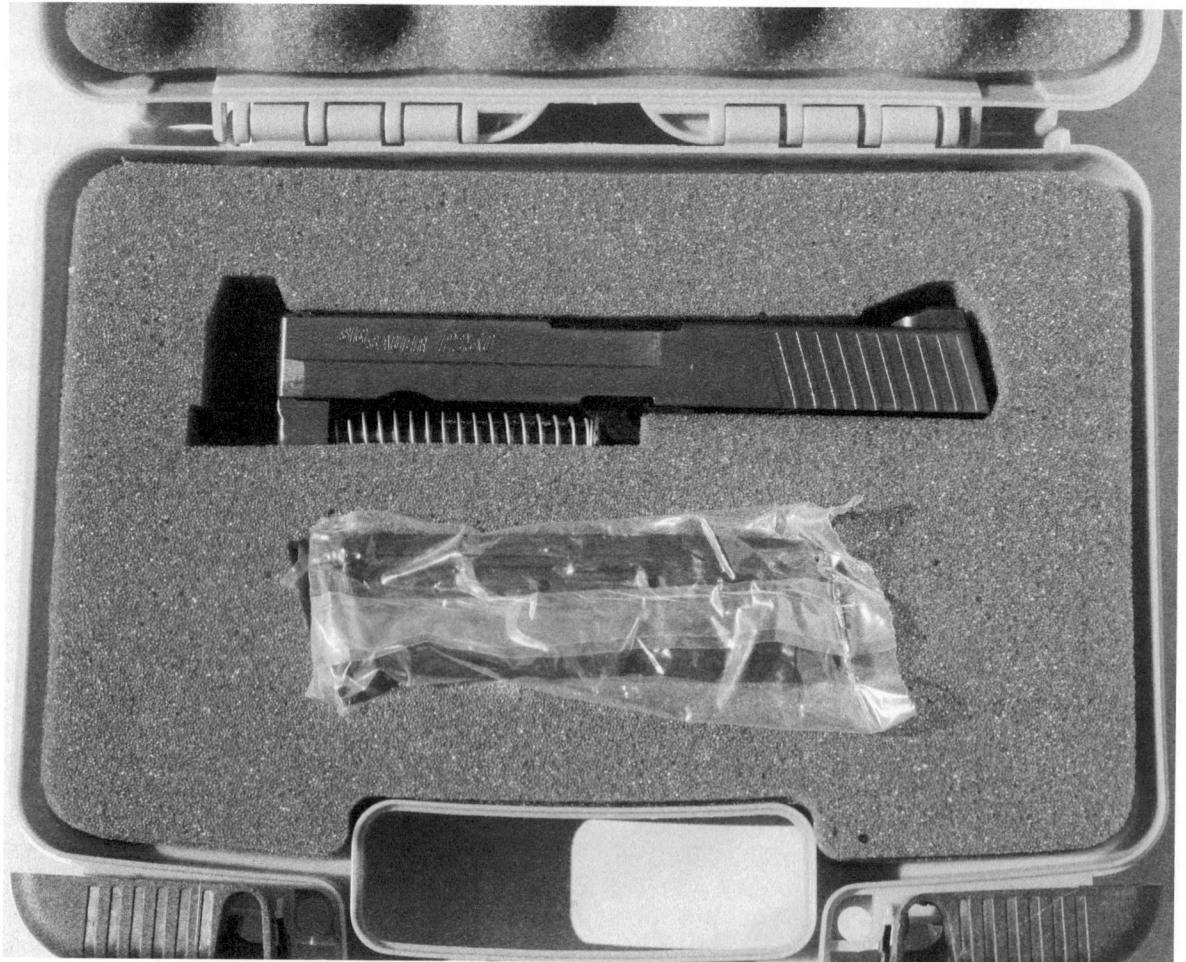

Right: Caliber change kit for a SIG P250.

THE SIG 2-SUM: MORE THAN THE SUM OF ITS PARTS?

SIG-Sauer offers a two-guns-in-one kit which offers fascinating options.

The P250 pistol has generated quite a bit of interest since its introduction here a few years ago. SIG-Sauer continues to advance the concept. It's presently available in compact to full size configurations, and in a range of four calibers including 9mm Luger, .357 SIG, .40 S&W, and .45 ACP. This year alone, we've seen two distinctly new variations of the P250 offered.

One is a manual safety version, its ambidextrous levers mounted at the rear of the frame. It was developed initially upon the request of a Peruvian agency, but will be appreciated by us old traditionalists who just grew up expecting semiautomatic pistols to have manual thumb safeties. It will also appeal to those at risk of being disarmed, since on-safe pistols have a history of confusing those who snatch them and try to murder the legitimate owners, for long enough that said original owner has more time to rectify the problem.

The other big news in the P250 line is the subject of this article: the 2-SUM, so called because it is basically two guns sold as one.

Well, make that two potential handguns sold as one, since between them, there is only one fire control mechanism. What is unique about the P250

This handy kit is the P250 2SUM.

2-SUM was tested in both formats (subcompact shown here) with loads of known accuracy in the three most popular 9mm bullet weights.

119

platform is not only that it is modular, but that the heart of the beast is a serial-numbered hammer-and-trigger assembly which legally constitutes the gun itself. This assembly sits inside the chassis of a polymer pistol frame which the company calls a grip shell. It takes a paradigm shift for us old gun geezers to wrap our heads around this disembodied hammer-trigger linkage being a "frame" or "receiver," but that's just how it is, and we have to get used to it.

The design – for which we can thank Michael Mayerl, Thomas Metzger, Adrian Thomele, and the brilliant American Ethan Lessard – brings handgun modularity to a new level. Compact or full-size "handle." Big grip, small grip. Long barrel or short, each of course with commensurate length slide. Short-reach or standard-reach triggers. Caliber choices. Woot!

A MATTER OF NEED

Some people need multiple gun capability on one serial number more than others. Let's say you are a citizen in the Republic of South Africa, where firearms restrictions have become increasingly Draconian over the years since the current government there came into power. You may be allowed to own but one handgun for self-defense. If it's a SIG 2-SUM, you have a compact and a full-size, and are technically in legal compliance. Let's say you're one of those privileged citizens of New York City who has been fortunate enough to obtain an unrestricted concealed carry permit. The general custom there seems to be to put one specific gun on the permit, by serial number. Some few permit holders have been able to extend theirs to a second firearm, I'm told, but more than that is extremely rare. You just got the permit, and the city has basically told you, "Pick one carry gun," and will record its serial number. With the SIG 2-SUM, at least theoretically, you have your compact 13-round warm weather carry gun, and your full size, longer barrel, 18-round pistol in the same 9mm chambering for carry under more concealment-friendly cold weather garb.

One is reminded of the Dan Wesson revolver, a double action that burst on the scene in the late 1960s and was chambered initially for .38 Special/.357 Magnum. The namesake designer, a descendant of S&W co-founder Daniel Baird Wesson, crafted the gun with interchangeable

sleeved barrels. The deluxe outfit was the Dan Wesson Pistol Pac, which came with multiple length barrels and the changing tools...kinda like a SIG 2-SUM, except that the latter doesn't need proprietary tools to change configurations.

SIG's hope was that departments and individual cops would buy P250s, as well as private citizens, for the versatility. The theory was that a police officer would wear the pistol to work in full size duty configuration, and then change it out to compact configuration in the locker room or at home, for off duty concealed carry. Looking at the Dan Wesson experience with the same market decades ago, we know that it didn't work out that way. After an exhausting eight- to twelve-hour tour of duty, the last thing a tired cop wants to do is unload his gun, take it apart, reassemble it differently, and reload before going about his business on his own time. Thus, cops of the period simply invested in a second, smaller revolver for off duty, which could also be carried as backup to their service revolver at work.

Those of us who learned to appreciate the Dan Wesson for its fine accuracy and its potential for an extremely smooth action, and desired them in different barrel lengths, found that changing barrels on one wasn't like changing lenses on a single lens reflex camera. The revolver had to be sighted in again after each barrel change, or there could be subtle changes in point of aim/point of impact. It was something of a hassle, and serious shooters who liked the Dan Wesson

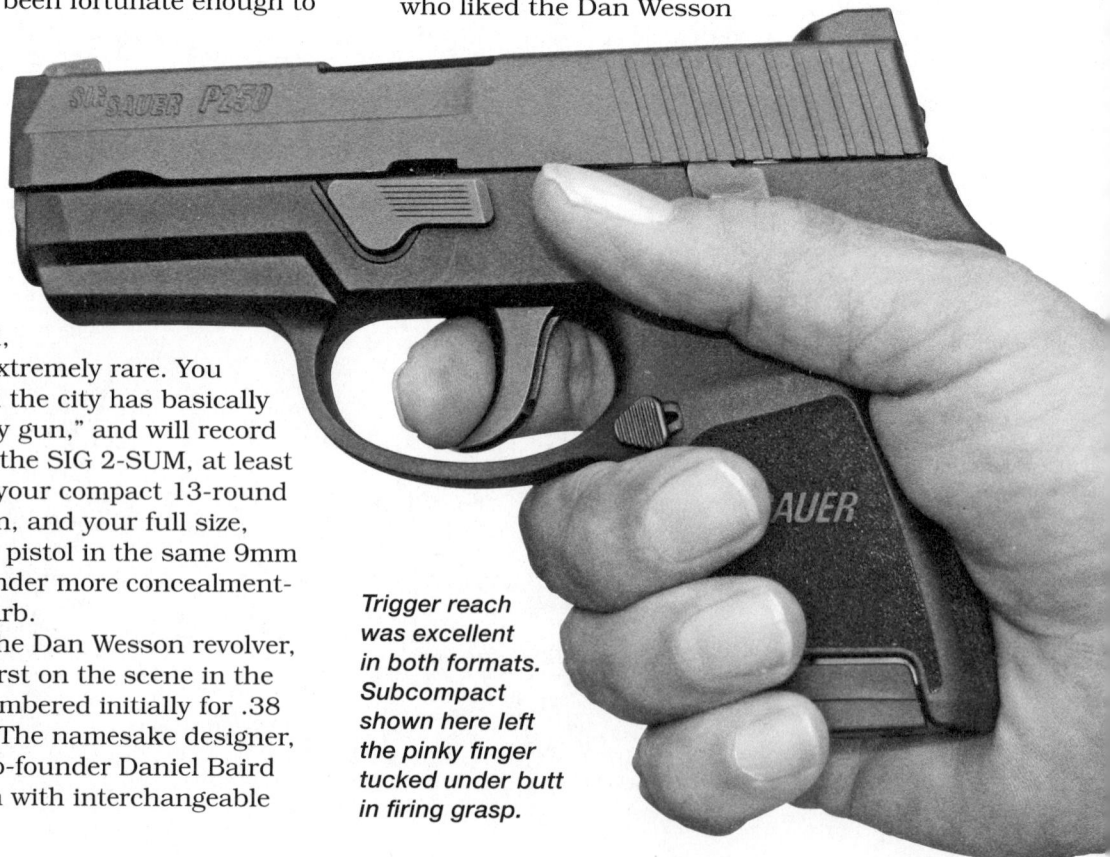

Trigger reach was excellent in both formats. Subcompact shown here left the pinky finger tucked under butt in firing grasp.

Mas with 2-SUM set up as subcompact, and 25-yard target. Shorter version delivered tighter groups: go figure.

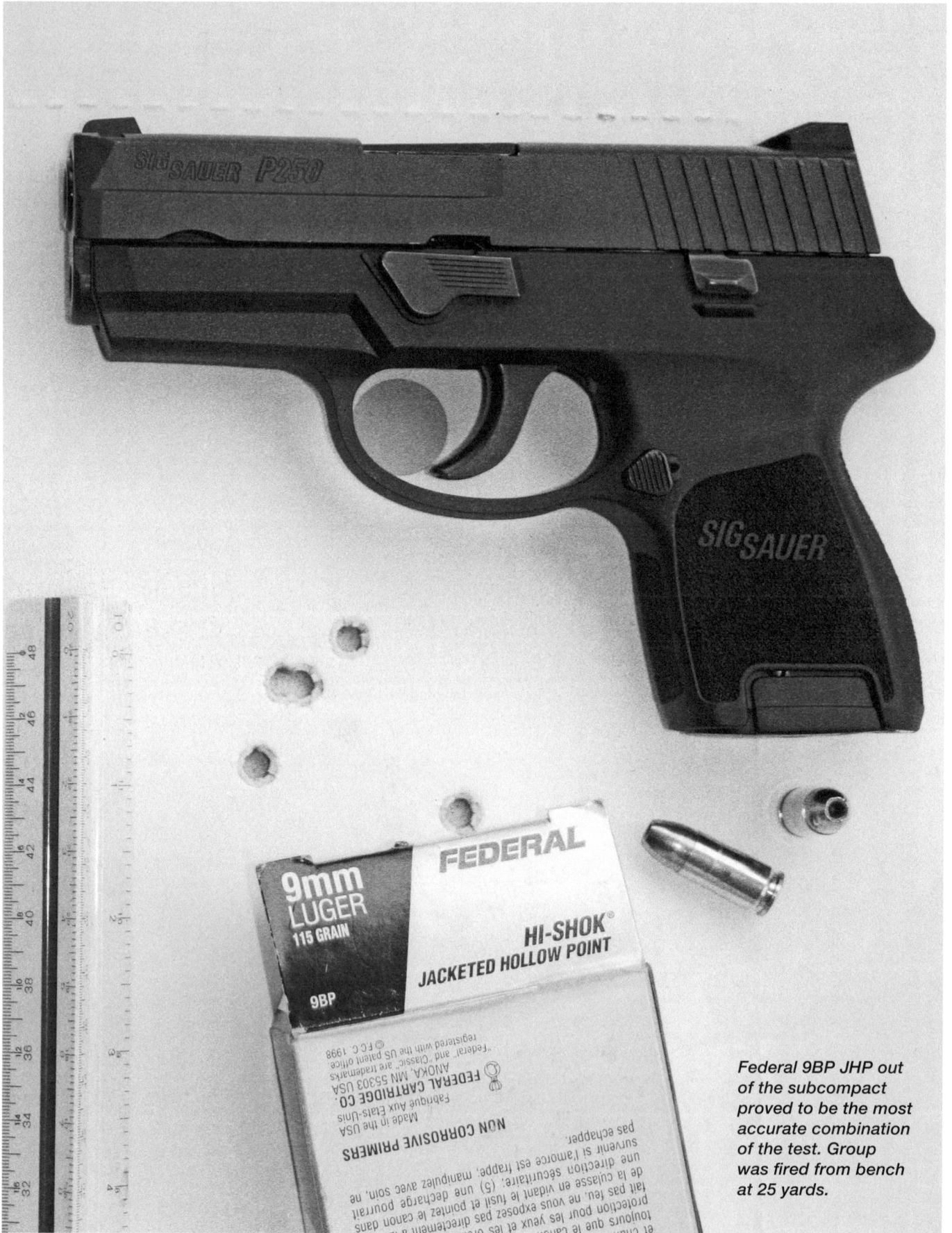

Federal 9BP JHP out of the subcompact proved to be the most accurate combination of the test. Group was fired from bench at 25 yards.

simply bought another one in the additional barrel length they wanted.

I mention that, because I see the same happening with the P250. One friend of mine who likes the P250 now has two of the whole guns, plus two change-out kits. The fact is, the majority of P250 owners I know like the gun just as it is, as a stand-alone pistol, and the modularity element just didn't factor into their purchasing decision that much.

2-SUM ON THE FIRING LINE

Our test 2-SUM came in 9mm, with a compact/subcompact grip module with smooth dust cover, and a full-size one replete with light rail. The little one came with a short slide assembly housing a 3.6-inch barrel, and with a single 12-round magazine. The larger came with a 4.7-inch barrel, proportional slide, and a seventeen-round magazine. Both slides were equipped with three-dot tritium night sights, generously proportioned to give a good, fast sight picture in daylight or dark.

Each gun was tested for grouping from the bench, using an MTM handgun rest. Every five shot group was measured once overall, center to center of the farthest-apart bullet holes to the nearest 0.05 inch, and then again for the best three shots. The second measurement factors out enough unnoticed human error to give a good approximation of the gun's inherent accuracy with the same ammo for all five shots from a machine rest, while the whole five-shot group offers a good preview of practical

Longer version also shot its best with the Federal 115 grain JHP.

accuracy in experienced human hands, given calm conditions and a braced firing position.

The 2-SUM was tried in each configuration with the three most popular 9mm bullet weights. For 124 grain, I picked the very accurate Black Hills 124 grain JHP. Out of the longer "kit," that load gave us 2.95 inches for five shots, with the best three in 1.2 inches. In the subcompact, the overall Black Hills group was actually a smidgen tighter: 2.90 inches, with a 1.35-inch measurement for the best three.

For 115 grain, the choice was Federal's famously accurate 9BP, a standard pressure jacketed hollow point. It lived up to its reputation with the best groups, irrespective of gun configuration. The service-size half of the 2-SUM twosome gave a 2.10-inch five-shot group, while the best three (including a double) went into 1.8inches. When morphed into subcompact form, the P250 shot the best group of the test with the Federal 9BP: 1.7 inches for all five shots, and a sweet 0.65 inch for the best three, a cluster which also included a double.

The 147 grain subsonic entry was a low-priced generic, but one that has proven to be an IDPA match-winner for me: Remington's UMC full metal jacket truncated cone. It delivered a 3.8-inch five-shot group, with most of the spread horizontal, and a 1.85-inch best-three group, with the long top end in place. But the subcompact "kit" completed its clean sweep of the accuracy testing, with a group that measured 3.25 inches for five shots and 1.2 inches for best three.

Why the counterintuitive outcome? I had expected the longer kit to outshoot the shorter if only because of the longer sight radius. However, it's not the first time I've seen a shorter polymer-framed auto outshoot its longer sibling. My subcompact Glock 26 9mm groups better from the bench than my full size Glock 17 with the same ammo; my little Glock 27 is dramatically more accurate than my service size Glock 22 with the same .40 ammo; and in .45 ACP, I've found the stubby Glock 30 to consistently outperform the full size Glock 21. Only in caliber .357 SIG have I found the opposite, with my full size Glock 31 consistently outshooting my "baby Glock" 33. It is theorized that in the shorter guns, there is proportionally more rigidity in the barrel/slide area, enhancing inherent accuracy.

With the P250 2-SUM, I noticed that "lighter was tighter" with the 115 grain ahead of the 124 and well ahead of the 147 grain in both barrel lengths. I've seen some early P250s that didn't "shoot where they looked" because the sights were wrong, but SIG seems to have this squared away, if the test 2-SUM is any indication. The long one grouped a tad right and the short one, a bit left with some loads, but either gun would have shot a perfect police qualification score at 25 yards, out of the box with a center hold.

The 2-SUM in full size format, with 4.7-inch barrel and light rail.

The 2-SUM is attractively and conveniently packaged.

RELIABILITY

The P250 recently passed a torture test by a large West Coast agency with flying colors, and insiders there tell me it will soon be approved for their personnel; they're just waiting to test a striker fired version of the P250 now in development. I've tested several P250s in three of the four calibers; haven't shot the .357 SIG yet, but Federal Air Marshals have adopted that .357 version of the P250, and FAM has very high reliability testing standards. The several P250s I've seen in the hands of my students in classes and fellow shooters at matches have all worked fine.

Imagine my surprise, then, when one of my staff testers had the 2-SUM break while he was shooting it in full-size mode. He called to tell me the trigger was no longer raising the hammer. A phone call to Bud Fini at SIG got fast delivery of a replacement. Dissecting the failed "receiver" module, our resident SIG armorer found that the trigger draw bar had become rounded at a critical point and was slipping, causing the problem. I emailed close-up pix to the production manager Eric von Bosse at SIG, who confirmed our diagnosis. He determined a small number of trigger bars had come in out-of-spec from the vendor. Problem caught and solved.

That said, I consider it an anomaly. The failure occurred at around the 180th shot. The part was replaced, and both long and short configurations ran fine, as they had before the failure: no misfires, no failures to feed or extract or eject.

VALUE

MSRP on the 2-SUM set is $945. Buying each individual P250, the compact and the full-size each with their own firing mechanism, would cost you $640 per gun. Buying the 2-SUM gives you a $335 savings. This includes the $100 per gun price cut that SIG gave the P250 pistols in late 2009. A $335 saving when you buy one good small gun and one good larger one is a nice taste of savings: it makes the 2-SUM a toothsome twosome. Just bear in mind that you won't have both formats working together at any one time.

The choice is yours. SIG has given you that choice. And choice is good.

Chapter 12

The SIG P290

SIG P290RS

A *year after its introduction, SIG's smallest 9mm gets some meaningful design changes.*

The guns I call "slim-nines," 9mm carry pistols made thin and ultra-compact, are a hot item today. SIG's entry is the P290. I first saw it in the fall of 2010 at the IACP (International Association of Chiefs of Police) conference. It was introduced in January 2011 at the SHOT Show.

Some concerns showed up in its first year in the field. There were reports of occasional misfires. Because a lot of buyers were fans of traditional double action SIG-Sauer pistols, they didn't appreciate the fact that, like so many striker-fired autos,

these new guns wouldn't let you just pull the trigger again if you got a misfire, one SIG exec later informed me. The folks at SIG-Sauer in Exeter, NH, came up with a few other tweaks that could be wrought on the P290, too.

As a result, the redesigned P290RS was introduced right at a year after the original P290, at the 2012 SHOT Show. It's not another option, it's a total replacement of the older gun.

KEY FEATURES

The trigger mechanism is the defining new feature – but not the only one – on the P290 RS. The suffix in its designation stands for **R**e-**S**trike. SIG-Sauer's Product Manager at the Exeter plant, Tim Butler, tells me that the change involved a redesign of trigger bar, sear, and hammer. The result is a long, conventional double action only trigger stroke. The trigger goes much farther back before sear release than on the first iteration, but has proportionally less backlash.

The obvious advantage is that it gives an immediate second "shot" at a recalcitrant primer in the event of a misfire. Some don't see this as a big deal, because they follow the doctrine that a bad round that's failed them once doesn't get a second chance, and their preferred response to a "click" instead of a "bang" is a fast "tap-rack-assess the situation in front of you."

An absolutely undeniable advantage of the P290RS over its predecessor, however, is

Accuracy testing was done at 25 yards with these three loads.

that it's much more friendly for dry fire. Instead of having to interrupt your trigger pulling practice by breaking your hold and retracting the slide between dry "shots," the P290RS owner can roll the trigger continuously.

Spent case is visible above and behind hammer area, with P290RS at peak of recoil in Mas' hands. Recoil wasn't bad at all.

There have been four other changes. Apparently some folks had hands beefy enough that the web of their palm could ride up and get pinched by the bottom of the external hammer during the slide cycle. (That never happened to this writer with the P290, but this writer doesn't have the world's biggest hands, either.) In any case a subtle, rounded beavertail has been added at the rear of the grip tang. For smaller-handed shooters, it won't hurt anything; for those with meatier paws, it could be a deal-sealer for this little 9mm.

The lower rear edge on slide lock lever of the earlier P290 had a rather sharp corner, and I can see where that would have been a problem for those who shoot with straight thumbs. That corner has been very nicely rounded. Good for you, SIG! There's another manufacturer of powerful subcompact pistols which has long ignored a similar well-founded criticism.

On the first variation, the magazine release button stood up "loud and proud." The good news was, when you were doing a speed reload, that big button was easy to hit. The bad news was, when you *weren't* trying to dump the mag, it was still easy to hit. There were reports of some buyers carrying it inside their waistband, along with a personal "spare tire," whose excess flesh accidentally popped the

Size comparison: above, SIG's previous smallest 9mm, the aluminum-framed "personal size" nine-shot P239. Below, the seven-shot P290RS with polymer frame.

Top, original P290; below, the P290RS which replaces it. Differences are visible at grip tang, mag release, slide lock lever, and magazine floorplate.

magazines. For the P290RS, the mag release button was trimmed down some in hopes of curing that problem.

Finally, for some users, the super-small profile that was the P290's *raison d'etre* proved to be *too* small. Those consumers felt they couldn't get enough hand on the gun when shooting. A lengthened lip on the P290RS magazine created enough additional frontal length for both middle finger and ring finger to gain a secure purchase. (For those who *want* minimum butt size in every dimension, the P290RS comes with a flush-bottom floorplate that can be installed on the new magazine which, like the old, holds six rounds. Older mags will work in the new version of the P290, and vice versa.)

Moreover, the P290RS comes with an additional eight-round magazine featuring grip extension. The thing was a test of strength insofar as getting the eighth round in, but it worked fine, and didn't bind upon insertion even with the slide closed.

The slide stop on the first P290 had a sharp edge at the lower rear. It is rounded on the P290RS. Test sample SN 20C008078.

TRIGGER PULL

P290s in their first generation had a trigger pull somewhere between nine pounds and off-the-chart, the latter referring to the fact that the most popular pull gauge hits its limit at about 12 pounds. The test

Seven fast head shots at seven yards. The P290RS is a controllable little 9mm.

P290RS with five-shot group from 25 yard bench. Ammo is Hornady 124 grain XTP 9mm.

Best P290RS group at 25 yards, by small margin, was with Federal 115 grain JHP. Note the tight "best three" cluster.

P290RS when tested on a Lyman digital trigger pull gauge from Brownell's averaged 9.23 pounds of pull weight, when leaving the slide forward throughout and just pulling the gauge on the trigger. However, when cocking the slide to duplicate live fire cycling between each test trigger pull, the average weight went up to 9.60 pounds of average pull.

ACCURACY

Strangely enough, over the years it has become common to test short-barrel handguns at short ranges – five, seven, ten, or fifteen yards – instead of at the 25-yard line, which is where fighting handgun accuracy has been judged ever since this old man

Economy-priced Remington UMC 147 grain FMJ delivered this group at 25 yards from P290RS.

Below: P290RS comes with extra, extended magazine: two more shots, and a much better "hold."

came on the scene. Not yet having "gotten the memo" that people with short-barrel hand guns will be "given a handicap" in a gunfight across a parking lot, this writer continues to test short barrel and longer-barrel defensive handguns alike at the traditional distance of 25 yards.

Working hand-held off a Matrix rest on a concrete bench at a measured 75 feet, I tried out the P290RS with the three most popular bullet weights in 9mm Luger/9mmParabellum/9X19. (You know the cartridge has been around for a while when there are at least three different designations for the same darn thing.) I used my standard protocol: measuring each five-shot group center to center between the farthest hits, and then taking a second measurement of the best three hits. A test done for *American Handgunner* a decade ago, with me and Charles Petty, confirmed that the "best three" measurement under these circumstances would come remarkably close to what the same gun and cartridge would do from a properly adjusted Ransom machine rest. It's a useful tool, because most folks don't have access to a machine rest, but most of

them *can* test their hardware from a solid bench rest, to compare their results with what the gun writer might be getting.

147 grain subsonic 9mm rounds became trendy in the late 1980s. Winchester developed the concept with their original

OSM (Olin Super Match), created at the behest of Special Forces personnel who wanted super-accurate 9mm rounds that could center an enemy sentry's head from a suppressed MP5 submachine gun. The exemplar of the concept for this test was the inexpensive Remington-UMC 147 grain full metal jacket round, which this writer has seen win many a pistol match. From the SIG-Sauer P290RS, it put five shots into 4.25 inches from 25 yards. It must be noted that four of those five shots were in 2.45 inches, and the significant "best three" shots created a tight group of 1.10 inches. (Measurements were to the nearest 0.05 inch.)

For most of the epoch of the 9mm Luger cartridge, the 124 grain bullet was

P290TT with Laser Attachment

the heaviest load available. For this test, our 124 grain exemplar was the Hornady XTP load, using a deep-penetrating jacketed hollow point projectile. The five shots went into 4.35 inches, and the best three of those formed a 2.80-inch group.

When this writer was a young puppy cop, if you wanted a hollow point 9mm round, it was going to weigh 115 grains. Our test load in that bullet weight was the Federal Classic, coded by its manufacturer as "9BP," which over the decades proved itself to be one of the most accurate loads ever produced in its caliber. It re-proved that in this test, with a five-shot group measuring 4.05 inches. Four of those shots were a mere two and a quarter inches apart, and the "best three hits" measurement was "the best of the test," 65/100ths of one inch center to center. That is simply amazing performance from a short barrel pocket pistol with a heavy trigger pull at, remember, 25 *yards*, not 25 *feet*.

P290TT Black Diamond Plate

P290TT Grip Inserts

*P290 Extended
Magazine*

*P290TT Black
Diamond Plate*

P290 Nitron

290RS-9-RB

For a very long time now, "conventional gun wisdom" has held that a 4-inch group at 25 yards was "acceptable combat accuracy" from a full-size 9mm service pistol. The P290RS, an itty bitty *pocket* pistol, came achingly close to that: 4.15 inches with 147 grain, 4.35 inches with 124 grain, and 4.05 inches with 115 grain averages under four and a quarter inches. By that standard, we have in the SIG P290RS a pocket-size 9mm that needs to make no apologies at all in terms of accuracy. This was, after all, a small, light gun with a long trigger pull much heavier than the gun's own weight. I have no doubt that its intrinsic accuracy is much greater than what I was able to wring out of it in five-shot groups.

SHOOTING AND CARRYING THE P290RS

I wore the little SIG 9mm for a while on my non-dominant-side hip as a backup, in the useful new Remora holster. Comfort was exquisite: no sharp edges anywhere.

Because of the long trigger pull and concomitantly long trigger return, I wasn't able to get the speed in rapid fire that I'd expect from some other fire control mechanisms. Recoil had a bit of a snap for 9mm Parabellum, but nothing I could call uncomfortable. The shape of the P290RS causes it to point low for me, but that's subjective: dry handling in the gun shop will quickly show whether it'll be a problem for *you*, before you put your money on the counter.

This little pistol passed through a lot of hands among my test group. Only one shooter had a problem: a man with very long fingers found his middle finger (and particularly his thumb, in the thumb-down grasp he prefers) rode the magazine release and three times caused the mag to drop when he didn't want it to. The long, heavy trigger pull didn't make a lot of friends, but the little SIG's comfortable size and rounded edges were both unanimously appreciated. Several also liked the fact that by putting their thumb on its flat hammer, they could holster the P290RS without fear of an unintended discharge if a drawstring from a warm-up jacket or something like that got fouled in the trigger area.

Throughout the whole test, there were only two malfunctions. One was a 12 o'clock misfeed with a 147 grain load, quickly rectified with a tug on the slide. The other was a misfire (on a Federal round, of all things, famous for sensitive primers). As per the "RS" design, I just pulled the trigger again, and the shot went downrange. Both malfs occurred early in the first 50 shots during "break-in." There were no further mechanical malfunctions.

All in all, despite a manufacturer's suggested retail price of $758, this handy little 20.5-ounce 7-shooter is a definite contender in the currently hot niche of subcompact 9mm carry pistols.

Chapter 13
The SIG P320

THE SIG P320

For several years now, traditional double action police service pistols such as the SIG P-series have been pushed out of the spotlight by polymer-frame, striker fired pistols, a revolution begun by Glock in the 1980s. SIG had entered the polymer pistol market twice, both times with polymer frame guns that were hammer-fired with double action triggers.

The SIG Pro, introduced some twenty years ago, is still in the line as the Model 2022, currently produced in 9mm Luger, .40 S&W, and .357 SIG. A perfectly good pistol, it is seen largely as a budget-priced version of the P-series guns, and is not on the radar screen of buyers – individual *or* institutional – who are locked into Glock or Glock's arch competitor in that market, the Smith & Wesson Military & Police pistol.

SIG's next foray into the polymer pistol market was the P250. Its selling point of interchangeable frame sizes, calibers, etc. was not what the law enforcement market was looking for. While it had an excellent double action only trigger, it was markedly different from the short-throw triggers cops were being trained on with Glocks and M&Ps at their departments, and police interest was scant.

SIG finally decided to meet the striker-fired polymer pistols on their own ground.

P320 DEVELOPMENT

Superstar engineer Ethan Lessard led the project of what would become the P320 pistol. The early versions were done on the P250 format, with the first two prototypes being a "straight drop in" for the P250 production line. A button takedown was designed: Lessard told me, "SIG protocol is for the user to HAVE to remove the magazine and HAVE to lock the slide to the rear to begin disassembly."

Prototype of P320 photographed during author's visit to SIG in summer 2013.

Prototype P320 seen from the rear.

GAIL PEPIN.

GAIL PEPIN.

GAIL PEPIN.

Stagnant for a time, the striker-fired pistol project resumed in 2011. One prototype was, said Lessard, "Way, *way* outside the norm for striker-fired guns because it cocked on opening like a hammer-fired pistol. Most striker-fired pistols cock on closing." Eventually, Lessard and SIG chose to make their new pistol cock on closing, too.

The result is a good-feeling pistol with its own distinctive look, lively in the hand, with the relatively low bore axis which the striker-fired concept promotes. This results in less muzzle rise and therefore less time between accurate shots.

Prototype 320's derivation is obvious: note "P250" on dust cover of polymer frame.

GAIL PEPIN.

As was necessary for the market SIG wants to penetrate with it, the P320 has a consistent trigger pull for every shot. Lessard tells me that trigger pulls will be able to be adjusted for weight by replacing parts, giving end-users and departments the option of trigger pulls in the 5.5-pound to 7.5 pound range. Price should be competitive with the Glock and the M&P.

I handled the early model in June of 2013, but did not have the opportunity to test-fire it. Introduction of the P320 took place at the SHOT Show in January of 2014. This pistol will definitely be an important chapter in the history of SIG-Sauer.

The P320 is a modular pistol. It has a serialized sub-frame — what SIG calls the Fire Control Unit, or FCU — that for legal purposes is the firearm.

Chapter 14
The SIG X-Six

SIG-SAUER MASTERSHOP SERIES: THE X-SIX

In-house factory custom centers have a long tradition in the firearms industry. Here, enhanced high-performance versions of standard line products are crafted, usually by the hands of the company's most skilled and experienced smiths and artisans. SIG is on board with this concept, too.

They call it the Mastershop series of pistols. The one selected to represent the program for this book was the new X-Six SIG in 9mm. I was so impressed with it that I wrote it up for the 2014 edition of my annual *Complete Book of Handguns* for Harris Publications. Here's what I had to say about it there.

PRESTIGE PRECISION PISTOL: SIG'S NEW X-SIX 9MM

If great workmanship and simply awesome "shootability" pulls your trigger, you'll want to take a deep breath, reach for your credit card, and become the proud owner of a SIG X-Six.

The front sight of the heavy stainless pistol in your hand settles on the tiny spot about a hundred yards downrange. It's a Styrofoam drink cup, drained of every purpose but to be a target. You apply a gentle touch to the light trigger, and you see the sights move back and forth on the slide, though the pistol itself barely elevates at the shot. The cup jumps, surrounded by a nimbus of sand from the backstop. Well, that went well. You try it again. Another hit. And another.

You on-safe the pistol, your trigger finger in register on the frame. You are *liking* this pistol.

For almost three thousand dollars retail, you bloody well should be.

BACKGROUND

So, there we were at a shooting session at the fabulous SIG Academy range in New Hampshire. I was there to do an update on the company for the second edition of the *Gun Digest Book of SIG-Sauer*. We had shot a variety of new SIGs: the suppressed models with silencers produced in-house, demanded for some government contracts. The P227, a very sweet higher-capacity version of their great old P220 .45. The single action only version of their classic P226 9mm, and more.

If you were touring Ford, do you think your hosts might give you a ride in their highest performance offering, the Mustang Boss? SIG did something similar (though they're generally more often compared to Mercedes than to Ford), and trotted out their new X-Six 9mm target pistol.

I understand why they did. SIG-Sauer is a company proud of both their design and their workmanship...and the X-Six pistol is a veritable showpiece of both. It was a fitting *piece de resistance.*

Left: The SIG X-Six (right side).

Below: Fittingly, the X-Six is displayed along with the revered old P210 at the SIG Academy.

THE X-SERIES

For a while now, SIG-Sauer's answer to Smith & Wesson's Performance Center and Springfield Armory's Custom Shop has been the Mastershop series. Here's how SIG explains the concept:

"Be unique. Take advantage of SIG-Sauer's experience in top-class shooting sports and passion for technology. Let our experts create a masterpiece just for you. Individual creation is our most valuable skill. Our dedication to perfection is legendary, and our Mastershop takes it one step further. The pistols created here are fully customized to suit the needs and personality of their owner in terms of quality, precision and performance. Thanks to the most elaborate craftsmanship, a one-of-a-kind pistol is born. Distinctive and extraordinary modifications

226 X5 SCANDIC
9MM
226X5-9-SCANDICGD
GOLDEN DRAGON

MSRP: $3,199.00
Academy Price: $2,879.10
Student Price: $2,559.20

X-5 and X-Six pistols are available in a wide variety of finishes and configurations.

P210 SUPER TARGET
9 MM
210-9-LEGEND-STGT
6" BARREL

MSRP: $3,626.00
Academy Price: $3,263.40
Student Price: $2,900.80

Here's a recent variation of the P210, SIG's earlier and classic target grade 9mm.

are made to the trigger, sights, barrel weights, grip plates, compensators and finish to create a top class, state-of-the-art, eye-catching firearm. One that is in a league of its own.

"Each Mastershop pistol is hand-built to order by the highly skilled Master Gunsmiths at SIG-Sauer in Eckernforde, Germany. Each is a unique example of the gun-makers art. Once available only in Europe, the Mastershop Series are available as a special order through your local SIG-Sauer dealer.

"Lead times vary depending on model and work load but average 12 – 16 weeks."

The X-Six follows the celebrated X-5. No one had an explanation for why they went from the numeric X-5 to the spelled-out X-Six, but its primary distinction from the X-5 is its six-inch barrel with proportional-length slide. This gives a human error-reducing sight radius of 8.1 inches. Caliber is 9mm Luger, and it comes with nineteen-round magazines

and a long "handle" to accommodate same. Other specs for the X-Six, known as "Item Number 226X6-9-L1" on SIG's inventory sheets: overall height of 5.9 inches and overall length of 9.8 inches. As might be expected from its P226 derivation, it is not SIG's slimmest pistol, and is 1.7 inches wide. Weight is a bit over 43 ounces.

TRIGGER

The heart of the beast is a simply wonderful target trigger. Though the frame tracks back to the double action P226, the X-Six is a single action pistol. Naturally, there is an ambidextrous thumb safety, and if you're comfortable with a 1911, Browning High Power, or CZ75 type pistol, you'll be comfortable with this one.

Factory spec for trigger pull weight on the X-Six is 2.2 to 3.5 pounds. That pull range doesn't mean

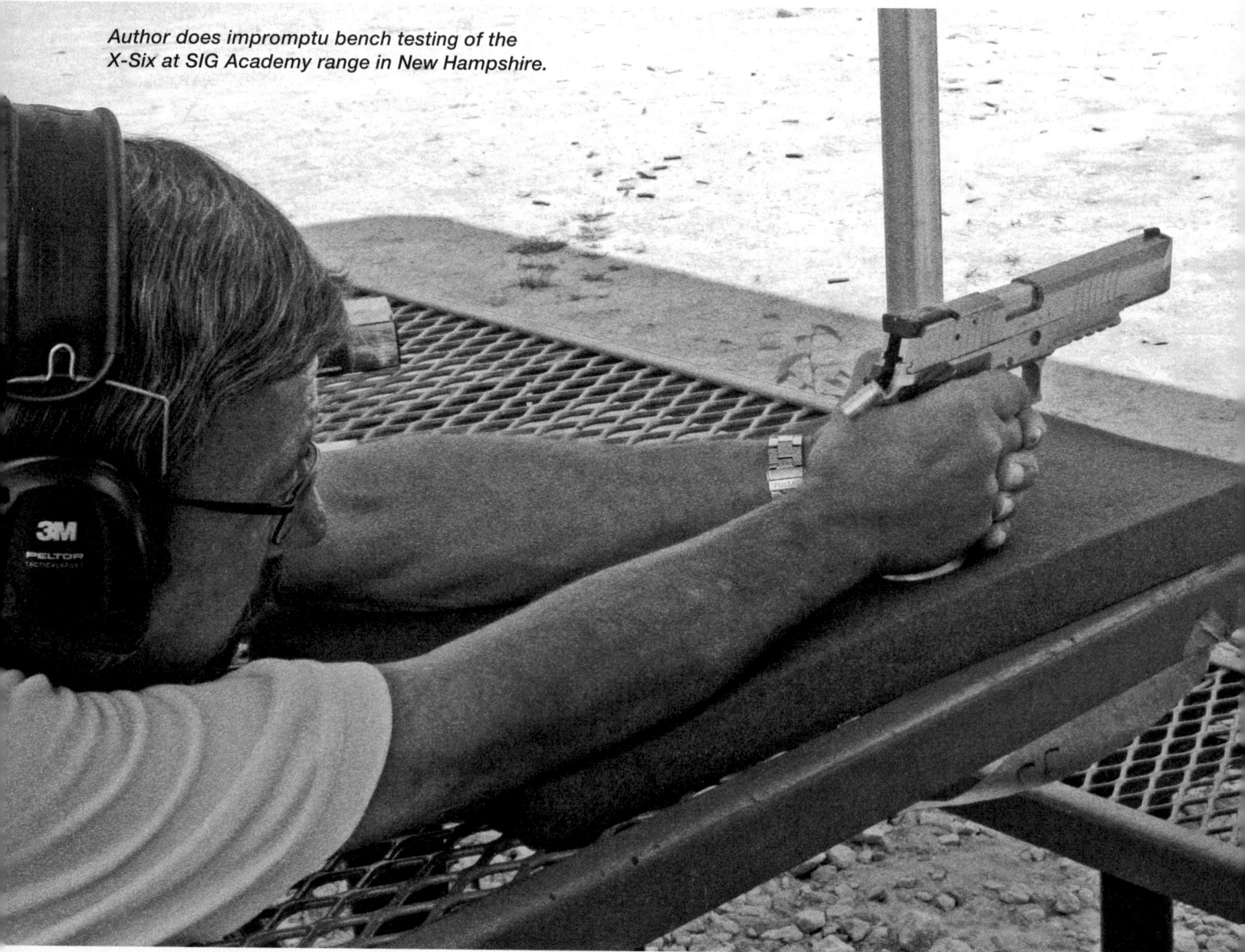

Author does impromptu bench testing of the X-Six at SIG Academy range in New Hampshire.

This heavy 9mm target pistol is easy to control in rapid fire, as author demonstrates on the SIG Academy range.

Arrow shows brass, but petite Gail Pepin is still on target with the easy shooting X-Six.

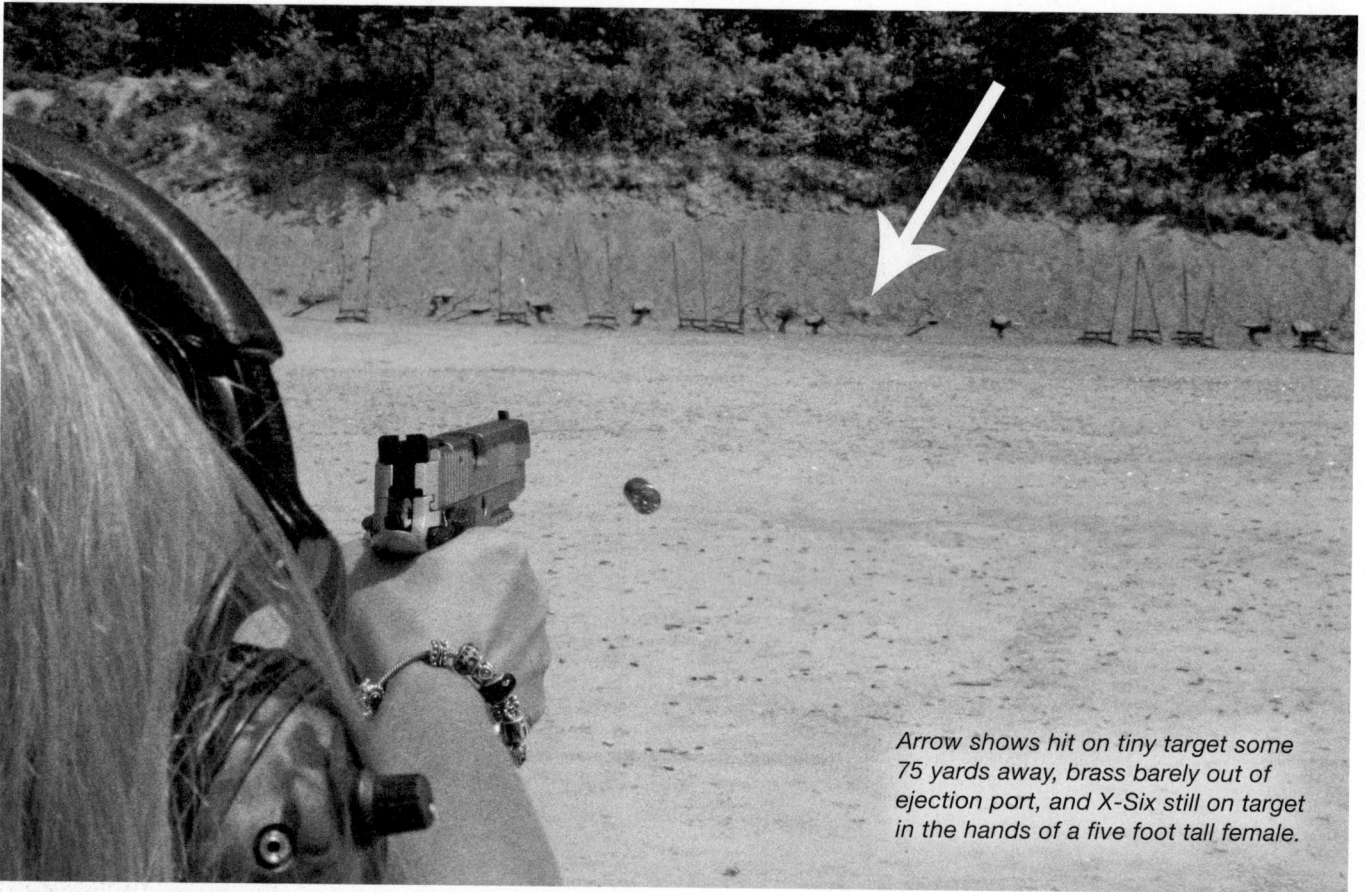

Arrow shows hit on tiny target some 75 yards away, brass barely out of ejection port, and X-Six still on target in the hands of a five foot tall female.

Brass bubbles out of the ejection port as author "races" X-Six.

Tapered magazine plus generous magazine chute equaled very fast reloads with the SIG X-Six.

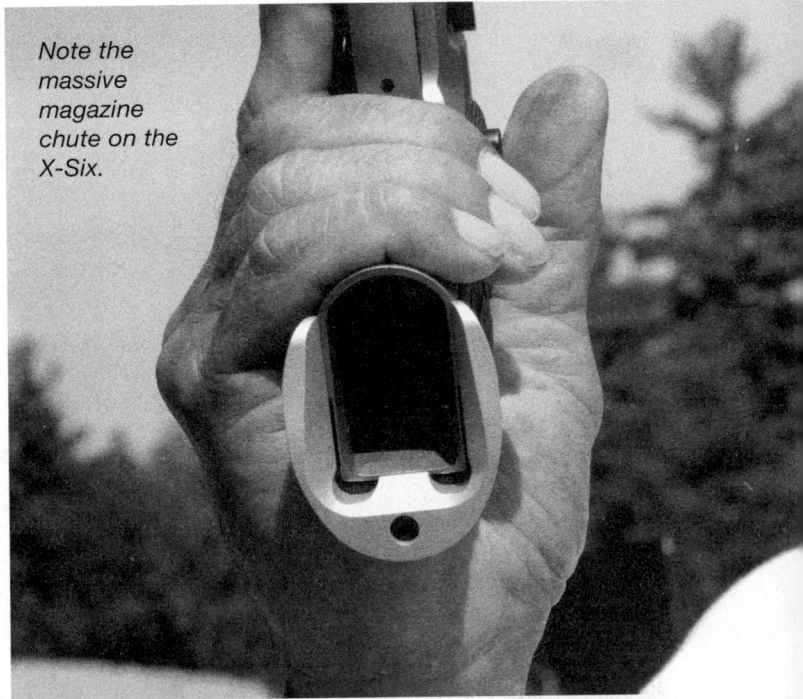

Note the massive magazine chute on the X-Six.

all five shots out of a machine rest. With a group that measured four-fifths of one inch, the X-Six was obviously living up to its advertising.

Federal 9BP, in my opinion the most dynamic of the old-school 115 grain "cup and core" 9mm police hollow points, has always been a remarkably accurate round. It proved so once again this nice summer day in 2013, drilling five holes a measured 1.45 inches apart at the same 25 yards where we did all the accuracy testing. Not only did the X-Six put every shot into less than an inch and a half – the best five-shot group of the day, under less than optimum circumstances – but it put the best three in under an inch. That measurement went 0.90 inch.

Finally, the Remington-UMC – that maker's economy ammo line – gave a group of 2.5 inches on the nose. However, the best three of those were nested in barely more than half of that, 1.30 inches.

As noted, we didn't have a solid enough bench rest to fairly test for accuracy. However, given the groups we got from what we did hastily rig up, I was left with the impression that this pistol is every bit as precisely accurate as its manufacturer claims it to be.

To eke out the most of that accuracy, the X-Six buyer has a list of sight options from which to choose. Adjustable, of course. Fiber optic front if you want speed. Patridge-style if you want bulls-eye accuracy. Night sights are on the option list, too.

HANDLING

The long, distinctively sculptured grip of the X-Six sat well in my hand, and did not present any

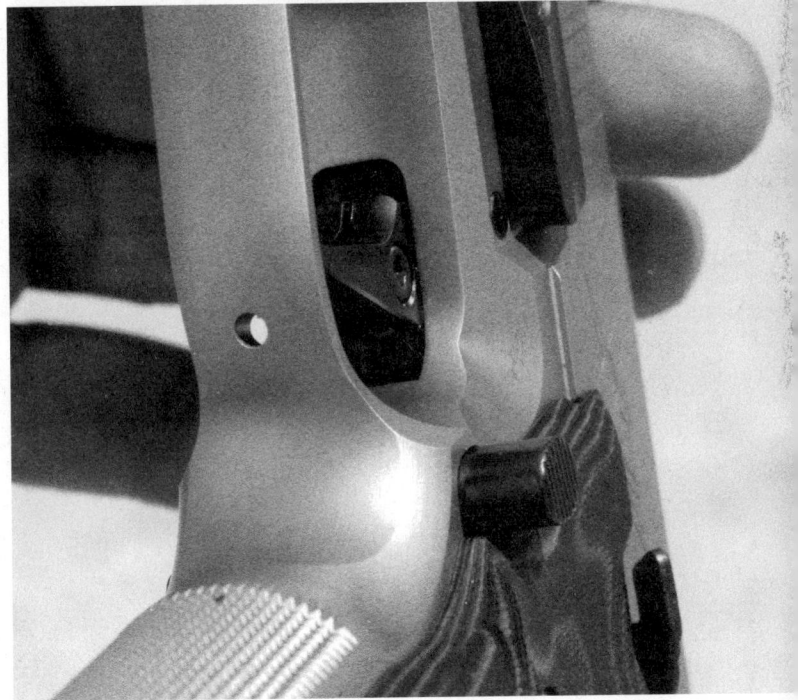

With a wide range of adjustment, the X-Six trigger was designed to please the most demanding precision pistol shooter.

problem to the one petite female who shot it on the range that day. The large magazine release button was easy to reach with the thumb. The generously-proportioned shelf of the manual safety invited the shooter's thumb to rest upon it. The left-side lever for right-handed operation was perfectly adjusted: it went on and off easily but positively. It was a

Inexpensive Rem-UMC ammo gave this 25 yard group from imperfect bench rest.

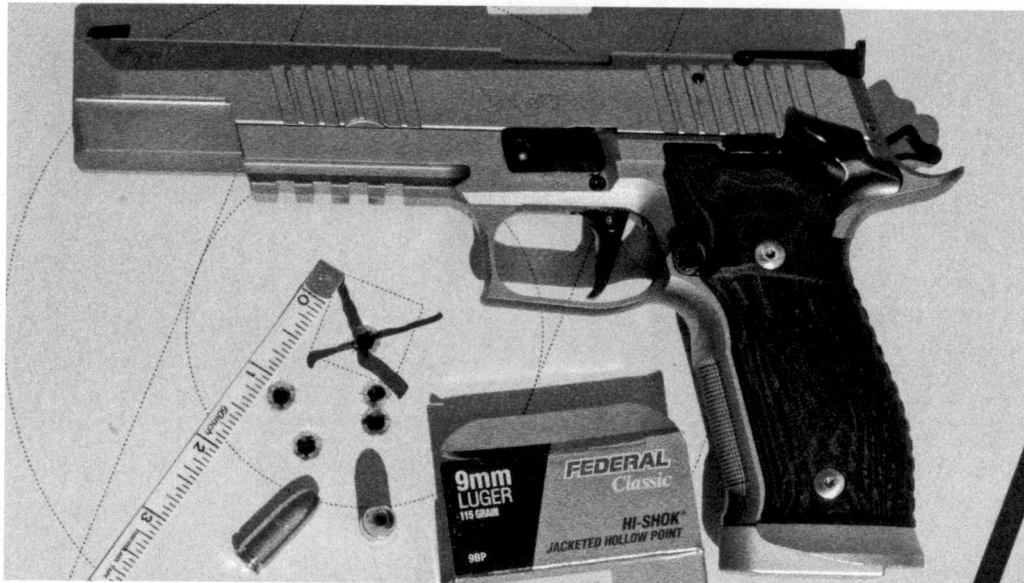

X-Six proves southpaw-friendly as SIG's Tim Butler runs a fast, well-controlled double tap.

Federal American Eagle 124 grain FMJ, SIG X-Six, 25 yards.

X-Six proves southpaw-friendly as SIG's Tim Butler runs a fast, well-controlled double tap.

Note proximity of thumb safety to slide stop/ slide release lever on X-Six frame.

tiny bit stiff on the opposite side of the ambi safety, however. I've found this to be true of most of the "double action frames built as single action" in the SIG-Sauer line.

At the butt is a flared magazine chute that could double as a vase for flowers if you set the pistol upside-down. This greatly speeds reloading in the competition environment. This requires extended base pads on the magazine, of course. SIG well knows this, and provides exactly such magazines with the pistol. As expected, reloads were fast and sure.

When SIG and Sauer designed the original P-series pistols, they were double action and no frame-mounted manual safety was contemplated, they put the slide stop/slide release lever well back on the left side of the frame. With that manual safety now present on single action variations

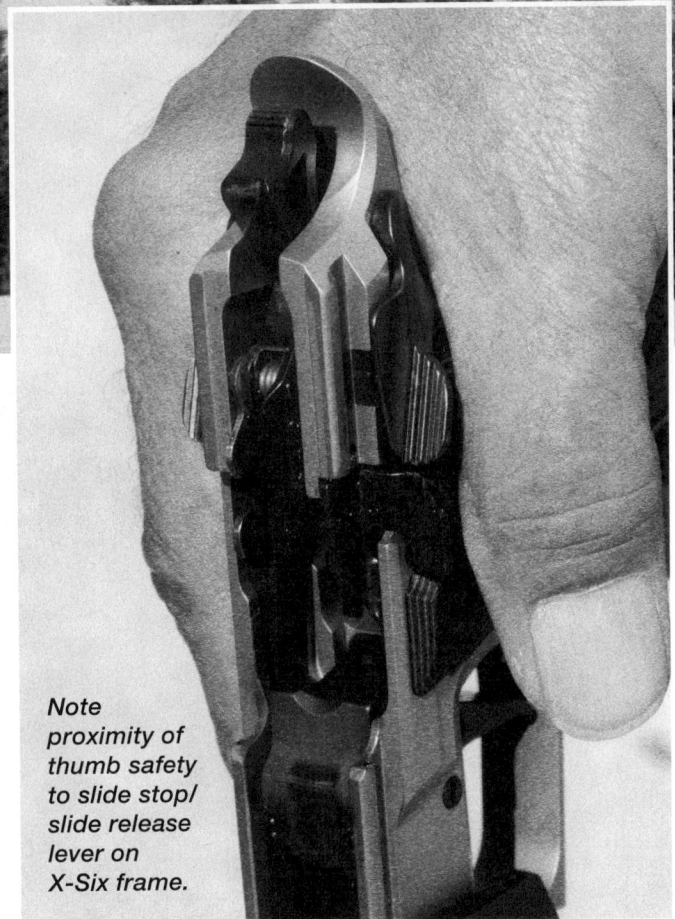

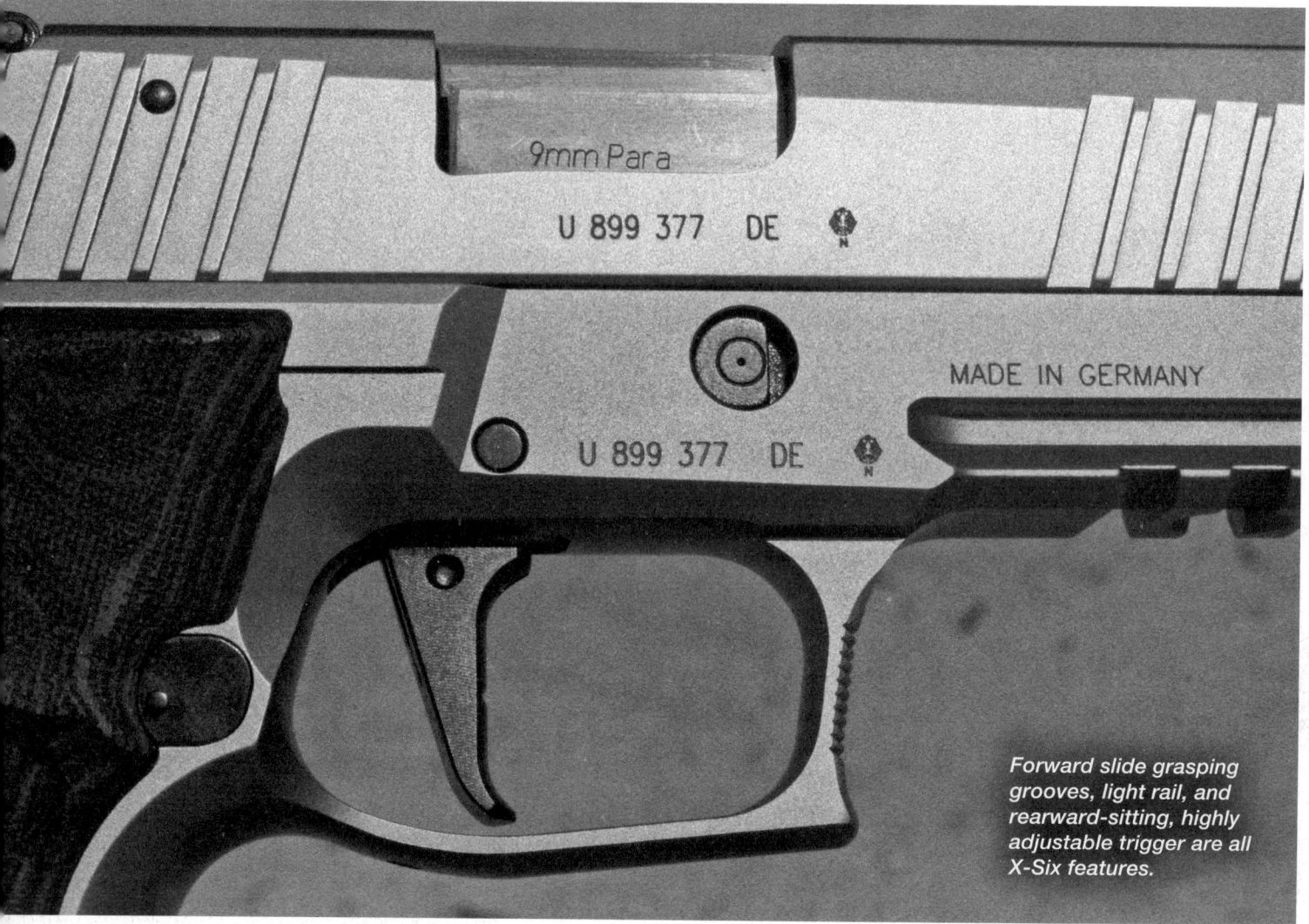

9mm Para

U 899 377   DE

U 899 377   DE

MADE IN GERMANY

Forward slide grasping grooves, light rail, and rearward-sitting, highly adjustable trigger are all X-Six features.

such as this one, the photos will show that those two levers are relatively close together. This may be problematic for some shooters. A couple of generations of handgunners have learned that the currently popular straight thumbs pistol grasp

will often cause the right-handed shooter's thumb to over-ride the slide stop, holding it down. This, of course, makes it incapable for that part to rise and lock the slide back after the last round is fired. Blame the shooter, not the gun.

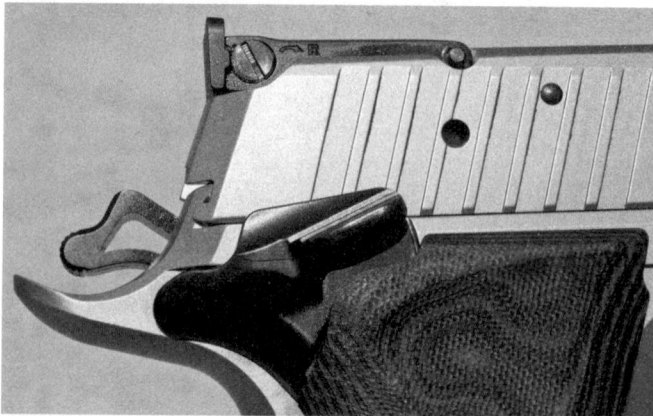

Here we see the low-mounted adjustable rear sight, ambidextrous safety lever, beavertail grip, and skeletonized hammer of X-Six.

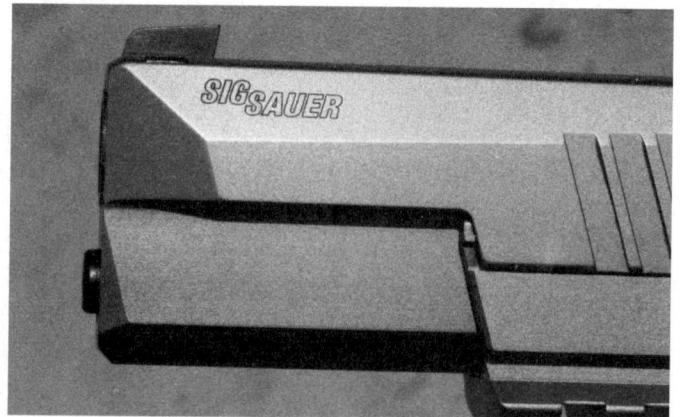

The long slide of the X-Six adds steadying weight and more sight radius.

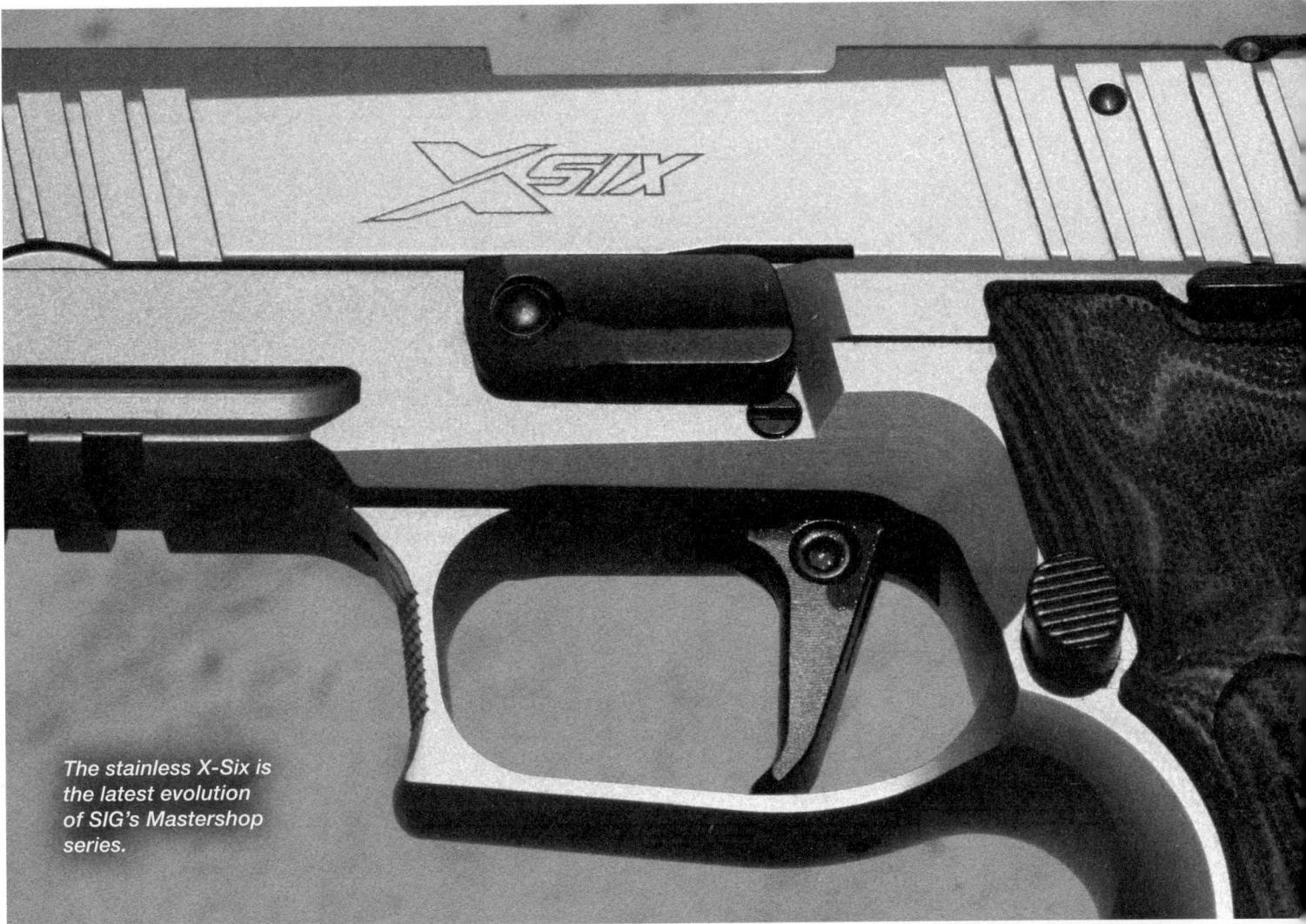

The stainless X-Six is the latest evolution of SIG's Mastershop series.

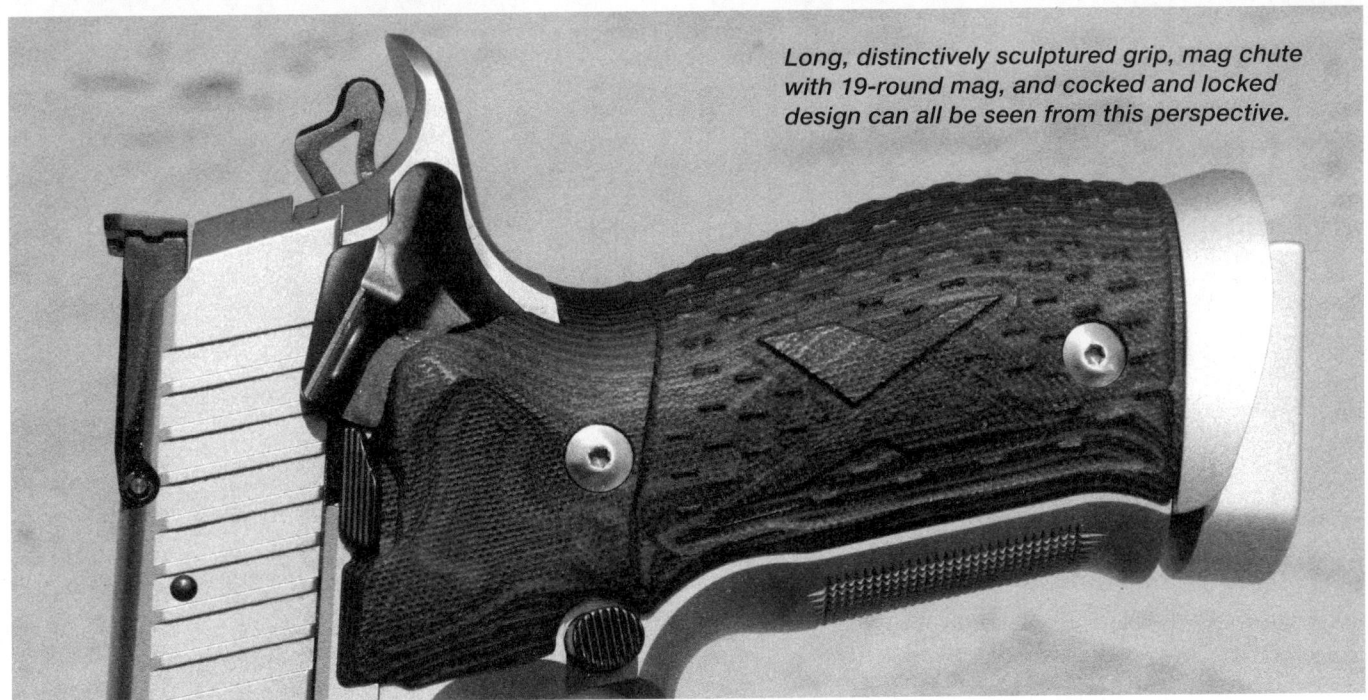

Long, distinctively sculptured grip, mag chute with 19-round mag, and cocked and locked design can all be seen from this perspective.

X-Six feels great in a wide variety of hands.

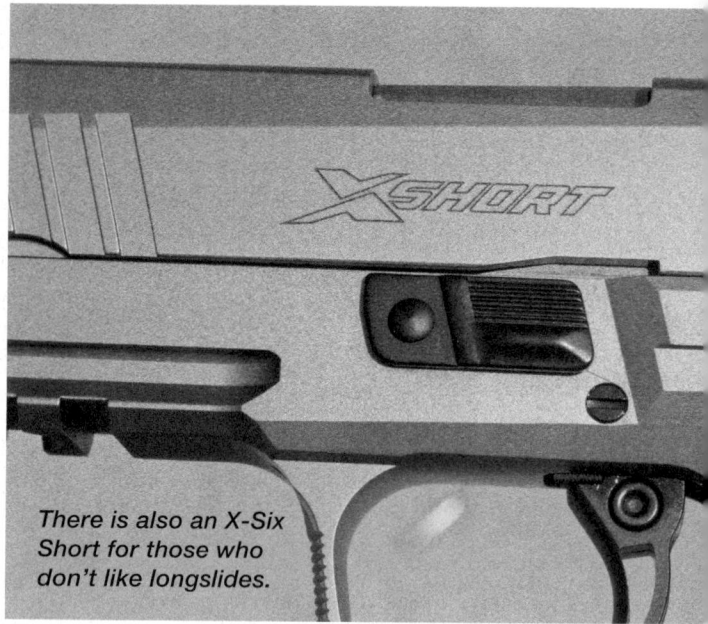

There is also an X-Six Short for those who don't like longslides.

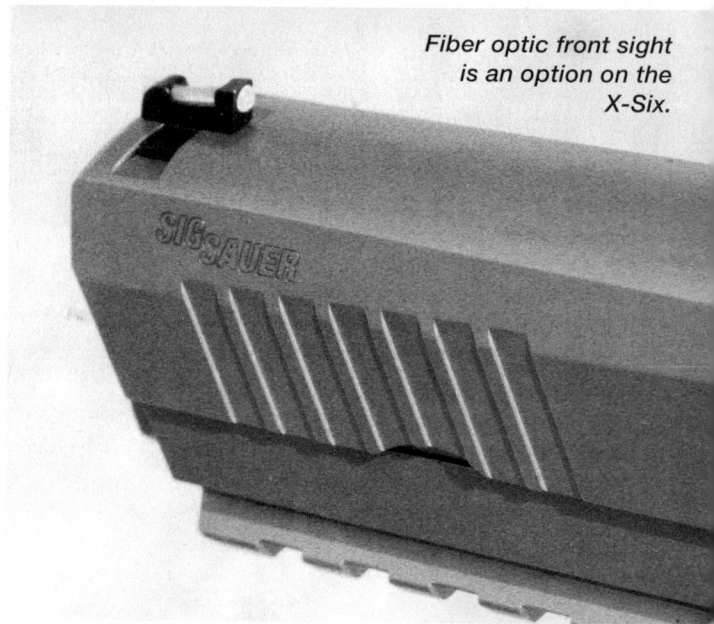

Fiber optic front sight is an option on the X-Six.

A muzzle-on view of the X-Six.

For those who find the longslide X-Six (top) too muzzle-heavy, there is the X-Six Short, below.

Some shooters may find that riding the X-Six's safety with the thumb exacerbates this. Those with shorter thumbs may find that riding the safety has the opposite effect and cures that problem. It's going to be up to the shooter, in my view. However, if you have a chance to handle the pistol in the gun shop before you lay your money down, you should be able to tell immediately whether it is going to be a problem or not.

VALUE

With MSRP of $2,950 at this writing, the X-Six certainly isn't cheap. However, perspective is necessary. We live in a world in which shooters are happy to pay $1800 to $3600 for a 1911 pistol that shoots as well as the X-Six. That level of accuracy, reliability, build quality and pride of ownership is absolutely present in the X-Six. It just doesn't *look* like a 1911. Of course, nowhere is it written that a fine pistol *needs* to look like a 1911, either.

Though its frame rail will take a white light or light-and-laser unit, and a low-recoil 20-shot "built to last forever" 9mm would be a good thing to have for home defense, the super-light trigger pull in my view disqualifies the X-Six from that mission. I see it as a fun gun, a top-grade competition quality target pistol, and simply a fine specimen of gunmaking for any firearms *aficionado* to own.

It is significant that in the museum-like display section at SIG Academy, the X-Six and its predecessor the X-5 are displayed with that great old classic, the still-manufactured P210. Both are made in Europe, even now at a time when most SIG-Sauers are produced at the New Hampshire facility. Both have always been high-priced luxury machines which also are purpose-built high performance devices. A SIG is rather like a Leica camera in that respect.

The X-Six fits squarely within that corporate tradition. Yes, it is more expensive.

But, to the demanding *connoisseur,* it's worth it.

Chapter 15
The SIG Pro

In June of 1998, I attended the conference at which SIGARMS' new *sig pro* pistol (a.k.a. SP2340) made its debut to the firearms press. As the speakers explained the gun, my forearm touched the SIG P226 under my coat, and I wondered what the cheaper-looking new pistol would do that my reliable "old" pistol would not. The answers were quick in coming. It had a frame rail for light attachment, first seen on the HK USP. It had a polymer frame for light weight, recoil-absorbing flexion, and reduced cost, a concept popularized by the Glock. It offered a changeable grip size, a feature pioneered by Walther on their high-tech new service pistol that barely preceded the *sig pro.* The flat-wire coiled springs were already proven by SIGARMS on the compact P239 they had introduced a couple of years earlier.

Our first test guns were in the most popular current police caliber, .40 S&W, with .357 SIG to follow and, possibly, a 9mm if demand warranted. Apparently it did. The *sig pro* in .357 SIG, also designated SP2340, was not long in coming, and thereafter SIG introduced the 9mm version, dubbed the SP2009. While a simple change of barrels would convert the SP2340 from .40 to .357 or from .357 to .40, the 9mm variation had no interchangeability potential due to the smaller case head of its cartridge. The .357 SIG and .40 S&W are identical in that respect.

These guns say "SIGARMS" on them, not SIG-Sauer. That said they have "SIG-Sauer" written all over them in other ways. The manual of arms is *exactly* the same as on the pistols SIGARMS began calling "the Classic line" upon the introduction of the *sig pro.*

From the first, the *sig pro* proved to be an accurate pistol, particularly in the two more powerful calibers. I recently benched one of each from the 25-yard line of the Manchester, New Hampshire Indoor Firing Line, with the following results:

A lot of cops have bought *sig pro* pistols. Those who have them seem very pleased with them. Where I live, the state law enforcement academy has bought DAO SP2340s in .40 S&W for their armed personnel, and one of the most gun-wise chiefs in the state has bought *sig pro* .357s for all his troops. I'm told the DEA has approved the *sig pro*. The Richmond, Virginia Police Department had these guns for many years in .357 SIG. They worked out very well. When they 'aged out,' the department found the money to upgrade to more expensive classic SIGs in the same caliber.

"Will it stand up?" "Will it shoot like the SIGs we know?" These were the questions that were asked when the gun came out. They have been answered by time and extensive field experience: "Yes" and "Yes."

Witness the fact that J. P. Sauer & Sohn GmbH was in 2003 awarded what may be the largest

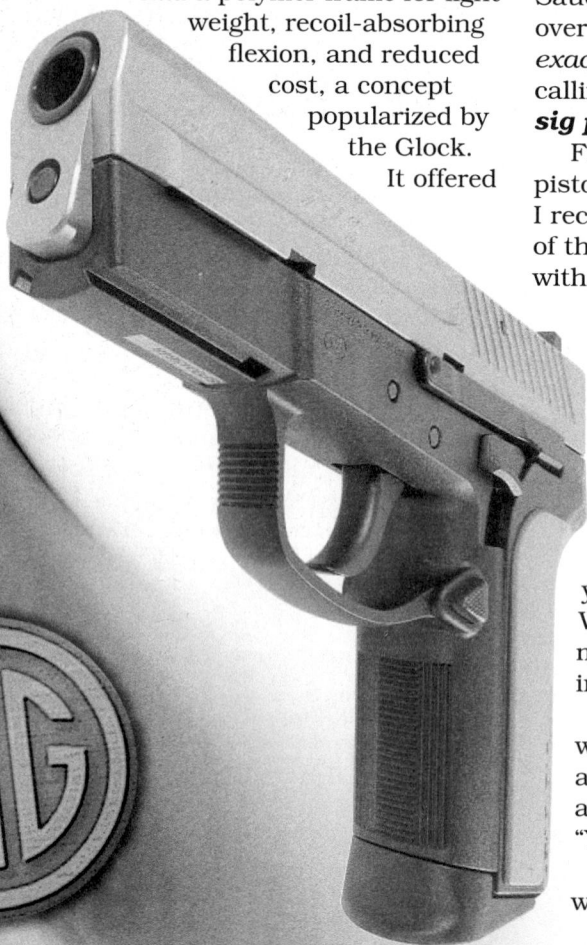

Pistol / Caliber	Manufacturer	Load	5-Shot Group	Best 3 Shots
Sig Pro SP2009, 9mm Parabellum	Federal Classic	9BP 115-grain JHP	2-5/8"	2-1/2"
	Remington +P	115-grain JHP	1-3/4"	1-3/16"
	Winchester Subsonic	147-grain JHP	2-7/8"	1-1/2"
Sig Pro SP2340, .40 Smith & Wesson	Black Hills	180-grain JHP	2-9/16"	1-3/8"
	Remmington	180-grain JHP	3-3/8"* (* 4 of 5 shots in 1-7/8")	1-5/8"
	Winchester Silvertip	155-grain JHP	4-1/16"** (** 4 of 5 shots in 1-3/4")	1-1/4"
Sig Pro SP2340, .357 SIG	CCI Speer Gold Dot	125-grain JHP	2-15/16"	1-3/16"
	Federal Classic	125-grain JHP	2-1/2"	1-3/8"
	Winchester Ranger	125-grain JHP	4-5/16"	2-7/16"

contract for new service handguns signed since World War II. It was for **sig pro** pistols. It was a joint purchase by French agencies including the Ministry of Defense (Gendarmerie Nationale, Ministry of Interior (Police Nationale), and Ministry of Finance (Customs). The order called for more than 200,000 **sig pro** pistols.

The background and rationale of the **sig pro** were fresher and closer to the source when, immediately after the 1998 introduction, I wrote an article on these guns that appeared in the 1999 "Complete Book of Handguns." It is reprinted immediately hereafter, with the original publisher's permission.

SIGARMS GOES POLYMER

This is not your father's SIGARMS pistol...

In June of 1998, I was among a handful of industry professionals invited by SIGARMS to the debut of their newest handgun, the **sig pro**. The event was concurrent with the National Rifle Association's annual meeting in Philadelphia. I think it's safe to say that all of us who enjoyed the hospitality of the hosting range were impressed.

First, some points on terminology. Why did a brand that went from "SIG-Sauer" to "SIGARMS" in all caps decide to use not only all lower case letters, but both *italicized* and **boldface** lower case letters for the name of their newest product? I'm not really the guy to ask. I figured at first it was just a Madison Avenue thing. No, we were told, it was simply an assurance that the market would see from the beginning that this was something really new from a company that hadn't offered this type of

A randomly selected .357 sig pro put five Federal JHPs into 2.5 inches, and five Gold Dots in under 3 inches at 25 yards.

pistol before. It was their way of saying, "this isn't your father's SIG-Sauer," nor is it your grandfather's SIG-Neuhausen.

OLD QUALITY, NEW TECHNOLOGY

Seen as the top-quality, top-price BMW of service handguns, the conventional SIG pistols (known as the Classic models since the coming of the **sig pro**) had priced themselves out of certain markets. This included many law enforcement agencies that bought on bid. It included the ordinary working stiff that Bill Clinton (but not, to their credit, SIGARMS) has been known to call "Joe Sixpack." Believing, unlike Clinton, that rank-and-file law-abiding citizens have a right to fine quality defensive handguns, the decision-makers at SIG wanted a pistol they could sell one at a time, as well as bid a department at a time, for less.

A polymer frame was chosen for light weight and reduced cost of manufacture. Working on a clean sheet of blueprint, SIG designers were able to design in the best features of some of their competitors, and try for the occasional "first."

HK had, with the USP, been the first to mold rails on the front of the frame for flashlights and other attachments. They were followed by Walther (P99), Glock and, of course, the **sig pro.** Wilcox Technologies were first out with the attachments, ranging from white light to laser to night vision-compatible infrared.

The above-mentioned Walther had interchangeable grips to allow for different hand sizes. So does the **sig pro.**

They may look different, but the sig pro slide stop and decocking lever are in the same places and operate the same way as on "classic" SIGs.

The Glock has quick-change trigger options that let an armorer bring the gun from heavy DAO to ultralight target configuration and many things in between. The HK USP can be altered between trigger system variants, though it's not something the manufacturer overtly encourages. The **sig pro** is the first pistol to my knowledge that allows an armorer to quickly switch from conventional DA first shot/SA followup/decocker design to double-action-only, simply by switching the ingenious "fire control units."

Finally, as one who likes to think of himself as a connoisseur of trigger pulls, my compliments to the chef. I have seen

Interchangeable "grip shells" allow fit adjustment to hands of different sizes.

the rare case of the same company's less expensive guns being slightly more accurate than their analogous full-price ones (i.e., the excellent S&W Value Series). However, not until this new pistol have I seen a case of the same company's cheap gun having a better trigger pull than its expensive one.

SHOOTING THE SP2340

On that day in June, only the .40 caliber specimens (SP2340) were in this country. We shot them in both DA/SA and DAO mode. Sights were fixed, in the Von Stavenhagen ("dot the i") pattern that has become a trademark of the SIG Classics. Three-dot night sights are available at extra cost. These are all fixed sights. Some were spot on, and some were a little off here and there, but all were close enough for Government work.

The only ammo provided was Federal's recently introduced Hydra-Shok 155-grain hollow-point. The caliber, of course, was .40 S&W. A compliment here to SIGARMS for sportsmanship. More than one rival manufacturer of pistols in the caliber Smith & Wesson and Winchester jointly created in 1990 simply mark their pistols

With Black Hills .40 ammo, SP2340 put five rounds in just over 2.5 inches at 25 yards.

".40." This one says boldly on the barrel, ".40 S&W." It is good to see professional courtesy.

The guns proved accurate. From impromptu bench rest positions at 25 yards, I tried five-shot groups with both a DA/SA and a DAO specimen. Having found over the years that what I shoot hand-held for five rounds with no called flyers will generally have in it a "best three" hits that roughly equal what all five would have done from a machine rest. As a result I make two measurements. "All five" shows me what I could have done firing over an auto hood in an emergency, and the "best three" gives a fairer prediction of the pistol's inherent mechanical accuracy.

Pistol	5 Shots	Best 3 Shots
SP2340 DA/SA module	1-31/32"	1-1/8"
SP2340 DAO module	2-3/4"	1-1/8"

By the fall of the year, SIGARMS was able to send me an SP2340 to test on my own. While I didn't have any of that fine 155-grain Hydra-Shok on hand, I tried several other brands in varying weights. None did as well, running 3- to 4-inch five-shot groups on the average. The most accurate in this test pistol (DA/SA module, serial #SP0002546) was the 180-grain Remington Golden Saber. Its overall group size was similar to the others, 3-7/8 inches, but the best three were just 1-5/8 inches

apart, center to center. I noticed throughout that the first, hand-chambered round tended to go a bit wide from the rest in SP0002546. It could be that the gun was new and needed breaking in. I suspect that the ones we shot in Philadelphia had been thoroughly "seasoned" in prior testing.

RELATIVE ACCURACY

I've owned my share of SIG-Sauer pistols in calibers .380, 9mm, .40 S&W, and .45 ACP. In all but the .40 S&W caliber, they have tied for top honors as the most accurate double-action defense pistols in their calibers. The P229 .40 simply does not shoot as well as the self-same P229 in either of its other calibers (9mm or .357 SIG) and that tells me it's the caliber, not the gun, that's causing the mediocre if still acceptable accuracy.

The *sig pro* is also produced in .357 SIG, though it wasn't available at the Philadelphia debut. I had my choice of chamberings when ordering my test gun, and the fault is mine in that I ordered the .40. I have seen enough case neck separations in multiple brands of .357 SIG ammunition to be leery of the caliber. The ammo makers assure me that this is all sorted out now. I suspect the .357 SIG would be exquisitely accurate in the *sig pro.* It has been so in every other .357 SIG pistol (P229, P239, P229 Sport, and P226) that I have tested thus far.

In any case, the accuracy of the SP2340, while not something you'd pick for the national championships at Camp Perry, fulfills the acceptable standard for a service pistol by virtually every such criterion.

If you want more accuracy, just switch to .357 SIG. It's easy enough. The *sig pro* requires only a simple user-accomplished barrel swap to change caliber. The same magazines, springs, and extractor will function with either round.

The latest test gun shot to the left with its fixed sights. I see more and more of this lately. It's an industry-wide trend that needs attention. Yes, the SIG sight-pushing tool can easily drift the rear sight back to true, but that should have been done at the factory.

ERGONONOMICS

George Harris, the knowledgeable instructor at SIGARMS Academy, told me the SP2340 was deliberately engineered to point naturally with a grip-to-barrel angle of approximately 16 degrees. We're all a little different, but I have no reason to doubt him. I close my eyes and bring my SP2340 up where I want it, and open my eyes to find the gun right on target.

Though I'm not personally a big fan of "point shooting," those who are desperately need a gun that will naturally follow the extension of their arm. For me, at least, this one does. As someone who wants at least a coarse visual index of the gun's orientation to the target before I press the trigger, I still appreciate the SP2340's "pointability." It gets me on target quicker and requires no physical adjustment after the eye has verified to the brain that the pistol is where it needs to be and "we have a green light."

I have a couple of those "average sized adult male hands" you read about. Mine fit the *sig pro* particularly well with the smaller of the two "grip shells" (for want of a better term) that it is provided with. Still, I can get by with either.

Trigger reach on the *sig pro* is right to give good control in both double-and single-action modes of fire. The surface of the trigger is smooth, as it should be.

The trigger stroke in double-action is *excellent.* Better than on any P229 I've shot save for the fancy Sport model. Resistance is smooth and absolutely even, from the beginning of the press to the breaking of the shot. On my specimen I'd estimate the pull weight at 10 to 11 pounds. The sights stay dead on target while the trigger comes back for that first, all-important shot.

In the double-action-only model I shot in Philadelphia, that same excellent pull was there for every shot. I found it no problem at all. The people who tell you that you can't shoot worth a damn with a DAO auto either haven't shot this one, or haven't mastered the double-action trigger stroke.

The SIG duty pistols tend to have a long reset after the previous shot, the better to prevent an unintentional second round being fired by a hand that is predictably nervous after a shot needed to be fired at all. Starting with the single-action trigger as far forward as it resets, there's about a quarter inch of movement before the shot. I found some "good creep" in the test sample.

Remington's 115-grain +P proved accurate in the 9mm sig pro, delivering five hits in 1-3/4 inches at 25 yards.

There is good and bad trigger creep in the same sense that there is "good and bad" cholesterol. Bad creep is friction drag so sharp that it can move the gun you are trying desperately to hold on target while trying to get off the shot. "Good creep" doesn't move the gun, it just gives you a felt awareness that the trigger is coming back. It's sort of saying, "Hey, brain, we're about to fire this pistol again. Has the decision to do so truly been made?" In a service as opposed to target gun, this isn't a bad thing.

I would estimate the single-action pull on my test SP2340 as about 6 pounds, which is pretty mainstream in a military/police/armed citizen gun these days.

The decock lever and the slide release are shaped differently than on the Classic SIGs, but they're in essentially the same place and work the same way. The decocking mechanism on the SP2340 is particularly crisp and clean in its function. If your hand is habituated to the standard SIG-Sauer type pistol, it will have no problem whatsoever adapting to the *sig pro.*

THE PRICE IS RIGHT

Designed to sell at a suggested retail of around $600, the SP2340 delivers the same performance as the P229 of the same caliber that sells for $800 or more in some gun shops. My specimen is about as accurate as any P229 .40 I've tried, and the well-broken in ones I shot in Philadelphia were more accurate. The *sig pro* is a fraction of an inch longer than the Classic gun and a couple of ounces lighter. I like its double-action better than that of the more expensive model.

CONTROLLABILITY

Recoil is no problem with the SP2340. Even with snappy Triton rounds, the front sight rebounds right back onto the target. In Philadelphia, I accepted Walt Rauch's challenge to shoot these guns standing on one leg. There wasn't enough recoil to interfere with balance.

In looking at the pictures from the test of the new sample, I noticed a two-shot sequence. In the first, I'm braced on the bench and asking the photographer if she's ready for me to shoot. In the second, the shot has been fired, the spent casing is spinning toward the camera – and the SP2340's muzzle is already back on target. Photographic proof: the pistol is controllable.

RELIABILITY

We shot a helluva lot of that Federal ammo at the Philadelphia intro — cases of it. Giving gunwriters access to free ammo is like giving Warren Beatty a trip to Mustang Ranch on your chargecard: it's gonna add up. I fired several hundred rounds at the intro. Later, after I got a test weapon, I fired a few hundred more: Black Hills in 180- and 155-grain hollow-point; CCI Blazer 180-grain FMJ; Winchester in Silvertip 155-grain and 180-grain Subsonic and Ranger Talon; Remington 155-grain JHP and Golden Saber 180-grain; and the hot Triton in both 135-grain and 165-grain hollow-points. I've probably got over 1,000 rounds through SP2340s myself, and have seen a whole lot more fired through them. One observation sticks out in my mind.

I have not yet seen an SP2340 malfunction.

Harris told us that multiple pistols had been fired for 20,000 rounds; being cleaned every 500, with zero malfunctions save for defective cartridges. I can believe it.

SUMMARY

In my "Self Defense and the Law" column in *Combat Handguns* magazine, I focused on the *sig pro* as an example of how modern designers of duty guns are engineering them to respond to civil liability attacks. The guns need to be able to deliver good hits in predictable circumstances. They need to be resistant to unintentional discharge. They need to be natural and ergonomic to deploy. They need to be utterly reliable.

One reader sent a letter noting his displeasure. The article had sounded to him like a thinly disguised ad for the *sig pro.*

Actually, that wasn't the case. I'll be sending my sample gun back to the factory. There's nothing wrong with it. It's just that a .40 S&W pistol with roughly a dozen rounds "in gun" (you're down to 10+1 if you're a citizen buying a new gun in a limited magazine capacity jurisdiction) always struck me as a compromise between the 16-shot P226 in 9mm Parabellum and the P220 in .45 ACP. I have a P226 with a sufficient number of standard full-capacity magazines for when I need lots of bullets, and I have my pet P220 for the rest of the time. I simply don't need the *sig pro.*

But that's not the point. The point is that a lot of people do need a gun like this. SIG engineered this new concept pistol for those people and for civil liability concerns *and* for surviving gunfights with criminals.

If making that point sounds like an ad for SIGARMS, all I can say is, it probably means SIGARMS got it right when they developed and produced the *sig pro.* The sig pro line is now sold by SIG under the model designation of 2022.

Chapter 16
SIG's That Are Sweet, Not Sauer

This book is about SIG-Sauer pistols; the double-action semiautomatics with no manual safeties. The SIG name has also appeared, but without any Sauer input, on three fine single-action semiautomatics which do have manual safeties. As such, we will treat them separately here.

My story on the "Americanized" SIG Neuhausen P210, the P210-8, appeared in the 2002 edition of *The Complete Book of Handguns*. A story on the neat little SIG/Hammerli Trailside .22 was published in the 2001 edition of the same title. Both are used here with the original publisher's permission.

SIG'S NEW P210-8

A famous 9mm pistol is back, with the touches American combat shooters favor. Will the makeover warrant its extremely high price?

The SIG P210, often called the SIG-Neuhausen after the city of its birth in Switzerland, is a shadowy mystery gun to many shooters. Often read about because of its almost legendary quality of manufacture, it is rarely seen on the shooting ranges because of its equally legendary high price. The service-grade 210-2 lists at $1,680, the fancier 210-5 and 6 at $2,325 and $2,089 respectively.

Licensing the Petter System, a modification of John Browning's 1911 concepts developed by Charles Gabriel Petter for the French Modele 1935 7.65mm service pistol, SIG began work on this gun in 1938. Its preview version was the Model 44/16. The P210 as we know it made its debut in 1949 and was immediately adopted by the Swiss Army, which designated it the SP47/8. It would become better known as the *Pistole 49*.

Gun experts have had little but praise for this firearm. In the current issue of the authoritative *Small Arms of the World*, we hear this from W.H.B. Smith and Edward Clinton Ezell: "Nearly 200,000 *Pistole 49* were made for the Swiss Army, most are still in use... This weapon is beautifully made in the finest Swiss tradition. Because of the care taken in fitting the barrel, it demonstrates considerable accuracy." [1]

In the *Gun Digest Book of 9mm Handguns* by Dean Grennell and Wiley Clapp, the latter stated flatly, "The best 9mm pistol made is the SIG 210, for a variety of reasons and with only a small qualification or two." [2] Jan Stevenson, the man the late Major George Nonte called the most articulate of firearms journalists, was always a big fan of the P210. Ditto Leroy Thompson, who has said that he so appreciates its accuracy, he carries it when he thinks he'll encounter long distance shooting but won't have access to a rifle.

The gun simply reeks of quality. You feel it as soon as you rack the slide. Among mass-produced auto pistols, only the Beretta 92/96

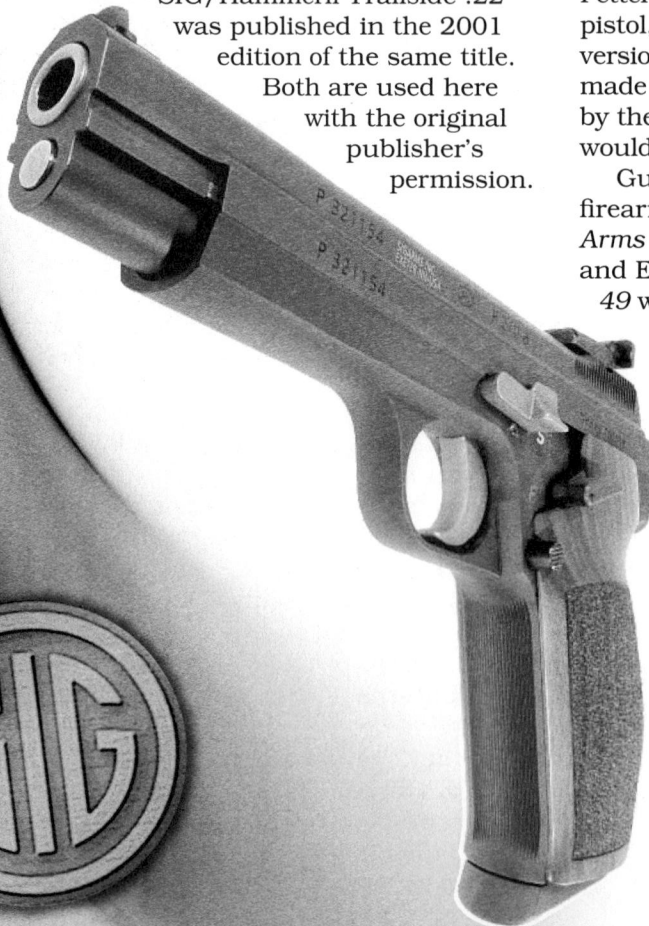

can equal the glassy smoothness of the action as the slide runs inside its frame rails, a design feature that was copied in the much more popular CZ75 and numerous other auto pistols subsequently. When you stroke the trigger of a P-210, you get the proverbial "glass rod break" of a .22 target pistol. According to handgunner's lore, the pistol is polished inside and out, even on non-contact surfaces, like the premium-priced Patek-Phillippe wristwatch that shares the P210's country of origin.

Why was it not more popular? Price was certainly a big part of it. There was also concern that the finely fitted parts would not stand up to grit, muck, and dirt in hostile environments, or to neglect in the hands of what Mark Moritz called NDPs (Non-Dedicated Personnel). Noted Clapp, "I wonder how well the 210 would perform when it gets unavoidably dirty. It would seem that the very tight fit of parts, which make the gun all that it truly is, would gum up and cause jams in extended firing sessions in rough service. Despite these considerations, I still feel that the pistol is the best in the world."(3)

Given the American handgun enthusiast's predilection for costly custom handguns, I suspect that neither price nor sensitivity to maintenance was the real problem. Yanks want their auto pistols to reload fast. The P210 for 51 years had a butt-heel magazine that required considerable effort to activate. Its slim, single-stack magazine only held eight rounds, and Americans want a 9mm of that capacity to be just about down to pocket size, or they want a 9mm the size of this SIG to hold buckets of bullets, but they have scant love for a 9mm that's both big and low on round-count. Also, the sliding safety catch behind the trigger guard on the left was awkward for many to reach, and often stiff to operate. The gun was classy and accurate, but it was slow. In the most affordable military models, the sights were too small to see quickly and sharply.

Sales languished, and eventually SIGARMS stopped importing the P210. Imports resumed in 1998, with SIGARMS bringing in a limited number, but the firm ran into the same problems of selling an expensive Old World design in the New World.

So, you can understand how intrigued I was when SIGARMS' public relations liaison Laura Burgess showed me the P-210-8. I handled it, and said enthusiastically, "Sign me up!"

"DASH-EIGHT" IMPROVEMENTS

The "dash-eight" could be called "the Americanized P210." It comes with adjustable sights that give a good sight picture. A white three-dot pattern is superimposed, presumably on the assumption that the Yank version will be used for fast practical shooting. The thumb safety has been enlarged to the rear and widened considerably. I found it fast and comfortable, though the placement took just a little getting used to. The slide stop lever has always been easy to operate, and this feature has been retained on the "-8".

Perhaps most important, a generously-sized push-button magazine release has been placed behind the trigger on the left of the frame in what we call here "the right place." The button protrudes sufficiently that I thought the trigger finger in left handed shooting might accidentally release it, but this never happened in testing. The magazines dropped cleanly and freely. Curiously, the magazine well was not beveled. I would have expected that in a gun built for fast American-style speedloads.

The grip has been re-shaped, and is the best-feeling P210 "handle" I've ever grasped. The wooden stock is top quality in looks, shape, and execution of its stippling (in lieu of their usual grooving). It fills the palm and locks into the grasp nicely.

The glassy smooth running of the slide that I remembered from older P210s was still there. The super-light trigger I remembered from P210s past was replaced in the "-8" with a smooth-rolling unit whose let-off weight felt like an also Americanized 4 pounds. SIG's Laura Burgess advised me that while the usual P210 lets off at 3.31 pounds, the 210-2 service model breaks at 3.92 lb. The test 210-8 feels all of that. The gun has an internal firing pin safety as well.

The big difference is price. The 210-8 carries a suggested retail of – a drum roll here, please – $4,289. Spare magazines are $100 apiece.

ACCURACY

The pistol came out of the box with a test target purportedly fired at 50 meters. The six-shot group measured 4.2 inches. (The best five were in 2.55 inches, the best three in 1.1 inches). It did not say whether the gun had been fired from a bench rest or a machine rest.

Now, 2-1/2 inches at 50 paces is *very* good handgun accuracy, though there are guns that will beat that standard. Four inches at the same distance is pretty mundane if you're talking about target guns. Being snowed in, I found long-range testing out of the question and ran targets out to the 25-yard line at the Manchester Indoor Firing Line range. I brought with me three batches of ammo known for accuracy.

Federal 9BP, the 115-grain hollow-point from their Classic line, long ago set the standard for accuracy in the 9mm cartridge. Right up there with it is the Winchester 147-grain subsonic round, originally introduced as the Olin Super Match (OSM) for good reason. Finally, I had some of the last of a cherished lot of particularly accurate Federal

Manufacturer	Load	Nominal Velocity	5-Shot Group	Best 3 Shots
Federal 9AP	123-grain FMJ	1120 fps	2.15"	0.90"
Federal 9BP	115-grain JHP	1160 fps	2.25"	0.80"
Winchester Subsonic	147-grain JHP	990 fps	2.10"	0.75"
		Average	2.166"	0.817"

9AP, their standard (not generic) full metal jacket 123-grain "ball" ammo. The gun was fired from the bench using a Millett rest. Each five-shot group was measured once overall, and again for the best three shots, the latter to help factor out human error. All measurements were center-to-center of the farthest bullet holes in question, rounded off to the nearest 0.05 inches. (See chart above.)

Now, this is very good accuracy indeed. The potential shown by the best three-shot measurements is particularly intriguing. But what really struck me was the *consistency* of the pistol. There was no more than fifteen thousandths of an inch difference in the three five-shot group measurements or, for that matter, the three-shot group measurements! Consistency may be the hobgoblin of little minds, but it is also an indication of top quality in any machine.

For perspective on the accuracy of this particular shooting machine, we can look to other tests. Wiley Clapp and Dean Grennell in their 1986 *Gun Digest Book of 9mm Handguns* tested

two of the three loads I used at the same distance. Their gun was a P210-6, and the fiveshot groups measured 1.5 inches with 9BP and 1.75 inches with 9AP. Results had been 3/4inch apart with the hollow-point and less than half an inch different with the ball round. (4)

The proof target indicated that it had been fired from a machine rest at 50 meters. It would follow that 4.2 inches at roughly 50 yards should translate to 2.1 inches at half the distance, and this is just what we got. It should extrapolate in the opposite direction to roughly 8.5 inches at 100 yards. I didn't have a place to do that at the time, but I had a copy of the article in which Leroy Thompson had called his P210 "a rifle on the hip" because of its accuracy. A photo of a 100-yard target Leroy had shot with an early production, 50-year-old P210 indicated a group size of just under 8 inches.

That, ladies and gentlemen, is consistency. Three P210s, the oldest and newest half a century apart, all grouping to virtually the same point on the graph.

PERSPECTIVES

Clearly, the SIG P210 in its latest incarnation is accurate. But is it as super-accurate as the lore of the handgun would have us believe? Is it accurate enough for its huge price tag?

Just 35 years ago, the P210 was priced exactly the same, to the dollar, as the S&W Model 52 Master target pistol built for the .38 Special wadcutter cartridge. That gun's descendant, the Model 952 from the Performance Center, sells for $1,200 and fires the same 9mm round as the SIG, but into groups averaging around 1.5 inches. The same company's PC 5906 has been known to put five rounds into an inch at 25 yards, and 1-inch groups at that distance are *guaranteed* for the PPC-9 that the Center builds for police pistol teams.

It may be unfair to compare the P210 to other brands. It's certainly unnecessary. One need look no farther than the SIGARMS catalog itself.

I've shot sub-1-inch groups on two occasions with the P220, one European and one American style, both using Federal Match 185-grain .45 ACP hollow-point ammo. I've lost count of how many times I've seen the P226 shoot 2-inch groups or better with good 9mm Parabellum ammo. In 1998, testing the then-new *sig pro* near Philadelphia with Walt Rauch and some other gun writers, I got a sub 2-inch group using Federal 155-grain Hydra-Shok .40 S&W ammo. (Under by all of 1/32 of an inch, mind you, but still under the 2-inch mark.) In testing the P-245 compact .45 ACP, we got 2 1/8-inch groups with Federal Match 185-grain JHP, 2 3/8 inches with Pro-Load 230-grain ball, and 2.5 inches with Winchester 185-grain Silvertip. Finally, while touring the SIGARMS plant in Exeter, New Hampshire in 1998, I had the privilege of watching SIG's Casey McCarthy shoot an entire magazine of 125-grain CCI Lawman into less than an inch with a .357 SIG P229 Sport model. All shooting mentioned in this paragraph was at 25 yards. All were five-shot groups except for Casey's superb marathon performance.

All the modern SIGARMS pistols just mentioned are modern guns, drop-safe, and utterly reliable with virtually any cartridge within the range of what they're chambered for. Best of all, they don't cost you the price of a good used car.

DISAPPOINTMENTS

For a pistol that costs $4,289, I would have expected more. Night sights. Ambidextrous controls. Given all the effort put into making this "speed-load friendly," I would like to see a beveled magazine. It reloads faster than it did, but not quite as fast as a regular SIG-Sauer or *sig pro.*

Older magazines will not be compatible, lacking the cutout for the push button release. Conversely, new mags won't fit older guns, the way American style P220 magazines will fit a European style P220 .45, but not vice versa. The reason is the mags for the P210-8 have a polymer extension. This does aid somewhat in speed and positive reloading, and with a very large hand, may give a welcome additional grasping surface. However, it probably won't allow the butt heel release to lock in.

The accuracy? It's "plenty good," but it's not the true "1-inch super match-grade" of handgun accuracy that you expect for the money, and expect from the P210 legend.

Workmanship? Fit was almost flawless. The safety catch did score a nasty drag mark into the bluing of the frame almost immediately once I started shooting the gun. In disassembling it, I discovered that there *were* tool marks on the inside. Darn. Another handgun myth bites the dust. Actually, there were some minor tool marks on the bottom front of the slide, just ahead of the dust cover. Nothing that would impair the smooth function, though.

Finish was what SIG calls a matte black. It was nice. It wasn't fancy. It didn't look like what you'd expect on $4,000 pistol.

Finally, *this gun bites!* Not in the figurative sense, but literally. The sharp little hammer spur pinched the web of my hand each time the slide re-cocked it after a shot. It wouldn't take much to re-shape the hammer and make it more user-friendly.

A MATTER OF VALUE

According to the 1966 *Gun Digest* The P210 went for $165 that year with polished blue finish and wooden stocks, three bucks less with plastic grips and matte finish. At the time, a Colt Government .45 was $90, A Python was $135, and a Ruger Standard .22 auto, $41.50. S&W's deluxe .38 target pistol, the Model 52 Master, sold for the exact same $165 retail as the SIG.

By the 1986 edition of the same publication, the fixed-sight P210-1 or -2 cost $1,275 to $1,600 depending on which of the two importers had brought it in. The target-sighted -6 model was $1,580 as imported by Osborne's Supplies, and $1,750 from Mandall's Shooting Supplies. By contrast, the Python started at $577.50 and the Government Model .45 at $459.50, Ruger's .22 pistol was at $168, and the S&W M-52 was a relative bargain at $573.50. The super-accurate HK P9S Sport Target, its fanciest version, retailed for $990. The SIG P220, which had replaced the P210 as Switzerland's national military pistol, was $585.

In the 1991 edition of *Gun Digest*, which had SIG-Sauers on the cover, a P226 and a P228, the price on the P226 was $780. The P220 was $720 in the American style with the push-button mag release, $695 in the Euro style. Other prices: Python, $759.95. Ruger .22, $224.75. Colt Government:

$624.95. S&W M-52 Master: $832. The P210-6 was now $1,900, imported only by Mandall.

Little more than a decade later, "American style" renovations still cost more at SIG. Roughly (choke) twice as much. The P210-6 carries a suggested retail of $2,089. The Model 52's descendant, the PC 952, is $1,200. That gun has all the features of the P210-8 except a firing pin lock, and has a beveled mag well.

My own idea of a good buy in a medium-caliber pistol outfit for almost $4,300 is a *sig pro* and something to carry it in. Like, oh, the glove box of a perfectly functional 1993 Nissan Sentra for $3,500 (6), which leaves money for ammo.

A new P226 lists at $851; for the price of the P210-8, you can arm five people with a classic SIG that shoots about as well. Or you can arm seven good people with a *sig pro* each ($602 per) and ammo. That primo P229 Sport (whole mag, 1-inch, 25 yards) is $1,353. Meaning you could get one each for yourself, your significant other, and your oldest kid, plus some .357 SIG ammo, for the cost of a single P210-8.

But where's the prestige in that? They're importing a Rolex-quality gun with a Rolex-quality price from the land of the Rolex, and isn't that all about prestige?

Let's talk about that. My old daddy was a jeweler and watchmaker. He was licensed to repair the Rolex. I learned from him. The watch I wear now has an "E-X" at the end of its name. However, its first three letters are "T-I-M." The main function of the Rolex, in addition to telling time as well as the best Timex but no better, is to show the world the wearer has made money.

How do you do that with a P210, which (a) will be unrecognizable as anything but "a gun" to 99 out of 100 people you meet, and which (b) unlike the Rolex, won't be flashed in public. If the Rolex was carried concealed, would anyone but watch collectors buy them?

You can earn prestige and show you've made it by buying the excellent SIGARMS pistols. You just bypass the P210-8. For what it would cost, you can purchase nine of the unquestionably "best buy" SIG/Hammerli Trailside target pistols. Amply accurate and lightweight, they are ideal for a junior pistol team, and in league matches nine guns gives you enough to simultaneously field two four-person teams and

have a spare gun. There'll be money left over for buckets of .22 LR ammo, and for the team shirts that can bear your name.

That, dammit, would buy more respect from any of our peers than owning an admittedly very nice, but unquestionably and grotesquely overpriced, 9mm pistol.

Update for second edition: the pistol just discussed is today available as the P210-9 Legend, at a somewhat more reasonable price of $3993.

References

1. (1) Smith, W.H.B., and Ezell, Edward, *Small Arms of the World, 12th edition*, 1983. Harrisonburg, PA: Stackpole Books. P. 673.
2. (2) Grennell, Dean A., and Clapp, Wiley, *Gun Digest Book of 9mm Handguns*, 1986. Northbrook, IL., DBI Books. P. 226.
3. (3) *Ibid*, P. 227.
4. (4) *Ibid*, P. 206.
5. (5) Thompson, Leroy, "Swiss Perfection for Y2K," *Handguns* magazine, October 1999, P. 69.
6. (6) *Boston Globe*, Classifieds, 3/12/01

Chapter 17
SIGARMS'
Hammerli Trailside

This slim, light, handy .22 pistol is more accurate than you'd think it had a right to be!

I wasn't the first gun writer to get my hands on a SIG Trailside. I write mostly about self-defense guns and police gear, not recreational handguns, and probably wasn't even on the radar screen for test samples of this sporting pistol. Like you, I read about it in the NRA magazine *American Rifleman* and elsewhere. My eyebrows rose at the glowing reviews, especially when they talked about its phenomenal accuracy.

I was interested and called SIGARMS in Exeter, New Hampshire to ask for a test sample. It was a difficult task since demand is so great they can't keep these guns in stock.

You've been told the truth. I'm happy to report that this gun is every bit as accurate as the reports have promised.

A SPECIFIC NICHE

Since the long-ago and much-lamented departure of the Colt Woodsman, there has been an empty niche in the sport handgun market. The Woodsman .22 auto was flat and easy to carry, even tucked in the outdoorsman's waistband. It had a very good trigger pull, and was so inherently accurate that target shooters hung barrel weights on them, fitted them with new sights, and took them to matches. Colt paid more attention to the market then than in more recent decades, and they picked up on this. Soon they introduced a match target version. For decades, the Colt Woodsman dominated the .22 stages of bull's-eye shooting, then the only real handgun competition game in the country, until the coming of heavier and more sophisticated .22 target pistols like the High Standard Supermatic and the Smith & Wesson Model 41.

Let's look at what the 1940 Stoeger *Gun Bible* had to say about the Woodsman. "Graceful in appearance and beautifully finished. It is furnished with an unusually comfortable grip that fits the hand snugly and securely...Fast and certain action...a trigger pull that is smooth and crisp. Ten-shot magazine and slide-lock safety."

There have been numerous nice sporting .22 autos since. Some had the lightness of the old Woodsman, but few had its combination of good inherent accuracy and excellent *practical* accuracy. "Inherent accuracy" is what is mechanically built into the gun. Sometimes, though, the human engineering of the pistol is so poor that only a device like a Ransom machine rest will be able to deliver that accuracy downrange. "Practical accuracy" is what the gun can do in our hands, and it encompasses ergonomics as well as inherent accuracy.

There was the Woodsman. Now there is the Trailside.

"Graceful in appearance and beautifully finished"? Check. "Furnished with an unusually comfortable grip that fits the hand snugly and securely"? Check. "Fast and certain action"? Check. "A trigger pull that is smooth and crisp"? Check. "Ten-shot magazine and slide-lock safety"? CHECK!

TRAILSIDE FEATURES

SIG's affiliate, Hammerli, morphed the splendid Model 208 series, designed for demanding International Standard Pistol competition, into this "field model." They did the reverse of what Colt had done some 60 years earlier. Where the American firm had built up their accurate sporting pistol into a full-fledged target model, the Swiss company essentially downscaled their magnificent target gun into a field sidearm.

The original Woodsman with 4-1/2-inch barrel weighed some 27 ounces. In its first competition incarnation, the Woodsman Match Target of 1940 had a 6-1/2-inch barrel and weighed 36 ounces. In the 1950s, updated variations with an underlug barrel went to about 38 ounces, still with the 6-1/2-inch barrel length.

The Hammerli 208S pistol weighs 37-1/2 ounces unloaded and has a substantially constructed barrel a tenth of an inch under 6 inches. The Trailside weighs 28 ounces with a 43/4-inch barrel. Great efforts have been made to transfer the 208's action to the Trailside, and to incorporate Hammerli's legendary ability to produce accurate barrels. These efforts, as we shall see, have come to a happy fruition.

Two models are available, an adjustable-sighted version with laminated wooden grips and a plastic-stocked plain-Jane version with fixed sights. We got the latter. The simple fixed sights gave

Trigger stop on target variation of Hammerli Trailside adjusts to limit overtravel.

Orthopedic target grips come on the high-end version of the Trailside target .22.

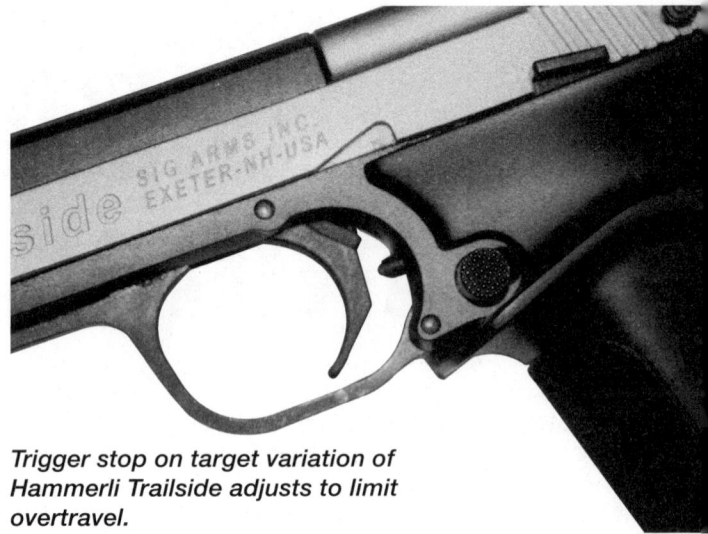

an excellent picture to the eye: big, blocky rear and big, highly visible front with lots of light on either side as you aim the pistol.

Magazine release is the usual "American style," a push button behind the trigger guard. The magazine does not drop free, but falls slightly downward for easy retrieval by hand from the magazine well. This is not a problem and probably an advantage. The magazine won't be accidentally dropped to the floor in a bull'seye match when you meant to withdraw it and set it on the shooting bench, and there aren't many competition venues where you need a speed reload of a .22 sporting pistol.

The magazine itself is an ingenious thing, almost weightless, made purely of polymer except for the magazine spring. It has a hollow in the bottom of its base, something you see with the 10-round "Clinton" magazines SIG makes for its big "Classic" series auto pistols. I can't stand that. It can falsely tell a finger probing in the dark that the magazine is out of the gun when in fact it's still in there. It wouldn't hurt anything to add an ounce and fill this hollow.

The plastic stocks on the test gun felt very nice in the hand, widening toward the bottom. They may not be perfect for those with the tiniest hands and the shortest fingers. In a natural grasp, my index finger reached the trigger at the pad of the last phalange. I have that "average-sized adult male hand" that gun designers talk about. This means the reach to the trigger will be short for very small hands.

This is a single-action pistol with an excellent trigger pull. I would make it right at 4 pounds. It is not the pure "glass rod" break of a 208 Hammerli or other world-class match target pistols. The release is soft, but it is still clean and doesn't pull the sights off target. A surprise break is easily attainable.

I could not feel any "backlash." This is the annoying movement that happens after you've released the sear and broken the shot, and the weight your index finger is applying to the trigger

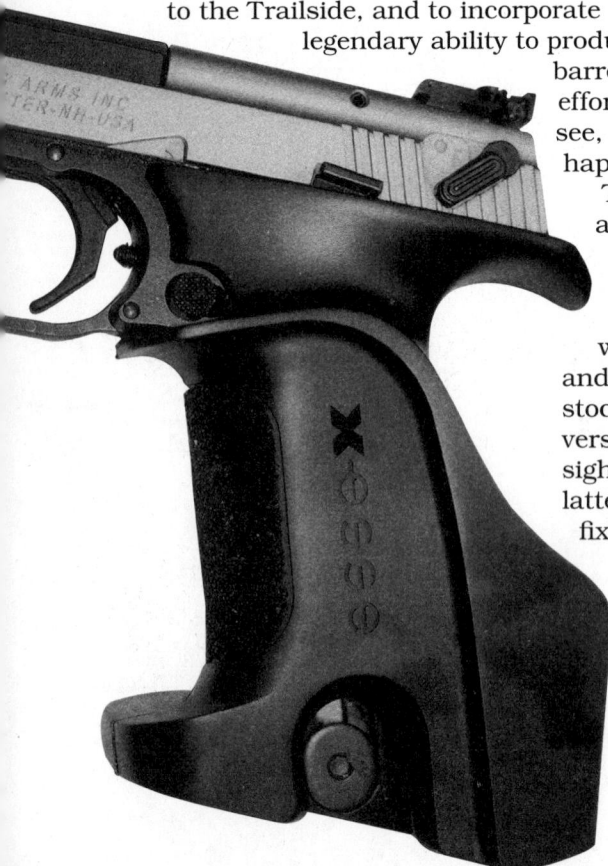

is no longer resisted. This causes the trigger to slam back against the frame, jarring the gun. A "trigger-stop," sometimes called just as descriptively an "anti-backlash device," is affixed to the frame inside the guard behind the trigger. The one on the Trailside has an ingenious spring-loaded ball. It effectively stops extraneous, aim-disturbing rearward movement of the trigger, yet it would leave enough movement possible to fire the gun if it got out of adjustment and stopped the trigger prematurely when a shot *needed* to be fired.

A manual safety, set up for right-hand use only, is found at the left rear of the slide. It differs from the usual slide-mounted safety lever in that "up" is "Safe" and "down" is "Fire." A conspicuous red dot appears along with a capital "F" when the gun is ready to go, and a large "S" is visible when the safety catch is locked on.

I had no trouble releasing the safety with a downward swipe of the thumb. However, when trying to "on safe" the Trailside, the upward movement was stiff enough that I had to either shift the gun in my hand to do it with the gun hand thumb, or simply use the free hand to push the lever up into the "on safe" position.

The slide stop is where it should be: readily accessible to the right thumb or left index finger of the right- or left-handed shooter respectively. However, it is in a position where if the shooter uses a high-thumb grasp in right-handed shooting, the thumb will ride that lever and keep it from locking the slide open after the last shot is fired. The same is true of the SIG Classic centerfire service pistols. Perhaps the always-practical Swiss simply assumed that smart shooters would curl their thumbs down for maximum grip strength and not impinge on the working parts of their pistol.

The butt of the pistol flares widely. This creates a flat-bottom surface that rests beautifully on a bench, or on the ground when you shoot prone. It's not as if the Trailside was a concealment gun and you had to worry about this as a bulge point. For "rested shooting" when there's time to stabilize the gun for the shot, it's an advantage.

Finally, the gun has rails atop the barrel for attaching a scope or a red dot sight. My shooting buddy Walter Carlson donated the use of a Leupold 4X pistol scope with appropriate mounts. This excellent piece of handgun optics aided greatly in wringing out the Trailside pistol's surprisingly good accuracy.

SHOOTING THE TRAILSIDE

Accuracy testing was done outdoors in cold weather, from the bench in a two-handed hold. Five-shot groups were fired with each type of ammo, and measured center-to-center of the farthest bullet holes for all shots (a good test of what the gun can do in a solid field position when the handgunner is not experiencing, or at least not affected by, stress). They were measured again for the best three shots, which if an experienced shooter is firing the gun will come remarkably close to what the pistol can yield for a five- or even 10-shot group from a machine rest. That's a "shorthand test" that saves a lot of set-up time and a lot of inserts for your Ransom Rest. Because of the good things I'd heard about its accuracy, I tested the Trailside more with target ammo than plinking ammo.

The following results were gained at 25 yards, with the Leupold 4X scope in place.

Right: Slim, graceful, and light, the Trailside is the best .22 target pistol for the small-statured shooter since the old pre-war Colt Woodsman Match Target, in the author's opinion.

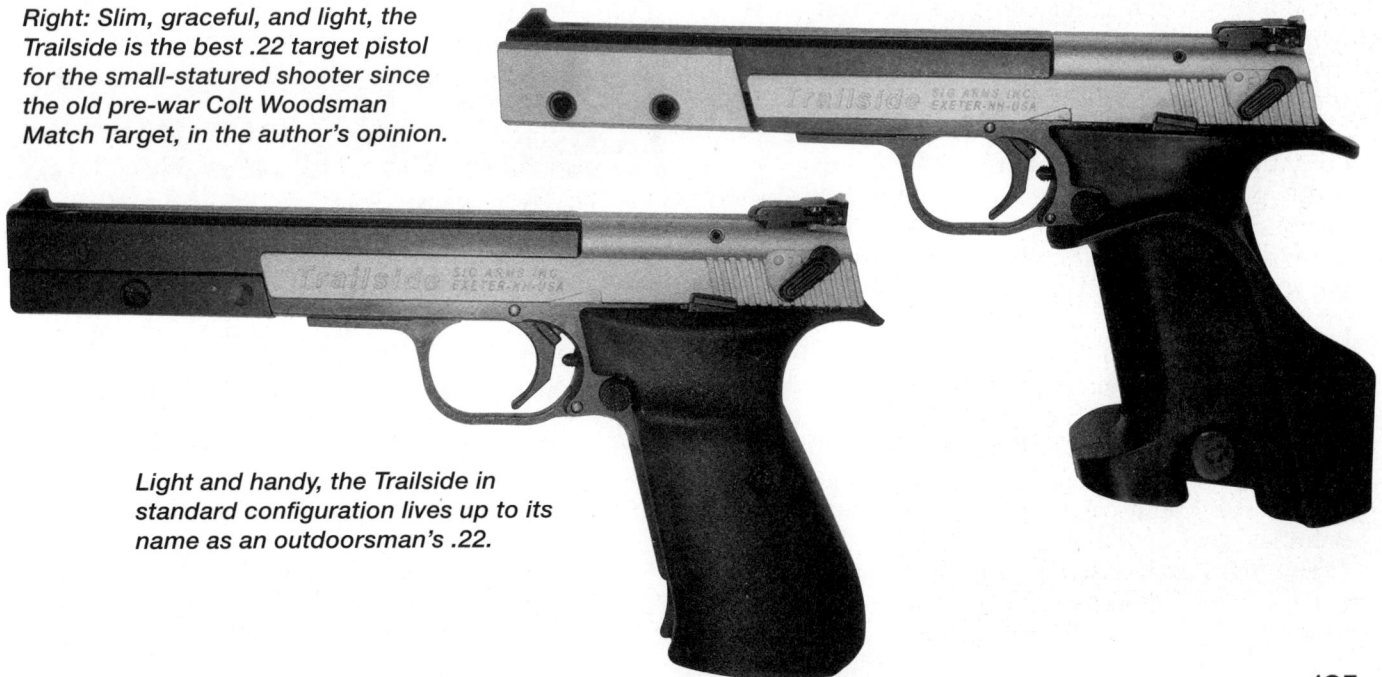

Light and handy, the Trailside in standard configuration lives up to its name as an outdoorsman's .22.

Jaskiel MacDowell was 11 when this photo was taken while he won the National Junior Handgun Championships in sub-junior class.

Cartridge	5 Shots Group	Best 3 Shots
CCI Green Tag	1.2"	.7"
CCI Pistol Match	1.2"	.7"
Eley Pistol Match	1.9"	.75"
Winchester T-22	2.15"	1.0"
Remington Hi-Speed	2.1"	.65"

The above does not tell the entire story. All three of the match-grade rounds shot pretty consistently spread five-shot groups. However, the Remington Hi-Speed solid, a "standard .22 plinking load" if you will, and the Winchester T-22, kind of a cross between a cheap target round and a practice round, both suffered "4+1 syndrome" in this pistol. First commented upon in print by my colleague Wiley Clapp, this is the tendency of certain semiautomatic firearms to place their first shot in one spot and subsequent rounds in another. What we think is happening is that the parts of the gun wind up in a very subtly different "battery," or position vis-à-vis one another when the gun is ready to fire, when the first cartridge is hand-cycled into the chamber. Another "battery" is in alignment when the mechanism automatically cycles subsequent cartridges into the same firing chamber.

The Remington load had four of its five shots in three-quarters of an inch, a group spoiled by the first shot that spread the total to 2.1 inches. The

Winchester load had a 2.15-inch spread counting the first shot, but put its last four into exactly an inch and a half.

Two other accuracy tests were done. Because the temperature was below freezing and it was necessary to "shoot a group, go back to the car and warm the hands at the heater, and shoot the next group," each was limited to two types of ammunition.

If the Trailside was this accurate at 25 yards, what would it do at two thirds that distance, 50 feet? The reason this was an issue was that a stronghold of .22 target pistol shooting is the so-called "gallery match," done indoors at a regulation distance of 50 feet. The results were:

Cartridge	5 Shots Group	Best 3 Shots
Eley Pistol Match	.75"	.30"
Winchester T-22	.7"	.25"

I chose those two cartridges because the pricey Eley is the standard against which other .22 rimfire target ammunition is judged, at the highest levels of competition. You see the results in an accompanying photograph. The pattern of the five shots was such that all five would have hit a single .22 Long Rifle cartridge, if only on the edge, at that 50-foot distance. *This is accuracy!*

The T-22 is an affordable standard-velocity cartridge of an accuracy level suitable for club competition, and less than world-class tournaments, or so Winchester's modest advertising would imply. Yet I couldn't help but notice that this "economy" round produced in the USA *outshot the expensive British cartridge.*

If I seem a little too exultant about that, forgive me. It's not a xenophobe thing or a chauvinist thing. I love and respect my brothers and sisters who formerly owned handguns in Great Britain. I used to teach handgun classes there every year until the Tony Blair government disempowered its subjects and made them turn in all their pistols and revolvers. The surviving Spitfire pilots, and their aging relatives who remember standing guard duty on British shores with handguns, rifles, and shotguns donated by American citizens when a Nazi invasion seemed imminent only a little more than half a century ago, will understand. So will the yeoman archers of Agincourt, who must be restless in their ancient graves at the recent turn of events in Mother England.

Back on track, though, another question remained unanswered with the Trailside pistol. How

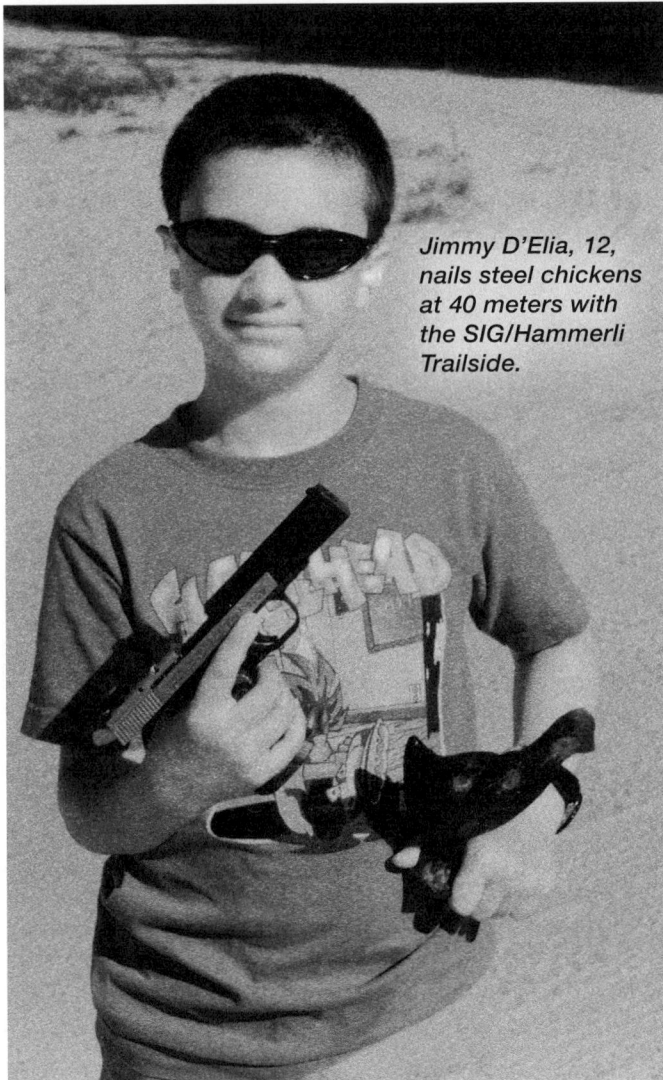

Jimmy D'Elia, 12, nails steel chickens at 40 meters with the SIG/Hammerli Trailside.

well does it shoot with those fixed, "iron sights"? Again, only two loads were selected to tell the tale:

Cartridge	5 Shots Group	Best 3 Shots
CCI Pistol Match	2.4"	1.1"
CCI Green Tag	1.7"	1.05"

Both groups were evenly distributed. Both, unfortunately, also grouped about four inches to the left at 9 o'clock. This is nothing that couldn't be fixed by moving the rear sight slightly in its dovetail, but the gun belonged to SIGARMS instead of me, so I didn't try. It did, however, tell me that the adjustable-sight version might just be worth a look. For my own needs, I'd register the fixed sights for my favorite load and never look back.

RELIABILITY

My friends and I put a thousand-some rounds of all manner of .22 Long Rifle through this neat little pistol. There were only three malfunctions.

This gun had a love/hate relationship with the Winchester T-22 round. Love: it shot it very accurately. Hate: in a couple hundred rounds, there were three malfunctions with this cartridge and this one alone. Two were misfires. Each time there appeared to be a solid hit on the rim of the cartridge by the firing pin. Each was given a second try. One fired at that point, and one didn't. There was also one malfunction of a spent casing caught in the ejection port. It looked to me as if it had possibly hit the scope on the ejection arc and bounced back into the open-top feedway. It happened to be a Winchester also. I turned the gun over, jacked the slide, and kept shooting.

There were no other malfunctions. Veteran shooters well know that .22 pistols are idiosyncratic about what ammo they like and what ammo they don't, more so than larger caliber guns firing centerfire cartridges. One possible ammo incompatibility in one particular specimen doesn't exactly torque me out.

VALUE FACTOR

What's this new gun good for? It replaces the long-lost Woodsman – the light, accurate, reliable .22 auto that Ernest Hemingway and Gary Cooper and Charles Askins Jr. swore by. It comprises efficiency, convenience, and quality rolled into one compact, accurate small-bore auto pistol package.

For those getting started in one-hand bull's-eye shooting, the .22 is the place to start. Buy a Trailside. Put on optical sights like everyone you're shooting

The electronic timer is running behind them as Jaskiel MacDowell, foreground, and his dad James vie for the National Champion Parent/Child Team victory at the National Junior Handgun Championships, 2002. Both are shooting Trailsides.

against, and you'll have accuracy you can take to the bank, and to the winner's circle. SIGARMS ads say modestly that you may not take this model to the Olympics like you would its big brother the Model 208S. Maybe not, but let me tell you something. The 50-foot slow-fire 10-ring on a gallery pistol target measures about 9/10 of an inch in diameter. The 10-ring of the timed and rapid fire target is twice as big. This pistol has shown me it can shoot a perfect score on those targets at that distance.

Long strings of fire with the pistol extended at the end of one arm can be tiring until the shooter has developed the muscles for it, muscles not normally used for other things in life. New shooters in this sport thus benefit from pistols that are light but accurate. Pistols that weigh perhaps 28 ounces and can shoot five shots for five into three-quarters of an inch. Pistols like, oh, the Hammerli Trailside.

At the time Colt upgraded their sporting .22 auto pistol to a competition model, the 1940 Stoeger *Gun Bible* listed the standard Woodsman at $32.75 and the new Match Target Woodsman at $41.75. Now, at the dawn of the new Millennium, Hammerli has taken their world-class match grade target pistol, the Model 208S that retails for $1,925, and made it available in a lightweight sportsman's model for about $400. Our fixed-sight test gun can be duplicated at a suggested retail of $398. Adjustable sights and fancier grips will run the price somewhat (but not unreasonably) higher.

I recently had to hire an economist as an expert witness in a hard-fought legal battle. The time for his research and testimony cost our side about $20,000. I didn't ask him about Colt Woodsman and Match Target Woodsman versus Hammerli 208S and Hammerli Trailside. If I had, I suspect he would have told me it was a hell of a deal, maybe the deal of the year in the world of value for your money when buying a new handgun.

Basically, six decades ago a plain-Jane Colt Woodsman cost 75 percent as much as its competition-grade sibling, the Match Target. Today, the Hammerli Trailside costs *20 percent* as much as its sibling in full match trim, the Model 208S.

But I suspect you figured that out already without paying an economist 20 grand.

At the end of the article reprinted above, I thanked SIG for bringing us the Trailside. SIG later parted from Hammerli and stopped importing it. While most buyers loved their Trailsides, a few high-volume league match shooters eventually ran into breakage issues. Hammerli discontinued the Trailside, replacing it with the updated but very similar Hammerli Exesse.

Chapter 18
GSR: The SIG 1911

To understand the SIG 1911 line as it exists today, we need to go back to its roots. The following appeared in the first edition of Gun Digest Book of SIG-Sauer, *when the SIG 1911 was new...*

In November 2003, SIGARMS announced their new 1911 pistol at the national sporting goods wholesalers' show. It stirred so much interest that their website almost crashed from the unprecedented number of hits.

Dubbed the GSR for Granite Series Rail, this is the first all-American SIG with no European design input. In February 2003, SIGARMS' Mark Kresser talked with former IPSC World and USPSA National pistol champion Matt McLearn, an accomplished 1911 pistolsmith, about what he'd like to see on a 1911 if SIG was to produce one. For one thing, Matt told Mark, "Make it look like a SIG."

The "granite" in the title presumably draws from the Granite State, as New Hampshire (where SIGARMS is located) is known. More Granite Staters got into the act as SIGARMS' own New Hampshire-based crew approached Makers, an engineering firm in Manchester, for assistance. Mechanical engineer Kevin Webber and industrial designer Chris Aiston weren't gun guys, at least not to start, but their input brought a fresh outlook to the project. Meanwhile, McLearn was hired for three months as a consultant on the project, and that worked out so well that he became a SIGARMS employee in late October. By then, the design was pretty much finalized.

The formula, says Matt, is strictly "made in USA." Caspian produces the frame, with integral light attachment rail, in neighboring Vermont, as are the slides; Caspian makes both for Wilson Combat, and these are pretty much the same. In a logical *quid pro quo*, the superior outside extractor is made by Wilson and used by Caspian, and of course, now by SIGARMS. Caspian also makes the firing pin, firing pin stop, beavertail grip safety, and ejector. Wilson makes the GSR's mainspring housing (steel on the silver guns, aluminum on the blue ones), and the thumb safety.

The bushing and sear come from George Smith at EGW, the appropriately named Evolution Gun Works. The distinctive trigger – and the slide stop, magazine catch, and plunger tube – come from Grieder Precision. Performance Engineering is the vendor the for hammer, grip screws and bushings for same, and the 11 pins involved in assembling the classic 1911.

Wolff is providing the springs: An 18-pound recoil spring, 19-pound mainspring, extra power firing pin spring and plunger tube springs, heavy-duty extractor spring, and standard strength on everything else, is the prescription there.

Storm Lake did the barrels, with a one turn in 16 rifling twist (actually, 1:15.75, not to put too fine a point on it). They're made of 416 stainless. In fact, the whole gun is stainless, 416 alloy on the slide and 415 on the frame, according to Matt. The blued

A 1911 with a "SIG look."

version is Nitron over the stainless; the "regular" is a pleasant silver color. Stock options are nicely checkered wood from Herrett, and businesslike black plastic from Falcon. The Italian ACT eight-round magazines, and the three-dot streamlined fixed sights, both come from Novak's.

The contributors to the effort read like a "who's who" of the best in custom 1911 components. McLearn is in charge of assembly and production. The question was, how well did it all come together?

ON THE FIRING LINE

For testing Dana Owen of SIGARMS' law enforcement/military sales wing joined Matt, IDPA Master Steve Sager, and me at the SIGARMS Academy facility. We received a welcome break in the rotten weather and were able to use the outdoor range. Our samples were production guns, two of the first to come off an assembly line commanded by McLearn and four skilled workers on his staff, along with the entire deburring and polishing crew available to them. One blue and one silver, the test pistols were both in .45 ACP; this is the initial chambering and can safely be predicted to be the most popular. However, there are plans to produce this gun in 9mm Luger, .40 S&W, .38 Super, and .357 SIG if all goes well. The Academy had PMC hardball and Speer Lawman ball on hand; I had some Winchester hardball, Winchester 230-grain

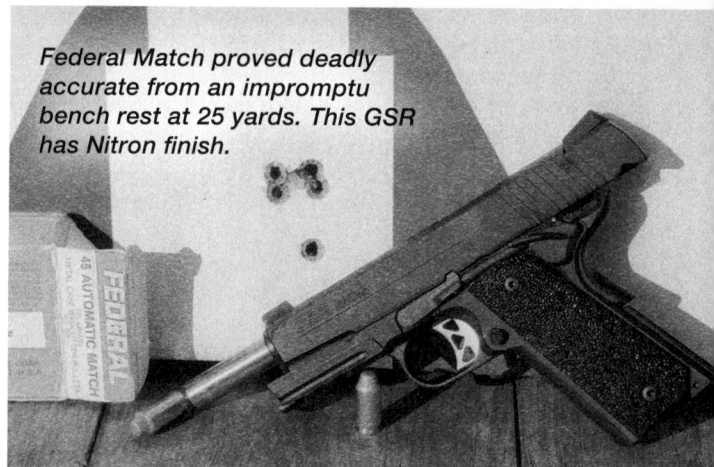

Federal Match proved deadly accurate from an impromptu bench rest at 25 yards. This GSR has Nitron finish.

JHP, and an old box of Federal Match 185-grain mid-range SWC in the car. We set up a wooden bench at the 25-yard line.

The silver specimen was spanking new, and it wasn't fair to accuracy-test a gun that hadn't been broken in, so I benched the Nitron sample that had been shot some. Each group was measured for all five shots, of course, and then again for the best three hits. The latter measurement is a good way to factor out human error when you don't have a machine rest on hand, and get a better idea of the pistol's inherent accuracy.

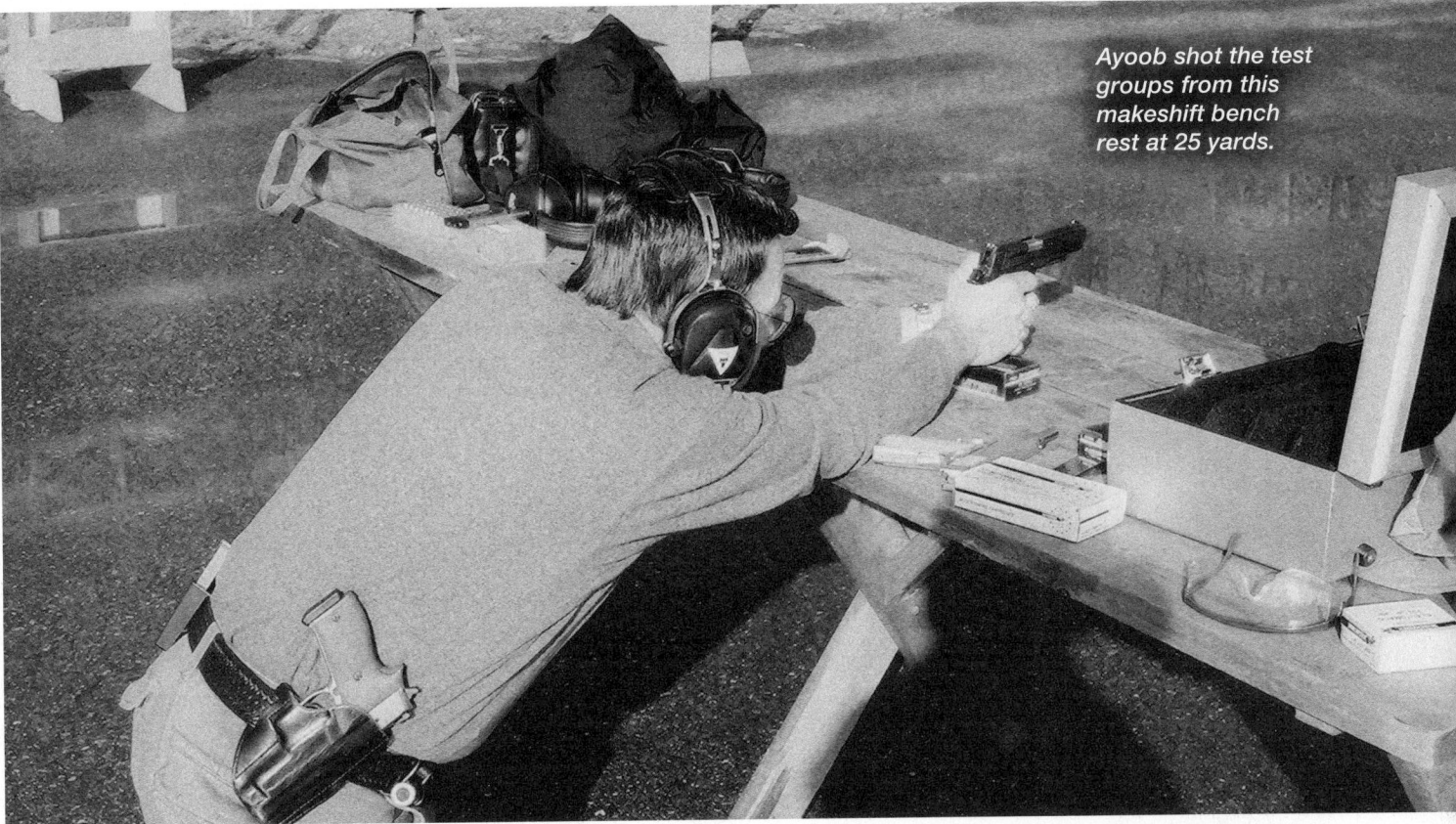

Ayoob shot the test groups from this makeshift bench rest at 25 yards.

Overall, this was excellent performance. The gun didn't group well with CleanFire, but that's common with lead-free primers. It's because of their erratic ignition, which is why CCI/Speer doesn't use them in their famously accurate Gold Dot line, which we unfortunately did not have on hand. The Winchester hollow-point actually outshot the Federal Match. This 230-grain JHP is uncommonly accurate ammunition.

My box was from a law enforcement lot, but Winchester is now running essentially the same load in the generic, low-priced USA line. It is good to see a pistol that delivers champagne performance at beer prices. Note particularly the extraordinary inherent accuracy potential promised by the "best three shot" measurements, with three out of five under an inch.

With none of these rounds did the GSR exhibit the common auto pistol idiosyncrasy known as "4 + 1 syndrome." This is believed to occur when the first hand-cycled round sends its bullet to a different point of impact vis-à-vis point of aim

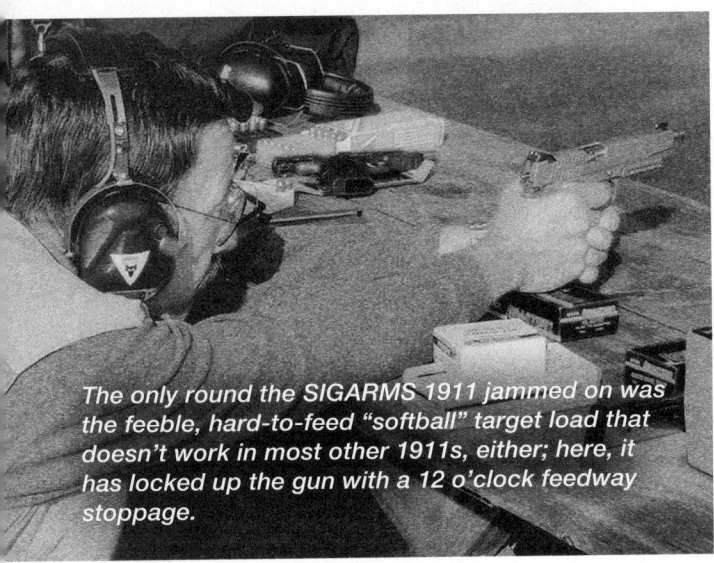

The only round the SIGARMS 1911 jammed on was the feeble, hard-to-feed "softball" target load that doesn't work in most other 1911s, either; here, it has locked up the gun with a 12 o'clock feedway stoppage.

The GSR is very controllable with .45 hardball. World Champ Matt McLearn has a spent casing over his head in mid-air, but is still dead on target.

Manufacturer	Load	5-Shot Group	Best 3 Shots
CCI/Speer Lawman CleanFire	230-grain FMJ	4-5/8"	2-1/4"
Federal Match Midrange	185-grain SWC	1-5/8"	3/4"
PMC	230-grain FMJ	2-1/16"	5/8"
Winchester	230-grain JHP	1-1/4"	3/4"
Winchester USA	230-grain FMJ	1-7/8"	1-1/8"

Even with El Cheapo generic hardball ammo, the GSR delivered this impressive group at 25 yards.

than the subsequent shots. The latter rounds are automatically cycled into the chamber and therefore are fired when the parts have, very subtly, come into a different alignment of firing position, or "battery."

When "4 + 1" doesn't happen with a 1911, you know that there has been some truly superb fitting of parts. This is the case here. "We specify a .752 inch maximum width on the frame rails, and .752 inch *minimum* width on the slide grooves," explains McLearn. The GSR's barrel bushings are fitted snugly, but hand-tight.

The polish is equal in quality to the fit. The slide moves back and forth like a much more expensive semi-custom gun, not a mass-produced one. There is almost no palpable play in the mechanism.

GSR ON THE GSR

In my world, "GSR" stands for "gunshot residue." The SIGARMS GSR pistols were coated with GSR when we were done putting hundreds of rounds through them, often as fast as we could pull the triggers. That might not sound like much until you remember that one of the people running those triggers was former World Champion Matt McLearn, who runs at a speed most shooters can only dream of.

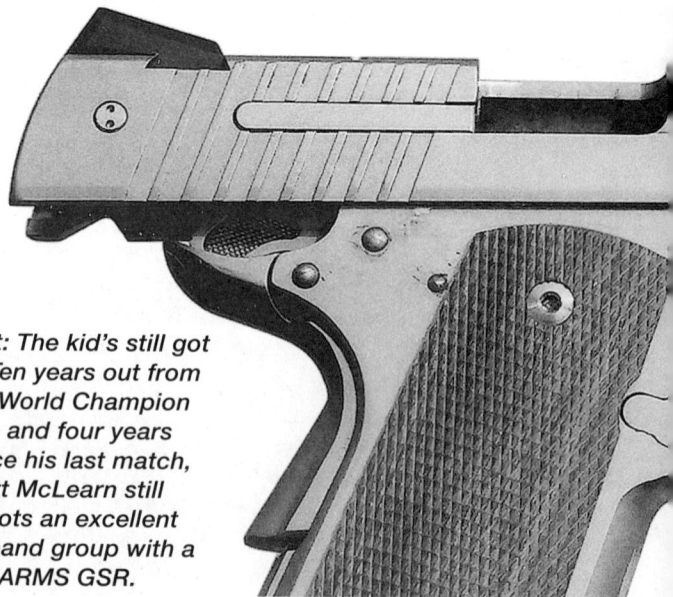

Left: The kid's still got it. Ten years out from his World Champion title and four years since his last match, Matt McLearn still shoots an excellent offhand group with a SIGARMS GSR.

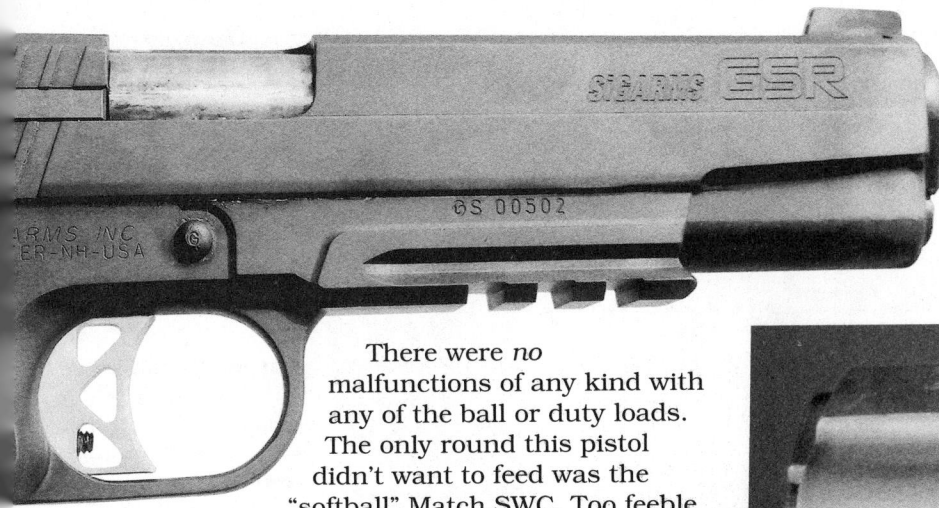

Left: GSR on the GSR. Covered with gunshot residue and filthy from hundreds of rounds, the SIGARMS 1911 was still 100 percent reliable.

Below: The "R" in GSR is the rail machined into the dust cover of the frame.

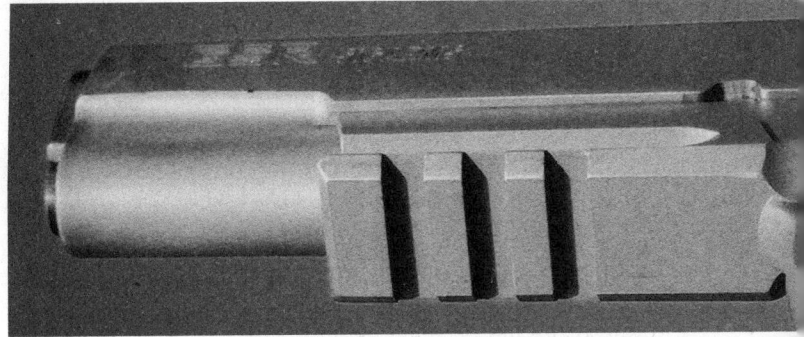

There were *no* malfunctions of any kind with any of the ball or duty loads. The only round this pistol didn't want to feed was the "softball" Match SWC. Too feeble with its low velocity to cycle a pistol with an 18-pound recoil spring, this round is also a nightmare to feed because of its strange button-nosed shape. It was hell for accurate, though. Frankly, I don't see anyone buying this gun to shoot light loads in. It's a defensive piece.

THAT "SIG" LOOK

McLearn's suggestion, "Make this gun look like a SIG," has become a reality. The shape of the slide, narrow above and widening in a band at the bottom, at the middle of the gun, looks "SIG-ish" indeed. The grasping grooves on the slide put you in mind of the extremely ergonomic pattern found on the little P232 .380. It was easy to manipulate. The GSR's trigger guard has a thick, squarish, heavy duty look that is also rather SIG-like, to this reviewer's eye.

Matt says he weighed the GSR on a digital scale and got the standard "Government Model" 39 ounces. Most all steel 1911 "rail guns" are distinctly heavier than that. Sounds as if the reshaping of the

Above: From this perspective we can see the absence of front slide serrations, the absence of a fulllength recoil spring guide, the presence of a light rail on the frame, Novak sights and a Wilson-designed heavy-duty extractor on the slide. These are all good things.

slide has taken some weight off on top, despite the massive look. If you thought the original 1911 was "Old Slabsides," this rendition is more so. Still, the weight saving will be appreciated.

Like other SIGs, and thankfully unlike the current spate of 1911s including even most Colts, this gun did *not* have trendy grasping grooves at the front of the slide. Quite apart from "good looks" and tradition, grooves in that spot encourage shooters to manipulate the slide from the business end, altogether too close to where the bullet comes out. John Browning was wise enough to put the original 1911 grasping grooves at the rear of the slide, where the operating hand will be out of harm's way. I am grateful to McLearn, George Smith (who had a lot of input into the SIGARMS 1911 project), and the company itself for leaving the damn grooves off the front.

The same goes for the welcome absence of a full-length recoil spring guide rod. McLearn and the engineers tested intensively with and without a full-length guide rod, and concluded that it was unnecessary and had no function except to make the gun much more difficult to take apart and reassemble. I had come to that conclusion a long time ago. So had master 1911-smiths like Bill Wilson and Les Baer, and so had gun experts like Charles Petty and Chuck Taylor. So had the 1911 guru, Col. Jeff Cooper, before the rest of us. I, for one appreciate, SIGARMS dispensing with the full-length guide rod.

SIGARMS does not produce a pistol that isn't drop-safe. This one won't change the paradigm. The proven Colt Series 80 passive firing pin lock is employed. I asked if it was licensed from Colt. The reply came with a shrug: "Their patent ran out."

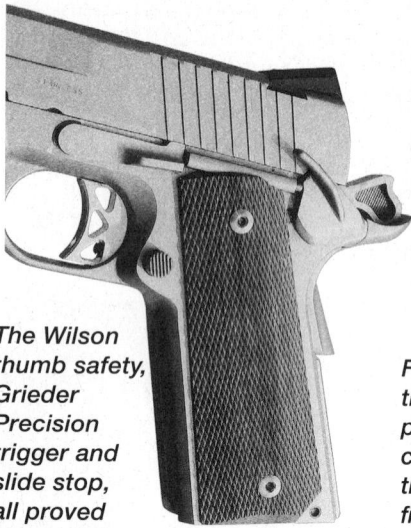

The Wilson thumb safety, Grieder Precision trigger and slide stop, all proved ergonomic.

Falcon high-traction plastic grips complement the Nitron finish of this GSR.

Not your grandfather's 1911, this silvery stainless SIG sports an improved slide grasping groove configuration, Herrett stocks, a state-of-the-art trigger and hammer.

McLearn expanded upon the subtleties of the firing pin safety. "Proper heat treating is important to its function," he said. "Experimentally, we put in a set without hardening the parts and shot hell out of the gun. By 10,000 rounds, we were seeing burrs on the plunger that compromised function. Then we tried again, with the parts properly hardened. There was no change in shape or dimension."

Speaking of parts, most everything will be interchangeable with standard 1911 components. Not the extractor obviously, and not the plunger tube. "We machine a .015" slot into the frame, then stake it on," McLearn explains. "The slot takes all the stress off the tube." Having seen my share of conventionally-staked 1911 plunger tubes come loose and screw up the gun – and having one integral plunger tube on another manufacturer's 1911 break, which effectively killed the frame and required a new frame – this sounds like an improvement to me.

Trigger pull weight is specified at 4.5 to 5.5 pounds, which is just right for a duty or personal protection gun designed to be used under high stress, as opposed to a target pistol. The two we

Below: From this perspective we can see the massive front of the frame, and conventional recoil spring cap.

The classic 1911 "feel" is all there. With a lighter slide, the pistol balances like a standard Government Model despite added frontal weight of the flashlight rail on frame's dust cover.

Right: The manual of arms with the GSR is exactly the same as with John Browning's first 1911. All the controls are in the same place as 92 years before.

The Italian ACT magazines, like the sights, come from Wayne Novak. They work.

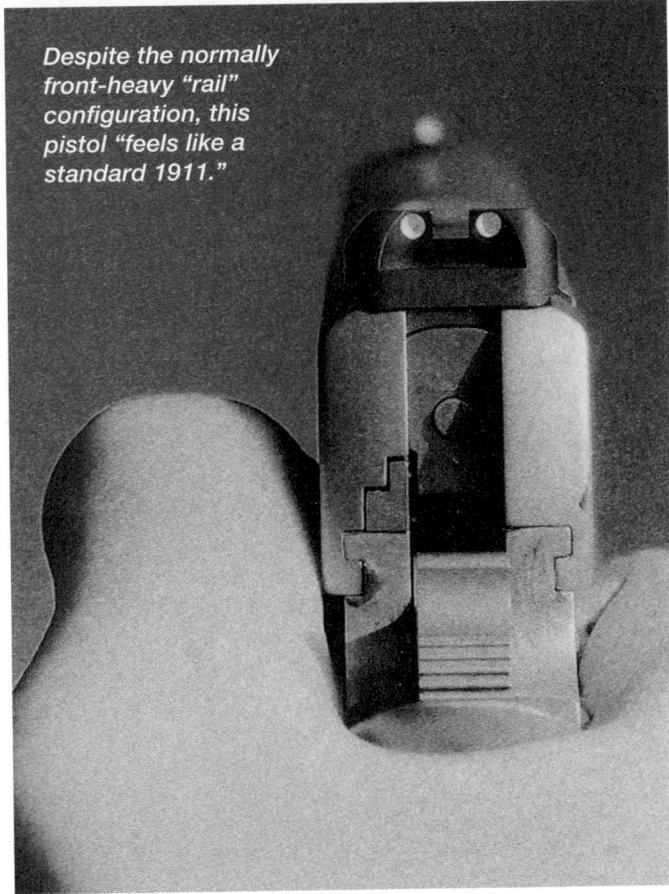

Despite the normally front-heavy "rail" configuration, this pistol "feels like a standard 1911."

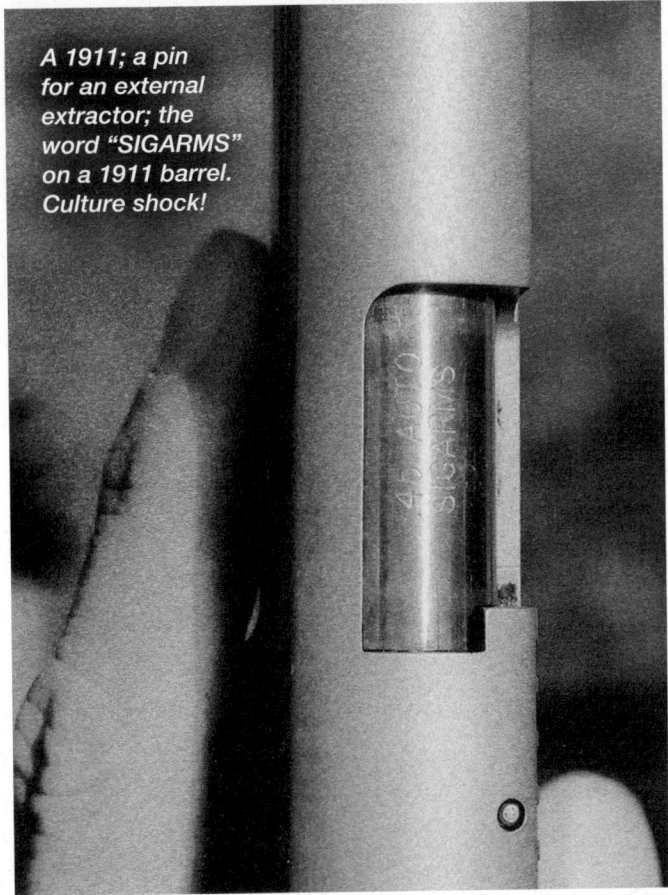

A 1911; a pin for an external extractor; the word "SIGARMS" on a 1911 barrel. Culture shock!

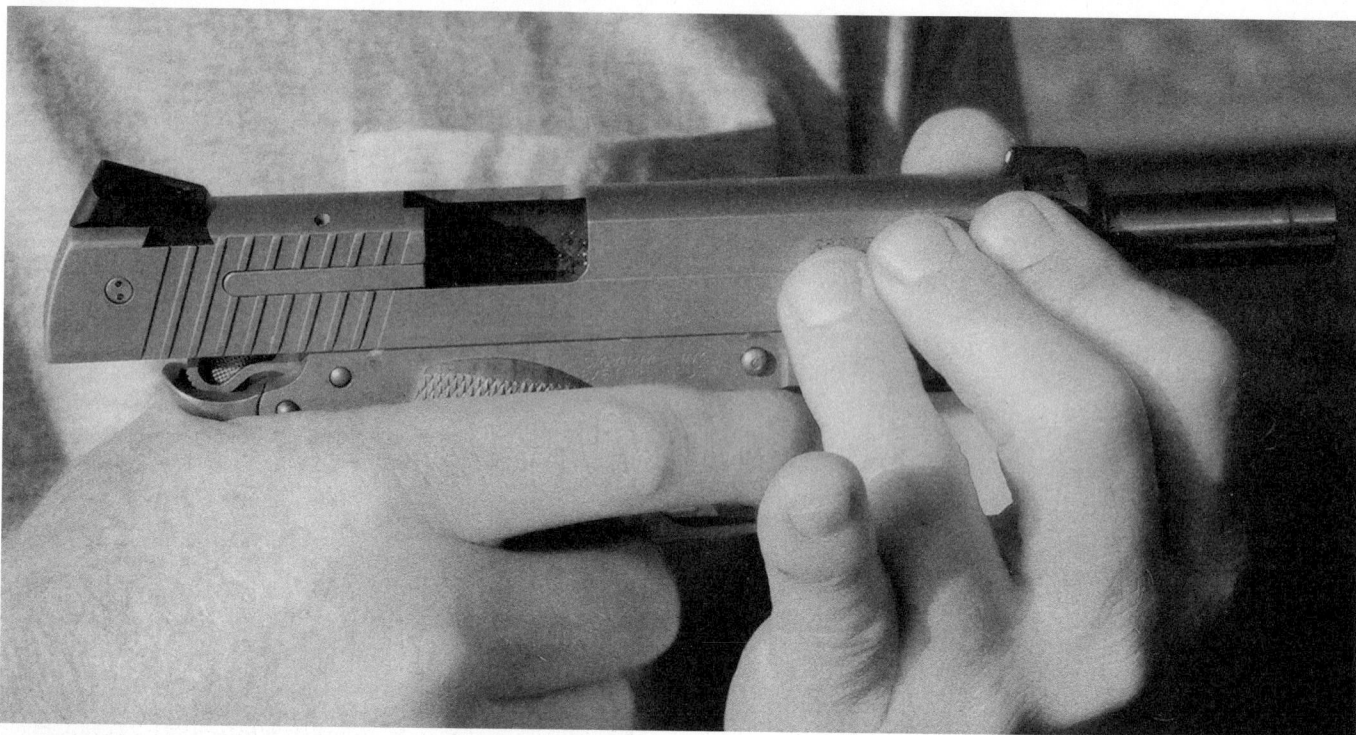

GSR's action is extremely smooth. It can easily be worked from the front even without forward slide serrations.

fired were right in the middle, and felt like about 5 pounds even. Trigger breaks were smooth and clean, and conducive to good hits without the sort of anticipation that makes the shooter jerk the trigger.

Having been an enthusiastic 1911 shooter for some 43 years, I was very impressed with the SIG GSR. Sager, who has been shooting 1911s almost forever, is extremely picky about them, having been spoiled by Wilson Combat and Kimber deluxe target .45s and .38 Supers. He fell in love with the SIGARMS GSR, if not at first sight, certainly at about his first 100 rounds or so.

With a suggested 2004 retail price of $1,077, this gun's smoothness, reliability, and accuracy will make it *extremely* competitive with other top-line 1911 pistols. It equals the performance of some others that cost much more.

The GSR is more than a 1911 story. It ushers in a new period and a new paradigm at SIGARMS, a time when an increasingly Americanized company has now taken a major step away from the European designers at Sauer and Hammerli who once defined what SIG would sell in the United States. This SIG is sweet, but it isn't Sauer.

Yes, GSR stands for **G**ranite **S**eries **R**ail. But in its effective and startling new interpretation of John Browning's classic design, it could also stand for **G**rand **S**IG **R**etro. And, in terms of the company's fast-changing identity, it may also be the first shot in the **G**reat **S**IGARMS **R**evolution.

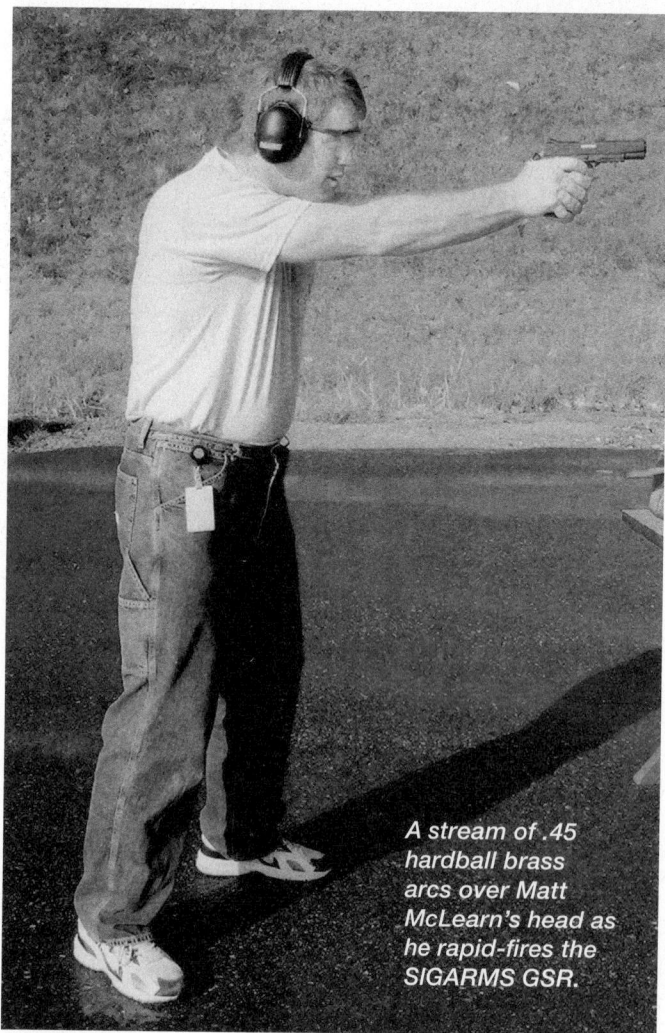

A stream of .45 hardball brass arcs over Matt McLearn's head as he rapid-fires the SIGARMS GSR.

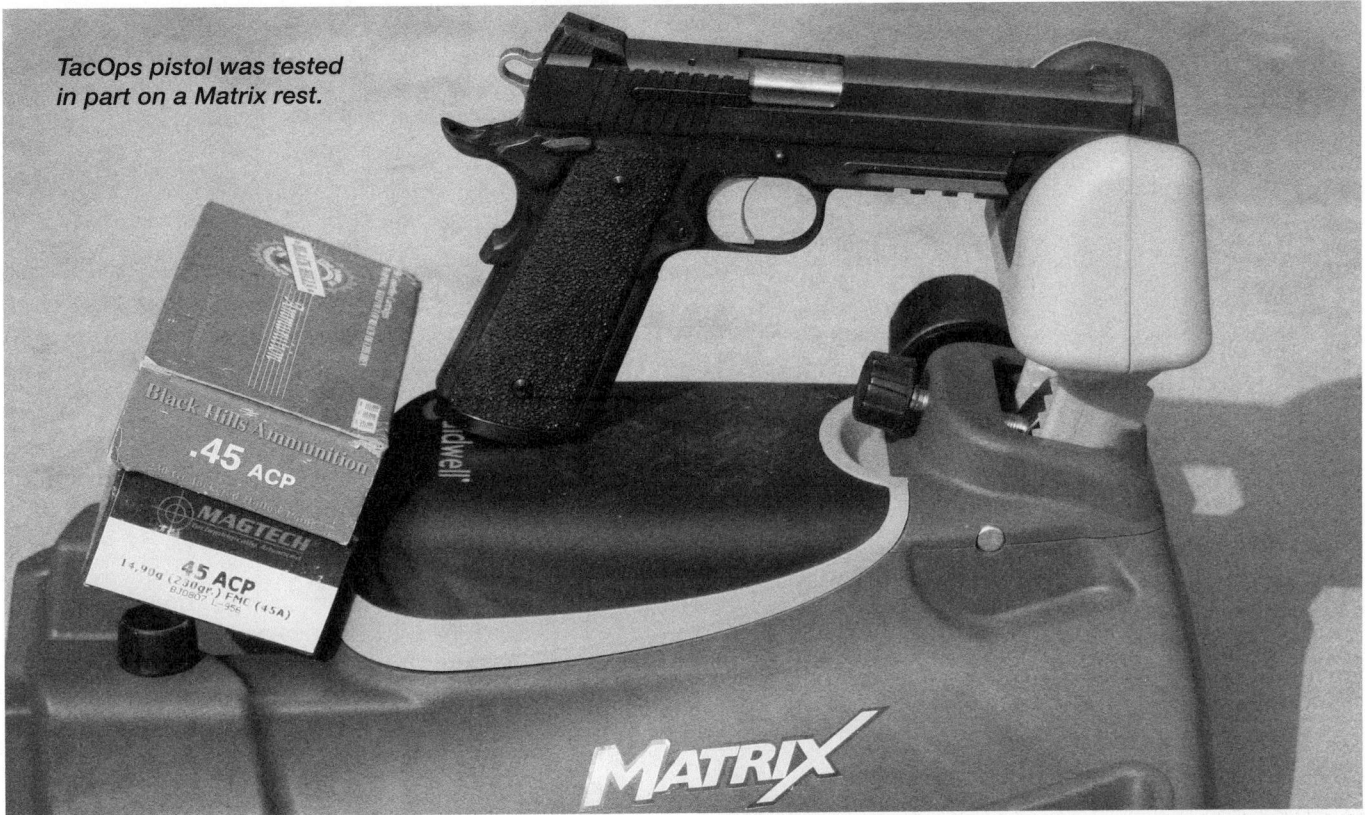

TacOps pistol was tested in part on a Matrix rest.

A PAIR OF SIG PISTOLS, LARGE AND SMALL

As time went on, SIG more and more got away from using vendor components, and more and more toward consolidating production of the line in-house at their New Hampshire plant. The author wrote the following article much later on, assessing later production samples:

Back around 2002, when I wrote up the first SIG 1911 pistol, I called it a SIG that was sweet, and not Sauer. It wasn't just a play on words. Created by USPSA champ and master gunsmith Matt McLearn (www.mattmclearn.com), the SIG-ized 1911 that they introduced as the GSR was the first real, indigenous American SIG. Influenced by neither SIG of Switzerland nor Sauer of Germany, this firstborn of the American entity then known as SIGARMS was fittingly cloned from a uniquely American pistol.

Matt McLearn has gone on to greener pastures in the gun world, and the US arm of SIG has gone from assembling parts from top makers in other parts of the USA to making more and more of their 1911 in-house at their plant in Exeter, NH. New Hampshire is of course the Granite State, and the first iteration of the SIG 1911 was called the GSR to denote Granite State/Rail. It came with an integral light rail as part of the frame's dust cover.

As the photos will show, the passing years have given us versions that are more Granite State than before, being manufactured right there in

The test gun came with FOUR eight-round magazines.

Exeter, but less Rail. Not everyone *wants* a light rail, particularly on a carry gun, since even now concealment holsters for "rail guns" are relatively hard to come by. There are many 1911 enthusiasts who can accept the less-classic lines of SIG's interpretation of the all-American 1911 pistol, but just draw the line at the rail.

It's also well established that the .45 auto is just too big for some people to carry. Call it workplace dress code or complacency, it's a fact of life. That's why small .380s are so popular...and it's why SIG in January '09 introduced a tiny 1911 clone in the

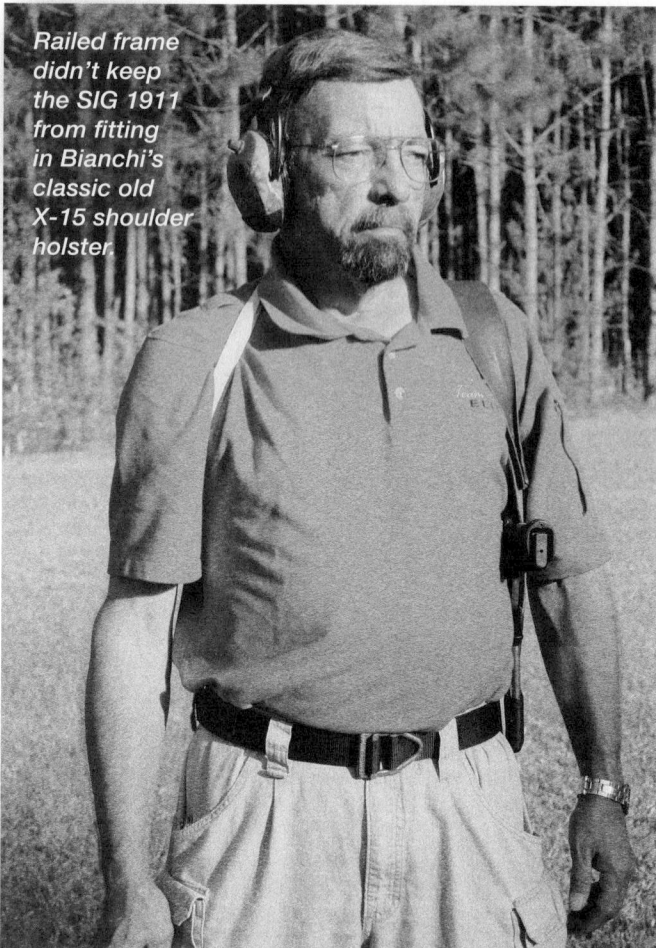

Railed frame didn't keep the SIG 1911 from fitting in Bianchi's classic old X-15 shoulder holster.

short 9mm chambering. If nothing else, the scaled down model makes sense for hideout backup.

THE .45

I took the test pistols to the 25-yard berm on my range, set an MTM rest on the concrete bench there, and proceeded to fire five-shot groups. Over the years I've learned that if an experienced shooter cranks off five braced rounds slow fire and doesn't "feel" anything go bad, the best three shots in the group he or she produces will come remarkably close to what the same gun/ammo combination would have produced from a machine rest. The five-shot group has its own value as a predictor of what one can hope to do on a good day with a solid rest, human error and all, while taking the best three eliminates enough "human factor frailty" to teach a second lesson with the group.

Each group was measured center to center of the farthest-apart holes, to the nearest 0.05 inch. In the big SIG I used three popular brands of .45 ACP ammo, all of proven high quality, that ran the gamut from the lightest to the heaviest in widespread use with this caliber. In alphabetical order:

Black Hills ammunition is famous for its quality control and accuracy. I've won matches with it in 9mm, .40 S&W, .38 Special, and .45 ACP. For the latter, I went with 230 grain jacketed hollow point. With a post-in-notch sight picture (as opposed to using the three-dot image, which will generally send

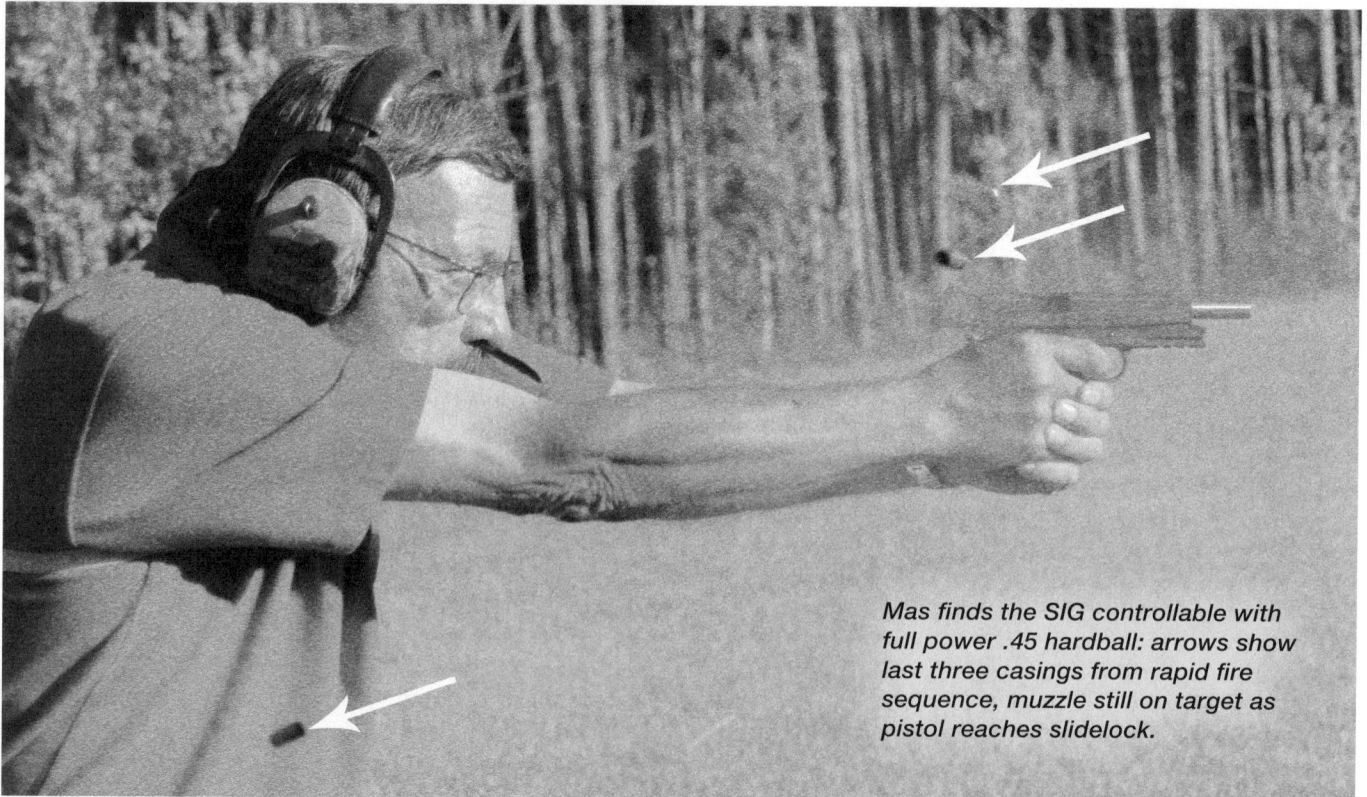

Mas finds the SIG controllable with full power .45 hardball: arrows show last three casings from rapid fire sequence, muzzle still on target as pistol reaches slidelock.

Group at 25 yards was quite satisfactory with Black Hills 230 grain JHP.

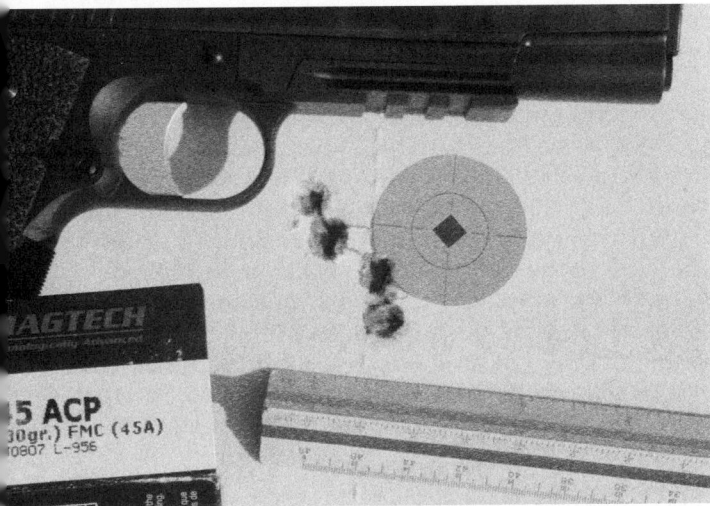

Pleasing group was fired at 25 yards from Matrix rest with MagTech 230 grain FMJ. Note the outstanding "best 3" cluster, including a tight double.

the shots higher), the Black Hills 230 grain JHP centered its group a little over an inch left of point of aim, but pretty much on for elevation. The five shot group measured 2.75 inches, with four of the shots in 1.60 inches and the best three in 1.55 inches.

Hornady XTP ammunition is designed for relatively deep penetration with controlled bullet expansion, a good thing in the light 185 grain bullet weight we chose. Recoil was particularly mild, and the accuracy was the best of the test: five shots in 2.15 inches, with the best three hits 1.75 inches apart. These shots went a little higher than the 230 grain loads tested, but were center for windage.

Winchester Ranger-T ammo is one of the most dynamic high-tech self-defense bullets available today. I've seen its 230 grain .45 ACP version expand to nearly an inch in diameter in ballistic gelatin, and it does fine in the FBI tests through auto glass, fabric, and so forth. In the SIG .45 it

delivered five hits in a cluster that went 2.95 inches, with four of those hits in only 1.80 inches and the best three in a mere 1.35 inches. A crisp trigger in the mid-four pound range helped here. Price is under $1200 at this writing.

RELIABILITY

Only one "jam" occurred in testing the .45, a 6 o'clock misfeed with a Ranger-T round, which was instantly corrected with a slide tug. One of the magazines that came with the pistol started failing to lock the slide open in the middle of the testing, and also became stuck in the pistol during a reload. This did not occur with the other factory magazine, nor did it occur with Wilson and Dave Lauck magazines that were also tested.

SIG P238 .380

This new SIG single action .380 looks so much like the old Colt Mustang that some on the Internet

Fixed sights sent 230 grain rounds a little high, but centered for windage, at 25 yards.

SIG now produces a huge variety of 1911s.

theorize SIG bought the rights from Colt. Bud Fini of SIG says, "We bought nothing from Colt. Although the Mustang was the inspiration, we designed the internals and gave it the SIG look."

Designed for cocked and locked carry, its thumb safety is set up for right hand use only. Ours came with big, blocky night sights that are easy to see in all light conditions, with MSRP of $686; price would be $543 without the Tritium sights. Notes Fini, "Trigger is metal (MIM part)...grips are or will be in future models made of plastic, aluminum and rosewood...Aluminum frame, machined right here from a solid billet...Recoil spring weight is approximately 10.5 pounds."

With that light spring, and the hammer cocked to relieve mainspring pressure, this pistol's slide should be the easiest to manipulate among the current crop of very small .380s. The P238 was designed as a six-plus-one shot pistol, but some magazines have gotten out that won't lock into the gun with the slide forward unless downloaded to five rounds.

Factory sources say that magazine follower design is being addressed. There was a recall of some 1400 early production P238s because, if the trigger was pulled with the thumb safety engaged, the hammer could fall to half cock when the safety lever was pressed down. By the time you read this, all new P238s on dealer shelves will likely have the safety problem squared away, and be equipped with true six-round magazines. Mine ran fine loaded all the way up to seven, by the way.

SHOOTING THE P238

On the Lyman trigger pull gauge, this pistol's average pull weight was seven and three-quarter pounds but frankly, felt like half that or a little more. The trigger is close-coupled to the small frame, with a very short reach. This makes it perfect for short-fingered folk, and for those with average length fingers like mine, it gets the finger deep into the trigger for lots of leverage, which makes it *feel* lighter. The pull has a very short take-up, then a smooth, rolling release conducive to the desirable surprise trigger break.

ACCURACY

Alas, this .380 test sample came out of the box with its front sight way left in its dovetail, and its rear fixed night sight, way right. Either of these by itself would make the pistol shoot to the right, and in tandem the effect was such that shots aimed at the center hit the right edge of the IPSC silhouette or missed it entirely. Lacking the proper sight-pushing tool on the range, I resorted to the expedient of turning the targets horizontal and putting the aiming dots on the far left.

One of many stylized limited runs of SIG 1911s.

Colt/Browning style slide treatment, as shown here, is seen on some 20% of SIG's 1911s.

In bright sunlight, however, the angle of the front sight was such that glare on its face caused the silhouette of the front sight to disappear. The circle of the Tritium module was still visible, of course, but that made it a one-dot sight in a rear notch, or three dots. The latter is a good expedient for close, fast shooting but neither sight picture is conducive to accurate hits at 25 yards. So, I used a movie title as a strategy ("Wait Until Dark") and put high beam headlights on the target, which now gave me a silhouetted sight picture.

It was in the midst of the Great Ammo Drought of Ought-Nine, and few mainstream calibers were scarcer than .380. I had managed to get my hands on two loads, 88 grain **CCI Blazer** jacketed hollow point, and some generic round-nose 90 grain full metal jacket. The FMJ shot atrociously, putting three or so reasonably close together and then sending a couple of bullets far, far away. The best I could get with it was a three-shot group of 1.65 inches within a five-

shot group that would have been better measured with a yardstick than a ruler. However, the low-price aluminum case Blazer JHP punched five shots into 5.35 inches, with four of those in 2.05 inches and the best three in an inch and three quarters. I have a feeling it will shoot better than that under better circumstances. The sights were part of it: we later installed some of the way cool Advantage Tactical sights on this gun, but deadline came upon us before we could repeat the accuracy test with them. Suffice to say that the P238 will group "minute of brain stem" at seven yards.

Recoil was negligible. You could practically watch this .380's sights go back and forth. No pinching of the web of the hand by the hammer, as a couple of European designs are infamous for.

In 100 rounds (half 88 grain JHP, half 95 grain FMJ), no malfunctions of any kind occurred in actual firing. With the hollow point, we noticed that when reloading from slide-lock, there would sometimes be a six o'clock misfeed, which was always easily cleared by tugging the slide all the way back and releasing it. That never happened with the FMJ (more tapered feeding profile) and never happened with either round when the slide was tugged all the way rearward (giving it a slightly longer, stronger throw) to chamber the first round.

The left thumb got dinged by the sharp edge of the protruding slide stop when firing right hand/two hand with thumbs straight forward. This grasp also sometimes caused the thumb to "ride" the slide stop and prevent it from locking open in firing. Neither problem occurred when shooting southpaw or with the thumb(s) curled down.

My friend Jim McLoud has over 3000 rounds through his P238 without a malfunction, and loves the little thing. For those in the market for a very small, reasonably light .380, the SIG P238 has a lot to recommend it.

THE SIG 1911 MARCHES ON

When the first edition of this book appeared, the 1911 line was still very new with SIG. A decade later, it has become the fifth biggest seller in the SIG-Sauer catalog. Here's my test of a TACOPS model in 2011, from **On Target.**

SIG 1911-R-TACOPS .45

For most of a decade, SIG has been upgrading their US-made 1911s...and this specimen shows it.

Early in the first decade of the 21st Century, SIGARMS brought in pistol champion and master 1911 pistolsmith Matt McLearn to build a uniquely SIG-ish pistol for them in the classic American style. Since it came from the company's American factory in Exeter, New Hampshire, the Granite State, they called the gun the GSR for Granite State/Rail. The last part of the appellation denoted the fact that it had an integral light rail on its dust cover, something of a radical departure for a 1911 style pistol at that time.

The original plan was to have as many components as possible built by fine-quality US makers: after all; 1911 parts had become a cottage industry. Alas, there was instance after instance of cases where vendor parts were out of spec, resulting in guns that weren't up to the standards of either SIG or their customers. The company moved toward making more of their own components, in house. Soon, the problems seemed to fade away.

Now, years later, we have the SIG 1911-R-TACOPS, the "R" of course for the still-present rail (though in deference to popular American tastes, SIG has also made slimmer variations without the rail for some time), and the "TACOPS" for "tactical operations." That includes working in darkness, hence the rail for the light, and also the Novak night sights that come standard.

Our test sample at *On Target*, serial numberGS30934, came with an ambidextrous safety whose twin levers were exactly the right size (subjective opinion) for this tester, and perfectly adjusted (objective opinion). Hard stippled grip panels (Ergo XT) that felt a bit like skateboard tape, and fine checkering on frontstrap and backstrap. An integral magazine funnel for swift loading/reloading. A solid-configuration "long trigger" (this shooter, with average adult male size hands, had to contact the trigger with the pad of the index finger, and couldn't do it comfortably with the distal joint). No forward slide serrations, and no full length guide rod, both good things in this reviewer's subjective opinion developed over half a century of shooting 1911 .45s.

This first time shooter is very happy with her SIG P238.

Action smoothness in terms of running the slide was sweet: not quite the "oiled ball bearing feel" of a pre-war Colt National Match, but fairly close. The trigger pull averaged six pounds, 1.5 ounces with a very little bit of takeup and no significant backlash, but was so well executed it felt lighter. The beavertail grip safety proved very comfortable in every hand that held it. And, wonder of wonders, the test sample came with four, count them, *four* stainless eight round magazines with bumper pads. Clearly, SIG has been listening to its serious end-users!

ON THE FIRING LINE

With its 40-ounce (on my scale, anyway) solid steel weight, and well-thought-out grip configuration, this 5-inch barrel .45 didn't move at all in the hand in firing, and its recoil allowed double taps and longer "bursts" to stay on target. None of the testers found it unpleasant to shoot.

From the 25 yard line, with a Caldwell Matrix rest from Battenfeld Technologies on a concrete bench, I tested for accuracy with two flavors of the .45 ACP's most popular "food group," the 230 grain standard velocity load. Black Hills red box jacketed hollow point plunked five rounds into 1.40 inches measured center to center, with the best three of them in nine-tenths of one inch. MagTech 230 grain full metal jacket was almost as tight for five shots, at 1.65 inches, but even tighter for the best three, at half an inch even for that measurement. The years have taught me that the "best three" measurement factors out enough human error in hand-held fire from a bench to give a very good idea of what all five rounds might have done from a machine rest.

Thanks to the funnel, reloads were fast and smooth. However, the funnel's bottom edges were a little too sharp toward the front and could stand to be rounded. Hits were reasonably centered for windage at 25 yards and about two and a half inches high, meaning that with a six-o'clock hold the gun came out of the box shooting spot on.

Reliability, of course, is the key thing...and in the course of the test, there were no malfunctions of any kind. 100% reliability is the baseline for anything serious, and the SIG 1911-R-TACOPS seemed to deliver that, right out of the starting gate.

SUMMARY

One downside of an integral rail 1911 is that there aren't nearly as many holsters available for it as for more common railed guns like the Glock. This one fit reasonably well in an old Bianchi X-15 shoulder holster, and a Quad Concealment holster from Elmer McEvoy's Leather Arsenal (www.leatherarsenal.com) that was made specifically for a railed SIG 1911. It concealed fine under a

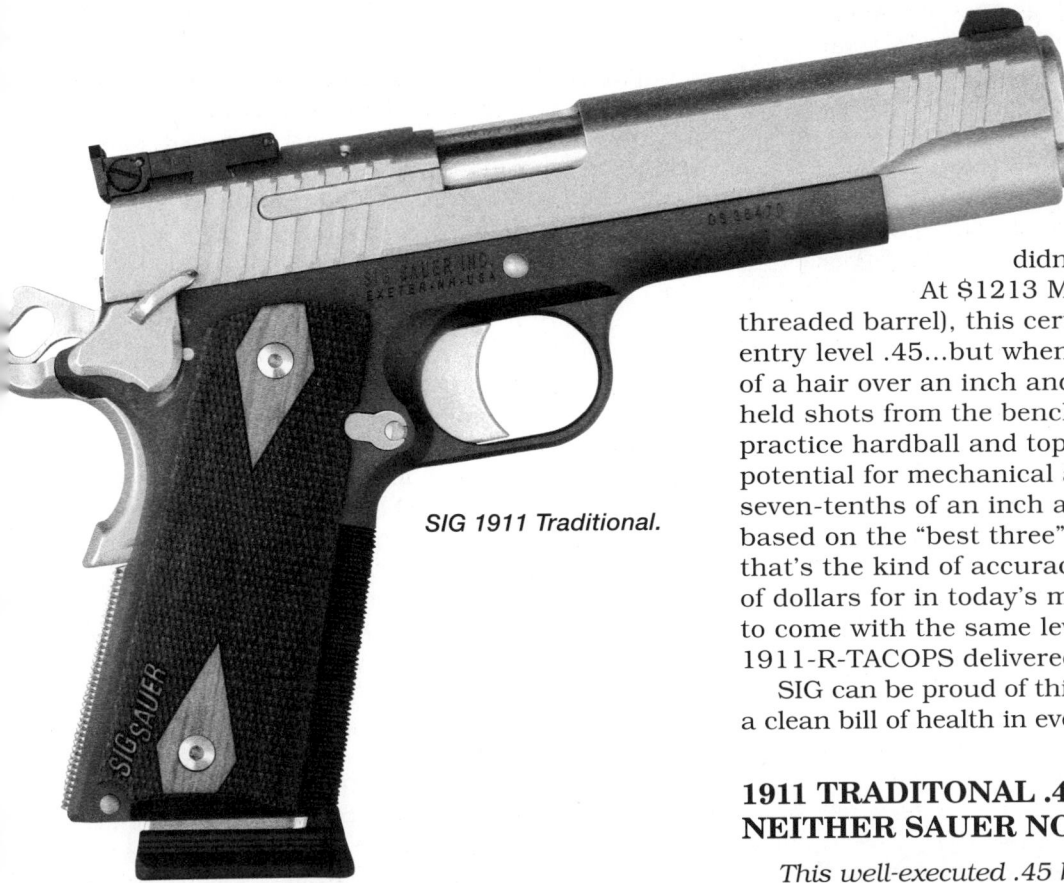

SIG 1911 Traditional.

photographer's vest or unbuttoned, untucked safari shirt. With the rough-surface grips, it might have been a little less comfortable in deep concealment against bare skin. I dunno...I didn't try that.

At $1213 MSRP ($1235 with threaded barrel), this certainly isn't a low-priced entry level .45...but when you look at an average of a hair over an inch and a half for five hand-held shots from the bench, with economy brand practice hardball and top quality JHP, *and a* potential for mechanical accuracy averaging seven-tenths of an inch at the same distance based on the "best three" measurements...well, that's the kind of accuracy you pay thousands of dollars for in today's market, if you expect it to come with the same level of reliability the SIG 1911-R-TACOPS delivered.

SIG can be proud of this one. Our sample earned a clean bill of health in every respect.

1911 TRADITONAL .45: A SIG THAT'S NEITHER SAUER NOR SOUR

This well-executed .45 brings SIG's 1911 back to a more conventional look.

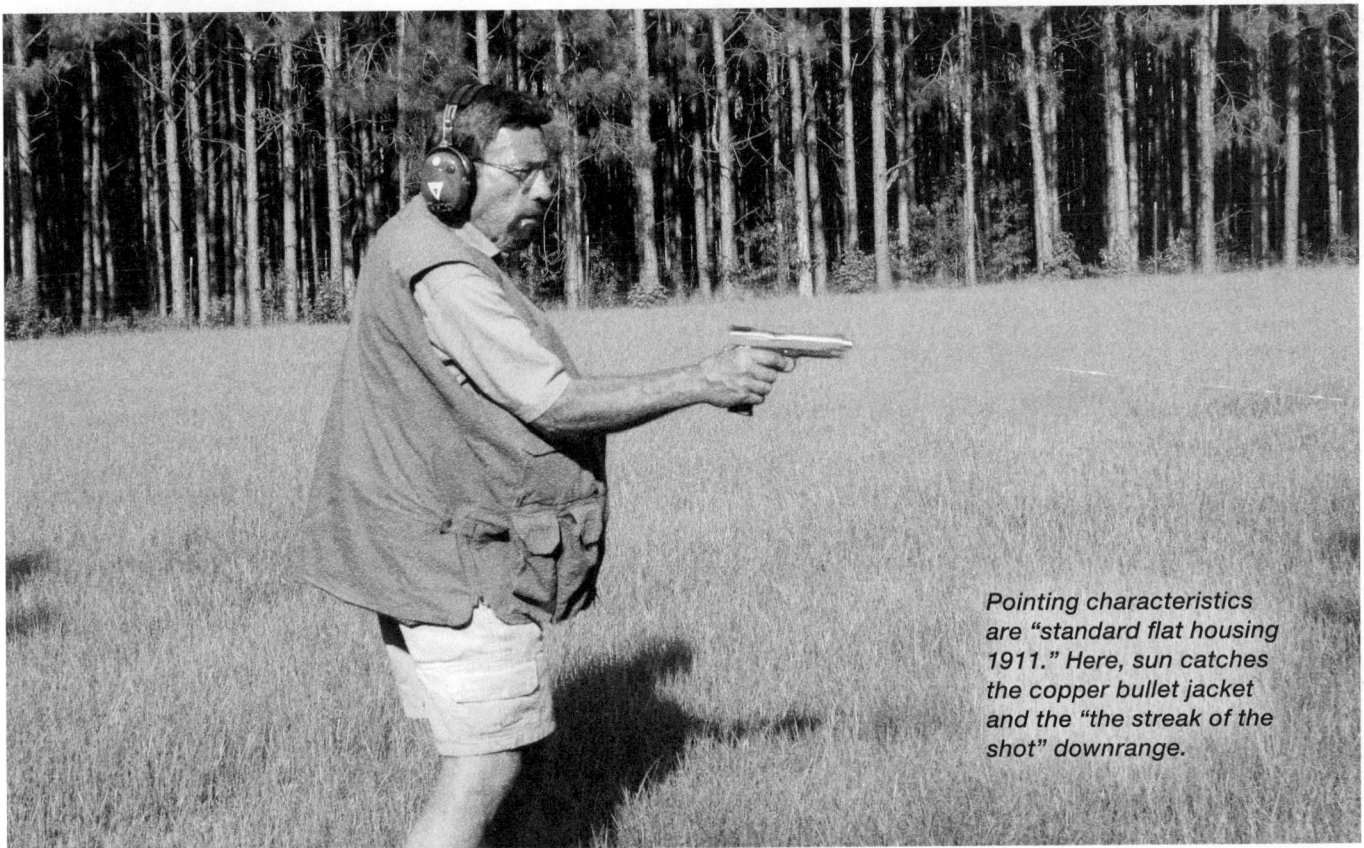

Pointing characteristics are "standard flat housing 1911." Here, sun catches the copper bullet jacket and the "the streak of the shot" downrange.

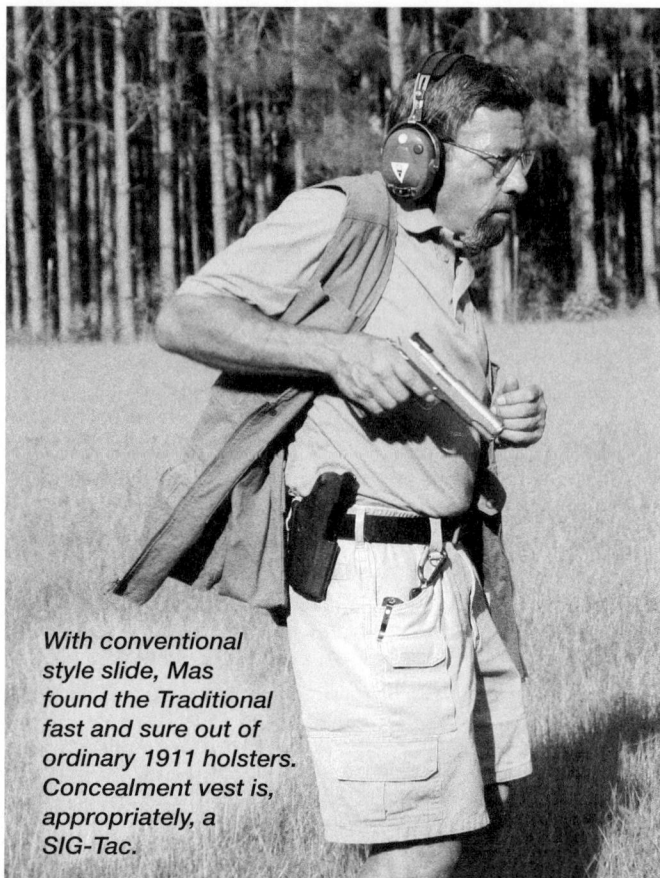

With conventional style slide, Mas found the Traditional fast and sure out of ordinary 1911 holsters. Concealment vest is, appropriately, a SIG-Tac.

When SIG introduced their 1911 in 2003, it didn't exactly *look* like a 1911. SIG's Mark Kresser had brought in Matt McLearn to lead the project, and instructed him, "Make it look like a SIG." Matt was a top 1911-smith as well as a world champion shooter, and what he brought forth along with industrial designer Chris Aiston and mechanical engineer Kevin Webber was a 1911 that was...different.

It was among the first 1911s to have a light rail machined right into the frame, helping to give it the name SIG GSR. Produced in Exeter, NH, the Granite State, the GSR's name stood for **G**ranite **S**tate **R**ail. The slide was sculpted in the fashion of the P-226 and P-220 pistols that had justly earned fame for the joint Swiss-German efforts of SIG and Sauer. As a result, there were few 1911 holsters the pistol would fit...and some 1911 enthusiasts for whom "the look" would just never be right.

Under CEO Ron Cohen, SIG has learned to listen intently to the end-users of its products, and one result of that is a new variation of the SIG 1911. Called the Traditional for obvious reasons, it fits both the old holsters and the old image of the classic John M. Browning design, and its introduction in 2011 seems an appropriate *homage* to the centennial of this grand old handgun. The company is now called SIG-SAUER in all caps, and that's what's marked on the slide, but that's the only Sauer vestige in this SIG-made 1911.

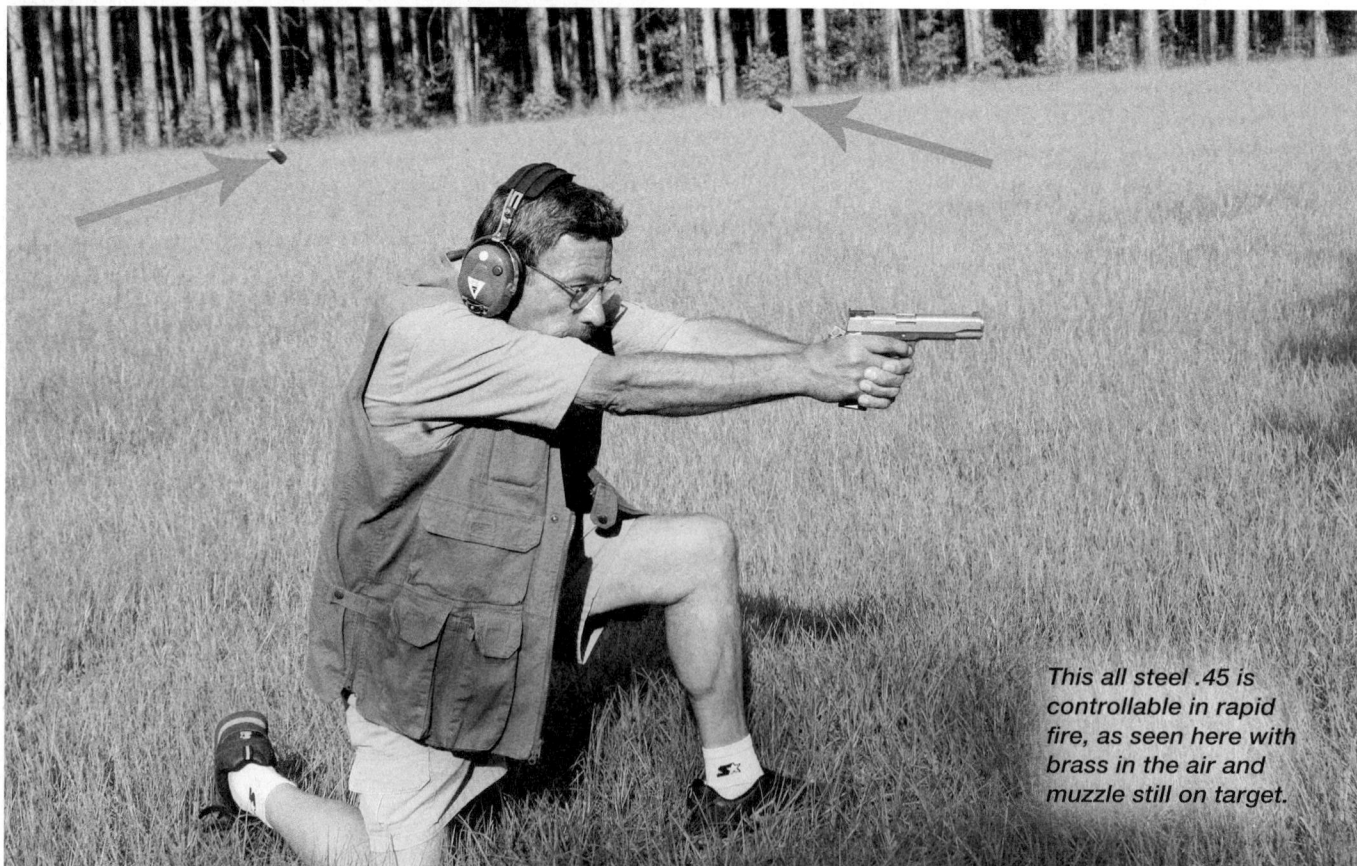

This all steel .45 is controllable in rapid fire, as seen here with brass in the air and muzzle still on target.

FIRST LOOK

All steel with a two-tone finish, the Traditional lives up to its name with standard JMB bushing and short recoil spring guide rod. Keng's adjustable sights ride atop it, with three white dots inset. Front strap and back strap, the latter with flat mainspring housing, are nicely checkered, as are the walnut stocks, also traditional with diamond-cuts around the screw holes. Non-traditional, however, are the subtle raised letters on the stock panels that spell "SIG-SAUER." The same is true of the forward slide grooves everyone seems to demand today.

The ambidextrous thumb safety features levers shorter than are popular today, but still amply sized for fast handling. More to the point, they're not so big that a forearm brushes them unintentionally into the "fire" position while walking down the street with the gun in the holster. I liked this feature very much.

Harkening back to the pistol the US Government adopted in March of 1911, we have not only that flat housing, but also a long, solid trigger, though this one is adjustable via Allen wrench. The magazine well is lightly beveled. The one feature that would probably raise JMB's eyebrows would be the externally mounted extractor, a signature of the SIG 1911 since its inception. A handsome two-tone finish, something that became popular among 1911 aficionados in the last half of the 20th century, completes the package.

ON THE FIRING LINE

From the first chamber check, it was apparent that this pistol had a pleasingly smooth-running slide. The only sharp edges were on the lower edge of the right portion of the ambidextrous thumb safety, and the rear sight. Rather than rounding the sharp corners of the old BoMar target sight it brings to mind, the Keng's rear adjustable on this gun has corners cut at 45-degree angles. There are

still edges that can be hostile to the hand in rapid slide manipulation, such as practicing malfunction clearance drills. (Fortunately, we didn't have to do that. The pistol ran fine with everything from light loads to full power, and with magazines ranging

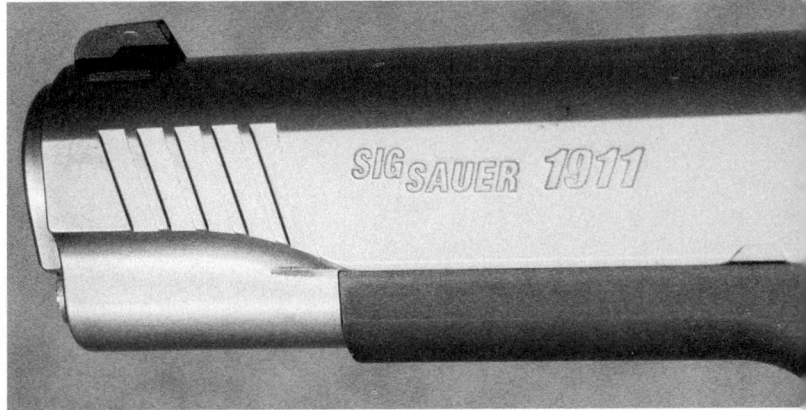

The only real "Sauer" influence on this all-American SIG, author feels, is the name on the slide.

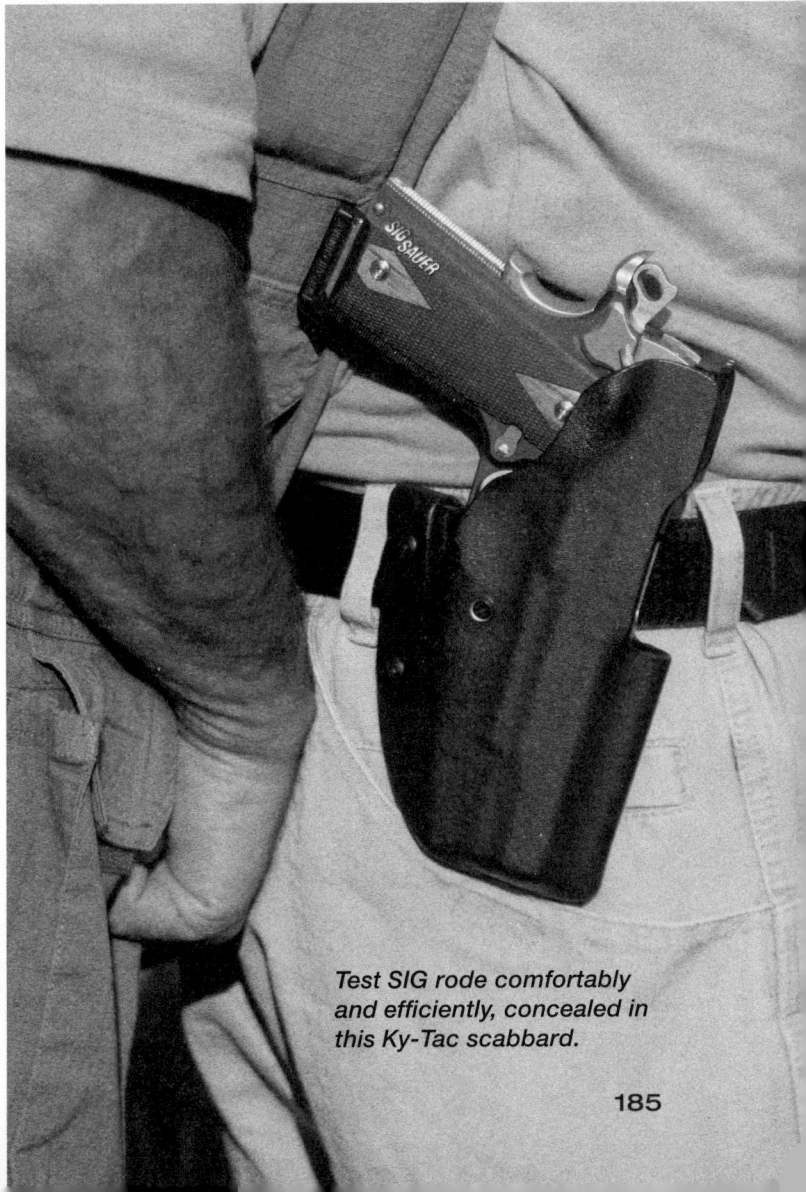

Test SIG rode comfortably and efficiently, concealed in this Ky-Tac scabbard.

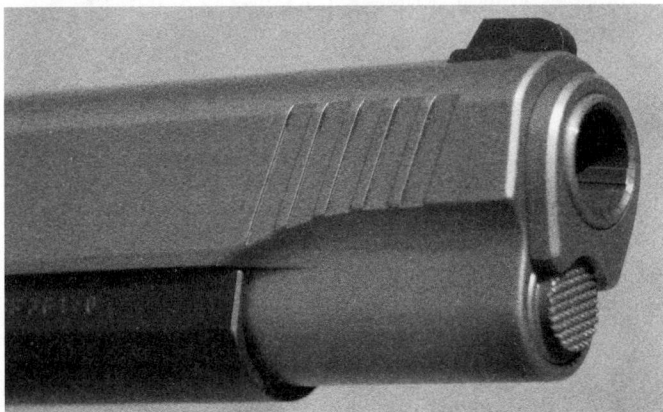

Old and new: here we see "JMB traditional" bushing and recoil spring plug, but also the currently trendy forward slide grooves on the SIG Traditional.

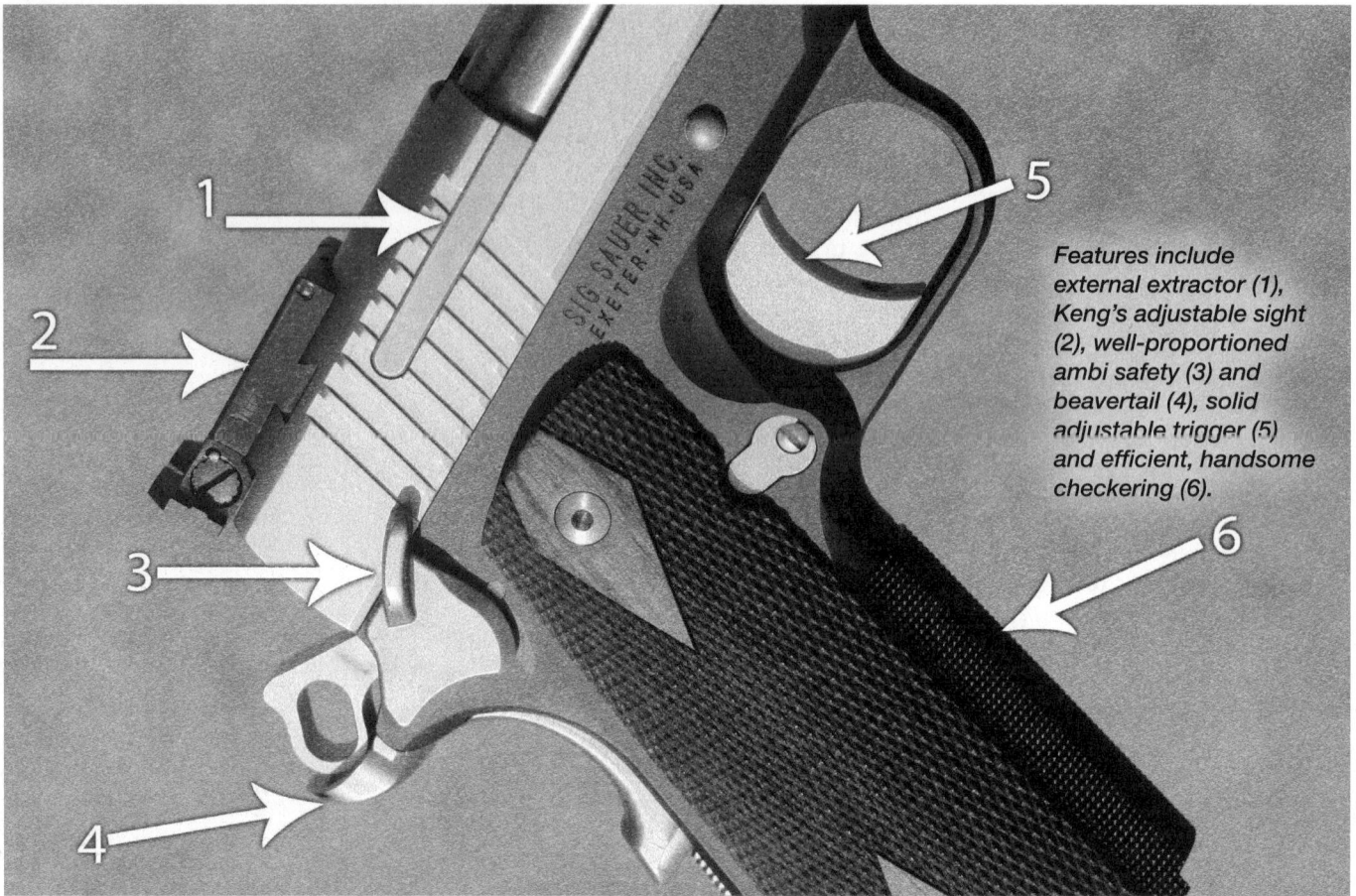

Features include external extractor (1), Keng's adjustable sight (2), well-proportioned ambi safety (3) and beavertail (4), solid adjustable trigger (5) and efficient, handsome checkering (6).

from the two Mec-Gars that came with it, to my own Wilson EDMs. There were no malfunctions whatever in the course of a few hundred rounds.)

In 2003, the plan had been to assemble the guns in Exeter with top-quality parts from famous vendors. Following the short historical trail of the SIG 1911, we find the occasional skid mark. SIG insiders confided to me that they were frustrated by how many vendor parts were not to spec, including one particular batch of those external extractors that got SIG some bad reviews for reliability by shooters. SIG eventually moved more of the

The Traditional has the traditional slimness of the 1911, and is well put together.

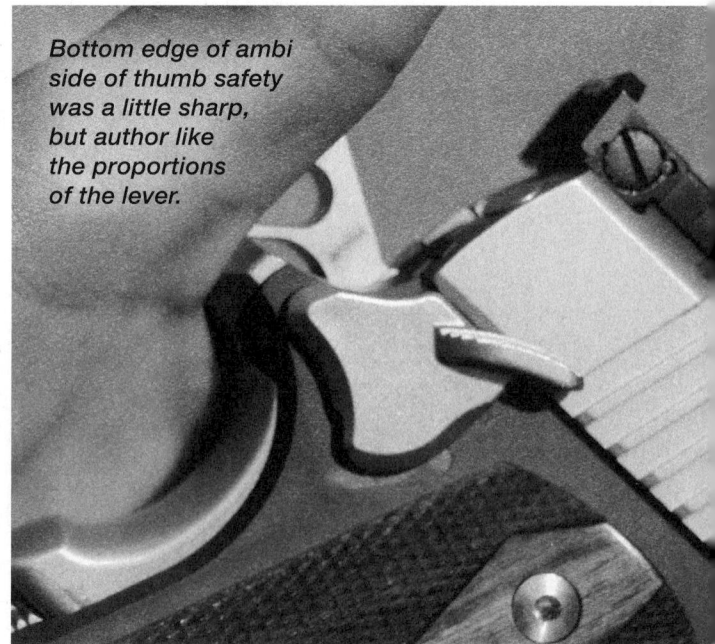

Bottom edge of ambi side of thumb safety was a little sharp, but author like the proportions of the lever.

component manufacture in-house, and that seems to have solved the problem. All I can say is, test gun number GS 36470 ran flawlessly.

On the Lyman digital trigger scale from Brownell's, average pull weight proved to be five pounds, 9.3 ounces. (Original GI spec for the 1911, if memory serves, was a pull weight of five to seven pounds...it's that Traditional thing again.) This is actually a pretty logical pull weight for a defensive handgun that might be used in hands that are shaking from adrenaline dump. The pull has a touch of "good creep," by which I mean you can feel it starting to move, but it's a smooth movement with no fits and starts, and conducive to the "surprise break" marksmen strive for.

On a Matrix rest at 25 yards, Winchester's light 185 grain total metal jacket target load ran five shots into a 2.45-inch group, four of those in under two inches (1.95), and the best three in just 1.05 inches. The 1911's natural food, you might say, is 230 grain .45 ACP hardball, and that was represented here by Winchester's USA brand "white box," the single load I see .45 shooters bring most often to class and to IDPA and GSSF matches. The SIG Traditional put five of these in 2.40 inches, with four of those in 1.10 inches and the best three, in 1.05 inches.

In modern defensive handgunning, of course, we use jacketed hollow points for what gun writers used

Keng's rear sight is angled on corners rather than rounded, and serrated to prevent reflection.

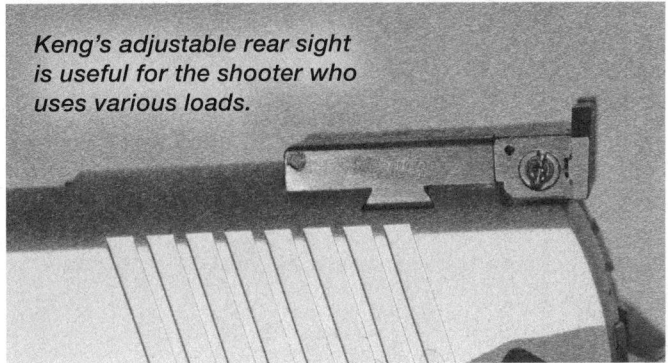

Keng's adjustable rear sight is useful for the shooter who uses various loads.

These were the three loads selected for accuracy testing.

to euphemistically call "serious social purposes." We tested with Black Hills 230 grain JHP, and got the best group of the day: five shots in 1.60 inches. Four of those five were in 1.30 inches, and the best three were all under an inch at 0.90 inch.

For many years, I've taken that "best three" measurement along with the whole five-shot group (center to center between the farthest-apart hits, to the nearest 0.05 inch) because testing has taught me that this second measurement eliminates enough unnoticed human error from the equation to roughly equal what the same gun/load combination will usually do from a machine rest. Thus, the "best three" group is the predictor of the gun's inherent grouping ability. With "best three" measurements of 1.05 inches with both of the low price practice loads, and under an inch with hollow point service ammo, I think it's safe to say that the Traditional can be expected to be a "one inch gun" at 25 yards.

All these loads grouped way low left of point of aim. Yes, that's what adjustable sights are for, but on a pistol with a suggested retail of $1,128, you'd expect someone to have taken the time to make sure it shot to the sights before it went into the shipping box.

CARRYING THE SIG TRADITIONAL .45

I wore this gun cocked and locked for a couple of days in a Ky-Tac concealment hip holster. It was no more uncomfortable to carry than any other full-size, all steel 1911 .45. Those sharp edges on the center front top of the rear sight, while unfriendly to the manipulating hand, are out of the way of concealing garments and do not snag or slice the fabric.

BOTTOM LINE

While on the West Coast recently doing a case for a sheriff's department, I learned that the agency had tired of their previous "carry what you want" policy and given their deputies a choice between one of two very different SIG pistols. One choice was the double action SIG-Sauer P229 in .357 SIG. The other option was the SIG 1911 in .45 ACP. The firearms instructors told me the department split right down the middle, with the two styles proving equally popular among the troops. The agency seems happy with this protocol.

If the customers are happy, SIG is happy. The Traditional is definitely worth a look for anyone interested in an accurate, reliable, well-made 1911 .45 auto that combines modern performance with classic styling.

Soft-loaded 185 grain Winchester delivered this group at 25 yards. Note the best three hits.

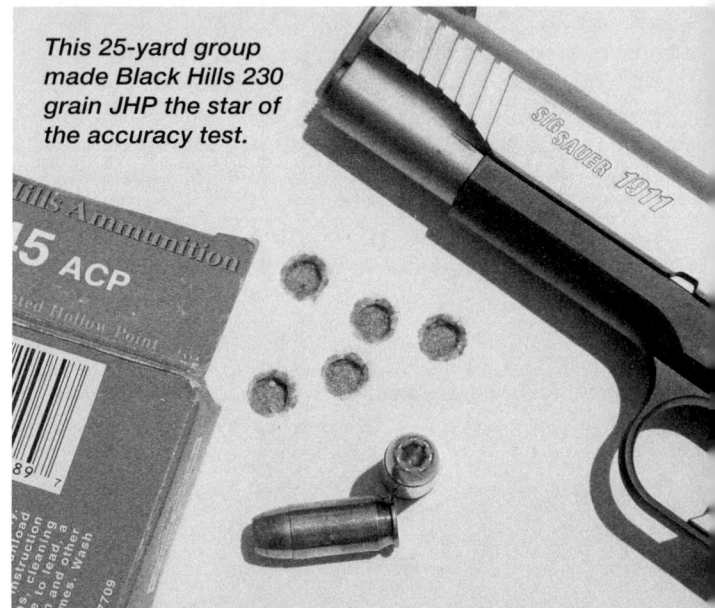

This 25-yard group made Black Hills 230 grain JHP the star of the accuracy test.

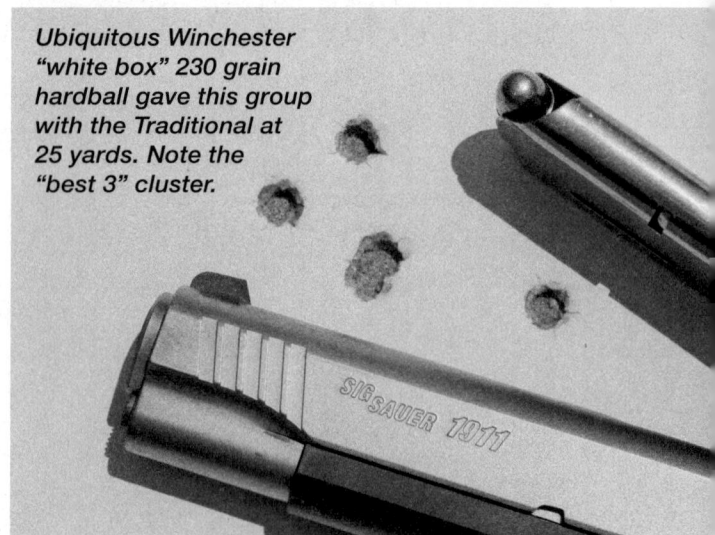

Ubiquitous Winchester "white box" 230 grain hardball gave this group with the Traditional at 25 yards. Note the "best 3" cluster.

Chapter 19
Manipulation of the Pistol

Fans of the brand like to say, "SIG stands for **S**imple **I**s **G**ood." There is truth in that. One reason so many police departments chose the SIG-Sauer when the time came to switch from revolvers to autos was its relative ease of training.

What had roughly a century of policing with the double action revolver taught cops they needed to know about combat handguns? How to load and unload, both in conditions of calm and under stress at high speed. How to fire both single-action and double-action. How to cock and decock. How to take the gun apart was a topic that was *not* taught in police classes, because it was perceived, correctly, that any operator who hadn't spent at least a week at a factory-sponsored armorer's school might not be able to disassemble one and put it back together perfectly.

What needs to be taught to a new operator with the SIG-Sauer semiautomatic pistol? Well, see if this sounds familiar. There's how to load and unload, both in conditions of calm and under stress at high speed. How to fire both single-action and double-action. How to cock and decock, and frankly, you can leave out the "cocking" part because that will take place during the loading process. How to disassemble and reassemble the gun *is* a proper topic for the operator of a SIG-Sauer, because its mechanism is actually so much simpler than a revolver's that it can be taught to anyone competent enough to fire it.

Before we go on, it is important to make the distinction between *administrative* handling and *combat* handling, as the terms have been distinguished in law enforcement training. Administrative handling encompasses routine loading and unloading, checking, and assembly/disassembly. Combat handling is practice for what would likely take place in an actual gunfight. It includes shooting, speed reloading, tactical reloading, and drawing and holstering. Firing is actually treated separately from handling per se.

189

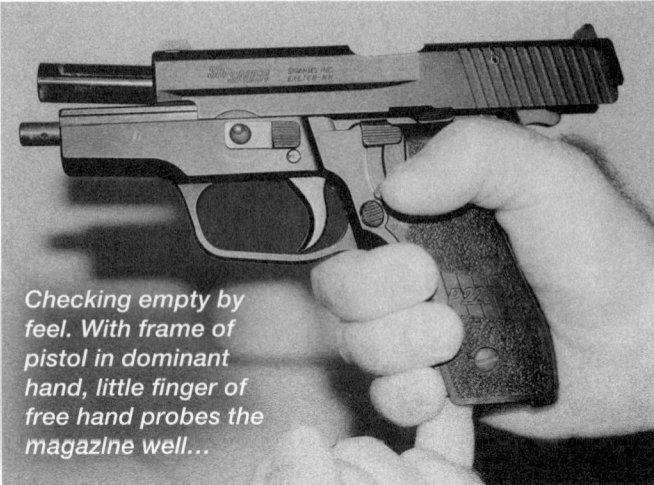

Checking empty by feel. With frame of pistol in dominant hand, little finger of free hand probes the magazine well...

... and then index finger probes firing chamber to make sure all is clear. Pistol is P228.

ADMINISTRATIVE HANDLING

LOADING typically begins with the slide closed on an empty chamber and no magazine in the pistol. Always hold the grip-frame in the dominant hand, and always allow the non-dominant hand ("support hand") to perform support functions such as loading. This prevents over-handling, switching the gun back and forth between hands, and other manipulations that can cause people to fumble or lose track of where the gun's muzzle is pointed.

With the SIG's frame in the firing hand, held in a firing position except for the trigger finger being outside of and away from the trigger guard, and in a firm grasp, take hold of the loaded magazine with the support hand. The strongest way to hold the magazine is with its floorplate, the bottom part, at the palm of the hand, and the middle finger and thumb supporting the sides of the magazine with the index finger up along the front and just under the nose of the topmost live cartridge.

Insert the magazine with its flat back making contact with the flat back of the magazine well inside the grip-frame. Insert firmly until you hear and feel the magazine click securely into place. The pistol is now in what is called "Condition Two," with loaded magazine in place but firing chamber still empty.

Since all SIG-Sauer pistols are "drop-safe," i.e., safe from accidental discharge due to inertia firing if the gun is struck or dropped, it is mechanically safe to chamber a round, which means to put a live cartridge in the firing chamber.

If the SIG's slide was locked to its rearward position before the loading process began, the slide

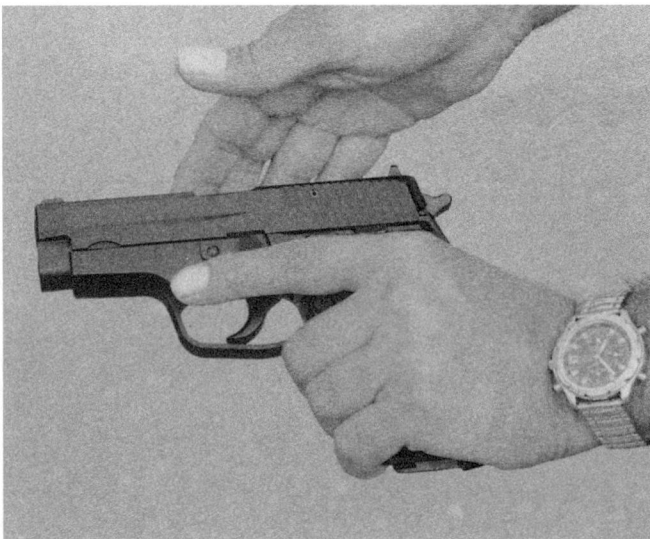

Administrative slide-lock for SIG-Sauer by lefties. Dominant left hand holds grip-frame, while support hand comes in Israeli-style...

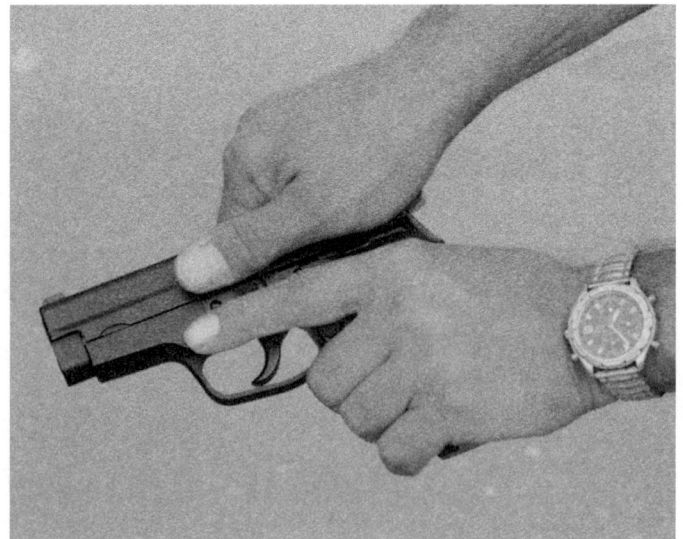

... shooter takes Israeli grasp, carefully placing right thumb parallel to ejection port on left side of slide...

can be closed either by pressing down on the slide release, or by tugging it to the rear and letting go. In either case, the slide will fly forward under the pressure of the recoil spring, which rides on a guide rod beneath the gun's barrel. Always let the slide snap forward on a live magazine with full force. This guarantees that the cartridge goes all the way into the firing chamber. Keeping a grip on the slide as it comes forward is a no-no called "riding the slide." You don't want to do it because it may keep the cartridge from chambering all the way. Just release the slide with either a downward press on the slide lock lever or a tug on the rear of the slide and let it snap forward full force. This is how the pistol was designed to be operated.

The pistol is now fully loaded, cocked, and ready to fire. Since this is administrative loading, not combat loading, it is presumed that we don't need to fire the gun at this exact moment. Therefore, in the interest of safety, we immediately decock the gun. This is done by pressing straight down on the decocking lever, located behind the trigger on the left side of the SIG-Sauer's frame. You will feel a release, and will see the hammer and trigger both come forward. A safety shelf has stopped the hammer. This automatic hammer lowering process is the only way to safely decock the gun! Despite well-intentioned but bad advice based on old, obsolete designs, you should *never* lower the hammer of a SIG-Sauer or any similar pistol by holding the hammer and pulling the trigger! First, this creates a great opportunity for human error. If the hand slips, and the trigger is being held back, the gun can and probably will discharge. Second, this ill-advised maneuver

prevents the pistol's hammer from taking its proper position vis-à-vis the safety shelf, and the gun is no longer drop safe. ALWAYS DECOCK YOUR SIG-SAUER BY USING THE DECOCKING LEVER, THE WAY IT WAS DESIGNED TO BE USED.

At this point, administrative loading is now complete.

UNLOADING means, by definition, that we are handling a loaded firearm which may be cocked. Always keep that in mind, and take due care. Make certain that the muzzle stays in a safe direction at all times. This is another good reason to get in the habit of always using the dominant hand to hold the gun, and the support hand to perform functions such as these.

Before unloading, make sure that the hammer is down and the trigger is forward, in double-action mode. While this is not mechanically necessary to the unloading process, it is one more safety step to reduce the danger of an unintentional discharge. It is axiomatic that a cocked pistol with a short, light trigger pull can be fired more easily than an uncocked pistol in double-action mode with a long, heavy trigger pull.

To unload, first remove the magazine. On most SIG-Sauers, this means pressing the magazine release button located on the frame behind the trigger guard, but on some models – the P230 and P232, and the early P220 style with the European release – there will be a lever at the rear of the butt. Push this lever rearward with the support hand's thumb, as the long, strong middle finger of that hand curls over the lip of the magazine at the front of the butt and pulls the magazine completely

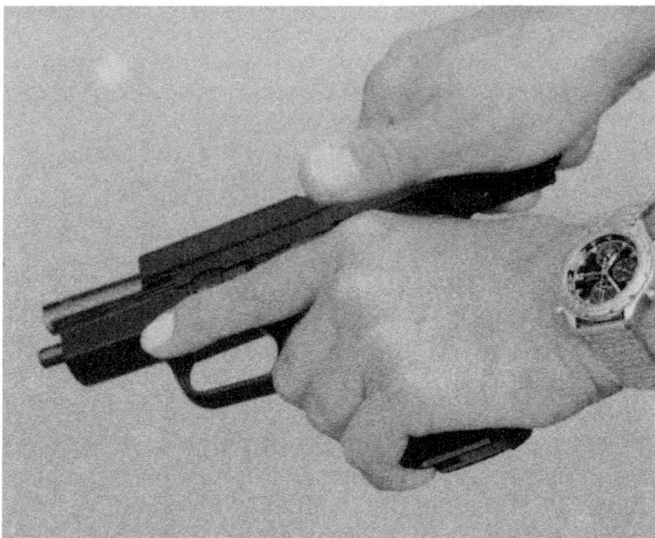

... and retracts slide. Right thumb is now perfectly positioned...

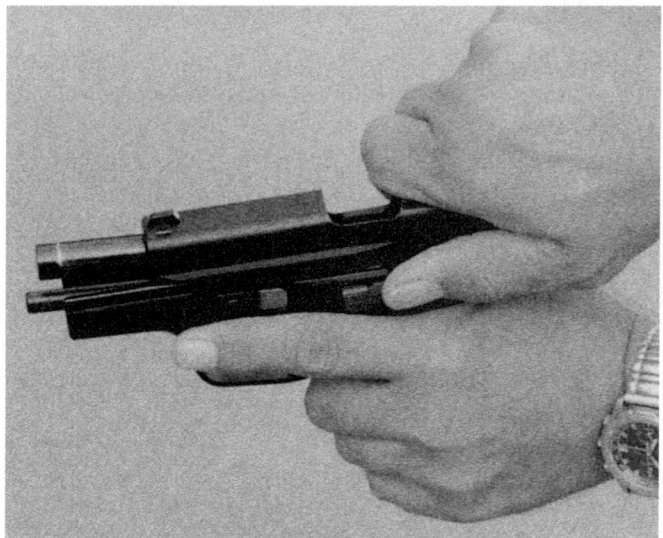

... to pull slide lock lever up and lock slide of empty pistol open.

Right handed shooter's manipulation of slide release lever. After inserting magazine as shown…

…shooter can depress slide lock lever with either right thumb…

… or left thumb, depending on which is faster, more natural, and more positive for the individual shooter…

…but in any case applying straight down pressure on the lever until the slide snaps forward, chambering the topmost round from the magazine.

out. Just pushing a button or a lever will not do it. You'll need to actually pull the magazine out if there is a butt-heel release, and if a cartridge has ridden forward a little at the top of the magazine, this may be true even for the SIG (or any other semiautomatic pistol) with a push-button mag release. A cartridge that has ridden forward between the feed lips will drag its bullet nose on the inside front of the frame, creating friction which may keep the magazine from falling free on its own.

Once the magazine is out of the pistol, *put the magazine away* before going any farther. You'll have your hands full, literally, as you clear the chamber. Holding the pistol steady against strong physical pressure as the slide is manipulated is an important job, and it is wise to completely dedicate

the dominant hand to it. Pulling the slide firmly back against the recoil spring without deviating the muzzle of a still-loaded gun is an important job, too, and it is just as wise to totally dedicate the support hand to performing that function.

This is why the magazine should be put away before manipulating the slide to unload the chambered round. Do NOT attempt to keep the magazine in either hand. The old military doctrine of putting the removed magazine into the little finger of the firing hand goes back to a time of "cold ranges," where the pistol was only loaded when there was about to be a "fire" command, and only unloaded when all shots in it had been fired. It may have been considered safe in the old days to hold an empty magazine in the little

Author recommends decocking with the firing hand, because the support hand may not always be available for the task. Right handed, it is done thus...

...making sure the movement is completed, bringing hammer safely down and trigger safely forward.

Left-handed decocking of SIG-Sauer. Flex index finger, place tip on decock lever, and push straight down toward butt of gun. Note how finger is flexed at distal joint to put more sectional density in direction of pressure...

... giving ample leverage to decock the gun properly.

finger of the hand grasping the gun when the chamber was certain to be empty, but it is a very dangerous habit to get into when you are going to be unloading live ammunition from a still-loaded firearm.

Once the magazine has been removed, it is time to immediately clear the remaining live cartridge out of the firing chamber. With the muzzle in a safe direction, use the support hand to retract the slide all the way back. The cartridge should now tumble out of the ejection port, or fall down through the now-empty magazine well.

DO NOT attempt to eject a live cartridge through the ejection port and into the palm of your hand! This technique goes back to before WWII. At that time, the predominant semiautomatic pistols in the Western world were the Colt 1911 .45 auto and the P-35 9mm. Both were constructed with short ejectors that were virtually incapable of hitting a cartridge primer during this maneuver. However, the technique is manifestly unsafe with modern semiautomatic pistols – the SIG as well as the Beretta, the Glock, the Ruger, the Smith & Wesson, and even many contemporary 1911 style pistols. The reason is that these guns all have long ejectors to more effectively kick empty shell casings out through the ejection port as the pistol cycles. It is possible, particularly if the slide of a dirty or un-lubricated pistol sticks a little during the attempt to retract, for the slide to come back in such a way that the head of the cartridge comes toward the ejector. If the ejector hits the exposed primer hard enough, the result can be an out-of-chamber discharge.

Normally, the ordnance steel of the chamber contains a cartridge's pressure as the powder burns. Outside the chamber, the cartridge literally explodes, and if the palm of the hand is over the ejection port, it takes the brunt of the blast. The result can be profound nerve damage to the hand.

Incompetent unloading techniques have led to accidental shootings, usually of the "I didn't know it was loaded" variety. Some of these were fatal. If the unloading is done out of sequence – "clear the chamber, remove the magazine" – the stage has been set for disaster. If the magazine is in place when the slide is drawn back to clear the round out of the chamber, as soon as the handler lets go of the slide it goes forward and chambers another live cartridge off the top of the magazine. If the handler takes the round out of the chamber and then removes the magazine, he has in fact left a live round in the launch tube.

With this in mind, always complete an administrative unload with the following ritual. Put away the removed magazine and the cartridge removed from the chamber. Then, as carefully as you would with a loaded gun, draw the slide rearward and lock it open. Peer carefully into the chamber to make certain that it is empty, and into the magazine well to make sure that a magazine is no longer in place. Get into the habit of holding the pistol in the dominant hand (in firing position, muzzle in a safe direction) as the little finger of the non-dominant hand, normally the narrowest of the ten digits, actually probes the firing chamber and the magazine well to confirm that both are empty.

Once the gun has been unloaded, don't leave it lying around unattended. In a training environment, you can put it back in the holster. There it will at once be available and secure from unauthorized hands. Or, it can be locked away in a vehicle, a locker, or a safe.

SLIDE MANIPULATION

For many shooters, the operating of the slide is the hard part of routine handgun manipulation. The slide is held closed or "in battery" by the strong recoil spring beneath the barrel. There is also the matter of the mainspring in the grip-frame, which is holding the hammer down and at rest when the gun is in battery in double-action mode. The firm push necessary to operate the slide can be difficult for anyone who has any limitations in upper limb strength.

Certain emergency techniques, such as working the slide when you only have one hand to work with, will be dealt with later in this chapter. The manipulations under discussion in this particular chapter require two hands. The dominant hand holds the grip-frame, and the support hand retracts the slide.

There are two basic techniques for doing this, each of which has advantages and disadvantages. Let's examine both, along with their pros and cons.

The *U.S. Method*, which draws its name from having been taught to American soldiers virtually since the adoption of the semiautomatic pistol in 1911, has also been called the "overhand" technique. Officer survival expert Dave Spaulding dubbed it the "saddle" method, because the hand sits astride the slide like a person astride a saddle. In this technique, the dominant hand holds the grip-frame; the support hand grasps the slide palm down, with the thumb pointing toward the shooter, and pulls the slide backward in the direction of the shooter's shoulder.

Many longtime shooters were originally trained in this technique, or self-taught shooters learned it from gun magazines and TV or movie screens. The

Overhand method of slide operation is known as "American style" or "saddle style." Grasp is seen here from the weak side...

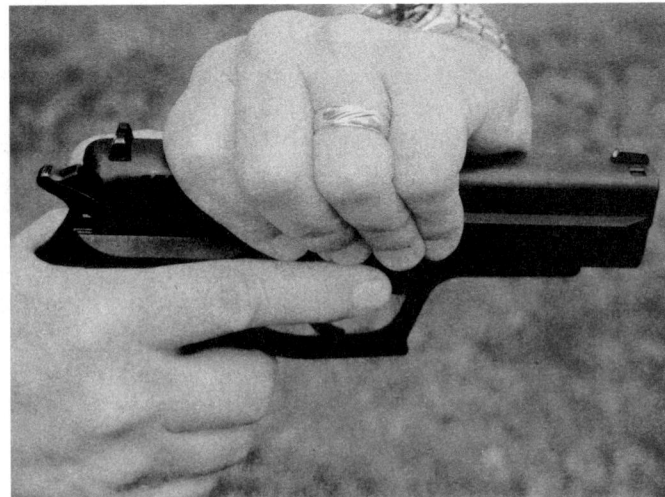

...and here from the strong side. Forearm is always kept perpendicular to slide at 90 degree angle, muzzle downrange, finger on frame. To activate...

...draw slide all the way back...

... then let it slam forward on its own power...

... and, if you're not going to instantly fire, decock the pistol. Instructor Steve Denney demonstrates with P220 American.

U.S. Method can be very fast, particularly when drawing a pistol which does not have a round in the chamber. In the latter situation, U.S. military personnel were taught for generations to thrust the gun hand forward to the target as the slide-operating hand snapped toward the gun arm's shoulder. This allowed an extremely fast draw-to-the-shot of a pistol that was in Condition Two, that is, with a loaded magazine but empty chamber.

However, Spaulding and other professionals before him identified problems with this technique. Since it involves a "hand-against-hand" movement, it requires upper body strength and is therefore sometimes less than optimal for those with limited strength. One shortcoming, which is irrelevant when the shooter uses a SIG, is that if the pistol has a slide-mounted safety and/or decocking lever, this

Slingshot method, also known as "Israeli style" operation of slide. All four fingers grasp weak hand side of slide, with dominant hand holding grip-frame...

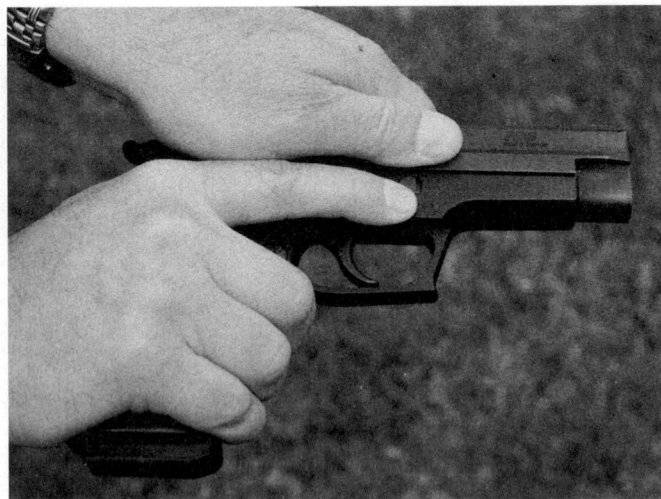

...and entire thumb, from drumstick to thumbprint, holding slide on strong hand side...

movement can inadvertently on-safe or decock the pistol.

There is another concern with this technique no matter what pistol it is employed with. Human beings instinctively tend to align their skeletal support structure in the direction in which they are exerting force. Thus, if attention is momentarily diverted, the shooter can end up bringing his elbow dangerously near the muzzle while performing this slide movement. For the same reason, a right-handed shooter may unintentionally point his muzzle to his left while doing this. (A southpaw may do the same thing, with the muzzle pointing to the right.) This is why many instructors suggest the student take a step back with the leg on their gun hand side before operating the slide. It keeps the muzzle downrange if either of those mistakes is made.

The *Israeli Method* is called that because Israeli firearms instructors have been teaching it for decades. It is also known as the "slingshot method" because it shares some biomechanics with the way that instrument is operated. In this technique, the dominant hand, as always, takes a firm hold on the grip-frame of the pistol with the trigger finger on the frame above the trigger guard. The support hand grasps the slide firmly, with the thumb pointed *away from* the shooter.

When properly executed, the Israeli method is extremely strong, fast, and natural. It works as well on a SIG as on anything else, but it is particularly advantageous with those other makes of pistol that have slide-mounted safety/decock levers. Its biomechanics are such that the thumb on one side of the slide and the index finger on the other tend to hold the slide-mounted safety lever where it is. In other words, if the pistol is off-safe when this

movement begins, it will remain off-safe when the slide operation is completed. If it is on-safe when the manipulation starts, it will be on-safe when the manipulation is completed.

With the Israeli Method, the muzzle always seems to stay downrange and never stray to either side or toward the elbow of the slide-manipulating hand. Some instructors prefer to teach this technique combined with a slight tilt of the top of the slide toward the weak-hand side, and some even turn the gun upside down while performing the maneuver. The latter is what you would want to do if you were trying to eject a casing or live round from the chamber. With the pistol upside down, gravity is working with you to help clear out the chamber. By operating the slide the same way all the time, the theory goes, no harm is done in administrative loading and the shooter learns to do one technique properly all the time.

To perform the Israeli or slingshot technique correctly, care must be taken with two things. First, the support hand should not just lightly grasp the slide with thumb and forefinger. It should take a very firm grip. If you are a right-handed shooter, you hold the SIG's grip-frame in your right hand as your left hand came down with the thumb on the right side of the slide and the fingers on the left side. The thumb would press firmly in contact to the slide all the way from the base of the "drumstick" to the tip of the thumb; all four fingers would likewise take a firm hold.

Second, the Israeli technique allows the shooter to use the power of his or her whole body in the slide operation. The movement looks like a karate practitioner performing a reverse punch. The heel of the strong side leg digs into the ground or floor as the shooter straightens that leg, turning the hip

...allowing shooter to use whole body strength with turn of hips to rack slide all the way back until it stops...

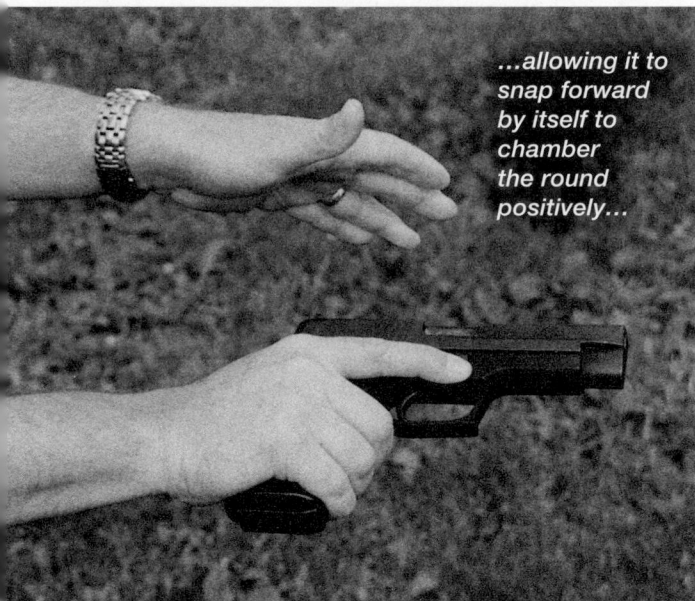

...allowing it to snap forward by itself to chamber the round positively...

... and then shooter can fire instantly as shown, or if that is not necessary, decock.

on the gun side forward. This in turn drives the gun arm very strongly forward. Simultaneously, the firmly grasping support hand pulls the slide to the rear. As with the overhand method, the slingshot method is complete when the slide reaches the rear extreme of its movement. The support hand lets go, allowing the slide to snap forward and chamber a round. The pistol is then decocked if shooting is not

to take place instantly.

Either of the above methods is safe if the shooter keeps the muzzle downrange and does not allow any body parts to approach the "business end" of the pistol. It has been this writer's experience over decades of teaching the handgun that the slingshot is the safest technique, and in many ways the more efficient.

HELPFUL HINTS

Some pistols have very strong recoil springs. Remember, too, that in a conventional pistol such as the SIG-Sauer, the shooter is also working against a hammer that is held forward by a very strong mainspring which runs vertically down the back of the grip-frame. Many shooters do not have as much upper body strength as they might like. When all these factors are taken into account, it is not surprising that some shooters have difficulty operating the slide of a semiautomatic pistol.

One way to make the job easier is to cock the hammer first. This is best done by holding the pistol firmly by the grip-frame in the dominant hand, and bringing the hammer back with the support hand. In a firing stance, this is generally done by applying the thumb of the supporting hand to the spur of the hammer. In administrative handling, the easiest way to do this is with the lower edge of the support hand, the part of the hand that would be the striking surface in a *shuto* or "karate chop." The movement resembles a cowboy actor "fanning" the hammer of an old-fashioned single-action revolver,

Tara Miller shows other petite females how to easily operate the slide. Here she takes the Israeli grasp on her P245 ...

...and digs in her right foot, driving right hip and gun hand forward as left shoulder and arm pull back...

...allowing her to easily retract slide, even starting with hammer down...

... by simply releasing support hand grasp, she allows slide to fly forward and chamber a .45 round...

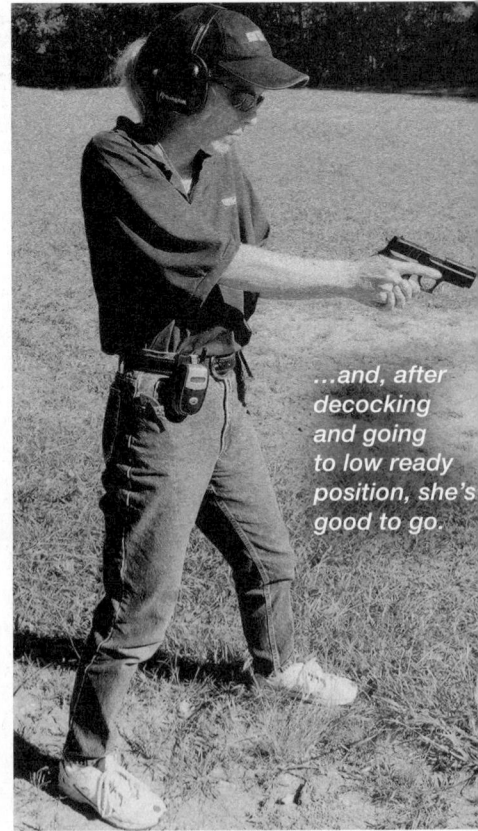

...and, after decocking and going to low ready position, she's good to go.

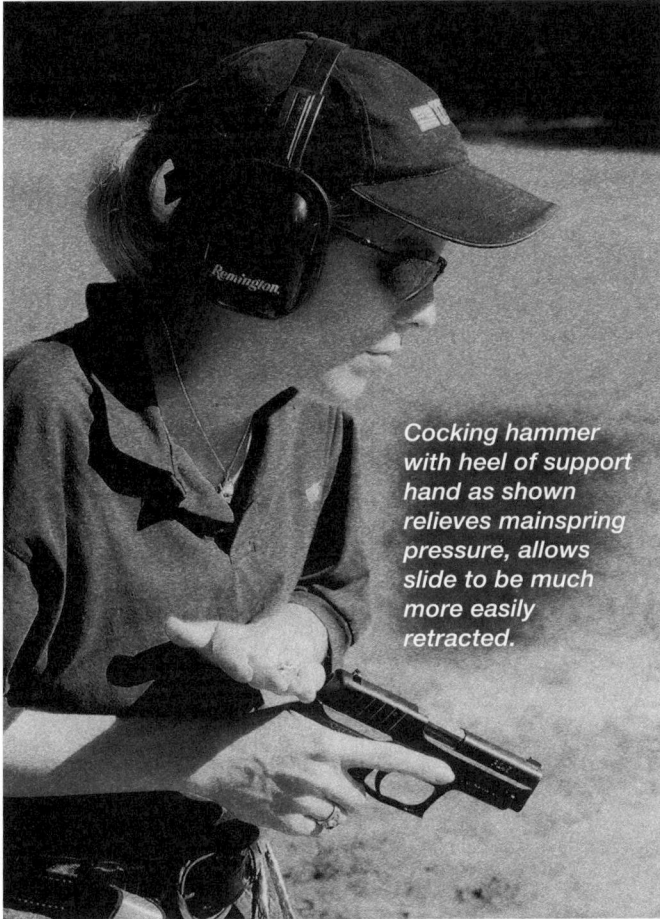

Cocking hammer with heel of support hand as shown relieves mainspring pressure, allows slide to be much more easily retracted.

though of course it is not done as a strike. The hand should touch, and then push the hammer back for maximum control.

This relieves all the pressure of the mainspring that the hammer has been applying against the slide while forward. With the hammer now back instead of forward, it will be much easier to draw the slide to the rear.

For maximum leverage, the shooter has two excellent techniques to choose from. One is the Israeli Method, done as described above: the body performing a karate-ka's forward punch from the ground up while drawing the slide to the rear. The other is a variation of the U.S. or "saddle" technique that has been attributed to former national speed shooting champion Mike Plaxco. The shooter, keeping the muzzle firmly downrange and trigger finger completely clear of the guard, pulls the gun in tight to the rib cage under the breast or pectoral muscle on the dominant hand side. The support hand grasps the slide firmly in the "saddle" grasp. Now, again, the "forward punch" element is added. The shooter digs in the rear heel on the gun hand side, driving hip and body forward toward the gun while the support hand holds the slide fixed in place so that the frame and barrel can push forward beneath it. As always, when the slide reaches its rearmost point of movement, the shooter should let go so that it can snap forward with full power to guarantee that a cartridge is properly chambered.

Tara demonstrates alternate technique for less strong people who prefer American style slide manipulation. Grasp as shown, forearm across chest and safely 90 degrees to gun muzzle...

...digging in rear heel and driving gun side hip forward, she pushes pistol against firmly holding hand until frame comes forward under slide...

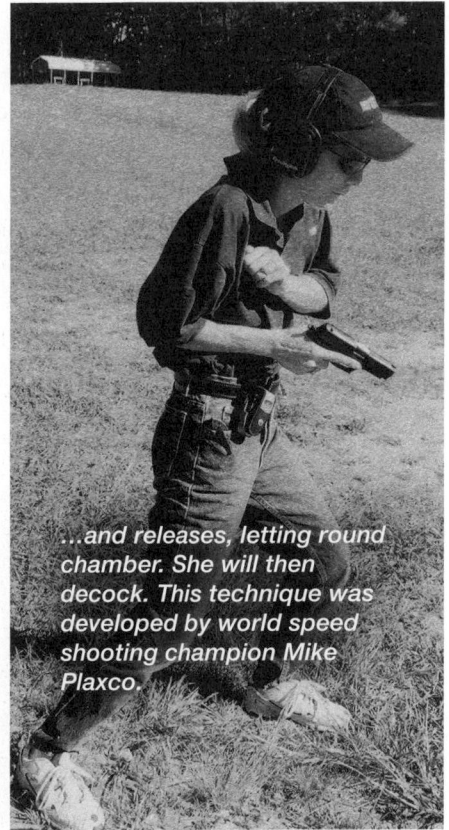

...and releases, letting round chamber. She will then decock. This technique was developed by world speed shooting champion Mike Plaxco.

LOCKING THE SLIDE OPEN

Not counting the slide locking itself back on an empty magazines, there are three ways to get the SIG-Sauer pistol opened up with the slide locked back and the magazine out, the condition it which it should be for inspection to confirm that it is unloaded. Note: only with an empty magazine can you lock back the slide of the blowback .380s, the P230 and P232, since neither has an external slide stop/slide release lever.

Option One: Hold the pistol in the right hand with the muzzle in a safe direction. Without allowing any part of the support hand or arm to get in front of the muzzle, and without letting the muzzle turn in an unsafe direction, draw the slide to the rear with the left hand while the right hand thumb pushes upward on the slide stop lever.

Option Two: Hold the pistol in the right hand with the muzzle in a safe direction. Place the left hand on the slide with the thumb pointing forward on the right side of the slide, and the index finger level with the front of the ejection port. As the slide is drawn to the rear by the left hand, the left index finger will find itself in proximity to the slide stop lever. Pull this upward with the tip of the left index finger, and the pistol will be locked open.

Option Three: (For left-handers) Hold the pistol in the left hand with the muzzle in a safe direction. Place the right hand on the slide with the right thumb on the left side, pointing forward, and level with the ejection port. Draw the slide back. The

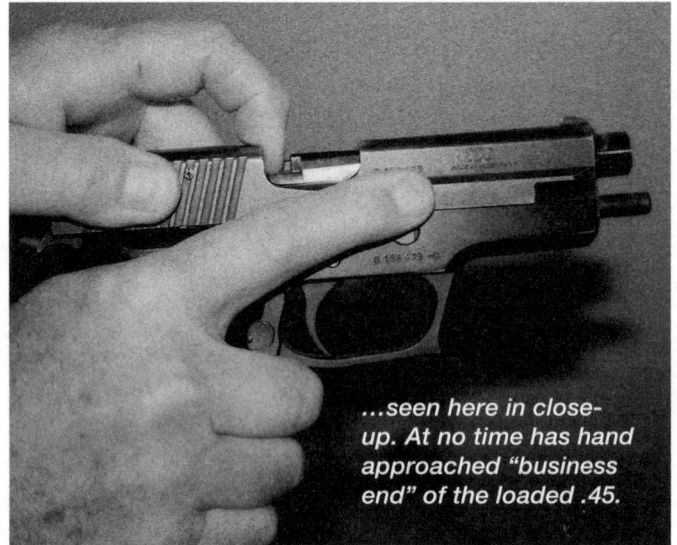

...seen here in close-up. At no time has hand approached "business end" of the loaded .45.

right thumb should now be in proximity to the slide stop, in position to pull that lever up and lock the slide open.

EASING THE SLIDE FORWARD WHEN THE PISTOL IS EMPTY

You do not want to store any semiautomatic pistol for a long time with the slide locked to the rear. This will put great, sustained pressure on the fully compressed recoil spring, which will soon take a set and lose tension prematurely. When the gun is stored, the slide should be forward and the hammer should be down in the double action position.

Once the gun has been checked and confirmed unloaded, you don't want to close the slide by letting it fly forward. The mechanism was designed to be cushioned by the resistance of a cartridge that is being stripped from the top of the magazine. Without that, the slide slams forward in a way that can damage the extractor and, on some other guns, can also ruin the sear.

Therefore, you want to hold the grip-frame firmly in the dominant hand and use the non-dominant hand to ease the slide forward. You can tug the locked-open slide to the rear, which will release the slide lock, and then hold it as it comes slowly forward with the support hand. If the shooter is holding the grip-frame in the right hand, he or she can also use the right thumb to release the slide stop while the left hand eases the firmly held slide forward.

If the gun is held with the grip-frame in the left hand, it is not wise to attempt to twist the left thumb around behind the gun to activate the slide stop. This weakens the primary grasp on the pistol. In that situation, just hold the grip-frame firmly with the left hand, and use the right hand to release

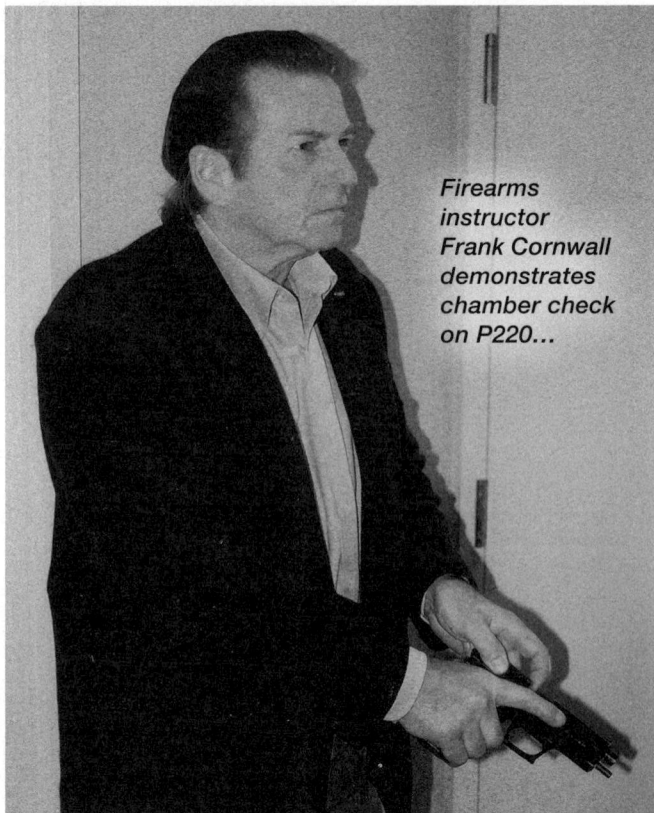

Firearms instructor Frank Cornwall demonstrates chamber check on P220...

the slide and let it come forward, as delineated above in Option Three.

CHAMBER CHECK

It's easy enough to check if the *magazine* of your pistol is loaded. Simply withdraw the magazine and examine it. Checking the chamber is a more difficult, dexterity-intensive task.

Do *not* reach up under the pistol and grasp the slide from underneath to push it back. The hand is now in too close proximity to the "business end" of a presumably loaded pistol. If the hand slips, you can shoot a finger off. Firearms instructor John Farnam recently reported the case of a man who shot two fingers off his own support hand while attempting to check his gun with this ill-advised technique. When he slipped, the gun discharged, costing him a finger. He was so shocked and startled that his hand convulsed, inadvertently pulling the trigger a second time...and shooting off the second finger.

There are other, better options. One is the *armorer's grasp.* The dominant hand takes its conventional hold on the grip frame, with all fingers completely clear of the trigger guard and the muzzle in a safe direction. The support hand stabilizes the frame at the dust cover area, just ahead of the trigger guard. Now, the firing hand pivots upward at the juncture of the web of that hand and the grip tang area, bringing the fingers of the firing hand up over the slide. Index and middle fingers squeeze; this contraction brings the slide slightly back, exposing the firing chamber. Depending on size, shape, and flexibility of the hand, the shooter can use the ring finger or little finger of the dominant hand to check the chamber by feel.

A still better method is seen in Andy Stanford's book, *Surgical Speed Shooting,* and demonstrated here by noted firearms instructor Frank Cornwall. With the trigger finger safely extended on the frame, retract the slide as in the Israeli method. While holding the slide just slightly out of battery, use the tip of the index finger to probe through the top of the now partially open firing chamber.

EMERGENCY TECHNIQUES

The SIG-Sauer pistol is a defensive handgun. It is intended to be emergency rescue equipment in a life-threatening crisis. As such, it must be operated swiftly and surely. We hope never to need the fire extinguisher or the lifeboat, but we drill in their use. The same is true of the defensive handgun. We hope never to need it, but we know that if we do ever need it, we shall need it badly indeed.

The separate chapter on shooting the SIG-Sauer is geared entirely toward its use under extreme stress. Adjunct skills will be addressed here. These include getting the gun out of the holster and into the fight in time to interdict a deadly threat;

Steve Denney demonstrates LFI draw from under an open-front concealing garment.

Both hands move. Support hand comes to centerline of body – edge out so it can ward off a close-range grab – as gun hand's fingertips all touch body centerline...

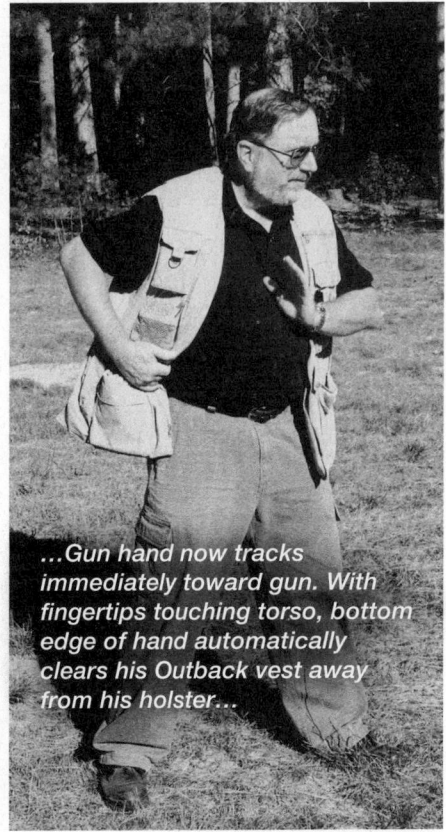

...Gun hand now tracks immediately toward gun. With fingertips touching torso, bottom edge of hand automatically clears his Outback vest away from his holster...

...gun hand takes firm firing hold on grip-frame with every digit but trigger finger, which is rigid outside the holster...

...and Steve executes "rock and lock," pulling gun up out of holster and snapping muzzle toward target as soon as it clears. Meanwhile, support hand is in position...

...to come in from behind muzzle and take its place. Gun is already on target, and can be fired from here if necessary...

...as Steve completes the draw by extending his P220 .45 into firing position. Note that finger is off the trigger; in the real world, most draws will end in "gunpoint" instead of shooting.

reloading if the emergency is so grave that the defender has emptied the gun and not yet resolved the crisis; tactical reloading after the shooting is over; and emergency manipulations that may be required if the user is wounded or otherwise injured.

THE DRAW

If we knew an armed attack was coming, the SIG we'd want in our hands would be their 550 rifle. The handgun is a reactive, defensive weapon, sufficiently compact to have always available to defend against surprise attacks. This means that the wearer needs to practice quickly deploying it in emergency situations. Going on the assumption that any officer wearing a pistol in uniform has police academy and in-service departmental training geared to the officer's specific uniform holster, we'll focus on bringing the lawfully concealed handgun to bear.

Lets start with a few rules.

• **Don't practice the draw to the shot more than 1/10th of the time.** Cop or citizen, most of the time you draw you'll be holding someone at gunpoint, not shooting him. If you condition yourself to reflexively fire as you complete the draw, that conditioning could result in tragedy and imprisonment.

• **Start slow.** With any physical skill, we should crawl before we walk, and walk

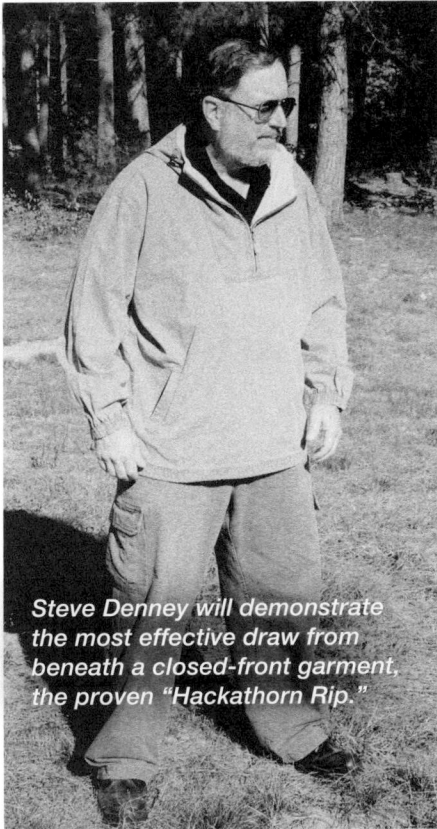

Steve Denney will demonstrate the most effective draw from beneath a closed-front garment, the proven "Hackathorn Rip."

Free hand goes to hem of anorak in appendix area, takes firm hold...

...and rips up toward shoulder to expose pistol, as gun hand begins reach. Garment may not reach shoulder, but attempting to get it there guarantees sufficent clearance for a draw...

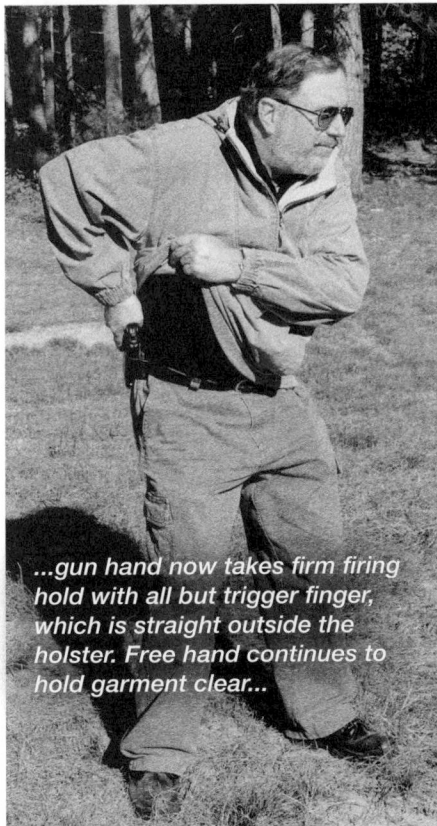

...gun hand now takes firm firing hold with all but trigger finger, which is straight outside the holster. Free hand continues to hold garment clear...

...and as gun hand "rocks and locks," support hand is naturally positioned to join it in two-hand grasp. Gun is already toward the threat...

...and gun is thrust toward target. Note that finger remains "in register" on frame unless intention to fire immediately has been formulated.

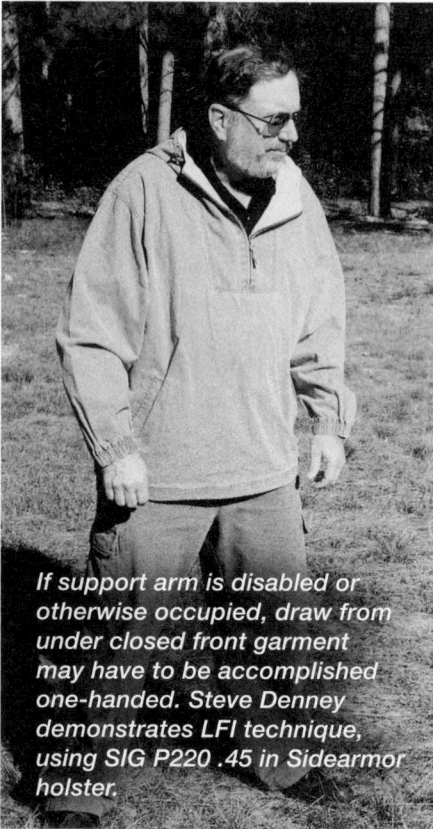

If support arm is disabled or otherwise occupied, draw from under closed front garment may have to be accomplished one-handed. Steve Denney demonstrates LFI technique, using SIG P220 .45 in Sidearmor holster.

Extended thumb of gun hand tracks up leg along trouser seam or common peroneal nerve, and digs under hem of garment...

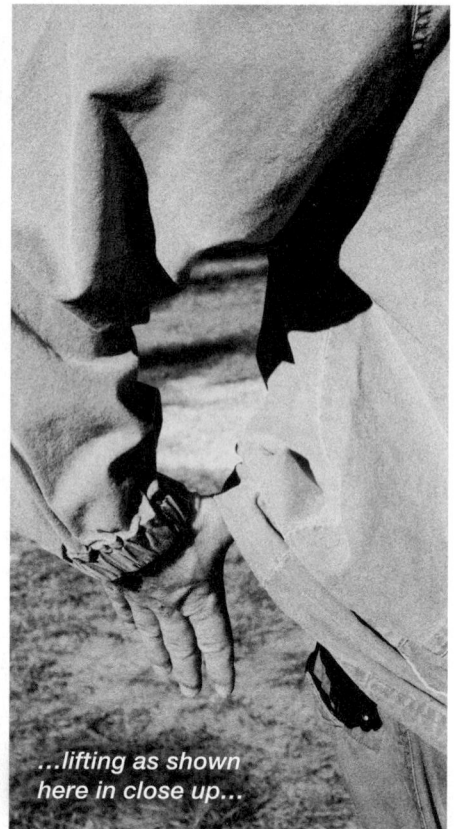

...lifting as shown here in close up...

...gun hand takes drawing grasp...

...being right handed, Steve now rocks his hips to the left, to give gun more range of movement with which to clear. He draws the SIG...

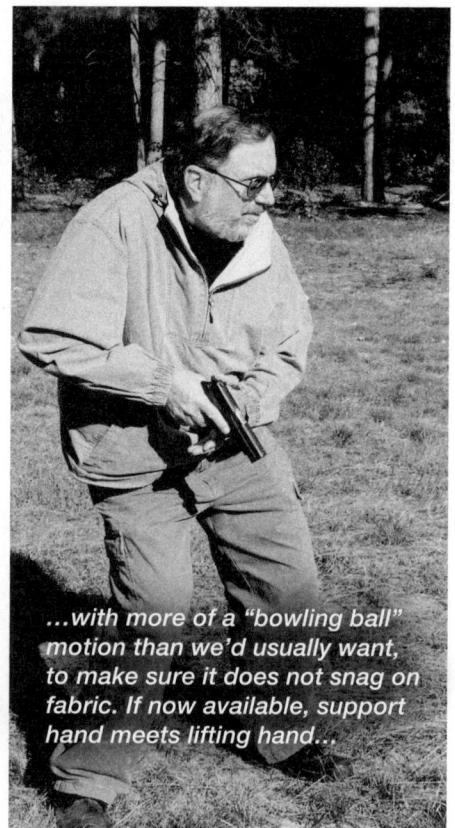

...with more of a "bowling ball" motion than we'd usually want, to make sure it does not snag on fabric. If now available, support hand meets lifting hand...

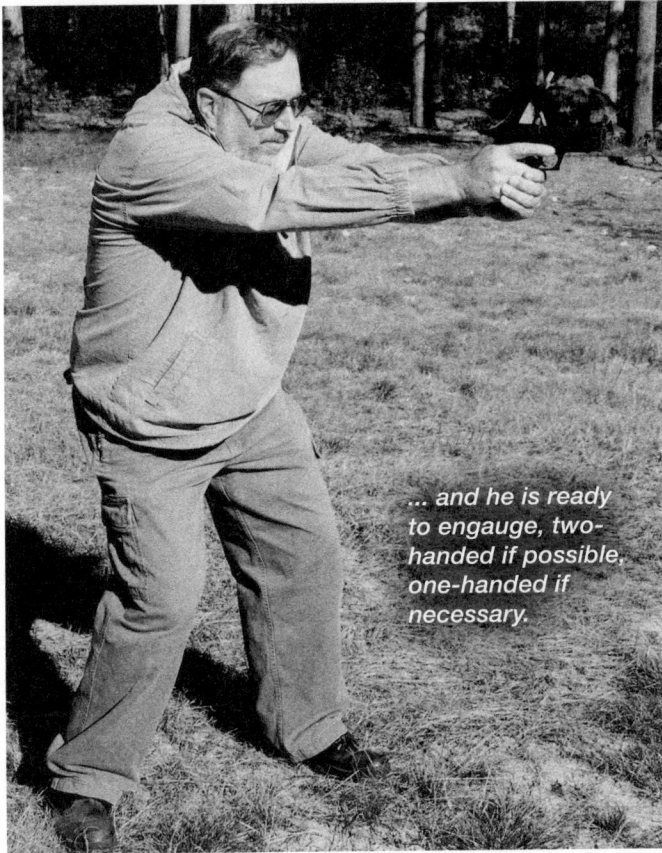

... and he is ready to engauge, two-handed if possible, one-handed if necessary.

before we run. The best way to learn to do anything swiftly is to start practicing it slowly. This programs the mind and body to get every nuance down correctly. As world combat pistol champ Ray Chapman always said, "Smoothness is five-sixths of speed."

• *Finger off the trigger.* Never let your trigger finger enter the trigger guard until the pistol is on target and you have formulated the immediate intent to shoot that target.

• *Control the muzzle.* Do not let the muzzle cross any part of your body during the draw. Practice to a high skill level with a dummy gun or unloaded gun before attempting these techniques with live ammunition in the weapon.

The draw breaks down into two key components, *access* and *presentation*. Access means getting the firing hand onto the gun properly. That tends to be the tough, dexterity-intensive part. The next step, presentation, is bringing the gun from the holster to the target. This tends to be easier, since it is more of a simple gross motor skill.

Illustrated here are the strong-side draw from under an open garment and shoulder-holster draw, neither of which should require both hands. Also demonstrated is the draw from beneath a closed-

Shoulder holster draw is demonstrated by Jeff Williams with .357 SIG P229 in Mitch Rosen Stylemaster rig.

Support arm rises in Najiola-style krate block, not only to ward off close-range attack but also to clear the arm from the muzzle's path. Elbow should be shoulder high as gun hand knifes through what would be opening in concealing garment...

...and takes drawing grasp. Thumb breaks safety strap. Trigger finger is "in register" outside holster...

...the P229 is rocked straight out across chest. Note that holster-side hip is slightly turned toward target...

...and gun is quickly on target, too. As gun hand thrusts forward, support hand can now safely come in from above and behind the gun muzzle...

...to fashion a strong two-handed stance.

front garment, which can be done one-handed but is much more effective when both hands are employed. The illustrations and captions should be self-explanatory.

SPEED RELOAD

The speed reload is sometimes called the "emergency reload." We can't quibble with the semantics. If you are in a situation that has required you to fire every round in your SIG pistol, and you're still under attack and need to fire more, "emergency" may be an understatement.

In the speed reload, the magazine is empty and the slide has locked back. Jeff Cooper credits the standard protocol illustrated here to Ray Chapman. However, to the best of my knowledge, the grasp of the magazine with the baseplate in the palm and the index finger up under the topmost cartridge nose is actually Jeff's idea.

Again, the illustrations are self-explanatory, but a few points bear emphasis. First, a righthanded shooter who insists on firing the SIG-Sauer with a high-thumb hold may have disabled his own slide lock lever, allowing the slide to fall on an empty chamber. In this case, the reload will be an insertion of the magazine and a brisk racking of the slide to recharge the chamber.

Second, most shooters are significantly faster and even more positive using the slide release

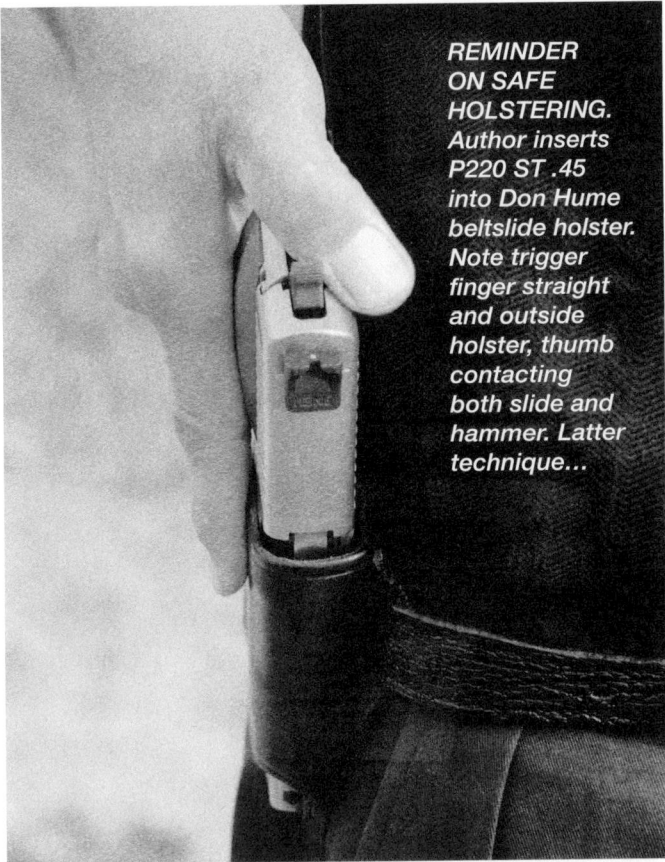

REMINDER ON SAFE HOLSTERING. Author inserts P220 ST .45 into Don Hume beltslide holster. Note trigger finger straight and outside holster, thumb contacting both slide and hammer. Latter technique...

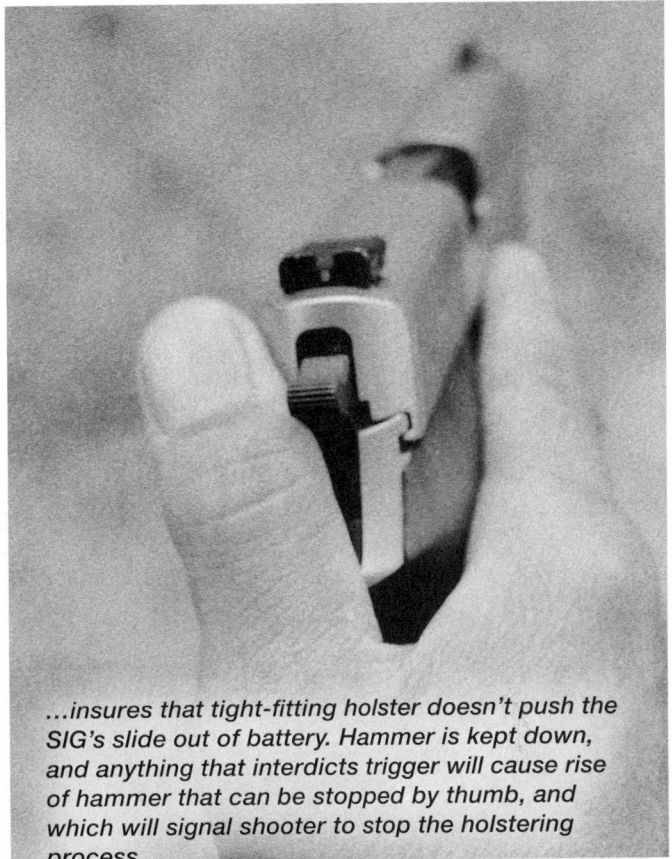

...insures that tight-fitting holster doesn't push the SIG's slide out of battery. Hammer is kept down, and anything that interdicts trigger will cause rise of hammer that can be stopped by thumb, and which will signal shooter to stop the holstering process.

Author demonstrates right-handed speed reload of SIGSauer. P220 ST is at slide lock. Support hand drops to mag pouch and seizes spare magazine...

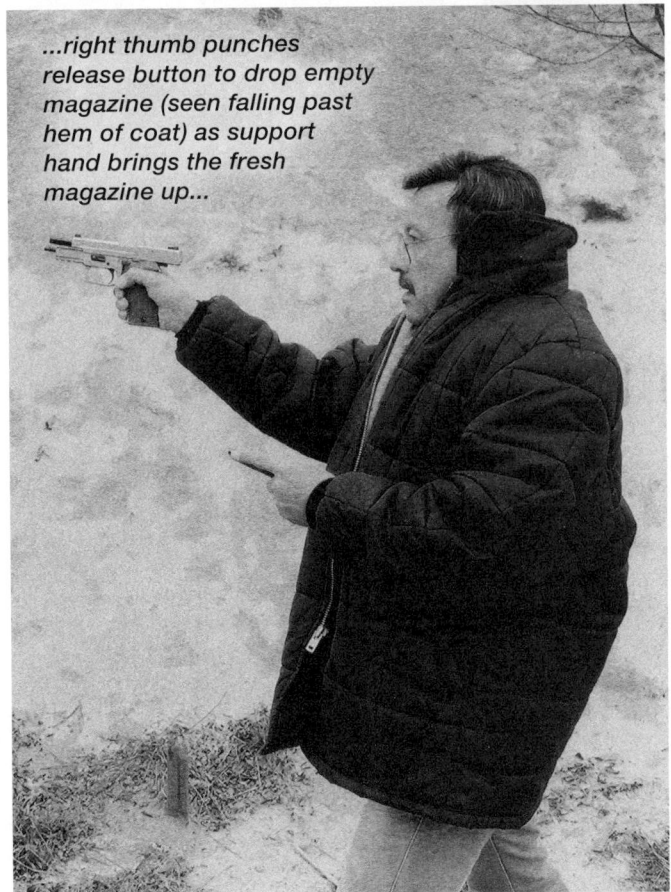

...right thumb punches release button to drop empty magazine (seen falling past hem of coat) as support hand brings the fresh magazine up...

...guided by index finger, beginning with flat back of magazine against back of magazine well opening, it is inserted...

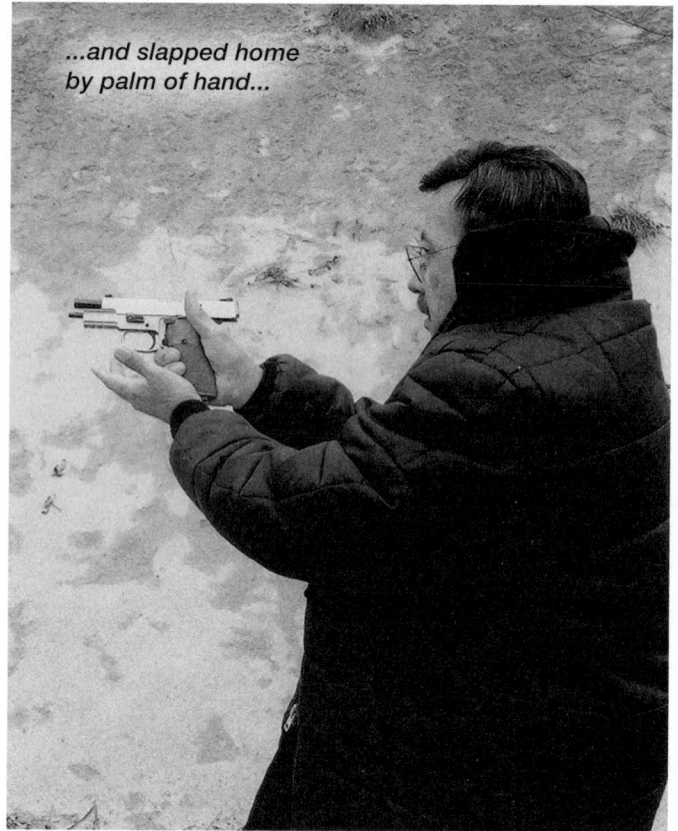

...and slapped home by palm of hand...

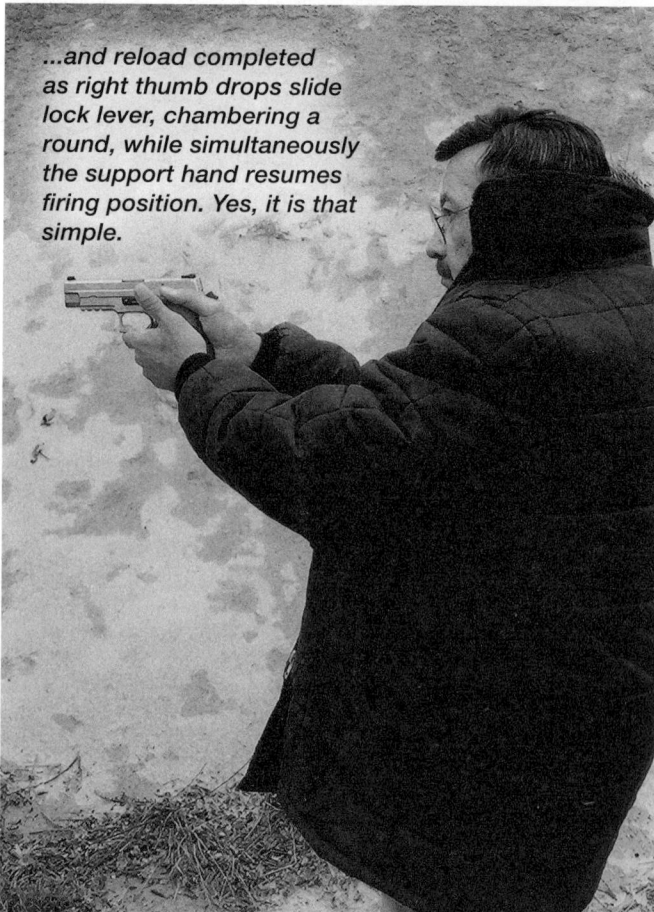

...and reload completed as right thumb drops slide lock lever, chambering a round, while simultaneously the support hand resumes firing position. Yes, it is that simple.

lever to drop the slide forward instead of making a separate tugging movement on the slide itself. If, however, *you* find that working the lever is difficult for *you* under stress, revert to the slide tug. (You will have to use that method anyway with a P230 or P232, since those models do not have slide lock/ slide release levers.)

Third, most SIG-Sauer pistols have a reversible magazine release. It makes sense for southpaws to take advantage of this and put the release button on the right side of the frame. The reason is the button is better protected when it's toward the body while holstered. I know some performance-oriented shooters who've moved the button to the same side as their dominant hand because they find it faster to dump the mag with their trigger finger than with their thumb. I understand their point, but on a defense gun, leaving the button to the outside invites bumps that can accidentally dislodge the magazine.

TACTICAL RELOADS

There are several different methods of rapidly retrieving a partial magazine from your pistol while inserting a full one. The theory of the tactical reload is that even when you think everything is over, it's a good idea to have a fully loaded magazine in your gun just in case your optimism

For the left-handed shooter... With SIG .45 at slide lock, trigger finger activates the magazine release button as free hand goes for spare mag...

...magazine insertion is accomplished...

...as magazine is slammed home, right hand continues upward movement, with fingers in "spear hand" configuration crossing up over back of firing hand behind knuckles. This brings fingertips to slide stop area...

was premature. It's also not a good idea to throw away perfectly good ammunition when you're still at a danger scene, and the tactical reload preserves that ammo.

Off the top of my head, I can think of at least five different tactical reload sequences, each of which has its strong adherents. It's at least a six-beer argument in the bar after the shooting session once the guns are locked away. For details on the various techniques, reference *The Gun Digest Book of Combat Handgunnery, Fifth Edition.* For now, we'll focus on the single technique that has proven most adaptable to the greatest number of combinations of hand, gun, and magazine sizes and shapes. It was developed by Col. Jeff Cooper, and is still taught today as the standard technique at Gunsite Training Center, Thunder Ranch, and some other schools.

In a speed reload, there is no need to decock a double-action or engage the safety of a single-action auto, because you are attempting to sustain fire as fast as possible. The tactical reload, however, is to be done during the proverbial "lull in the action," and it is a fumble-prone technique. For both reasons, it is important to *take your finger out of the trigger guard* of any pistol before you begin, and to *decock your double-action or engage the safety of your single-action* before you begin.

When you are done, put the partial magazine where it will be accessible, but where you won't mix it up with a full magazine. If you only carry one spare magazine and pouch, put it back in the pouch; with the only other magazine being the full one in the gun, there is nothing to mix it up with. Many shooters put it in a pocket, but beware of two problems. First, when you need those last precious rounds, you are probably not habituated to reaching for them in a pocket. Second, we tend to practice shooting while standing up on the range in casual BDU pants with capacious pockets.

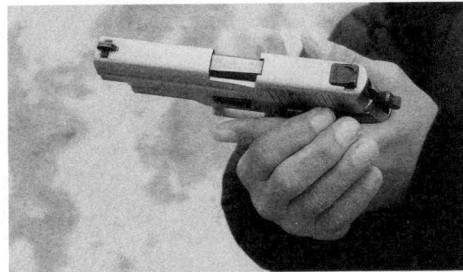

...and with simultaneous flexion of all four fingertips, one fingertip hits slide stop and chambers a round...

...and right hand pivots back into support grasp for firing. If this does not work after serious practice, revert to slower but simpler "slide tug" method to chamber the round....

Tactical reload begins with the pistol magazine still partially loaded, round chambered, and hammer cocked if your SIG is the most common TDA variety.

Top Left: Finger is removed from trigger guard and hammer decocked as support hand begins its descent to the magazine pouch...

Top Middle: ...support hand brings up fresh magazine exactly as it would for a speed reload...

Top Right: ...but as it approaches pistol, index finger slides from magazine an toward thumb, leaving fresh mag between middle finger and index finger creating a "pincer" between thumb and index finger...

Right: ...partly depleted magazine is removed by index finger and thumb...

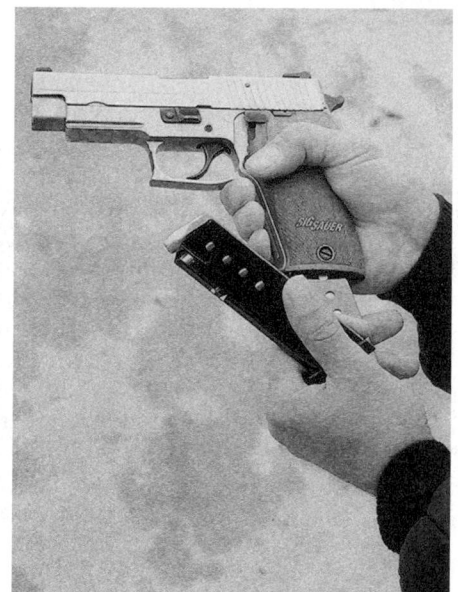

Far Right: ...and hand rotates slightly to align the full magazine with the gun butt. Magazine is now inserted...

...and slapped home by support hand, which now has three fingers free...

...to take a reasonably effective two-hand firing hold without "changing channels" and dropping magazine, should need to fire return at this point....

...and the partial magazine is now placed in pocket, waistband, or location of shooter's preference.

When we need this technique for real, we might be wearing a tailored uniform or tailored suit, and be kneeling or crouching with trouser fabric drawn taut. This could make it impossible for us to access the pocket. My preferred option is to simply shove the retrieved magazine into the waistband, but each practitioner needs to know what works for him or her, and practice accordingly.

WOUNDED OFFICER TECHNIQUES

I've always used the term "wounded officer" because I started teaching cops long before I trained civilians, and got stuck in the groove. The fact is, any good person in a gunfight needs to realize that their first indication that they're up against a really skilled bad guy may be when they take a bullet or catch a knife thrust. They need to be prepared to

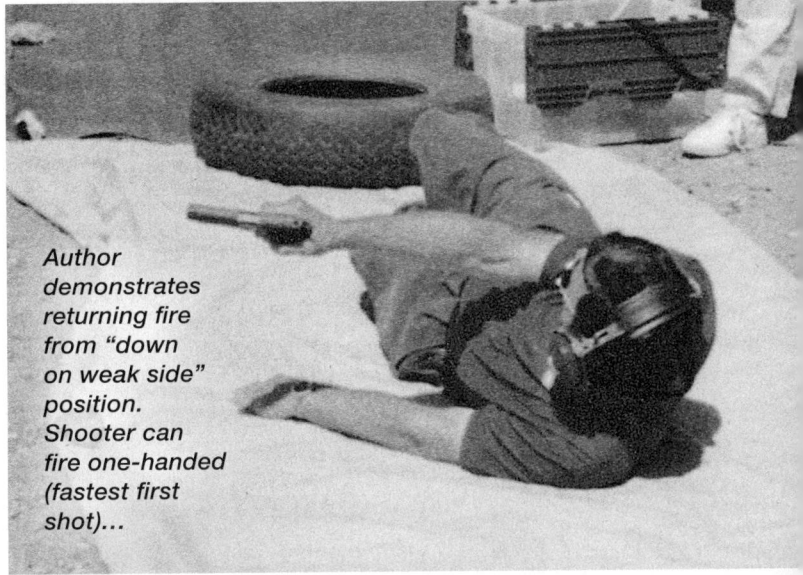

Author demonstrates returning fire from "down on weak side" position. Shooter can fire one-handed (fastest first shot)...

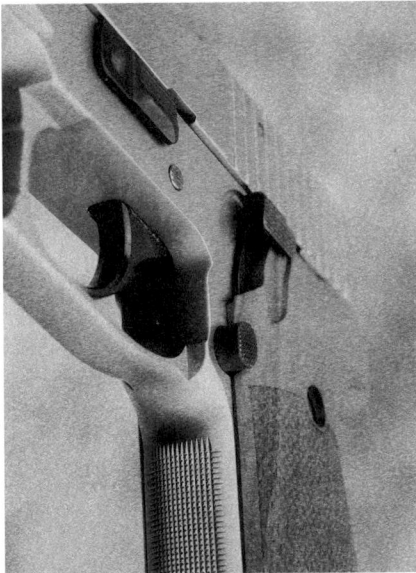

Slightly extended SIG magazine release from Langdon Tactical Technologies enhanced positive speed of reloading when tested by author, and did not seem to increase likelihood of unintentional magazine release, as is the case with some other such parts.

...two-handed extended (best control for rapid fire)...

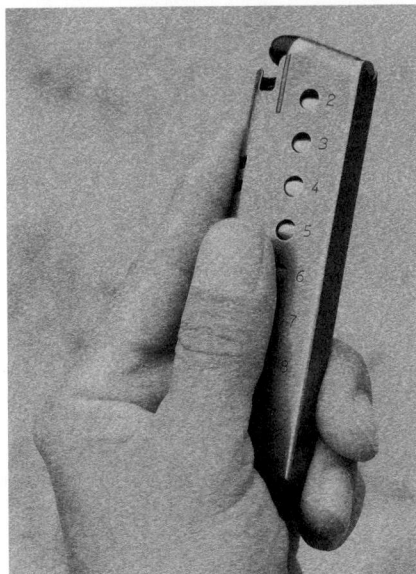

Here is the proper magazine grasp during any kind of reload. Floorplate is in contact with palm for maximum insertion strength. Index finger is in position to guide magazine into gun. Thumb and middle finger, the two strongest digits on the hand, take firm grasp.

...or with down elbow braced for single high-precision shot. Pistol is P226 9mm, scene is an LFI-II class in the Rockies.

Author uses P226 to demonstrate weak hand only reload. P226 starts with slide locked back...

...fresh magazine is accessed...

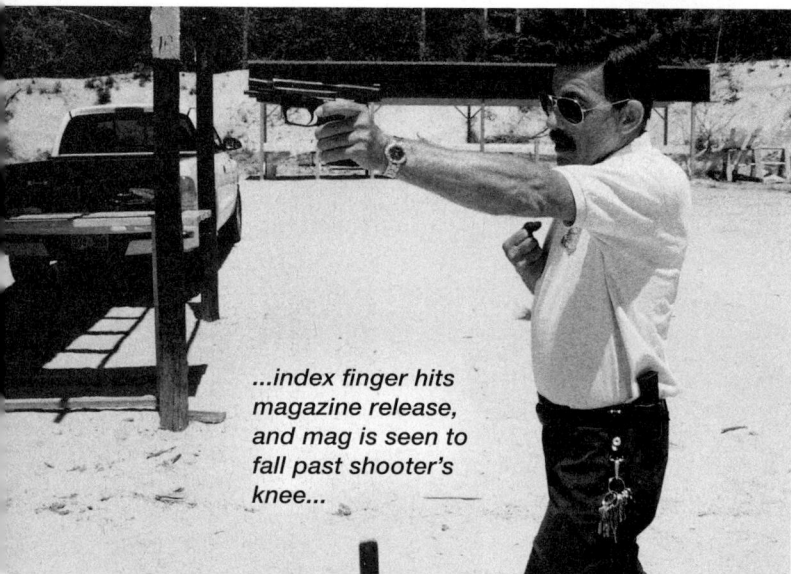

...index finger hits magazine release, and mag is seen to fall past shooter's knee...

...and inserted...

...pistol is inserted into Ted Blocker DA-2 holster butt-forward

...and locked in as shown. Thumb locks over backstrap of grip frame, palm over floorplate of magazine

...and close with a crush of the hand to ensure seating. Now...

...or with thumb as some others like, though author finds it a bit unstable...

...pistol is drawn cross-draw...

...or by catching sight against belt and thrusting forward and away from you, a variation of the "tug" method of slide release...

...and slide can be closed with trigger finger pressing straight down on slide release lever, as author prefers...

...and the shooter is now ready to get back to work.

Above: Author demonstrates his preferred one-handed-only reload on the strong-hand side. P226 is at slide lock. Thumb hits release button, and empty mag drops...

Right: ...gun is thrust into holster on this particular angle, because slide is locked back...

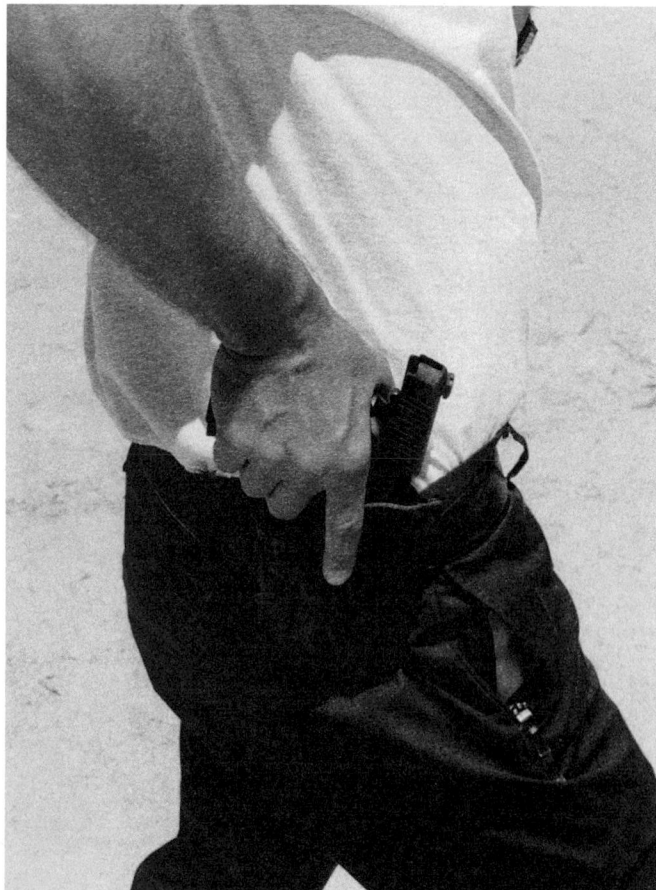

...then shoved securely home. Hand is now free...

...to reach around front and grab spare from duty belt, or around back as shown and grab spare mag from concealment pouch...

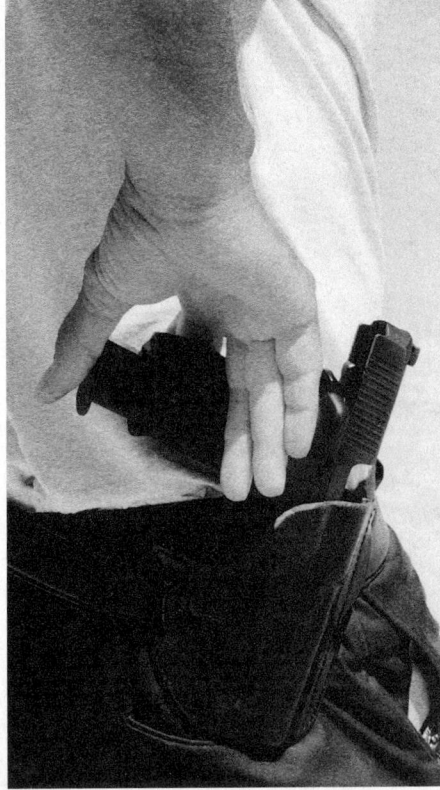

Top Left: ...insert into butt of holstered gun...

Top Middle: ...using index and middle fingers as pincers to stabilize locked-back gun in holster that no longer fits properly, thumb makes certain magazineis seated...

Top Right: ...gun is now drawn in conventional manner...

Left: ...and thumb hits slide lock release lever, putting shooter "back in business"

When face down with head toward an opponent, slapping the ground with your weak hand palm will give you the elevation you need to engage him.

keep fighting with the body parts that still work and finish the fight.

You can shoot a pistol with your weak hand or strong hand, right-side-up or upside-down and hanging from the chandelier, and anywhere in between. The key doing is successfully is to at least dry-fire from every conceivable position so your mind and body know how to do it. No, you may not have the accuracy or recoil control you'd have from an ideal, fully "enabled" position, but you can get the job done. It's important to have a plan ready to go when it happens, and dry-fire practice "programs your computer" for that.

Be extremely careful live-firing these techniques. A lot of downed officer positions can disorient the shooter and increase the chance of his gun muzzle crossing another good guy on the practice range. Take particular care when shooting from low on-the-ground positions that the angle is not such that your bullet will go over the backstop and escape the range. *It is recommended that these techniques be practiced with live ammunition only under close and competent supervision.*

Many of these positions make it difficult for the shooter to get a locked wrist behind the gun. This has been known to jam many semiautomatic pistols. Fortunately for the SIG-Sauer shooter, this brand is not particularly sensitive to weak wrists, though any autoloader can jam if held loosely enough.

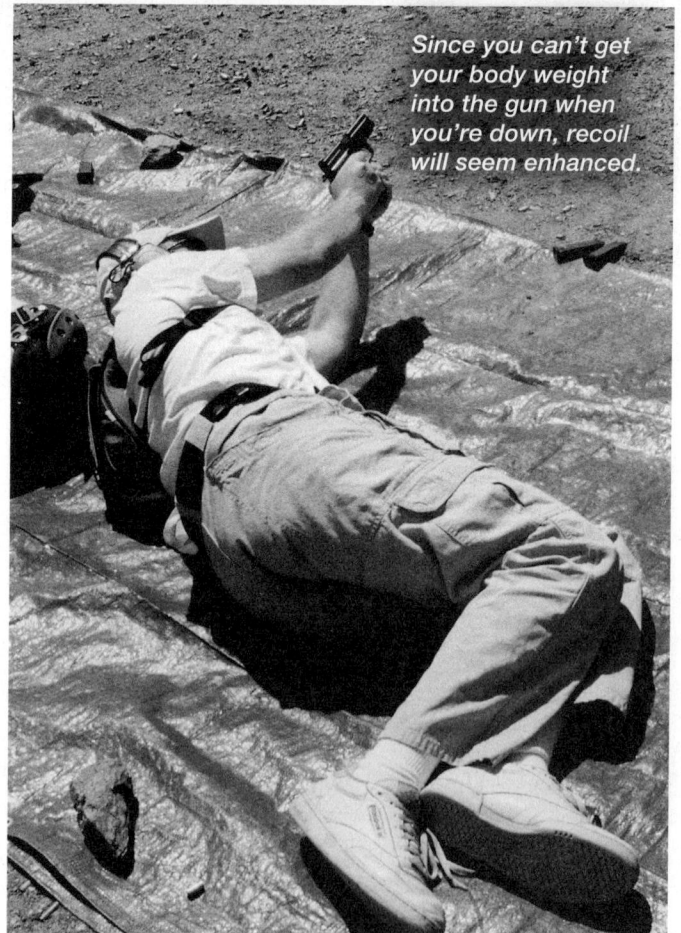

Since you can't get your body weight into the gun when you're down, recoil will seem enhanced.

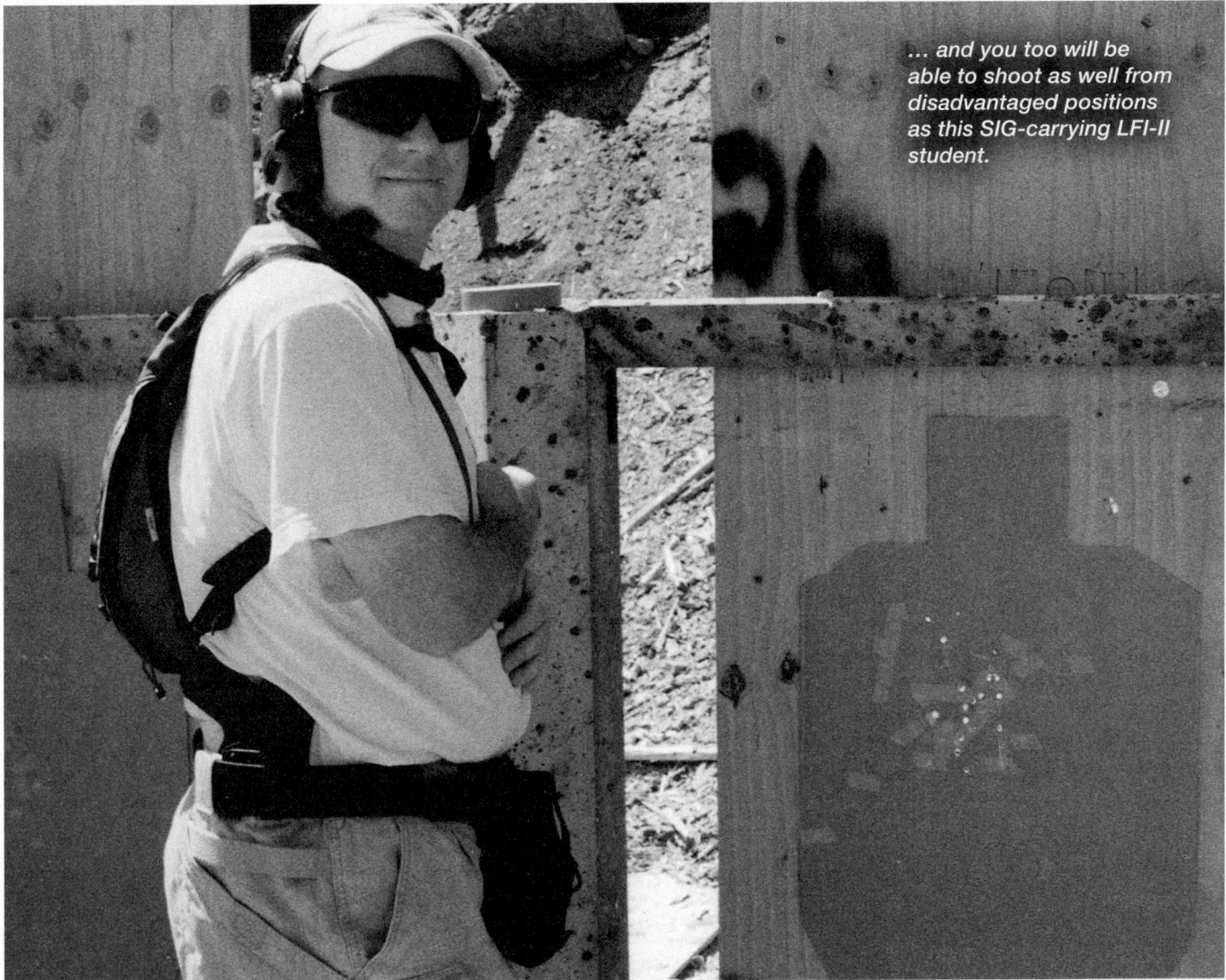

... and you too will be able to shoot as well from disadvantaged positions as this SIG-carrying LFI-II student.

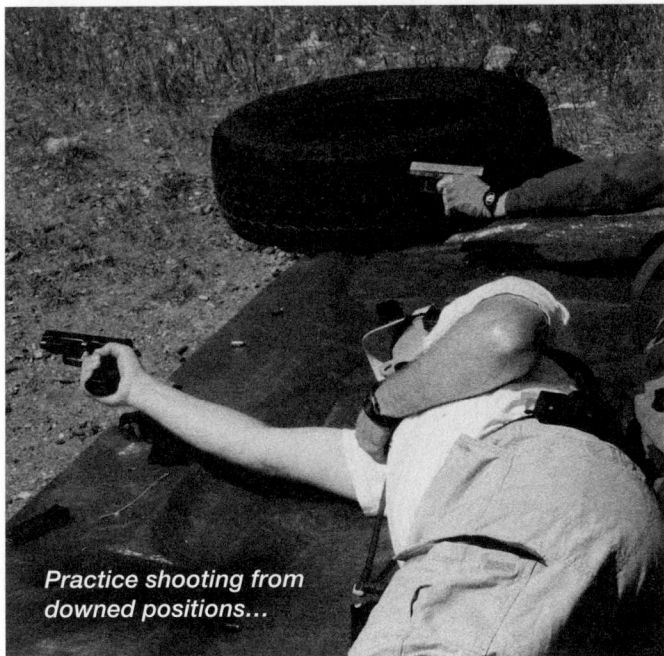

Practice shooting from downed positions...

...on either side, and prone and supine...

...two-handed and one-handed...

Chapter 20
Shooting the SIG-Sauer Pistol

The SIG-Sauer models are all accurate pistols. However, it is axiomatic that handguns are the most difficult firearms to shoot. The gun's inherent performance potential is one thing, but the shooter's actual performance lies mostly with himself. It's the driver, not the car, which wins the race.

Administrative handling is touched upon in an earlier chapter. Here, we'll address live fire techniques that have been proven to give the shooter faster, more accurate delivery of pistol fire. This will not be a reprise of the author's books *StressFire* or *The Gun Digest Book of Combat Handgunnery, Fifth Edition*, both of which go into shooting techniques with far greater depth. Rather, we'll simply touch on key elements of good, effective, safe practical shooting, with emphasis on how these elements may apply to the SIG-Sauer pistol.

GRASP

The grasp is the key interface between shooter and pistol. A target shooter may be able to get away with a light hold, but a combat gun will be rocked by the substantial recoil of powerful defense ammunition and needs to be held firmly. A target pistol with a 2-pound trigger pull may allow the shooter to get away with little grasping pressure. Not so a double-action pistol whose trigger pull weight on the first shot may be as much as 12 pounds. *That* task demands a firm hold or the pull itself can jerk the gun muzzle off target when the shot must be fired quickly.

Instructors agree on basic placement of the gun in the primary hand, but tend to debate such subtleties as thumb placement. There is consensus that the web of the hand should be high on the gun, pressed firmly against the bottom edge of the grip tang. This lowers the muzzle axis vis-à-vis the wrist axis as much as possible. This is good thing for several reasons. The high-hand grasp gives the gun less leverage with which to jump upon recoil. It helps keep trigger finger pressure coming straight back instead of relatively downward, where it could jerk a shot low. It also gives the slide a firm abutment against which to cycle, minimizing the chance of

Firearms instructor Wes Doss demonstrates marksman's kneeling position with SIG .45.

a malfunction. I like to grasp the pistol high enough that a little ripple of flesh shores up against the grip tang near the web of the hand.

The primary hand has basically four thumb placement options. The *vertical thumb* hold has this digit pointed straight up. I see nothing good whatsoever coming of this, only a weak hold and a thumb placement that can bind the slide, especially with a large or gloved hand. When I ask its proponents why they push the vertical thumb hold, the answer I always get back is, "High thumbs equal high scores." Sorry, that's a bumper sticker slogan, not a biomechanical explanation.

High thumb is a holdover from the old days of the 1911 pistol's renaissance. Back in the 1950s and 1960s, aftermarket gun parts makers had not yet figured out that the shelf of that gun's thumb safety needed to be curved. Otherwise, the middle knuckle of the thumb could hit the bottom edge and knock the lever back up into the "safe" position during a firing sequence. It became doctrine to "ride" the thumb safety with the shooting thumb to keep this from happening. This had some negative side effects, then and now. The thumb is placed where if it is large or gloved, it can contact the slide and bind it, jamming the gun. This hold also pulls the web of the hand away from the 1911's grip safety, which can cause the gun to fail to fire unless it has a correctly shaped grip safety as on the GSR 1911 pistol by SIGARMS.

Straight thumb grasp is the choice of most of the top modern shooters at the upper levels of competition. With the thumb pointing to the target, the index finger can pull back in a straighter line. It's something archers figured out before shooters did: the forward-pointing thumb aligns the skeleto-muscular support structure behind it in an advantageous way.

Low thumb, with the thumb curled – bent at the median joint, tip of thumb pulling downward – is seen by some as old-fashioned, but it remains the strongest grasp. It is particularly suitable for one-handed shooting, because of its added strength.

Right-handed shooters must be aware that HIGH-THUMB, VERTICAL-THUMB, OR STRAIGHT-THUMB GRASP CAN CAUSE THAT DIGIT TO RIDE A SIG-SAUER'S SLIDE STOP LEVER, DEACTIVATING IT. THIS MEANS THAT THE SLIDE CAN NO LONGER LOCK OPEN ON AN EMPTY MAGAZINE AS IT WAS DESIGNED TO DO. This will not occur with the left-handed shooter.

Some pistolsmiths, like Ernest Langdon, have attempted to cure this with a custom slide lock lever for the SIG-Sauer which has a smaller shelf. It has met with limited success at this writing. A high thumb can still over-ride the slide stop, and the smaller dimension only makes it more difficult to activate the slide stop.

Grasp options include "vertical thumb" hold, which author doesn't care for...

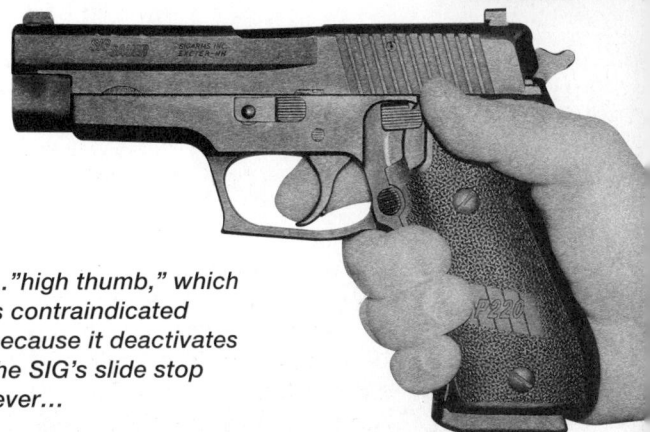

..."high thumb," which is contraindicated because it deactivates the SIG's slide stop lever...

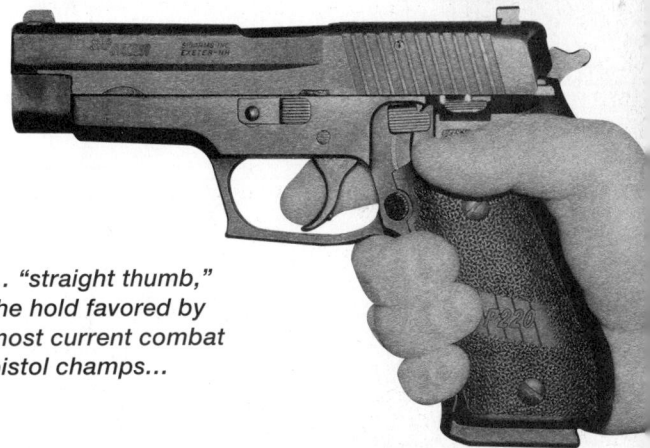

... "straight thumb," the hold favored by most current combat pistol champs...

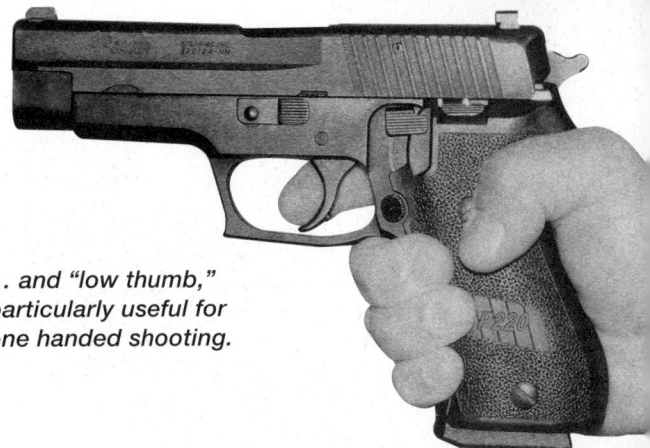

... and "low thumb," particularly useful for one handed shooting.

The simplest cure for this problem is to simply use the low thumb position. If that's not in the cards, use the straight-thumb grasp for two-handed shooting and adopt the "LE", or "Leatham/Enos" hold. Rob Leatham and Brian Enos, two of our most successful practical shooters, place the firing hand's straight thumb atop the support hand and out of contact with the pistol. Their support thumb is also pointed downrange toward the target.

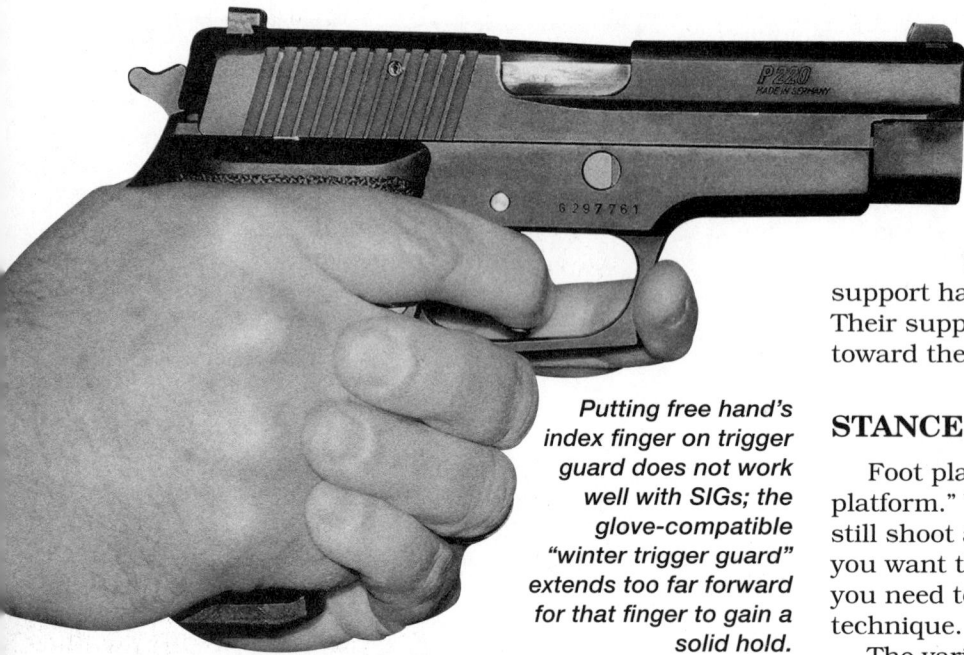

Putting free hand's index finger on trigger guard does not work well with SIGs; the glove-compatible "winter trigger guard" extends too far forward for that finger to gain a solid hold.

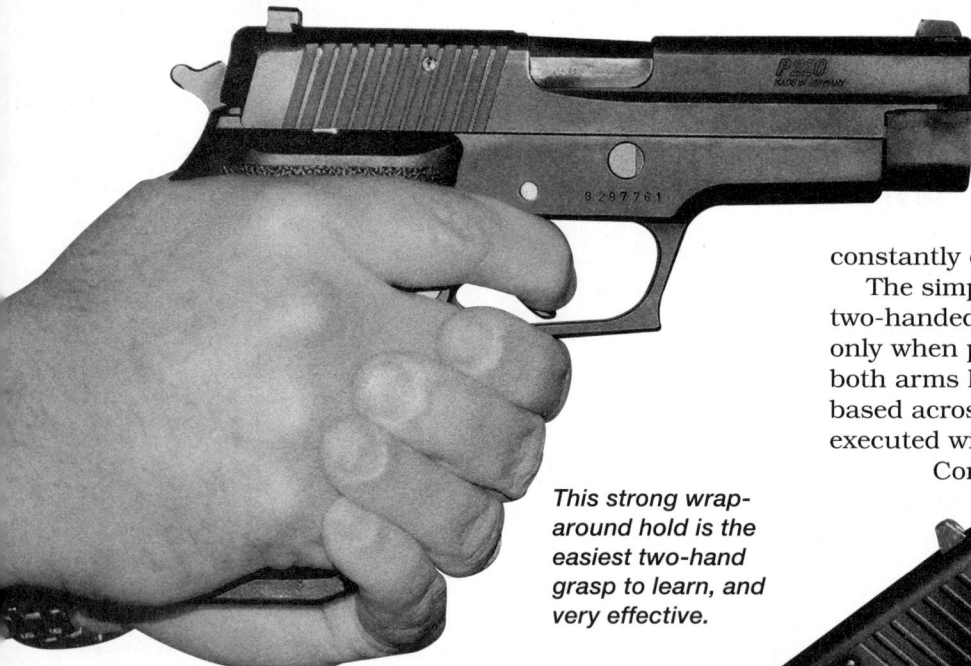

STANCE

Foot placement and body position create the "gun platform." You can be completely off balance and still shoot accurately, if you go slowly enough, but if you want the speed essential to defensive shooting, you need to get your whole body into the shooting technique.

The various stances are best taken collectively as parts of a system, rather than focusing on one to the exclusion of the others. Each has biomechanical advantages over the others in some situations, and a shooter with only one stance is like a fighter with only one punch: he won't last too long in the arena when everything starts moving and angles are constantly changing.

The simplest and in many ways the strongest two-handed shooting stance is the *Isosceles*, but only when properly executed. So-called because both arms lock out and form an Isosceles triangle based across the chest, this stance must be executed with the upper body forward of the hips.

Competitors who favor this style like to say, "Nose over toes." This writer has had the best luck with

This strong wrap-around hold is the easiest two-hand grasp to learn, and very effective.

Primary grasp is foundation of two-hand grasp. If shooter prefers thumb curled down...

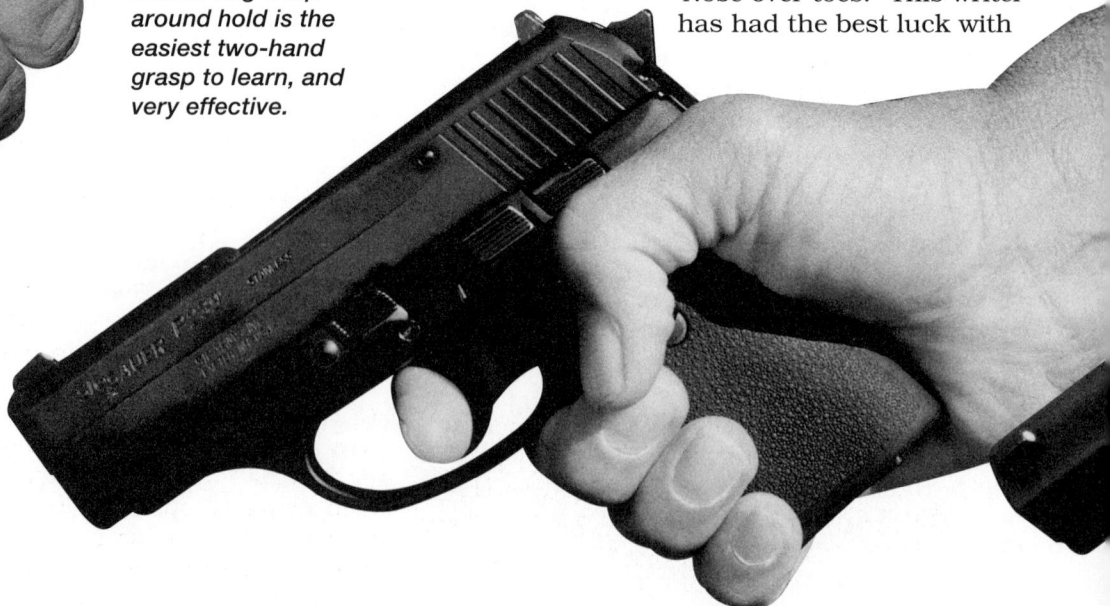

the extremely aggressive Isosceles stance developed in the StressFire ™ system. The rear leg digs into the ground hard with its knee just off a full lock, and the forward leg flexes distinctly to take the majority of body weight.

In Isosceles, the gun is at body center so it doesn't matter which foot is forward. The wide adaptability of foot position gives Isosceles the greatest range for swinging between different targets or threats at widely divergent angles, and the NYPD Firearms and Tactics Unit coined the term "turret stance" to describe this shooting posture, which they have taught and used successfully for decades. Even with feet parallel, the shooter can stay balanced if the knees are bent and the upper body is forward. Because the chest is square to the identified threat, this is the ideal stance to use when wearing body armor. The gun's placement at body center makes the Isosceles the ideal stance for the cross-dominant shooter (i.e., right handed with left master eye) and the most natural for darkness situations where the sights are not visible.

Downsides? While probably the most effective stance for pivoting toward your strong-hand side if you can't move your feet, Isosceles may give the least range of movement when pivoting toward your weak side. Some shooters are too muscular to use it without the muscles binding, and the same can happen with very tight shirts or coats and with some types of body armor and load-bearing vests. Requiring extended arms, it can be torture for shooters with elbow problems. If the shooter keeps

Author's preferred grasp of SIG. With no safety on slide to unlock, he likes to take advantage of the greater strength of the locked down thumb position, placing trigger finger on trigger at palmar surface of distal joint.

...doing the same with support hand, "thumb print over thumb nail," will work. Note that little of left hand actually touches gun. Doesn't much matter: strength of grasp is reinforcing right hand's grasp.

the torso straight up without forward lean, recoil control will be severely dissipated, and if the shooter leans back instead of forward, muzzle jump will go completely out of control.

The classic *Weaver* stance, popularized by Jeff Cooper and his colleague and inspiration Jack Weaver, uses isometric tension where Isosceles uses body weight and skeletal support structure. Best suited for those with good muscle tone and particularly good for those with great muscle strength, the true Weaver requires both elbows to be bent to some degree. The firing hand pushes forward and the support hand pulls back, with equal and opposite pressure. The tense, bent arms act as shock absorbers, flexing slightly at the wrists and noticeably at the elbows. This shock absorption effect allows the classic Weaver, alone among two-handed firing stances, to survive awkward positions in which the shoulders are back instead of forward, and is particularly suitable to shooting while moving. The feet need to be in a boxer's stance, weak side forward; if foot positions are reversed, the body binds at the hips and the lower back.

Because the body can generally turn more effectively to its weak side than its strong hand side, the bent arms of the Weaver afford great range of movement turning to the weak side, making it the stance choice in that situation. Conversely, it will be the poorest stance from which to pivot at the hips to fire toward the strong side if the feet cannot move. Tending to turn the body somewhat edgeways toward the target, the original Weaver stance compromises your protection when wearing body armor, which is of necessity partially cut away at the upper side of the torso to allow arm movement.

Author shows students the difference between classic Weaver and Chapman stances. In Weaver, both elbows are bent, with isometric push/pull, and stance will survive neutral or even rearward leaning torso position...

...while with Chapman's modified Weaver, gun arm is locked straight out and shoulder must be at least slightly forward.

Other shortcomings: The classic Weaver has poor adaptability to the cross dominant shooter, who must either tilt the gun sideways to align the sights with the dominant eye, or drop the head toward the gun-side shoulder, an awkward position which also compromises the ability to scan for danger. It does not work well for people of limited muscle mass, strength, and tone. It is a more complicated stance than Isosceles, more dexterity intensive, and more difficult to learn and teach. It requires extensive practice if it is to work in the dark without visible gun sights.

The *Chapman* stance, sometimes called a modified Weaver, employs the boxer's stance but with the gun arm locked straight toward the target, and the forward arm flexed and pulling the gun

arm back into the strong-side shoulder socket. Very compatible with long gun firing techniques, this posture's straight shooting arm brings the chest more forward and more effectively utilizes the shooter's body armor than does the original Weaver. Adaptation to the cross dominant shooter is easier, too. Simply bring the chin to the gun arm's bicep to align the sights with the opposite eye.

This stance, developed by world champion Ray Chapman, has few downsides. One is that, like Isosceles, it is greatly compromised if the shooter leans the shoulder back instead of forward. Another is that it doesn't offer as much range of movement to the weak hand side as the classic Weaver, nor to the strong hand side as the Isosceles.

For one-handed shooting, I use exclusively

the "punch" techniques of the StressFire system. The gun arm is locked straight out; the free hand curled up into a fist (preferably palm up for greater sympathetic upper body strength) in the region of the pectoral muscle, and the upper body is aggressively forward. Body weight is supported by a flexed forward leg, and body mass is driven forward by a slightly flexed rear leg or "drive leg" with its heel driven hard to the ground.

Avoid the street punk "gangsta" technique commonly seen in the movies in which the pistol is turned over flat on its side. Recoil control is poor and sighting is difficult. By turning the pistol somewhere between 15 and 45 degrees inward toward the weak hand side, however, gripping strength can be slightly increased. This variation was developed for precision match target shooting by the great Marine shooting champion Bill McMillan, and adapted and popularized by combat pistol champ Ray Chapman. Such great instructors as Clint Smith teach it today as their one-handed technique of choice.

Try this stance holding the gun straight up and with the "McMillan tilt," and see which works better for you. The tilt brings the gun's sights directly in line with the non-dominant eye, making

Ayoob demonstrates proper Isosceles with .45 hardball in a P220. Gun is still on target, but two spent casings in air show how quickly and recently the shots were fired. Note aggressive forward body posture. Grasp is a "wedge hold."

This tilt of the gun is one way to line up the sights for right handed, left eye dominant shooter who prefers Weaver stance. Demonstrated by Wes Doss at SIGARMS Academy range.

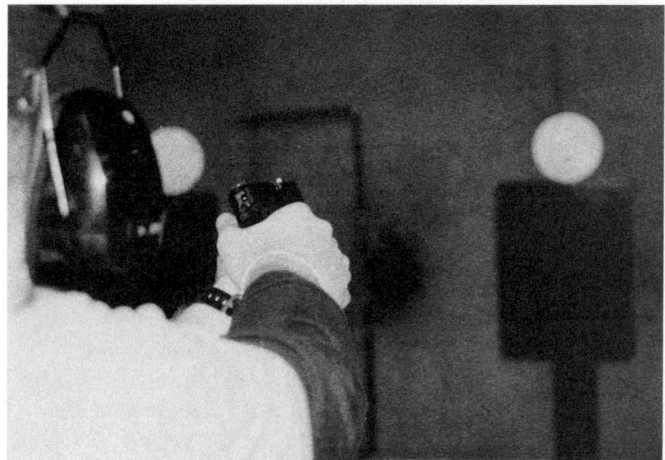

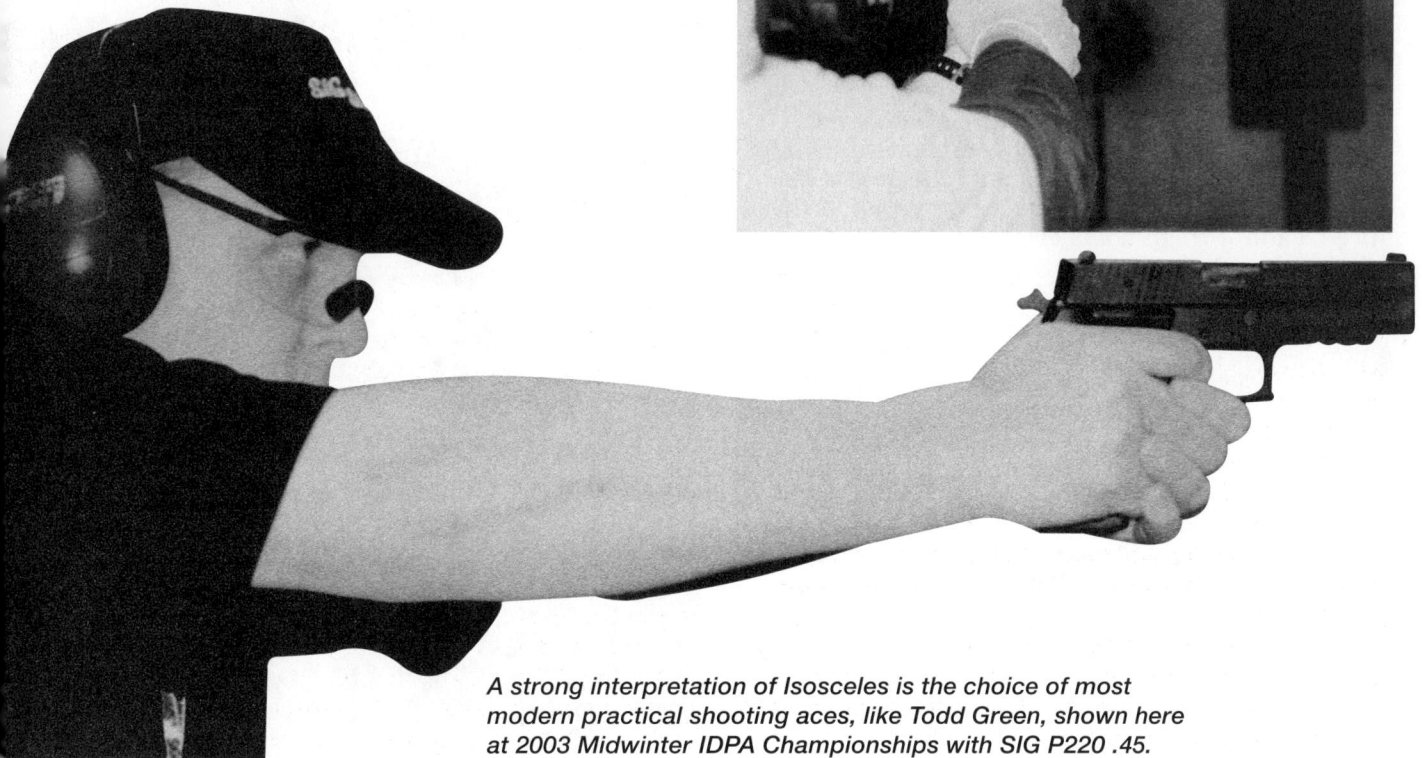

A strong interpretation of Isosceles is the choice of most modern practical shooting aces, like Todd Green, shown here at 2003 Midwinter IDPA Championships with SIG P220 .45.

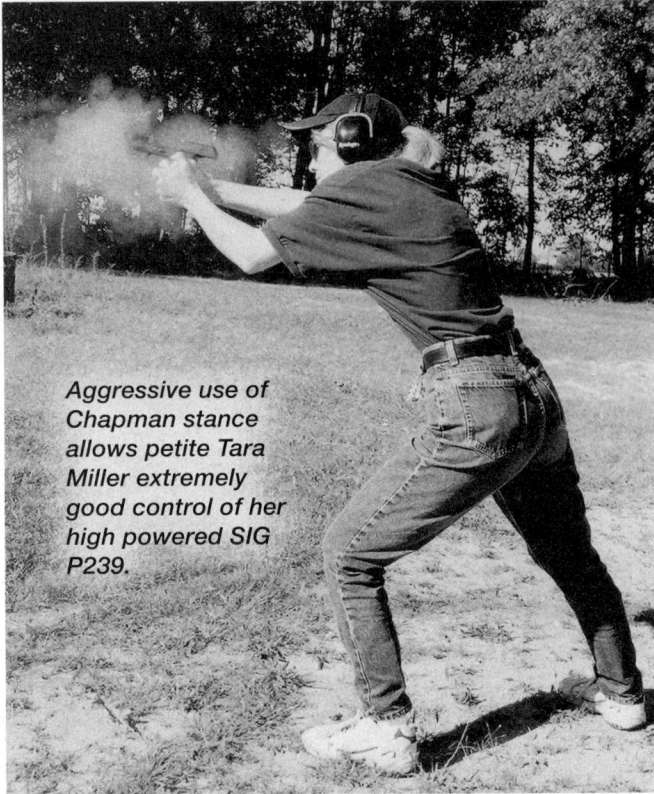

Aggressive use of Chapman stance allows petite Tara Miller extremely good control of her high powered SIG P239.

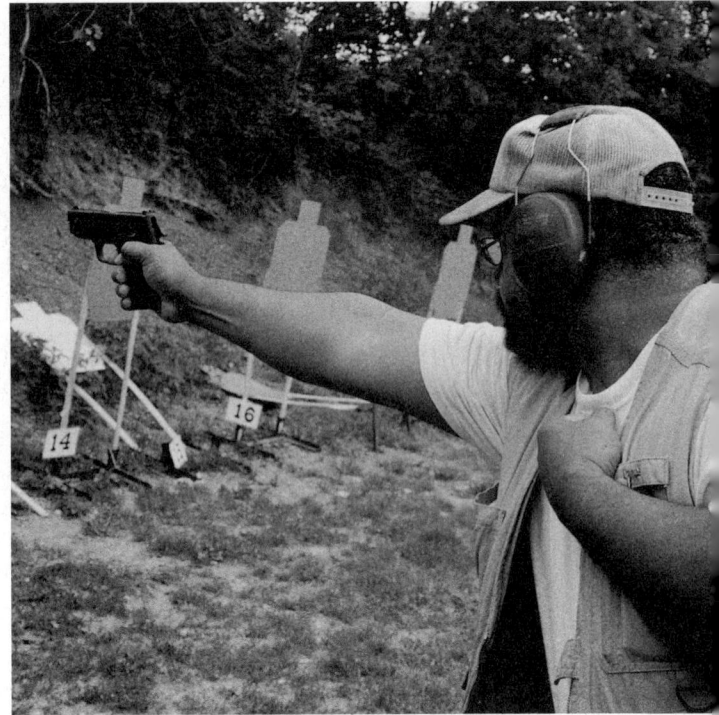

This LFI student demonstrates splendid control of his SIG with StressFire "punch" one-handed technique.

it the choice for cross dominant shooters. I tell my students to feel free to mix and match; many shoot one-hand-only with the McMillan on their non-dominant eye side and the sights straight up on their dominant eye side. It is important, of course, for the shooter to be well practiced with using either hand in one-hand-only firing.

NON-STANDING POSITIONS

The *roll-over prone* position developed by Ray Chapman is the strongest of shooting postures. The body rests on the earth, rolled onto the strong side of the torso with the weak side leg flexed up at the knee so a taut thigh holds everything in position without muscle tension. Be certain to let the heel of the support hand touch the ground for stability. Digging the butt of the extended magazine into the ground, contrary to popular myth, will help rather than harm accuracy. Try it yourself and see. (Don't do that if your pistol is has the European style butt heel release, however; recoil can move the latch of the pistol when the butt is in contact with the ground, causing an unintended dropping of the magazine.)

There are numerous *kneeling* positions from which to choose. The traditional marksman's kneeling rifle position can adapt to the handgun, with the lower inside edge of the upper arm against the front of the knee. Don't try to go "joint on joint" with ball of elbow on the kneecap; this will cause wobble, not stability.

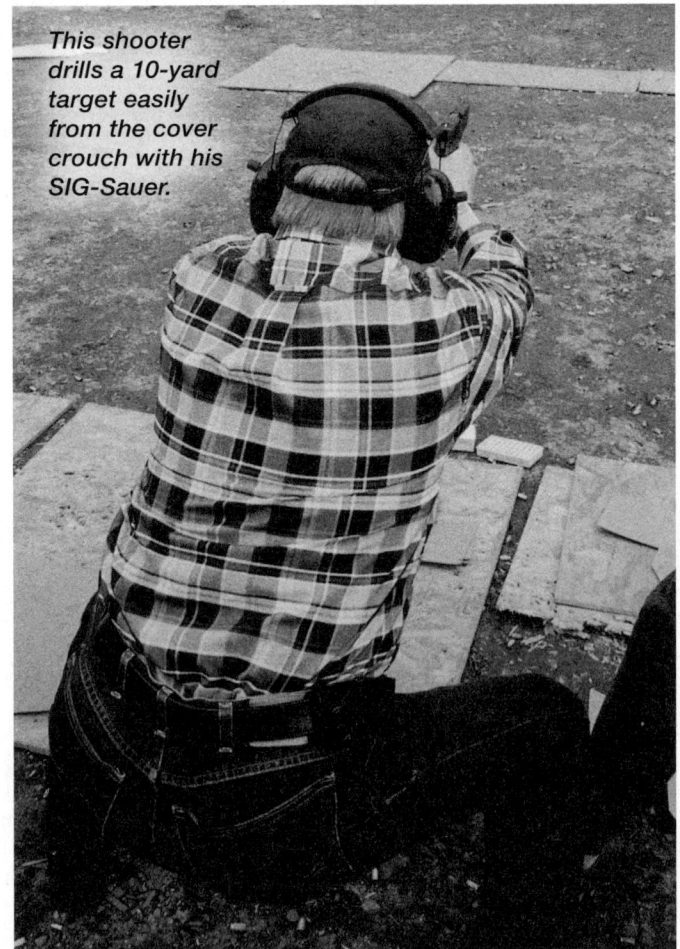

This shooter drills a 10-yard target easily from the cover crouch with his SIG-Sauer.

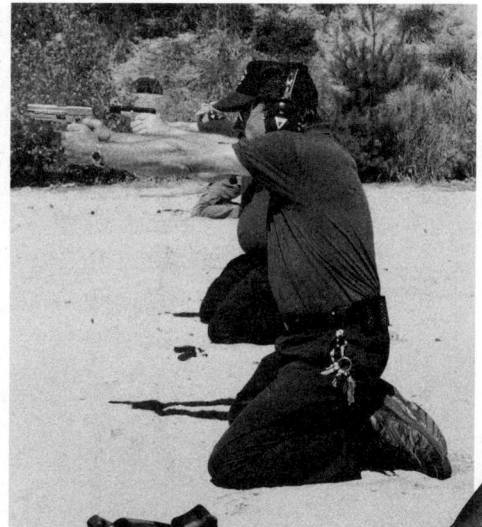

Top Left: Cover crouch… Top Middle: …high kneeling… Top Right: …and low kneeling may each have a place when behind low cover, depending on height of cover, angles of fire, and other circumstances.

At high speed, there often won't be time to get the elbow to the knee, and in any case that position brings the torso so far forward that breathing is compromised, as is vision through corrective eyeglasses. Elbow at knee also severely limits range of movement in terms of height and particularly in terms of the ability to traverse against running or multiple targets. Simply get a knee on the ground, keep the torso upright, and use an appropriate Weaver, Chapman, or Isosceles from the waist up if you want your shooting from the kneeling position to be fast as well as accurate.

For "high kneeling" as with shooting over a patrol car hood, you want to be down on the gun side knee only, with the other leg's knee up and foot flat. This will give you maximum balance. A high kneeling position on both knees positions the femurs as parallel vertical sticks, compromising balance and steadiness. If the target is at 12 o'clock and you are right handed, go down with the right knee on the ground pointing toward 2 o'clock and the left foot down flat, its toe pointing to 11 o'clock. For southpaws, reverse and put the left knee down, positioning the left knee toward 10 o'clock and the right foot toward 1 o'clock.

For low kneeling, keep the same stance and "rock back on your haunch," sitting on the strong side calf, or put both knees down and drop your buttocks. Be sure to flex at the waist to bring upper body weight forward to help to control recoil.

The *cover crouch* of StressFire is an alternative to kneeling. It is faster than going to kneeling, in terms of both getting into position and getting out of it to move to a safer location. It is also safer when

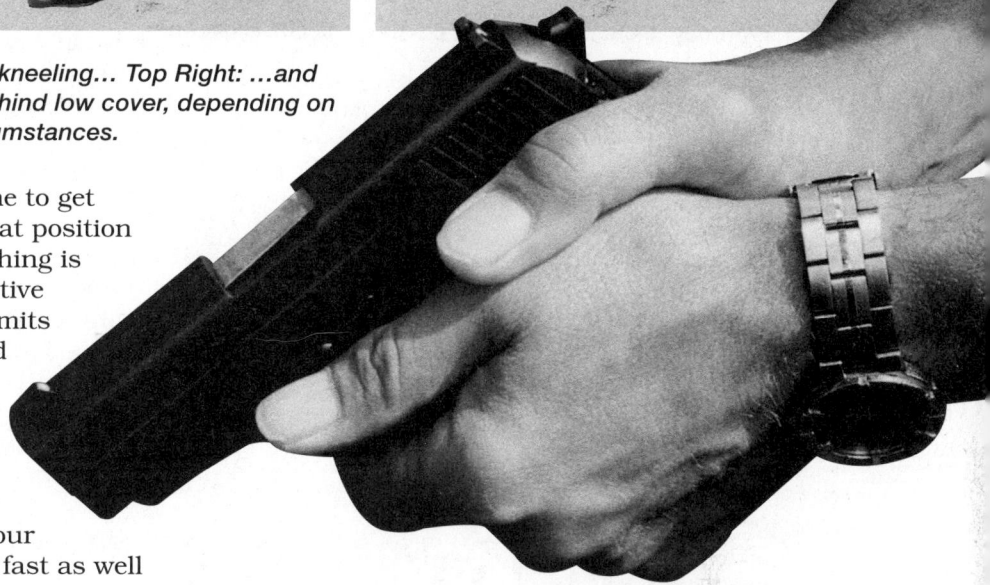

This Leatham/Enos grasp works very well, and applies pressure from drumstick of support hand to grip panel. If firing hand thumb is placed on support hand instead of frame, it won't over-ride this SIG P239's slide stop. Many shoot their best with this grasp.

the shooter may be on dangerous ground such as rocks, broken glass, punji stakes, or a rice paddy filled with *e coli* from "night soil" fertilizer. Unlike the skeletal support based "rice paddy squat" of the rifleman, this position is more similar to a martial artist's horse stance. The feet are wide, the knees are flexed deeply, the butt is low (at least knee level), and both feet are flat on the ground with upper body weight suspended equally between the two tense lower limbs. Not the most stable shooting technique, it is fast and safe and gets you to the same height as a high kneeling position.

Barricade shooting, or firing in proximity to cover, can be handled in different ways. Some advise getting back away from the cover. The problem with this is twofold. First is the geometric problem: the farther you are back from the barricade, the easier you are to

225

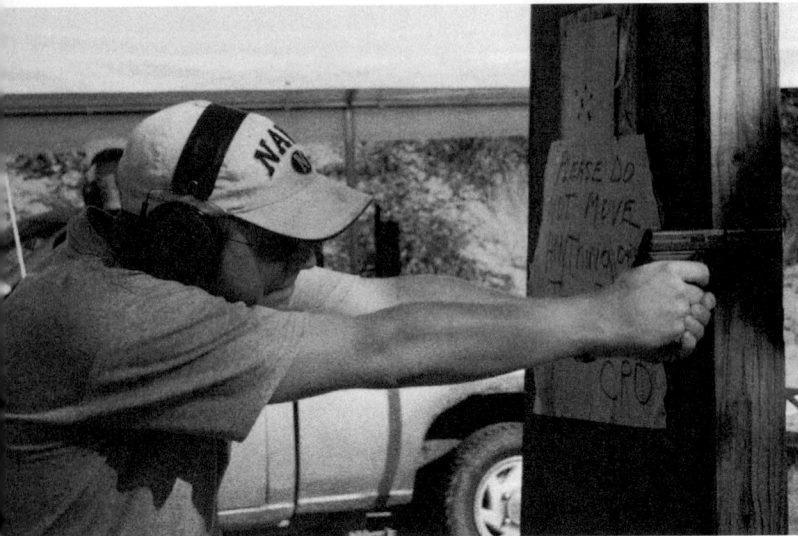

In barricade shooting, take care that your pistol's slide does not actually contact the cover, or friction bind can jam the gun.

Using techniques explained in this chapter, Ayoob has just shot this 60-round timed qualification target in front of his students to demonstrate. Pistol is P220 ST.

outflank. Second, it is less stable. Third, under stress you can hit your cover instead of your opponent. Not only does your cover now become your opponent's, but if it is something like a boulder or a steel beam, your own bullets could bounce back hard enough to take out an eye or knock you unconscious. Stay back from the walls, by all means, when *searching*, but when under fire it may actually make more sense to get closer to your protective barricade.

There is nothing unique to the SIG-Sauer to consider here. With any auto pistol, make sure that the slide is not in direct contact with the barricade, or it can bind and jam the pistol.

Your shooting posture will very likely end up being what the situation dictates when you need your SIG for real. The more familiarity you have with firing from the different positions, the more tools you'll have in your toolbag and the better a job you'll do.

Whichever your favorite shooting style may turn out to be, you'll always be able to apply to it the advice that countless students have learned from ace instructor George Harris at SIGARMS. "The three tenets to successful shooting are balance, mobility, and stability," according to Harris. "You must always balance the body, be mobile and therefore always able to improve your position, and stabilize the muzzle on the target. The trigger is always controlled in both directions when justified in shooting. The index finger never loses contact with the trigger. When fitting the pistol to the shooting hand, the muzzle should point naturally to where the eye is looking."[1]

ADVANCING THE BASICS

Don't focus so much on the fine points of style that you forget the basics. The finger should stay in contact with the trigger throughout the firing sequence, because if it comes off and then has to return, it strikes with impact. This is the often warned against "trigger slap" that pulls the muzzle off target. Some instructors will tell you to "catch the link" or "ride the link," meaning to let the trigger come just far enough forward from the previous shot to reset the sear. This can work in experienced hands in a shooting match, but tends to fall apart under pressure. It is a rare person who can actually do it in the heat of a life-threatening fight. Under stress, strength goes out of control and dexterity goes down the toilet. Flexor muscles being stronger than extensor muscles, it is highly likely that in a "fight or flight" situation the finger will be unable to feel the catching of the link and will fail to return the trigger sufficiently to reset it for the next shot. This could be disastrous. The defensive shooter is better served to allow the trigger to return all the way forward until it moves no more, without actually removing the finger from the trigger.

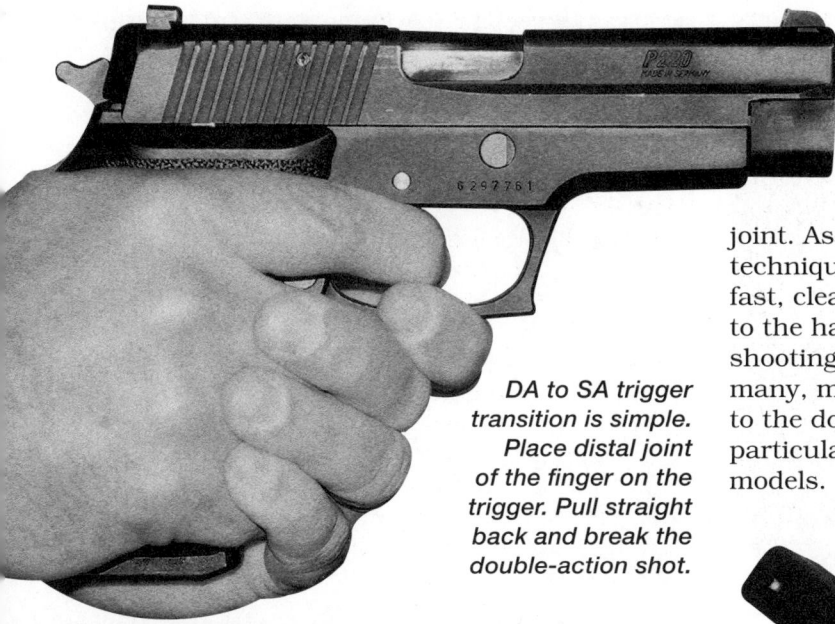

DA to SA trigger transition is simple. Place distal joint of the finger on the trigger. Pull straight back and break the double-action shot.

joint. As illustrated in accompanying pictures, this technique gives the finger maximum leverage for a fast, clean, straight pull with minimum disturbance to the handgun. Masters of double-action revolver shooting have known and valued this technique for many, many decades, and it translates perfectly to the double-action semiautomatic pistol, being particularly valuable with the double-action-only models.

Shooter will be strongest if gun's fit to hand allows barrel to be in line with center of forearm with wrist locked. If hand is too small or trigger reach too far...

...and, changing neither grasp nor finger placement, let the trigger come forward to stop and fire again in single-action. Yes, it is that simple. Pistol is P220 American.

...shooter is forced into this weak "h-grip," with only thumb in line behind recoil. A poor adaptation with a powerful combat gun, this is called the "h-grip"...

SIG-Sauers come in two variations, traditional double-action (TDA) and double-action-only (DAO). The first double-action shot may require 10 or more pounds of pressure, though probably no more than seven with the DAK variation, but that's still a lot more than the weight of the gun. This means that the pistol must be held steadily and firmly throughout the trigger pressure. It also means that the shooter will benefit greatly from the maximum leverage he or she can exert against the trigger.

Instead of using the usual index finger placement with the pad or tip of the finger on the trigger, Lethal Force Institute teaches putting that finger on the trigger at the palmar crease of the distal

...because it causes the hand and arm to describe a lower case letter h.

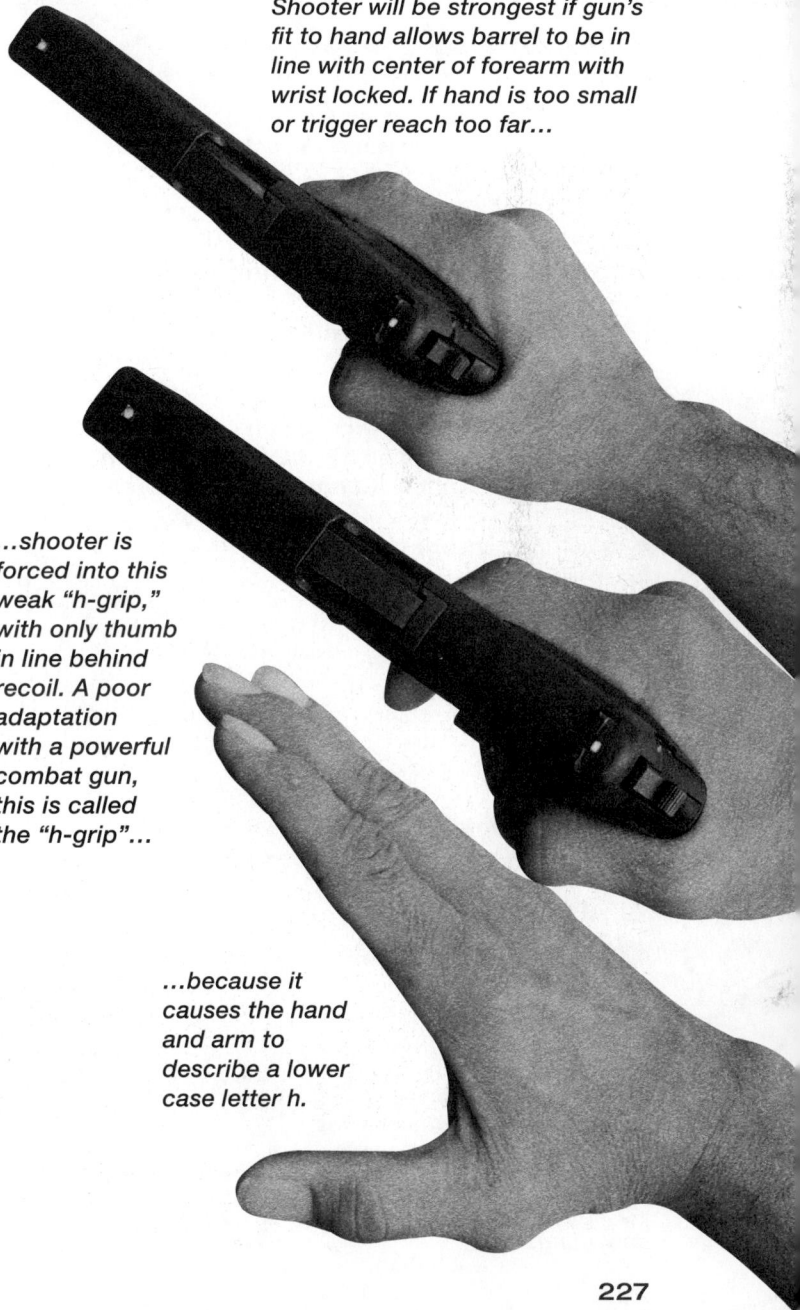

227

DA technique as recommended here has given author these five hits at seven yards, decocking after each shot...

... and it looks as if everything is under control. Double-action autos are not so hard to master as some would have you believe. Pistol is stock P220 ST.

Transition from double- to single-action, despite the confusion and misinformation that abounds, is simple. No change of grasp or finger placement is required. Here's the secret.

Grasp the handgun firmly, holding it on target. Place the distal joint of the index finger on the

Importance of firm hold. To make a point on the SIGARMS Academy range, George Harris deliberately fires a .45 with light grasp. Note high muzzle rise...

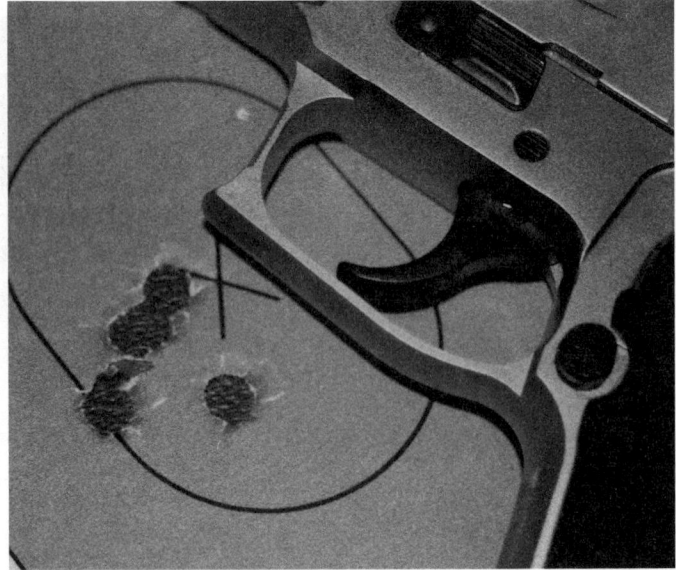

Right: ...but now, using strong stance, George demonstrates negligible muzzle jump as his XS-sighted P245 sends a .45 slug into the steel target downrange.

trigger. Draw it back until the shot breaks. *Keep the finger in contact in exactly the same position at the distal joint.* Allow the trigger to return forward until it stops (or, if you insist, until it catches the link). Repeat the process, firing the subsequent shot(s). Yes, it *is* that simple.

The gun is like a long-range drill with the bullet as the drill bit. If the drill is not indexed, the holes will not appear in the intended place. The gun's sights are the most precise index. A hard focus on the front sight, once it is properly aligned with the rear sight, is critical to precision accuracy. At very close range and at high speed, a coarser visual index will still get you on target. This writer prefers the StressPoint Index of the StressFire system, with the front sight atop the rear sight. Even with the eyes locked onto the threat in "target focus," this alignment is coarse enough to be seen in secondary or tertiary focus and recognized by the mind as the signal to shoot right now. Looking over the top of the gun or superimposing the whole gun over the whole target can also work. Sometimes called "point shooting," these actually comprise quick and dirty aiming.

Good luck. The key to your development of defensive skill will be your training. With the SIG-Sauer pistol, you'll be well equipped in that environment, and we'll explore that shortly.

References

1. (1) "Training Tips" by George Harris, *Velocity* magazine, February 2003, P. 5.

Chapter 21
Holstering the SIG-Sauer

Developed originally for the soldier, the SIG-Sauer design was swiftly adopted by many armed citizens and by domestic police of many nations. All three categories of end user had one thing in common: they had these pistols for self-defense, and that meant that they had to be carried.

The soldier with his web belt, the cop with his Sam Browne rig, and the citizen with the concealment holster all know what an inconvenience it can be to "carry" for somewhere between eight and 24 hours a day. Selection of the holster and its related accoutrements becomes critical. If it's uncomfortable or, in concealment, too obvious, the wearer will find excuses to go without it, and will be helpless when the day comes that the gun is needed for its intended purpose.

Today, we are blessed with a better and more efficient selection of holsters, belts and ammo pouches than ever in the history of the handgun. There's no good excuse for leaving your SIG at home when you go in harm's way. Yes, you can carry a .25 auto or a miniature .22 revolver instead of, say, a P239. You can carry a Band-Aid in your first aid kit, too, instead of trauma dressings and Quick-Clot. But then you have to ask yourself why you have emergency gear in the first place.

The answer is simple: in case of an emergency. If someone is hemorrhaging, the Band-Aid isn't going to stanch the massive bleeding. But with a

good pressure dressing and a fist full of Quick-Clot, the victim has a fighting chance to survive. A mouse gun is convenient to carry. However, I've had occasion to show my students the death scene photos of a despondent and suicidal old man. He shot himself three times with a .25 auto before he died, pausing after each of the first two shots to go into the bathroom and examine himself in the mirror to find out why he was still up and running. After the third and finally fatal shot, he had time to carefully set the gun down and fold his hands across his chest in the classic "resting in the coffin" position. I explain to the students, "This is the effect of three muzzle-contact small-caliber pistol wounds on a frail, elderly man who wants to die. It shouldn't be hard to extrapolate what the effects of that low-powered gunfire might have been on a huge, enraged, drug-fueled attacker who wanted *you* to die."

BREAKING IT DOWN

A couple of things need to be broken down and treated separately here. There are holsters that work for large pistols but not for small ones, and there are holsters that make sense for large pistols that would be ludicrous when filled with little guns. Also,

Inspect your holster as carefully as your gun. This old Safariland duty thumb-break's leather safety strap is cracked with age, disqualifying it from future use.

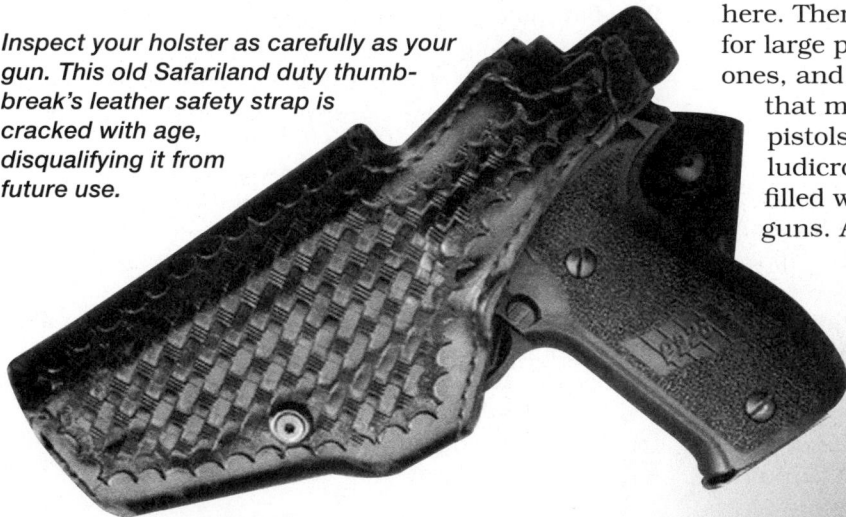

Quality is always worth it. This is the splendidly made, high performance #55BN by Milt Sparks Leather, designed by Bruce Nelson.

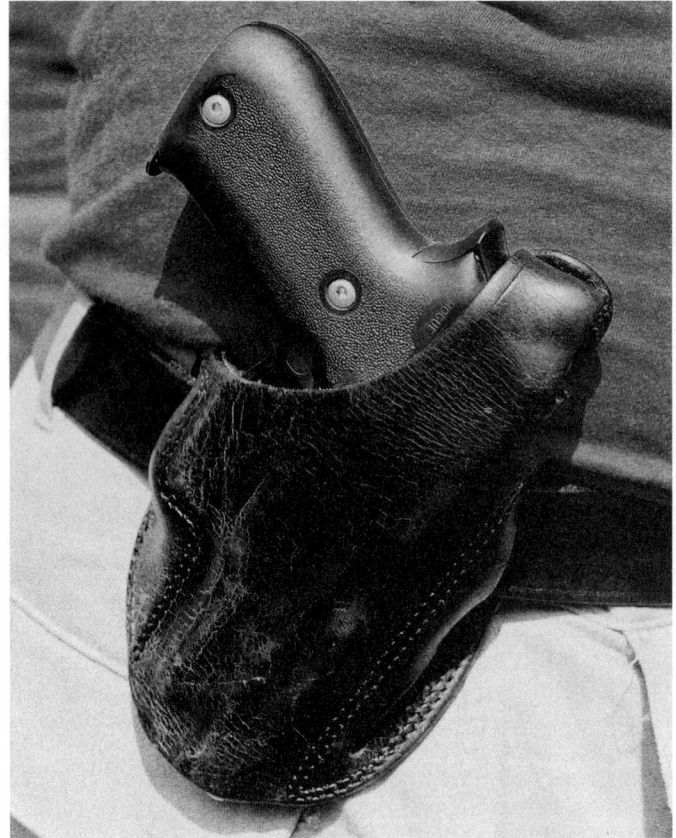

A safety strap makes sense even on plainclothes/off duty holsters, like this one carrying a Chicago officer's P220 DAO .45.

just semantically, the chapter title "Holstering the SIG-Sauer" can be taken two ways. It can mean "picking a holster," and we'll get to that momentarily. But it can also mean "putting your gun in the holster." You're going to have to do that no matter what size your pistol may be, so let's discuss that first.

SAFELY INTO THE HOLSTER

The newcomer to this gun-carrying business worries about being too quick on the trigger and shooting his foot off when he draws the gun. Actually, what seems to happen more often is that a careless shooter accidentally discharges the weapon while putting it into the holster.

In Southern California, one officer became understandably rattled after shooting a large, vicious dog that attacked him. It took a good part of a high-capacity magazine of department-issue 147-grain subsonic 9mm JHP to put the animal down for good. He forgot to decock his traditional double-action service pistol, which did not happen to be a SIG, and he also forgot to remove his index finger from the trigger of his still-cocked and still-loaded pistol. He thrust the weapon into the holster. His finger hit the edge of the holster and stopped. The rest of the gun kept going.

BANG! He shot himself in the leg. Startled and terrified, also understandably, he went into

that endless loop mode people enter when they're confused, and kept trying to do what he had been doing. The issue holster, designed by his department and made to their specifications by the gunleather company, was open in the front and had allowed the slide to cycle, ejecting the fired round and feeding another into the firing chamber. As he attempted to holster again, the same thing happened. BANG!

Along about then, he connected the cause and effect, and stopped. However, he now had two bullet holes in his leg. He survived, and interestingly enough, sued the holster company...

All of which leads us to a holstering principle I have been teaching for years and years. HOLSTER YOUR PISTOL WITH YOUR THUMB ON THE HAMMER, HOLDING IT IN PLACE, AND WITH YOUR TRIGGER FINGER EXTENDED OUTSIDE THE TRIGGER GUARD! The index finger is called the "pointing finger" for a reason: in this case, it points the gun into the holster and will make the task smoother, faster, and altogether more professionally accomplished. They call it the index finger, after all, because it *indexes*. As you holster, you want to feel the surface of the gun's scabbard beneath your trigger finger: another felt index that the finger is safely out of the way.

Twin "J-hooks" effectively secure this Kydex holster by Sidearmor inside the waistband. Pistol is P229.

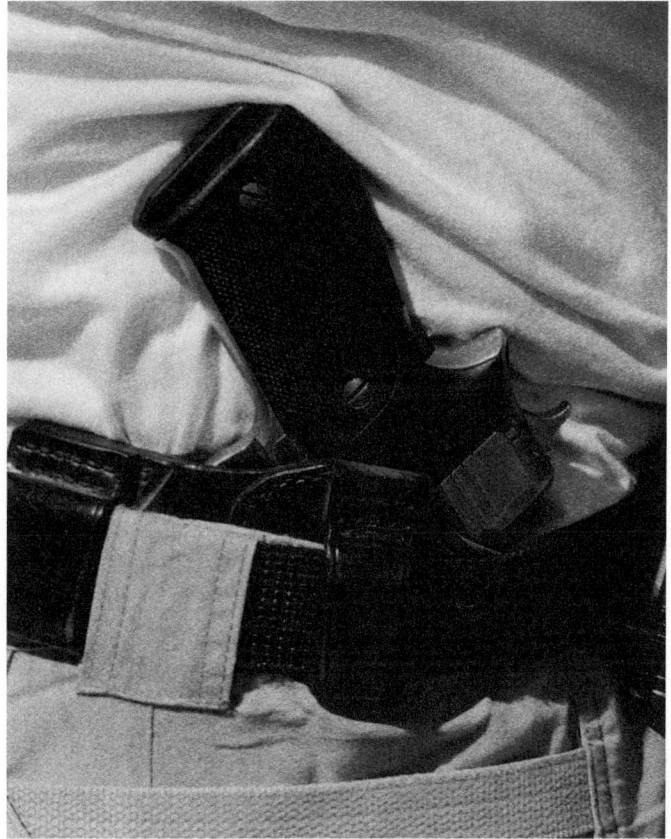

With a second belt loop as suggested by Mark Morris, this ARG-M inside-the-waistband holster locks its P220 firmly in position.

The thumb on the hammer verifies that the double-action pistol is in fact decocked. If the trigger finger or anything else catches the trigger, the thumb will feel the hammer start back in time to stop everything and prevent an unintentional discharge from taking place. The thumb is, after all, holding the hammer down. If you are holstering a cocked and locked 1911 or P35 pistol, and something trips the hammer forward, your thumb is in position to interdict the hammer's fall before the gun can fire.

Do not "palm" the gun when doing this. The way you do an "administrative" holstering while calm is the way you will have programmed yourself to do it when you have to holster after the gun has been drawn in a high-stress situation. In the latter scenario, if you realize in mid-process that you have begun to holster too soon, you can simply bring the thumb back into firing position as you raise the gun again. In holstering, nothing changes in the grasp except that the thumb goes to the hammer and, of course, the trigger finger is kept clear of the trigger guard. The remaining three grasping fingers *should not change their positions at all.*

This is a generic technique that will work with any handgun, even a striker-fired Glock, Kahr, or

what have you. The thumb on the back of the slide holds the slide forward, preventing a tight holster from pushing the slide back and out of battery. When the gun is drawn, there is no guarantee that the tight holster will pull the gun back into battery again, and a gun out of battery is a gun that will not fire when you need it to fire. The thumb on the back of the slide of the striker-fired pistol ensures that the gun is in battery while in the holster, and therefore will be in battery and ready to do what it's there for when it is drawn.

With the SIG-Sauer pistol, I suggest that you modify the technique very slightly. The easy-working slide of the typical SIG-Sauer can, in fact, push back slightly out of battery when inserted into a too-tight holster. This is because the safety shelf on which the hammer sits (erroneously called a "half-cock notch" by some) holds the hammer slightly back from the rear face of the SIG's slide. To keep that from happening, simply place the thumb diagonally at the back of the slide as shown in the accompanying photographs, so that the thumb at once is holding the hammer *and* the slide of the SIG in the appropriate forward position.

Use this "holstering grasp" while inserting your pistol into any receptacle. And when you

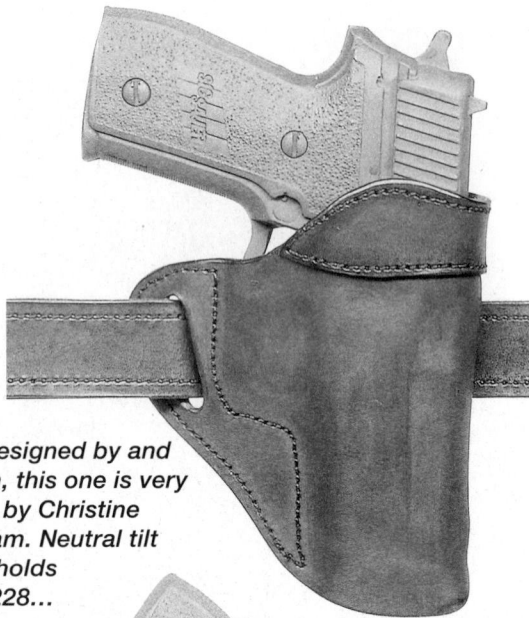

Holsters designed by and for women, this one is very well made by Christine Cunningham. Neutral tilt scabbard holds dummy P228...

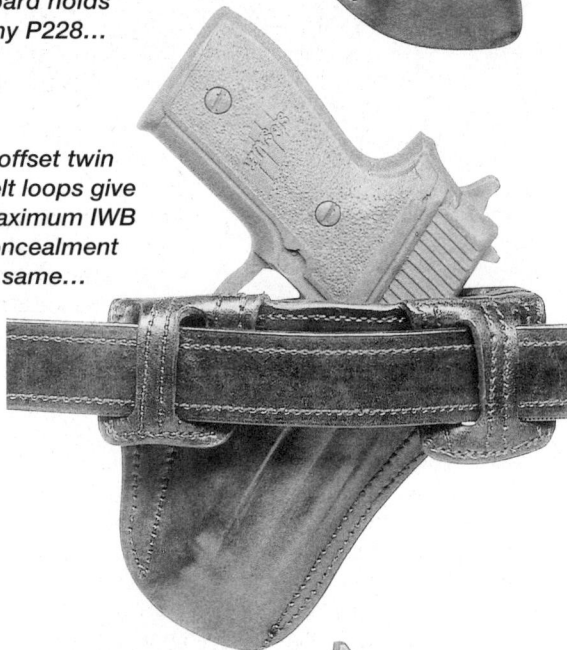

...offset twin belt loops give maximum IWB concealment of same...

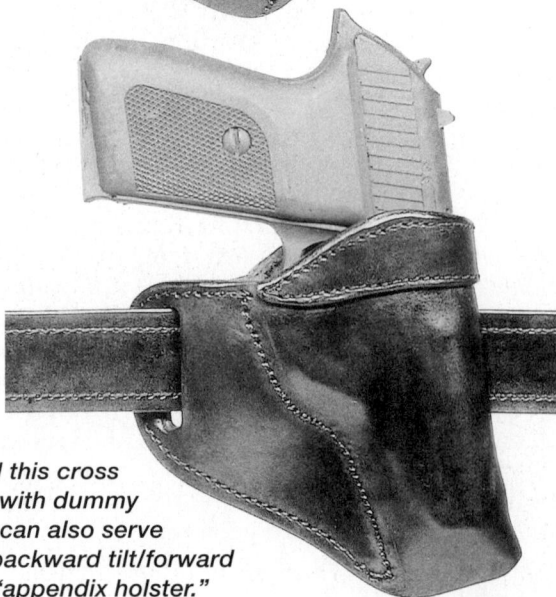

...and this cross draw with dummy P230 can also serve as a backward tilt/forward rake "appendix holster."

put a gun in a drawer or lock box, remember the admonition we all give our kids and "Watch what you're doing!" Many years ago in Alaska, a police officer became distracted in conversation with a brother officer as he put his pistol in a lock box while entering a secure area. He did not realize that as his P220 entered the metal receptacle on an angle, its hammer caught on the edge of the door and became cocked as he thrust the gun in. Later, without looking at the gun, he retrieved the cocked pistol and shoved it in his holster. (Safety straps on some holsters for double-action pistols are cut in such a way that they can snap with the hammer back instead of properly forward.) The stage was set for an injury-producing accidental discharge that occurred later that night. Fortunately, it was not fatal.

BEST RIGS FOR SMALL SIGS

The smaller the gun, the easier it is to hide in a concealment holster. No one reading this needed to pay the price of this book to figure *that* one out. The fact is, however, that what's small for one isn't that small for another. I'm sure there are guys out there with legs the size of The Incredible Hulk's and pants huge enough for me to cut off and use as T-shirts, who can wear SIG P228s or P229s in ankle holsters. I've met guys who have carried the P239 in an ankle rig. But the fact is, I can't hide a gun that big there, and neither can most people.

Even the little P230 and P232 pistols are a bit on the long side in both barrel length and slide top-to-gun butt height for ankle wear. In any case, I wouldn't recommend either the SIG or the Walther .380 for that type of carry. They are finely fitted pistols, and do not well survive the dust and grit with which an "ankle gun" is covered after just a day of being carried a few inches above where the soles of the shoes are kicking up dirt with every step. I've run across cases of ankle-carried SIG and Walther .380s that were drawn and fired in self-defense and jammed in the midst of the firefight because they choked on that grit. A P239 or larger SIG will cope with that, but those guns are just a *little* too thick and just a *little* too heavy to be practical for all day, every day carry strapped to most people's ankles.

Shoulder rigs, particularly the horizontal styles, work great with the smaller guns since the shorter gun doesn't require as much depth of chest to conceal when slung under the arm. The fact is, however, that most folks who have experimented a lot with the different gun/holster combinations find that the shoulder rig is actually more suitable for larger pistols in most applications.

The vest holster favors a gun with a short butt and a slim profile. By "vest holster,"

I mean a scabbard that attaches to the side of the chest under the uniform shirt on the elastic Velcro-closing straps of a bullet-resistant vest. The slimness of the SIG .380 makes it a natural for this, but they you're back to that thing about "what do you really carry that backup gun *for?*" I confess that I carried a SIG P230 there for a while, but constant reminders from the field of the relative impotence of its .380 cartridge brought me back to something more powerful as my second gun. A P239 won't be that much more noticeable in the same kind of carry, and now you're talking about something really serious coming out of the muzzle when you really need what the late, great police instructor Bill Clede called "Onion Field Insurance."

If you want a pocket gun, you may want a revolver instead of *any* semiautomatic pistol. Again and again I've tried different small autos in the side pocket, from the ingenious little Seecamp and NAA Guardian .32s up to the baby Glock, and after each period of experiment I've come back to the snub-nosed .38 Special revolver loaded with +P ammunition. It's not so much a "power thing" as an "accessibility thing." True, the revolver with shrouded hammer will fire every shot through a coat pocket and the auto pistol will probably jam on the first shot when the slide binds in the fabric and the lining of the pocket blocks the ejecting casing. However, in a pants pocket you're not going to shoot through the clothing anyway, unless your plan is to shoot yourself in the kneecap. Physical human dynamics get in the way.

The "pocket problem" with autos is, the very flatness of the pistol that made it so comfortable to carry there holds the inner side of the gun tight against your thigh, and when you reach for the gun your fingers have to claw to get a hold. The rounded grip-frame of the small revolver guides the reaching fingers into a drawing position much more rapidly. My own bottom line on this can be stated simply: I don't carry my SIGs in pants pockets.

The belly band, on the other hand, makes huge sense for small autos such as the shorter SIGs. Developed originally by John Bianchi in the 1960s and first produced by the MMGR

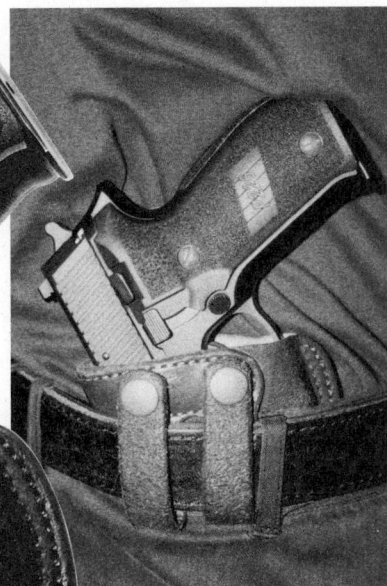

First designed by the late Bruce Nelson and known as the Summer Special, this is the most-copied style of IWB holster and is as fast and concealable today as it ever was.

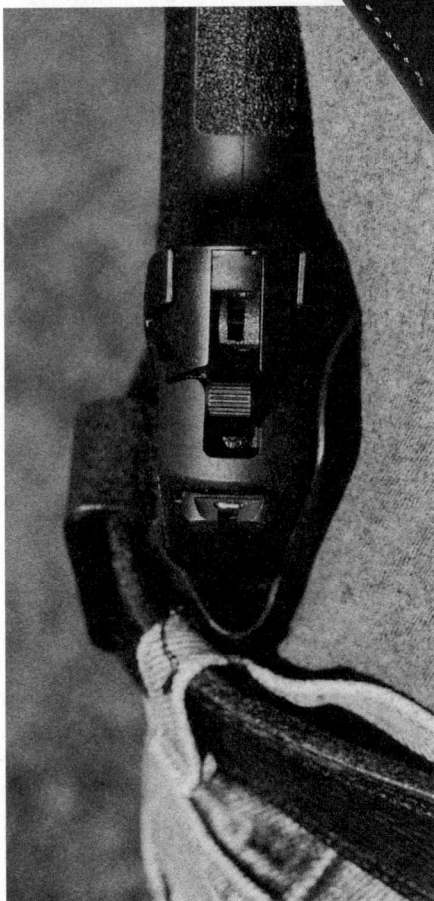

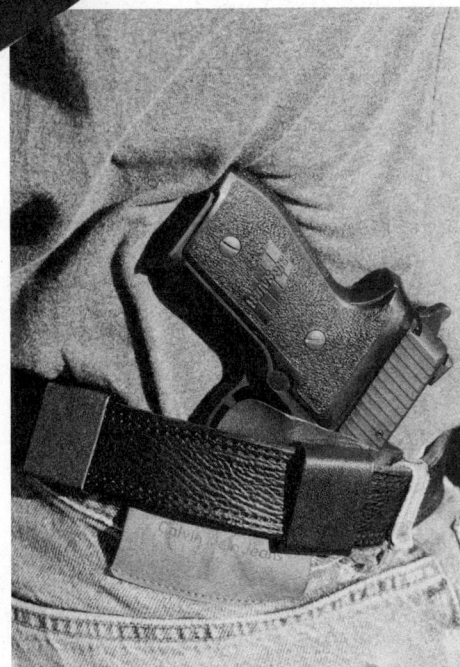

This Ky-Tac IWB is extraordinarily fast, comfortable, and concealable and its waterproof material helps to shield this P228 from wearer's perspiration.

Company in New York, the belly band is a 4-inch-wide elastic belt with a gun pouch. It rides very nicely under a tucked in shirt, "inside the outerwear but outside the underwear." Holster catalogues show these things worn wrong, across the lower rib cage. That can work for buxom women if the pistol butt is centered in the midst of the cleavage, but for anyone else, it's going to look as if they're wearing a colostomy bag in the wrong place. The belly band should be at belt level.

With a short automatic or a snub-nosed revolver, it can be particularly effective to carry the gun at the front of the abdomen. Most males find that wearing it to the left of the navel if they are right handed, vice versa for southpaws, puts the gun in a very accessible cross-draw position. The hand can access it quickly through the front of the shirt. I personally find that anything bigger than a P230/P232, P239, or snubby revolver will, when I sit down, dig into the femoral artery where my leg joins my torso. Taller men with higher waists don't seem to have that problem. Neither do women, who have higher waists in any case and seem to be much more comfortable with the pistol at centerline of the abdomen.

My older daughter, a tall and slim young woman, found this the optimal place to carry a P239-size gun. She found she could conceal it under almost anything. She also discovered that this location made the gun very accessible even under winter clothing. She proved it one snowy night when two would-be rapists came after her. The gun was out so fast that one of them almost fell trying to backtrack away from her as he and his accomplice fled her drawn pistol. I was damn glad that she had that gun. I sincerely hope that both of those punks still wake up screaming with nightmare recollections of the muzzle of her 9mm pointing at them.

If the belly band doesn't feel comfortable with the gun in the front cross draw position, the wearer can always slide it around to put the gun toward the strong side hip. In fact, this works particularly well for larger pistols that must be hidden deep, as will be discussed in greater depth shortly.

Women who wear regular belt scabbards often find that wearing the gun in front of the hip, instead of behind it where most of their brothers carry, works better for them. The cross draw and shoulder holsters that men find awkward tend to be ideal for women who tend to have narrower torsos, higher waists, and proportionally longer and more limber arms. Conversely, the high-ride hip holsters that work so well for men can be torture for many females, with the discomfort increasing in proportion to their curves. The wider female pelvis pushes the gun muzzle out, which means it pushes the higher-mounted gun butt *in*, and a gun butt that on the male is at kidney level is, even on his

sister of the same height, at lower rib cage level. This not only impedes the draw but can be hellishly uncomfortable in all-day wear.

We've been talking about the smaller pistols here. There are a great many of us who prefer the full-size SIGs for our particular needs. Can these be carried concealed? Most certainly! So we'll now segue to that topic.

BEST RIGS FOR BIG SIGS

If you want a top quality fighting handgun in a sufficiently potent caliber – 9mm and up – the SIG-Sauer catalog should be one of your first stops. If concealment is what you want, you can't do better than the P239, offered in 9mm, .357 SIG, and .40 S&W. Countless cops and citizens alike, as well as the U.S. Army Criminal Investigation Division, use the compact high-capacity P228 9mm, which is also extremely popular with the FBI. About the same size, but heavier in the slide, is the P229. It's a light-kicking joy to shoot in 9mm, but most prefer it in its more potent chamberings, the .40 S&W and the .357 SIG. Even trimmer for concealed carry is the 9mm P225, originally developed for German police and still widely used by them. This fine little 9mm is favored as their uniform duty weapon by two of the nation's top officer survival instructors, Dave Spaulding of the Montgomery County Sheriff's Department (Dayton, OH) and Roy Huntington of the San Diego Police Department.

Yet there are those of us who prefer the larger SIG-Sauer pistols. Some just can't resist the 16-round capacity of the 9mm P226. The high-capacity magazines are still available on the secondary and gun show market for private citizens and from licensed dealers for police officers. For some others, the reason is caliber: the .38 Super and .45 ACP are available only in the service-size P220 models. Being a fan of the .45 ACP, that's important to me. Besides, I've determined that the P220 .45 European model with flat backstrap and butt-heel magazine release works better in my hand than any other pistol when I'm encumbered with heavy gloves during the brutal winters of my northern New England home turf.

So it is that I've had a lot of occasion to carry full-size SIG-Sauer pistols concealed. For many years, SIGs were my teaching guns at Lethal Force Institute, and the P226 or P220 would be with me even in tropical climes, still carried concealed as my personal defense weapon after work. Thus, I learned to carry the full-sized SIGs under anything from a polo shirt to a winter mackinaw.

I have learned from people who came to similar decisions through much, much harder expedients. Most reading this will recall the April 11, 1986 gunfight in Miami in which two FBI agents were killed and three crippled for life in a harrowing gunfight before the two cop killers were shot dead. One of the maimed FBI men was supervisory special agent Gordon McNeill. In the opening moments of the fight, McNeill emptied his six-shot revolver and shot one suspect but was wounded, in the gun hand. Unable to reload or otherwise continue firing, he turned to run to his vehicle for his shotgun, and at this helpless moment he was shot and crippled by cop killer Michael Platt. McNeill is no longer with us, but carried a 16-shot SIG P226 9mm to the end of his days with the FBI.

Special agent Edmundo Mireles is considered by most to be the hero of that terrible shootout. His left arm nearly blown off by a .223 round, Ed cycled his 12 gauge pump one handed to shoot back and when it ran dry, emptied his six-shot revolver as he staggered into the kill zone, slaying the two gunmen with five hits out of six shots. Struck by how much lead these suspects had absorbed before they stopped fighting — including .38 and 9mm slugs and 00 buckshot — Mireles told me he had become one of the first FBI agents to switch to the SIG P220 .45 automatic when it subsequently became an option for field agents.

Carrying the SIG in uniform is simple enough. I carried the P226 for a while in a Don Hume Lynx, which I liked because the leather of this Level II security holster came up over the glowing Trijicon night sights, concealing them from view if I was sneaking up on a suspect in the dark. In time, however, I went to the P220 .45 in what I consider the best of all police duty holsters, the Security Level III Safariland 070, designed by Bill Rogers as the SS-III.

Concealed carry required more options, because four-season wear put a lot more cards in the game. Basically, it comes down to three sets of holsters and wardrobes, because spring and fall are pretty close.

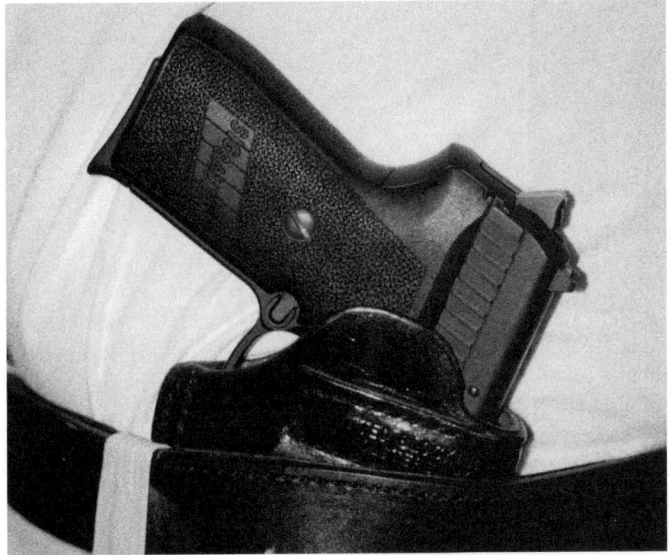

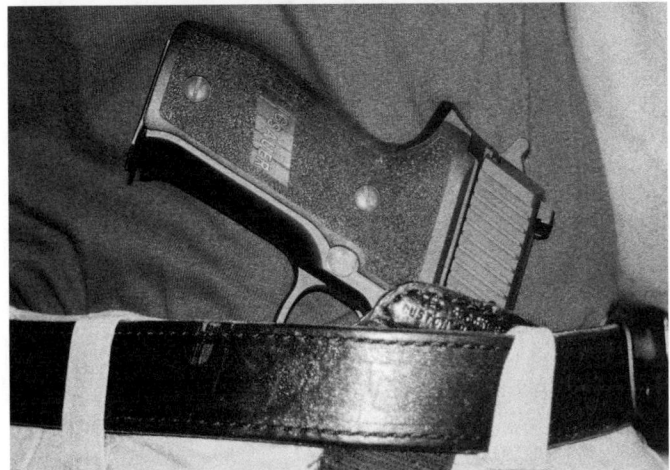

Above: Using Velcro tab mated with Velcro lining of matching dress gunbelt, the LFI Concealment Rig designed by manufacturer Ted Blocker and the author gives wide range of secure positioning, and easily conceals not only this subcompact P239, but also the full size P226 above.

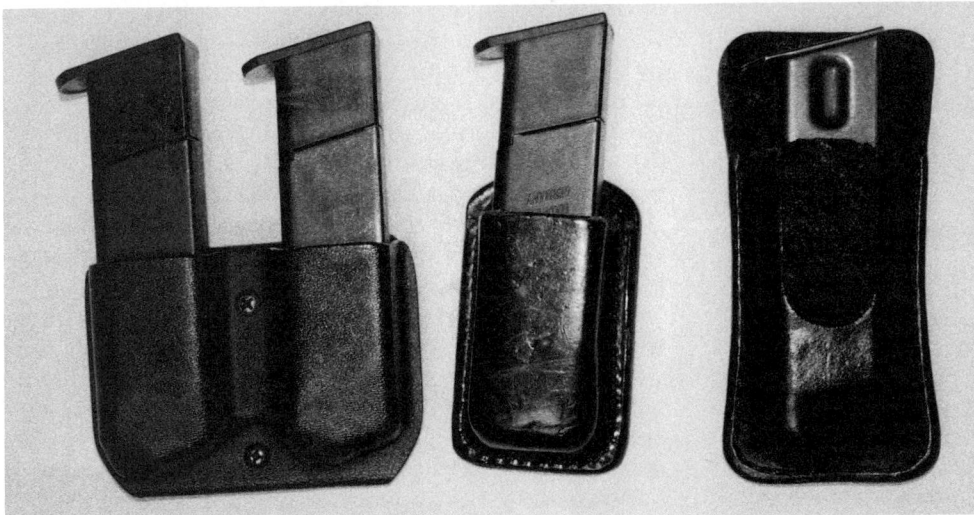

Three takes on magazine pouches. Left, the Blade-Tech double pouch made of Kydex is super-fast, reasonably concealable. Dillon leather single-cell pouch, center, is comfortable, affordable, and very fast. LFI Concealment Rig pouch, right, is slower but the most concealable; note the leather shield to protect body from magazine edge in IWB carry.

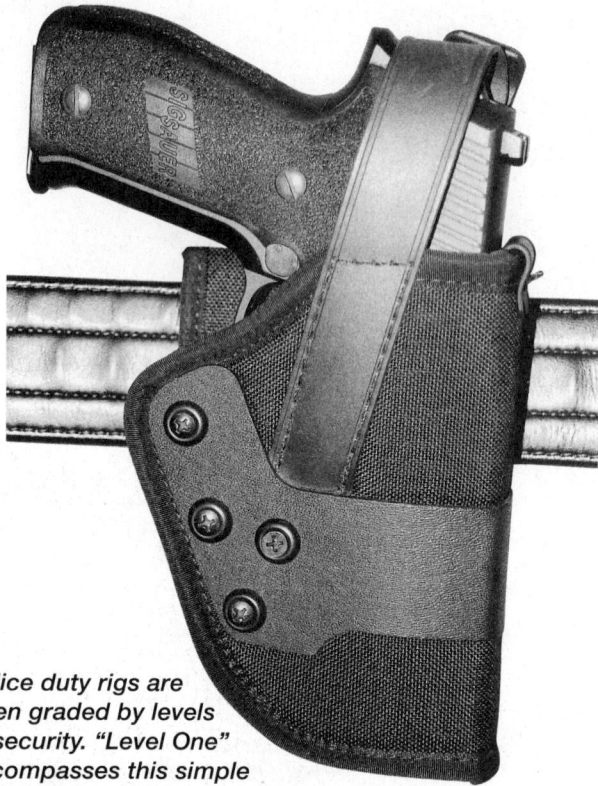

Police duty rigs are often graded by levels of security. "Level One" encompasses this simple Uncle Mike's rig, with a single thumb-break safety strap retaining the P226...

... "Level Two" is typified by this Safariland SLS (SelfLocking System) holster, here containing a .40 caliber SIG P229, which requires two moves to release the gun for draw...

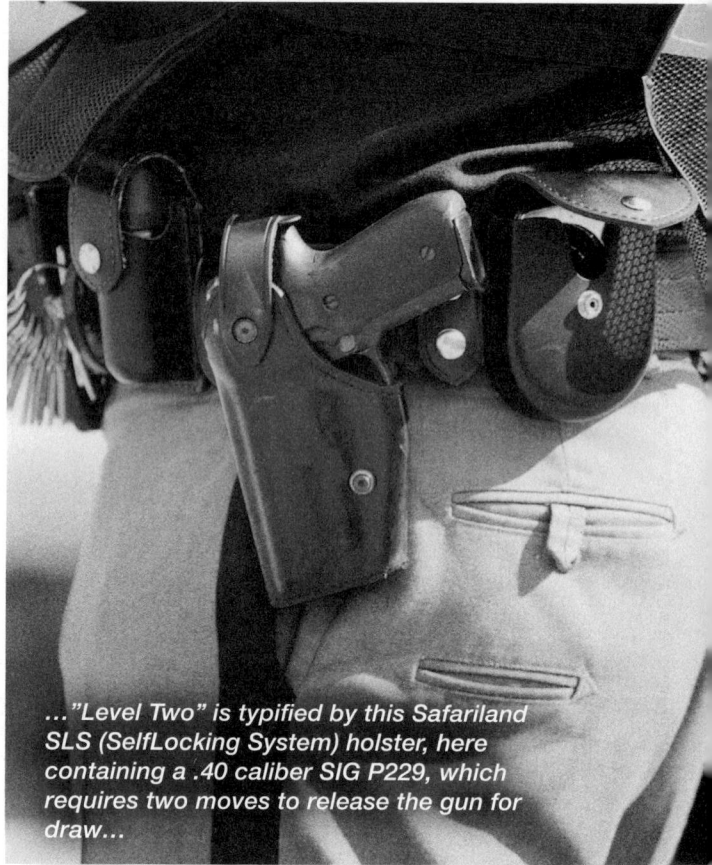

... and "Level Three" is exemplified by the author's favorite in uniform, this Safariland SS-III/070, which requires three retention elements to be cleared before draw is allowed.

HOT WEATHER CARRY

Summer means that, unless you're going in and out of formal environments in the course of your daily work, you won't have an outer garment like a suit coat on all the time. I recall one bodyguard assignment where my consultation with state law enforcement indicated that the client wasn't paranoid: the suspect *did* intend to kill him and had committed murder before. The locale was murderously hot and humid.

I wore body armor for that one, under a wardrobe of untucked square-bottom bowler's shirts, khaki bush shirts, and the guyaberra shirts popularized by Cubans in Miami. All were one size large, allowing for both the Second Chance vest and the P220 .45 loaded with CCI's famously effective 200-grain "flying ashtray" bullets, which it fed perfectly and shot with deadly match accuracy.

The holster was the LFI Concealment Rig that I had co-designed with Ted Blocker in the 1980s. It comes open-top or thumb-break. I have both. I wore the open-top on this job, because the small fraction of a second difference in drawing speed was likely to matter given the profile of the attacker, who would get to move first and would predictably come in shooting. I wore two spare magazines inside my waistband in the complementary carrier on the opposite side. Both mated with Velcro tabs to the

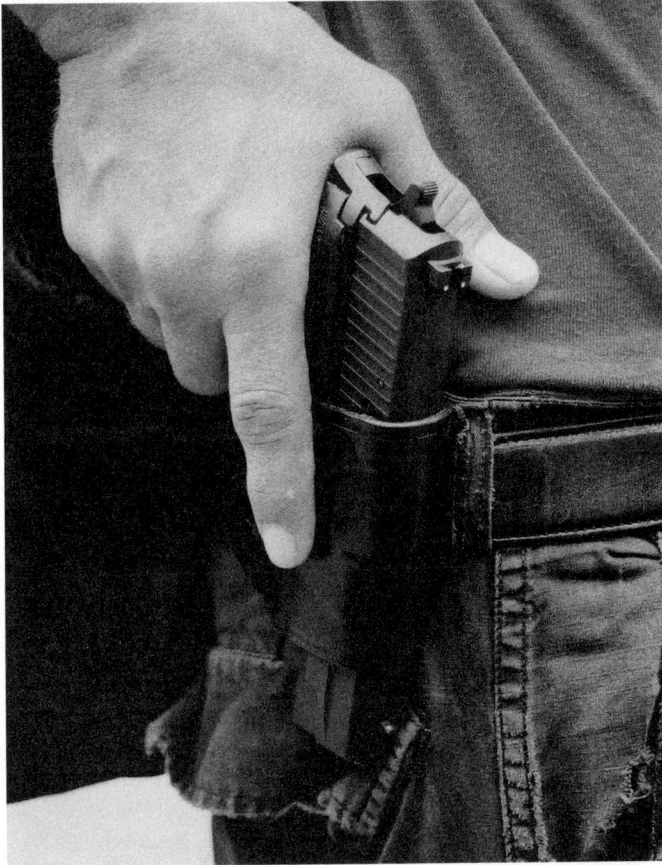

Author begins draw of P226 from comfortable, versatile Don Hume belt slide.

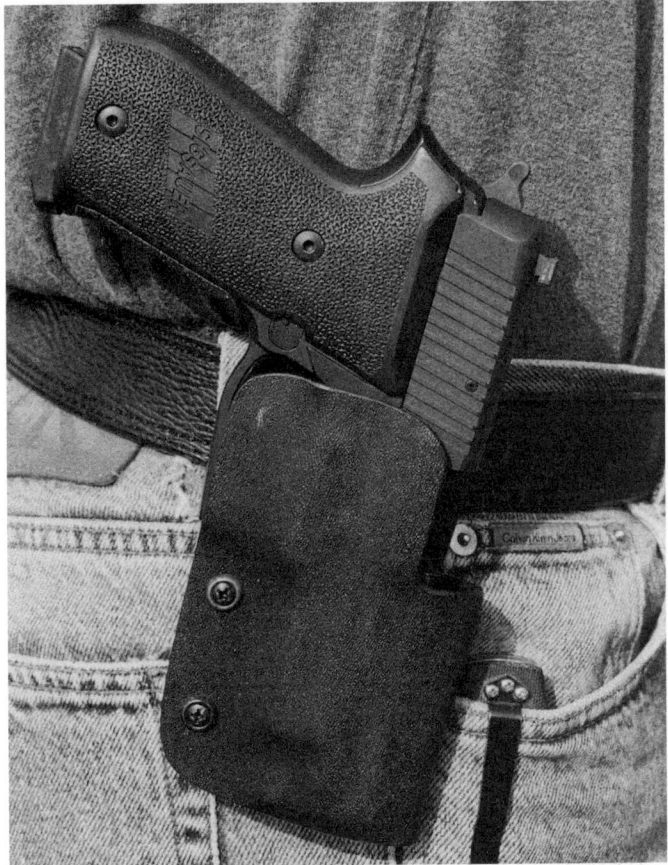

Kydex holsters are growing in popularity because they are inexpensive, fast, and comfortable, but some have been known to break off the belt during fights over the gun.

Velcro lining inside the dress gunbelt. The result was perfect concealment, all day comfort, and all the speed that was possible from under a concealing shirt. (The environment combined with the weather to make any garment but an untucked shirt out of the question).

In addition to the small backup revolvers in the side pocket and on the ankle, I also had with me my SIG P226, loaded with the 20-round extended magazine. This rode inside the Guardian Leather Portfolio, which looks like a lawyer's briefcase and has the additional advantage of containing a hidden Level II plate of bullet-resistant hardshell material. In the front seat of the principal's Mercedes I could access it quickly, and 21 rounds of 9mm were a comforting resource if one of the predictable threat profiles – the suspect pulling alongside us in traffic or at a stoplight while inside his own vehicle – should materialize.

The murderer never carried out his threat. The SIGs remained silent. But despite tropical weather, both the P226 and the P220 had hidden well, constantly and instantly ready to deliver maximum accuracy and downrange force. The big SIGs had been most comforting, more so for me than anything smaller would have been.

SIG-Sauer is one of the safest guns to carry "Mexican style," i.e., thrust into the waistband without a holster, but it's still not recommended. For one thing, it is insufficiently secure if there is strenuous activity.

Fast on and off, fast to draw from, and very concealable, this Safariland double-cell magazine pouch is one of the author's favorites. Magazines are the older style SIG P220.

Alessi CQC is the author's choice for a belt scabbard that is quick to take on and off.

Inside-the-waistband carry under untucked shirts works well for hiding full-size combat handguns like these. The key is that the shirt has to be one size larger to give enough drape to hide the full-size grip, and the trousers have to be 2 inches larger in the waist to allow comfortable long-term carry of both holstered gun and spare magazine(s).

For deepest concealment, I've found I can hide even these big SIGs – indeed, a 4-inch Smith & Wesson .44 Magnum – under a polo shirt in a "belly band" holster. There are several of these on the market; the one I keep coming back to for personal use is the Bianchi Ranger, which doubles as a money belt. It lets me bury the gun low into the waistband for maximum concealment. However, few such holsters give any protection to the gun from sweat or from body acids, and even though the standard phosphate finish on the full-size SIGs resists corrosion well, you might not want to push your luck. If you anticipate this carry, I'd suggest ordering your new SIG from the factory with the optional and excellent K-Kote finish, or refinishing the one you have with something like Birdsong Black-T, which has proven very effective on my Gunsite Custom P226.

One point on carrying these guns in deep concealment: The P239 and the other SIG compacts, designed for hidden wear, have magazines whose baseplates have plastic shields rounded at the edges for comfort in concealed carry. The P220 and P226 were designed as uniform police/military holster weapons, and their mags have sharp edges on the floorplates. You want to carry these spare mags in pouches that hold them a little away from the body, or concealment pouches like the Blocker or the Alessi, which put leather between the sharp edges and your body. How do I know this, you ask? Trust me, I know this.

COOL WEATHER

Spring and fall generally mean jacket or sweater weather, and these garments greatly ease the concealed carry task with full-size service pistols like the P226 and P220. The sweater should be a bulky knit, or a loose cardigan, ideally worn open. Just make sure that the latter is long enough that its hem drops well below the waist.

A Pendleton style "shirt-jac" is another great idea for hiding a full-size gun. Again, an inside-the-waistband holster works the best. If I'm not dealing with a "threat profile" where speed is of the essence, as in the executive protection situation mentioned above, I'll use the same style Blocker LFI Concealment Rig but with the thumb-break. I recently compared my open-top and thumb-break Concealment Rigs for my big SIGs (the P220 holster fits the P226 and vice versa) and couldn't help but

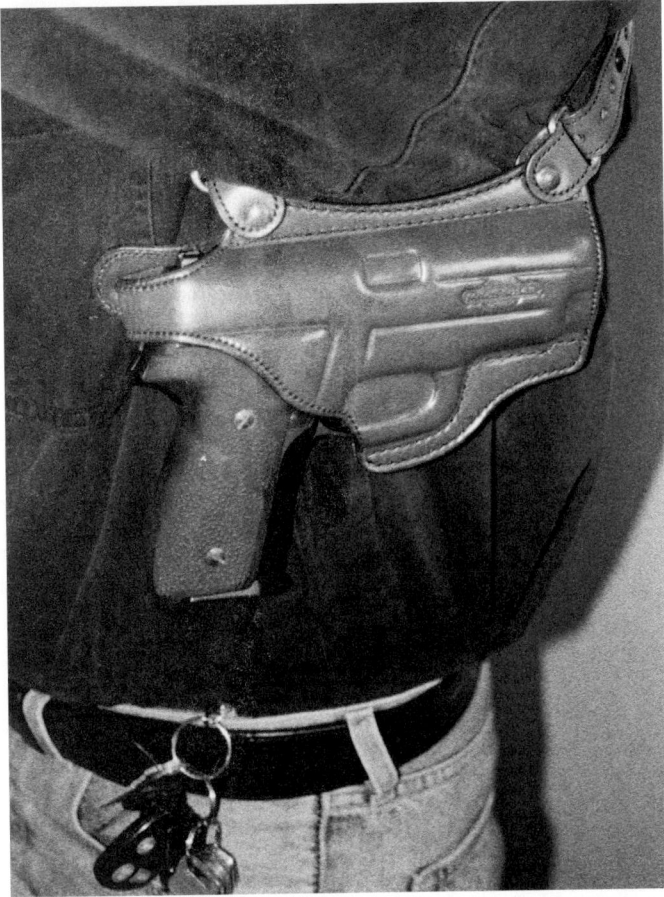

Above: This DA-2 belt scabbard, with about 15 years of wear, is one of the author's favorites, and moderately priced.

Left: The author believes horizontal carry is the fastest style of shoulder holster, as on this Mitch Rosen Stylemaster.

notice that over the years I'd put a helluva lot more wear on the one with the safety strap.

Remember, most physical confrontations are more likely to result in physical force struggles than in the need to resort to a lethal weapon. If a guy grabs me around the waist during a fight, he's going to feel my gun, and if he goes for it I'll appreciate anything that buys me a little more time to execute a counter-disarming, or weapon retention, technique. I say that as someone who learned the Kansas City method of handgun retention from its founder Jim Lindell in 1977, was certified to instruct in the discipline by Lindell at Smith & Wesson Academy in 1980, and became a trainer/certifier of other instructors in the same system through the National Law Enforcement Training Center in 1990.

Jackets, of course, are easier than sweaters. For one thing, they make outside-the-belt holsters much more viable as concealment wear. The sports coat or windbreaker also should be one size large if the holster for a gun this size is on the belt instead of inside it.

With any belt holster, it is critically important that the belt slots fit perfectly to the belt, and that the belt be sturdy enough to provide a solid drawing platform. Otherwise, you can expect the holster to come up a bit with the gun, slowing or even stalling an emergency draw. You wouldn't believe

how many people I run across carrying fine guns in junk holsters, or fine guns in fine holsters on junk belts. The SIG-Sauer is a superbly engineered piece of specialized equipment, as good and as reliable at what it's designed for as the Rolex is as a timepiece or the Mercedes-Benz is as an automobile. You wouldn't put your $10,000 Rolex Oyster on a $5 chicken-hide watchband, or mount two-ply retread tires on your Benz. Don't carry your SIG in crap leather, either.

The shrouded safety strap of the Don Hume Lynx duty holster shielded the night sights and kept them from giving officer's position away in the dark.

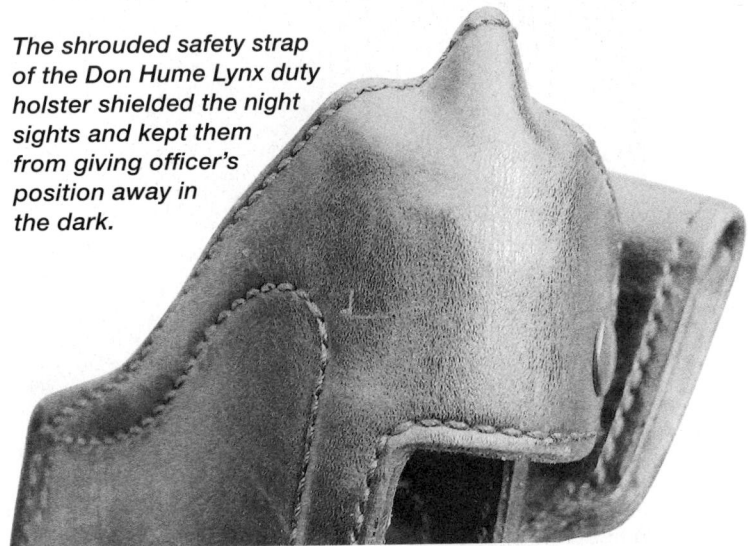

Blocker's DA-1 thumb-break hip scabbard is an excellent choice. If you need quick on and off capability, I haven't found anything better than Safariland's paddle holster, which will secure even on beltless slacks. It rides a bit high for me, but that's probably more a peculiarity of my build than of the holster.

COLD WEATHER

You wear heavy clothing, and lots of it, when it's cold. It would seem that this would solve the problem of gun concealment. Actually, as far as it goes, it does just that. But there are two things a lot of folks miss.

One is that you're not always wearing the outer garments. When the winter coat comes off, you probably still want the gun concealed.

The other is that you still have to be able to get to the damn thing... under all that clothing... and quite possibly with your gloves on! It terrifies me how many people carry guns in deep cold without practicing their deployment while

Safariland is one of the most popular paddle holster styles. It's convenient and can be comfortable with a proper orthopedic curve, but can be torn from the belt by a powerful assailant in a struggle for the gun.

wearing winter garb and gloves. Don't fall into that trap!

Once again, the police uniform is not the problem. I favor hip-length instead of waist-length winter patrol jackets to cover the glutes and the groin, but they are tailored with "gun-slits" on either side, and my Lynx and my Safariland 070 alike had "jacket slots" that kept the fabric from sliding over the holstered pistol. These holsters hold the gun out clear of the body. Even a gloved hand can pop the necessary safety straps and draw with more than sufficient speed to react to an emergency.

This is not necessarily so with a concealment holster that holds the gun tight to the body, with heavy fabric from one or two outer garments pressing inward from one side and what might be a heavier shirt pressing tighter against the thumb-break paddle of an inside-the-waistband holster from the other. Reaching under multiple garments with gloves on to grab a holstered pistol is hard enough. Of late, I've gone to concealment holsters without safety straps for deep cold wear.

If I need a high degree of concealment once the foul-weather coat comes off, it'll be my open-top LFI Concealment Rig inside the waistband. If the sports coat, suit coat, or untucked flannel shirt will remain as a covering garment when the heavy coat goes on the hook, I'm more likely to use my Rosen sharkskin beltslide or my DA-2, the ultrafast scabbard by Blocker with the open top. I have to say I haven't seen an outside-the-belt holster that allows the gun to be better concealed than the DA series. The holster is extremely secure; despite all manner of strenuous "sudden anaerobic activity" including running on ice and snow and occasionally falling on same, my John Quintrall "Jim Andrews Package" Custom P220 has never even *started* to come out of any of the holsters mentioned above.

A tip on drawing. I'll draw from under a closed, relatively short-waisted parka the way I would from under a sweater or a closed, untucked shirt. Plan A is the "Hackathorn Rip," Ken Hackathorn's technique of grabbing the hem of the garment in front of the holster and ripping it up toward the gun-side shoulder to clear a drawing path for the gun hand. Plan B, in case that hand is otherwise involved (with a flashlight or communications device, or warding off an assailant) is to run my gun hand's thumb up the trouser seam to catch and lift the garment, then grab the pistol and throw the hip to the side opposite the gun hand, creating an easy movement path for a one-handed draw.

It is important to *leave the under coat, if there is one, unbuttoned, and to button the outer coat no farther downward than just above the navel!* This allows you to sweep the edge of your hand in toward your center and back toward your strong-

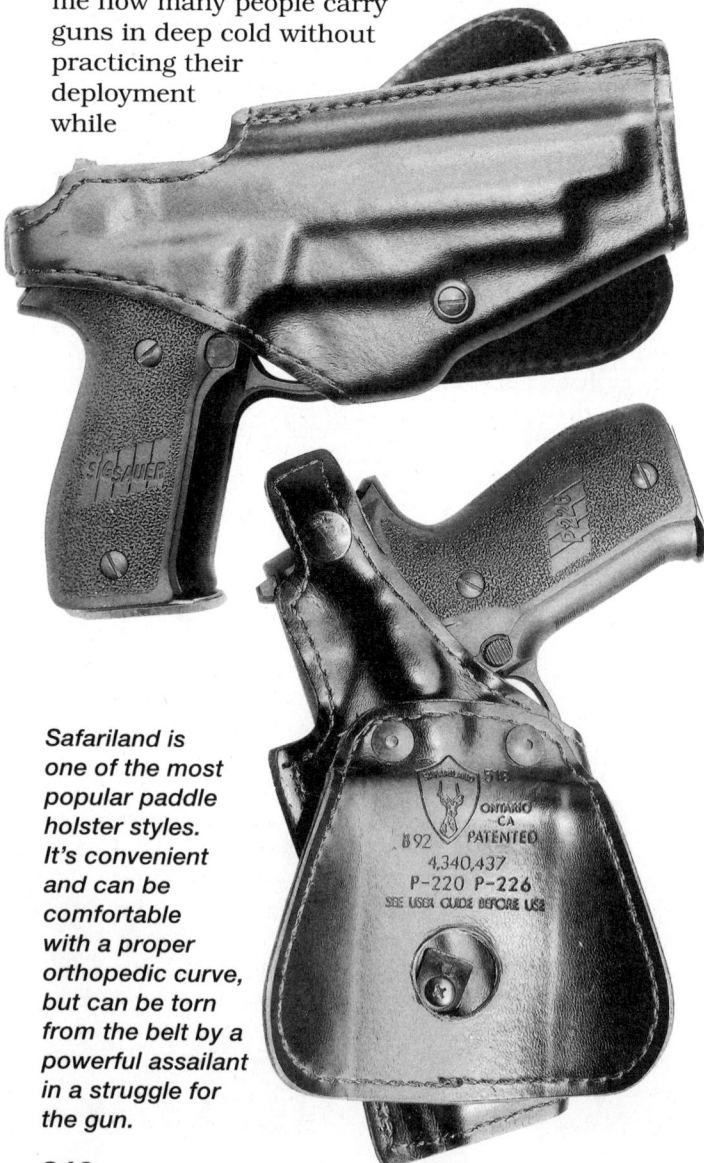

The belly band is a most useful option for deep concealment, especially under tucked-in shirts. This one, made by Bianchi, holds a SIG P228 and does double duty as a money belt.

side hip. A drop of the hip sideways (to the left, if you carry on the right) now facilitates a quick and easy strong-side draw from a belt holster.

What about shoulder holsters? Because of bulge factors, they make more sense for most people with guns this size under heavy coats in winter. In the most brutal weather, I'll wear one of Bianchi's holsters – the late, great X-15 or one of their later equivalents – that hold the big SIG muzzle down, butt up and forward under my non-dominant arm. Then the coat will be buttoned or zipped to a point a little way up the sternum. Since I'm right-handed and men's button lines fold to the right, the weight of the heavy fabric holds the rest of the garment warmly closed across my chest...but if I raise my right elbow high I can knife my hand down and in across my chest and execute a right hand draw with satisfying speed.

When it's cold but not truly arctic, I wear what I've found to be the most comfortable of shoulder holsters: Bianchi's sinfully comfortable Tuxedo, made of lightweight black nylon. I simply leave one button across the chest undone on the topcoat, and the right hand can spear-finger its way right under that and any other covering garment beneath for as fast a draw as I can execute. The P220 under my left armpit is partially balanced by a pair of full .45 magazines in the double-cell pouch suspended under my right axilla. As with a hip holster, I leave

the suit coat or sport coat under the outer garment unbuttoned to facilitate this draw.

A crossdraw can also work well for some people, depending on build and range of movement. Leave the undercoat unbuttoned, and button the overcoat in a manner that leaves undone the button in the path of the cross-body draw.

It should be noted that the standard SIG-Sauer pistol design is particularly well suited for use in a winter-gloved hand. The trigger guard of the big P220 and P226, originally designed for all-weather military use, is large enough to easily admit a gloved finger. The long, firm pull necessary to fire the first double-action shot is an effective answer to the problem of a numb or padded finger accidentally putting too much pressure on a trigger that could be too sensitive to that pressure in a stressful gunpoint encounter.

Once the shooting starts, you don't have to worry about a double-action-only trigger mechanism failing to return forward for the next necessary shot because a heavily gloved finger blocked it. Even with snowmobile gloves on, my SIGs keep shooting. When the need to fire has ended, the right-handed shooter can easily thumb down the ergonomically mounted SIG decocking lever, and a southpaw can do the same with the trigger finger.

PERSPECTIVES

Why do we carry a gun in the first place? In case we need to employ it in a worst-case scenario to prevent the imminent and otherwise unavoidable danger of death or great bodily harm to innocent people including ourselves! If you knew you were going to have to use the pistol you carry to defend your life, you'd want the most powerful one, with the most ammo and the longest sight radius and the most solid fit to your hand. This is why I prefer to carry a full-size SIG-Sauer for my own needs instead of one of the same firm's compacts expressly designed for concealed carry.

Obviously, the advice given above for the P220 and P226 works for any full size revolver or semiautomatic pistol at a power level that fits Jeff Cooper's classic description, "the fighting handgun."

Chapter 22
Don't Let Your SIG Go Sour

Anything created by man can fail, including our parents' children. The finest machine can break if given enough wear and/or abuse, and the finest machine deserves the finest maintenance.

The SIG-Sauer pistol is no exception. If I've learned anything in all these decades with handguns, it's that there isn't a one of them that can't break. The SIG-Sauer was developed as a combat pistol. As such, it's a life-saving emergency rescue tool. Learn from firefighters. When they're not actually putting their life on the line or training to do so, they're inspecting and maintaining the equipment to which at any moment they may have to entrust their lives. Treat your SIG-Sauer – and any other firearm – the same way, and you'll minimize the chances that it will ever let you down.

For this chapter, I am indebted to Rick Devoid, a certified SIG armorer since the mid-1990s and staff armorer for Lethal Force Institute. He is located at Tarnhelm, 431 High St., Boscawen, NH 03303, tel (603)796-2551, www.tarnhelm.com.

ROUTINE INSPECTION

Make sure your pistol is unloaded, checking by sight and feel. Lock the slide open. Now, with the muzzle in a safe direction, thumb down the slide release (or, on the P230 or P232, snap the slide to the rear) and let the slide fly forward. Watch the hammer. If it follows the slide down and is not double-action-only, your gun has a big problem.

Close the slide of the empty pistol. Drop a full-size #2 pencil down the bore, eraser first. Cock the hammer, point the pistol straight up, and activate the decocking lever. The pencil should only quiver when the hammer falls. If the pencil jumps, it means a firing pin got through when it shouldn't have and struck the eraser, which means the decocking mechanism is not working properly and the stage is set for an accidental discharge.

Re-insert the pencil down the barrel and point the empty gun straight up again. Pull the trigger. The pencil should go flying, propelled by the impact of the firing pin. If it doesn't, you probably have a broken firing pin. FOR THIS AND THE PREVIOUS TEST, MAKE SURE YOU AND ALL AROUND YOU ARE WEARING SAFETY GLASSES. THAT PENCIL CAN GO FLYING HARD AND FAST ENOUGH TO CAUSE EYE DAMAGE.

Cock the hammer of the unloaded pistol and, with your thumb, push forward on the hammer. If it snaps forward without the trigger or decocker having been activated, there is

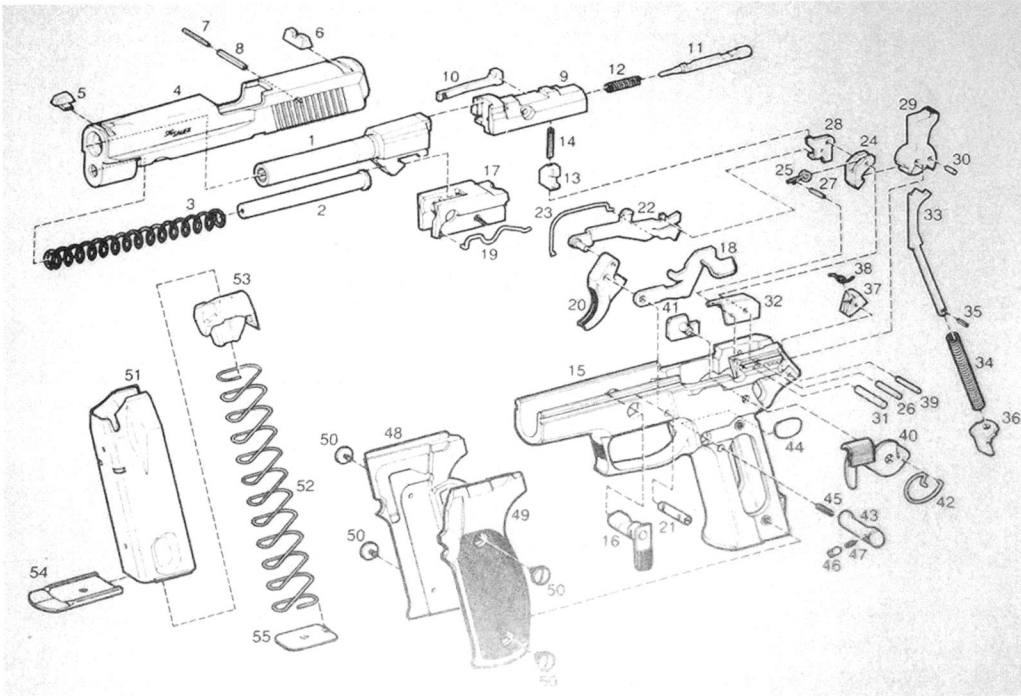

The SIG-Sauer is a proven and durable design.

Below: SIGARMS takes no chances on maintenance. This is their substantial armorer's guide.

some bad sear engagement that needs immediate attention.

Examine the extractor area to make sure it is clear of crud and debris. This is a weak point in every semiautomatic firearm. The SIG armorer's manual even makes a point of stating in all caps, "SPECIAL ATTENTION MUST BE GIVEN TO CLEANING THE EXTRACTOR."

Particularly if you have an older model 9mm and have been shooting a lot of hot ammo in it, check the frame very carefully. If the frame is going to crack, I've seen it most commonly on the left side toward the front, right along the slide rails.

CLEANING AND LUBRICATION

"SIG told us at armorer's school that the pistol should be cleaned every 200 rounds," notes Devoid. From a perfectionist's standpoint, this may be true, and neither I nor this publication will ever suggest more lax safety and maintenance standards than those of the firearm's manufacturer.

That said, I've seen SIG-Sauer service pistols go between 1,000 and 2,000 rounds without cleaning or lubrication, and still work fine. I put between 1,500 and 2,000 rounds through my P226 at Chapman Academy in their "big dogs" course in 2003 and don't recall cleaning it. The gun never jammed on me once. I see the same high order of reliability in the other SIG duty models, full-size and compact. The only SIG-Sauer I've found to be particularly sensitive to dirt and crud is the little .380.

Rick suggests that in an intensive training environment, it wouldn't hurt to at least lubricate

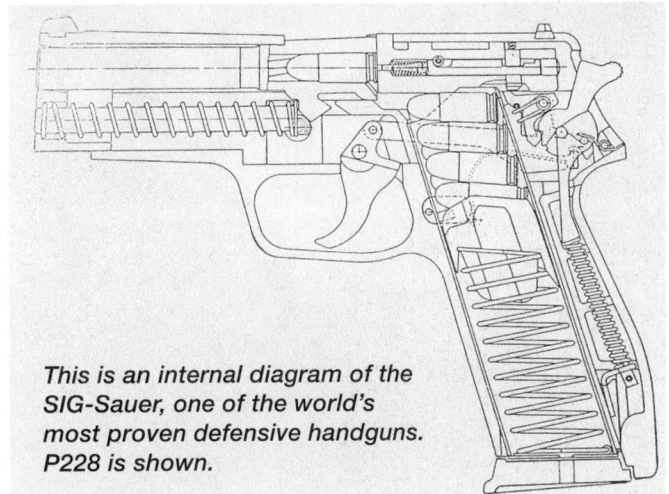

This is an internal diagram of the SIG-Sauer, one of the world's most proven defensive handguns. P228 is shown.

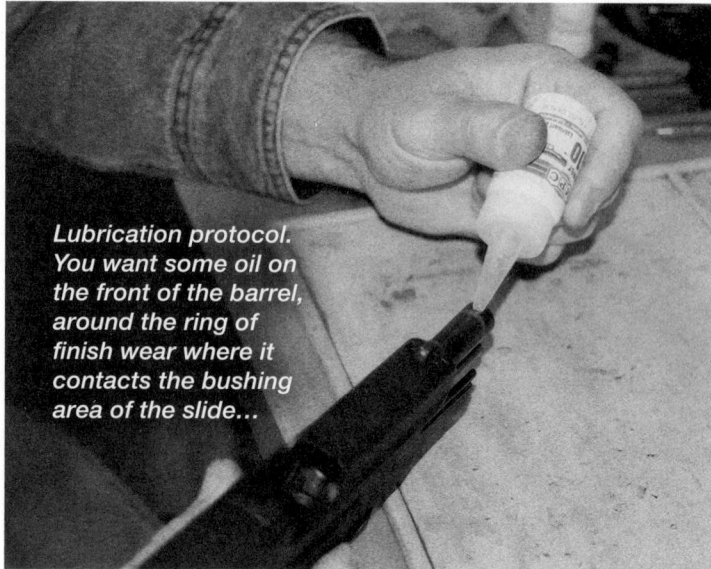

Lubrication protocol. You want some oil on the front of the barrel, around the ring of finish wear where it contacts the bushing area of the slide...

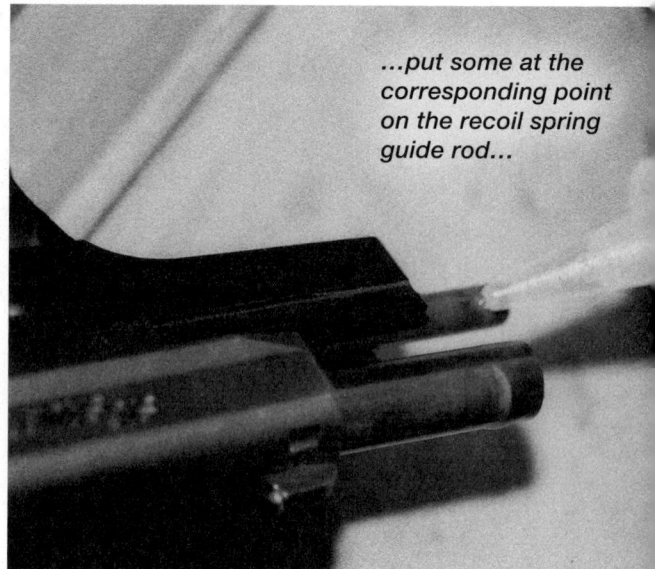

...put some at the corresponding point on the recoil spring guide rod...

the gun every few hundred rounds. If your intensive shooting schedule calls for 500 to 1,000 rounds a day, he recommends oiling at least once a day during lunch break. Of course, magazines that have fallen in sand should be attended to immediately. Ditto pistols exposed to sand or mud during grueling on-the-ground exercises.

There are more fine gun lubricants and solvents on the market today than ever before. Devoid is partial to Break-Free CLP, Firepower FP-10, and Sentry Solutions for lubrication. "At armorer's school, we were told that Gun Scrubber ™ was OK but generic brake cleaner wasn't," remembers Rick. "Their point was that if it wasn't marketed as a gun-cleaning product, it wasn't a great idea to use it for cleaning guns." Again, I won't attempt to gainsay the manufacturer's suggestions, but the writer can't help noting a long and satisfactory experience with the much

less expensive generic aerosol brake cleaner for getting the crud off.

Rick is a big fan of ultrasonic gun cleaning systems. I recall an article by Wiley Clapp in which his exhaustive testing proved that the use of such a device seemed to maintain maximum accuracy by sort of deep-cleaning the gun's barrel. Both the SIG Armorer's guide and Rick Devoid remind us that since this cleaning process will remove all lubrication, the pistol should be re-lubricated by an armorer after each ultrasonic cleaning. Shooters are reminded that brake cleaners do the same thing.

Devoid and LFI both recommend monthly field stripping, cleaning, and lubrication *even if the pistol has not been fired since its last cleaning.* Most lubricant is liquid; it can evaporate. Liquid has weight: the lubricant can drain from the gun, particularly when it is carried vertically all day in a

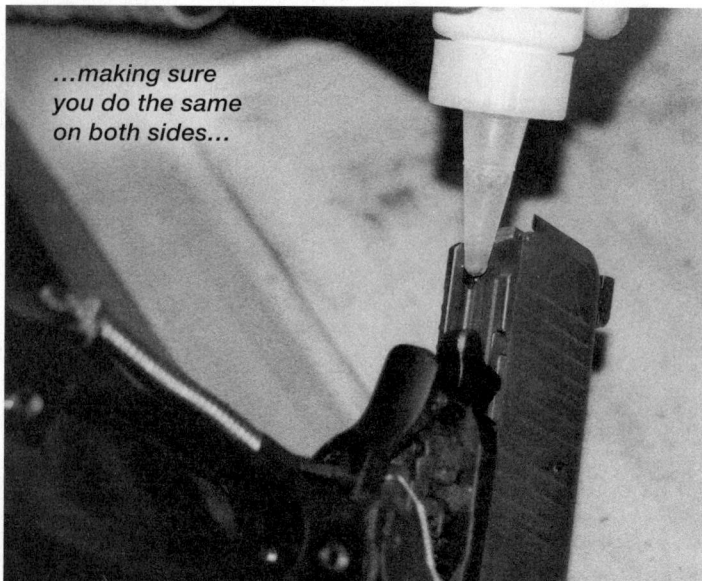

...making sure you do the same on both sides...

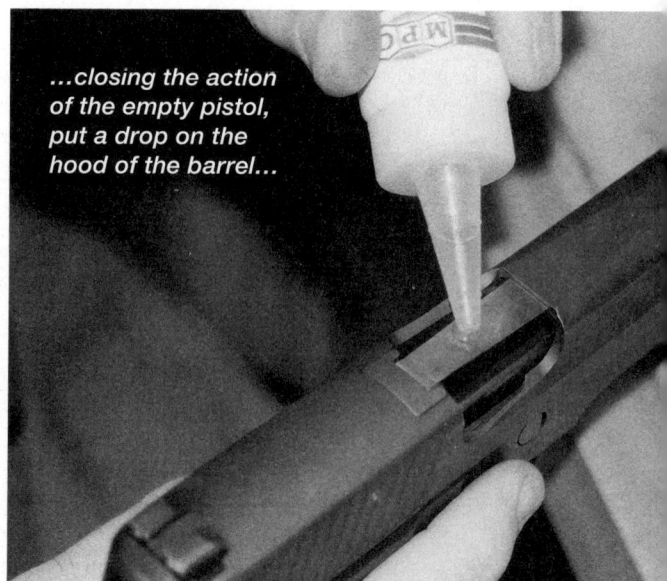

...closing the action of the empty pistol, put a drop on the hood of the barrel...

...now put a drop of oil on the side and bottom of the slide rails at contact points...

holster. A dry semiautomatic is a malfunction waiting to occur. "Lack of lubrication is the most common problem you see with a SIG," observes Rick from extensive experience.

Devoid suggests the following lubrication protocol for routine maintenance. "Put a bit of oil on the barrel, at the ring you see where it contacts the slide. Do the same to the recoil spring guide rod below it, at the corresponding point. Put a big drop on the hood of the barrel, and another on the front edge of the hammer where the slide rides over it. Then oil both the tops and the sides of the frame rails where the slide travels; those are the longest and perhaps most critical set of bearing surfaces on the pistol. Work the slide rapidly a few times, then wipe off the excess."

Devoid adds, "the factory says to lube it so you can see and feel the lube, and if you're going to be shooting hot and heavy, lube it so you can see it, feel it, and literally push the lubricant. The hotter the gun gets, the more lubrication it's going to need."

MAGAZINES

Anyone experienced with semiautomatic firearms can tell you that bad ammo and bad magazines are the two key causes of malfunctions. Devoid recommends only SIG factory magazines, period. I would extend that to include SIG and Mec-Gar brands, and the ACT-Mags for the P220 .45 imported by Wayne Novak from Italy. The latter are stiff at first when you try to load the stated capacity of eight rounds, but break in soon enough. I would avoid like the plague any other magazine in the SIG pistol.

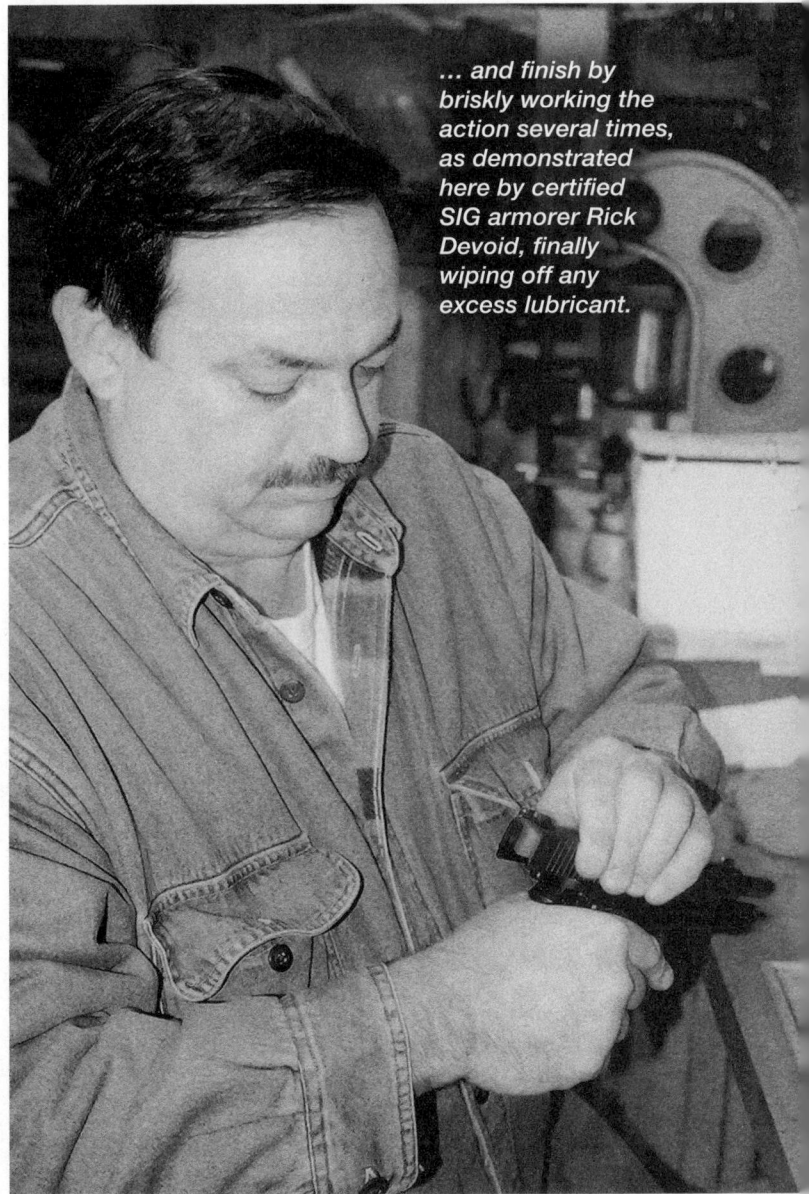

... and finish by briskly working the action several times, as demonstrated here by certified SIG armorer Rick Devoid, finally wiping off any excess lubricant.

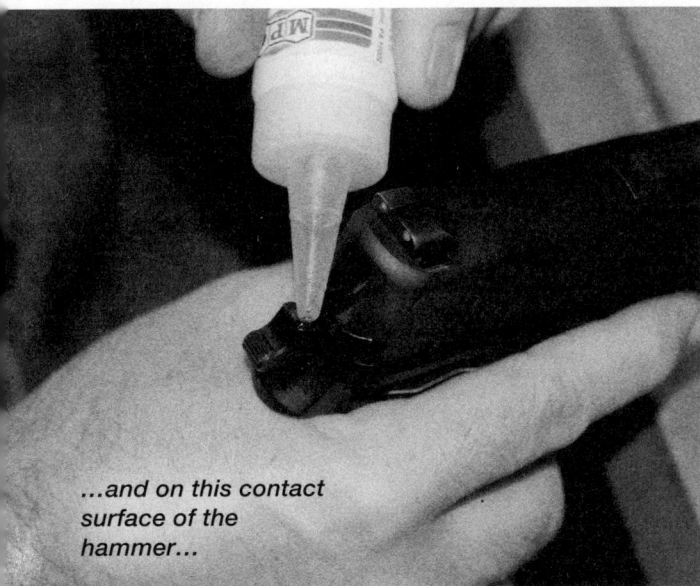

...and on this contact surface of the hammer...

If you want an eight-shot .45 magazine for your P220, get this current-production one, not the earlier "DPS" variation with flush floorplate and a cartridge stack that is tighter than optimal for some purposes.

Clean your magazines when you clean your pistol. Armorer Rick Devoid uses a punch to depress the button holding the floorplate of a P226 mag and slides floorplate forward and off...

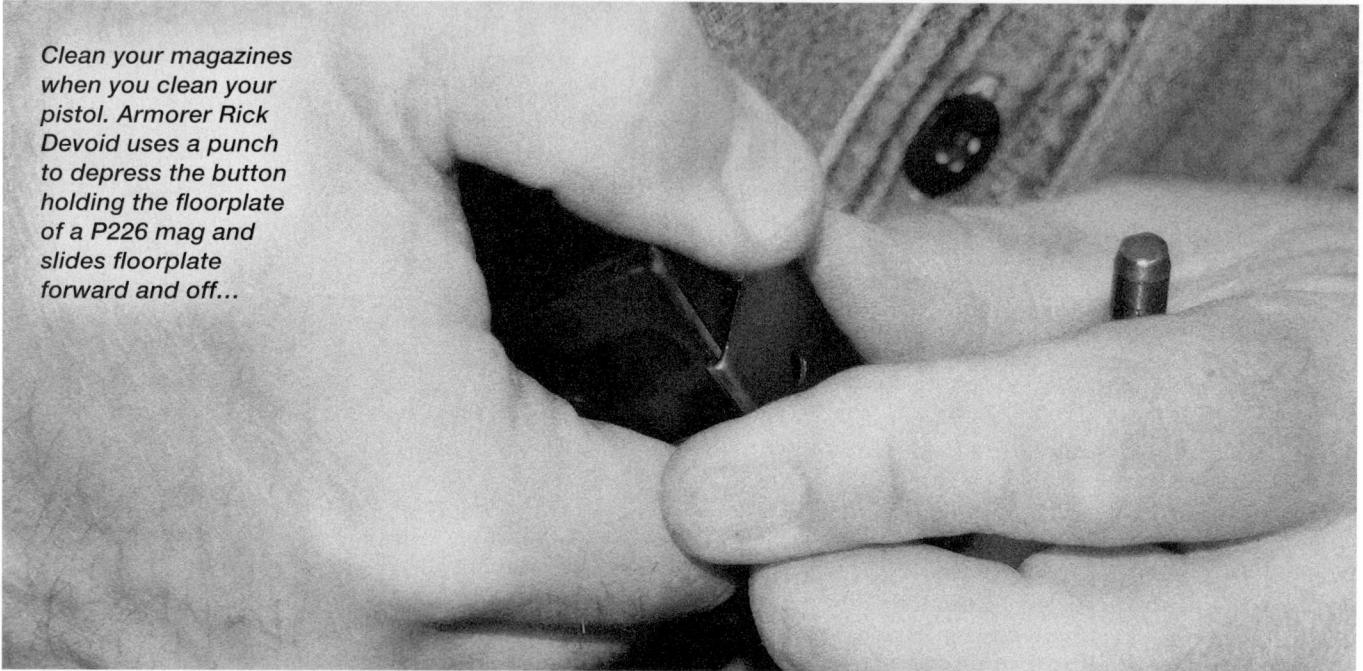

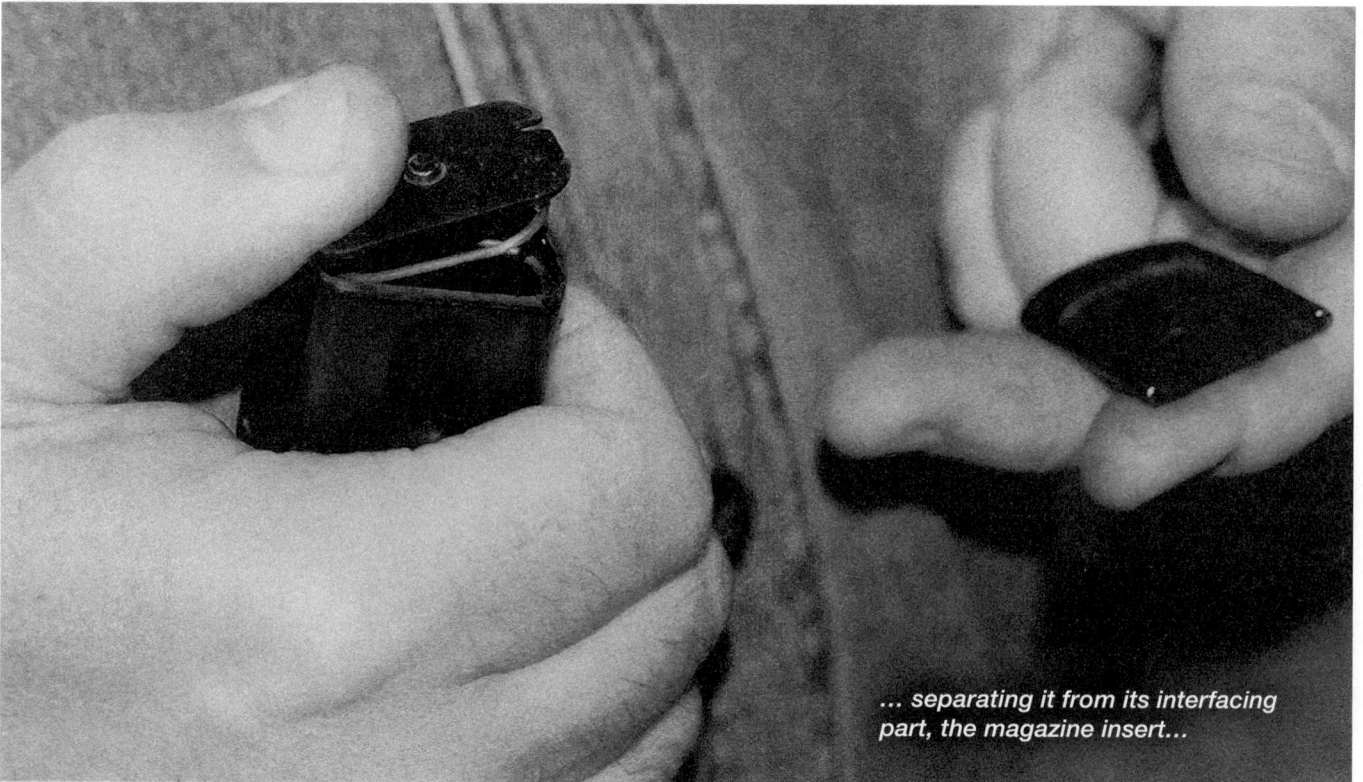

... separating it from its interfacing part, the magazine insert...

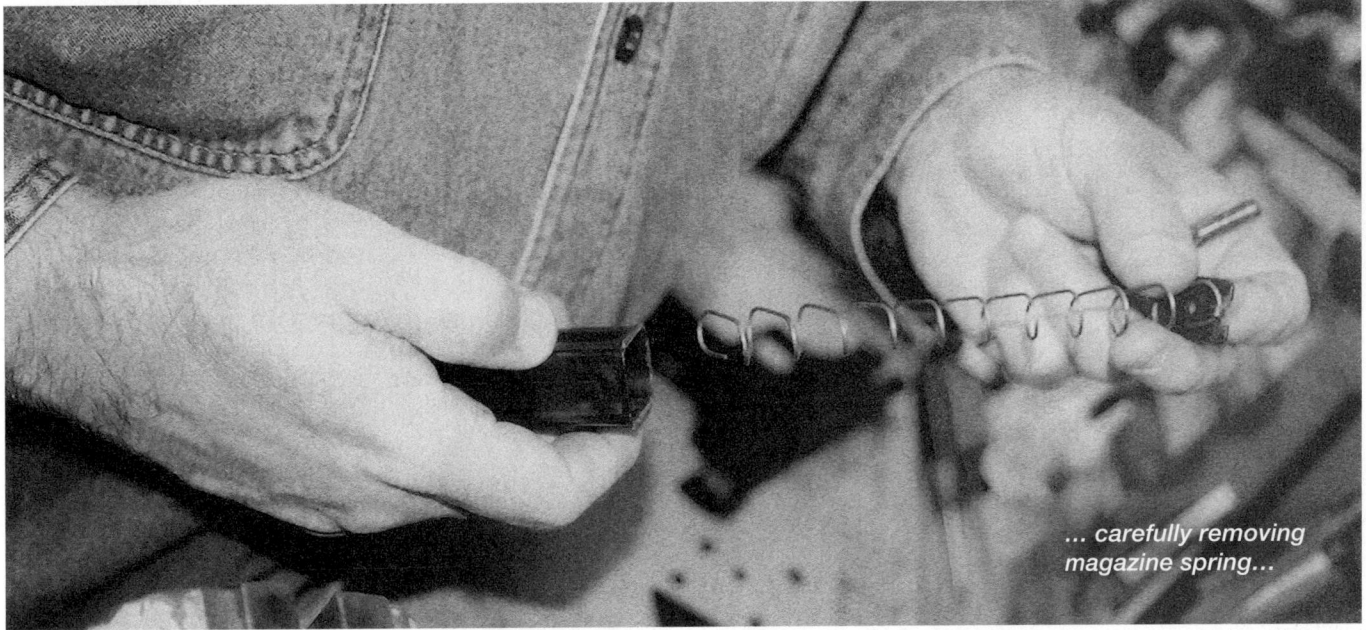

... carefully removing magazine spring...

Keep the magazines clean. There is something in the psychology of many shooters that tells them to clean their pistol as religiously as they would polish a Rolls-Royce, and to ignore their magazines and treat them like slaves and drones. Bad attitude. The magazine is the heart of the pistol's feeding system. As the SIG armorer's manual notes, "The pistol is not considered clean 'unless the magazine is clean also'!"

Do not overload the magazine. The 10-shot magazines for the double-stack 9mm pistols, guns designed for higher capacity, hold the stack of cartridges so tightly when fully loaded that there is no flex left inside the magazine when it is slammed home. If the slide is forward when the full 10-round magazine is inserted, it may not seat fully. This writer uses those magazines only for training (if for no other reason that I don't feel bad about ejecting

them into the mud) and loads them only with nine rounds to insure positive insertion. The same is true with the old DPS eight-round magazines for the P220. New P220 magazines with eight-shot capacity, distinguished by an extension on the floorplate, are fine when loaded all the way up: it's the payload they were carefully designed for.

Michael Izumi has been a top-level practical pistol competitor, a sworn law enforcement officer and a splendid part time firearms instructor, and works full time as an aerospace engineer with many patents to his credit. They say that you don't have to be a rocket scientist to figure certain things out, but it doesn't hurt, either. Mike literally *is* a rocket scientist, and he did an exhaustive study of fatigue in pistol magazine springs. He determined that it would be wisest to keep his SIG P220 duty .45's magazines downloaded by one round, and to

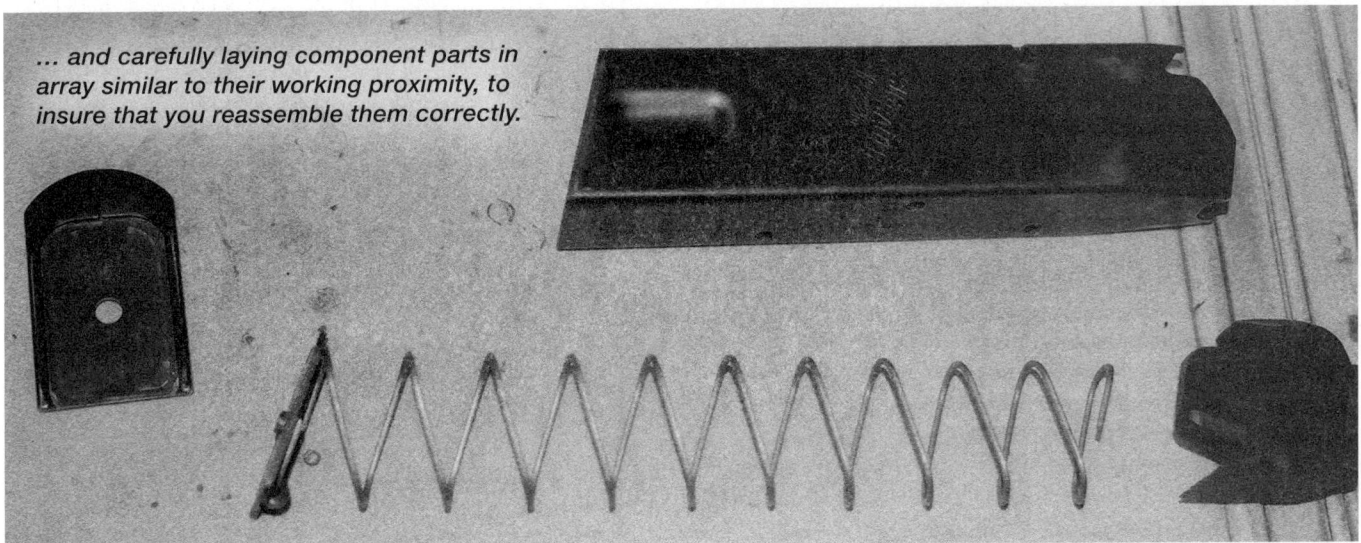

... and carefully laying component parts in array similar to their working proximity, to insure that you reassemble them correctly.

OTHER MAINTENANCE TIPS

Ammunition in the gun should be changed out annually at an absolute minimum. Twice a year is better, quarterly is better yet, and monthly is best of all. Ammo carried on your person, both in the gun and in the spare magazine pouch, is being jiggled around every step you take. Each time a round is jacked into the firing chamber, the bullet is being pressed back toward the inside of the case. It doesn't take long to break the seal, which means the round is no longer waterproof. The bullet can also set back into the case, which will create feeding problems its next time through the magazine. A set-back bullet can also cause pressure to reach a catastrophic point, blowing up the gun. Rounds with the bullets set back visibly should not be fired; collect them, soak them in metal penetrating oil to kill their powder charges, and bury them somewhere safe. Rounds that have been jacked in and out of the chamber repeatedly which do not show shortening can be set aside for practice later.

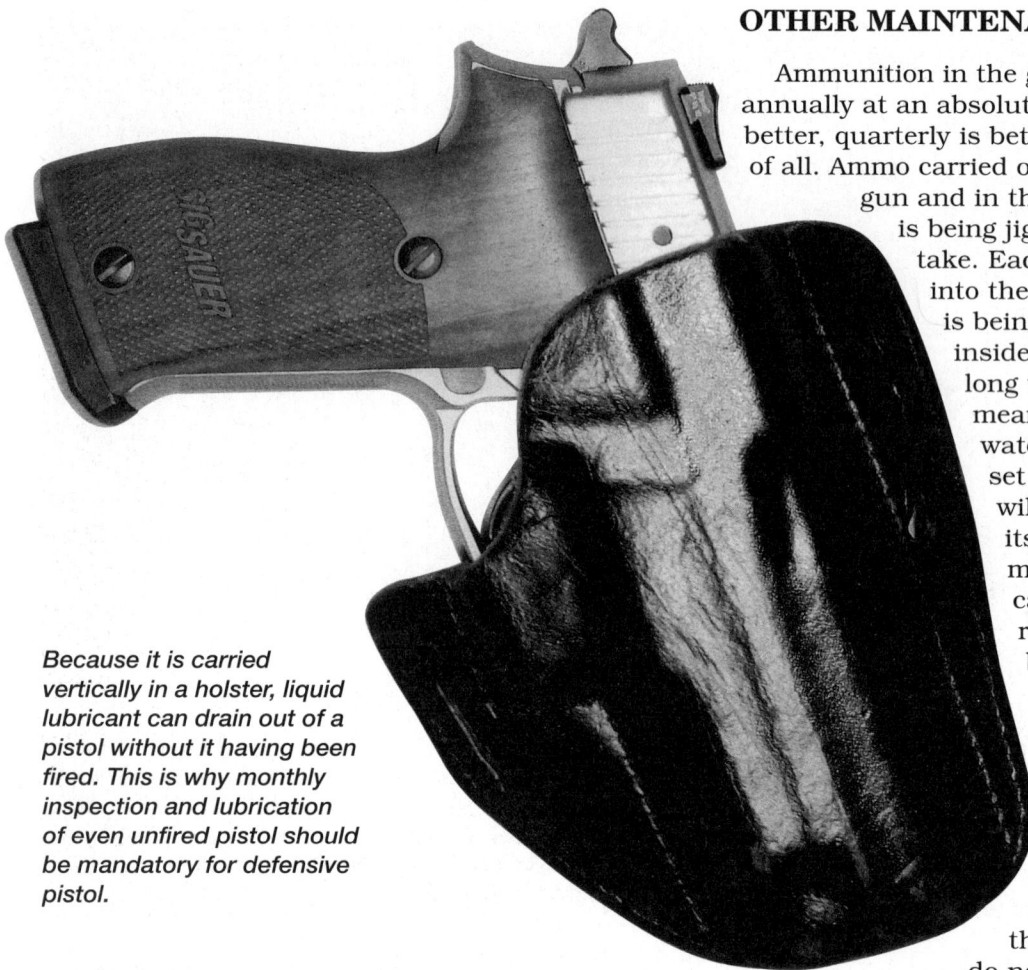

Because it is carried vertically in a holster, liquid lubricant can drain out of a pistol without it having been fired. This is why monthly inspection and lubrication of even unfired pistol should be mandatory for defensive pistol.

load them all the way up only when he was about to go on duty. He determined that the majority of magazine spring fatigue came from being loaded to full capacity. He likes to download by two rounds when storing loaded high capacity magazines.

When Mike Izumi talks, I listen. I've also gotten into the habit of keeping at least half a dozen magazines for each of my carry guns, since I normally carry three magazines at a time: one in the pistol, and two spares on the belt. Whenever daylight savings time rolls around, I do the bit where we change the smoke alarm batteries when we change the clocks. I also change the batteries in my flashlights, *and I also rotate the magazines of my carry guns.* The ones that have been loaded until now I unload to rest; the ones which have been resting now have their turn to be loaded and carried. You can color code the magazines with little dots on the floorplates: sunshine yellow for summer, snow white for winter.

Clean the magazines when you clean the gun. The armorer's guide suggests a light coat of oil. Personally, I prefer the inside of the magazine to be clean and smooth but absolutely dry. Oil in a magazine, in my experience, becomes a suspension medium for dirt, sand particles, and other debris.

Remember that each time you cycle a live round through your pistol, an extractor slides over a rim, the slide hammers the cartridge home, then the extractor pulls it back again and the ejector kicks the cartridge out of the pistol. Little burrs have been made in the soft brass of the cartridge case. These can impair feeding later. Ditto dings on the bullet nose. Remember that "life saving emergency rescue" thing. Ammo that is getting "used up" should be consigned to the training bin, not carried for the protection of innocent human life.

Don't blame the gun for human error. A limp-wristed grasp is notorious for jamming semiautomatic pistols. The SIG-Sauer is much more forgiving than most brands in this respect, but that doesn't make it immune.

The single biggest complaint I hear, always from right-handed shooters, is "My slide won't lock back when the gun is empty." Nine times out of 10, it turns out that they are using a high-thumb grasp in which their own thumb is holding down the slide lock lever and preventing it from engaging when the pistol runs dry. Lowering the thumb will solve this problem, and may even enhance shooting with the stronger grasp it provides.

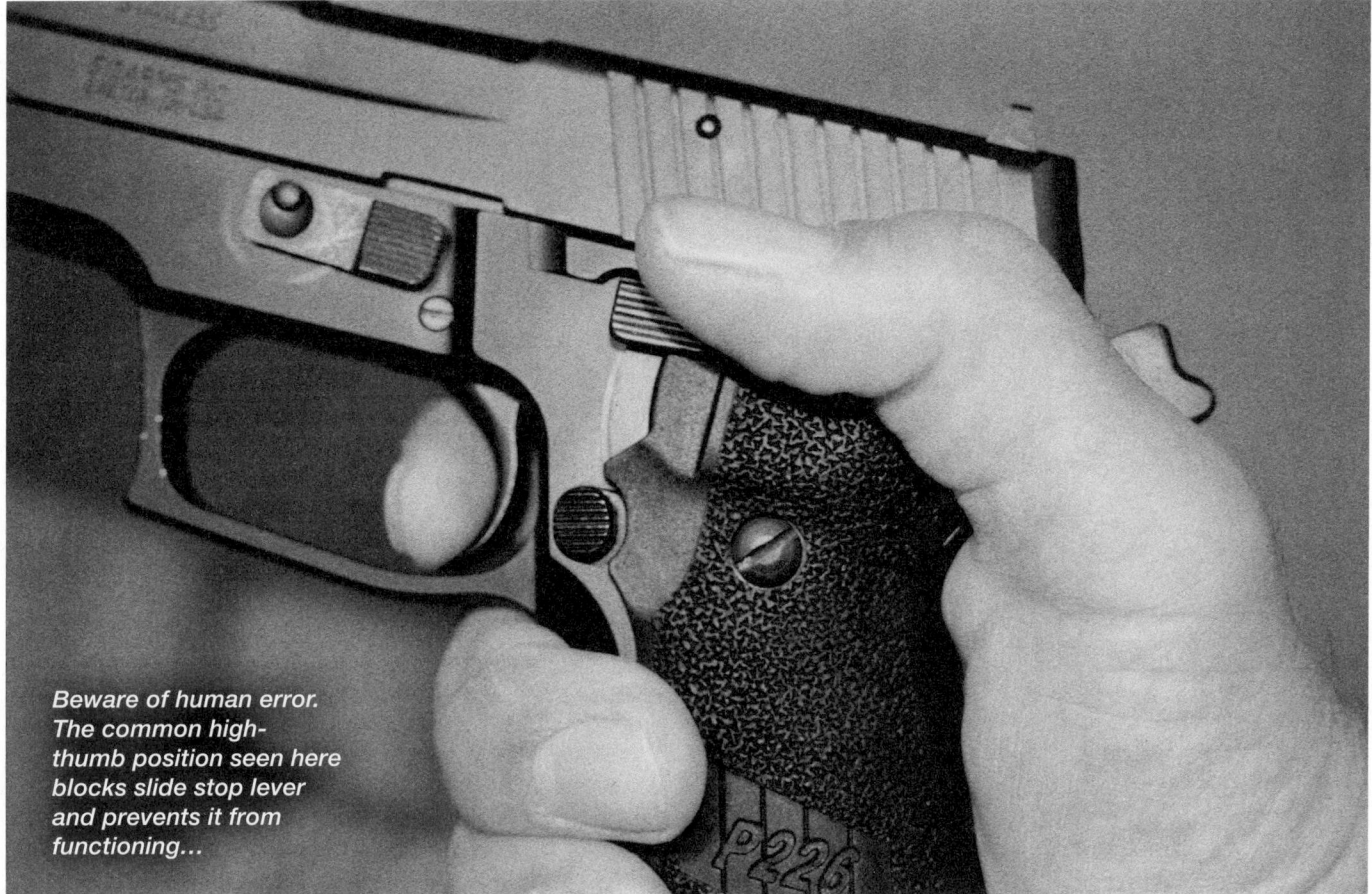

Beware of human error. The common high-thumb position seen here blocks slide stop lever and prevents it from functioning...

... a problem cured by simply going to this low-thumb grasp.

Use proper size screwdrivers. This grip screw has been "boogered" by using a screwdriver with too small a head.

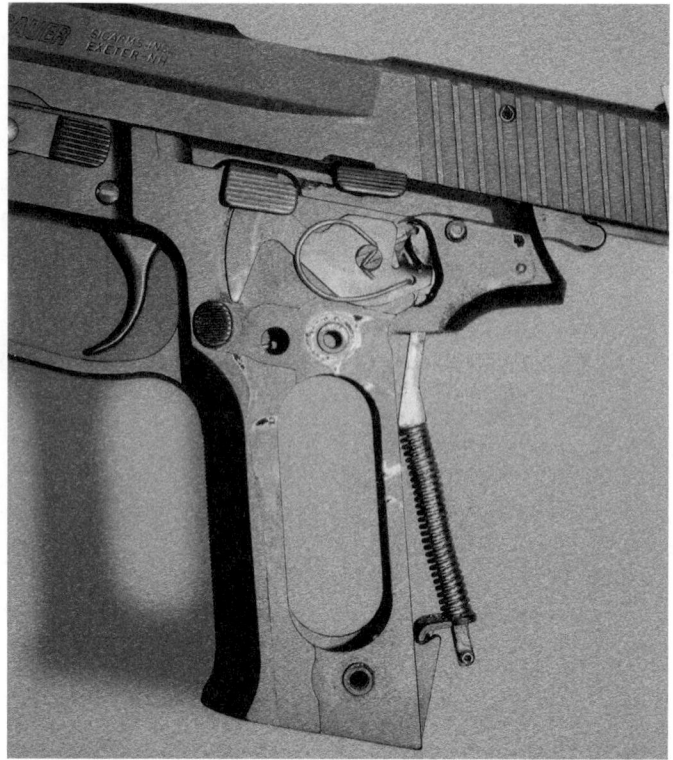

Note that the SIG-Sauer mechanism has springs that flex in places between the frame and the stocks. Aftermarket stocks with improper inside dimensions can compromise the function of the mechanism.

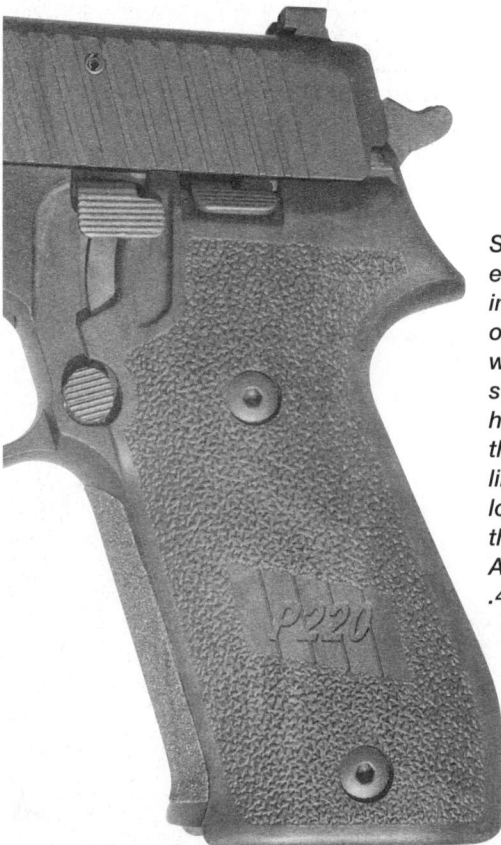

Some SIG enthusiasts install their own screws with factory stocks in hopes that they'll be less likely to work loose, as on this P220 American .45ACP.

Use screwdrivers of the proper size for removing stocks. Improper head size can lead to ugly, "boogered up" screw heads. The SIG armorer's manual stresses the importance of using a short screwdriver for this task, since long ones can generate enough torque to strip threads.

One irritating idiosyncrasy in all SIG-Sauer pistols, though somewhat less common in the most recent ones, is the tendency for the grip screws to work loose. Check regularly to make sure they're reasonably tight, and do so several times a day in a heavy training session on the range. Some enthusiasts tell me that hex-head aftermarket screws solve the problem. If you go that route, be sure to keep a hex-head screwdriver handy on a keychain or multi-tool.

Be advised that some aftermarket grips can impinge on the function of the springs that flex between frame and stock. One particular brand of "rubber" grips has been implicated in this. If you prefer this type of grip, I would recommend the Hogue brand for the SIG, never having seen it cause any problem with these guns.

If you neglect or abuse the finest human, dog, or horse, it can turn on you. Ditto the finest machine. Give your SIG-Sauer pistol the professional level of care and maintenance it deserves. You take care of it, and it will take care of you.

Chapter 23
The Custom SIG

When we try to improve on the truly beautiful, we are said to be gilding the lily, and it is implied that this is a bad thing. Well, we can debate that. Certainly, gilding the lily is probably an unnecessary thing. But sometimes, a master craftsman can take something that is excellent and enhance it until it is truly sublime.

There are a very few craftsmen who can do that with SIG-Sauer pistols.

WHAT COULD BE BETTER?

You'll find those enthusiasts on internet chat rooms like SIG Forum who feel that the pistol in question is the *ne plus ultra* as it comes out of the box. The fact is, though, there aren't a whole lot of things that can't be made better. That includes the SIG-Sauer pistol.

SIGHT

Sights are a highly subjective topic. SIGARMS has offered a decent adjustable sight, excellent fixed night sights, and even the XS, as Ashley Emerson's "express" pistol sight is now known. Most models are compatible with some sort of laser sight if that's what pulls the given purchaser's trigger. The P226 and P220 ST are produced with an attachment rail for white light and laser units, and the white light in particular makes eminent good sense for certain tactical situations, including the home-defense gun. But there are some other, more conventional sights that some of us prefer. The excellent fixed night sights by Heinie are my personal favorites. I know experts who prefer the MMC adjustable night sights. Many of my SIGs wear Trijicon fixed night sights, and I've found them to be excellent. I've also had good luck over the years with IWI night sights, and recently, with the Meprolight. Novak fixed sights are the choice of a number of professionals. I've even seen oversize target pistol sights fitted to SIGs, though for concealed carry or duty use I think they go past the point of diminishing returns.

One under-recognized advantage of night sights is that if you are awakened in the darkness by home invaders, the glowing sight dots catch your eye instantly and guide your hand to the pistol like airstrip landing lights. SIGARMS offers their own night sight options, factory order or retrofit, under their trade name "SIGlite."

When the mission profile indicates pure close-range shooting done very fast, the XS sights originally designed

Stocks by Nill. Sights by Heinie. Slide stop, magazine release, and magnificently reworked trigger and action by Ernest Langdon. Result: The SIG the author most often carries on his own time.

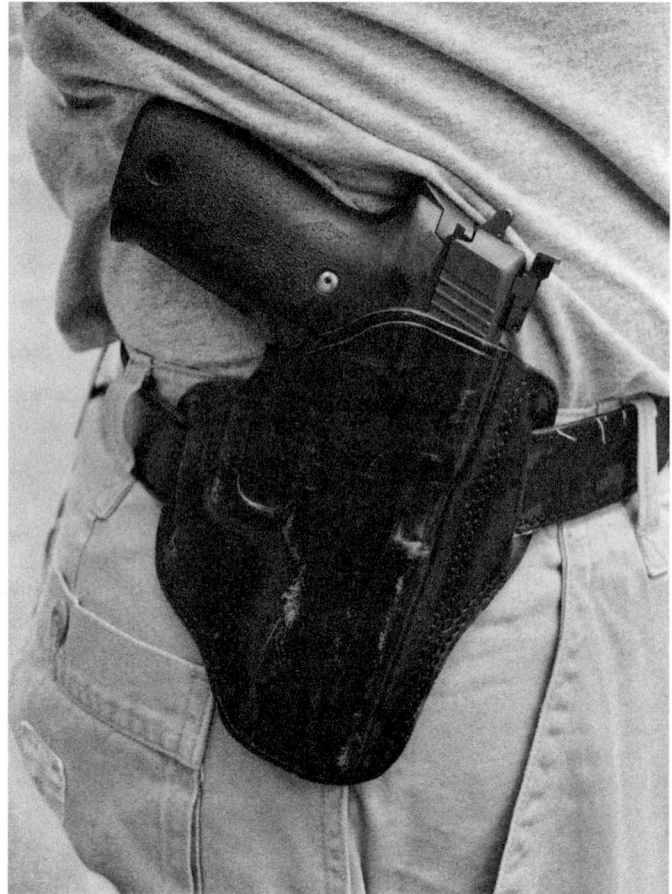

These high-tech adjustable target sights would be great for a bull's-eye match, but notice the sharp edges and protrusion: not terribly practical for defensive carry.

Note the rounded surface and edges of the short SIG trigger installed in this P220 ST by Ernest Langdon. For maximum performance when hand meets machine, little things mean a lot.

by my friend and student Ashley Emerson as the Ashley Express are a useful special-purpose option. Not what you want for a 25-yard medulla shot, these get you into the vital zone very fast even with the eye focused on the opponent when you're in close. SIGARMS has recognized this, producing one special run of P245 pistols with XS sights.

Laser sights? I think they're over-rated in terms of their ability to deter a violent aggressor by simply putting a red dot on his body, though there is ample testimony that this has indeed happened on some occasions.

They are ideal, however, for shooting from behind a hand-carried ballistic shield, or "body bunker." They can be a valuable adjunct in a wounded officer situation where the gun can't be raised to line of sight, and can be the answer for the small number of people whose vision is such that they can identify their target but can't focus on conventional gun sights.

Laser sights are great for marksmanship training, because they show the student in dry fire if he is jerking the trigger. Working in reverse, laser sights can help teach good trigger control when the student learns to hold the dot motionless on the target while the index finger strokes the trigger back. In live fire the bouncing of the red dot on the target, particularly at night, has what I call a "graph effect" to gauge recoil control, because the bouncing red dot traces a red line downrange as the pistol kicks.

SIG-Sauers have traditionally come standard with these fixed sights in the Von Stavenhagen pattern: white vertical dot at the back...

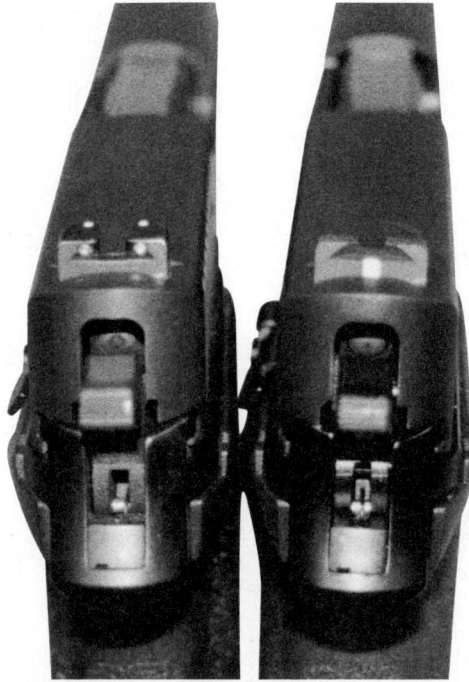

...and round white dot at the front. The quick-sighting principle is to "dot the i." Of course, a conventional post-in-notch marksman's sight picture is also possible with these.

Above: two of the three glowing green dots of Trijicon replacement sights, which author loves. Right, the not-yet-dotted "i" of the "dot the i" Von Stavenhagen sights. Pistols are P226 9mms.

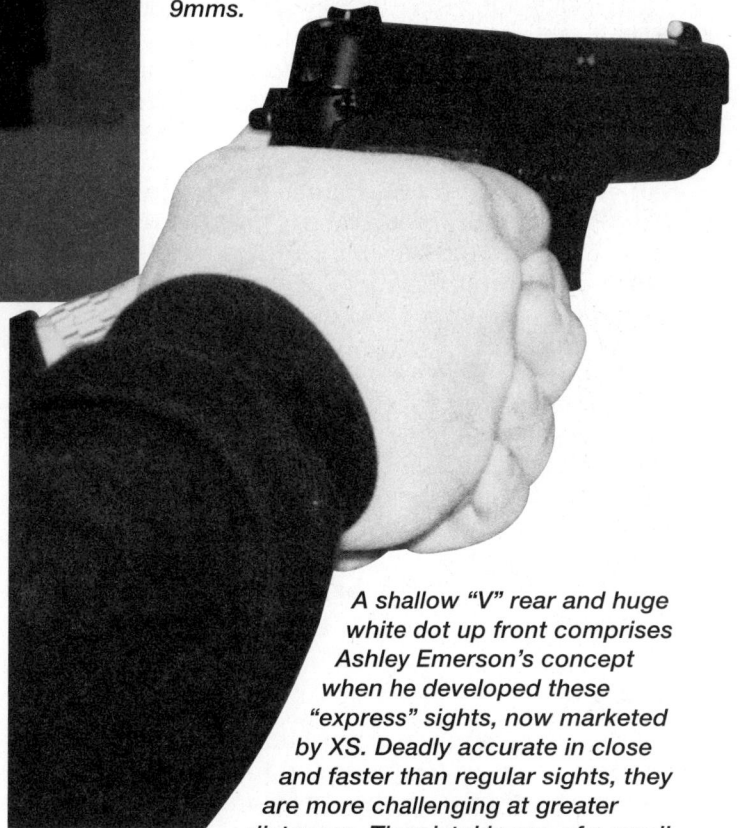

The Big Dot™ of the XS sight comes quickly in line with the eye as George Harris cracks off a .45 round at close range from a P245. Note his excellent control of recoil.

A shallow "V" rear and huge white dot up front comprises Ashley Emerson's concept when he developed these "express" sights, now marketed by XS. Deadly accurate in close and faster than regular sights, they are more challenging at greater distances. The pistol is one of a small number of P245s equipped with XS sights at the SIGARMS factory.

The P245 at left has the standard three-dot SIGlite night sights. The P245 at right has XS sights. SIGARMS Academy's ace instructor and shooter George Harris has shot slightly better with the XS sights on the steel targets.

A LaserMax unit replaces the recoil spring guide on this SIG P228.

IDPA Stock Service Pistol Master Steve Sager demonstrates the use of the Crimson Trace LaserGrip for dry fire practice and diagnostics with a P226.

The SIG rail guns can take lock-on accessories such as the InSights M6, a combination white light and laser sight unit. Most of the SIG pistols will accept the LaserMax, which replaces the recoil spring guide and projects its dot from beneath the muzzle. It is activated by a push button on either side of the frame, thanks to a module that replaces the takedown lever. Crimson Trace makes its excellent LaserGrips for a variety of SIG-Sauer pistols. This unit replaces the stocks and projects its beam from the upper portion of the right grip panel. It is adjustable.

I adjust mine to send the red dot parallel to the barrel, which is above and to the left of the projecting lamp. I now know that the bullet will always strike about an inch above the dot and half an inch left. Sighting in any laser sight to exact point of aim point of impact will put the bullet on the dot only at the same, exact distance at which it was sighted in. Closer or farther, dot will diverge from bullet strike.

GRIPS

Hogue grips may give the shooter a better interface between operator and machine. SIGARMS apparently thinks so; they've equipped some of their pistols with them from the factory. So might a rubbery grip sleeve, as produced by Uncle Mike's, Hogue, and others. With that attachment, be careful

that it doesn't work its way down the grip-frame to where it can block insertion or ejection of a magazine. You want fancy yet functional? Can't beat K.G. Nill's handsome checkered wooden stocks from Europe. SIGARMS thought enough of 'em that they had some made with the company logo.

OTHER ACCESSORIES

Magazine extensions can be useful and SIG offers some. Let's say you have a compact SIG and want to use the longer, more capacious magazines of its larger counterpart. A P228 will take a P226 magazine. However, some worry about it overtraveling and locking up the gun. This happens to single-stack magazines, but not to double stack SIGs in my experience, because the taper of the mag at the top prevents it. So, maybe you worry about using your P220 mag in your P245 compact, or maybe you just don't like the feel of a too-long magazine hanging out under your pinkie finger.

Solution: SIG inserts that encircle the body of the longer magazine above the floorplate, filling out the grip shape to the exact dimension of the larger pistol. These also give you the advantage of having "two grips in one." Let's say you are comfortable accepting a six-round .45 mag in your P245 or a 13-round mag in your P228 in return for a lower concealed carry profile. But, you would really rather have a full-length grip for more comfort and control when you come home and turn your carry gun into a home-defense pistol. No prob. A simple tactical reload, and the insert-equipped longer magazine is now inside your "bedside home companion," which has assumed the configuration of a full size pistol with a shorter barrel and slide.

PISTOLSMITHING

Some gunsmiths offer a "dehorning" or "melting" job on auto pistols. There are some that can certainly use it. About the only part of a SIG-Sauer that ever seems to need smoothing is the lower outside edge of the trigger guard, and then only for certain hands where it bites in after long, *long* shooting sessions.

Many auto pistols need to be "throated" to feed blunt-nosed rounds. Fortunately, this is not normally the case with SIG-Sauer pistols. That's taken care of at the factory. I can only think of two exceptions. If you wanted to set up a SIGARMS GSR 1911 as a target pistol with the odd-shaped 185-grain mid-range wadcutter bullet, then in addition to a new, much lighter recoil spring, you would probably need a little more radiusing at the top of the feedway. The 1911 pistol has a more angled feedway than the almost straight-line feed of the SIG-Sauer, and this may have to

Heinie Straight Eight™ front sights, here installed by LTT, encompass the superb Trijicon night sight concept.

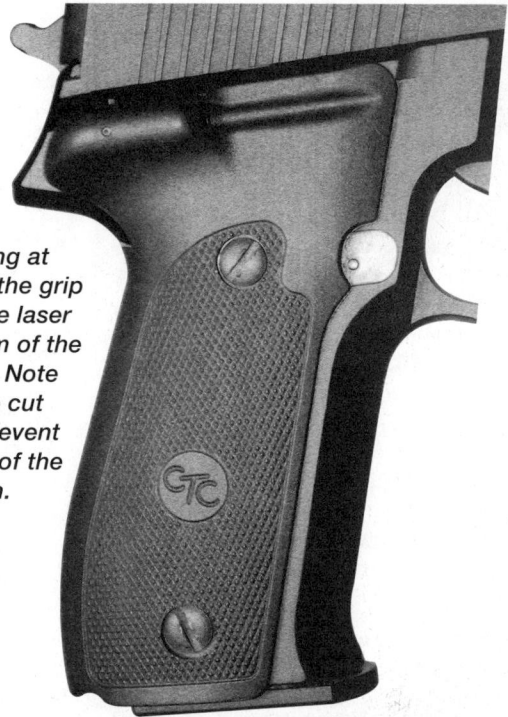

The swelling at the top of the grip panel is the laser mechanism of the LaserGrip. Note the groove cut away to prevent deflection of the laser beam.

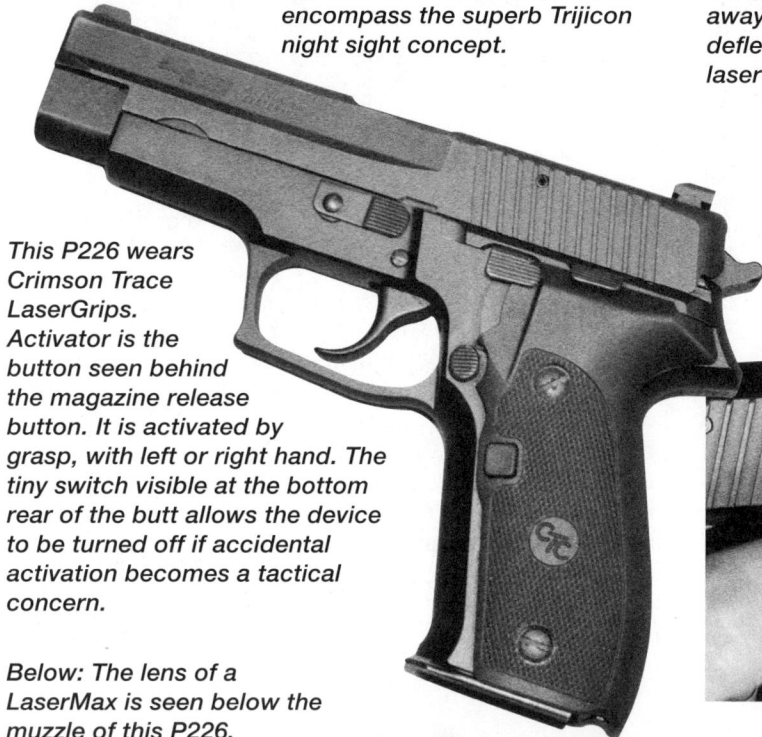

This P226 wears Crimson Trace LaserGrips. Activator is the button seen behind the magazine release button. It is activated by grasp, with left or right hand. The tiny switch visible at the bottom rear of the butt allows the device to be turned off if accidental activation becomes a tactical concern.

Below: The lens of a LaserMax is seen below the muzzle of this P226.

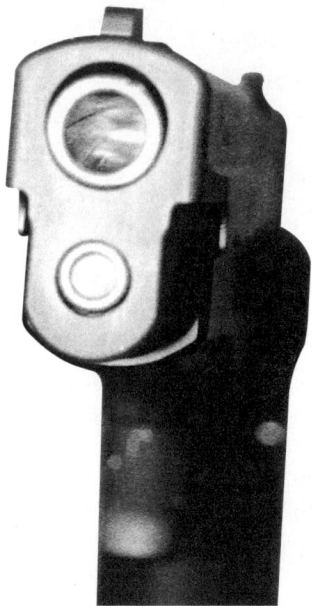

A press of the button on the replacement takedown lever activates this P228's LaserMax dot.

Hogue grips have been popular for a long time among SIG shooters, and have been provided by the factory on some models.

Below: Nill stocks fill out the shape of a P220's grip-frame nicely.

Smart, purpose-driven accessorizing in action. Pre-ban extended SIG magazine, M3 light, and SIGlite night sights have turned this P226 "rail gun" into a 21-shot weapon which enhances the holder's tactical control capability. Light attachment and tactical reload together take only a few seconds to change the face of the firearm.

be compensated for. On the older P220s with the early seven-round magazines, it would occasionally happen that a reload from slide-lock with a very wide-mouthed bullet such as the 200-grain Speer "flying ashtray" would cause a 6 o'clock misfeed. This seems to have cleared up with the new P220 magazines built by Mec Gar, but if you have a P220-E or Browning BDA whose butt-mounted magazine release restricts it to firstgeneration magazines, some additional throating may be necessary to speedload with very short, very wide .45 ammo.

Finish is a concern. SIG has addressed this. The original phosphate-finished steel and anodized aluminum frame worked well enough for most. However, some combinations of user, carry method, and environment were such that brown spots would appear on the barrel and slide, and constant wear would take the finish off the frame. Robar, Accurate Plating and Weaponry, and countless other aftermarket vendors can give you superb

If your standard P228 is a little short in the grip, the optional magazine from SIGARMS shown next to the gun can give you more to grasp.

finishes that resist the elements and look great. Hard chrome, Teflon, you name it. SIG itself has offered its guns with electroless nickel finishes, and late in the SIGARMS epoch offered stainless. I never particularly cared for the slick "K-Kote" finish SIG offered, but many thought it was the cat's meow, and I certainly have no problem with it. I appreciate stainless steel as much as the next guy, but frankly, for this writer's needs the standard factory finish has always sufficed. Still, particularly in the case of finishes, whether or not a golden lily is more visually appealing than a natural one, it will probably prove to be longer lasting.

The extended floorplate available from SIGARMS better fits this P228 to a larger hand.

A P245 with a six-shot magazine in place is next to an eight-shot P220 mag with SIGARMS optional insert.

For many, this is the most important accessory. Left, short trigger; right, standard trigger, both produced by SIG.

With one of SIG's "rail guns," home-defense capability is enhanced with the easily attached and detached InSight M3 high-intensity flashlight. The rocker switch at the rear activates the light in "dead man's switch burst mode," or it can be locked on.

Below: The short trigger rests atop the long one. In the hand, the difference feels like much more than what it appears to the eye.

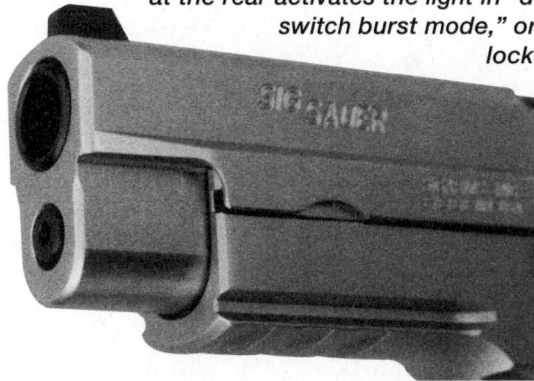

The author is perfectly happy with grips currently provided on SIGSauer pistols.

The "business end" of the author's Langdon Custom P220 ST .45. Jeff Cooper's formula of DVC – "Diligencia, Vis, Celeritas" or "accuracy, power, speed" – are all there.

George Harris demonstrates the advantages of a laser-sighted pistol from behind a body bunker. Note the almost complete absence of body exposure, while he can effectively target the opponent by watching the P226's LaserMax-dot through the bullet-resistant viewing port. Photo taken at SIGARMS Academy.

Some handgun grips are not compatible with the SIG's mechanism. These Hogues are compatible and factory-approved.

Custom barrels for greater accuracy? I tried that… once. John Quintrall expertly fitted one of Bar-Sto's superb barrels on my favorite P220-E. It was very accurate indeed…but I can't say it was more accurate than the typical P220 barrel new from the factory, because that is also match-accurate. I have numerous 1911 and other pistols with Bar-Sto, Jarvis, and Storm Lake barrels, and the fact is that the properly fitted aftermarket match barrel improved the accuracy of every one. A Bar-Sto or other top-quality match barrel might improve the accuracy of some SIG-Sauer pistols. It's your choice.

To my mind, the trigger mechanism was where custom attention seemed most important. Given that historically, the SIG has been the traditional double-action auto pistol by which the trigger pulls of others were judged, this seemed to be *truly* gilding the lily. The fact is, however, the best trigger somehow never feels good enough for the truly driven pistol shooter. The SIG-Sauer is a mass-produced firearm. Intensive polishing and certain subtle changes in parts geometry can indeed give both a smoother and a lighter pull to what is already the gold standard. If the out-of-the-box SIG is the gold standard, the very best custom jobs might be called the "platinum standard."

One aftermarket touch that can be critical to many shooters is the installation of SIG's own short trigger. This does not involve a change in the mechanism per se; the part in question is simply the standard trigger with more metal taken off the front so the finger does not have as far to reach. It is a Godsend to petite females, and a huge advantage to anyone with short fingers. This writer has "average adult male hand dimensions" according to the $100,000 study commissioned by Smith & Wesson for their Sigma project in the early 1990s. I have found that I shoot better with the distal joint of my trigger finger making contact with the trigger, particularly in double-action

An important accessory for any handgun is a matching dummy gun. Odin Press in Kansas City produces this heavy-duty metal duplication of the P226. It shows years of constant wear and tear.

pistols and revolvers. This means that for me the shorter trigger is the logical choice. Give one a try; you may discover the same. Any qualified SIG armorer can install one. If you don't have one handy, feel free to use the highly experienced armorer I work with, Rick Devoid at Tarnhelm Supply, (603)795-2551, www.tarnhelm.com. SIG also offers a short re-set trigger option.

Let's take a look at the work of one true master craftsman of the SIG-Sauer custom duty pistol. Ernest Langdon is in practice as I write this, and he offers many insights to those who want maximum performance from a SIG.

Before we segue in that direction, though, let's touch on one more accessory that isn't even part of the gun. It's always smart to own a dummy duplicate of your carry/defense pistol. Use it for practicing disarming and handgun retention. Use it for initial practice with draws, new techniques, and other complicated maneuvers. Use it for introducing new shooters to your gun. If they accidentally "cross" you with the muzzle of even an unloaded real gun, they can find it traumatizing; the dummy gun gets both instructor and student through such growing pains. Finally, when water-soaking your fine leather holster to a perfect fit on your pet gun, you'll almost wake up screaming as if you could hear your gun rusting in the other room, grease and Saran Wrap notwithstanding. Wet-mold your new holster to your dummy gun instead, and take the worry away. Ring's makes the best plastic dummy guns I've seen, but I prefer the more "real gun" heft of the rugged metal ones from Odin Press of Kansas City.

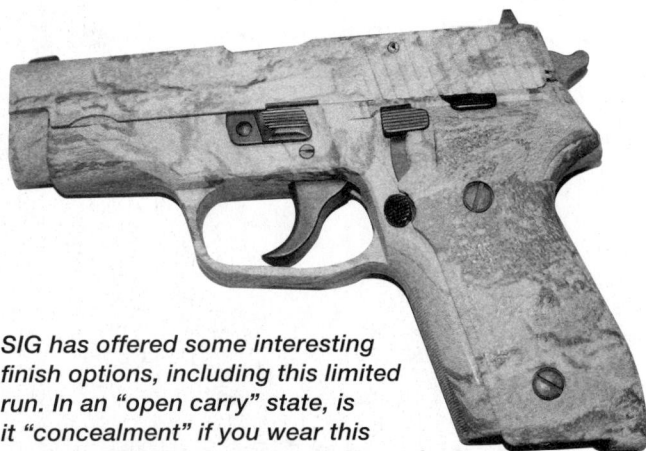

SIG has offered some interesting finish options, including this limited run. In an "open carry" state, is it "concealment" if you wear this particular P228 exposed and dressed in matching camo? Do not tell the author that SIGARMS does not have a sense of humor.

Chapter 24
Competing with the SIG

The SIG-Sauer pistols were designed for service, not sport. That said, they have performed remarkably well in the practical pistol competition arena.

The guns were built to be accurate, reliable, and ergonomic. If you think about it, those are three essentials for winning a match, too. With the clock running, you don't have time to re-grip a pistol that doesn't fit your hand; the SIG is a natural pointer and famous for its good feel in the hand. With the sights on target and that same clock still running, you can't afford a crappy trigger pull that might pull your shot off the center of the mark and cost you so many points that you lose. The SIGSauer designs are famous for the quality of their trigger pulls both double-action and single. And, if you have to stop to clear a malfunction, you're in the tank *big* time. The same reliability that makes the SIG a favorite among the cops makes this pistol a top choice for any shooting match the competitor takes seriously.

Let's look at how the SIG-Sauers have performed in various "combat competitions." Not designed for bull's-eye or Olympic sports, these guns are not seen there. It is in the martial arts side of shooting tournaments where you'll find the SIG-Sauers in play.

IDPA

The International Defensive Pistol Association is in many ways what Jeff Cooper originally intended IPSC to be. Only "street guns" are used, in practical holsters, generally worn concealed. The most popular of IDPA's four different gun categories is Stock Service Pistol, encompassing double-action autoloaders such as the SIG-Sauer as well as pistols like the Glock.

The man who has won the national championship in this category more than any other is Ernest Langdon, formerly a Marine teaching in the high-risk personnel program. He began with the Beretta 9mm auto, just like the one the Marine Corps had issued him, but in 2003 he switched to the SIG P220 ST .45. Now, in IDPA cocked and locked 1911 .45s are seen as easier to shoot than TDAs with the first shot double-action, and they are shot in separate categories: Custom Defense Pistol for 10mm and .45 1911s, and Enhanced Service Pistol for such guns chambered in 9mm or .40. Marksmanship categories are adjusted accordingly.

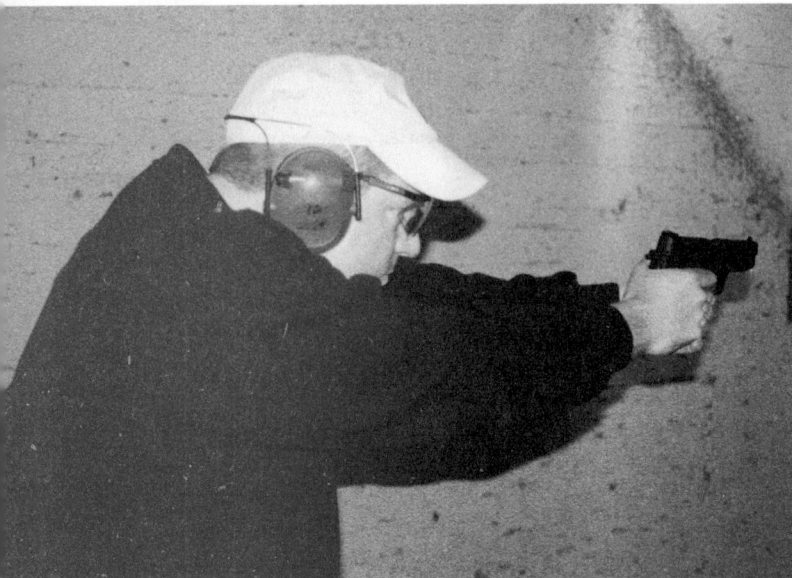

Street cop, SWAT trainer, and adjunct SIGARMS Academy instructor Scott Reidy wields a 9mm P226 to good effect at 2003 IDPA Mid-Winter Championships.

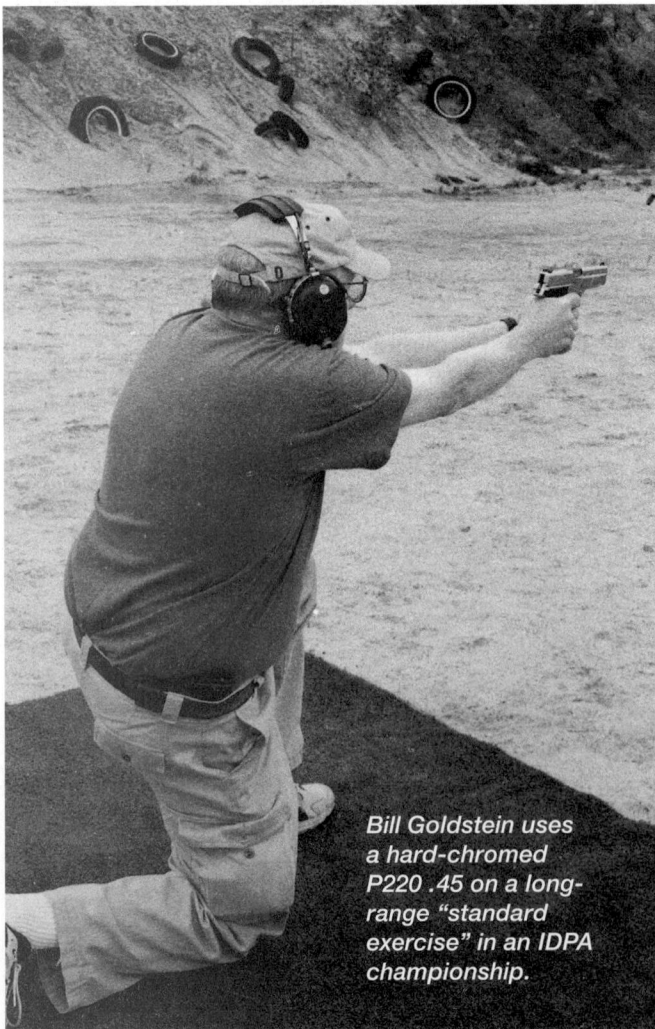

Bill Goldstein uses a hard-chromed P220 .45 on a long-range "standard exercise" in an IDPA championship.

To qualify as a Master in Stock Service Pistol, you need to complete the tough 90-shot Classifier course in 91.00 seconds or less. However, in Custom Defense Pistol, you need to race your single-action .45 auto in 92.00 seconds or less, and in Enhanced Service Pistol, 89.00 seconds or less.

This reflects the conventional wisdom, and collective experience, that one can shoot faster and straighter with the short, easy trigger pull of a pistol that is cocked for the first shot than with one that must be trigger-cocked by a long, heavy double-action pull. However, Ernest Langdon has defied that conventional wisdom.

Throughout 2003, he shot his SIG P220 ST .45 in CDP class, against the cocked and locked 1911 automatics. He came in First Master at the Mid-Winter IDPA Championships hosted by Smith & Wesson in Springfield, Massachusetts, and stayed on a roll for the rest of the year. He romped all of us at the New Hampshire State IDPA championships and won pretty much every other IDPA match he shot. His winning streak culminated in October of 2003 when, still shooting his SIG, he won National Champion CDP at the IDPA Nationals.

Ernest did this firing double-action for the first shot every time he drew the big SIG from his Kydex holster. You see Langdon has discovered something that a lot of people who use a light, easy trigger pull as a crutch have missed. So long as the trigger pull is smooth, a double-action gives you more of a surprise break than does the "glass-rod-breaking" let-off of a cocked target pistol. This is why the best PPC masters shoot their revolvers double-action all the way through their course, including the 50-yard stage where they are allowed to cock their hammers to single-action mode if they choose. Why not go double-action-only? Langdon goes for speed, and the longer trigger return plus the longer pull for the next shot add up to more distance traveled

Todd Green is one of IDPA's consistent top shooters. His match pistol is the same P220 .45 he is licensed to carry on the street.

This shooter uses her SIG P229 .40 to good effect in the New England Regional Championships of IDPA, 2003, on a weak-hand-only stage.

by the trigger finger, which in turn adds up to more time consumed. With traditional double-action, Langdon squeezes off the first double-action shot starting as soon as the muzzle is downrange. The trigger is thus "prepped" as he is coming up

on the target, and that first double-action shot breaks at about the time the sights have arrived where he wants them. Now the relatively short travel of his trigger re-setting to single-action for each subsequent shot can be taken advantage of for an extremely fast string of fire. Ernest adjusts his guns at about 6 or 7 pounds pull weight for double-action, and 3 pounds for single-action in a match gun. For the street, a Langdon SIG action will have the same sweet double-action pull, and about a 4-pound let-off in single-action.

IPSC

The International Practical Shooting Confederation, developed in 1976 by Jeff Cooper, has turned into "track and field with a pistol" in the open class events. One needs a tricked out target pistol with an extremely light single-action trigger pull to be competitive in this arena. However, in a return to its roots, IPSC has begun a factory-production gun category that initially is proving extremely popular. Shooters are limited to double-action guns, including Glocks.

Here, too, Langdon has done well with his P220 ST. In a typical match, it ould come down to Dave Sevigny with his Glock 34 9mm target gun dueling

IDPA often makes you start in awkward everyday positions, like leaning back in a chair with a bottle of water...

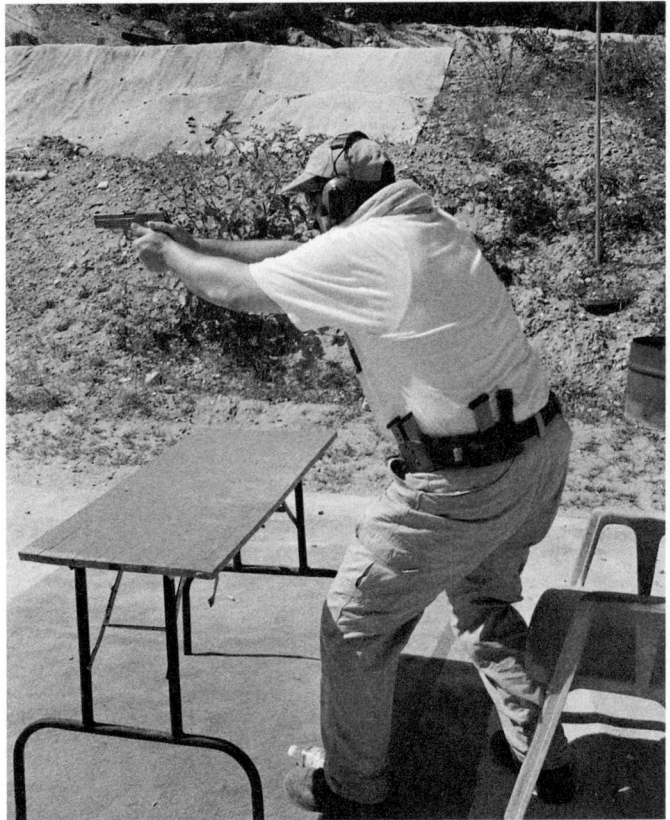

...before you have to react and engage with your carry gun, in this case a SIG P220 .45 auto. Scene is New Hampshire State IDPA Championships, 2002.

with Ernest Langdon and his double-action SIG .45 for determination of the overall winner.

PPC

Once the realm of purpose-built custom target guns with massive heavy barrels and sight ribs, the Police Pistol Course as run by the NRA Competitions Division has evolved much more toward semiautomatic pistols. Of particular interest is the Service Automatic event, which forbids sight ribs, recoil compensators, and other "game" paraphernalia.

In 2000 Mike Talbert, a SWAT sniper, joined the Richmond (VA) Police Department Pistol Team to compete at the NRA's National Police Shooting Championships in Jackson, Mississippi. For the open class events the team used 1911 9mm target pistols custom built by the department's own Jerry Keefer, who is truly a master pistolsmith. They kicked butt with these guns. However, the story on point to this book is that Talbert also won the Police

P226 9mm has easily "cleaned" the 7-yard stage, 12 shots in 20 seconds, at Boston Gun and Rifle Club indoor PPC match.

Service Automatic National Championship.

The gun Mike Talbert used to become national champion was a bone-stock, out-of-the-box *sig pro* in .357 SIG. The ammunition, like the gun, was out-of-the-box department-issue: the 125-grain Speer Gold Dot jacketed hollow-point. He outshot men with custom-barreled Glocks and S&W Performance Center 5906 PC pistols costing two or three times as much as the *sig pro.*

In PPC, the time constraints are not so tight as in IPSC or IDPA. One works on a fixed time schedule for each stage. Not slow fire, but not quite hyper-speed either. There certainly isn't time to clear a serious malfunction and still get a winning score. The extreme reliability of the SIG came through for Mike Talbert, and so did the excellent factory trigger pull, and so in particular did the inherent accuracy of the SIG pistol.

It should be noted that in IDPA, the standard target is a cardboard silhouette whose maximum five-point zone is a circle in the chest measuring 8 inches in diameter. In IPSC, the standard target is similar in configuration but with a center five-point zone measuring about 6 inches across by 11 inches in height. But in PPC, the target is the B-27, whose center X ring is an oval measuring only 2 inches wide by 3 inches high.

This PPC stage required six shots from the leather at 50 feet in 12 seconds. Winning target is shown, 58 points out of 60 with only one hit outside the 10-ring of miniature silhouette. Pistol is 9mm P226.

REPORT FROM THE ARENA

When I test a gun for a gun magazine I like to shoot a match with it. The score measures the

Barricade shooting is a key component of PPC, with the left hand always controlling the gun on the lefthand side. SIG's controllability is a big help here.

Sitting position is part of the PPC course of fire, accomplished here with 9mm P226.

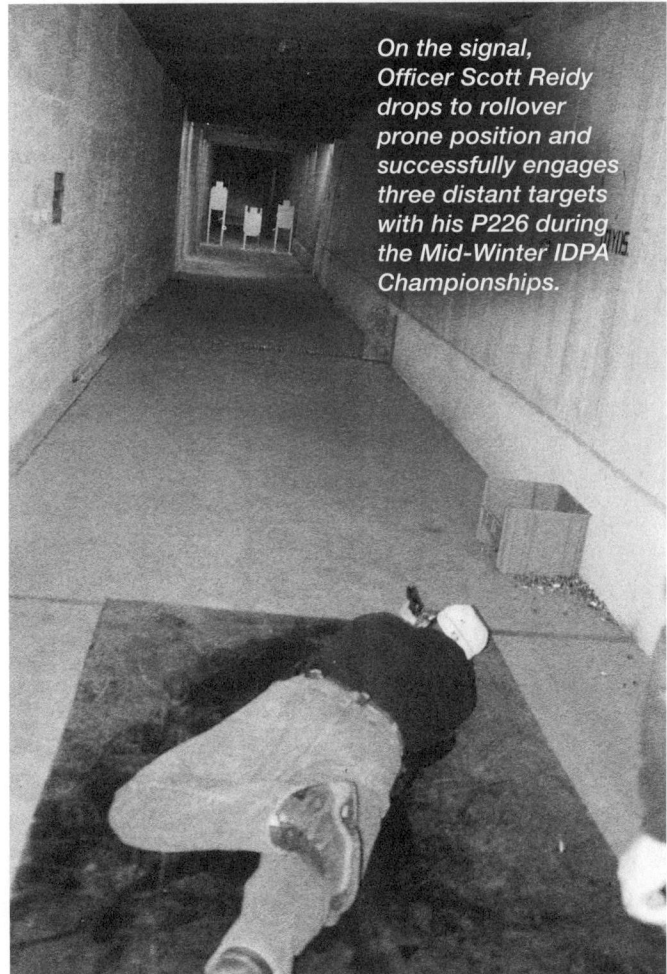

On the signal, Officer Scott Reidy drops to rollover prone position and successfully engages three distant targets with his P226 during the Mid-Winter IDPA Championships.

shooter subjectively more than it measures the capability of the gun objectively, but even so, a good combat match is a microcosm of a gunfight and teaches you things about a given pistol's handling.

One thing the matches have taught me about SIG-Sauer pistols is that they are reliable and consistent, and built for good handling under stress. I remember the day when legendary modern gunfighter Jim Cirillo and I were on the same squad at the first Bianchi Cup and walking from the Barricade Event to the Moving Target Event. Jimmy commented that he was feeling more stress than he ever felt in any of his gunfights. The reason was that here, as opposed to the street, there was ample time for the pressure to build, and the prize-rich Bianchi Cup, which became known as "the Wimbledon of pistol shooting," was nothing less than a pressure cooker.

The Bianchi Cup was geared more for target guns than street guns, but the SIG was capable of doing well there. Ernest Langdon proved it in the Stock Gun class, and years before, gun writer and U.S. Customs Agent Seth Nadel proved it when he shot his SIG .45 there and did quite well. Seth's gun was either a P220-E or a Browning BDA if memory serves. Since there are no speed-reloading stages in the Bianchi Cup, the butt-heel release of his older-style SIG .45 did not slow him down at all.

Another event that could raise the blood pressure was the old National Tactical Invitational, which was partly a contest and partly a training experience. The demands were so intense that it

The author bolts from a chair as the timer behind him starts a "home invasion" drill. The finger can safely enter trigger guard as he brings the downrange-pointed P226 up...

...rapid firing on the run...

...and nailing targets close and far. Scene is 2002 Southwest Regional Championships of IDPA.

could get a little dangerous – one year, a range officer was accidentally shot by a contestant, fortunately surviving – and usually three out of ten scenarios would involve live role-playing in which contestants and training role-players shot at each other with Simunitions™. Those paint pellets stung and drew blood, and a day at the NTI always gave you your daily adrenaline requirement. For many years, SIGSauer pistols were what we were issued for Simunitions sessions, and the gun's shootability and good human engineering for use under stress was reinforced in that environment. At least one year, military spec-ops instructor John Hoelschen won the event, using his personal SIG P228 in the live fire portions of the program.

In September of 2002, in Phoenix to speak at the Gun Rights Policy Conference, I learned that the IDPA Southwest Regional Championships were going on in the city. My friend Kate Alexander was one of the people running it, and I sneaked away Friday afternoon to shoot the match with her and the range officers before it was opened to contestants over the weekend, days I did not have free. The carry gun I had brought with me was a SIG P226. The plan was that I would buy some 9mm ball ammo from shooters who hopefully had some extra, since I didn't have enough of my Winchester SXT Ranger 127-grain +P+ carry loads to shoot through the whole tournament.

Phoenix is home turf for some of the best practical shooters in the world. Robbie Leatham and Brian Enos are two legendary names that come to mind. Would I be able to shoot an out-of-the-box SIG service pistol creditably against such lofty competition as I could expect there? I was about to find out.

The first stage I found myself on began with the shooter seated when home invaders kicked in the doors. Since this was a home-defense scenario, it was one of the few stages where a concealment garment didn't need to be worn over my inside-the-waistband holster, a Ted Blocker LFI Concealment Rig. As the buzzer of the electronic timer signaled the start, I sprang from the chair, moving forward as I drew and fired. With the double-action pull of the SIG, I felt safe in prepping the trigger as soon as the muzzle was downrange, and I cracked off the first shot as the front sight hit the middle of the silhouette. The second shot came instantly behind it. With the trigger finger placed on the trigger at the distal joint for maximum leverage, transition from the double-action first shot to the single-action follow-up was instantaneous. Most of the rest of the targets I shot on the move, saving time. To keep the gun from bouncing, I bent my arms into an approximation of a Weaver stance, creating a shock absorption effect that kept my sight picture on the targets as I ran. This bends the wrists, and some auto pistols jam when held with anything but a locked wrist. Fortunately, a SIG-Sauer doesn't. I finished the stage in good shape.

And so it went. The P226 had come out of the box with its fixed SIGlite night sights dead on for point of aim/point of impact. This helped a great deal on some tough shots where the bad guy was behind the good guy and only a sliver of the "opponent's" head was visible. The SIG's sweet trigger did the rest: when the pistol barked, the shot went true.

Unfortunately, no pistol comes with a tactical computer installed. On one stage I shot the targets in the wrong sequence, costing me a relatively huge penalty of time added to my score. My fault, not the SIG's.

Night fell. The range crew was trying to shoot in an afternoon a long course of fire intended for a whole day's shooting. They would complete the rest during breaks over the next couple of days. However, I couldn't get back to do that, so it was decided that I'd finish shooting in the dark.

There were three stages left. On one of them, there was still enough light in the heavy dusk to distinguish the target array. The glowing green tritium dots of the SIGlite sights allowed me to

An extended magazine and attachable M3 light make this P226 9mm "rail gun" ideal for certain tactical competitions.

pretty much clean the targets, with a nearly perfect score accomplished in a decent time. By the time they were scored, though, the sun was truly below the horizon, and it was unscheduled night shooting from there on.

My SIG P226 was the latest model with frame rail for attaching flashlights. Since this was supposed to be a daylight stage, allowances were made. I set my InSight M3 attachable light on a table to light up the left side of the range, and took the SureFire 6P high-intensity flashlight from its belt holder and lay it down to illuminate the right side. I was able to finish this next to the last stage with a decent score.

The final stage required the shooter to pick up the gun from the table. Since this was not designed as a night shooting stage and would be fired in daylight by the other competitors, I was allowed to start with the M3 light already attached to the P226. The illumination was bright enough that I felt as if I was shooting in daylight, and the intense white light on the target gave me a silhouetted sight picture that was crystal-clear.

We finished the match. I reloaded for the street with +P+, being legal to carry in Arizona, and thanked everyone for a splendid shooting tournament. A few days later, when it was over, Katie Alexander told me I had come in fourth. Against the high level of competition there and under the circumstances, I was grateful for that finish.

But the bottom line was, the SIG pistol had proven to me yet again that, although built for the battlefield and proven on the street, it was also absolutely "match-worthy" for practical pistol competition, right out of the factory box.

From behind replicated cover, the author returns to a ready position and decocks after completing a stage in the dark at Southwest Regional Championships. On the table is his InSight M3 light used to illuminate the target array.

Chapter 25
The SIG in Training

Any tool requiring a responsible hand at the controls is a tool that cries out for training. The handgun is no exception. While the SIG-Sauer pistols are easier to learn to operate safely than many others, this doesn't mean that their selection eliminates any need for training.

I have observed these pistols in the training environment for hundreds of thousands of rounds. An instructor since the early 1970s and for more than 20 years full time, seeing 10,000 bullets or more go downrange in a given week, I've had the opportunity to examine the SIG-Sauer in training from every perspective; as the instructor, as the student, and as the evaluator of the class. I've learned some interesting things about these guns and how they interface with the students who learn their use.

TEACHING WITH THE SIG

Back in the 1970s, I taught with either the department-issue service revolver or the Colt 1911 .45 auto. Time went on. The serious police switch to autos began in the 1980s, with the SIG P226 taking an early

lead in popularity in many parts of the country. I was seeing more of them in classes, so I picked one up. Nice little gun. The trigger reach was longer than I liked, but overall I was quite happy with the pistol, and taught with it for quite a while. Then I bought a P220 .45 and liked it even better.

By the 1990s, I had gotten into my current habit of using different guns on each road trip or "teaching cycle." The students after all had Beretta, Glock, H&K, Ruger, SIG, and S&W pistols for the most part, along with revolvers and 1911s, and I had to stay current with all of them. In no particular order I'd do a couple of weeks on the road with a Beretta, then come home and switch to the SIG for the next cycle, and so on, including the revolver at least one week a year. I learned that any week I was teaching with a SIG

would be a week when I wasn't going to have gun trouble. I learned that when I shot a demonstration for the students, the gun would never embarrass me, and neither would the score.

It's worth emphasizing that last point a little bit. I've paid my dues in the competition arena. I've shot in several Bianchi Cups – fired the first shot at the first one, as a matter of fact, and have the "Silver Bullet Award" to prove it – and when commentators called it the "pressure cooker" of competitive handgun shooting, I never argued the point. But I can tell you, the pressure you feel when a bunch of students, who paid you to teach them to shoot, are looking at you on the firing line and thinking, "Let's see if he can practice what he preaches" challenges the pressure of The Cup. At moments like that, you *do* want a gun that works, and you *do* want a gun that always delivers.

There are some things with a gun – the draw, for instance – that are best seen from the front, and for that I bring a dummy gun with which to demonstrate. But there are some things you can't teach with a dummy gun, such as speed or tactical reloading. For that, I simply fieldstrip my teaching handgun. An advantage of the SIG-Sauer for this is that it comes apart *en bloc* into two main sections that stay together. I can simply put the top half of the gun in the pocket of my BDUs and use the bottom half for the demo. Unlike some other autos, there's no slide stop that's going to get lost or misplaced, and the parts won't fall out of the assembly and into the sand or mud of the range.

The instructor's teaching gun is his carry gun when he is on the road doing this work. I put mine on when I dress in the morning, and don't take it off until I go to bed at night, except to shower and change between the end of class and supper. If I go out for dinner, I don't leave guns in an unattended hotel room. The modest weight of the typical SIG-Sauer makes it easy to wear constantly. Similarly, its lack of sharp edges provides for all-day carry comfort.

Over the last few years, I've gotten into the habit of wearing the SIG P220 .45 to class when I'm on my home turf, and carrying the SIG P226 9mm instead when I'm on the road. A box of 115-grain 9mm rounds simply weighs less than a box of 230-grain .45 cartridges, for one thing, and I put at least my carry ammo in the luggage. When I buy practice ammo locally, 9mm is distinctly cheaper than .45.

Since 9/11/01, I've had another concern. We recall how long the airports were shut down after the nightmare at the Twin Towers. My wife and older daughter were on vacation and stranded for some time in Las Vegas. There were no cars to rent, and trains and buses were instantly overbooked. It took them a long time to get back home. Many people in that situation hitchhiked. I figure if I have to do that in the wake of another terrorist attack,

Author finds en bloc disassembly of SIG-Sauer lends itself to certain learning points...

... such as the tactical reload...

... because students can see what's going on from the front, safely, without being "crossed" by an actual gun.

267

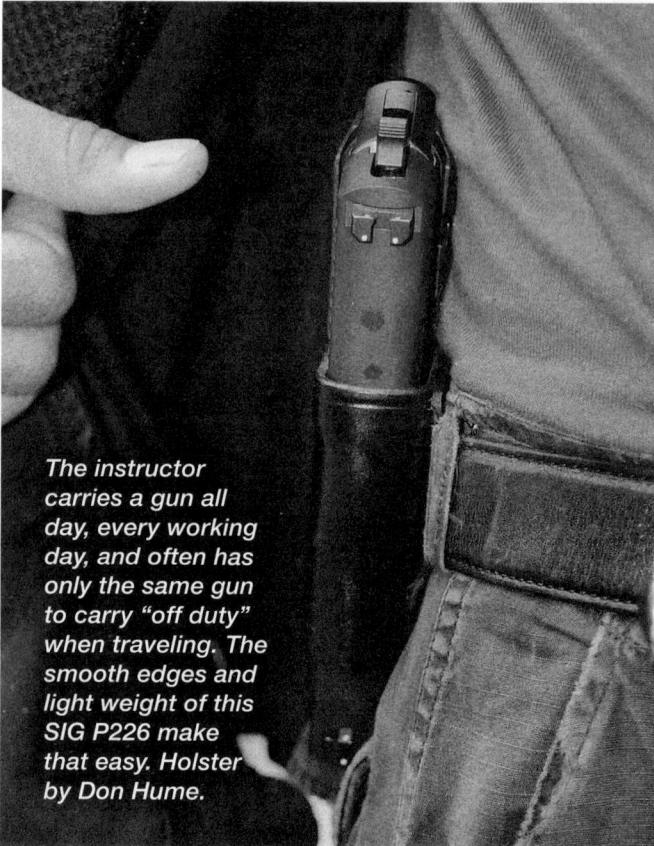

The instructor carries a gun all day, every working day, and often has only the same gun to carry "off duty" when traveling. The smooth edges and light weight of this SIG P226 make that easy. Holster by Don Hume.

I want my journey of what may be thousands of miles to see me carrying a gun and enough ammo to get me through whatever may come. The fact is, I can carry more 9mm ammo than .45 ACP ammo. A similar argument was used for the 5.56mm rifle cartridge of the M-16 over the 7.62 mm ammo of the M-14 it replaced, the same logic prevails here.

LEARNING WITH THE SIG

If you don't read, you won't be able to write well; if you never take the student's role, you'll eventually stultify in the teacher's role. That's why I try to take a major class related to what I teach at least once a year, more if I can. Being someone else's student has taught me how to make the training experience more pleasant, meaningful, and rewarding for my own students.

While preparing the first edition of this book, I signed on for what was nicknamed "The Big Dogs' Course" at Chapman Academy in Columbia, Missouri. Founded by Ray Chapman, the famed world champion of IPSC, that legendary firearms training school was then run by Ray's hand-picked successor, the extremely capable John Skaggs. I got to know John well when he and I both taught at Chapman Academy, and he's one of the best in the business.

The "Big Dogs" class with the Chapman Academy staff who taught it. At far left front is John Skaggs, then-chief instructor.

When you run with the "Big Dogs," you want fangs as sharp as theirs. Six of 16 in the class at Chapman Academy were state or regional handgun champions. Left to right: Rick Staples, Jim Williams, Trent Taylor, Mas Ayoob, Dennis Reichard, Gary Hartzel.

The Chapman Academy staff makes a point of teaching with different guns and not having one "trademark pistol." From left, Ray Chapman himself is most likely to take a student's gun to demonstrate. Rich Greiner uses a high-end 1911. John Skaggs prefers the Beretta 92. John Leveron carries a Glock Tactical/Practical, and Mark Spedale teaches with the same P220DAO he wears to work as a street cop.

Mild recoil of the 9mm SIG makes shooting thousands of rounds in five days no chore at all.

The Chapman Academy advanced course includes a lot of one-handed shooting at 7 yards with either hand; they recommend this angled hold adapted by Ray Chapman from target shooting champ Bill McMillan...

SIGlite night sights in action. Camera's flash has caught ejected spent casing and the bullet splash at 9 o'clock on the Pepper Popper downrange as the author nails it in the dark from behind cover with his out-of-the-box SIG during a night "assault course" at Chapman Academy.

Above: Firing from The Barricades at 35 yards at Chapman Academy. Here, a SIG's accuracy and "shootability" manifests itself.

Below: ...and the SIG has put all its bullets into the 4-inch center X ring, even in rapid fire. This Bianchi Cup target is standard (except for steel) at Chapman Academy.

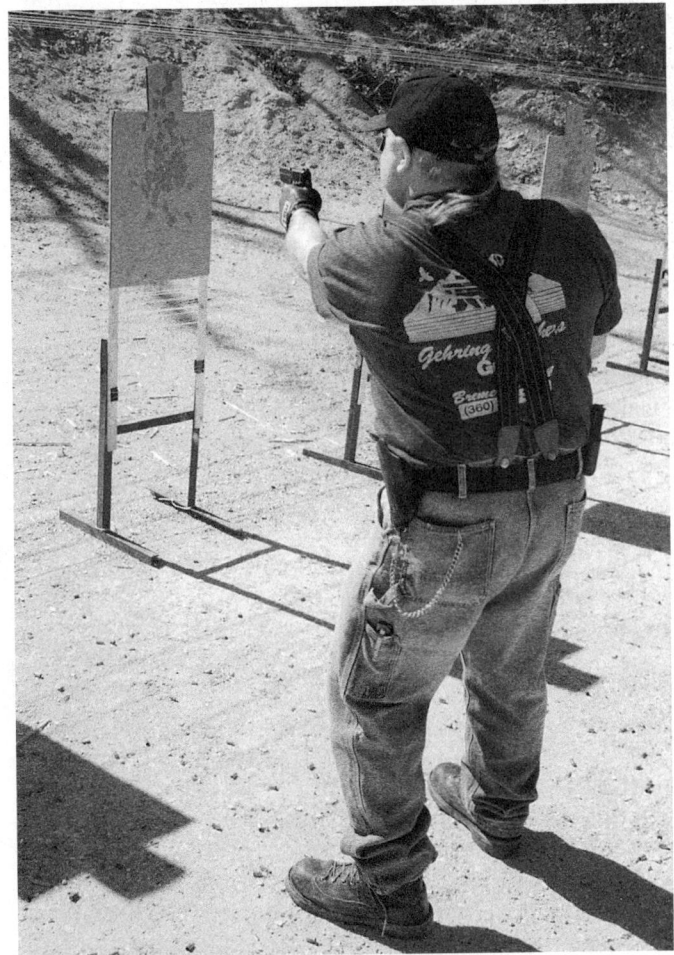

Chapman Academy emphasizes shooting below the line of sight at close range. Here, Brad Gehring engages the second of two targets with his P229 .40.

By the third day of the intensive shooting course at Chapman's, half a dozen students had bandaged hands...but were still lovin' the class. Note, however, that neither of the SIG shooters needed dressings.

We were warned that this class could go over 2,500 rounds of pistol alone, with shotgun, rifle, and perhaps some full-auto thrown in. Custom tailored as a combination of the famous Chapman Advanced course with some of the stuff the Academy reserves for SEALs and other heavy hitters who train there, this one-time course got its "Big Dogs" nickname from the fact that 14 of the 16 attendees were certified firearms instructors. Moreover, six were combat pistol champions at state or regional levels, and there had been a national title or two among the collective accomplishments of the student body. Ray Chapman himself had come out of retirement to be present for three of the five days.

Not wanting to stay on the porch while the big dogs ran, I knew I'd need some top-notch hardware to keep up. The rifle and shotgun I used came from Al Greco's shop, Al's Custom (1701 Conway Wallrose Road, PO Box 205, Freedom, Penn. 15042). The rifle was a race-tuned DPMS AR-15 with minute-of-angle accuracy, and the shotgun an 870 so tricked out with recoil reduction modifications that it felt like

shooting a 20-gauge. My pistols, by contrast, were ordinary, out-of-the-box SIG P226s. Out of habit, I brought two so I'd have a spare. It turned out I never needed the second one.

Knowing you can deliver a group like this at 25 yards gives confidence to instructor and student alike. Ayoob shot this group in front of a Virginia class, Pro-Load +P 115-grain 9mm duty ammo from P226.

"Shootability" of the SIG is appreciated when a student has to fire from awkward positions like this one at a Chapman Academy advanced course.

Certainly, the 9mm ammo – Black Hills' accurate remanufactured 115-grain JHP – was lighter than .45 ACP to lug around the many ranges on the complex. But with a promised 1,500 to 2,500 rounds of shooting on the menu, the light recoil of the 9mm made a lot of sense. When I was younger, all I brought to places like Chapman's were .45s, and I could literally shoot them all day. Hell, back then I'd shoot a .44 Magnum until the ammo ran out. But that was then, and this was now. Arthritis had crept up on me, and I had discovered that a whole week of intensively shooting .45s could leave me with a wrist so sore it was almost crippling. If that made me a pussy, I could only say, "Meow."

The week wore on. Only two of us, Brad Gehring and I, brought SIGs. Brad switched back and forth between a P229 .40 and a P220 .45. Since we are both geezers old enough to remember the "Fabulous Furry Freak Brothers" of the underground comix of the 1960s, and since we both had facial hair, we became known as "the fabulous furry SIG brothers" for the week.

During that arduous week, the SIGs performed brilliantly. In exercises that demanded unsighted point shooting, their natural pointing qualities kept them on target. Shooting prone at 50 yards, the high accuracy of the SIG combined with the minimal

bullet drop of the 115-grain 9mm made consistent center hits easy from the roll-over prone position that Chapman developed and made famous many years ago.

Moving targets? No sweat: the gun tracked them easily. Tight grouping drills? My P226 does an inch and a half at 25 yards, and its smooth trigger pull in both single- and double-action allows the shooter to deliver as much as he can earn from that promised accuracy.

The final qualification course was tougher than the Bianchi Cup course of fire. I make that statement having shot the Bianchi Cup 11 times. When it was over, the many target pistols, the one target-grade revolver in evidence, and the many super-expensive custom handguns had all been beaten by a SIG-Sauer. Brad and I both finished in the top five with our SIGs, the only two such guns in the class. I didn't keep track on Brad, but I had fired between 1,500 and 2,000 rounds through my P226 and hadn't cleaned it once during the week. It never jammed once.

Let me tell you something. That "first-in-class" certificate from Chapman Academy is framed and displayed along with a handful of other awards that really, *really* mean a lot to me. It was a hard-fought battle against "them big dogs."

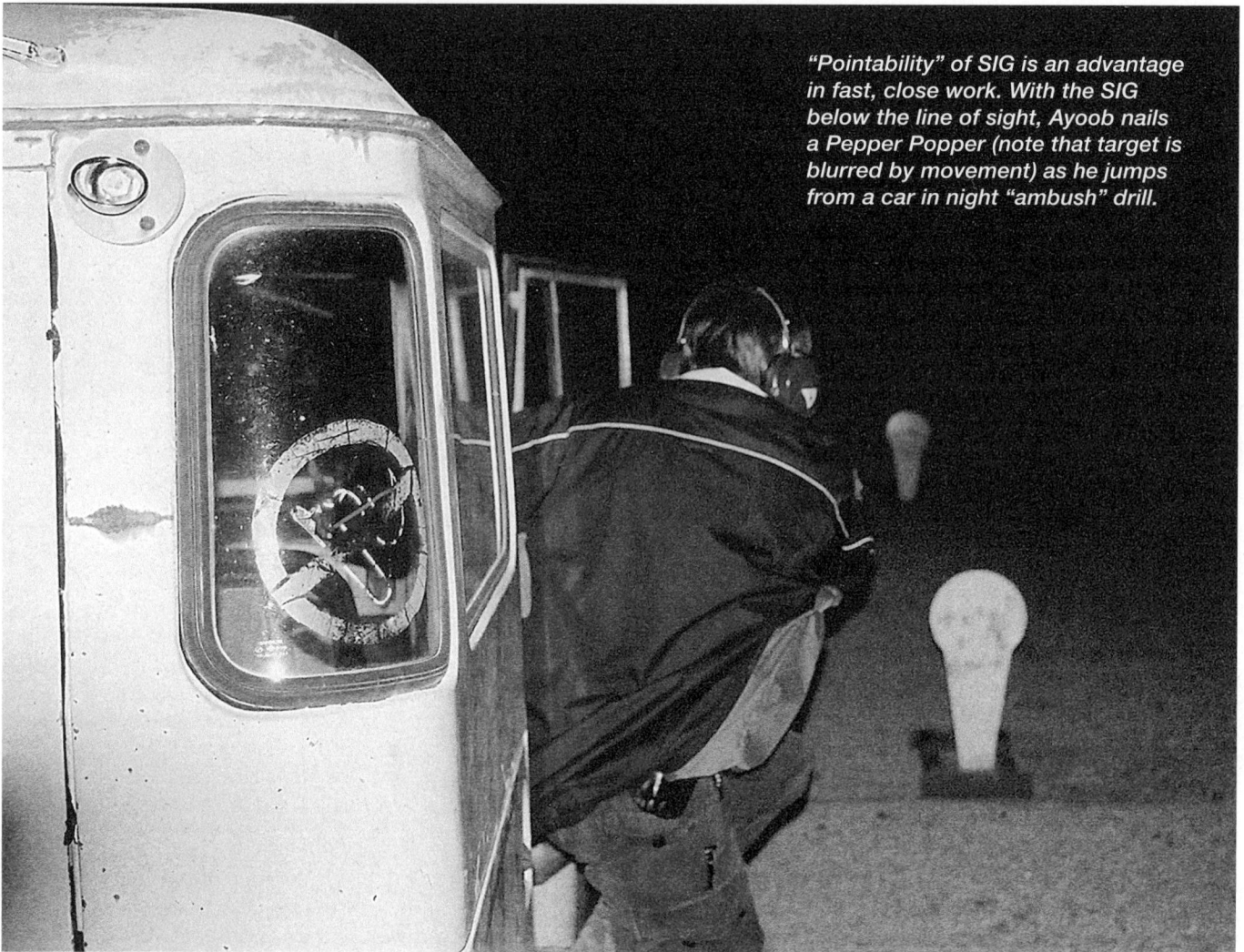

"Pointability" of SIG is an advantage in fast, close work. With the SIG below the line of sight, Ayoob nails a Pepper Popper (note that target is blurred by movement) as he jumps from a car in night "ambush" drill.

Night shooting? The factory-optional SIGlite night sights did fine. One-handed shooting proves easy with the SIG when the other hand is manipulating a flashlight. And easiest of all – mercy, it's almost cheating – was slipping an InSight M3 light onto the P226's light rail.

Along about mid-week, we had noticed an epidemic of what John Skaggs calls "Chapman's Disease." The symptoms are hands abraded by sharp-edged guns fired day in and day out. One of the students was not only a state IDPA champion but an emergency room physician, and by Tuesday was either bandaging injuries or taping shooters' hands to prevent such injuries. Mine needed nothing: The SIG hadn't left a mark on 'em.

A few years earlier, I had gone to Clint Smith's Thunder Ranch and taken the Advanced Pistol Course with my older daughter. We had both shot 9mm Berettas. With a similar round expenditure of the fine Black Hills ammo (FMJ ball that time), we were also jam-free with those guns, but by the second day my thumb bore twin lacerations from the feed lips of the magazines we were constantly

reloading. That did not happen with the SIG magazines.

I shot most of the Chapman course with 10-round "post-Ban" SIG mags. I don't like to put wear on my pre-ban high-capacity magazines if there's no need. Since the 10-rounders bespeak a stupid and disingenuous gesture toward crime control anyway, dropping these "Clinton magazines" in the dirt is pleasing rather than disturbing. I found the 10th round in these magazines a pain to put in. Fearful of making a magazine that could get them in trouble with the government, most manufacturers take pains to be certain an eleventh cartridge can't be inserted. Once fully loaded, the cartridge stack has no flex left, and has to be really hammered into the butt of the SIG if it's going to seat properly. For all those reasons, I just loaded them with nine rounds. When there was an "assault course," I would break out the 15-rounders or my extended 20-round magazine.

Excellent performance. Non-fatiguing. Trouble-free. Sends the student to the head of his class. What more could a student at gun school ask of a pistol?

Chapter 26

Ammunition for the SIG-Sauer

Many pistols designed originally for military-specification ammunition would feed *only* milspec ammunition. Round-nose, full-metal-jacket bullets would taper themselves into the chambers, but the high-performance hollow-point rounds needed by police and armed citizens might fail to feed. Not so the SIG-Sauers, whose virtually straight-line feed angles and good internal polishing have made them extraordinarily reliable with the best defense ammo.

Let's look at these service pistols caliber by caliber, watching for incompatibility and looking at the substantial collective history of these guns to determine what works best in them. Comments will be limited to conventional ammo. Exotic ammunition, usually with very light bullets at very high velocity, is notoriously unreliable in semiautomatic pistols because it does not operate at the same pressure curve for which the guns were designed. These loads also tend to be woefully inaccurate. Besides, with some of them costing $3 per cartridge, the tab will be about $600 to see if they work in your pistol or not. As a rule of thumb, *never carry a pistol with ammunition that hasn't been fired 200 rounds straight, in that gun and those magazines, without a single malfunction.* The defensive handgun is emergency life-saving rescue equipment, and reliability is a non-negotiable baseline requirement.

.380 ACP

The smallest caliber service pistol SIGARMS brings to the U.S., the .380 is at best marginal in power. Some of us would say submarginal. .380 ACP (**A**utomatic **C**olt **P**istol) is known overseas variously as 9X17, 9mm Kurz, or 9mm Corto. The latter two words mean "short." The little thing comes up short not only in length, but in power.

In this book's chapter on the SIG .380s, three actual shootings are recounted. In those incidents a total of 10 shots were fired, and all struck the

offenders. Scoring 100 percent hits in actual combat is nothing to sneeze at, and the shootability under stress of the P230 and P232 are the reason they are widely considered "the thinking man's .380s." However, you will notice that the only one-shot stop of the three was a brain shot. In the other two incidents, the offenders made a rather leisurely thing of stopping their hostilities after sustaining fatal wounds from .380 JHP rounds.

Evan Marshall's studies show the Winchester 85-grain Silvertip, Federal 90-grain Hydra-Shok, and 88-grain Federal Classic hollow-points to work the best. I've also seen significant disruption of soft tissue with the El Dorado StarFire .380 JHP which, like the Hydra-Shok, was designed by my friend Tom Burszynski. All these rounds should be reasonably close to one another in terminal performance. Winchester with the SXT designed by Alan Corzine, and Remington with their Golden Saber designed by Dave Schluckebier, tried the combination of a slightly heavier bullet with a bonded-jacket high-tech hollow-point to get deeper penetration and better overall wound effect. Marshall's colleague Ed Sanow, a very knowledgeable man who has completed much testing in ballistic gelatin, loads the Golden Saber in the .380 he carries for backup. In the slaughterhouse, I found even the 102-grain Golden Saber lacking in penetration, one reason I prefer not to carry a .380 at all. (Marshall, a gunfight survivor, at one time carried a SIG P230 for backup, but later went to a

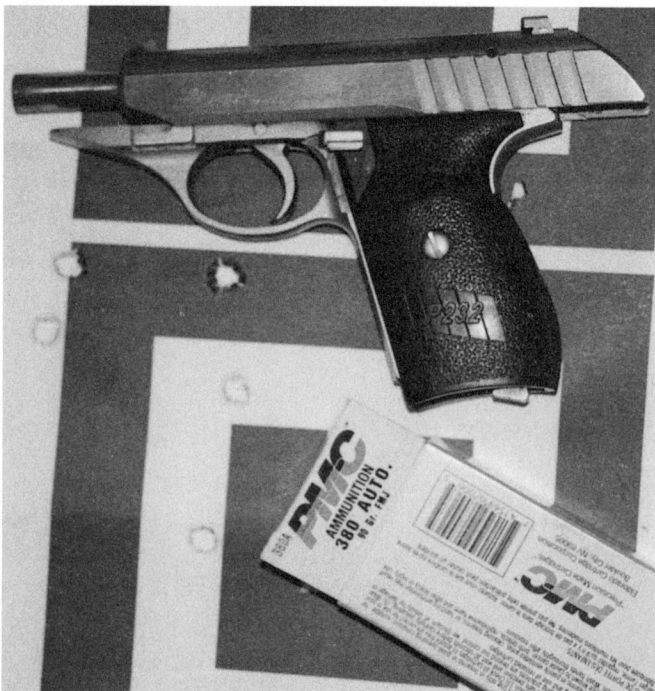

The author knows a prominent gunshot wound authority who carries a SIG .380 loaded with ball ammo. The trick is putting the bullet in exactly the right place.

more potent caliber for his second gun, and neither he nor Sanow ever advocated carrying a .380 as a primary weapon.)

One of the top medical examiners in this country carries a SIG P230. He and I were talking shop in the witness's waiting room waiting to testify for the defense in the case of a cop wrongfully charged with murder and got to talking about carry guns. He explained that having to wear a tailored suit for court all the time, he needed the flattest, smallest gun possible. His extensive gunshot autopsy experience had shown him that all .380 JHP rounds fell short of the penetration depth he felt was necessary, so he carried FMJ ammo and trusted his anatomic knowledge and not inconsiderable marksmanship skill to put the little SIG's .380 bullet in the right place if ever needed. (The accused officer, by the way, was found not guilty. He had stopped a deadly knife attack with two .40 S&W 180-grain Hydra-Shok bullets to the knife-wielder's chest, dropping the man instantly.)

I've found no particular round among the conventional .380 loads that causes problems in the SIGs. If you run across the rare P230 or P232 that jams, send it back to SIGARMS and they'll square the problem away for you.

9MM PARABELLUM

Also known as 9X19, 9mm Luger, and 9mm NATO, this is the most popular SIG-Sauer caliber in the world. It was once the most popular in the U.S., but has been eclipsed by the .40 Smith & Wesson.

The hottest loads (anything in the 1,300 feet per second velocity range) have been known to cycle the light slide of a P225 so fast that it did not pick up the next round on the cartridge stack. I would load the P225 only with standard-pressure loads. Prior to the 1996 beefed-up redesign, the P226 was known to suffer cracked frames with frequent shooting of these very hot rounds. It hasn't been a problem with the later models, nor with the P239 or the *sig pro.*

Ball ammunition is impotent in stopping power and dangerously over-penetrative for defense use. You definitely want hollow-point rounds. Whether heavy slow bullets or light fast ones work best has been the subject of much debate.

The 115-grain JHPs at 1,300 or so feet per second proved to be the top "stoppers" in Evan Marshall's controversial study of actual gunfights. Illinois State Troopers shot many felons with that ammunition, and never had a case of one absorbing bullet after bullet and staying up and running, as has been common with many other 9mm rounds. It was used with much success in the optional 9mm pistols of the Border Patrol, and in the SIG P228s of

P226 9mm gives remarkably consistent accuracy, and 100 percent reliability, with a wide range of ammunition.

the Secret Service and the Air Marshals. The latter two agencies were so impressed with 9mm +P+ performance that they opted for more of the same, trading up to SIG P229s in .357 SIG and loading with CCI Gold Dot and Winchester SXT 125-grain JHPs at 1,350 feet per second. ISP and the Border Patrol both later standardized on .40s.

On the other end of the scale we find the 147grain subsonic JHP. Once touted as the ultimate 9mm load, its potency in the field proved so spotty that most agencies that adopted it either went to

lighter, faster 9mm ammo (Las Vegas, Jacksonville), or simply traded up to more powerful calibers. Some chose .45s (Chicago, LAPD, Los Angeles County). Some went to .40s (Michigan State Police, Indianapolis PD, New Orleans PD) or .357 SIGs (Richmond PD, and Virginia and Delaware State Police). It was FBI that popularized the 147-grain subsonic, and one of the ranking agents responsible later told me he was disappointed with how many times it took (in his words) "multiple, *multiple*" 147-grain bullets to stop an attacker. Today, we

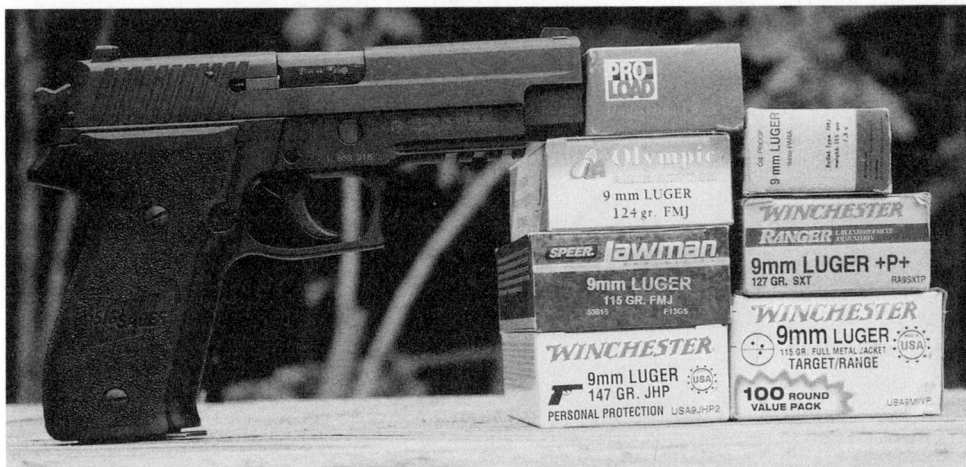

This broad array of 9mm ammo all works fine in author's late model P226; for personal needs, he picks the 115-grain +P Pro-Load Tactical or the 127-grain +P+ Winchester Ranger.

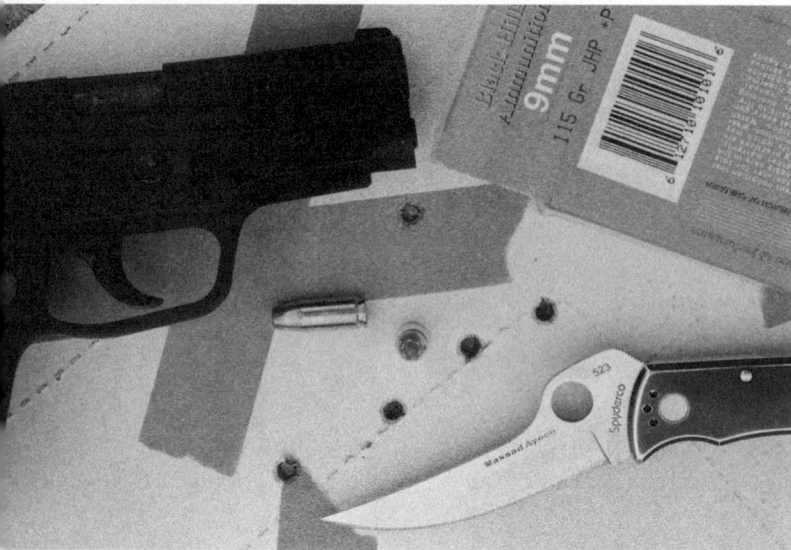

Using a knife blade for perspective shows a sub4inch group at 25 yards with the Black Hills version of the 9mm Illinois State Police load, available to the public. Pistol is P228.

have highly evolved 147 grain loads such as Federal HST and Winchester Ranger, which are far more effective than their predecessors.

A middle ground compromise in the eyes of some is the 124-grain +P at 1,250 feet per second. In the Gold Dot configuration from CCI Speer, this is the standard load of NYPD for their SIG, S&W, and Glock service pistols, and they report excellent results. This round is available to the public in gun shops. Winchester's Ranger-T 127-grain +P+ has

earned a splendid reputation in the SIG P226s of Orlando PD and other agencies. Unfortunately, this load is sold to police only, as are the "Illinois State Police Loads" (115-grain/1,300 fps) produced by Federal, Remington, and Winchester.

OEMs (original equipment manufacturers) load 115/1,300 fps 9mm JHP for public consumption, but their products are not always available at gunshops and in some cases have substandard quality control. One brand I can strongly recommend, fore both ample power and excellent QC in a +P load, is Black Hills EXP.

Personally, I keep my SIG 9mms loaded with Ranger 127 grain +P+, Speer Gold Dot 124 grain +P, or Black Hills 115 grain +P. P225 owners and others more comfortable with standard-pressure rounds, can do no better than the Federal Classic 115-grain JHP, coded "9BP." It topped the standard-pressure 9mm list in the Marshall Study, and I've seen the same results. In one of my cases, an officer's single 9BP from a P226 struck the suspect in the chest and dropped him like a rock. In another, two such rounds in the thorax stopped a knife-wielder in his tracks. In both cases, every bullet was found lodged in the back at the end of a dynamic wound track, fully mushroomed. Winchester Ranger or Federal HST 147 grain are also good choices in a standard pressure 9mm defense load.

.40 SMITH & WESSON

Introduced in 1990, conceptualized by experts Paul Liebenberg and Tom Campbell as a

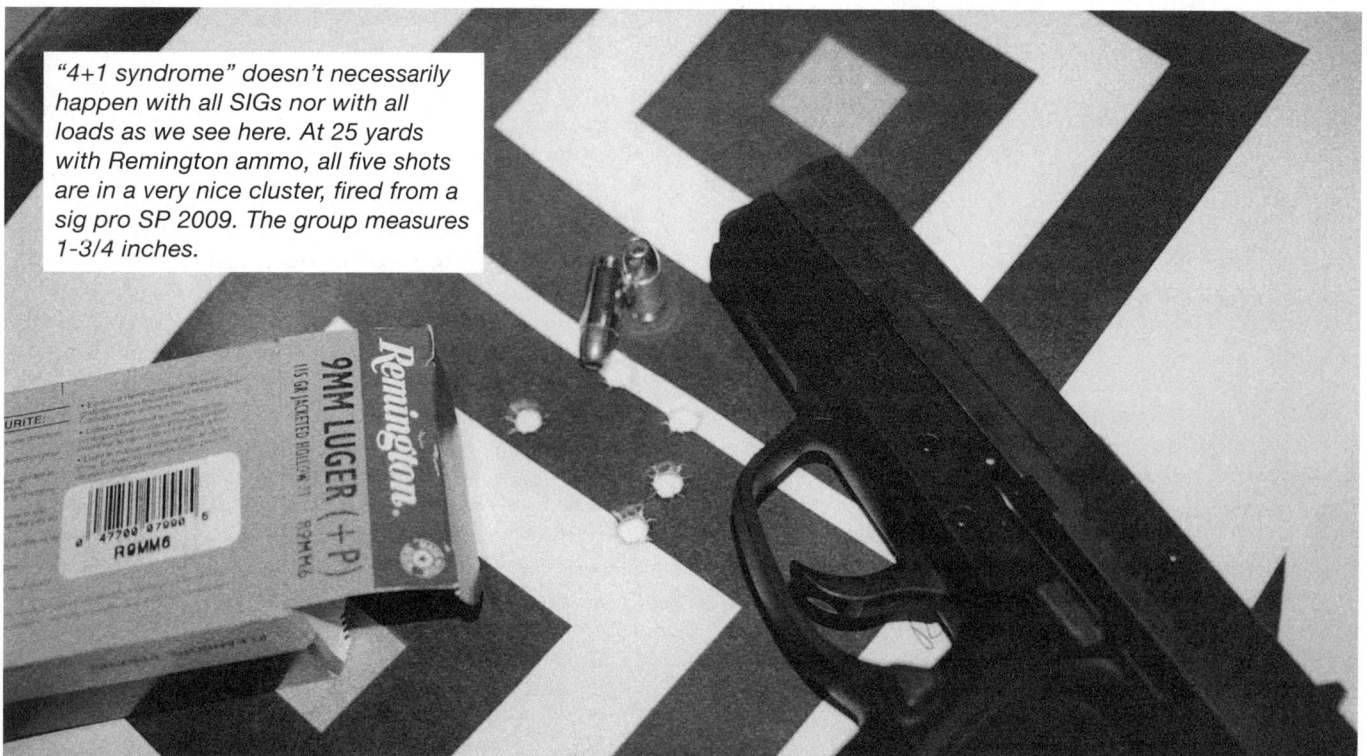

"4+1 syndrome" doesn't necessarily happen with all SIGs nor with all loads as we see here. At 25 yards with Remington ammo, all five shots are in a very nice cluster, fired from a sig pro SP 2009. The group measures 1-3/4 inches.

compromise between the firepower of a 16-shot 9mm and the power of an eight-shot .45, this cartridge was instantly embraced by the police and almost as quickly by the armed citizens. It is by far the largest selling police handgun caliber today. It has proven to be a better manstopper than any of us dared hope it would at the time of its introduction, thanks in large part to high-tech ammo and improved generations of loads.

First generation was the 180-grain subsonic JHP at 950 to 980 fps. It is the ballistic twin of the Old West's .38/40 Winchester round, albeit with a more efficient projectile. Standard JHPs seem prone to shooting through the opponent; the higher-tech hollow-points seem more likely to stay in the body. Milwaukee PD reports splendid performance from their 180-grain Gold Dots; Evan Marshall ranked the Federal Hydra-Shok tops; and Dr. Martin Fackler touted the Winchester Ranger 180-grain. I would tend to go with the Ranger; almost every case I've seen of it striking a human body has resulted in a fully mushroomed projectile lodged in the opposite side of the torso.

Second generation was the 155- to 165-grain transonic, with the former at about 1,200 fps and the latter at around 1,150. This is very close to the performance of the 158-grain .357 Magnum bullet at 1,200 foot-seconds, but without that revolver load's tendency to almost always shoot through the human body. It has worked out very well in police shootings and seems to be a more dynamic combination than the first generation subsonic. I did one case where the officer shot the attacker five times in about a second with 155-grain Winchester Silvertips at 1,200 fps. The assailant instantly collapsed and dropped his weapon, dying moments later. All the bullets were recovered from the opposite side of the torso, widely mushroomed, at the end of impressive wound tracks. In another case, an ambusher shot a cop in the face with a .38, and the officer reflexively lit him up with a stream of 165-grain CCI Gold Dots at 1,150 fps. The assailant dropped his gun and fell, convulsing. Bullet performance of the Gold Dots was as advertised. This round passes all the FBI protocols for penetration through various barriers. Winchester's Ranger load in this 165-grain format has performed splendidly in multiple shootings in Nashville and elsewhere. Alaska State Troopers, who issue high-tech 180-grain subsonics to road troopers, chose the 155-grain Hydra-Shok for their SWAT team.

Third generation was the 135-grain supersonic bullet at 1,300 fps, very similar in performance to the .357 SIG and the .357 Magnum 125-grain rounds. Salt Lake City ballistics experimenter Richard Kelton developed it. In Louisiana, a man charged a cop with a knife and the officer fired one

The exquisite accuracy of Black Hills .40 S&W ammo is seen with this subcompact SIG P239, twice over from 25 yards.

round of this from the hip out of his SIG P229. Only feet away, the man stopped as if he had hit an invisible wall, fell heavily onto his back, tried to roll over, sighed, and died. The bullet had struck him in the abdomen. The wound was truly massive in width. Medically, the attacker should not have died so quickly from an abdominal hit, but I've talked to the involved officer and seen the official reports.

The 135-grain supersonic, unfortunately, is limited to a very few OEMs. I am not impressed with Federal's much slower personal defense loading in this bullet weight. The bullet mushrooms, but it does very little corollary damage beyond the width of the bullet itself. At 1,300 fps, such bullets shred tissue massively around the wound track. The only brand of 135-grain .40 I could recommend in good conscience, with unblemished quality control and full velocity, would be the Pro-Load Tactical.

Another variation of .40 S&W is the 165-grain subsonic developed for the FBI. It has mild recoil and is very accurate, delivering roughly the paper ballistics of a .38 Special or a little better, but hasn't earned much of a track record in actual shootings.

I'm not aware of any conventional .40 S&W round that causes any problem in the SIG-Sauers chambered for it.

.45 ACP

The first of the SIGs to really "make it" in this country, the P220 chambered for the .45 **A**utomatic **C**olt **P**istol cartridge is a perennial steady seller for SIGARMS, though their compact P245 hasn't taken off as much sales-wise as many of us expected. Having been the service pistol cartridge of the United States from 1911 through well into the 1980s – and still in service with a number of Special Forces units – the .45 caliber is a trusted American institution. Generations of soldiers came back from war speaking in awe of its potent effect, especially in contrast to that of the 9mm Luger, and it is rare to read an article on the .45 automatic which does not contain the phrase "legendary stopping power."

There is substance to the legend. There has been the occasional case of a human being who stood up to multiple .45 hits and stayed in the fight, but that occurrence is rare. In slaughterhouse testing of defensive handgun ammunition, we noticed that the .45 was the most consistent quick killer of large animals, more so even than the sometimes more spectacular .357 Magnum. A low-pressure cartridge, the .45 is not particularly difficult to control, and some people with small hands shoot the P220 .45 better than the lighter kicking P226 or P228 9mm simply because its slimmer grip-frame is a better fit for their hands.

The larger the caliber, the more forgiving the gun in terms of ammunition. The .45 is big enough in diameter that even with the least efficient bullet type, non-expanding full-metal-jacket with around nose, it earned that "legendary stopping power" reputation. With modern hollow-points, it works even better.

Standard-pressure 185-grain loads in the 900 to 1,000 fps range were once most popular in law enforcement, but have lately given way

This all-steel P220 ST easily handles Winchester's police-only Ranger +P 230-grain .45 ACP at 950 fps.

to the 230-grain. Of the 185s, Winchester's Silvertip earned the reputation for virtually always expanding, and for staying within 8 to 10 inches of flesh. This makes it particularly suitable for home defense or situations where one can predict a "bystander-rich environment." At +P velocity, a concept pioneered by Remington, the 185-grain bullet reaches 1,150 feet per second. Now it will do every bit as much damage as a 230-grain JHP, and will have a flatter trajectory for more effective long-range shooting, making it a good choice in a rural environment where long shots might be more likely. The Remington 185-grain +P. JHP is available in standard and Golden Saber configurations, and Federal offers it in Hydra-Shok form.

The 200-grain bullet pioneered by Speer has such a short, wide configuration it was originally nicknamed "the flying ashtray" by gun expert Dean Grennell. It earned an excellent record in actual shootings, generally dropping the bad guys with one or two shots even if the bullets didn't expand, which often happened when they were fired from short barrels. This cartridge configuration was very difficult to feed in 1911s. It would work fine in the loaded SIG P220 .45, but when reloaded into a P220 that had gone to slide-lock, the topmost round would sometimes catch on the feed ramp at six o'clock. This seems to have been pretty much cured in current generations of SIG P220 magazines and pistols. A department near me issues the 200-grain +P CCI Gold Dot for their agency-standard P220s and reports no feeding problems. Denver PD has issued that round for all their .45s, including the many SIGs carried by their officers. The Gold Dot bullet expands more consistently and reliably, even at lower velocity, than its predecessor and in the +P loading offers 1,050 feet per second velocity. Pro-Load offers the same load with the same bullet in their Tactical series, and this ammunition delivers exquisite accuracy.

A brief digression. Avoid low-velocity mid-range Match 185-grain semi-wadcutter target ammo. Its bullet profile is difficult to feed, and its recoil impulse is too feeble to cycle aluminum-frame P220 and P245 pistols in which I've tried it. Strangely enough, it will work fine in my all-steel P220 ST. Apparently, the gun is moving less with lighter recoil because of greater weight, and the slide on the all-steel gun therefore is losing less momentum. I found that the brass would sort of dribble out of the ejection port and onto my feet. In any case, these competition loads are not relevant to defense guns like the SIG.

The most popular duty ammo in .45 ACP today is in the 230-grain weight. A standard-pressure load will duplicate the recoil, muzzle blast, and trajectory of inexpensive generic 230-grain hardball. This allows relevant training, once it has been established that the gun will feed the JHP round, and is extremely cost effective.

The "high-tech" JHPs have earned a reputation for almost always expanding, unless they are plugged, even when fired from shorter barrels. Federal's Hydra-Shok has been around the longest, and has been called the gold standard. I noticed in P220s that it wasn't as accurate as it is in most other guns, and that most P220s would shoot other JHPs tighter. I never got to the bottom of that. It's not a big deal, in any case. The P220s I've fired with Hydra would print it into 3 inches or so at 25 yards, 4 inches at worst, and that's still acceptable police service accuracy by most standards. However, when the same gun would put Federal's exquisitely accurate 185-grain JHP or 230 Match hardball into an inch or so, I had to wonder. Many departments have had great luck in the field with 230 Hydra-Shok in their P220s, however.

Winchester's 230-grain Ranger is the choice of LAPD and LASD for their optional .45s, and the civilian version of this load, known as the SXT, also works well. Remington's Golden Saber 230-grain JHP does not seem to expand quite as much, but the FBI is very happy with it and uses it exclusively in their SWAT team and Hostage Rescue Team handguns. El Dorado/PMC StarFire 230-grain JHP expanded very dynamically in our slaughterhouse testing and caused massive wounds. CCI/Speer 230-grain Gold Dot expands very consistently in .45 ACP.

Shooters can also find +P 230-grain loads. Hornady's XTP in this configuration penetrates deeper than I'd like and doesn't mushroom as early in the wound track as some others. While it might be ideal for hunting javelina or deer within range using a P220, I'd hesitate to use it in a crowded environment. One of the best 230-grain +Ps I've seen is the Winchester Ranger, as issued to San Bernardino County Sheriff's Department. In one shooting, two deputies faced a gunman with a pistol in each hand. The first deputy shot him in the stomach with a blast of 12 gauge 00 tactical buckshot, and the suspect showed no response whatever. The second deputy shot him in the upper arm with a 230 Ranger +P from his privately owned, department-approved SIG P220, and the man instantly dropped his guns and fell. The perpetrator survived. The detective who interviewed him after surgery said the gunman told him, "Something (12 gauge shotgun) hit me in the stomach. Then something like to tore my arm off, and it hurt so bad I thought I'd better give up." His words were prophetic. The Ranger .45 bullet caused so much damage, surgeons had to amputate the arm at the shoulder.

SIGARMS recommends that +P be used sparingly, if at all, in aluminum-frame pistols.

Three particularly accurate loads in the author's stainless SIG .45: 185-grain Gold Dot, 230-grain Pro-Load ball, and 185-grain Winchester Match. Curiously, the latter works in his all-steel P220 but often not in aluminum guns.

Personally, I keep my all-steel P220 ST loaded with either Pro-Load Tactical +P 200-grain, or Winchester Ranger 230-grain +P.

As noted, you rarely get complaints about bad guys going down too slowly when hit with .45s. But, it does happen. In Texas, the Department of Public Safety was delighted with their SIG P220s and had good results with a wide range of .45 ammo, from 185- to 230-grain. Some said, however, that the big, slow bullets didn't seem to have what one called "the lightning bolt effect" of the 125-grain .357 Magnum ammo they'd used when they carried revolvers. Multiple West Coast agencies have also had splendid performance from Federal 230 grain +P, in both Tactical and HST variations.

SIGARMS was listening. The result was the next cartridge we'll discuss

.357 SIG

The Texans weren't the only ones who missed their 125-grain .357 Magnum revolver ammo when law enforcement switched from sixguns to auto pistols. Running at 1,450 feet per second from 4- inch barrel, this round had delivered awesome stopping power in countless shootings involving departments from Indianapolis PD to the Kentucky State Police. Even with the substantial drop in velocity that occurred in the shorter barrel of an Indianapolis detective's 3inch S&W Model 65 or a KSP detective's S&W 2.5-inch Model 66, the effect seemed to be the same and the bad guys couldn't tell the difference.

SIGARMS in general, and then-SIGARMS executive Ted Rowe in particular, decided to do something about it. The result was the .357 SIG cartridge. Resembling a .40 S&W necked down to 9mm, although in detail it was much more than that, Federal Cartridge had developed a round that

An abundance of ammo is now available for the .357 SIG. 125-grain JHP is the proven choice.

would give an honest 1,350 feet per second with a 125-grain bullet. It was 100 fps short of what was expected from a 4-inch service revolver, but as noted above, that didn't seem to matter much. Rowe and others went out and shot deer with it. The deer promptly fell down and died. The gun was tested for accuracy, and proved to be inherently more accurate than the .40 S&W in most pistols.

Introduced in 1994, first in the P229 and later in the P226, P239, and *sig pro,* it was an instant hit. Delaware State Police kicked off a long list of major departments that adopted it. That list would soon include the Texas Department of Public Safety, which quickly developed a track record with it in actual shootings.

In one incident during the transition from .45 SIGs to the P226 in .357, two Texas state troopers engaged a gunman ensconced inside the cab of a tractor trailer. The senior officer's .45 fire from his P220 was accurate, but the short, wide bullets did not penetrate the cab. His rookie trainee fired his newly issue P226 into the same spot, and the 125-grain Gold Dot bullet went through the heavy steel and into the brain of the gunman, killing him instantly.

While .357 SIG ammunition has been produced by all the serious makers and has been made in 115- to 147-grain configurations, virtually all the actual shootings on record have involved the 125-grain JHP for which it was designed. Though Federal got there first, CCI's Gold Dot and Winchester's Ranger seem to have won most of the law enforcement agency ammo bids, and it's what the cops carry that gets documented in the field first as to "what actually works on the street."

The results, to make a long story short, virtually equal those of the great old 125-grain Magnum. They do so with *much* less muzzle flash and with dramatically less recoil. Bob Forker's excellent book *Ammo & Ballistics* lists the .357 SIG as generating 0.76 "relative recoil factor" with a 125-grain bullet at 1,350 fps, and the .357 Magnum revolver as generating a relative recoil factor of 0.89.(1) Subjectively, in the hand, the difference seems more than that. It feels to me as if the .357 SIG in an auto kicks about half as much as a .357 Magnum in a service revolver, and I say that having shot a *hell* of a lot with the latter during 30 years of wearing a badge and teaching the gun.

There is no particular downside to this cartridge in the SIG-Sauer pistol; after all, SIG designed it with Federal to be used in SIGs! The one problem I've seen with the cartridge is separation at the case neck. This seems to be specific to the ammunition manufacturers. I've seen it over the years mostly with Remington and Starline, very rarely with CCI or Winchester, and *never* with Federal. I've seen it happen with the .357 SIG round in other makes of pistol, not just SIG.

The ammo makers and the folks at SIGARMS all assure me that this is in the past, and I don't know of an instance where a case neck separation has occurred anywhere except in training. Nonetheless, it did put me off from the caliber for a while.

Accuracy is superb, power is undeniable, and recoil is controlled in trained hands. The .357 SIG is an excellent cartridge, and more and more police departments are adopting it. The round's design makes the gun chambered for it interchangeable with the .40 S&W by simply swapping barrels. This can be a good thing or a bad thing. I know armed citizens who travel a lot who really appreciate this. They keep the .357 barrel in their SIG most of the time, but put the .40 barrel in the suitcase just in case they wind up someplace where they want to do a lot of shooting but can't find .357 SIG ammo. On the other hand, the cops in a town adjoining the city where I live issued their officers P229s in their choice of .40 S&W and .357 SIG. The cops split almost down the middle. After a couple of years, there were enough instances of .357 SIG ammo finding its way into the magazines of officers carrying .40s, or vice versa, that the agency simply put .357 SIG barrels into all the guns and standardized on that caliber.

During the Presidency of Barack Obama, America experienced a severe ammo shortage which impacted police as well as the public. Ammo shortage and expense, and also a trend toward lighter kicking ammo, led some departments to downscale from .357 SIG back to 9mm. Among them was Texas DPS, which at least allowed troopers who already had SIG .357s to keep the guns they loved.

THE RARE CALIBERS

While they've been made experimentally or in very short production runs in a variety of calibers, the only unusual or "exotic" calibers in which you are likely to encounter in a SIG-Sauer pistol are .38 Super and .30 Luger.

The .38 Super in the P220 was the first accurate pistol in its caliber, because it was the first to headspace that semi-rimmed cartridge on the case mouth instead of the rim. Secret Service looked at .38 Super SIGs very seriously and ended up going with the .357 SIG instead, simply because it offered more velocity in a more accurate package that held more cartridges. (The .38 Super's length is such that it requires a larger frame; the .357 SIG, like the .40 S&W, was expressly engineered to fit a more compact 9mm-size platform.)

For decades, the .38 Super was the gun of choice when going legally armed in South America, where many countries forbade possession of military-

Controllability is important in ammo selection. With proper stance and focus, Tara Miller has no problem with rapid fire of .40, .45, or .357 SIG.

caliber handguns by any but their own soldiers or police. Today, the .357 SIG and .40 S&W cartridges fill that need more effectively. The rarely-encountered .38 Super SIG is generally carried today by American shooting enthusiasts who (a) use a .38 Super "race gun" in competition, (b) therefore have buckets of practice ammo in that caliber, (c) recognize the practical and civil liability of using a double-action pistol for self-defense, and (d) want to practice with the cheap ammo already in hand.

The .38 Super will equal, or at best, only slightly exceed the ballistics and wound potential of the fastest 9mm +P+ ammo of the same bullet weight. Because so few of the guns are out there, researchers encounter few actual shootings with the .38 Super. Most of those occur near the Mexican border with 130-grain ball ammo, which is nearly identical to 9mm unless it hits heavy bone, in which case its greater power may have some increased effect. Winchester Silvertip appears to be the defensive load of choice in .38 Super and it should present no problems in a SIG P220 so chambered.

The .30 Luger (7.65 mm Parabellum) is generally considered obsolete and an anomaly. It was introduced in 1900. Resembling a miniature .357 SIG round with its bottleneck case, it was basically "necked up" to form the hugely popular 9mm Parabellum cartridge. It has a reputation for being particularly accurate, and in the Luger pistol was for decades the service handgun cartridge of Switzerland. This is why the classic SIG-Neuhausen P210 has been available in .30 Luger as well as 9mm Luger since its inception, and why SIG offers it in that caliber (and a conversion unit) to this day.

While I've heard of P220 and P226 pistols being made in this caliber, I've never actually seen one, let alone shot one. The time came when I was invited to teach in a South American country where carry permits were available even for qualified foreigners, but where no one but indigenous police and military could possess a handgun larger than .32 caliber. When scanning available guns, .30 Luger was the obvious choice. Finding the P210 ergonomically unsuitable and ridiculously expensive, unable to find a .30 Luger barrel for a SIG-Sauer (or for anything else), I bought a Browning High Power in that caliber. No JHP ammo has been made for .30 Luger since Fiocchi ran a few thousand rounds a long time ago, so I went with handloads, specifically the Hornady 90-grain XTP bullet at 1,400 feet per second. In South America, handloaded ammunition does not present the problems it creates in American courts.

References

1. (1) Forker, Bob, *Ammo & Ballistics*, Long Beach, CA: Safari Press, 2000, PP. 218 & 226.

Chapter 27

Seasons of the SIG

Born in the land of ski troops, the SIG pistol obviously works in cold weather environmentsÖbut it seems equally at home in the deserts.

The SIG pistol's roots are in alpine Switzerland and in Germany, both of whose armies are famous for the skill of their ski troops. It's not surprising that the engineering parameters of the P-series SIGs work well for cold and gloved hands, and that they are not disadvantaged by icy temperatures. However, they've also been proven to work in the desert sands.

In the United States, you don't find a whole lot of places where there's more desert than in Arizona. That state's Department of Public Safety has issued SIG-Sauer pistols since they consigned their .38 Special service revolvers to the law enforcement museum. The Arizona Highway Patrol has found SIGs in .45, 9mm, and .40 to be so reliable that SIGs still ride in their holsters to this day.

Texas has no shortage of hot and sandy environments, either. The SIG P226 in .357 SIG has long been standard issue for the Texas Department of Public Safety, and the Texas State Highway Patrol and the legendary Texas Rangers are issued SIG .357s to this day.

Still and all, once you learn that the firearm platform in question will operate in hostile temperatures and will survive sand and mud and heat and cold and precipitation as much as is possible, it comes down to how the weather effects the user as much as opposed to how it affects the machine. And, in that analysis, it is in cold weather that the SIG really comes into its own.

COLD WEATHER ADVANTAGES

The New England states are well known for their frigid winters. In five of the six of those states, SIG pistols have at various times been chosen for their respective State Police agencies. When nor'easter storms howl in from the Atlantic in the most bitterly cold winter months, Rhode Island state troopers will be carrying SIG pistols, chambered for the .357 SIG cartridge. Not far away, Connecticut State Troopers will be carrying SIG-Sauer P220 pistols, loaded with .45 ACP ammunition.

In Oklahoma, where as in the namesake song "the wind comes sweeping down the plain" and songwriter

With heavy glove, this P227 is unlikely to be prematurely discharged in double action mode and easy to fire in single action follow-up, with no fear of glove material blocking trigger return.

On warm days, this compact SIG P239 conceals easily and comfortably under a Hawaiian shirt.

Oscar Hammerstein probably never had to do a midnight manhunt in the snow, state troopers are issued SIG P226 pistols in .357 SIG. SIGs are also the choice for troopers in the notoriously frigid Dakotas. North Dakota issues the same P226 .357 as Oklahoma, and South Dakota standardized the P226 in .40 S&W, SIG's Tom Jankiewicz tells me. Montana is none too warm in winter, either, and there the troopers carry the SIG P229 in .357 SIG.

Let's look at some explanations for that popularity.

The SIG-SAUER P-series pistols – P220, P226, P229, etc. – all have large trigger guards. The same is true of the more recent polymer-frame P250. This feature accommodates gloved hands.

A gloved hand presents two problems to the user. First, the thickness of the glove material fattens the hand to an appreciable degree. (That degree, of course, depends on how thick the glove material is, which in turn depends on how much protection from weather the given climate demands of the human out and about in it.) It also deadens feel, and that effect likewise increases proportionally to the thickness and material/ construction of the glove.

Many double action only pistols have small trigger guards. This, of course, leaves limited space between the contact face of the trigger and the inside of the trigger guard at the front. Too cramped a guard, and the thickened finger can now be applying premature, unintended pressure on the trigger the moment it enters the trigger guard. Moreover, if the pistol is indeed double action only, the artificially-added thickness of the gloved finger can *prevent a full trigger return forward after the first shot*. This in turn can render the six-shot revolver *or*

the twenty-shot pistol a single-shot handgun after the first round is fired. That can leave you dead in the cold, with your only consolation being that your corpse won't begin to rot quite as soon, given the temperature.

If your SIG is the traditional double action (TDA) configuration, in which the hammer is cocked and the trigger stays to the rear after the shot is fired, you won't have this problem. The SIG will keep shooting for you until it runs empty at slide-lock, at which time you simply reload it and keep shooting. Once the shooting is done, you hit the easy-to-reach de-cocking lever, and the fight is over.

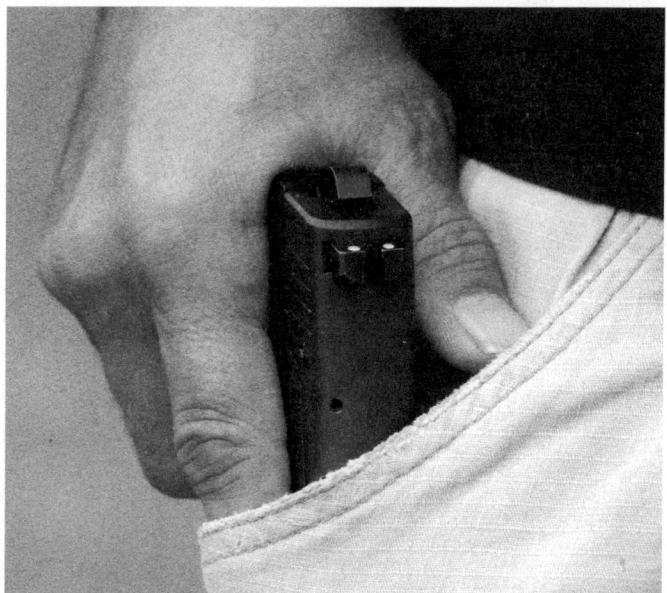

SIG 9mm P290 conceals easily in pocket holster, in lightweight warm weather cargo pants.

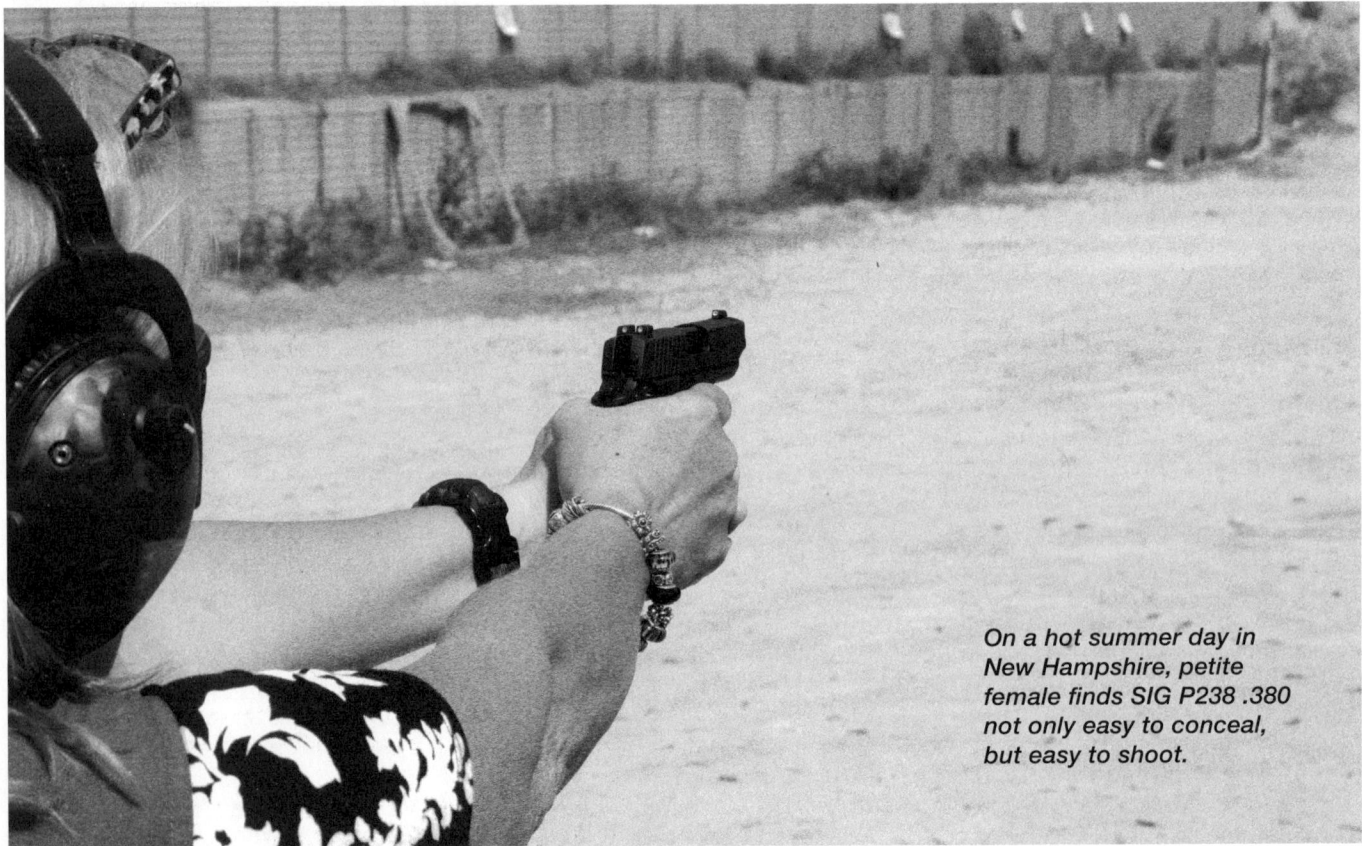

On a hot summer day in New Hampshire, petite female finds SIG P238 .380 not only easy to conceal, but easy to shoot.

If your SIG is DAK (double action, Kellerman) persuasion, you'd have to have fingers the size of King Kong's to keep the trigger from returning forward to re-set to keep shooting. And once you're done, you don't even need to de-cock.

If your SIG is a P250, room has also been designed in to allow a full trigger return after every shot.

Is your SIG the newest of all, the striker-fired P320? It looked to me when I handled the prototype at the SIG factory in Exeter, NH, as if it would be gloved hand-compatible.

The wide range of SIG calibers helps to make a weather-related choice, too. Note that those cops mentioned above who patrol frozen wastelands were carrying either .45 caliber SIGs, or SIGs chambered for the .357 SIG cartridge. Winter means heavy clothing;; even the home defender comfortably indoors can expect to be facing people who came in from the outside, who are dressed for the outside temperature. Here are the facts:

- Almost since the dawn of handguns, it was noted that all other things being equal, bigger bullets stopped fights faster than slower bullets.
- With the coming of hollow point bullets, it was noted that if their hollow cavities were plugged with inert material – such as thick layers of heavy fabric – they could fail to expand and turn into flat-nosed ball configuration by the time they hit the underlying tissue.
- It was also noted that faster-moving bullets were less likely to plug than slow-moving bullets, and were thus more likely to expand.

Running at 1350 feet per second and often into the mid-1400 foot-second range, 125 grain .357 SIG rounds turned out to handle heavy clothing quite nicely and still expand once they were through; hence, their adoption by cold-clime cops who remain quite comfortable with them after having had them in the field for quite some time.

The *very* long history of wide, heavy bullets getting the job done better than narrower, faster-moving bullets *when neither expand in flesh*, militates in favor of the larger bore diameters. When you think ìcold,î you think ìAlaska.î It's a rare department in that state which issues 9mm; .40 and .45 caliber are the most commonly seen, the .40 S&W round being standard issue for Alaska State Troopers, and the .45 ACP being standard for the Anchorage, Alaska Police Department, which will issue nothing smaller than a .40 to officers with hands too small to be comfortable with a .45.

It should be noted that SIG service pistols are available in 9mm, .40 S&W, .357 SIG, and .45 ACP. That pretty much covers the waterfront of calibers to tailor for the given season.

Snow line is visible in background on bitterly cold November day in Iowa as author fires P227. With bare hands numbed by cold, double action first shot is seen by many as an advantage in terms of safety.

There is no weather-specific downside to SIG pistols in any of the ìserious calibersî in warm weather, presuming that top-quality defensive ammunition is available for the given choice. However, when the weather is bitterly cold, there is much to be said for both SIG-Sauer design features in most of their models, and in the broad availability of calibers. Both .357 SIG rounds and .45 ACP rounds have no ballistic *disadvantages* in warmer weather against ìthinly-clad targets.î If one has to select a single ìgun and cartridge for all seasons,î eminently suitable pistols and calibers can be found in the .357 SIG and .45 ACP sections of the SIG-Sauer catalog.

I am writing this in Tucson, Arizona, in November, and am perfectly comfortable in that Eden-like temperature with a 9mm pistol loaded with Winchester 127 grain +P+ Ranger-T hollow point. However, I'm only a bit more than a week out from having to travel to the Midwest during what is shaping up to be an unseasonably cold and snowy early winter there.

When I head out on that journey, I'll be packing on a SIG P227 pistol, in .45 ACP.